DK SUCCESSFUL MANAGER'S HANDBOOK

DK SUCCESSFUL MANAGER'S HANDBOOK

MOI ALI, GEORGE BOULDEN, TERENCE BRAKE,
ANDY BRUCE, JOHN EATON, ROBERT HOLDEN,
ROY JOHNSON, KEN LANGDON, CHRISTINA OSBORNE,
BEN RENSHAW, JOHN SEYMOUR,
MARTIN SHERVINGTON, REBECCA TEE

DK

LONDON, NEW YORK, MUNICH,
MELBOURNE, DELHI

Project Editor Richard Gilbert
Senior Art Editor Edward Kinsey
DTP Designer Rajen Shah
Production Controller Sarah Sherlock

Managing Editor Adèle Hayward
Managing Art Editor Marianne Markham
Category Publisher Stephanie Jackson

First published in Great Britain in 2002
by Dorling Kindersley Limited
80 Strand, London WC2R 0RL

A Penguin company

2 4 6 8 10 9 7 5 3 1

A CIP catalogue record for this book is available
from the British Library

ISBN 0 7513 3735 8

Reproduced by Colourscan, Singapore
Printed in Slovakia by TBB

see our complete catalogue at
www.dk.com

CONTENTS

INTRODUCTION

BUILDING ON SUCCESS

The ability to welcome both change and development is a key asset for today's successful managers. In the modern, ever-changing world, what is satisfactory today will need constant advancement to cope with the demands of tomorrow. Pressures build from fast-footed competitors operating in an economic environment more volatile than ever before. Customers demand quicker improvements to services they find unacceptable, while technological change presents both new opportunities to adabtable organizations on an almost daily basis, and threats to the very survival of the poorly prepared.

To be successful in such a world, you have to maintain both your personal skills and knowledge, and use the latest techniques to motivate and encourage others to accept your leadership and ideas. *Successful Manager's Handbook* will provide you with all the assistance youneed to stay ahead. Concentrating on key areas of self-development and people skills – effective methods of organization, written and verbal communication,

thinking, relating to others, avoiding conflict, appraising staff, career development, and job satisfaction – it builds your competence in each of the areas crucial to the success of every manager and team leader in the private or public sector. Here in one book are the topics, tips, and techniques you need to achieve peak performance.

DEVELOPING YOURSELF

There is no immediate precedent for the challenges that face you as a manager today. You will find yourself in situations that no one has faced before, but you can call on the experience of other successful people to help you thrive in whatever direction an unpredictable world takes you, and in whatever direction you decide to go. How do you get organized so that procrastination, that thief of time, never stops you getting things done? What is the key to making sure that your written communication supports rather than hinders your ability to make things happen? After all, crucial decisions may depend on letters, reports, and e-mails. How do you think creatively so that you deserve to be known as an innovator who challenges accepted ideas? *Successful Manager's Handbook* explains the answers to these questions, and shows you how to take a team and an organization forward while improving your ability to organize your affairs, communicate with others, and generate ideas.

SUCCEEDING WITH PEOPLE

Your success depends largely on the ability and desire of other people to play their part in your plans. You will only arrive at your view of the future if you can persuade people to follow the same course. Improve your techniques of Neuro-Linguistic Programming to sway opinions and influence senior managers so that your good ideas get heard. Use the most up-to-date and proven methods to help everyone think about performance and then improve it – today and every day. Real professionals know that the key to winning people over is not what is said, but how it is articulated.

You can achieve success by helping others to improve and work towards common goals, but there are people barriers to be overcome as well. Some people will present particular challenges through internal values that may be different to yours. Understanding why people are difficult helps you to anticipate their behaviour and take action to prevent problems and reduce conflict.

As well as leadership, of course, people need appraisal processes. If they do not understand what is expected of them, how can they deliver? You need an effective appraisal system that can incorporate clear and comprehensive personal development plans to enable everyone to understand what success means to them, and that can be used to polish strengths and work on weaknesses.

THE WIDER PICTURE

Equally important to individual and corporate success are the stakeholders outside your organization. Successful managers make customers, the real drivers of the organization, feel part of the team. Put them first as you think about the way ahead. However, your task is not only to deliver your promises, but also to be seen to be delivering your promises. You need practical skills and strategies to enhance the reputation of your organization. This reputation depends on your publicity and media coverage as well as your service, so to win support you must send out the right message to your key audiences.

Dealing with the outside world today means dealing in an integrated, worldwide economy. To become a successful global manager, you must develop a global outlook by understanding the customs and norms of different cultures, and overcoming communication barriers. You need clear systems and approaches to achieve success with global networks and teams.

ENJOYING YOUR CAREER

There is an all-too-common trap facing successful and ambitious professionals: the trap of working excessively long hours. You may achieve, in financial and material terms at least, a higher standard of living, but in the process

neglect relationships, self-development, leisure pursuits, and personal happiness. You need to think through and sustain a balance between work and life. *Successful Manager's Handbook* shows you how to live life to the full, and in so-doing, increase your vitality and effectiveness at work.

Take this "working smarter, not harder" attitude and use it to map both your career and your future. Appraise what the work market can offer you, and fully explore all your options to develop a dynamic career and a broad portfolio of skills.

USING THIS BOOK

Successful Manager's Handbook is packed full of step-by-step diagrams, checklists, charts, easy-to-follow annotated photographs, and detailed instructions in each skill area. Case studies taken from real life illustrate the points being made, while Dos and Don'ts and Questions to Ask Yourself add to the practicality of the advice. Over 1,200 tips pass on the insights that successful managers have discovered in their own careers.

The *Handbook* uses clear, straightforward language throughout, avoiding jargon and specialist terms to allow for rapid understanding. Equally suited to experienced managers and those looking to learn or consolidate new skills, it acts as an invaluable source of reference material that can be used when faced with a variety of unfamiliar situations.

The first three sections cover the essential techniques of effective management – communication and innovation (Getting Organized, Writing Effectively, and Thinking Creatively). The next four show you how to lead and influence others, master techniques of controlling emotional intelligence, turn difficult people into team players, and assess the performance of individuals and teams (Influencing People, Developing NLP Skills, Dealing with Difficult People, and Appraising Staff). The *Handbook* then shows you how to deal with the outside world – getting an organization's message across, focusing on the customer, and operating in the global dimension (Managing Public Relations, Putting Customers First, and Managing Globally). Finally, the book turns to the art of achieving satisfaction in your work and personal lives, and planning your route to the top (Balancing Work and Life and Managing Your Career).

Success comes to managers who can confidently analyze their professional performance and take the necessary measures to improve it. Improvement brings results, and *Successful Manager's Handbook* will start or accelerate this process. Every manager with aspirations for the future will find it a valuable reference work for the problems and opportunities that confront today's professionals on a day-to-day basis. It puts good managers on a fast track to becoming outstanding performers who welcome change and thrive through development.

GETTING ORGANIZED

INTRODUCTION

*A*chieving objectives on schedule and within budget is crucial to the success of any organization. Getting Organized *considers the main causes of delay and inefficiency in a business environment, and offers practical ways to help you and your team identify objectives, prioritize actions, organize time efficiently, tackle issues as they arise, and use experience as an element of the decision-making process. Adopting a do-it-now approach will enable you to maximize the performance of your organization while allowing you to optimize your leisure time, making you more efficient in all aspects of your life. Throughout this section, 101 tips offer practical advice to help you improve working routines, while a self-assessment questionnaire allows you to evaluate your performance and keep track of your progress.*

PREPARING TO DO IT NOW

People who operate on a do-it-now basis focus on the important activities they need to complete in order to meet their objectives. Make a start on working more effectively.

DEFINING THE TERM

A do-it-now person can be relied on to get work done on time. Such people do not put anything off until later, whether the issue involves taking immediate action, thinking matters through, or gathering the facts necessary to make a decision.

I Understand that proactive people do the right things on time.

▲ CREATING TEAM SPIRIT
Do-it-now people create and maintain excellent relationships with their team, colleagues, and business partners.

WHY DO IT NOW?

Some business people consistently meet their performance targets by dealing with the right issues in the right order. They are in control of both their personal and business lives and their colleagues rely on them. Do-it-now people have to cope with stress in their business lives like everyone else, but their well-organized approach and ability to cope with the issues of the day in a timely fashion allow them to keep stress to a minimum. Finally, when do-it-now people go home, they leave work behind them entirely, knowing that their tasks are under control.

2 Make sure that you keep everyone informed about when a task will be completed.

▼ **WORKING PROACTIVELY**
A proactive person reviews a task on receipt, schedules it, and then informs the relevant parties of a completion date.

ANALYZING OTHERS

Think about the people you work with. Divide them into do-it-now people and the put-it-off gang. Think about what distinguishes one group from the other. Do-it-now people will never need reminding that they have a task to complete, and they will tell you when to expect the task to be done. Conversely, you never know where you are with people who put things off. If, for example, they are having difficulty with a task, they fail to inform you and you find out that something has gone wrong only when the completion date has passed. Decide which category of person your colleagues would put you into.

| Review | Schedule | Inform |

RESOLVING TO CHANGE

Decide now to become a do-it-now person. This may require you to make significant changes to the way you work. Getting organized may involve, for example, changing your filing systems, using a new system for making decisions, or implementing a new way of prioritizing actions. Remember, however, that it is also a matter of getting your attitude right when taking control of your work.

Communicates effectively
Takes initiative
Responds efficiently
Improves processes
Prioritizes actions

3 Be a proactive person who initiates actions, rather than a reactive one who waits to be prompted.

▲ **AIMING TO DO IT NOW**
The qualities that a do-it-now person possesses lead to a reputation for reliability and for being able to complete actions successfully, on time, and with the minimum of stress.

KNOWING YOUR OBJECTIVES

A do-it-now person is quite clear about what his or her goals are. Decide what your objectives are and begin to separate what you must do to achieve these objectives from any other matters that call on your time. Be ruthless in avoiding unnecessary work.

> **4** Prepare specific objectives and agree them with your team leader.

> **5** Sort the important tasks from any unnecessary ones.

> **6** Make sure your job description is up to date and still relevant.

FOCUSING ON YOUR AIMS

Other tasks often distract you from your real responsibilities. Distinguish between the actions and information that directly contribute to your business success and the other issues that infringe on your workload. Be quite clear about your objectives and remind yourself of what you are aiming for. Refer to your job description, if you have one, or ask your team leader for their view of your job and use this as a basis for your job description so that you can set your objectives.

▼ ANALYZING YOUR ROLE

In this example, an employee is discussing his role with his manager so that he can begin to set his short- and long-term objectives and start to form definite goals to work towards.

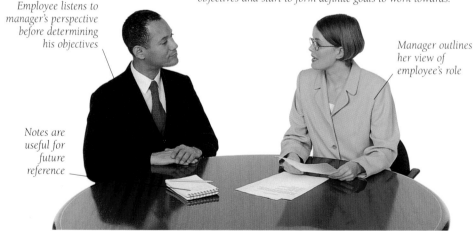

Employee listens to manager's perspective before determining his objectives

Manager outlines her view of employee's role

Notes are useful for future reference

SETTING YOUR OBJECTIVES

Work out your objectives by listing the key areas of your job in order of importance. Limit the number of objective areas to six and choose active words to describe your objectives. Add the percentage of time you need to put into each area. Make sure that you can measure your achievements in each area, and consider the best ways to monitor your performance, for example, through customer feedback or regular reviews.

List objectives

Set amount of time

Objective	Measure	Percentage of time
To maintain customer satisfaction.	Reduction in complaints received from 10% of sales to 5%.	20%
To answer telephones promptly.	90% of calls to be answered within three rings.	30%
To train new team member.	New team member can work on their own.	50% of time for first two months, then review.

Agree performance measures

▲ DOCUMENTING OBJECTIVES

The more specific and clear you make your objectives, the more focused your work will be. Make sure you include performance measures that you and your team leader have agreed.

7 Remember, once you have identified your objectives, you can focus your mind on them.

POINTS TO REMEMBER

● Objectives can be restated by the team leader to clarify precisely what is expected of all team members.

● Urgent tasks are not always the most important tasks.

● It is important to take the time to analyze all your routines.

BEING CRITICAL

List all the things that you do currently and put them into the order in which they impact on your performance. The clearer your vision of what you are trying to achieve, the easier it will be to get things into the right order. Now create a second list, using your calendar or your activity reporting system, of your work activities in order of the time you spend on each one. Compare the two lists. If they are both in the same order, you are focusing on what is important for achieving your objectives.

Compares lists against diary

COMPARING LISTS ▶

If you find that the list of your objective priority ratings is very different to your daily schedule, you are going to have to change your priorities and methods.

CHOOSING TO ACT

Sometimes it is best to deal with an issue immediately, and other times it is better to leave it for a more appropriate time. Choose whether to act immediately, deal with it later, or decide to delay action while you gather more information.

8 Recognize the routine triggers you should react automatically to.

STIMULATING ACTION

Think about what stimulates you to act. It may be a customer, your manager, or a stimulus such as an order form. Some triggers are regularly going to be more important to the achievement of your objectives than others. Work out which these are. Make sure these triggers happen early enough for you to be able to deal with them in time. If you are ordering materials from a supplier, for example, ensure the system gives you enough time to allow for timely delivery.

▼ RECEIVING TRIGGERS
In this example, an administrator found that a trigger for action came too late for her to be able to achieve her objectives efficiently, and this affected her colleagues.

CASE STUDY
Sally took on the responsibility of moving people's belongings from one workplace to another when they moved office or department. To do this she had to organize the provision of crates to movers before the actual move was due. She then had to get removal people to handle the move. The removal people were contractors and it cost Sally's organization money if their work was postponed.

Although she organized the delivery of the boxes as soon as she had notice of a move, many people complained that they did not have enough time to pack their things. Sally talked it over with her colleague in Human Resources who changed their system to make sure that Sally was informed earlier of an impending move. This gave Sally the opportunity to get the boxes to the right place and give the movers at least a week to pack.

QUESTIONS TO ASK YOURSELF

Q Do I know which triggers prompt me to take action?

Q Do I recognize these triggers early enough to be able to take effective action?

Q How can I get an earlier trigger in areas that require an urgent response?

ACTING IMMEDIATELY

On receiving a trigger, it may be appropriate to act immediately. You may have encountered the situation before or there may be a set procedure in place. In these circumstances, you should act now rather than putting the action off. Act now when you have all the information you need to respond to the trigger, and you do not need any thinking time to decide what needs to be done.

MAKING DECISIONS

Some triggers offer you options of what action to take and, in this situation, the correct response to the stimulus is to make a decision. Suppose a team member reports a problem with a computer terminal. If you know that they are inexperienced with the terminal, you may choose to go and see if you can make it work. If you know the team member to be expert in using the terminal, you may choose to call for technical help immediately.

POINTS TO REMEMBER

● Many decisions are complex, and there may be numerous options that could be taken.

● Gathering more information can be an important stage in a decision-making process.

● The right decision can be taken in less time if a decision-making process is used.

9 Act now if you already know what needs to be done.

10 Gather relevant data before you make a decision.

GETTING INFORMATION

With some stimuli, it may be impossible to act immediately. In fact, an immediate response can cause problems if you make the wrong decision. It may also be impossible to act if you do not have all the information. Recognize when this is the case. Initiate actions to gather the facts you need to make a decision. Often, the best response is to gather as much information as you can.

▼ RESPONDING TO TRIGGERS
It is not always right to act immediately. There may be more than one possible response, or you may need to spend time gathering more information in order to take appropriate action.

RECEIVE TRIGGER
You receive a memo

GATHER DATA
It may be necessary to gather more details before you act

TAKE ACTION
It is sometimes appropriate to act immediately

CHOOSE OPTION
You may need to choose from a number of possible options

ACTING EFFECTIVELY

*I*t is not enough to make a decision on whether to act immediately based solely on triggers. Take the time to think about acting in a way that gets the most effective results in the future, and look continuously for ways to improve procedures.

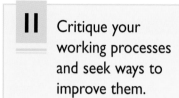

11 Critique your working processes and seek ways to improve them.

THINGS TO DO

1. Look at your working procedures.
2. Check whether all the tasks you carry out are necessary.
3. Decide which actions are repetitive and unnecessary.
4. Think about how you could start to work differently.

ANALYZING PROCESSES

Whenever something prompts you to action, take time to analyze it. If it is routine, check that the routine is still the best way to get things done. Think about it as though you were your team leader. Would you change the process involved in dealing with the issue? Is there a better way of acting? If the stimulus is not routine, decide whether an initiative from you would have improved the situation. Even when you are acting on an instruction, make sure that it contributes to your objectives. Discuss an issue if you consider it to be a distraction from your main task.

IMPROVING PROCESSES

Many actions are part of normal business processes. Such processes evolve over time and, sometimes, this evolution introduces actions or paperwork that are not directly necessary to any critical part of the process. Think about the processes that you are involved in. What parts of them are critical? What parts could you cut out with no adverse effects? Re-examine all your routines in this way. Consider new processes that could help you achieve the same goal in less time. Get rid of any unnecessary routines.

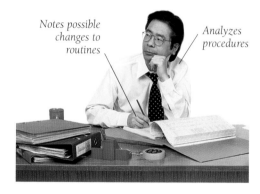

Notes possible changes to routines

Analyzes procedures

▲ ANALYZING EFFECTIVENESS
Take the time to think through your routines and methods of working. Continuously seek ways to improve your effectiveness and efficiency.

IMPROVING A ROUTINE PROCEDURE TO BOOST PERFORMANCE

A sales assistant needs to arrange a courier delivery

Old System　　**New System**

Sales assistant contacts the logistics department

It is agreed that a courier can be ordered directly if under £50, leaving staff free to deal with other work

Logistics administrator obtains three quotes

Sales assistant seeks approval for the expenditure

Courier collects parcel

BECOMING PROACTIVE

How much of your time is taken up responding to stimuli, and how much is spent in activities that you have planned? Work towards a point where most of your actions are planned. If you spend a lot of time "fire-fighting", consider the cause of the delay. Always take action at the right time, irrespective of whether or not the task is difficult. Resolve to deal with the causes of problems even if you then delay your reaction to an issue others consider to be urgent. This means that, as well as reacting to events, you are starting the process of making a crisis less likely in the future.

12 Look at whether or not you put off difficult tasks.

13 Remember, if you put things off, a problem can turn into a crisis.

STARTING TO ACT NOW

The do-it-now culture is a way of life. Think about other people's reactions to the way you work and start adopting proactive habits. Learn to deal with information in the most effective way and work on your reputation for reliability.

14 Note down ideas that might lead you to better ways of doing things.

RECORDING IDEAS

A magazine article or a conversation with one of your friends can spark off ideas about how you go about your work. Carry a notebook or a personal organizer to capture these ideas. These insights may help you to achieve your objectives or improve the way that you work. Remember, once a great idea is recorded it can never die.

Colleague discusses how he dealt with a difficult customer

Team member keeps notepad to hand to write down ideas

COLLECTING INSIGHTS ▶
Listen to your friends and colleagues talking about their work. You may find that they have habits that you could adopt yourself. Note down any good ideas for your own reference.

QUESTIONS TO ASK YOURSELF

Q Do I let people know when I have heard from them?

Q Do I tell people how and by when I will react?

Q Do I take charge of meeting other people's expectations?

Q Do I let people know when they have sent me material that is not relevant to me?

KEEPING IN TOUCH

Most people have had the experience of sending finished work to a person and hearing nothing in reply. If you receive no reaction, you wonder first of all whether the work was received, and then you start to worry that the recipient does not like your work. Remember that other people feel the same way when they correspond with you. Start to respond immediately to every communication you receive. If you do not need the material you have been sent, tell the sender in a response.

RESPONDING TO A COMMUNICATION

ACTIONS REQUIRED	APPROPRIATE RESPONSE
RESPOND AND ACT NOW	Act immediately if you know what the correct action is, and have all the necessary information to hand.
RESPOND AND SCHEDULE	If immediate action is impossible, schedule when you will carry out the action and inform the appropriate people.
RESPOND AND REFER	If you are not the appropriate recipient, refer the communication on and advise the sender.
RESPOND AND FILE	If the information received is useful but requires no action, advise the sender and file for future reference.
RESPOND AND DISCARD	If the communication is irrelevant, inform the sender. Take steps to prevent irrelevant material reaching you in future.

WORKING WITH OTHERS

Just as you want other people to understand what they should expect from you, you need to know what you should expect from other people. Make sure you understand the responsibilities of the people in your team. When you delegate an action, make sure you are referring it to the appropriate person and that he or she will accept responsibility for it. Realize that it is not enough to ask someone to do something and use this as an excuse if nothing happens.

15 Set people's expectations at an achievable level.

Supplies schedule to team member via e-mail

Telephones team member to emphasize the deadline

FOLLOWING UP ▶
If you delegate work, make it clear what you expect others to do. Follow up actions to make sure that they are successfully completed.

DEALING WITH DATA

Everyone is beset by incoming data. Look around at the desks in your place of work. Notice the sense of order about the desktops of proactive colleagues. When you receive new data, aim to deal with it immediately by making a decision to act, filing it in an accessible place for future use, or by discarding any irrelevant material. If you need to keep an in-tray, make sure that it does not become a permanent resting place for old, unfiled paperwork.

16 Keep filing up to date and easily accessible.

Diary and notepad are within reach

Electronic filing is orderly

In-tray is tidy and free of filing

Unnecessary data is discarded

Frequently used files are accessible

BEING ORDERLY ▶
Keep your working area and filing systems orderly so that you can access and make good use of information easily.

PRESENTING E-MAILS

It is best to keep e-mail correspondence short and to the point. Make sure that your messages are clear and leave no room for misinterpretation. If a matter requires a lot of explanation, it may be better to communicate it by telephone or face-to-face. Although you can flag e-mails as "urgent", use this device sparingly. Remember to keep formatting, such as bullet points or hyphenation, to a minimum, as this can be altered in transmission to other people's systems.

IMPROVING PRESENTATION

Consider the data that you receive from other parts of your organization. Ask yourself in every case whether the current method of presentation makes the data useful to you, or do you have to do some work to find out what you need? This is often the case. Solve this problem by talking to the sender of the data. If it is easy for them to change the presentation to suit your needs, it will save you time. Look at data you usually ignore and assess whether it could be presented in a way you might find useful.

AVOIDING PERFECTIONISM

Try to avoid analysis paralysis. Many decisions are based on less than perfect information. Avoid waiting for more information if it means that you will decide or take action too late. Time is money and waiting for data is counterproductive if the delay costs more than taking action earlier. If you put something off, you have to go through material again in order to remember the details. If you take action immediately on a matter that, with the benefit of hindsight, was not strictly necessary, the waste of energy is compensated for by the time you saved in acting quickly.

17 Recognize that the perfect answer can arrive too late.

18 Remember that acting immediately takes less time than putting actions off.

POINTS TO REMEMBER

● It is only useful to gather more information if you use it to increase your understanding.

● You should avoid collecting and filing information if it is not actually of use to you personally.

● A large percentage of filed papers are never referred to because they were not required in the first place.

● As your job changes, so does your need for information.

DISTINGUISHING BETWEEN INFORMATION AND DATA

Whenever data arrives at your workspace, always assess what is information and what is simply data. Data is a series of available facts or opinions. Information is made up of facts that will help you in your operational life or offer insights into your strategic thinking. For data to be information, it must have value to you. Make this clear in your mind so that you begin to look for data to increase your effectiveness, rather than merely close gaps. Think about this as you strive to reduce clutter.

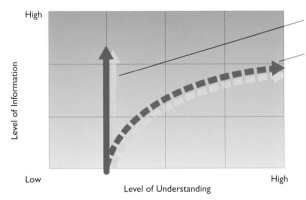

High

Level of Information

Low

Level of Understanding

High

Data is collected without aiding understanding

Information is used to develop new insights

◀ **USING DATA**

When you start a project, it is tempting to gather a lot of data. Instead, focus on information that you actually require so that you can start working on the project and learn how to make improvements. Here, the red-dotted line shows that data is being used to increase understanding.

DECIDING NOT TO ACT

The proactive choice can be deciding not to do something. If an action that you are about to undertake is not relevant to your objectives, consider not doing it. Make and explain your choice rather than ignoring what others see as a commitment.

19 Realize that it is sometimes more effective to decide not to take action.

QUESTIONS TO ASK YOURSELF

Q Have I checked that there is a real problem that needs to be acted on?

Q What would be the effect if I did nothing about this?

Q Who should I ask so that I can ascertain whether action is really necessary?

Q Am I the right person to act on this?

Q If I do nothing and it becomes important, will I be able to do it later?

ASKING "SO WHAT?"

When action is called for, make sure you respond immediately. Sometimes that response will be to ask yourself, "So what?". Suppose, for example, a supplier fails to deliver the computer equipment that you were due to install in another department. Rather than sourcing the equipment immediately from somewhere else, ask yourself what the delay actually means. Check that there are no other actions concerned with the project that mean that the late delivery will delay the completion of the installation. You may decide you do need to take action, but check first.

CASE STUDY

In a training course on decision making, a sales assistant, Alice, raised the point: "Whilst I understand the elements of the decision-making process you are giving us, I do not see where I would be able to use them in my work." Andrew, the trainer, tried to ask questions and make suggestions to solve this problem. After 20 unsuccessful minutes, the group moved on from this point.

During the coffee break, Andrew explained what had happened to his team leader. The leader suggested that rather than immediately answering such a question, Andrew should try "doing nothing". On the next occasion that a person expressed a similar doubt, Andrew deliberately did nothing and, within a few seconds, other course delegates explained how they used the tool with their own real examples.

◀ **GETTING THE RIGHT RESPONSE**
In this example, a trainer conducting a training course realized that it is sometimes better not to try to solve a problem immediately, but to leave it for a more appropriate moment. He saw that, in some instances, problems can resolve themselves.

DOING NOTHING

There are occasions when, after asking the "So what?" question, the right response to a stimulus may be to do nothing. If you suspect that something could harm your performance, but you believe the risk that it will happen to be small, then taking action to counter the threat may be a poor use of your time. Realize that some problems simply go away. This may be, for example, because someone else tackles them. Some problems will be easy to recover from even if they persist.

DECIDING WHETHER TO DO NOTHING ▼

Analyze a problem when it arises and check whether it could cause damage to the achievement of your objectives. If it will not have an adverse effect, decide to do nothing.

20 Check that you are taking action because you actually need to.

21 Remember, if you do decide to do nothing, tell the relevant people.

Analyze ➡ **Check** ➡ **Do Nothing**

▲ **COMMUNICATING A DECISION**
Discuss a decision not to act with your customer. Your customer may agree with you, suggest a possible solution, or point out the reasons why it is important that you do take action.

INFORMING PEOPLE

The key to a decision not to act is to ensure that you inform the people involved. Deciding not to act is then a proactive choice. If you do not inform others of your decision, they may expect action and feel let down when nothing happens. A salesman, for example, who thinks that a customer is unlikely to prefer his solution to his competitor's, may decide not to take part in a tender. He must tell his client. The reaction of colleagues or clients can be interesting. They may well agree with the decision.

TAKING ACTION NOW

Action now is often more effective than action later. Decide what needs to be done, make sure that your decision is based on a good understanding of the facts, then do it now.

CREATING A TO-DO LIST

The starting point for getting organized is your action list, or to-do list. This document controls what you do and when you do it. Draw up a to-do list with all the entries relevant to your operational responsibilities, and prioritize your time.

22 Be ruthless in taking irrelevant actions off your to-do list.

Forward-thinking

Organized

Receptive

Efficient

Focused

▲ **THINKING PROACTIVELY**
Do-it-now people are efficient not only because they focus on objectives, but also because they recognize the need to review and change their working processes.

MAKING YOUR LIST

Start by making a to-do list that is up to date. Make sure that it is comprehensive and incorporates all the operational matters that need to be done, while also including what you need to do to plan ahead. Your list will then include actions that are important for the present as well as the long term. Go through the list looking for actions that make no contribution towards achieving your objectives. Assess these actions and whether they must remain on your list.

ALLOCATING STATUS

Sort the list according to the status of the activity. If the action is straightforward, and you have all the information you require to carry it out, allocate it status "green". If you are unsure how to carry out the action, or you need further information, allocate that action "amber". "Red" status actions are those that you know are going to give you a problem. For example, if you know that an activity involves expenditure that will cause you to exceed your budget, give it status "red". Discard any unnecessary actions.

23 See if there are any tasks that you could delegate.

24 Make sure you are not doing other people's work.

◀ COMPILING A TO-DO LIST

In this example of a to-do list, the tasks involved in planning a conference are subdivided into their relevant categories.

Use categories to clarify areas of action

List all tasks involved

Topic	Actions	Status	Date
Book facilities	1. Get three quotes	Green	19th June
	2. Check with speakers what visual aids they need	Green	
	3. Place order with full requirement described	Green	
Brief participants	1. Agree joining instructions with conference leader	Green	25th June
	2. Issue joining instructions	Green	
Secure budget	1. Calculate travel and subsistence budget	Amber	30th June
	2. Prepare total budget	Green	
	3. Present and agree with Finance Director	Red	

Schedule date that actions should be completed by

Allocate status for each action on list

25 Review your to-do list frequently and discuss it with your team on a regular basis.

DISCUSSING THE LIST

Your to-do list now reflects what you think needs to be done and what problems you are going to have to overcome. Now talk through your list with the members of your team so that you get another perspective on your main aims. They may help you to see that some actions are unnecessary. The status of an action may be reduced by a change in your objectives – for example, by the allocation of extra funds to your budget from a source that is known to be underspent.

USING ABC ANALYSIS

Assess the priority of each action. Rate actions that are crucial to the achievement of your performance objectives as category "A", and include difficult actions that are still critical. Label actions that will have a lesser impact on your performance, or ones that are not yet urgent, as category "B". Each day, prioritize the "A"-rated actions first and, when you can make no more progress with them, go on to the "B"-rated activities. Allocate "C" to the rest of the to-do list.

DOS AND DON'TS

✔ Do be analytical and honest with your priority ratings.

✔ Do test all "C"-rated actions to make sure they are relevant.

✔ Do act on difficult actions first rather than delaying them.

✘ Don't give priority to actions just because you enjoy them.

✘ Don't be afraid to discard actions on your list.

✘ Don't concentrate on one task to the detriment of others.

ASSESSING YOUR PRIORITIES

Decide which actions are critical to your objectives

↓

Consider which actions have a lesser impact or are not urgent

↓

Allocate a priority rating to each item on your list

↓

Concentrate your actions each day on your top priorities

26 Use your priority ratings to schedule your work.

Each action on to-do list is allocated priority rating A, B, or C

Topic	Actions	Status	Priority	Date
Book facilities	1. Get three quotes	Green	A	19th June
	2. Check with speakers what visual aids they need	Green	B	
	3. Place order with full requirement described	Green	B	
Brief participants	1. Agree joining instructions with conference leader	Green	C	25th June
	2. Issue joining instructions	Green	C	
Secure budget	1. Calculate travel and subsistence budget	Amber	B	30th June
	2. Prepare total budget	Green	B	
	3. Present and agree with Finance Director	Red	B	

◀ SCHEDULING YOUR ACTIONS
Concentrate on category "A" actions first, followed by category "B" actions. Work on category "C" actions when you can make no further progress with the "A" and "B" categories, or when the urgency of a "C"-rated action increases and you have to re-rate it.

Date is set for when actions need to be completed by

27 Ensure your team understands the difference between what is important and what is urgent.

TAKING CONTROL

Some actions will be considered urgent by you or your colleagues. Make sure that they are also important before you agree to do them urgently. An urgent action is one that needs to be done now, but an important action is one that is vital to achieving your objectives. Explain to your manager if a task he or she thinks is urgent is actually not important to you. Your manager may delegate the action to someone else, or change your objectives to reflect a new business requirement.

KEEPING CONTROL

In the long term, take such good control of your business life that you reduce the number of urgent actions on your list, even though you are unlikely to remove them completely. If you find yourself regularly dealing with things that have high urgency and high impact, then you are still in fire-fighting mode. The ideal is to look ahead and foresee problems and opportunities before they become urgent. When you find that much of your time is spent on actions that are high impact but low urgency, you have got things under control.

28 Give yourself the time to take up opportunities.

29 Predict and prevent problems before they occur.

BEING SELFISH WITH YOUR TIME

Many people may make demands on your time. It is important that you, not they, make the decisions about what is high priority and what is low priority. If someone is putting pressure on you to complete an action that you consider to be low priority, explain to them why you have set your priorities as you have. Selfishly guard your time. Avoid acting on low-priority activities when you have more important things on your to-do list. This can be difficult if the person who is putting you under pressure is senior to you. You must still explain your priorities and let your senior know that they are jeopardizing your performance by insisting you carry out a low-priority task. It is preferable to be open and honest about conflicting pressures by regularly discussing priorities with your team.

USING TIME WISELY

The key to using time wisely is to have a good plan that recognizes not only what you have to do, but also how long it will take to carry it out. Set deadlines for the actions on your to-do list so that you allow enough time to complete them.

30 Refer to your to-do list to check you are meeting your deadlines.

31 Add contingency time to projects, so that you can cope with unforeseen delays.

ESTIMATING DURATION

Being in control means being able to complete the required actions on schedule. Work out what is involved in each activity and how long it will take. Put the high-priority ones first. Forecasting the duration of an action is vital, but it is often not easy – especially when the activity is new or reliant on others. Break actions down into stages and then estimate the time required for each task. Use historical data to help you. If someone has done a similar task before, ask them how long it took.

ACTING LOGICALLY

When you have estimated the time the actions on your to-do list will take, and have split them into manageable tasks, decide what to do first. Always bear in mind your top "A"-rated priorities and be careful to make an accurate estimate of the time it will take to carry them out. Now look at the relationship between the activities. For example, if you are organizing a training workshop, check the availability of the facilities before finding out when the participants are available.

Manager asks his colleagues to clarify several issues

WORKING SIMULTANEOUSLY ▶
See if there are any actions on your to-do list that could be resolved at a short meeting where queries can be addressed simultaneously and the job completed faster.

RELATING TASKS

Where a task is complex, take the time to draw a simple workflow diagram. Also called a network diagram, this reveals the order in which tasks must be completed. It also clarifies which tasks have the greatest time pressure. If there is a single task that has to be done before others can start, the network diagram will show you this and will allow you to trigger early action in this area. Look at the logic of the network diagram and see if it brings you some insight into how the tasks could be simplified and done faster.

POINTS TO REMEMBER

● It is always worth taking the time to schedule tasks.

● You should examine what tasks need to be completed before you begin work on the next tasks.

● You need to recognize which actions cannot be delayed.

▼ CONSIDERING ORDER
Analyze the tasks on your list; recognize some actions can only begin when others are complete; then schedule your tasks.

Look at the critical tasks on your list → **Decide on their natural order** → **Finalize the schedule for the project**

32 Make realistic estimates of how long tasks will take.

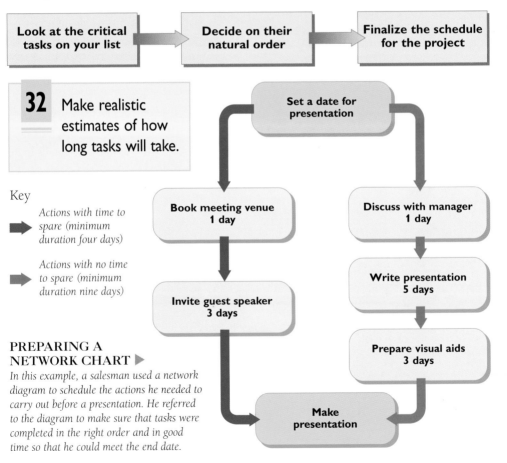

Key

Actions with time to spare (minimum duration four days)

Actions with no time to spare (minimum duration nine days)

PREPARING A
NETWORK CHART ▶
In this example, a salesman used a network diagram to schedule the actions he needed to carry out before a presentation. He referred to the diagram to make sure that tasks were completed in the right order and in good time so that he could meet the end date.

37

AVOIDING PROCRASTINATION

Procrastination is the first obstacle to overcome when you begin to tackle the tasks on your to-do list. Resolve never to put anything off and always start activities as early as possible. Be realistic about your schedules and your workload.

33 Get into the habit of tackling difficult issues first thing in the morning.

34 Analyze the reason why you are postponing a task.

35 Remember that procrastination only makes matters worse.

TACKLING HARD ISSUES

You may put a task off because you believe that completing it is going to be difficult. However, activities that cause you concern frequently turn out to be easier than you expected if you act immediately. For example, you may procrastinate when you realize that a deadline is going to be impossible to keep. Instead, contact the person who is expecting you to finish the task on time and tell them of the potential problem. Acting in advance of missing a deadline may either get you more time, or result in a suggestion as to how the matter could be handled differently and in time.

DELIVERING PROMISES

A reputation for delivering on time will make your colleagues regard you as dependable. It is one of the best reputations to have. Live by the slogan "Under-promise and over-deliver". Add contingency time when you are scheduling. Offer dates that you are confident you can meet and, if possible, deliver early.

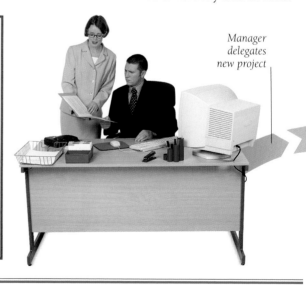

Manager delegates new project

STARTING EARLY

Learn to start activities as early as you can. Even if the deadline is far enough in the future to make starting now unnecessary, it is good practice to "front-end load". This means doing as much as you can as early as possible. The opposite of front-end loading is leaving everything until the last minute. People who do that are much more likely to miss deadlines. They cut away all the time they might need to handle the unexpected. Suppose you are moving offices: if you leave packing until the day before the move, you make it impossible to do any other work that day. You have no contingency time to deal with any unforseen problems or issues that might arise.

THINGS TO DO

1. Look at your action list and decide which activities you could start on immediately.

2. Start on these tasks as soon as possible, even though the end date is some time in the future.

3. Make sure you plan contingency time in your new schedules.

BEING REALISTIC ▶
Encourage your team to alert you to any problems that are likely to affect your deadlines, and then you will be able to take any necessary action.

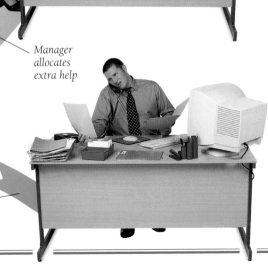

Employee has too much work to do

Employee explains situation

Manager allocates extra help

Employee is overloaded and schedule is jeopardized

MAKING THINGS HAPPEN

People accept the leadership of colleagues who make a plan and keep control of it during its implementation. Be proactive and use your strengths to initiate action. Keep others informed of what you are doing and be flexible enough to adapt to the unexpected.

36 Gain a reputation for being decisive and acting with initiative.

▲ BUILDING TEAMS
At the start of a project, create a unified team. Hold a team meeting and turn it into a social occasion afterwards to enable people to get to know each other.

LEADING WITH INITIATIVE

When you are approaching a new task or a series of tasks, work out what needs to be done and start decisively. When you are operating in a new area, it is easy to lack confidence and act hesitantly. Such hesitancy, however, passes itself on to others and leads to a loss of momentum. Think things through, then act decisively with leadership and authority. Work hard to get it right first time. When a project begins, build up team spirit and make sure that everyone knows what their role in a new project will be.

POINTS TO REMEMBER

● Project objectives should be put in writing and circulated to all team members.

● All the team members should have a copy of current schedules.

● From time to time, get everyone together to monitor progress and share ideas and feedback.

TAKING LEADERSHIP ▶
It is essential that team members are aware of their roles. They will remain focused if they are kept informed.

| Take the initiative and form a project plan with clear milestones | ▶ | Call a team meeting to introduce the plan |

| Make sure that everyone is working to the same goals | ▶ | Ensure that everyone knows what their role is |

| Keep the team focused on the main objectives and build a team spirit | ▶ | Keep everyone informed of progress |

USING YOUR STRENGTHS

Remember that putting a wrong action right can take twice as long as getting it right the first time. Recognize your weaknesses and build on your strengths. Understand that in today's changing business environment more and more is expected of people. New tasks will feel uncomfortable and you will lack confidence – recognize and accept this as a natural human trait, but avoid letting it stop you from completing tasks. Maximize your chances of success, but also accept challenges.

37 Be involved in tasks that use your strengths.

▼ ANALYZING YOURSELF
Never let your weaknesses stop you from accepting new challenges. Learn to recognize your weaknesses and eliminate or get round them if necessary. It is possible to counteract your weak points by planning ahead.

RECOGNIZING WEAKNESSES

WORKING WITH WEAKNESSES

Your technical knowledge is limited

Consult a technical expert for advice

You get nervous when people ask questions

Anticipate possible questions beforehand

You find it hard to do visuals spontaneously

Prepare visual aids before a presentation

38 Remain flexible so that you can adapt to new situations.

39 Change the plan if you anticipate a possible problem.

PLANNING FLEXIBILITY

No matter how well you have planned, some things will go wrong. There is an adage used in the military that goes, "No plan ever survives contact with the enemy". This also applies to the business environment. Make sure you do not let your to-do list become set in stone. Review it regularly. Check whether or not the actions are still relevant, or if you need to change the list to reflect circumstances you were not expecting. Be open, admit problems when they occur, and remain flexible enough to respond to difficulties.

INVOLVING OTHERS

You may have to answer a call to action through the work of others as well as your own endeavours. Make sure that everyone involved in your to-do list understands their responsibilities, and aim to empower them to excel in their work.

40 Ensure that all team members are working towards the same goals.

41 Ask your team members to keep reviewing their actions with the customer in mind.

ALIGNING PEOPLE

If a team is to work together to improve overall performance, each member must agree on a group aim. A split in focus can cause conflict and adversely affect performance, particularly when team members come from different parts of the organization. Get them to understand and agree to the objectives of the team. Align the team towards the customer so that the team has the right focus and all members are focused on the same goal.

TEAM PLANNING

Your to-do list includes the priority you have set on each task, an estimate of how long it is going to take, and a schedule for when it is due to be completed. Ensure your team adopts the same planning method. Allocate responsibility for each specific task to one person. Make sure that people know the schedule and have agreed dates – they should know when you expect them to finish a task. Each team member's to-do list must show who will do what and by when.

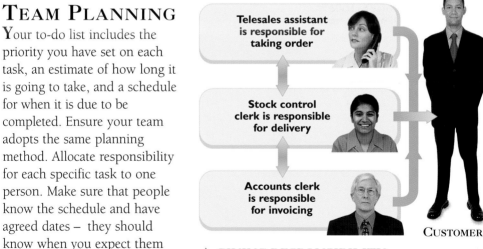

Telesales assistant is responsible for taking order

Stock control clerk is responsible for delivery

Accounts clerk is responsible for invoicing

CUSTOMER

▲ GIVING RESPONSIBILITY

In this example, the team members each have separate roles and responsibilities, but they are all working towards the same objective of getting the right product to the customer on time.

MOTIVATING TEAMS

ANALYZE
Take the time to look at the issues of a project yourself

↓

QUESTION
Ask the team questions and gather relevant facts

↓

LISTEN
Listen to your team members' points of view and opinions

↓

RESOLVE
Work to resolve any conflicts or obstacles to action

↓

INFLUENCE
Act as a leader to build consensus and motivate action

DO-IT-NOW LEADERSHIP

Leadership is the skill of persuading people to co-operate willingly to achieve a result. If you want people to join you in taking action now, you have to motivate them. Listen to them and understand what makes them enthusiastic about certain parts of their job. Your ability to have an impact through others is limited only by your ability to influence others to do it now. There are different leadership styles to motivate different people. Adopt the correct style, from dictatorial to consensus-based, to meet the needs of a situation.

DOS AND DON'TS

✔ Do ask questions to make sure the team is co-operating willingly.

✔ Do find out if there are any obstacles preventing an action being carried out.

✔ Do check that no-one is hiding resentment.

✘ Don't assume that your team will agree with your plan.

✘ Don't delegate and then relinquish all responsibility for the actions.

✘ Don't ignore the value of your team's ideas.

EMPOWERING PEOPLE

Most people want to do a good job. Delegate actions in such a way that the person to whom you are giving the task feels a sense of ownership. Encourage this by showing people that, once the task of delegation is complete, you have full confidence that they will achieve their objectives and complete the task on time and within budget. Understand that if you treat people as though they want to succeed and improve their performance, you will produce a strong environment of willing co-operation.

Manager expresses confidence

Employee takes ownership of task

▲ **DELEGATING TASKS**
Your staff will be motivated to achieve objectives on time and within budget if you show them you are confident in their ability to complete their tasks.

DECIDING LOGICALLY

If faced with several choices of initiatives, do-it-now people stop, think critically, and go through a decision-making process. Organize your thinking and improve your decisions.

VALUING THINKING

Good decision makers organize their thinking so that they can improve the speed and quality of the decisions they make. Spend time on analytical and creative thinking so that you can balance issues and make decisions that result in effective action.

> **42** Remember that good decisions are the result of effective thinking.

Perceptive

Resourceful

Practical

Original

Logical

▲ QUALITIES OF A GOOD THINKER
A do-it-now person is able to approach and think through issues effectively, in order to reach the best conclusions and make the most productive decisions.

THINKING CLEARLY

A logical decision-making process will enable you to become quicker at thinking things through and reaching "right-first-time" decisions. If you approach a decision in an organized manner and then meet the same situation again, the value of your original thinking is repaid. Well-organized thinking will be of benefit to other people in your organization. Make sure others can make use of the thinking that you have put into a decision by taking notes about how you reached your conclusion.

43 Schedule time to think in your weekly diary.

44 Realize it is not a sign of weakness to admit you do not have an answer.

STARTING THE PROCESS

Take immediate and decisive action whenever possible, but do not act immediately if you are unclear how to choose the right option. Learn to think things through right to the conclusion of a project or activity before you set off on a course of action. Follow a consistent process that leads to a decision and a list of activities that will achieve your objectives quickly and efficiently. Do not put off making a decision, even a difficult one. Deal with it now and start the decision-making process. Even if you do not have the time to do all the thinking connected with a decision, remember the benefits to be gained from an early start.

FOCUSING CORRECTLY

Just as do-it-now people spend time and energy deciding what actions have a high impact on performance before they set priorities, they also make sure that they invest time thinking about and discussing the things that matter. There is no point in thinking of better ways of doing things if they do not have much impact on performance. Keep asking yourself, "So what?" to make sure you are on target.

45 Practise the decision-making process until it is automatic.

REMAINING ▶ FOCUSED
In this example, a manager found that he ran out of time to tackle the most important issues on his agenda during a meeting he had called. He realized how important it was to always keep his main objectives in mind.

CASE STUDY
A manager called a team meeting, intending to cover five agenda items. The last two items related to actions that would directly affect the team's performance. The team members all contributed towards the first few items on the agenda, which were about the layout of the new office accommodation. The manager spent time listening to every team member's view of the new layout. When the fourth item on the agenda was reached, a decision about entry to a new market, three team members had to leave for other appointments because the meeting had already overrun its time. The manager resolved to call another meeting to focus solely on the items which significantly affected the performance of the team. By keeping the main aims constantly in mind, the next meeting was more productive.

DEFINING FOCUS

Making a decision that will ensure the most effective outcome the first time relies on a good understanding of what is the best choice. Sometimes "best" means "within budget". In this case, you can only make a decision based on cost. In other instances, time is the crucial factor. Sometimes "best" means the best way to fix a problem or to exploit an opportunity. If your reputation is based on the quality and design of your product, you will need to spend the money and take the time necessary to get the best design.

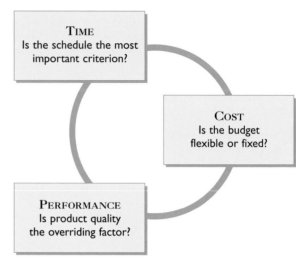

TIME
Is the schedule the most important criterion?

COST
Is the budget flexible or fixed?

PERFORMANCE
Is product quality the overriding factor?

▲ FOCUSING ON OUTCOMES

All projects have issues in terms of time, cost, and performance that must be balanced. There is little point producing results on schedule if the budget is exceeded or quality is jeopardized.

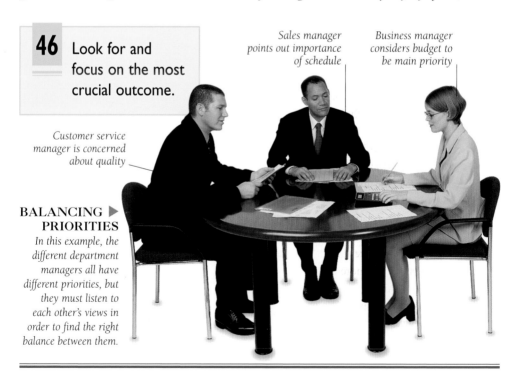

46 Look for and focus on the most crucial outcome.

Sales manager points out importance of schedule

Business manager considers budget to be main priority

Customer service manager is concerned about quality

BALANCING ▶ PRIORITIES
In this example, the different department managers all have different priorities, but they must listen to each other's views in order to find the right balance between them.

THE EFFECTS OF EXTERNAL PRESSURES

PRESSURES	POSSIBLE IMPACT
The introduction of a new corporate computer operating system.	Current projects or tasks may be delayed while systems are put into place.
The implementation of new government regulations.	Procedures and projects may have to be adapted to fit new regulations, causing delays.
A change in the demands and expectations of a customer.	Customer demands may take a project over the expected budget and timescale.
Unexpected environmental elements, which disrupt schedules or damage products.	All resources may have to be diverted to deal with the unexpected issue.

CULTURAL DIFFERENCES

Many Japanese organizations adopt a technique called *nemawashi*. The term comes from horticulture, and means "to prepare the ground". *Nemawashi* aims to get every person who is involved in a project to support a strategy individually, long before the final decision is made. For example, this may involve inviting individuals to comment on recommendations. The process of resolving conflict and gaining consensus takes time, but means you are more likely to gain unanimous agreement with your decision from your colleagues.

ANTICIPATING PRESSURES

There are many external pressures that can affect your decisions, such as changes in software or the needs of a new customer. Many organizations are also affected by the pressure to create the quickest route a product or service takes to reach customers and to reduce the time each activity takes. Even if your job is to support those directly responsible for getting new products or services from inception to delivery, always recognize the effects of outside influences and make them influence your decision making. Take the time to check and think about every decision you make. Assess whether your decisions actually reduce the impact of external pressure.

47 Remember that the perfect solution produced late is a free gift to the competition.

UNDERSTANDING CAUSES

Decision making is aimed at eliminating problems or removing barriers to opportunities. Understand the real causes of a problem in order to find solutions and make the best decision quickly, otherwise you may act but not solve the real issue.

48 Make sure you understand the real cause of recurring problems.

POINTS TO REMEMBER

- Team meetings should be arranged to identify problems and possible solutions.

- Temporary staff can be employed to cover for people on training.

- Your IT department should ensure that office software is compatible and problem-free.

IDENTIFYING THE CAUSE

Before you can make the best decision on how to eliminate a problem, you need to be very clear about what the roots of the problem are. There are five possible areas where the roots of problems may lie: Environment, Manpower, Machine, Method, and Material. When you are assessing a problem, ask yourself a series of questions to help you identify the area where the problem lies.

ASSESSING POSSIBLE PROBLEM AREAS

PROBLEM AREA	EXAMPLES
ENVIRONMENT Consider all aspects of working conditions.	Temperature; lack of space; difficulties in internal communication.
MANPOWER Assess your staff's level of skill and support.	Inadequate number of staff; poor skills; lack of training opportunities.
MACHINES Check the tools used for doing the job.	Poor state of repair; difficulty in getting spares; incompatible machinery.
METHODS Analyze how the business process works.	Inefficient department structures; tasks not done in the most effective order.
MATERIALS Examine supplies and suppliers.	Inadequate stock-level checks; inappropriate materials; reliance on one supplier.

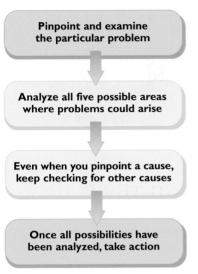

Pinpoint and examine the particular problem

⬇

Analyze all five possible areas where problems could arise

⬇

Even when you pinpoint a cause, keep checking for other causes

⬇

Once all possibilities have been analyzed, take action

FINDING MULTIPLE CAUSES

Analyze the problem until you have been through all five possible problem areas. If you find and act on the first cause, you may find that the problem persists because there is another root cause you had overlooked. If, for example, sales are down in a particular region and you find out that the sales people do not have all the appropriate brochures, provide them with the correct brochures, but keep checking for other possible causes. You may find that the region has less demand for the product.

◀ **COMPLETING THE ANALYSIS**
It is tempting, when you have discovered a cause of a problem, to take action to resolve it. However, keep analyzing all eventualities to make sure you have looked at all possible causes.

GETTING HELP

In any organization there is a huge amount of historical data about past performance. Consult this before making your decision. Do not disregard the opinions of your colleagues, who may have tackled a similar problem before. They may be able to give you a short-cut to finding a cause. Determine whether the problem is permanent or temporary. If it is a temporary issue and you make a decision to do nothing about it, will the problem simply disappear?

49 Consider asking customers for help in analyzing causes.

50 Avoid assuming the obvious cause is the only one.

Makes notes as colleague describes similar experience

◀ **TAKING ADVICE**
If you are trying to resolve an issue, you can get help from all sorts of people apart from your colleagues in the same organization. Ask your suppliers or friends who may have met the issue before.

USING A PROCESS

There is a process for making decisions that has helped many do-it-now people get to the right choice quickly. Use this analytical decision-making process so that, with practice, you will be able to make good, effective decisions quickly.

51 Tell your team members and colleagues the process you use.

52 Discuss issues with others to help with your decision.

PROCESSING DECISIONS

An analytical decision-making process has three parts. The input element is the stimulus to action and the facts or knowledge a person has to go on. The second element is the processing time, when the person uses a methodology to process input. The third element, the output, is the quality and speed with which a decision is made. For better output, improve the information on which a decision is based, and the quality of the thinking.

MAKING A DECISION ▼
There are three stages in the decision-making process: receive a trigger, consider all the issues involved, and then make a decision and carry it through.

| Receive information | Think it through | Decide and act |

UNDERSTANDING PURPOSE

The start of the decision-making process is understanding exactly what your decision aims to achieve. For example, if someone has left your team, the purpose of your decision is not simply to decide who to appoint to replace the person you have lost. Taking that decision ignores the opportunity you have to evaluate and improve. Recognize that the purpose of your decision is how to get the person's work done. You may decide to appoint a replacement, but consider all the possibilities. Ask yourself if you could outsource the work or delegate it to another team.

53 Look at all the issues before you make a decision.

54 Analyze the purpose of the decisions you have to make.

LISTING YOUR CRITERIA

The quality of your decision depends on how well you understand the issues involved. Make a comprehensive list of these issues, or "decision criteria". If, for example, you are deciding between computer suppliers, your decision concerns not only their products, but also implementation, training, and support. Cost is also a criterion, although it is not always the best decision to buy the cheapest if there are other criteria on the list. Put criteria in order of importance by using a form of weighting such as one to ten or "low", "medium", and "high".

POINTS TO REMEMBER

- Decision criteria should cover the issues thoroughly.
- Weighting can be used to pinpoint the key criteria that will have the most impact on the decision process.
- The ideal outcome should be identified even if you cannot be certain of meeting it.

55 Make a complete list of your decision criteria.

PRIORITIZING CRITERIA ▼

Most decisions are a trade-off between competing criteria. List the decision criteria involved and note what your ideal solution would be. When selecting a training seminar on decision making, for example, consider time, cost, and the flexibility of the approach.

List criteria

Criteria	Ideal	Weighting 1–10
Minimize time to implement	Workshops over summer shutdown	5
Maximize effectiveness of approach	Improve quality and speed of decision making	10
Make sure it is easy to transfer skills back in the workplace	Tailored approach	8
Minimize cost	Within current budget	2
Offer opportunities for cross-functional team work	Generic and usable across functions	8
Allow for flexibility for part-time workers	Taught by coaches in the field	4

Give highest weighting to most crucial factor

Low weighting indicates area of flexibility

Consider implications for all team members

Note down ideal solution

GENERATING OPTIONS

Consider first the option of continuing with the current solution. For example, suppose a painter has left the workshop. You could simply replace that person – a "manpower" solution. But look at your "materials" and see if there is an alternative that would enable you to buy components ready painted. Look at the other elements of cause and effect: "Method", "Machine", and "Environment". Involve other people inside and outside your organization when you are looking for options.

Read trade journal for ideas on options

▲ GATHERING DATA
Gather as much information as possible. Browse trade magazines or the internet before you form a list of alternatives.

56 Aim to generate creative ideas with your team.

57 Make sure that new ideas are achievable.

CREATIVE THINKING

Rational thinking helps to ensure that you consider all logical options and make the "best" choice. However, if you do not look for creative alternatives at this stage in the process, you may find that your decision-making skills are not progressing. Creative thinking challenges the status quo. It helps you and your team to identify new ways of working that improve both quality and the time taken to get things done. Take the time to brainstorm with your team so that you can come up with new and innovative insights.

INSPIRING CREATIVE THOUGHT

The most effective individuals and teams combine rational and creative thinking. Help your team members improve their creative thinking skills. Ask probing questions that will provoke creative thought, different perspectives, and new ideas:

❝ *If the current way of doing things becomes unusable, what would we do?* ❞

❝ *How, if you were the team leader, would you start to make improvements?* ❞

❝ *Could we begin to examine our objectives in a more productive or creative way?* ❞

❝ *What do you think our competitors do in this area that we could aim to do better?* ❞

MAKING THE DECISION

Evaluate the options against each of the weighted criteria. At this stage, one or two of the options will be obviously less suitable. Drop the least suitable options. Remember you are looking for the best choice, not the first satisfactory one you find. Make a decision. Now think about how you "feel". If the decision "feels" wrong, check the criteria and weighting to make sure you have missed nothing out.

POINTS TO REMEMBER

● You should make sure that the decision is being driven by the right issues.

● It is not always possible to get total consensus before the time has come to make a decision.

● Your team may need help to understand why you have to decide now.

Manager explains option

Weighs up advantages and disadvantages

Points out a possible problem

DOS AND DON'TS

✔ Do read widely to find as many options as possible.

✔ Do look at the options others have discovered in similar circumstances.

✔ Do reject options if their disadvantages have become clear.

✘ Don't deal with too many options – create a short list.

✘ Don't assume that options that were viable in the past are still viable now.

✘ Don't keep an option open if most people have rejected it.

▲ CONSIDERING OPTIONS

In this example, a team discusses a new option put forward by a supplier. The manager encourages the whole team to discuss and weigh up the options, before making a final decision.

58 Plan when you will make a decision and do it then.

TAKING SHORT-CUTS

When you have gone through the decision-making process a few times, it becomes your natural way of working. Learn how to short-circuit the thinking process when necessary, because some situations give you very little time to think.

59 Create an environment that encourages timely decision making.

60 Encourage your team to look for the best decision rather than take an easy option.

DECIDING NOW

You have to make a decision in time for it to be implemented – do not wait for perfect information if the delay will impact performance. Remember that the worst decision can often be to make no decision at all. When the time comes, make the decision and confidently inform those who need to know. In some organizations, a "blame" or "fear-of-failure" culture leads to employees making low-risk decisions rather than the best decisions.

DECIDING QUICKLY

If there is no time to adopt an analytical approach, use the VSAFE method of quick decision making. Look at the value each of the options gives you and consider how they would impact on your key performance measures. Then, consider how suitable the options are and how acceptable they are to those involved. It may be that some people will not welcome the decision. Be prepared to put off explaining it to them and try to get their agreement after the decision is made. Check the option is feasible and long-lasting.

VALUE
Check option aids objectives

SUITABLE
Check option fits strategy

ACCEPTABLE
Check option is acceptable

FEASIBLE
Check option is achievable

ENDURING
Check option is long-term

USING THE VSAFE PROCESS ▶
Test your chosen option against the VSAFE model. If you do not get a positive answer to all of the criteria, look for another option or modify the chosen action plan. Encourage your team to adopt the same checking process.

CHOOSING A NEW SUPPLIER

CRITERIA	FACTORS TO CONSIDER
VALUE	Consider whether the option offers a significant reduction in operating costs.
SUITABLE	Analyze whether the option fits in with your overall business strategy of forming supplier partnerships.
ACCEPTABLE	Find out whether the supplier is already accepted and used in other parts of your organization.
FEASIBLE	Assess whether the supplier has the experience and capacity to deliver on time and within budget.
ENDURING	Consider whether any further change is required to lengthen the life of the product line.

61 Remember that if a decision is not an enduring solution, it can lead to a recurrence of a problem.

EVALUATING RECOMMENDATIONS

Use other peoples' experience by welcoming recommendations. Check how they came to the decision by asking them what process they went through. If the process was thorough, your confidence in the recommendation will be higher than if no thought was given to it at all. Use the VSAFE generic questions to evaluate other people's suggestions. Think about a decision you have to make or a recommendation you have to decide on, and examine the possible options by using the VSAFE technique right now.

USING INTUITION

Start to consider your thinking process. Intuitive thinking or "gut feeling" has a place in every successful person's toolkit. Intuition is the result of accumulated experience as well as skill, and the more experienced people are, the more they can rely on their intuition – or the subconscious mind. However, there are times when the thought process needs to take place in the conscious mind. In either case, if the answer is not clear, then stop and think.

TURNING A DECISION INTO ACTION

*O*nce you have thought through and made a decision using a combination of analytical process and creative thinking, put the decision into action now. Remember that until everyone involved has agreed to do their part, the decision is incomplete.

62 Remember, never take for granted another person's agreement to act.

63 Check how new commitments affect existing ones.

64 Make sure your decision will make an impact on your objectives.

COMMITTING TO ACT

Be aware that a decision to do something is different from a commitment to act. Put your action on your to-do list, give it the right priority, work out how long it will take, and allocate the time in your schedule for when you are going to do it. Check that the decision to act does not conflict with the other actions on your list. Does it mean that timings and priorities should change? Look at the to-do list as a whole, as well as a series of separate tasks. Finally, having checked the decision, make sure that, in its current form, it is going to address the underlying need.

IMPLEMENTING ▶ DECISIONS
In this example, a sales manager decided to send his assistant on a course. However, the training manager was unsure that the assistant was ready for the training. There was a risk that the decision would be left unimplemented.

CASE STUDY
A sales manager decided to send his sales assistant on a customer-care course in order to improve his customer-liaison skills. To get on the course, the sales assistant had to explain to the training manager why he should be considered for the training. Places on the course were limited because of budgetary restraints and the training manager was not convinced that the sales assistant merited a place on

the course. The training manager explained to the sales manager that the sales assistant had not sounded convinced that the training course was right for him. The sales manager and his assistant then reviewed the decision together and agreed that it was still the right course of action. The assistant made a more confident presentation of his need for the training, and was offered a place on the next available customer-care course.

THINGS TO DO

1. Brief your team on the decision you have made.
2. Make sure everyone involved agrees with it.
3. Ask your team to prepare a plan of action.
4. Make sure the decision is carried through effectively.

GETTING OTHERS TO ACT

Communicate your decision to anyone who is involved and get their commitment to carry out their role. Often the right decision is rejected at the implementation stage because others do not fully understand the reasoning behind it. Improving the speed and quality of your thinking will have little impact if this happens. Spend time before and after making a decision to make sure the implementation goes smoothly. Speak to other people to make sure they understand the logical process involved in reaching your decision.

TAKING ACTION WITH CONFIDENCE

Your ability to get others to commit to an action is much stronger when you can support it with the reasoning of a logical process. But remember that enthusiasm and your own commitment and confidence will persuade others of the merits of your recommendations as much as logical or rational argument – one without the other is likely to result in rejection. Recognize that once someone has rejected a decision, it is much more difficult to persuade them to change their minds.

65 Take time to prepare your communications.

66 Combine rational arguments with enthusiasm.

CARRYING THROUGH A DECISION

When an appraisal meeting is held, a manager and an employee often agree a number of actions to improve the employee's standard of work and job skills. After an appraisal, however, when there are other demands on everyone's time, good intentions are often forgotten. Learn to be realistic when planning for an appraisal, and be persistent in ensuring that all targets are worked towards and met.

AGREEING ACTIONS ▶
A manager discusses and agrees a realistic action plan with the team member, and sets achievable dates for targets to be met.

Employee agrees objectives and actions

MANAGING INFORMATION

Do-it-now people act once they have made a decision based on the information they need. Organize your information so that you can maximize your overall productivity.

GATHERING FACTS

Learn to use an analytical, systematic process for gathering facts. Develop a network of people and systems that gives you the facts you require at the time you require them, and make sure that you always have information accessible.

67 Identify the information you need in order to make a decision.

68 Assess which contacts possess useful information.

69 Recognize the benefit of gathering the relevant facts before a meeting.

UNDERSTANDING YOUR NEEDS

The ability to make good decisions fast adds to the effectiveness of any team leader. Make sure that you recognize when you have insufficient knowledge to get to the right choice – no matter how hard and logically you think about it. Consider what the best sources of information are likely to be. When you know where you can get the information, you can estimate how much it will cost in money and in terms of your own time. Make sure that the advantage offered by the information is worth that time and cost.

USING YOUR NETWORK

When information is not available from your systems and archived files, it is often quickest and simplest just to ask your colleagues. It is an unfortunate fact that the best sources of information are often experts who are nearly always busy. Mail them or e-mail them with a concise list of the information you need to make it as quick and easy as possible for them to give you the information – but accept that you may need to invest time in a face-to-face meeting to get the real facts you are looking for.

DIRECTOR

Ask your directors for historical data on projects

Ensure director passes down his business overview

Share views and information with your suppliers and external partners

MANAGER

Pass down relevant information to front-line staff

Solicit feedback and comments from front-line colleagues

COLLEAGUES

BUILDING NETWORKS ▶
Take every opportunity to create good relationships with people who are able to provide information. Build a network of colleagues who can supply you with up-to-date and relevant information.

70 Realize that the person who draws up the agenda tends to be in control of the meeting.

PREPARING FOR MEETINGS

If you are organized before a meeting, it will be more effective. If there is no agenda for a meeting, it can often result in a lack of focus and may not lead to the outcome you were seeking. When you schedule a meeting, send out an agenda beforehand so that people can bring the relevant information needed to address the meeting objectives. During the meeting, you will then be able to gather the facts you need in order to make quick decisions.

STRUCTURING YOUR INFORMATION

The point of storing data is to build up a source of information that increases your effectiveness. Make sure that the way you structure your files turns it into useful and accessible business knowledge that you can find quickly when you need to.

71 Review your file structure to ensure it is appropriate.

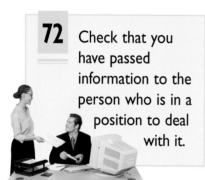

72 Check that you have passed information to the person who is in a position to deal with it.

HANDLING DATA ONCE

File new information as soon as it arrives. Recognize that it takes time to put data into one place only to have to find it again and deal with it later. When you receive data, ask yourself, "If I put this information here, will my colleagues and I be able to find it immediately if required?" The answer should be, "Yes". Check that data is passed to the relevant individual. This can be a problem in many offices, whether they are big or small.

CLASSIFYING INFORMATION TYPES

Prepare to structure your files by first classifying the information that you will file together by "type". These types are the main categories that you deal with, such as project information or customer data. Categorize your filing system by these types and then break them into sub-categories. For example, customer files will incorporate correspondence, such as proposals, and administration, such as order forms. This system applies to both paper-based or electronic filing.

Use folders to break down sub-categories

Use plastic folders as sub-files within folders

▲ STRUCTURING FILING

Identify your main information types, and consider how you will break down hanging files into folders and sub-files so that information is easily accessible.

DEFINING YOUR INFORMATION STRUCTURE

Decide on the hierarchy of your folders and files. The most appropriate structure is the one that enables you to find information easily. Time spent structuring information is rarely wasted. List the hanging file (sub-category) headings within each information type. Decide what folders you need in each file. You may need sub-files within these folders. Check that your list has a logical hierarchy. Keep reviewing your filing system to make sure that it is up to date and efficient.

73 Keep your file structure as simple as possible.

74 Encourage your team to adopt the same file structure.

CATEGORIZING YOUR FILING

INFORMATION TYPE	SUB-CATEGORIES	FOLDERS
INTERNAL Information relating to personal performance.	● Personal files ● Performance records	● Job description; contracts ● Appraisals; objectives; training records
CUSTOMER FILES Data relating to your customers.	● Correspondence ● Administration information	● Proposals; reports; letters ● Order forms; contracts; letters of agreement
BUSINESS ENVIRONMENT Details regarding business changes and movements.	● Technical information ● Business magazines	● Product brochures and updates; market research ● Trade journals
PROJECT INFORMATION Information on your current projects.	● Project plans ● Supplier information	● Minutes of review meetings ● Product specifications and prices
TEAM PERSONNEL Information relating to staff and recruitment.	● Team member personal details ● CV information	● Objectives; appraisals; personal-development plans ● CV backfiles
ARCHIVES Backfiles on completed material and projects.	● Internal ● Customer	● One to two years' backfiles ● Three years' backfiles

NAMING YOUR FILES

Give your files and folders simple, generic names. For example, if you want to check the costs of your company car for the year, you will find a file called "Car costs" more quickly than a file with the name of the garage that services your car. For folders, use general labels such as "Invoices". Use a noun as the first word of a file or folder name. You will find a folder called "Prospects, current" more easily than one called "Current prospects". Aim to have a small number of large files rather than a large number of small files.

QUESTIONS TO ASK YOURSELF

Q What will I be thinking when I try to find this file?

Q Is this the most sensible category for me to file this folder in?

Q Am I going to need to access this information very frequently?

Q Does this fit logically with the other data in this file?

Store files in alphabetical order

Align tabs so that you can see them all at a glance

TECHNICAL
PROJECTS
PERSONNEL
CUSTOMERS
ACCOUNTING

Leave space within the drawer for ease of access

Use colour coding to categorize hanging files

ARRANGING FILES ▲
Keep your files and folders in alphabetical order and arrange them so that their tabs are aligned, rather than staggered, so that you can remove a file without disrupting the filing system.

75 Make sure you can see the file label as soon as you open the filing cabinet.

ORGANIZING YOUR PHYSICAL FILES

In a hanging-file system, use colour to distinguish information types or the frequency of use. Clearly label the inserted folders and sub-files within the hanging files. The position of the label depends on how you see the hanging files as you open your desk or filing cabinet. You will not have to change hanging files very frequently, but you will have to move the insert folders as they become obsolete. You may also prefer to move a frequently used file to the front of the filing area.

76 Print out the list of your electronic filing for reference.

77 Make sure that all your information is easily available.

FILING ELECTRONICALLY

One of the benefits of storing files electronically is that the computer automatically produces your filing list. Match your e-mail filing hierarchy to the one in your filing system. When you receive e-mail, there are several ways to deal with it: act on it immediately and delete it; decide when you are going to deal with it and leave it in your inbox until complete; forward it to someone else for action and file it; or file it for future reading. Keep basic messages in your e-mail filing system and transfer attached files into your master folder.

ARRANGING INFORMATION

Think about the frequency that you access types of files. Arrange your files so that you can access easily the ones you refer to most frequently. For regularly accessed electronic files, create a short-cut to them and keep them on your desktop. Analyze which files you need less often, such as technical information. Finally, when information is finished with, put it into an archive area.

78 Remember that you access some information daily.

▼ ACCESSING DATA
You will access some information, such as your address book, on a daily and weekly basis. Put manual files where they are easy to get to.

Electronic files are easily accessible

Small stationery items are kept in a divided drawer

Contact numbers are to hand

Keep paperwork in your in-tray to a minimum

Notelets are kept by the phone

Files and folders are labelled for quick identification

UNDERSTANDING TECHNOLOGY OPTIONS

As technology continues to leap forward, learn to make the most of the electronic tools that can increase your efficiency. Plan how you are going to use technology to increase your effectiveness and help you meet your performance objectives.

79 Take the time to design a logical electronic filing system.

80 Set aside time to learn new skills from training disks and computer tutorials.

ORGANIZING YOUR TOOLS

The personal computer has dramatically changed the way we work. Think about how it can work for you. Look at the tasks you use it for and analyze the benefits of using a computer for tasks that you normally do manually. Be critical – if using a computer does not help in a situation, do not use it. Some teams find it useful to have an office "write on, wipe off" board to write down thoughts for their colleagues' reference or input – a board can be a useful part of a team's knowledge centre. Put the team's diaries or to-do list on it.

NEW SOFTWARE ▼
Take time to learn how to use software that can help you work more efficiently. Find out how spreadsheets can help you to organize data in order to make quick and effective decisions.

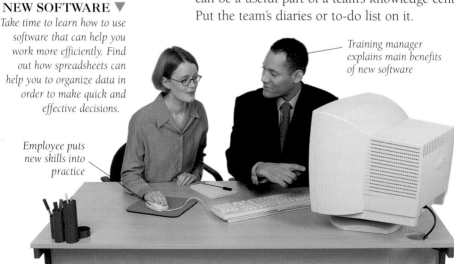

Training manager explains main benefits of new software

Employee puts new skills into practice

COMPUTERIZING YOUR SCHEDULE

The most basic of tools is the to-do list. It lists what you are intending to do, the priority of each task, and the date for completion. Since it lies at the core of the do-it-now person's planning-and-control system, keep it as a short-cut on your desktop. It is also a good idea to keep an electronic diary. This has the advantage of being able to display dates when, for example, the whole team will be available for a meeting. Be careful not to let it become a disadvantage by losing control of how you allocate your time. Remember to allow time for unexpected events. Consider blocking out parts of your diary, even if you are not sure what you will be doing during that time, so that you can remain flexible.

81 Make your diary accessible to your team on computer.

82 Block out time in your diary for unexpected issues.

▼ **ELECTRONIC DIARY**
The electronic diary is an excellent communications medium, provided that it is kept up to date with changes to your to-do list and appointments.

Refer to your to-do list	Schedule your time	Update your electronic diary

USING A PERSONAL DIGITAL ASSISTANT

When you are away from your desk, a Personal Digital Assistant (PDA) makes it possible to "take your office with you" and remain organized. It can contain a copy of your electronic diary and has the ability to go on-line so that you can bring the master diary back at the office up to date. It also allows you to access the internet and your e-mails wherever you are. Use a PDA successfully by working out where you will keep your data and how using the PDA can make you more effective. Make sure the rest of your team knows your system.

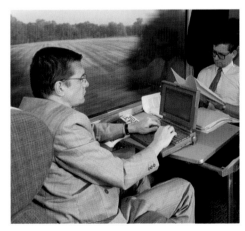

▲ **KEEPING ORGANIZED**
If you spend a lot of time travelling, a laptop computer is a useful device. It allows you to keep your to-do list and other data with you all the time.

HARNESSING TECHNOLOGIES

Successful people stay on the leading edge of technology. Understand that an effective and stress-free business life depends on keeping up with the opportunities offered by available technologies so that you are able to increase your proactivity.

83 Understand how new technologies can help maximize your performance.

USING TECHNOLOGY EFFECTIVELY

Become aware of the choices your organization has made in using technologies such as the internet. You do not need to understand how they work, just what they can do for you. Access the internet when you need to gather information quickly. Find out if your organization has an intranet. This is a network that uses the same technology as the internet but is restricted to one organization.

Sales manager researches competitors' products on internet

▲ RESEARCHING ON THE INTERNET
Information technologies have transformed the ways in which organizations can do business. Use the internet or intranet to access information from external and internal sources.

USING TECHNOLOGY WITHIN YOUR ORGANIZATION

TECHNOLOGY	USES WITHIN ORGANIZATION
E-MAIL	Quick communication of messages; transference of electronic files
INTRANET	Access to organizational databases; shared corporate information
INTERNET	On-line transactions; access to the world wide web
VIDEO CONFERENCING	Reduced travel budgets; improved global "team" communication

E-PROCUREMENT

Many suppliers offer an electronic procurement service. This is efficient because on-line product information can be kept up to date. When you order on-line, you normally receive an immediate e-mail saying precisely what you have ordered. This identifies errors quickly, and is preferable to waiting for written confirmation of the order or the delivery of the goods themselves.

USING SEARCH ENGINES

Search engines find information quickly, so that you can make efficient decisions and act. For example, if you have to buy computer supplies, use the internet to find the cheapest local supplier and place your order. Try different search engines to find the one that best suits your organization. Be careful not to waste time searching for data. View the internet as a vast library with an index system that can confuse users as well as assist them.

84 Take care to use your time on the internet efficiently when you are searching for data.

PUSHING AND PULLING

Become familiar with technologies that can work effectively for you. Use e-mail to "push" information out to all the people on specified lists. Make sub-sets of lists for information that you need to send out and review them when requirements change. Use search engines to find information and "pull" the required data from the sources that they find. Set up an automatic search to inform you if new information has become available in the places you have asked it to look.

▼ USING TECHNOLOGY
In this example, a salesman receives an e-mail. Before he replies, he "pulls" information he needs from the company intranet and decides which appropriate parties he needs to copy his e-mail reply to.

PUSH
Sends out to all necessary parties

A customer sends an e-mail to a salesman

Salesman prepares a response

PUSH/PULL
Tells others response is available

PULL
Searches intranet for information

HELPING OTHERS TO DO IT NOW

In the do-it-now culture, people pass on information for a purpose. Recognize that you are an important source of information for other people and that giving them information is not an end in itself, but part of the process of getting things done.

85 Make sure you send information only to the relevant people.

Look at the received information and decide on the necessary action to take

↓

Consider whether to circulate this information to your team and colleagues

↓

Think about whether it will help or hinder the other parties if they receive this information

↓

Review the process to check you are sending data to the appropriate people

86 Ask people if they receive information that you send them from other parties.

CHOOSING WHAT TO SEND

The information you receive will enable you to think things through and take the necessary action. However, sometimes it is necessary to pass it on to others for their attention and action. Look at information critically as it arrives and get into the habit of asking, "Who else might benefit from these details?" Make sure that you do not add to other people's "information overload" by unnecessarily circulating paperwork.

◀ ASSESSING RECIPIENTS
When deciding on a communication list, make sure that the information you are sending will have an impact on the receiver's ability to achieve their objectives.

DOS AND DON'TS

✔ Do keep information flow to the minimum.

✔ Do check with people that they want information you are sending them.

✔ Do communicate in the most effective style for each individual.

✘ Don't keep information flowing as a routine.

✘ Don't assume that everyone needs the same level of detail that you do.

✘ Don't keep sending data to a person if they do not read it.

WORKING WITH PEOPLE'S PREFERRED STYLE

Take into account the individual when you are sending information rather than using one method for all. Remember that everyone has a preferred style of receiving information. Try to work to the other person's preference whenever possible to increase the probability that the information will be received and understood. Some people prefer you to speak to them. Others prefer to receive e-mails that they can read when it is convenient, rather than be interrupted by a conversation.

▲ COMMUNICATING WELL
Some people prefer information to be presented face-to-face rather than in writing. Adapt your method accordingly.

87 Remember that it is often favourable to summarize information rather than present it all.

PRESENTING KNOWLEDGE

Concentrate on the purpose of presenting knowledge rather than the knowledge itself. Do not necessarily pass on all the information you have. Think about what will happen afterwards. If you are presenting information to senior people, for example, do not go into more detail than they need. A management summary may be all that is required to get them to accept your recommendations. Too much information or jargon can be counterproductive.

BEING OPEN TO QUESTIONS

People get a message when you present information at a meeting most effectively if they interact and ask questions. Cut the amount of information you present to the minimum, but make sure that people realize that you are expecting them to ask questions:

❝ *I am available to answer any questions you may have on this subject.* ❞

❝ *I have reduced these facts to the bare bones, if you need more details, please ask.* ❞

❝ *Please feel free to ask questions at any time during the presentation, or at the end.* ❞

❝ *If some people want further details, I am available for questions after the meeting.* ❞

LEARNING FROM EXPERIENCE

One way to become more organized is to capture
all the lessons you have learnt from past experience. Think
about how to make the best use of your experience.

FOCUSING ON IMPROVING

*The pressures of modern business life
mean that you can never relax and
think that you are working as effectively as
possible. Always be on the look-out for ways
to improve. Remember, you have to change
as fast as the business world is changing.*

88 Realize that if
you stop learning,
you will soon stop
being effective.

QUESTIONS TO ASK YOURSELF

Q Do I regularly ask customers if they are satisfied?

Q How could we adapt the service we offer?

Q Do I continually review processes to see how to change them for the better?

Q Do I keep up to date with changes in business?

Q Do I listen to other people's views?

ADAPTING TO CHANGE

Recognize that the business climate in which your organization operates changes continuously. Your customers expect more from you, and competitors frequently improve their performance and try to prove that they offer a better service than you. It is no longer satisfactory to turn up to work to do the same job that you did yesterday – you must continuously improve what you do and the way that you do it. For example, seek regular feedback from your customers to keep abreast of their requirements and to assess their levels of satisfaction with your performance.

PLAN Get into the habit of planning actions thoroughly	⫸	Work out how you are going to achieve an objective
EXECUTE Carry out the plan and adapt it where necessary	⫸	Make sure you keep your focus on your objective
REFLECT Think about how you could improve processes in future	⫸	Assess the implications of all your actions
LEARN Make sure you learn lessons from your past actions	⫸	Look at procedures you could change

▲ USING THE PERL CYCLE

If you adopt the PERL-cycle principle, you will become more and more effective, and you will be equipped to avoid the repetition of mistakes and the recurrence of problems.

USING THE PERL CYCLE

The four stages of the PERL cycle – plan, execute, reflect, and learn – allow you to make the most of and learn from experience. Once you have planned and executed some of the activities on your to-do list, reflect on how well you have achieved your aims and what you could have improved. Suppose you have just completed the installation of equipment. Was the customer happy? What could you have done better? Always aim to plan time into your schedule to reflect.

89 Put time aside to reflect on ways to improve processes.

KEEPING A WINNING METHOD

If you and the team have achieved a good result, put yourself in the best position to repeat the process. The PERL process gives the do-it-now person the opportunity to reapply the things that worked and eliminate those that did not. The time you spend on reflecting at the end of a successful activity will be repaid next time you do something similar. Keep the successful project plans for future reference.

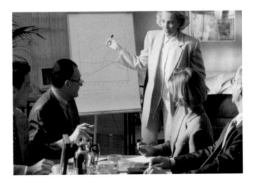

▲ REVIEWING A PROJECT

Meet with your customer at the end of a project to review how it went and to analyze procedures to see if there are any you would change next time.

CAPTURING BEST PRACTICES

As well as learning from experience, it is possible for whole teams or organizations to learn from each other. Experiences can be documented and distributed – often called "capturing best practices" – as templates for future projects.

90 Build on past experiences and benefit from improved decisions.

91 Encourage your team to work with templates.

92 Record successful decisions as templates.

USING TEMPLATES

You can formalize the process of reflecting and learning by documenting successful methods in the form of templates. A template provides standard ways of doing things and lists methods that have worked in the past. For example, all organizations select suppliers of goods and services from time to time. Some members of the team may prioritize quality, while others consider after-sales service to be of paramount importance. All factors common to purchasing decisions could be captured in the creation of a "Supplier Selection Template".

Notes down actions that worked well

▼ **ANALYZING PROCESSES**
In this example, a production team meet to discuss their standard processes, so that they can form a template.

Production manager describes how he handled a past project

THINGS TO DO

1. Look at how you could improve your routines.
2. Use a consistent approach to templates so that your team gets used to them.
3. Build a library of completed templates that you can learn from.

INSTITUTING ROUTINES

Once you have identified best-practice approaches, make sure you and your team follow them. They are useful in many instances, from preparing course material to building a system of fault recording. You will find that once you have followed the routine a number of times, you will no longer have to consciously think about how you are working. You will have internalized the template and will be automatically following best practice. To get consistency, encourage the use of these routines throughout the team.

USING TECHNOLOGY

Capturing and sharing best practices can be streamlined. Put the template on a spreadsheet and use examples that others can easily follow. Make it available in a file that everyone can access or send it out by e-mail. For example, suppose you have recently recruited two new people. One has worked out well and the other finds the job difficult. You can capture the differences between the two and build a template that lists the attributes future candidates will have to demonstrate.

93 Make sure that your team can access templates on a file server quickly and easily.

Risks presented by training programme

Impact on organization rated 1–10

Issues rated as "red", "amber", "green"

RISKS	PROBABILITY	IMPACT	ACTION	STATUS
Programme may not address needs of participants	5	6	Conduct a joint audit (interviews with representatives of staff groups affected)	A
Trainer may not have knowledge of our specific processes	6	2	Confirm trainer selection before signing contract and insist they know our processes	G
Participants may reject the approach and concepts	10	7	Involve representatives in understanding general needs and conduct a pilot	R
Train-the-trainer option may take the programme over budget	2	3	Build in contingency to allow flexibility of approach after the main programme	A

◀ **USING TEMPLATES**
This template reflects the risk analysis that was followed for gauging how likely a training course was to achieve its objectives. Knowledge was then shared across the organization.

Likelihood of risk weighted 1–10

Record of previous action in similar situations

SHARING INSIGHTS

W*hen people are achieving results, they sometimes have completely new ideas that can improve their performance and productivity. These can be real breakthrough ideas. Make sure that you take advantage of new ideas and insights.*

94 Share winning insights with your team and business partners.

POINTS TO REMEMBER

- Your ideas and insights may be of value to your colleagues.
- Information technologies have made it possible for insights to be shared globally.
- Technology allows the sharing of insights in "real-time" and can be acted on immediately.

95 Thank people for insights so that they share more.

FILING INSIGHTS

As people complete tasks, they often find that they have gained information that may be of value to others. This information is called an "insight". It is different from a template in that it comes from an understanding that a task can be done better. For example, a salesman in London loses an order because he pitched the wrong Unique Selling Proposition (USP) against a particular competitor. He now has an insight into how to sell against that competitor. If he logs this in an electronic "insights file" the next day, his colleague in Oslo, about to make the same mistake, can check the file and adapt his proposition to win an order.

CASE STUDY
Bill was the project leader of a mobile-telephone production line in the US. His manager noticed that the European manufacturers of the same product had a significantly lower production cost. He asked Bill to get in touch with the relevant project leader. Bill discussed the matter on the telephone with Olga, the person responsible in Germany, and discovered that she had found a source of materials in Asia that was much cheaper than the supplier Bill was currently using. Bill switched suppliers and his costs came down to match those in Germany. Bill and Olga agreed to set up a shared file on the organization's intranet recording the changes that they made to their production methods. This meant that both sites could share insights and they both improved their performance over time.

◀ **LEARNING FROM OTHERS**
The systematic sharing of new ideas and insights helps to spread best practice around an entire organization, even on a global basis. The benefits are outlined here by the interaction between a project leader in the US and his European counterpart in Germany.

CLOSING THE LOOP

In a time of increasing staff turnover and mobility, it is vital that insights are formally captured in an accessible file and shared. For example, use your team's accumulated knowledge to maintain customer satisfaction or stay ahead of the competition. Take time to write down and share insights with others. Give people access to insights by allocating key words that will make it easy for others to find information.

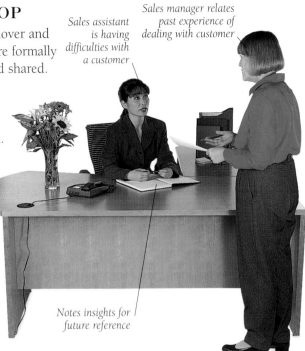

Sales assistant is having difficulties with a customer

Sales manager relates past experience of dealing with customer

Notes insights for future reference

COMMUNICATING ▶ EXPERIENCES

By talking to your colleagues about your experiences, you can significantly impact on the overall performance of the team.

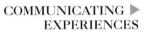

96 Make sure your team members record and file information.

INVOLVING THE TEAM ▼

Sharing insights with your team means that all team members have access to information and are therefore in a better position to make quicker decisions and act immediately and efficiently.

PASSING INSIGHTS ON

Aim to present insights to the team in an interesting way. An old but effective method of sharing information is to present it in the form of a story that everyone can understand and relate to. This approach is useful for coaching and mentoring. Avoid just telling the member of staff what the rule is, give them a real example. For example, a manual on setting up exhibition stands will include a precise specification for the handrails. This is less likely to communicate what needs to be done than telling the story of an accident caused by ineffective handrails.

Team share insights	▶	**Information is accessible**	▶	**Decisions can be made quickly**

LEADING A BALANCED LIFE

All work and no play is a recipe for becoming less productive at work and less fulfilled at play. If you are to continue to build on and develop your efficiency at work, it is important to maintain a healthy balance between work and leisure.

97 Remember that discussing matters with others reduces stress.

98 Use a separate room for work at home if possible.

99 Schedule time in your week for regular exercise.

WORKING FROM HOME

As an effective member of a team, you develop good methods for taking action, thinking things through, and gathering information. It is equally important to be an effective member of a family or a circle of friends. Avoid being a "workaholic". Take time to reflect on the balance in your life – how much time do you spend at work and how much at play? There are ways of adjusting this: you may be able to work from home one or two days a week; or perhaps your workload has increased so much that you can justify another team member.

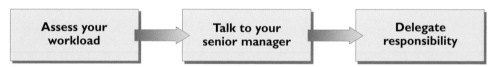

| Assess your workload | Talk to your senior manager | Delegate responsibility |

KEEPING FIT

Some people put things off because they are not feeling completely healthy. There is increasing evidence that people who are physically fit cope with the challenges of modern business life better than those whose work programmes leave them little time for exercise. This does not mean that you have to run marathons but that you should take some exercise at least twice a week. Try to put aside a regular time for this so that people know when you are not available.

▲ DISCUSSING OPTIONS
If your workload is too heavy, talk to your senior manager. The problem could be solved by delegating tasks and agreeing to lose responsibility for certain tasks.

100 Remember that exercise increases your energy levels.

▲ MAKING TIME TO RELAX

Develop one of the most important abilities any working person needs – the ability to go out of the workplace door and leave their business stress and worry where they belong.

101 Realize that overwork and stress can impair your ability to make effective decisions.

MANAGING STRESS

Your efficiency will increase rather than go down if you take regular breaks from intense activity. People who maintain their effectiveness develop the ability to take fifteen minutes in the middle of the day to unwind and prepare themselves for the challenges of the afternoon. Aim to really get away from it – do not spend this time with your colleagues. Of course, there are times in even the best-regulated lives when long periods of hard work are required. If this is happening to you on a regular basis, re-evaluate your working processes to find and deal with the underlying causes.

HEALTHY EATING

Always have a nutritious breakfast so that you are able to start the day feeling full of energy and ready to face the most difficult tasks on your to-do list first. During the day, make sure you take breaks to recharge your batteries, and then you will be able to work at your optimum efficiency. If you are in the habit of snacking, take fruit to work with you, because it is rich in vitamins and fibre. Quick-fixes of sugar-rich chocolate can boost your energy momentarily, but leave you feeling tired and prone to procrastination later, which can have an effect on your effeciency. Get into the habit of drinking plenty of refreshing water during the day and avoid stimulants such as tea or coffee, which can heighten stress.

EATING WELL ▶

A healthy, balanced diet will give you the energy to face the challenges of modern life.

ASSESSING YOUR SKILLS AS A DO-IT-NOW PERSON

Evaluate your ability to act effectively and on time by responding to the following statements, marking the option closest to your experience. Be as honest as you can: if your answer is "Never", circle option 1; if it is "Always", circle option 4, and so on. Add your scores together, and refer to the Analysis to see how well you scored. Use your answers to identify the areas that most need improvement.

OPTIONS
1 Never
2 Occasionally
3 Frequently
4 Always

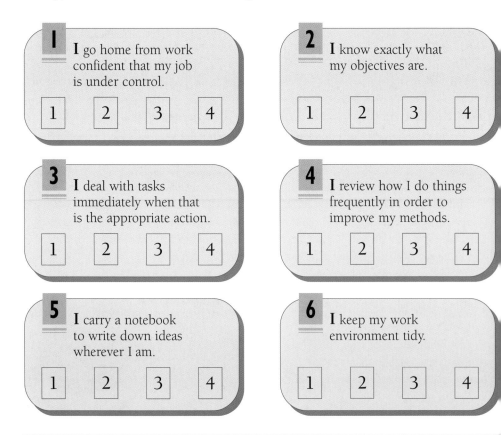

1 I go home from work confident that my job is under control.

1 2 3 4

2 I know exactly what my objectives are.

1 2 3 4

3 I deal with tasks immediately when that is the appropriate action.

1 2 3 4

4 I review how I do things frequently in order to improve my methods.

1 2 3 4

5 I carry a notebook to write down ideas wherever I am.

1 2 3 4

6 I keep my work environment tidy.

1 2 3 4

7 I respond to all incoming communications immediately.

1 2 3 4

8 I tell people if I have decided not to take action on something.

1 2 3 4

9 I allocate an up-to-date status to all the actions on my to-do list.

1 2 3 4

10 I deal with matters that are important before they become urgent.

1 2 3 4

11 I know what actions need to be done first.

1 2 3 4

12 I under-promise and over-deliver.

1 2 3 4

13 I make plans that take account of my weaknesses.

1 2 3 4

14 I use appropriate styles of leadership.

1 2 3 4

15 I make decisions at the right time.

1 2 3 4

16 I obtain other people's agreement to my decisions on an individual basis.

1 2 3 4

17 I look for all the causes of problems.

1 2 3 4

18 I list my decision-making criteria before I make a decision.

1 2 3 4

19 I think creatively as well as rationally.

1 2 3 4

20 I make use of a checking procedure to make sure I have made the right decision.

1 2 3 4

21 I follow up decisions by adding the actions to my to-do list.

1 2 3 4

22 I take time to prepare before I communicate with other people.

1 2 3 4

23 I find the information I need on a regular basis.

1 2 3 4

24 I keep the structure of my filing system up to date.

1 2 3 4

25 I file things as I go along.

1 2 3 4

26 I use technology when it is appropriate.

1 2 3 4

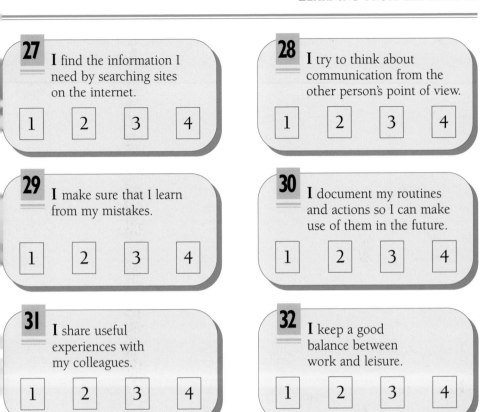

27 I find the information I need by searching sites on the internet.

1 2 3 4

28 I try to think about communication from the other person's point of view.

1 2 3 4

29 I make sure that I learn from my mistakes.

1 2 3 4

30 I document my routines and actions so I can make use of them in the future.

1 2 3 4

31 I share useful experiences with my colleagues.

1 2 3 4

32 I keep a good balance between work and leisure.

1 2 3 4

ANALYSIS

Now that you have completed the self-assessment, add up your total score and check your performance by reading the corresponding evaluation. Whichever level of skill you have reached in getting organized, it is important to remember that there is always room for improvement. Identify your weakest areas, and refer to the relevant chapters for practical advice and tips to help you develop and refine your skills.

32–64: There are areas you need to improve to be a do-it-now person. Implement some of the suggestions in this section now.

65–95: You are good at getting things done on time, but certain areas need improvement.

96–128: You are reliable and effective, but do not become complacent. Keep striving to improve your performance.

WRITING EFFECTIVELY

INTRODUCTION

K nowing how to communicate effectively through writing is essential for anybody who wants to progress in today's competitive business environment. Writing Effectively is a valuable tool that will help you meet that challenge. This section is divided into four chapters, each outlining key requirements for good writing: a clear and concise style, knowledge of grammar and structure, and how to apply basic formats to everyday communication. It also shows how to project the right image, choose the kind of language best suited to your reader, and write succinct e-mails, reports, and letters.

Information and advice are given that will help you to become a skilled communicator. In addition, 101 concise tips highlight the secrets of good writing, and a self-assessment test at the end of the section will enable you to evaluate the progress you have made.

WRITING CLEARLY

In this age of mass information and communication, being able to write clearly is fundamental to business success. Crucial decisions may depend on the written word in letters, reports, and e-mails.

COMMUNICATING CLEARLY

Knowing how to communicate efficiently in the current employment market is an enormous competitive advantage. The ability to take on board, change, and process information – mostly in written form – is a formidable business skill.

1 A clear style projects an efficient image, so choose words carefully.

2 For electronic communications, always write in simple language.

3 Writing positively and directly can influence and motivate others.

WRITING IN A PROFESSIONAL WAY

The written word projects your professional image to your boss, colleagues, clients, and suppliers. Your values, beliefs, ideologies, and personality all come through in the material that you produce. And it does not end there. Your knowledge, training, education, organizational skills, and creativity are also shown in the words you use and how you convey information. This information must be credible and supported by facts, because the people receiving it must have confidence in you and what you have written.

CHANGING OLD BELIEFS

Many professionals feel that writing is an old-fashioned form of communication. But in this electronic age, writing is a day-to-day necessity, and perhaps even more important than ever before. Another belief that needs to be corrected is that it is not possible to write inspirational text. With the right skills, methods, models, and lots of practice, everyone can write creatively. A third belief is that it is the quality of the writing that is important, not how it is read and received. The fact is that if a communication is badly written, it will not be clearly understood by its recipient, particularly if they are unfamiliar with, or do not have, in-depth knowledge of the subject matter.

4 Sometimes a special phrase or word is all that is needed.

5 Learn how to use the most up-to-date methods of communication.

UPDATING METHODS

In many established companies, old-fashioned or bureaucratic methods or styles of communication are often used, which can hinder rather than promote clear understanding between colleagues or suppliers. Memos or letters using an outmoded structure, or templates with pedantic or convoluted language are often used, which can sometimes confuse the recipients. But all of us can become involved in suggesting how to change and improve these old-fashioned methods and styles, so that clear, concise writing becomes the main form of communication. The aim is to produce communications that are well-written, interesting to read, and which will motivate and inspire.

▼ **USING NEW TECHNOLOGY**
The electronic age enables us to take a laptop computer with us anywhere. You can work on a train, at someone else's desk, or make notes in a meeting.

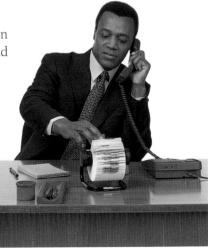

DEVELOPING WRITING SKILLS

To understand the importance of written language and the best way to use it, it is helpful to know something about how we write. Nowadays, with the speed of electronic communication, all text needs to be brief and focused.

6 Write all informal communications in a modern, lively style.

POINTS TO REMEMBER

- Written language is increasingly important in today's business.
- Direct mail lists, databases, and the internet are strategic activators and motivators in business operations.
- E-mail is becoming an extremely important tool, often replacing phone contact because of its speed and the records it provides.
- Written information is often circulated before filing, so extra care needs to be taken with text presentation.

WRITING THROUGH THE AGES

Society has moved through three major stages: the agricultural age, the industrial age, and now the electronic age (also known as the information age). Each period has brought changes in the methods and styles in which people communicated for business. The most recent and significant change in our current information age has been a transition from the more formal business language of the past to the informal approach used today, particularly in e-mails.

An electric keyboard for easier and faster typing

▶ **TECHNOLOGICAL DEVELOPMENTS**
How we impart information has changed over the years, from using a basic manual typewriter through a faster electric version to the modern computer where people write directly "on screen."

Manual keys

MANUAL TYPEWRITER

ELECTRIC TYPEWRITER

USING VISUAL AIDS

For today's young generation, highly visual resources such as television, the internet, video games, and multimedia resources are part of their normal day-to-day life. The visual presentation of materials as a business aid is also becoming increasingly important. Try using schematics – classifying information under specific headings alongside other visual aids, such as graphics, tables, charts, and colour. These can all be applied to the material to make its presentation more interesting and focused.

7 With large sections of text, use headings and boxes to break them up.

8 Reduce information overload by restricting the text on each page.

TARGETING YOUR MATERIAL

In modern business communications, the written material that is sent out must be targeted carefully. For example, in a letter to an interested party, you must state clearly what benefits there are to the consumer of your products and services, rather than just describing them. Present all the information in a clear, simple, but dynamic style using persuasive terminology that will capture the client's attention.

A screen for faster text changes

New machines come with diverse functions, are quicker, and have more memory

Basic word processing

OLD COMPUTER

MODERN COMPUTER

RECOGNIZING GOOD WRITING

*A*ll business professionals need to become *good communicators to succeed. To do this, it is essential to recognize, and correct, any bad or lazy writing habits that have developed, and establish good habits such as organization and focus.*

9 In day-to-day business, adopt a friendly but elegant style.

10 When supplying information, keep to the points you are trying to make.

▼ CHANGING WAYS OF WORKING
There are marked differences between how a bad and good communicator operates, but it is possible to change negative ways of working into positive ones.

GETTING ORGANIZED
Good commmunicators are easy to identify because they get themselves organized before they write any material. They research the subject matter to be discussed, and have defined objectives to motivate their readers to action. They always consider what information the reader needs, and review and rework their written work for increased clarity and sense. Bad communicators write in a hurried, disordered way without any prior thought or planning. They leave the reader to work out what they are trying to say.

Writes in a pompous way with little regard for the reader

Blames the reader for not understanding the text received

Claims there is no time to get to know the subject matter well

Sends off information without any structure or forethought

THE BAD COMMUNICATOR

Uses language that is understood by the reader

Makes notes before starting

Controls quantity and quality of information sent

Carefully revises a draft of the text before sending

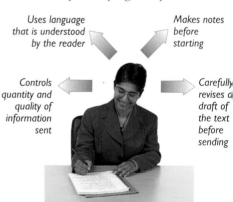

THE GOOD COMMUNICATOR

FOCUSING YOUR WRITING

When writing your text, be focused about what message you are trying to get across. In a marketing letter, for example, present the information in a punchy, positive style to encourage the maximum reader response. Be careful not to obscure your message with a dull and pedantic writing style.

 Check the tone of your text by reading it out loud.

◀ **WRITING WITHOUT FOCUS**

This marketing letter contains the information about the Small Business Programme at Zedcom, but it is not written or presented in a style that projects it positively to the reader. The text comes across as stilted and bland, leaving the reader with no desire to join Zedcom.

31 March 2000

Subject: Small Business Programme at Zedcom

Dear Sir,

The Small Business Programme at Zedcom aims to offer all participants the unique opportunity to set up and manage their own business.

All participants will receive essential information on the management and marketing of products, price setting, quality and stock control, and the training of colleagues, as well as learning other management skills.

Zedcom hopes through this initiative to offer participants, at no expense to themselves, increased opportunities, income, and an improved standard of living.

If this programme interests you, information can be obtained by telephoning 0800 000000.

ARE YOU SEEKING NEW OPPORTUNITIES, MORE MONEY, AND A HIGHER STANDARD OF LIVING?

If this is what you are looking for, then take part in the Small Business Programme – a new initiative run by Zedcom.

The programme will teach you how to start up and run your own business.

You'll learn, in a simple and practical way, how to:
✔ manage and market products
✔ work out pricing levels
✔ improve the quality of products and services
✔ control stock
✔ train and involve colleagues

You will also learn basic management skills and techniques.

The programme is free of charge, so call 0800 000000 to register your place now.

Don't miss out – this is just the opportunity you have been waiting for.

WRITING WITH FOCUS ▶

This marketing letter has been planned well. It advertises the programme run by Zedcom, selling its merits to the reader in a short and punchy style. The focus is on the reader, and the text is broken up into accessible paragraphs.

PREPARING TO WRITE

A good writing style has several different elements. It should give a positive message, show the writer's familiarity with the subject matter, relate the right information in a concise, friendly manner, and, if necessary, motivate the reader.

12 Always write in terms that your reader can understand.

ASSESSING YOUR STYLE

UNHELPFUL
"We are not able to assist you…"

or

CO-OPERATIVE
"We are willing to look at…"

UNDERMINING
"I am not sure you can do this job…"

or

SUPPORTIVE
"I think you are doing this job well…"

AUTHORITARIAN
"You must complete this job now…"

or

DEMOCRATIC
"When you have time, could you…"

ABRUPT
"Well, if you cannot handle the project…"

or

PERSUASIVE
"I really think this is your project…"

POMPOUS
"I have worked on many jobs like this…"

or

UNASSUMING
"I will do my best on this job…"

PROJECTING THE RIGHT IMAGE

The style and tone that you use for writing project your image, and can also reflect your credibility in the workplace. They give an indication of your personality and confidence in yourself in the work environment. A letter or e-mail that is written in an abrupt or unhelpful style will not inspire a client or colleague to respond as you wish – they are far more likely to reply in a similar vein. Using a persuasive or co-operative tone will instantly engage the recipient, making them much more likely to respond in a positive, helpful manner. The way someone reacts to the tone of a letter is very personal, but always try to be clear, objective, and polite in everything you write.

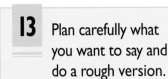

13 Plan carefully what you want to say and do a rough version.

Well-structured text is fundamental to achieving good communication with any client

PLANNING YOUR WORK

Before you start writing, structure a plan of what you are trying to say: this can be in note or bullet form. If you do not know what your objectives are, the people receiving your communication will also be confused and wonder what you need from them. A good piece of writing conveys the intended message with clearly defined objectives so that the recipients respond positively and take the necessary action. Make the text clear and precise, so that they know what decisions are required of them, and detail any time scale that is involved.

AIMING FOR GOOD TEXT

Project the right image

Follow an outline

Use language suited to the recipient

Show prior knowledge of the recipient

Provide all the necessary information

USING THE RIGHT LANGUAGE

When you are writing to clients or associates, you will need to vary your style to suit your relationship with them. Today's writing style is far more relaxed than that of a few years ago, but if you are addressing a new client or contact, for example, a degree of formality is still appropriate, out of politeness. Also, if you are writing to a person who is much older than yourself, again they may well appreciate a more formal approach. However, with someone that you regularly communicate with and know well, a relaxed, friendly style will be well received. You also need to use the right tone for the situation. If you are producing minutes of a meeting going to several people, for example, the tone needs to be informative and concise; concentrate on the key points that occurred. Remember, the aim is always to impart the message in an accessible way.

KNOWING YOUR SUBJECT

If you are preparing a report, make sure that all the information it contains is well researched. Gather together all the facts and figures by researching in reference books and magazines, looking at CD-ROMs and surfing the internet. Make sure you have a wealth of data, so that you can eliminate what seems superfluous and keep in the essentials. If you are unsure of the accuracy of some material, check it with two or three other sources to make sure it is correct.

14 Make sure all your information is well researched and substantiated.

Do not rely on your memory for facts – always take notes

When you do research, use as many resources as you can – such as source books or magazines, CD-ROMs, and the internet

▲ SORTING THE FACTS
When you have completed your research, sort the information that you have collected into three categories: essential, important, and miscellaneous.

15 Only start writing when you know what you want to say.

ALLOWING FOR RESEARCH TIME

When you are researching, set yourself a time limit as it is easy to spend far longer than you intended. You can easily waste time on the internet, for example, if you are directed to sites that end up being of little use for your needs. Always aim for the most relevant information. Find out in advance from colleagues the best sites to use, or be very specific with the key words you use with your favourite search engine.

PROVIDING THE RIGHT AMOUNT OF INFORMATION

Only give your readers the amount of information that is needed to make a decision or take action. Writers with a traditional science background can write very precisely, while those in the arts tend to have a more fluid style. However, you need to establish a style that is concise in its approach, but also allows for more descriptive paragraphs where a subject needs more elaboration or explanation. If, for example, you try to reduce a report from 15 pages to three, it inevitably means that some vital information will be left out. Cutting out too much information can make the text very bland to read, so that there is not enough descriptive language or clarification of the essential facts. Conversely, sending a long report, written in a convoluted style, will soon lose the interest of the recipients.

16 Make sure that your research is focused.

17 Tailor reports to suit what you know about the recipients.

QUESTIONS TO ASK YOURSELF

Q What does the reader need to know?

Q Why does the reader need this information?

Q What background knowledge does the reader already have?

Q What is the text going to be used for?

Q Who is the intended reader of the text?

Q Are the language and the vocabulary used suitable for the intended reader?

Q Has all the necessary information been included?

PLANNING AND STRUCTURING

When we read something that is written well, it is easy to see its plan and structure. The facts that you are presenting in your text need to be backed up with research material showing how you came to these conclusions, or how you arrived at those statistics. It is also needed to lend substance and credibility to the text that you are presenting. Always make sure that the source of your information is up to date. The financial position of companies or their share price, for example, constantly changes.

Producing good text takes a lot of work, but provided that you have planned well, and put the basic framework into place, you will find that the task is well within your capabilities.

DEFINING YOUR STYLE

If your letter or report is poorly constructed, ambiguously worded, and has grammatical errors, the impression you give of yourself and your skills is not very positive. You need to work on improving your writing style to present an upbeat image.

18 Good writing helps form a relationship between the writer and the reader.

19 Poor writing projects a negative image of both writer and company.

DEVELOPING A CLEAR STYLE

Generally, poor writers have problems developing a clear and concise style. Often their writing technique is old-fashioned and stilted, and the construction of their communications is badly thought out. Poor writers often fall down in their choice of language, using overly formal or technical jargon, or conversely, using language that is too familiar, colloquial, or "slangy". Sentence construction is also a problem, usually because too many words are used when fewer would make the sentence more succinct. Another common problem is using words inappropriately.

► **AVOIDING BAD WRITING HABITS**
There are a number of common communication faults, which usually encompass several, if not all, of the stylistic errors described here.

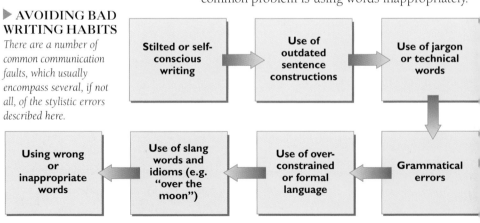

Stilted or self-conscious writing → Use of outdated sentence constructions → Use of jargon or technical words → Grammatical errors → Use of over-constrained or formal language → Use of slang words and idioms (e.g. "over the moon") → Using wrong or inappropriate words

WRITING GOOD TEXT

Poorly written work documents are usually the result of being produced in a hurry without too much thought for the content. As you write, ask yourself:

- Who is this letter written for?
- What is its aim?
- What does the reader need to know?
- Why does the reader need this information?
- What does the reader already know about this subject?

20 Before you start writing, define your target reader and your objectives.

▶ SHOWING COURTESY AND RESPECT

This is an example of a poorly written letter that does not even detail the student's full name. The content is confusing, not giving a clear explanation of why the letter is being written.

Using a student number, rather than name, causes offence

Pay the person you are writing to the compliment of addressing them by name

The actual letter does not contain enough information for the reader

The writer signs with initials so there is no contact name

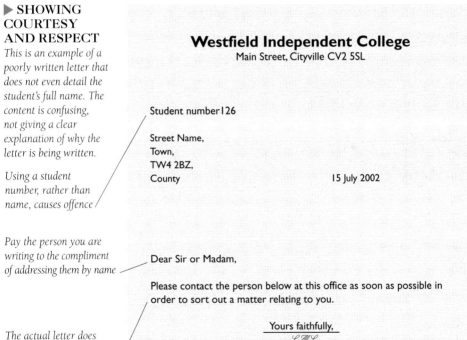

Westfield Independent College
Main Street, Cityville CV2 5SL

Student number 126

Street Name,
Town,
TW4 2BZ,
County 15 July 2002

Dear Sir or Madam,

Please contact the person below at this office as soon as possible in order to sort out a matter relating to you.

Yours faithfully,
LML

Secretary

SOUNDING VERBOSE

Some people write in such a way that it becomes apparent to the reader that they are only interested in telling you what they know. This is conveyed in the text by the addition of obscure or redundant information. Rather than engage with the reader, know-it-all writers try to project their own knowledge, effort, and competence. The end result is writing that is verbose and full of irrelevant information that just serves to irritate or annoy the people who are receiving the communication.

RIGHT	WRONG
BUYING IN/ CONTRACTING SERVICES	BUYING IN/ CONTRACTING SERVICES
These procedures conform to legislative requirements.	We have analyzed these items exhaustively and found, at the end of our investigations, that the procedures adopted with regard to the buying in or contracting of services are in line with current legislative requirements.

▲ **GETTING TO THE POINT**
The first text gets straight to the point. The second takes an unnecessarily circuitous route to say the same thing.

CORRECT AND INCORRECT

✔ The aim is to…

✔ I can inform you…

✔ I can let you know that…

✔ I am submitting for your approval…

✔ A decision is requested…

✔ Thank you for assisting…

✘ The desired end is to…

✘ We are in the proud position to inform you…

✘ We are taking the opportunity of letting you know that…

✘ We would like to submit for your approval…

✘ We would like to hereby…

✘ We are truly grateful for…

USING CLICHÉD LANGUAGE

Deferential writers know their place within their organization's hierarchy. They use language that is predictable, sounds false and verbose, and reflects their preoccupation with hierarchical levels. Such writers also tend to write in well-worn clichés. They may overuse phrases such as, "I will leave this to your better judgment". They have a tendency to use "we" often, which relieves them of the responsibility for their writing, and also indicates a lack of decision-making skills.

SOUNDING INSINCERE

Writers who use jargon extensively are a variation on the know-it-all writer. Jargon-lovers want to convey an image of being up-to-date with the latest business ideas supposedly from top personal development people. Some writers use and repeat sentences and phrases littered with "buzzwords" in the hope that it gives the impression that they are at the cutting edge of what is going on in their particular industry. These unusual, newly-created words and jargon are mostly incomprehensible to a wider audience. This writing style is consciously designed to impress and is quite commonly used where there is competition between individuals within a company. However, to the reader it often sounds insincere and reeks of self-promotion.

21 Resist using "buzzwords" as they weaken communication.

22 Some words have several meanings or nuances. Try to avoid ambiguity.

| Using new words not yet to be found in the dictionary | Using jargon to sell an idea | Creates text that is designed to impress rather than inform | The result is a writing style that is insincere and self-promoting |

▲ PROMOTING SELF IMPORTANCE
Writing that tries to project an up-to-the-minute feel through the use of new words can make it harder for some readers to understand the writer's meaning.

SPOTTING THE PITFALLS

There are several phrases that can irritate rather than impress the reader, so avoid using any of the following where you:

- "Attain ceilings".
- "Step up processes".
- "Engage" with others rather than "talk to" or "work with" them.
- Have marketing activities that "impact on" business instead of "have an impact on it".
- "Develop proactive outlooks".
- "Optimize results".
- "Arrive at decisions".
- "Prioritize spaces".
- "Find solutions on a countrywide scale".
- Are "proactive".

WRITING IN A FAKE STYLE

Some people will be impressed with elaborate text, and may even consider it to be creative. However, the more discerning reader will recognize it as fake. Generally speaking, avoid writing embellished texts that bring in certain ethical values and create emphatic views, which can lead to copy full of unsubstantiated statements. Usually this style is adapted to any type of writing, without showing where or how the "supposed" facts originated. So it is a way for the writer who lacks knowledge or ability to hide his personal failings.

The Importance of Thermonuclear Energy

A subject that is talked about very widely nowadays, not only here but also abroad, is the inestimable source of energy provided by thermonuclear power.

Thermonuclear energy is of fundamental importance to modern societies. Without it, humanity would not have experienced the developments that it has made over the last few decades.

This kind of energy, much used in the industrialized world, offers a giant step for mankind towards a peaceful 21st century, with harmony and union between different nations.

In our industrialized and globalized world, the absence of this wonderful source of energy would have led to an impasse with few alternatives for a harmonious relationship between human beings and mother nature – or maybe even survival. We should, therefore, be aware of this gift provided by the genius of man, an everlasting source, which should be used economically or we may run the risk of returning to being simply "king of the beasts".

▲ **SOUNDING SELF-IMPORTANT**
Writing styles that sustain the author's unquestioned views, rather than a sound perspective, are found frequently in business reports.

▶ **QUESTIONING VALUES**
As a writer, do not lose your credibility by adopting emphatic views to show you lack knowledge and information on a subject.

Look through your writing and correct any elaborate or unnecessary phrases

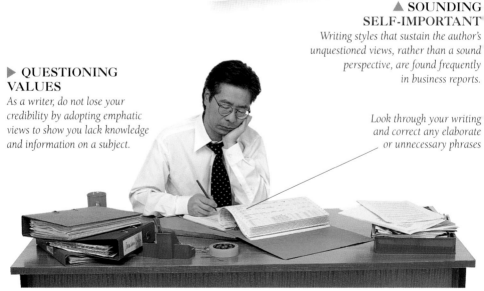

23 Be aware of your reader's level of expertise and write with that in mind.

24 Simplicity always impresses more than "trying to impress" text.

USING CONFUSING LANGUAGE

Technical language exists to aid communication between those who work in the same field of expertise. When writing in specialized areas avoid causing confusion, which sometimes happens when a writer uses language that is incomprehensible to most, including those in the same discipline.

The letter below does not communicate its message, other than conveying the "cleverness" of the author. Sentences are convoluted, and aim to show off the writer's education and knowledge of Latin. The author confuses the reader and it is not clear that he disagrees with a decision made by the people to whom he is writing.

◀ **GIVING INFORMATION**
The writer of this quirky style does not communicate well. The writer is more interested in demonstrating his or her own education than in objectively conveying facts.

Distinguished Sirs,

Although keen to express my warmest felicitations and acknowledge the deep honour your request bestows upon me, I feel that the reasoning behind your policy decision, which is enough to make wise men quick to cry out like the furies of ancient times, angers me beyond belief.

Your decision occasions the *onus probandi* to lie firmly on my shoulders, yet in these parlous times, those beings of limited ability are inseparable from those with superior knowledge, many of the latter residing so near to Mt. Olympus as to be unreachable.

For these reasons I regret that I am forced into declining your most felicitous invitation.

Your most honoured servant,

Evidence that the writer is trying to show off a knowledge of Latin in the text

This text may only irritate the reader

UNDERSTANDING THE BASICS

Once you know the basic techniques, you have the tools to write well. It is worthwhile spending time building a wide vocabulary and developing a flowing style with good sentence construction.

TAKING THE FIRST STEPS

Writing in a good style comes from three main activities: reading, writing, and rewriting. Reading provides you with the background vocabulary for writing; writing itself develops your style; rewriting helps refine your technique.

25 Reading different materials helps you write creatively.

26 As you gain more knowledge, your writing style will benefit.

READING WIDELY

When you read extensively you can discover useful information, develop your vocabulary, and learn about different writing styles. Reading newspapers, magazines, and a variety of books helps you gain as much information as possible. Absorbing different writing styles will enrich your own vocabulary, show you how different people write, and deepen your knowledge of many subject areas. By becoming well-read, you will feel more confident in how you write, and be better able to relate information and express your opinions in an informed manner.

IMPROVING YOUR WRITING

Writing should not be seen as a chore. With advance planning and careful thought, letters, memos, reports, and proposals can be produced to a high standard. Before starting, think about what you are trying to achieve: letters need to be polite because they represent the good image of the company, reports summarise many hours of research, interviews, and data collection, while proposals show the final presentation of a developing idea. Draft out the information you wish to convey, leave it for a while, then read it aloud to yourself to see how it sounds. Look for any awkward phrasing, bad sentence construction, or colloquialisms that may be inappropriate.

27 Always look critically at everything you write.

28 Find out how other professionals write in your subject area.

Manager and employee discuss informally how the department report should look

ACCEPTING ADVICE

When writing, think carefully about your attitude to your written work. Remember that whenever you write something, someone else may want to change it. If you show a draft report to your boss, for example, do not think it is a reflection on your abilities or intelligence if he or she suggests making several changes or additions. Instead, try to look at the comments in a constructive way, seeing how they are improving or enhancing the structure or content of your text. Often people who have more distance can give a better judgment and more objective assessment of what you have written.

◀ **TAKING ON CRITICISM**
After you have written something, be prepared to discuss it frankly and receive comments or changes from your manager or an office colleague.

COMPOSING GOOD SENTENCES

The sentence is the central part of any piece of writing, and needs to contain a subject, verb, and an object. Think about the correct vocabulary for the subject you are writing about, and beware of making grammatical mistakes.

29 Structure sentences well, so that the reader does not lose interest.

30 Avoid using empty phrases or including any superfluous information that sounds imprecise.

WRITING CONCISELY

When writing you will often find that using one word is more effective than using two or three together. Always write concisely, concentrating on the essential information you want to impart. Flowery or superfluous language will only irritate the reader or detract from the main points you are trying to make. The letter, report, or other document that you are sending will then take less time to read, which the reader will appreciate.

CONSTRUCTING CONCISE SENTENCES

AVOID	USE
During the year 2002	In 2002
Fines were applied in line with the relevant regulations	The regulatory fines were applied
We wish to make the most of this opportunity to inform you...	We would like to tell you...
We would like to request that you proceed to collect the debts...	Please collect the debts now...

USING THE RIGHT WORD

Finding the right word for what you want to convey needs a wide vocabulary and an awareness of the possible connotations in language. If in doubt check your dictionary. Here are a few pitfalls from using the wrong choice of words:

- Words that have several meanings just make the reader laugh. For example, "The cook gently laid the eggs in the fridge." Chickens lay eggs, but people "place" eggs in the fridge.
- When words are used out of context it can cause confusion. For example, "The fireman committed an act of bravery." People commit robberies, but "perform" acts of bravery.
- Words that are not used correctly can cause confusion. For example, "The accusations will be received by Procon." Accusations in this context are "heard", not received.
- Avoid unintentional puns. For example, "Dracula knew there was a lot at stake over what happened next."

QUESTIONS TO ASK YOURSELF

Q Is the word used known to everyone, or is it a strictly technical term?

Q Even though it is in the dictionary, is this word commonly used?

Q Is the chosen word the best one to use in this particular context?

Q Does the word help inform the reader, or are you using it to show off your vocabulary?

Q Are any foreign terms used appropriate in the context, and will they be readily understood by the reader?

31 Check the meaning of words and your vocabulary will improve.

32 Avoid contextual mistakes or people may laugh at you, not with you.

AVOIDING REPETITION

Try not to write in a repetitious way or use tautology. As well as padding out the text unnecessarily, these stylistic mistakes will only make the reader laugh. Look at the following examples (redundant words are in heavy type):

- It is necessary to start **the initialization** of the project.
- We want to keep the **same** payment conditions.
- The **highly** unique award was given to an employee in accounts.
- It was **an unexpected** surprise to receive an invitation to the opening of the **new** shop.
- Full-time dedication to the project is expected **at all times**.

USING DIFFERENT VOICES

There are different kinds of language that you can use in day-to-day business. These include: the "active voice", which can make your communications more effective, and the "passive voice", if you want to sound polite or avoid sounding aggressive.

33 Writing in the passive voice generates a less aggressive approach.

34 Short sentences are useful for conveying certain information.

BEING ACTIVE

Sentences in the active voice are shorter and livelier. In this type of sentence, the subject does something, for example, "The department requests the information". With sentences in the passive tense something happens to the subject, for example, "Information was requested by the department". However, using the passive voice too much can make text seem flabby and flat. When referring to your company, or to those who work for it, the active voice conveys real assertiveness and a direct style.

CORRECT AND INCORRECT

✔ Zedcom is building new laboratories.

✔ Zedcom is launching three new promotions in April.

✔ Zedcom is developing a social assistance programme for those on a low income.

✗ New laboratories are being built by Zedcom.

✗ Three new promotions are being launched by Zedcom in April.

✗ Social assistance programmes are being developed by Zedcom for those on a low income.

35 The active voice is best if you want to be assertive or inspirational.

BEING DIPLOMATIC

Although the active voice is normally recommended for most communications, there are times when a more diplomatic, passive style is preferred, so that the negative impact of certain information is reduced. There are occasions when you may need to deal with an ongoing conflict, for example, turn down an exployee for promotion, point out mistakes, or reprimand a member of staff, and a friendly but firm writing style is preferred. The secret is knowing how to pass on the necessary information in a way that will not cause upset between employees or other departments in the company. Using the passive voice on these occasions can make the information you are sending seem less abrupt or aggressive, softening the impact of what you are obliged to say.

36 Saying "no" to someone sounds better in the passive voice.

37 To adopt a diplomatic writing style, imagine the person is standing in front of you.

EMPLOYING THE PASSIVE VOICE

ABRUPT TONE	LESS AGGRESSIVE TONE
The clinic cannot tell you your result because you have not paid last month's bill.	Your result cannot be provided as there is a payment outstanding.
This is the estimate for the repairs to the window that your son broke last Thursday.	Here is the estimate for the repairs to the window that was broken last Thursday.
We are going to dismiss three workers tomorrow.	Three workers are going to be dismissed tomorrow.
The auditor handling the inspection noticed fraudulent activity in the company accounts.	Fraudulent activity has been noted in the company accounts by the auditor.

CHOOSING WORDS FOR EMPHASIS

When you are writing to clients or colleagues, you need to make it clear what you want them to do. Indicate whether the task is essential or if there is some choice involved. The verbs "may/can", "must", and "should" are recognized as being the most suitable for expressing what you require of the person to whom you are writing.

38 When giving instructions, always avoid ambiguous terms.

▼ IN PRACTICE

The examples below show how you can express your requirements with the right emphasis.

KNOW WHEN TO USE "MUST", "MAY/CAN", AND "SHOULD"

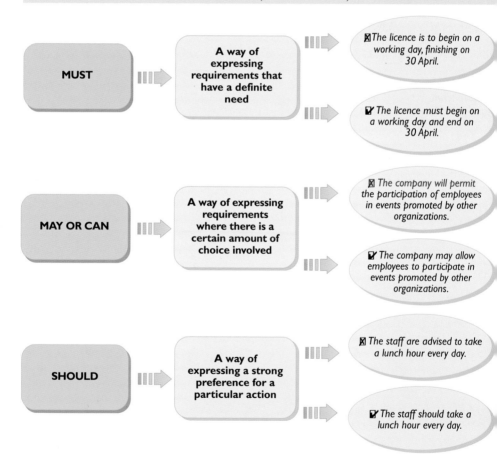

MUST → A way of expressing requirements that have a definite need →

☒ The licence is to begin on a working day, finishing on 30 April.

☑ The licence must begin on a working day and end on 30 April.

MAY OR CAN → A way of expressing requirements where there is a certain amount of choice involved →

☒ The company will permit the participation of employees in events promoted by other organizations.

☑ The company may allow employees to participate in events promoted by other organizations.

SHOULD → A way of expressing a strong preference for a particular action →

☒ The staff are advised to take a lunch hour every day.

☑ The staff should take a lunch hour every day.

USING PLAIN ENGLISH

Many people overcomplicate their writing in the belief that the reader will be impressed by unusual words or complex language. However, plain language is easier to follow and will keep the reader's interest. Remember that you are writing to communicate, so a good rule is to try to write as you speak. Aim to avoid overly formal language or officialese. Archaic language and very complex sentences are confusing and mostly redundant. Use concise phrases that get straight to the point.

39 Be accurate. Use nouns rather than several pronouns.

AVOIDING AMBIGUITY

AMBIGUOUS SENTENCE	SPECIFIC SENTENCE
Before leaving, check that the lift has stopped at the right floor.	Before leaving the lift, check that it has stopped at the right floor.
Attention, passengers for Flight 168! We would like to inform you that when boarding is announced, it will be through gate nine.	Attention, passengers! Boarding for Flight 168 will be through gate nine. Listen for the announcement.
During the assault, the thieves used knives and two guns. They were later found in the river.	During the assault, the thieves used knives and two guns. The weapons were later found in the river.
There were a lot of visitors to the Olympic Games. To put them up, the hotel network had to be expanded.	To accommodate the high number of visitors to the Olympic Games, the hotel network had to be expanded.
The film contains sex, bad language, and violence, which is unsuitable for children.	The film contains sex, bad language, and violence. It is unsuitable for children.

KNOWING THE RULES

A *sound knowledge of grammar will lend credibility to your writing, although it will not necessarily improve your style. Do not allow yourself to become preoccupied with different points of grammar, as it is important to maintain your creative flow.*

40 Use a dictionary and check your grammar when rewriting.

41 Write freely at first, but reread and correct later.

WRITING FREELY

You should not worry too much about the grammar you are using when you are in the act of writing. If you hesitate for too long over the right tense to use, where to put apostrophes, or whether it is a single or plural noun you will never write anything. Write a first draft of what you want to say and then appraise it later, correcting any obvious mistakes that you have made.

PROJECTING AN IMAGE

If you do send out communications that contain grammatical errors, it can compromise not only the quality of the information being presented, but it will also reflect on your professional image. Spelling mistakes can occur because of laziness, careless writing, or simply lack of knowledge. If you know that you have a problem with spelling or sentence construction, check what you have written carefully. Also consider getting a colleague, who you think has a good grasp of grammar, to look over what you have done and make useful comments.

Nick Eccles
Lawyer

Foster and Harding Co. Ltd.,
Civil, Crimnal, and Family Law
11 Street Square, Ardean, Perthshire
Telephone: 02131 333 5455

▲ **CREATING A GOOD IMPRESSION**
Making a spelling error on your business card does not promote a positive or professional image to potential clients.

110

MAKING USE OF OTHER RESOURCES

When you are writing, make use of all the information resources available on the Internet. You can use different search engines to source directories or other research material for the subject on which you are writing. Many successful writers create their own thesaurus of different words to use, and you may find this works for you. This can be particularly useful if you have to write or report regularly on the same subject. You can add in interesting quotations, extracts, or maybe cartoons, if these are appropriate.

USING A DICTIONARY REGULARLY

If you need to use a dictionary regularly to check your spelling or to look up the actual meaning of a word, you should not feel embarrassed. In fact, it reflects well on you as it shows that you are concerned about the standard of your writing and want to present it to the people concerned in the best possible way.

42 Knowing basic grammar rules is just the start of writing well.

43 Correct spelling is essential for credible communications.

44 Explore the dictionary widely to improve your vocabulary.

USING REFERENCE BOOKS

When you write regularly, it is a good idea to have several reference books to hand to check your content. Generally, an extensive dictionary and a book on grammar usage are the most useful. Look in bookshops and libraries for the best ones available, and ask which ones are preferred by editors and writers. If you are writing about specific subjects, you might also think about getting some encyclopedias and other reference guides that will help you find other information.

USING CORRECT GRAMMAR

Clear and grammatical writing is mainly a matter of common sense. If you can read and understand this book, then you are already familiar with basic grammar and how it helps to get your message across clearly and concisely. Start by forgetting about grammar. Just relax and write as if you were talking to another person and trying to explain something. You can then rewrite your text and correct the spelling and syntax as you edit. Syntax just means the grammatical structure of the sentence that gives it precision and meaning.

45 Keep your use of foreign words and phrases to a minimum.

46 Cut down on slang, jargon, clichés, and "buzzwords".

PARTS OF SPEECH

- ADJECTIVES are words that describe a noun or a pronoun.
- ADVERBS are words or phrases qualifying verbs, adjectives, sentences or clauses.
- NOUNS name or identify a thing or a person.
- PREPOSITIONS show the relation of one word to another, e.g. position, direction, and time.
- PRONOUNS take the place of a noun or a word group. There are five types: personal (I, you, he, we), relative (that, what, which, whose), interrogative (who, which, what), demonstrative (that, this, those), indefinite (both, each, many, one, other).
- VERBS express action or a state of being.

IMPROVING YOUR TEXT

It is a good idea to read what you have written out loud afterwards. Good writing has a rhythm just like music. You will know if your style is good if it flows together and does not sound awkward. If any part of your text sounds unintelligible, unnecessarily formal, pretentous, or is difficult to read without catching your breath (which means that your sentences are too long!), you will need to change it. Try breaking up the longer sentences into two or three shorter ones, each conveying a key point. To help you brush up on your basic grammar and give yourself confidence, look at the tips on grammar and usage in the tables opposite. Read as much good writing as you can from books, newspapers, magazines, and published reports. The more you read, the more you will subconsciously learn about good grammar, vocabulary, and style. Remember, English is a living, breathing language, so you are bound to use many everyday words to get your message across.

AVOIDING TYPICAL ERRORS

COMMON ERRORS	CORRECTED ERRORS
ADJECTIVES	
...the **principle** reason for...	...the **principal** reason for...
...the recently **floating** company...	...the recently **floated** company...
Managers' incompetence means that...	**Managerial** incompetence means that...
SUPERLATIVES	
His results were **worst** than hers.	His results were **worse** than hers.
My leg hurts **bad.**	My leg hurts **badly.**
...a **sound,** written constitution...	...a **soundly** written constitution...
CAPITALIZATION	
If you look in the **Preface**...	If you look in the **preface**...
The **Queen** of England...	The **queen** of England...
The **chairman of the board** announced...	The **Chairman of the Board** announced...
CONJUNCTIONS	
The next picture **that** is shown here...	The next picture, **which** is shown here...
Neither the book **or** the pen were found.	Neither the book **nor** the pen were found.
Insomnia is **because** you cannot sleep.	Insomnia is **when** you cannot sleep.
NOUNS	
He was treated by a **councillor**.	He was treated by a **counsellor**.
...the **smile** on the **face** of the staff...	...the **smiles** on the **faces** of the staff...
The **seller** was very helpful.	The **salesperson** was very helpful.
PREPOSITIONS	
My term of office is **for** six months.	My term of office is six months.
...my interest and concern for the staff...	...my interest **in** and concern for the staff...
...diplomacy **among** EU members...	...diplomacy **between** EU members...
PRONOUNS	
I do not know **whom** is stealing from **who**.	I do not know **who** is stealing from **whom**.
I solved the problem **with** my PC.	I solved the problem **on** my PC.
Between you and **I**, the office is a mess!	Between you and **me**, the office is a mess!
PUNCTUATION	
So to conclude; **We** must work harder!	So to conclude: **we** must work harder!
For more details see Chapter 10.	For more details, see Chapter 10.
The firm held **it's** AGM on...	The firm held **its** AGM on...
VERBS	
...bad weather **effected** deliveries...	...bad weather **affected** deliveries...
...the manager and his staff **is** coming...	...the manager and his staff **are** coming...
I looked to see if he **were** there...	I looked to see if he **was** there...

113

PRESENTING YOUR WORK

G enerally, anything that is produced *without effort must be read with great effort. It's not enough to simply write well. Knowing a little about fonts, colours, and layout can help you produce printed materials that are more interesting and attractive for the reader.*

47 Try not to use too many different typefaces as it will confuse the reader.

USING FONTS TO MAKE AN IMPACT

FONTS	EXAMPLES
SERIF FONTS Serif lines are little lines that finish off strokes of individual letters and lead the eye across the line. These fonts are usually used in the body of a text.	This report must be sent out to all our customers as soon as possible.
FONTS WITHOUT SERIFS (SANS SERIFS) These are modern-looking fonts. Using uppercase and bold, a title with impact can be created. They are often used in headings, margins, posters, and so on.	**HOW TO WRITE CLEARLY**
SUBHEADS WITHOUT SERIFS Subheads within a text that use a font without a serif are used to provide a distinctive contrast.	**Technical-Scientific Report** A document that formally details the results or developments obtained through in-depth investigations, or that describes the current thinking on a technical or scientific question.

CHOOSING THE RIGHT FONT

Do you want to write a text that grabs the reader's attention or one that is elegant and serious? You can create the impression you want by choosing an appropriate type style, or font. All modern word-processing packages are set up so that you can produce texts that are visually attractive, using a wide choice of different fonts. Remember to keep it simple. In general, the best ideas are those that make the reader stop and think for a second, with a little envy, "Why didn't I think of that?"

48 Write the text first, then think about how you want it to look.

FONTS	EXAMPLES
SCRIPT FONTS These fonts produce letters that look handwritten but are old-fashioned. They are ideal for personalized texts such as letterheads and invitations. If used as an opening to a business proposal, they can lend a touch of elegance.	*These fonts produce letters that look handwritten. They are ideal for personalized texts such as letterheads and invitations.*
UNUSUAL FONTS You can vary the look of your text by using unusual fonts that will grab the reader's attention. But be careful: overuse of this method may make the text appear less serious. When sending faxes, avoid elaborate fonts and background colours.	PERSPECTIVES FOR UNDERSTANDING ORGANIZATIONS
THINK ABOUT THE SIZE OF THE FONTS YOU USE Between 10 and 12 points is usual, although this varies for headers, posters, and so on.	8 points 10 points 12 points 14 points

49 Choose colours that suit the content of your text and your reader.

50 Use colours subtly so that you do not turn your text into a gaudy, showy document.

DISTRACTING THE READER ▶

Reproduce titles and figures in their simplest font. If you italicize them, take them out of focus, or place them over text, you will destroy them. Make sure that whatever image or figure you use attracts the reader's attention to the text, not away from it.

ADDING IMAGES

Using photos, drawings, and figures adds life to a text and can make it easier to understand. However, if you use too many, you will do the opposite and confuse and distract the reader. If you are using colour, apply it consistently. Applying different colours to headings within a single text is more appropriate for text aimed at children than adults.

WRONG

RIGHT

SPACING AND TYPE

When leaflets or reports have a long heading, make the text bold to stand out, and also try increasing the spacing between words as this can make it easier to read. The body text should be in a clear, easy-to-read type, centred under the heading to give it more prominence.

THE TOURIST ENTERTAINMENT ROUTE —— *Expanded heading in a bold type*

A route of bars, beaches, discotheques, and restaurants to help —— *Clear typeface with copy centred under heading* you enjoy yourself in ten capitals.

51 Visual aids help grab the reader's attention.

ILLUSTRATING YOUR TEXT

Charts and tables are of considerable value when explaining certain concepts, statistics, or demonstrating facts. Often, large amounts of plain text are not as good as illustrated text because the reader becomes confused or bored when they are inundated with so much solid information. Charts and tables allow the reader to understand the whole concept being discussed, and show visual examples of different points.

▼ IMPORTING CHARTS
There are a number of pre-programmed charts available on most computers. The most common are pie and bar charts.

Columns or bars show the percentage of respondents

Each "portion" of the pie represents a percentage

PIE CHART

BAR CHART

MAKING USE OF LABELS

Get the most out of any images you have included by adding labels or captions that add emphasis to what is being shown visually. Write these descriptions carefully so that they add to the visual impact of the illustration. Bear in mind that you are trying to arouse the reader's interest in the topic, so write points that are punchy, and that add interesting facts.

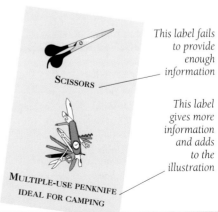

This label fails to provide enough information

SCISSORS

This label gives more information and adds to the illustration

MULTIPLE-USE PENKNIFE IDEAL FOR CAMPING

WRITING POSITIVELY

*P*roducing text that emphasizes the positive aspects of the information you are generating will make a stronger impression on your recipients. Also, be careful to write in a way that avoids any form of discrimination.

52 Good writers always present the positives, rather than the negatives.

53 Always ensure that you write in a non-discriminatory way.

BEING SUBTLE

A text which has a positive rather than negative emphasis will always be better received. Instead of writing, "Do not forget", write, "Remember". Rather than writing, "The container should not be boarded with the cooling equipment", write, "The container should be boarded without the cooling equipment".

As well as being negative, this communication confuses the reader

TAKING THE RIGHT ▶ APPROACH
The emphasis of this letter is quite negative, reflecting badly on the institute. The fact that a grant has been awarded, albeit for the following year, is only detailed in the last paragraph. By saying initially: "Your request for a grant has received approval...", the reader will feel positive, despite discovering later on in the letter that the date of approval is in fact later than originally requested.

CETED/PG
Street Name
Big City

Today's date

Ms. J Hartley
Street Name
Big City

Dear Ms. Hartley,

Re: Your application for an overseas study grant

Unfortunately, following a decision made by this foundation, all grant requests for overseas study not received by the date stated have been rejected. This decision relates to recent changes in government grants to this institution.

However, the budget for next year has been set, and your grant will be awarded early next year.

Yours sincerely,

Steven Milner

AVOIDING DISCRIMINATION

Be careful about adopting a discriminatory style when writing as it can:

- Render people invisible.
- Highlight physical or intellectual limitations rather than other positive personal characteristics.
- Describe people in stereotypical terms.
- Be insensitive to people's social position and needs, or be too focused on those aspects.
- Use terms that are considered negative, or are thought to be derogatory to certain groups of people.

CORRECT AND INCORRECT

✔ Black	✘ Coloured
✔ Low-income families	✘ Poor families
✔ Special needs	✘ Retarded
✔ Sensory impaired	✘ Deaf or blind
✔ Partner	✘ Boyfriend/girlfriend

Key

❶ *By not detailing who was involved, the majority of employees are discriminated against in this chairman's memo, even though they are not involved and probably should not be receiving it.*

❷ *This implies that Ms. Smith's disability makes her less competent than her able-bodied colleagues, even though she has broken the sales record.*

❸ *This is implicit discrimination, since it brings attention to Mr Brown's lack of qualifications. The wording makes an unnecessary comparison with those associates who have degrees.*

❹ *It is the wife's position as the co-ordinator that is relevant, not her husband's job, or her beauty.*

❺ *Mentioning skin colour is irrelevant and can be construed by many as discriminatory or racist.*

❶
We have been informed that two employees have been misappropriating company office materials.

❷
Our winner is Ms. Smith, who despite being a wheelchair user, managed to break the sales record in August. Well done, Ms Smith!

❸
We would like to congratulate Mr. Brown, who, despite not having a university degree, has been promoted to a managerial position.

❹
The Chief Engineer's beautiful wife was asked to speak in her role as co-ordinator of the SAC.

❺
Five people, one of them black, have been recruited to the department.

 USING DISCRIMINATORY LANGUAGE
These examples show five main types of language use which should be avoided at all costs.

COMMUNICATING WITH THE READER

When there is a tight deadline, the temptation is to write hurriedly, paying little attention to the way you express yourself. But this can often send a confusing or wrong message to the reader, so take time to write well and communicate clearly.

54 Your writing style should not upset the reader or lose their attention.

55 Have a final read of your text before you send it.

COMMUNICATING WELL

If a company is to have a friendly working environment, the communication channels, both spoken and written, between colleagues need to be amiable and efficient. When tense situations arise, this informal atmosphere can help when trying to resolve major problems or deadlocks. The same principles can be applied to existing clients and suppliers.

CASE STUDY

It was Andrea's birthday and she received a beautiful bouquet of flowers from her boss. The next day, she sent him a thank-you card, worded as follows:

Dear Robert,
Many thanks for my birthday flowers. I was really surprised at your kindness – it made me very happy.
Andrea

Andrea was a typical writer in a hurry and did not re-read what she had written. The text had an underlining meaning that Robert is normally rude and offensive, which is why she was surprised. If she had opted for "I was delighted" or "Your kindness was so thoughtful", she would have maintained the cordiality that needs to exist in all day-to-day situations.

◀ **WRITING IN HASTE**
In this example, Andrea did not take enough care when writing to thank her boss for the flowers. Andrea should have reread the text, noticed the unpleasant undertone, and then changed the style of the note so that it expressed her feelings more sincerely.

FINDING THE RIGHT TONE

In spoken language, what we say can often be softened and modified. You can say that you were misunderstood, that you did not say something, or that you were misheard. But everything we write down can sound stark and formal. Because of this, follow these simple rules:

- Avoid terse or impersonal phrases, as your reader will take offence.
- Present bad news in an objective manner. There is always a better way to say something.
- Do not think you are infallible; apologizing can be a good way forward in business.

LETTER OF COMPLAINT

INDIFFERENCE TO THE CUSTOMER

Dear Ms. Smith,

We have many customers using our internet service and inevitably some problems are experienced with our server from time to time. There has been no record of increased problems in your area, and other customers are able to access our helpline easily.

However, we have made a note of your complaint.

Yours sincerely,

J. Henry

PGF Customer Service

Dear PGF,

I am writing to complain about the internet service I am receiving in the Liverpool area. I often cannot get online because of server disruption, and when I call the customer helpline for an explanation it is always engaged.

I am totally frustrated and am considering changing providers. Can [...] st any positive changes you [...] g to improve the service and [...] ustom?

Yours sincerely,

Jane Smith

CONCERN FOR THE CUSTOMER

Dear Ms. Smith,

I am sorry for all the disruption you have been experiencing with our server. We aim to give the best service to our customers, and have started work on improving access and making the server more reliable.

We will contact you again in a few days, explaining the improvements we are making to our present system.

I do apologize once again.

Yours sincerely,

J. Henry

PGF Customer Service Department

Dear Mr. McManus,

Re: Account no: 12767899

I am sorry we cannot grant your request for a loan this month, but it will be reviewed in a few weeks' time.

I regret this inconvenience, but I am sure we will be able to accommodate your needs shortly.

Yours sincerely

D. O'Faolain

Bank Manager

▲ BEING PLEASANT

In this letter the loan has been refused, but only temporarily. In the tone of the letter the bank manager treats his client in a considerate manner.

▲ BEING UNHELPFUL

The tone of the first letter indicates that the Internet company is not interested in their customer's problem and does not offer any useful solutions. The second letter is more positive and addresses the problem immediately, offering to give further information on how they will improve their system.

STRUCTURING YOUR WRITING

Having learned the skills and techniques for writing readable text, you need to understand how to structure your work, and how to establish an efficient way of working.

ESTABLISHING PROCEDURES

There is no single way of getting your message across. Everyone has an individual method. However, there are a number of steps in the writing process through which every text needs to pass.

56 Ensure your text flows from section to section.

57 Think of your topic, then plan how to get the idea across.

58 Compose your text as a musician might write a piece of music.

PLANNING YOUR WORK

It is vital that your text makes sense from start to finish. So, before you begin to write, plan exactly how you are going to convey the various aspects of the topic in a straightforward way. Whether your text is a one-page memorandum or an extensive report, you will need a beginning, a middle, and an end. All your paragraphs need to flow from one to the other to create a whole. After an introductory paragraph, the second paragraph should flow onto the next, and so on, until a logical and effective conclusion is reached.

59 Connecting all of its parts logically will ensure your text makes sense.

ORGANIZING THE TEXT

For the text to work well, it must include:

- An introduction. This should outline the subject and clarify the aim of the text.
- Development. This longer section should set out new information and discuss, prove, compare, contradict, and justify the source of the information presented.
- Conclusion. This section will bring together and summarize the relevant points, reaffirming new information, and should also include the author's personal conclusions.

CONDUCTING RESEARCH

You must have in-depth knowledge of the subject you are going to write about. You will need to have relevant information to hand. To do this, gather together and organize your data. This task has been made easier by the internet, which can make massive amounts of knowledge and information accessible to all. Once you have finished your research, organize your results either as computer files or as documents in a filing cabinet.

Create computer files and make back-up copies of the most important documents

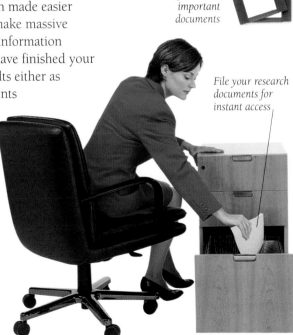

File your research documents for instant access

**STORING ▶
INFORMATION**
Set up a suitable filing system and ensure that it is efficient. The definitive test is always being able to find what you want quickly.

123

PRODUCING AN OUTLINE

Always prepare an outline of your text by listing all the ideas and information that you feel will be relevant to the document you are writing. At this stage, do not worry about the order in which you jot down your ideas. Just write everything down that comes into your head. When you have finished the list, read what you have written with a more critical eye and begin to eliminate irrelevant ideas, details, and questions. Use this method to get rid of everything that will be superfluous to the reader. Finally, you need to combine the ideas and information that you have decided to keep, listing them in order, from greatest to least importance. This is your outline.

60 With an outline by your side, you will not get lost.

61 Separate what the reader needs to know from what is merely of interest.

62 All new information needs to be backed up with evidence.

QUESTIONS TO ASK YOURSELF

Q Do I have enough background knowledge to deal with the subject in question?

Q Have I included all the relevant facts and information?

Q Have I recorded the sources of my information?

Q Have I given enough thought to the organization of the text?

Q Have I got my message over efficiently and effectively?

STARTING TO WRITE

Using your outline, write freely and do not be afraid to put down any thoughts, however imperfectly expressed. Do not necessarily start at the beginning. Begin by developing the ideas that you feel are easiest to deal with. You should not lose your way, because the outline will list all the ideas that you should cover in your text. It will take time to work out the paragraph structure. Once you have decided the subject for each paragraph, order them logically to follow the chosen structure and achieve a flowing text. Do not be tempted to read and rewrite the text as soon as you have finished your main points. Leave it alone for a short time. Then you will have the necessary critical distance to be able to revise what you have written more effectively and efficiently.

STEP-BY-STEP REVISION

Read the text right through

Make the first corrections

Ask somebody else to read your text

Make any corrections that you feel are necessary

Leave the text to "rest" for a while

Do a final reading

REVISING AND REWRITING

After a careful read-through, rewrite your text where necessary. Check to see whether or not the information is organized in the clearest way possible and also whether your use of vocabulary is appropriate. Then, make the required corrections, consulting dictionaries, a thesaurus, and grammar reference books. Look at, and revise the layout of all the information, including illustrations if they are being included. Once again, cut out anything that is not useful or which is not wholly relevant, so that what is left conveys your message perfectly and precisely. Then ask a colleague's opinion, add in any valid comments, and leave the text to "rest" for a while. Finally, have one last read-through before you send it out to colleagues or clients.

▼ **SHOWING YOUR TEXT TO A COLLEAGUE**

Accepting suggestions for changes made by colleagues is halfway to producing a good result. Be objective and open to new ideas and criticisms.

Colleagues point out any errors or problems they feel exist directly on screen.

ASKING FOR OPINIONS

Hearing the opinions of others on your text will help you to detect any of your faults. Often, what appears to be totally clear to you will be confusing for your reader, who may feel that the paragraphs are not clearly connected, or that the text does not make sense. It is difficult to spot such problems on your own.

USING THE INVERTED PYRAMID

The inverted pyramid system provides a logical structure for writing text. It enables you to write down information in an ordered sequence, according to what is most important. This structure is the one most frequently used by business writers.

63 The inverted pyramid format is ideal for executive summaries.

64 Put essential detail first, supporting data next, and additional data last.

APPLYING THE TECHNIQUE

The pyramid structure is ideal for writing general business communications and announcements, for example company results, invitations to participate in events, and employment notices. It is also ideal for producing executive summaries and other business documents that require you to provide condensed information in a report format that is understandable to everyone. Journalists also use this technique for writing news stories and reports.

Main information

Examples, back-up information, arguments that support essential information

Additional information

65 Do not confuse your reader with irrelevant details.

◀ PROVIDING A STRUCTURE
These are the three essential elements that comprise the structure of the pyramid and make for clearer, more concise writing.

66 Information should be competently, professionally, and politely presented.

67 Employment offers may be set out using the inverted pyramid structure.

WRITING BUSINESS MEMOS

This structure is ideal for in-house communications and memos. In the example below, Mr Prest receives a briefing from the Human Resources Department at InfoPower about his staff's standard working day. He finds the content difficult and confusing to read. The HR department is not practised at writing memos – and it shows. Had they used the pyramid structure, their memo would have been much shorter and clearer.

▼ BEING ORGANIZED
The memo on the left does not deliver its message because it is unclear, badly organized, and was not checked before it was sent out. The reader is left uncertain about what action to take. The memo below is clearer and more direct.

HUMAN RESOURCES DEPARTMENT

COMMUNICATION/WORKING DAY

As set out in Personnel Regulations, the working day at InfoPower is eight hours a day for all employees, apart from those in certain positions that have their own specific regulations (i.e., call-centre operators, after-sales service, and back-up staff) or when legal requirements state otherwise, such as those working as: doctors, dentists, engineers, work safety professionals, nurses, doctors, computer operators, and data-entry operators.
We therefore wish to alert those in management positions that basic company rulings must be adhered to on the standard working day and that no modifications may be made to the conditions set out in individual works contracts.

INCORRECT EXAMPLE

Support information

Essential information

Additional information

Watch the time!

The normal working day for InfoPower workers is an eight-hour day. This is clearly stated in everyone's work contract.

Managers are therefore requested to make sure that all employees work to these hours on a daily basis.

This rule does not apply to call-centre operators, after-sales service employees, and back-up workers; doctors, nurses, dentists; engineers; and any other professionals on our staff, all of whom are covered by specific regulations with respect to the working day.

USING THE PYRAMID STRUCTURE

WRITING BUSINESS REPORTS

There are three stages to writing a report. First, outline what your report will cover. Next, provide the details to back up your case. Finally, finish with a summary of the contents, or a list of conclusions based on the facts presented.

68 The essence of report writing is to make the facts clear and succinct.

COMMUNICATING FACTS

Report writing can cover many forms of communication. It is widely used in business for keeping managers and staff informed of developments in other departments, or between company and client. The report format is also used for making presentations.

Introduce subject areas

Elaborate on subject areas in more detail, breaking them down under subject headings

Provide a summary or conclusion

69 Your report should follow the outline of the introduction.

70 Reports should inform, clarify, and draw a conclusion.

◀ STRUCTURING THE REPORT
The report structure enables the writer to stick to the relevant points and provide a clear summary. Readers should not be in any doubt about the goals and suggested outcome detailed in the report.

Report title should clearly outline content

Report on Internet Requirements for Production Department

There is a requirement for quicker internet access within the Production Department. Access to research sources is vital for the smooth running of the department. We believe that we can provide an efficient service within the allocated budget.

Outline the problem clearly

We propose to do this in the following stages:

• Install ISDN lines for all seven staff.

• Upgrade seven PCs purchased three years ago to bring them in line with current working needs.

• Use redundant Production Department PCs in the stock-room, where computer speed is less important.

Use bullet points, numbers, or other graphic devices to emphasize each point

• An estimated 20% of the cost will be saved.

▲ UTILIZING THE REPORT STRUCTURE

Good report writing makes the facts clear, without any unnecessary padding. Use headings to highlight a change in subject and sub-headings for related themes. Make sure your page layout is clear and easy to follow.

71 Do not pass on unsubstantiated facts. Always make it clear if you are making a personal judgment, rather than relating facts.

USING QUESTIONS AND ANSWERS

You can use the question-and-answer format to provide information in a document by answering a number of questions that are frequently asked. When properly implemented, this style is extremely instructive and informative.

72 Anticipate the most common problems the reader might have.

73 Do not confuse by asking multiple questions. Just ask one at a time.

CONVEYING INFORMATION

The question-and-answer structure is very useful when you need to inform a varied public audience about something, or when you have a lot of information to convey, for example, to explain how to use a piece of equipment, fill in a form, or follow a set of instructions. By using this format, the reader is able to select the information they want, as you will have anticipated the most likely questions they may have when attempting to carry out your instructions.

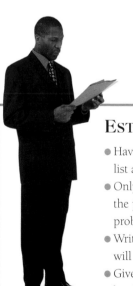

ESTABLISHING THE QUESTIONS

- Have a brainstorming session with colleagues so that you can try and list all the possible queries that a reader might have.
- Only select the most common problems or queries. If you mention all the possible areas of difficulty in your text, you may create more problems than most people would have.
- Write down the questions in the most colloquial manner possible. This will make the text feel more like a "conversation".
- Give answers that directly address the question so that the reader will be able to act on the information.

USING THE Q&A STRUCTURE

You will often find question-and-answer structure texts at visitor attractions. The Visitor Centre at Chandler Gardens in Wales, Britain, receives a large number of visitors every day who are interested in learning about the gardens. The number of questions asked by the visitors – all wanting to get the most out of their visit – is very high. The communications department, realizing that there were certain questions that were being asked over and over again, produced the leaflet shown below, as a way to answer these questions as clearly, efficiently, and effectively as possible.

74 Use Q&As when you have lots of data or information to convey.

75 Aim to provide vital information and avoid straying off the point.

ANTICIPATE ▶ CONCERNS
This model shows how the question-and-answer structure works in practice. Note that these questions and answers are short and succinct, covering all essential information.

CHANDLER GARDENS VISITOR CENTRE
Town, County
Motorway Junction

CHANDLER GARDENS

Q. How do I visit Chandler Gardens?
A. Come to the visitor centre by exiting the motorway junction. Chandler Gardens is 6 km (4 miles) away. Follow the signposts.

Q. How much does a visit cost?
A. All tours are free of charge.

Q. What is the Tourist Visit?
A. This tour covers the biodynamic, organic vegetable and fruit gardens, nature centre, and greenhouse where we grow non-hybridized plants. You will also be shown a documentary about Chandler Gardens. The tour and film will last about an hour.

Q. What is the Special Tour?
A. This tour is open to everyone above the age of 12, in groups of a maximum of 12 people. *You must book in advance.*

The Special Tour will cover the same area as the Tourist Visit, plus a visit to the Natural Pesticides Building. The tour lasts about two hours.

Q. What is the Technical Tour?
A. This tour is aimed at those working as horticulturalists, gardeners, scientists, students at universities and colleges, as well as specially invited government representatives. The tour covers the inside and outside of the centre as before, with the addition of a visit to the research areas. The tour lasts about two and a half hours.

Q. What are the opening hours?
A. Opening hours vary and are as follows:
Tourist Visit:
Monday to Saturday, hourly from 8am until 4pm.
Special Tour:
Monday to Friday, at 9am and 3pm.
Technical Tour:
Monday to Friday, at 8pm and 2pm.

Chandler Gardens will be shut on Christmas Eve, Christmas Day, Boxing Day and New Year's Day.

IDENTIFYING PROBLEMS AND PROPOSING SOLUTIONS

If you are writing a letter in relation to a situation in deadlock, the problem-and-solution format is the best to use. This offers several solutions to the other party, allowing you both to solve the existing problem in a practical and decisive manner.

76 A friendly writing style will always be well received.

77 Be rational in your writing style and avoid emotional words and phrases.

78 Make clear suggestions, but let the recipient choose the solution.

USING THE STRATEGY

The problem-and-solution strategy is ideal for solving situations with a colleague or company, that could otherwise cause the recipient to get angry, waste time, or lose patience. With this format, you detail a summary of the problem, and end with a proposal of the possible solutions. It is a tactic that shows that you are adopting a firm approach. You are in charge. So, rather than getting emotional and becoming angry, set out your position clearly and make it clear that you will not accept any further delays or excuses.

79 Your reader does not have time to waste, so focus on the points you wish to make and keep them succinct.

▼ **GETTING RESULTS**
The diagram below shows the three parts of the problem-and-solution structure. Be objective when you use it, as there is no point in denying the facts.

| Presentation of the problem | Clear analysis of possible solutions | Conclusion |

PROBLEM SOLVING

It is easy to see how the problem-and-solution format can help get you out of a difficult situation. In the example detailed below, Mr. Patel bought a latest generation computer for his small business, including all the necessary peripheral equipment. He paid for the goods at the time of ordering and received them punctually. The problems began soon after installation. After two months he was still not able to:

- Connect to the internet.
- Work for more than four hours consecutively without the operating system crashing.

Using a problem and solution structure letter, Mr. Patel obtained a satisfactory solution.

80 Write clearly, coherently, and with objectivity.

81 Present solutions with efficiency and politeness.

◄ **IDENTIFYING SOLUTIONS**
In this letter, Mr. Patel makes the problems he is experiencing quite clear and proposes definite options to resolve them. Presented with several solutions, all the supplier can really do is to accept one of them.

Today's date

Customer Services Department
Computer Company
Street Name
Big Town

Dear Sir/Madam,

The equipment I bought from your company two months ago is not working properly, and is stopping me from running my business efficiently. As the actions taken by your company have not given the desired results, I suggest that you implement one of the following three actions:

- Give me a full refund of the computer and the peripheral equipment.
- Replace all the equipment with a new system of the same configuration that is in perfect working order.
- Arrange a visit from a qualified engineer to reinstall the equipment so that it functions properly.

I am sure you understand that I cannot spend any more time waiting for a resolution of this problem. Please inform me which option you are going to implement by next week.

Yours faithfully,

S. Patel

Presents the problem and details what has happened

Clearly defines the options available to the company

Courteous tone is maintained throughout the text

USING EVERYDAY FORMATS

Achieving the right style of presentation is vital in most forms of communication. A few simple rules will help you structure effective letters, e-mails, direct mailings, and reports.

WRITING LETTERS

*L*etters form the basis of communication in business. A well-written, clearly laid-out letter that sticks to the point conveys the impression that your company knows what it does and does it well. Such letters are an important part of a company's public image.

82 Avoid waffle. Read through your letter and omit anything that is repetitive.

83 Check you have the right address and postcode when addressing letters.

ADDRESSING THE READER

A well-presented letter, with all the information set out clearly – and free of grammatical mistakes and spelling errors – is the minimum courtesy you should pay your recipient. Check the spelling of their name and their job title. When addressing a letter without knowledge of an individual's name, use "Dear Sir or Madam", followed by "Yours faithfully" when you sign off. If you know the recipient's name, address the letter "Dear Mr./Mrs./Ms. (add surname)" and sign off with "Yours sincerely". Do not confuse these forms of address.

THE LAYOUT OF A LETTER

Name of the company and document number

↓

Date sent

↓

Name of the recipient

↓

Address of the recipient

↓

Subject or reference

↓

Body of the text

↓

Closing

↓

Signature

USING A TEMPLATE

To make your letter easy to read, follow the template when you lay the letter out. If you are writing on a company letterhead, you do not need to add your address on the right-hand side again. Align all your details on the left-hand side, starting with the date and then the name and address of the person you are writing to.

● Identify the subject on a separate line.
● Do not indent your paragraphs. Leave a line space between each new paragraph.

Your name and address and telephone number are written at the top

Write the name of the recipient, followed by their company name and address

Identify the subject of the letter before going into detail in the body of the letter

Range your type on the left hand side. Do not indent paragraphs

The name of the author should be followed by your job description

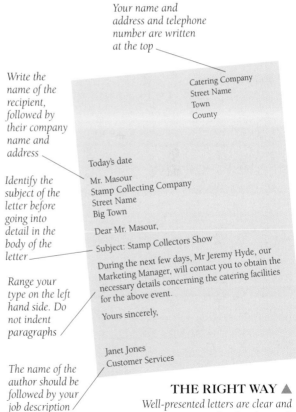

Catering Company
Street Name
Town
County

Today's date

Mr. Masour
Stamp Collecting Company
Street Name
Big Town

Dear Mr. Masour,

Subject: Stamp Collectors Show

During the next few days, Mr Jeremy Hyde, our Marketing Manager, will contact you to obtain the necessary details concerning the catering facilities for the above event.

Yours sincerely,

Janet Jones
Customer Services

THE RIGHT WAY ▲
Well-presented letters are clear and easy to read and understand.

ADDING TO A LETTER

When you want to attach documents or reports to your letter, or send your letter to other people as well as the recipient, you need to record this on the letter.

- When you are enclosing a document or report, write "Enc." at the bottom of your letter, two or three lines below where your job title appears.
- To inform the recipient that the letter is also being sent to others, write "cc" (carbon copy), followed by the names of the other people.

84 For clarity, use a reference code on letters about the same subject.

GOOD AND BAD STYLE

✔ 3 April 2000	✘ 3rd of April, 2000
✔ a.s.a.p.	✘ A.S.A.P.
✔ Page 9	✘ Page 09
✔ Yours sincerely,	✘ Yours truly,

85 Avoid casual endings such as "That's all for now".

SUBJECT AND REFERENCE CODES

Knowing how to use subject and reference codes correctly makes correspondence clearer. The subject of the letter needs to be clearly defined before the main text. When there are several letters on the same subject, a reference code is a good way to clarify which document your letter concerns. For example:
Subject: GM food products
Reference: 19/M; 19/5/2000

USING PUNCTUATION

Avoiding common errors, such as those listed below, will improve the quality of your letter.

- When abbreviating any terms, write them out first and follow with the letters in brackets. For example, United Nations (UN). The next time you refer to this, you can use the abbreviated form. However, if the organization's abbreviated form is widely known, use that instead. For example, CNN, BBC, SAS, and so on.
- Use an apostrophe to indicate the possessive, for example: Mrs. Lebrun's office is at the end the hall.
- Do not use an apostrophe when using a possessive pronoun, for example: The cat chased after its own tail.

ORGANIZING YOUR LETTER

Arrange your letter so that it is easier for the recipient to understand. Three general rules are listed below:

- Get straight to the point. The first paragraph should gain the attention of the reader by clearly outlining the key points of the letter.
- Repeat knowledge you share with your reader early on in your letter. However, it is important to express shared information concisely so as not to lose the reader's attention.
- Make sure that the reader knows your reasons for sending the letter and what action needs to follow.

86 Do not use "Kind regards" to end letters to people you do not know.

87 Repeat any shared knowledge in your letter as concisely as possible.

▼ GETTING IT RIGHT

The three points listed below provide the key to writing successful business letters.

| Get straight to the point | → | Repeat shared information | → | Make sure your requirements are clear |

WRITING IN A CONCISE STYLE

THE WORDY WAY

"With reference to the third term of the Business Quality course, due to take place from the 26–28th July at the Big Motel, Any Road, Phil Charles, Suzanne Page, and Lesley Storey, who were to complete the second term but could not due to their being busy with other work, we would like to request their registration for the third term of the course."

"With reference to your letter request of 23/5/01 in which you asked for the exchange of air conditioners supplied by this company, we will refer to 2334/DF for authorization to substitute…"

THE CONCISE WAY

"We are applying to register Phil Charles, Suzanne Page, and Lesley Storey for the third term of the Business Quality course. The absence of these employees from the second term of the course was due to…"

"In connection with your letter number 2334/DF of 23/5/01 requesting the exchange of faulty air-conditioners, we will send…"

WRITING E-MAILS

E-mail is an increasingly important tool in business and accounts for a growing portion of all internal and external messages. As fast as a telephone call, e-mail can also quickly pass on large amounts of written information via attachments.

88 Overusing capital letters and bold type makes e-mails hard to read.

89 Use the reply function to respond to e-mails within 24 hours.

USING E-MAIL

Simple to use and very fast, e-mail has proved enormously useful in business. Within companies e-mail enables instant communication with colleagues, saving quantities of paper in the process. Following a few simple guidelines makes using internal e-mails even easier. Always give your e-mail a clear "subject" heading. People receive a lot of e-mails every day, and it is helpful to be able to see which messages need to be answered immediately. Always edit what you have written before you send it. Check your grammar and make sure that the message you want to send is written in a clear, easy-to-read style.

COMPOSING E-MAILS

The speed of e-mail messages can lead to an inappropriate informality. Be careful to tailor the tone of your message to the prospective recipient and subject. Distinguish personal from business e-mails, and avoid using abbreviations, exclamation marks, and slang when writing to clients. Restrict the number of recipients to avoid overloading the system with superfluous messages. Respond to e-mails quickly, and with as brief a message as possible. If you are sending a lot of information, add file attachments to your basic message.

90 Be specific when defining the "subject" of your e-mail, making it clear to your recipient.

WRITING PRECISE E-MAILS

All your clients deserve a clear and professional response. Pay careful attention to what is being asked and respond precisely. Imprecision always doubles your workload because an incomplete answer will generate a further e-mail. However, do not lose control of the amount of information you send. If you provide more information than is requested, you may cause clients to worry needlessly about irrelevant problems. Remember, particularly when you are sending vital information, to keep a back-up copy of the e-mail so you will have a record of what has been said.

Your request of yesterday's date

Send Now Send Later Save as Draft Add Attachments Signature Contacts Check Names

Account: Helen Bennett Priority: Normal

To: Stephanie Brown
Cc:
Bcc:
Subject: Request for direct dial numbers

Size: Medium **B** *I* U T

Dear Ms. Brown

We received your e-mail requesting a list of all of the direct dial numbers in the country. Unfortunately, we are not able to deal with your request. Perhaps you could try Abatel, an agency that acts as an inspectorate for telephone services.

Their telephone number is: 0 800 099 000.

Yours sincerely

Helen Bennett
Customer Services Manager

▲ **USING THE RIGHT TONE**
Here, the writer has used a formal style, but it can be dispensed with in e-mail, as long as the tone is not overly familiar.

POINTS TO REMEMBER

● Around 95 per cent of e-mails are jokes, gossip, unwanted advertising, and anonymous files – often containing destructive viruses. Only five per cent contain information that should really be on the network. Make sure that your e-mails fall within the latter group.

● When you have a lot of information to send, put it in attachment files. E-mail text messages should always be brief.

● Avoid using exclamation marks and abbreviations in your professional e-mails.

KEEPING YOUR MESSAGES POSITIVE AND FOCUSED

The essential ingredients for using the e-mail system successfully are keeping a positive attitude towards your client and maintaining your focus on their needs. Try to be diplomatic in your e-mails – remember nothing that a client says is directed against you personally. Avoid using capital letters to emphasize a point – they may be interpreted as an angry or negative response. Quoting from your clients' e-mails in your response is helpful. Instead of "In response to your request, we are able to tell you…", you could write: "In response to your request for information about sponsoring the artistic event, we are able to tell you…" Never be afraid to apologize if the client is right. A well-phrased apology can work to your advantage.

COMPOSING DIRECT MAIL LETTERS

Direct mail – selling products or services to specific customers – allows you to select a target audience. Sending a carefully personalized letter is more likely to obtain a direct reply from the client, and to achieve a higher rate of response.

91 An internationally recognized good rate of response is three per cent.

92 Including a reply-paid envelope will increase the response rate.

USING DIFFERENT DIRECT MAIL METHODS

Post

Fax

E-mail

▲ GETTING RESULTS
Tailoring a mail shot to your target group will enable you to judge which medium to use. Post, fax, and e-mail can all be extremely effective.

ATTRACTING ATTENTION

When considering using direct mail, bear in mind that your first challenge is to grab the attention of your target consumer. A good direct mail needs to be interesting and convincing enough to provoke the recipient to open the envelope in the first place. Use a creative title and varied design elements such as different fonts and striking colours on the mailing envelope. If used well, these strategic elements will get the attention of your target readers and persuade them to open the envelope and see what is inside.

COMPILING DIRECT MAILS

There are five key elements involved in the structure of a successful direct mail:

- Attracting the attention of the reader by stating clearly your reason for writing.
- Arousing the reader's curiosity in the content.
- Making the product sound as attractive as possible to provoke the reader's interest.
- Using essential facts and guarantees to convince the reader of the quality of the product or service
- Gaining action from your reader by making it clear what response you expect from them.

PROVOKING INTEREST

The principal aim of the direct mail method is to provoke the recipient's interest in the product or services on offer. Whether you are sending a simple letter or a package containing leaflets and free samples, remember to make them as compelling as you can. A covering letter should be well-written. Good design can make all the difference to an envelope, encouraging the recipient to open it. Use bullet points to highlight any benefits such as economy, guarantees of good performance, and promises of adventure.

▼ MAKING SALES

By using a simply-written covering letter with clear, objective text, the company makes a convincing argument to the client. Here, the idea of economy, reliability, and smooth operation is combined with concrete benefits.

Panel Company
Street Name
Town

Today's date

Mr. Solenzky
Purchasing Manager
Building Company
Street Name
Big Town

Dear Mr. Solenzky,

Meeting your needs efficiently and providing quality and full satisfaction are our main goals at our company.

For us, this means:

- Producing panels that are durable and innovatively designed, for the best price on the market.
- Offering our clients the most convenient payment terms.
- Ensuring that our products always arrive as quickly as possible within agreed time limits.

Contact us and find out for yourself that our company is synonymous with quality and efficiency.

Yours sincerely,

Juanita Perez, Manager
Purchasing Division

93 Address the reader directly by using "you" to get their attention.

POINTS TO REMEMBER

- Including a freephone number or an e-mail address on your mail out makes it easy for potential clients to contact you and for them to update their details for your client mailing list.

- Without an up-to-date client list behind your direct mail shot, your marketing campaign will be less successful.

OFFERING INCENTIVES

All business communications benefit from a straightforward writing style. However, the strategies employed by direct mail are different from other types of advertising. Direct mail needs to provoke immediate action. A direct mail may offer one or more incentives such as discounts, small gifts, or attractive credit terms. It is also important to offer guarantees and user-satisfaction comments. A good client list means you can also benefit from knowing when to send the mail, such as on the client's birthday.

PRESENTING BUSINESS REPORTS

The size and format of your business report are determined by the complexity of the subject matter and your target audience. Some reports need be no longer than a single page, while the content of larger reports require more structure.

94 A well-presented title page on your report will create a good impression.

Company logo

Design Company

Title of the report

Recommendations for Improving Office Ergonomics at Design Company.

Author or authors of the report, plus their status

Carla Noble
Director of Human Resources
Design Company

Human Resources, Design Company

▲ **THE TITLE PAGE**
The title page is the first contact the reader has with the report. It should have impact and express the purpose of the document, together with the name, job title, and department of the author.

THE SUMMARY

The summary, or abstract as it is sometimes called, comprises a condensed version of the report. It states the aim of the report: what it looked at, what was found, and what action is required. Only the key points should be mentioned here.

CONTENTS PAGE

List the contents in sequence, with page number references. Provide a list of illustrations, if appropriate. Your reader will rely on this page to access the document, so make it very clear and keep the layout simple.

Title Page → Summary → Contents Page → Introduction

THE INTRODUCTION

The introduction, sometimes known as the preface, describes the background and format of the report. It should provide a broad overview of the subject, together with any necessary background details, such as the history leading up to the issue that the report addresses. The reader is told here how the discussion of the key points in the main text will be developed. If necessary, state what research methods were used.

95 Provide the key discussion points of the report in the introduction.

96 The summary is exactly that – a précis of the report's contents.

THE MAIN TEXT

This part of the report should focus on the information the reader needs to have. Here is where all the facts and evidence are laid out. Keep the development of your arguments logical, ensuring that the evidence is relevant and the arguments are clear. Present your key points first, followed by the back-up data. Order your points, making use of subheadings, bullet points, and other devices to help the reader follow your points.

CONCLUSION

The conclusion section is where you make your recommendations. It should draw upon the main text facts and your points should be both clear and precise. There should be a recommendation of action to be taken, as a result of the report's analysis of the data. However, if any issues or questions remain outstanding or unresolved, draw attention to them in the conclusion.

97 Put supporting material, such as data, in the Appendix.

Main Text	Conclusion	Appendices/References

◀ **THE STANDARD STRUCTURE**
Reports should contain seven elements. Sometimes the Appendices/References might not be necessary.

THE SUMMARY

The summary outlines the aims of the report before the detailed contents page. The introduction needs to give an overview of the subject matter with any relevant background details. The main text should provide facts and key points, plus supporting evidence, in a logical order. A good way of providing extra information is to expand specific topics. In your conclusion refer back to the main facts and, based on sound analysis, suggest what action to take.

98 In the report's introduction, summarize the objectives.

▼ **AN IDEAL SUMMARY**
A good summary will always detail the contents and main aim of the report, and highlight the key points, as shown in the example below.

THE SUMMARY

Identifies aim of the report ————— Following a request made by the Board of Directors, we have produced this report with the Engineering, Marketing, and Finance Departments, with the aim of finding the best location for the new company warehouse to replace the current hangar, which is now unusable, following the fire that occurred recently.

The problem it was investigating Research into new locations indicates that the Greater Manchester area is the most suitable site. This conclusion is based on the following:

● The site is in close proximity to Head Office.

What came out of the research ● A large warehouse site is needed, as more overseas customers are buying books directly from us to take advantage of the 20 per cent discount we offer over shop prices.

● We need to keep this stock in one warehouse site situated near our Head Office.

Key points that came out of analysis ————— ● Bus and train transport to the area is good.

● The road network in this area is excellent. There is also a rail freight yard, international airport, and ship canal nearby.

● Acquiring the warehouse involves a low initial investment.

● The region is densely populated and offers tax incentives for new corporations.

● There are at least three possible locations (see appendix B) that are for sale, and it seems there will be no problem recruiting local labour.

Conclusion on why the action is required ————— We realize that the location of the warehouse in Greater Manchester may generate some inconvenience with distribution to the south-east of the country, but this is a minor problem compared to the overall benefits to the company of a warehouse in this area.

HOW TO PRESENT A REPORT

Once you have put together your report, you need to think about how you are going to bind it up for final presentation to make the most impact on your clients or colleagues. You may decide to use coloured paper for your report cover so that it stands out. Choose a subtle shade, as a glaring colour may give the reader the wrong impression of the report's contents.

A plastic binder with a removable spine is the simplest option. Or you may have a printer that will heat-bind it for you.

PROFESSIONAL ▶ APPEARANCE
Using coloured paper for your cover, with an eye-catching title page, looks professional.

THE APPENDICES

An appendix is not always necessary, but if there is a large amount of reference material or further information that would weigh down the main text, they are best included in an appendix at the back of the report. Appendices are ideal for any supporting facts, giving necessary explanations, or any other relevant information that will help the reader to understand the report.

99 Include analytical information and useful suggestions in your reports.

100 Present reports in an interesting way to attract the reader's attention.

101 Put any supplementary information to your report in an appendix or set of appendices.

ASSESSING WRITING SKILLS

*P*ractice is the best way of developing and improving your writing. Analyze the statements below and evaluate your performance as a writer, selecting the options that match your level of expertise. Try to be totally honest. If your answer is "Never", circle 1; if it is "Sometimes", circle 2, and so on. Add up your score and then look at the Analysis box on page 149. Use the test to identify areas for improvement.

SCORING
1 Never
2 Sometimes
3 Often
4 Always

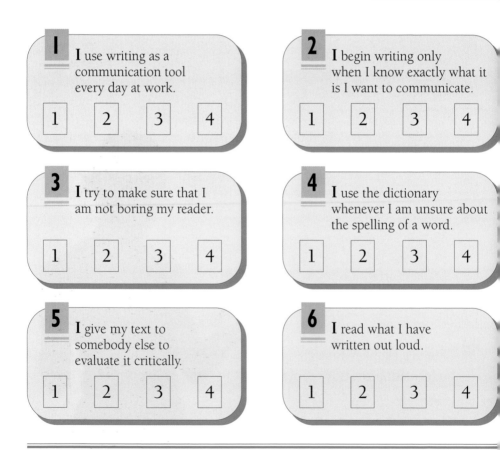

1 **I** use writing as a communication tool every day at work.

1 2 3 4

2 **I** begin writing only when I know exactly what it is I want to communicate.

1 2 3 4

3 **I** try to make sure that I am not boring my reader.

1 2 3 4

4 **I** use the dictionary whenever I am unsure about the spelling of a word.

1 2 3 4

5 **I** give my text to somebody else to evaluate it critically.

1 2 3 4

6 **I** read what I have written out loud.

1 2 3 4

7 I make my intentions totally clear to the reader.

| 1 | 2 | 3 | 4 |

8 I try to be pleasant and constructive when writing to people.

| 1 | 2 | 3 | 4 |

9 I use language that is suited to the person I am writing for.

| 1 | 2 | 3 | 4 |

10 I limit the information I include in my letters and documents to the essentials.

| 1 | 2 | 3 | 4 |

11 I respect my reader's level of knowledge of the subject I am writing about.

| 1 | 2 | 3 | 4 |

12 I clearly indicate the actions I recommend my reader should take.

| 1 | 2 | 3 | 4 |

13 I avoid the use of stilted language, slang, and unnecessary buzzwords.

| 1 | 2 | 3 | 4 |

14 I try not to "shout" at the reader by avoiding brash fonts and exclamation marks.

| 1 | 2 | 3 | 4 |

15 I always read my work afterwards to check for errors.

| 1 | 2 | 3 | 4 |

16 I make the information I supply as clear and easy to understand as possible.

| 1 | 2 | 3 | 4 |

17 I concentrate on making my text visually attractive.

1 2 3 4

18 I gather and organize my information before I start writing.

1 2 3 4

19 I identify my message first and then find the best way of explaining it.

1 2 3 4

20 I try not to write as though I am more important than my text.

1 2 3 4

21 I try to use language that is positive and optimistic – but not misleading.

1 2 3 4

22 When I reply to people, I let them know I have read their communications to me.

1 2 3 4

23 I read messages on the day I receive them and reply to them immediately.

1 2 3 4

24 I consider who should receive the information I want to pass on.

1 2 3 4

25 I try to avoid tired, overused, and clichéd phrases when writing.

1 2 3 4

26 I try to improve my knowledge through reading.

1 2 3 4

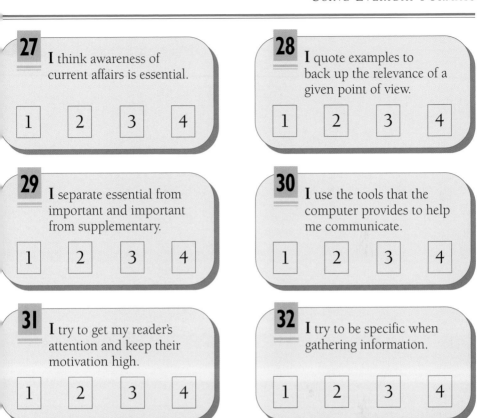

27 I think awareness of current affairs is essential.

1 2 3 4

28 I quote examples to back up the relevance of a given point of view.

1 2 3 4

29 I separate essential from important and important from supplementary.

1 2 3 4

30 I use the tools that the computer provides to help me communicate.

1 2 3 4

31 I try to get my reader's attention and keep their motivation high.

1 2 3 4

32 I try to be specific when gathering information.

1 2 3 4

ANALYSIS

Now that you have tested yourself, add up the points you scored and compare them to the performance analysis below. Whatever your score, remember that you can always improve. Identify your weakest areas and consult the relevant chapters of this section to find the practical advice and pointers that will help you improve your writing skills.
32–64: Your written communication skills could be improved. Read a little more and practise writing daily. Compare your own documents to those of others.
65–95: Your written work has its highs and lows. Practise more, concentrate on being clear and you'll soon see the benefit.
96–128: You write very well, but remember: there is always room for improvement.

THINKING CREATIVELY

INTRODUCTION

The ability to think creatively is an essential skill for every manager. By applying your creativity, it is possible to break out of your usual routines and patterns of behaviour and to increase your personal effectiveness. Thinking Creatively will show you how to tap into your innate creativity so that you can find innovative solutions to difficult problems. It will help you understand the process of generating and assessing ideas, and it will show you how to benefit from sharing ideas with others in order to build consensus and commitment. There are 101 tips throughout the section to give you practical advice, and self-assessment exercises enable you to evaluate your ability as a creative thinker. As you develop the techniques that will help you stimulate creativity in yourself and in others, you will find this section an invaluable guide.

UNDERSTANDING CREATIVITY

Thinking creatively helps you find ways to deal with challenges and form opportunities. Understand how creativity can help you become more successful in all areas of your life.

WHAT IS CREATIVITY?

Creativity is the process of challenging accepted ideas and ways of doing things in order to find new solutions or concepts. Be aware of the obstacles that stand in the way of the creative impulse and understand the benefits that creative thinking can bring you.

1 Recognize that everyone has the ability to be creative.

POINTS TO REMEMBER

- Our traditional approach to solving problems relies on logical, tried and tested methods.
- We can change our behaviour patterns only by looking at issues from different angles.
- Creative thinking involves changing your assumptions and beliefs.
- Creativity does not always produce better solutions, but it helps you generate more ideas and offers you new insights.

DEFINING CREATIVITY

Being creative means seeing ideas or objects in a different context, either by recognizing their inherent potential to be used in a different way or by putting previously unconnected ideas together to create something completely new. All of us have the ability to be creative. However, we tend to be constrained by culture and circumstances to do things the way we have always done them. Instead of seeing problems as opportunities to find new ways of doing things, we tend to see them as "hurdles" to be jumped. Use creative thinking to gain a new perspective on the world.

CREATIVE THINKING

Some people are naturally creative, but most of us accept things as they are. For example, a plastic bottle is only a bottle to some people. But to a creative thinker, it could also be a disposable container, a funnel, or a tiny greenhouse. Creative thinking starts with questioning. Are objects really just what we assume them to be? Or are they that way only because we see them like that?

◀ **BEING INVENTIVE**
We all instinctively use creative thinking to cope with daily situations, such as being caught in the rain. Learn to consciously tap into your creativity at work, too.

BENEFITING FROM CREATIVITY

Over the centuries, creative people have provided new solutions to the problems of their day. The ability of human beings to find creative solutions to problems is essential for the well-being of the human race. On a social level, collective creativity provides the opportunity to improve quality of life. In organizations, creativity is essential to ensure a firm's ongoing effectiveness in a changing world. On a personal level, creativity can help you break out of routines you dislike.

2 Change your current patterns of thinking.

3 Remember that change begins with questioning.

USING YOUR CREATIVITY

Take an everyday object, such as a paperclip. Ask yourself, "What can this be used for?" If your answer is "a paperclip", then you are responding "traditionally". If, however, you see it not only as a paperclip, but also as a piece of wire, then you are thinking creatively. From this perception, you will start to see that the paperclip has many uses. For example, it could be a fuse wire for an electric circuit, a marking instrument, or a clip for securing a box. Start noticing the potential in everything.

LOOKING AT OBJECTS ▶
When you look at an ordinary object such as a paperclip, think about the different uses it could have.

USING LOGICAL AND CREATIVE THINKING

We generate ideas by thinking creatively, and then we use logical thinking to help turn these thoughts into realistic actions. Understand the benefits of both logical and creative thinking, so that you can start to adapt the way you think.

4 Understand how logical and creative thinking are integral to each other.

5 Use your past experiences to find solutions.

6 Think creatively to increase your opportunities.

THINKING LOGICALLY

When we are faced with a familiar problem, logical thinking enables us to tap into our personal experiences and find a suitable solution with the minimum of effort. By assessing a situation against your relevant experience, you can choose the most appropriate path, and move towards a solution. This logical approach, also known as convergent thinking, is very efficient. However, it can become a barrier when you have little relevant experience; when there are a few potential solutions; or when you need a brand new solution.

CASE STUDY

John was a relatively inexperienced mechanic. During the course of his work, he regularly had to mend old cars that had problems starting. In his experience, the fault would usually be a flat battery or a damp spark plug. If he found that these were working, he would then deduce that there was a problem with the starter motor. Using logical thinking allowed him to get to the root of problems quickly.

As his experience increased, his boss allowed him to start working on newer cars. He found that it was harder to pinpoint the starting problems on the more modern cars, because they had more elaborate systems. Instead of relying on his past experiences, he started to ask the car owners for details about the problems they were experiencing. He relied on his creativity to help him find the roots of the problems.

◄ **ADAPTING YOUR THINKING**

In this example, a mechanic has learnt to deal with common problems in a logical way, using his past experiences to guide him to solutions. However, he is then faced with situations where he lacks experience, and he has to start thinking more creatively.

THINKING CREATIVELY

Divergent thinking, or creative thinking, involves opening up your mind to find new solutions and new ways of doing things. Instead of taking your usual, logical approach to a problem, learn to suspend your judgment and look for different, more inventive solutions. Once you have generated as many ideas as possible in this way, use a logical thinking process to refine your ideas and identify the best solution to the problem.

Manager identifies a problem

Takes a creative approach to the issue

Takes a logical approach. Refers to his past experiences of similar situations

Suspends judgment and generates ideas

Comes up with a variety of ideas

Analyzes his past experiences and comes up with possible solutions

Categorizes and prioritizes ideas

7 Explore possible options before making decisions.

Evaluates different solutions

SOLVING PROBLEMS ▶

Using either a logical or creative approach to a problem will produce solutions for you to analyze. However, creative thinking will generate a greater number of ideas to choose between.

Chooses the best possible solution to the problem

EXPLORING CREATIVITY

Most people are creative in their private lives, but tend to be less creative in their "public selves". Our conditioned behaviour encourages us to keep problems to ourselves and find quick fixes that involve as few people as possible. Start to break this habit. When you are faced with a problem, spend time exploring ideas, and involve other people in your search for solutions.

8 Think of possible solutions to a problem and then evaluate them using logical thinking.

BECOMING CREATIVE

We all have the ability to be creative, but this mindset is better developed in some people than in others. Examine how to overcome the conditioning that blocks your creativity, and learn to use your knowledge and experience more productively.

> **9** Use your imagination to find different solutions.

UNLOCKING CREATIVITY

We are brought up to believe that certain behaviours and thoughts are "right" and others are "wrong". This conditioning constrains our thinking and prevents us from finding new answers. Unlock your creativity. Empower yourself to question your ways of doing things.

Connects the unconnected

Generates new solutions

Remains open-minded

Challenges old ideas

Uses imagination

Asks question

THINKING CREATIVELY ▶
The person who is able to work outside the bounds of his or her experience and seek new solutions to problems will be more successful in the long run.

IDENTIFYING TYPES OF CONDITIONING

TYPE	POINTS TO NOTE
SOCIAL	This type of conditioning equips us to fit into the society in which we live. However, it discourages us from challenging the status quo.
LEARNING	We are taught to learn in a structured way. However, this means that we have a tendency to accept facts rather than challenging them.
FAMILY	Parental authority lays down our patterns and rules of behaviour at an early age – these become instinctive and are hard to break.
WORK PLACE	This conditioning sets the rules for behaviour at work. We have a tendency to accept procedures as they are and not to question those in authority.

THINGS TO DO

1. Identify something that you would like to change.

2. Think of the change you would like and identify what is holding you back.

3. Decide what action you could take, and then take it.

LOOKING AT INFORMATION

Our minds store vast amounts of information. When you receive an input signal, such as someone asking you a question, your mind will automatically access its relevant data store. Without this natural ability, you would spend a lot of time doing ordinary things. For example, finding your way to work would be a new experience every day. However, this mental process, which makes us very efficient in our everyday lives, is a barrier to creativity. Avoid making instant assumptions and connections.

11 Aim to look at information in more productive, insightful ways.

CHANGING THE BOX

We are conditioned not to think the unthinkable. For example, many people prefer not to ask for an explanation about an issue they do not understand, for fear of looking stupid. Let go of preconceived ideas and break the glass wall of conditioning in order to find your creative self. Avoid accepting procedures as they are, just because they have always been that way. Seek ways of doing things differently and always aim to increase your effectiveness and that of your organization.

10 Understand how conditioning forces you to think in a prescribed way and limits your potential.

THE CREATIVE PROCESS

Look at the diagram below. Where would the letter "F" go in the following sequence? Do you imagine that it will go above or below the line?:

A		E
	B C D	

There is in fact no obvious "right" answer. The "F" could go beside the "E" as part of a 1/3/2 sequence. Or it could go below the line as part of a 1/3/1/3 sequence. Alternatively, it could go next to the "E" so that all the letters that are made up of straight lines are above the line. Some people will dismiss this problem as not solvable, while others will assume that only one answer can be right. A creative person accepts that whatever he or she wants to believe is right and that there are lots of possibilities.

UNDERSTANDING THE CREATIVE PROCESS

When you bring together ideas that were not previously connected or see new ways of doing things, you are thinking creatively. Examine how the creative process works and start to change your current patterns of thinking.

12 Recognize that creativity is driven by the desire to improve processes.

USING HUMOUR

Humour provides an analogy to the creative process. The basic story line of a joke is logical and usually depicts an everyday situation. As the listener, you recognize the scenario and think you know how the story will progress. The punch line then destroys your preconceptions. You are "jumped" from one store of information to another.

▲ PLAYING ON PEOPLE'S ASSUMPTIONS
When a comedian tells a joke, the listeners make assumptions about what will happen next in the story – the punch line destroys these assumptions in a way that makes people laugh.

13 Bypass your assumptions and think creatively.

14 Believe that you can think of solutions.

DOS AND DON'TS

✔ Do be open-minded in your approach to situations and people.

✔ Do be ready to adapt your attitude to suit different occasions.

✔ Do break out of the box of past experience.

✘ Don't assume that what was right for yesterday is automatically right for today too.

✘ Don't be misled by your preconceptions.

✘ Don't just take the path of least resistance.

BREAKING PATTERNS

Learn to override your natural thinking processes and your tendency to rely on your usual way of doing things, so that you can find new solutions. Identify how you would normally deal with a difficult situation, and then deliberately adopt a different approach. For example, perhaps you are faced with a seemingly impossible deadline. Instead of deciding to work late to make sure that the work is finished on time, think about what would happen if the schedule was amended. Notice how changing your approach creates new opportunities.

15 Try not to be constrained by rules.

16 Accept that problems are the food of creativity.

◄ CHANGING YOUR APPROACH
In this example, a manager always felt anxious before negotiations – she disliked the feeling of confrontation. However, she learnt how to break this cycle by visualizing what she wanted to achieve from negotiations and by changing the way she viewed her customer relationships.

CASE STUDY
Joanna was a sales manager for a software company. She was good at her job, but she tended to get anxious about face-to-face negotiations.
She spoke to her boss about this, and he suggested that instead of looking at negotiations as potential confrontations, she should try to focus on them as opportunities to develop customer relationships and to meet mutual needs.

The next time Joanna was preparing for a negotiation, she began to visualize what she wanted to achieve from the discussion, and what the other party would want to gain too.
By approaching the situation from a new angle, she began to think of new possibilities that both parties could benefit from. She thought about how she could work in a collaborative way with the customer, and she began to look forward to meetings.

POINTS TO REMEMBER

● Imagination can free you from the chains of past experience.

● You need to use your imagination to ensure that you have the future you desire, not the future someone else has planned.

● Your imagination can help you to project yourself into "fantasy" situations. Then you can start making your dreams become achievable reality.

USING YOUR IMAGINATION

All creative thinking techniques work on the basis of imposing a condition on your thinking, for example, encouraging the use of your imagination. Imagination is the lifeblood of creativity. Use it to disrupt your natural thinking patterns. For example, when you are unsure about what you want from your job, visualize your desired future. Create a vision that you can work towards. Then, use your logical mind to work out how you can make this goal a reality.

IDENTIFYING THINKING PATTERNS

In order to become more creative, you need to be aware of how you usually respond to situations or issues. Notice your current behaviour patterns and ways of thinking and test how creative you really are – be honest with yourself.

17 Understand your thinking processes so that you are able to adapt them.

QUESTIONS TO ASK YOURSELF

Q If someone suggests a new way of doing something, do I embrace it or do I feel anxious about making changes?

Q Do I tend to stick to routines, or am I willing to be flexible?

Q Am I judgmental towards other people?

Q Am I able to see the whole problem or do I get caught up in the finer details?

UNDERSTANDING THE WAY YOU THINK

It is hard to generalize about people's thinking processes, because individuals tend to react to different situations in different ways. For example a manager may find that he or she works in a ver structured way at work, but is chaotic at home. Notice how you react to certain scenarios, so that you can start to change the way you think. Ask yourself searching questions. What do you think obstructs your creative impulses? For example, do you find that you are always so busy that you never make time to think creatively?

ANALYZING YOUR ▶ BEHAVIOUR PATTERNS
This manager always tries to cope with his workload instead of finding creative ways to work more efficiently.

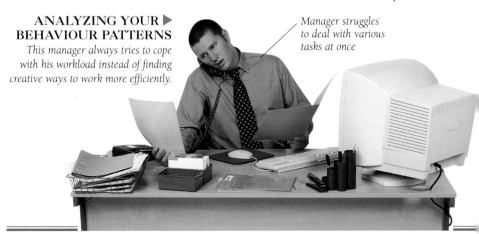

Manager struggles to deal with various tasks at once

ASSESSING YOUR CREATIVE POTENTIAL

The following statements are designed to provide you with some insight into your current level of creativity. On a piece of paper, make a note of your responses to each question (a, b, or c) and then assess your results.

1. You have been invited to join some friends for a holiday in the Alps. Do you:
a) Worry about who will look after things while you are away.
b) Doubt that you will have the time.
c) Accept it as a marvellous opportunity.

2. You are faced with a recurring problem at work. Do you:
a) Draw it to your manager's attention.
b) Immediately try to sort it out yourself.
c) Call a meeting with all involved.

3. You arrive home to find that the dog has destroyed your new shoes. Do you:
a) Blame yourself.
b) Punish the dog.
c) Go and buy a new pair.

4. You are on holiday and discover that the return flight is delayed. Do you:
a) Call work and say you will be late back.
b) Sit at the airport and wait.
c) Enjoy the extension of your holiday.

5. Part of your garden is very overgrown. Do you:
a) Clear it yourself.
b) Get somebody in to do the work.
c) Make a fun day of it with friends.

6. You are concerned about passing an exam. Do you:
a) Study hard.
b) Talk to someone who has already taken the exam and develop a revision strategy.
c) Organize private coaching with a tutor.

7. Your children are bored. Do you:
a) Promise to buy them some new toys.
b) Play with them.
c) Help them to find something they want to do and teach them how to do it.

8. You have a difficult relationship with a relative. Do you:
a) Pretend that there isn't a problem.
b) Try to minimize contact.
c) Find a common interest and build on it.

A high score in row "A" means that you are not thinking creatively

A high score in row "B" indicates average creativity

A high score in row "C" means you are very creative

UNDERSTANDING YOUR THOUGHT PROCESSES

Research indicates that the two hemispheres of the brain process information in different ways, and your natural thinking style will depend on the side of your brain you tend to be led by. Decide whether you are naturally creative.

18 Identify the side of the brain that you are naturally influenced by.

THINKING PATTERNS ▼
Organized people are more influenced by the left side of the brain, while intuitive people are influenced by the right side.

UNDERSTANDING HOW YOUR BRAIN WORKS

The left part of the brain processes information in a logical way, while the right part of your brain focuses on the creative, intuitive, part of your personality. Most people tend to be dominated by one or other side of their brains and have a distinct thinking style. Some people can adapt to both modes. People who are dominated by the right side of their brains are naturally creative but this does not mean that people who are dominated by the left side of their brains cannot be creative.

LEFT-BRAINED PERSON | RIGHT-BRAINED PERSON

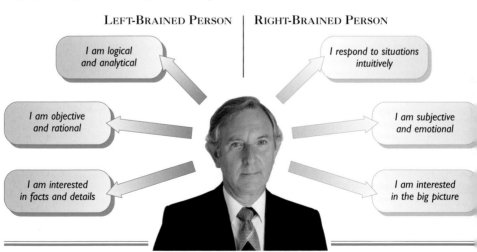

I am logical and analytical

I respond to situations intuitively

I am objective and rational

I am subjective and emotional

I am interested in facts and details

I am interested in the big picture

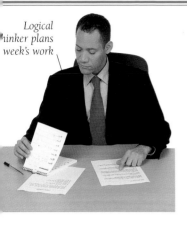

Logical thinker plans week's work

RECOGNIZING LEFT-BRAIN DOMINANCE

The left side of the brain processes information by taking small, separate pieces and building up a "big" picture from which it draws conclusions. Individuals who are more influenced by the left hemisphere of the brain work through problems logically. They are good at developing strategies and like to base their decisions on facts. They are articulate, good communicators. While they tend to conform to rules, they are also adaptable.

▲ BEING ORGANIZED

Left-brained people tend to work in a structured, routine-driven way. They tend to plan their daily schedules, and work through lists of tasks in a methodical, ordered way.

19 Notice how you approach problems, and think about whether you are naturally creative.

RECOGNIZING RIGHT-BRAIN DOMINANCE

People who are dominated by the right side of their brains are not happy to just follow an instruction and carry out a task, they need to know why they are doing it. These people like to see, hear, and feel, what is required of them. They trust their feelings and answer questions intuitively. Notice whether you tend to think in this way or not. Even if you are not naturally creative, you can learn how to change your approach.

NATURALLY CREATIVE ▶

People who are dominated by the right side of their brains like to find out the full picture before they start a project.

Manager discusses all the options with her team before making decisions

ASSESSING YOUR NATURAL CREATIVITY

Evaluate whether you are more influenced by the creative right side of your brain or the logical left side of your brain. Read the following statements and indicate whether you agree or disagree with them. Be as honest as you can. Check the Analysis below to see how you scored. Use your answers to identify how you could change your thinking processes and become more creative.

OPTIONS

A Agree

B Disagree

1 I read all the available information before meeting a new client.

A B

2 I like the challenges presented by new opportunities.

A B

3 I am happiest when I have the time to organize what I am doing.

A B

4 I normally use a logical approach when I solve problems.

A B

5 I am not happy making decisions unless I can consider all the facts.

A B

6 I like to visit new places and take every opportunity to do new things.

A B

7 I am at my best when I am working with ideas.

A B

8 I believe in investigating failures so that they do not happen again.

A B

9 I have learnt to trust my instincts and to rely on the way I feel about things.

A B

10 I invariably use a shopping list when I go shopping.

A B

11 I prefer it when people make formal presentations of their ideas.

A B

12 I am happiest when I am free to decide what should be done.

A B

ANALYSIS

Check your results against the following to see whether you are dominated by the right- or left-hand side of your brain:
1/ A=left, B=right **2/** A=right, B=left
3/ A=left, B=right **4/** A=left, B=right
5/ A=left, B=right **6/** A=right, B=left
7/ A=right, B=left **8/** A=left, B=right
9/ A=right, B=left **10/** A=left, B=right
11/ A=left, B=right **12/** A=right, B=left
If most of your answers were "left", this indicates that you are a left-brain thinker.

You like structure and logic and should concentrate on thinking more creatively. A near equal score suggests a balance between logical and creative thinking. If your score has a high percentage of "right", you are a right-brain thinker and are naturally creative. But remember, there is always room for improvement.

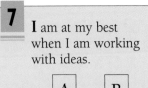

DEVELOPING CREATIVITY

In order to succeed in developing your innate creativity, you need to overcome the natural barriers in your mind. Start to challenge your usual approach to situations.

OVERCOMING BARRIERS

A big barrier to creative thinking is a tendency to seek quick solutions to problems. This may help you in the short term, but you will not excel in the long run. Look at the way you currently use your time, and start to spend more time being creative.

20 Recognize the advantages and pitfalls of different thinking patterns.

21 Structure your time so that it is more productive.

22 Generate lots of ideas before making decisions.

ADAPTING YOUR THINKING PROCESSES

Human beings have a natural tendency to seek quick and simple solutions to problems. We often know the answer we want and make sure the facts support our chosen solution. However, some situations require a different, more creative approach. Divergent thinking focuses on generating as many ideas as possible and opening up new opportunities in order to find a "best fit" solution. Make the time to think creatively, think about the big picture, and avoid rushing to quick conclusions.

MAKING THE TIME

The Japanese believe that there are four types of managerial time: "Operational time" – the time necessary to correct yesterday's errors; "Strategic time" – the time needed to plan for the future; "Innovative time" – the time needed to become more competitive tomorrow; and "Kaizen time" – the time needed for the continuous improvements that ensure that we will have a tomorrow. It is generally true that we do not devote enough time to finding better ways of doing things. Make the time to review what you could improve in your work and your life, and then take action.

▲ SCHEDULING WORK
Review your schedules and delegate work to your team, so that you have time to focus on long-term goals.

TIME ANALYSIS

Look at how you currently spend your time and highlight areas where you could improve. Firstly, keep a diary of what you do during a typical week. Divide your time into four categories: Operational (project work); Strategic (planning for the future); Innovative (seeking new approaches); Kaizen (making ongoing improvements). Then, review your findings. You will probably find that you spend a significant amount of time on operational issues. Aim to increase your creative time: identify the operational activities you could reduce in order to allow you to do this. For example, you could delegate more of your work.

THINGS TO DO

1. Look at how you could increase the time you spend creatively.
2. Review procedures and think about how they could be improved.
3. Take time out to find creative solutions.

MANAGING YOUR TIME

The Japanese believe that senior managers should spend no more than 25 per cent of their time on operational issues. The rest of their time should be spread across the other three categories. The more time senior managers spend on operational issues, the less time they can spend working creatively, and this reflects poor planning. Assess how you can restructure your time more effectively. Remember that the only way to manage time successfully is to set yourself realistic schedules, and then to stick to them.

BELIEVING IN CHANGE

We need to believe that we can think the unthinkable and believe the unbelievable. Challenge the accepted way of doing things. Overcome your fear of looking foolish in front of other people and have the courage to put forward your ideas.

23 Remember that there are many ways of looking at things.

24 Be ready to question the accepted.

25 View problems as an impetus to change.

CHALLENGING BELIEFS

Sometimes we have creative ideas, but we are reluctant to put them forward because they may create precedents that "go outside the box" of accepted beliefs. You may not like to say something that others may find challenging and thus reject. Being creative means not only having the ability to come up with ideas but also being willing to challenge the conventional wisdom. Realize that all creative solutions, by their very nature, involve change and change involves having the courage to challenge the status quo.

THINKING THE UNTHINKABLE

New ideas are essential for progress, yet most new ideas are initially perceived in a negative way. The unknown is seen as dangerous, and an individual's instinctive response to a new idea is often to reject it, because it is safer to stay with what he or she has already tried and tested. Have the courage to think the unthinkable. Persuade others that what seem like impossible ideas are possible.

▲ **CONSIDERING THE IMPOSSIBLE**
In the past, few people believed that sending a man to the moon would ever be possible. However, it became a reality because people had the courage to believe in it and make it happen.

BENEFITING FROM CHANGE

Most people are intuitively opposed to any idea that they see as "not being in their best interest". The problem is that one person opposing a new idea does not stop others benefiting from it. For example, deciding not to implement a technical innovation in your organization does not prevent a competitor from making that change. Recognize that those who fail to change will be left behind.

26 Ask questions, even if they seem ridiculous.

▼ ACCEPTING CHANGE
Change occurs when people recognize the potential advantages an idea can bring and work to put it into action.

Listen to ideas with an open mind	→	Accept that change is necessary	→	Implement creative solutions

POINTS TO REMEMBER

- Close-ended problems have one solution. For example, a flat battery will need to be replaced.
- Open-ended problems are those that have many possible answers, such as planning an office layout.
- A great barrier to creativity is the fear of looking foolish.

TAKING A NEW APPROACH

Being creative means using a different approach to the way you solve certain problems. This is not something you need to do all the time – this approach is time-consuming and irrelevant when the solution to the problem is clear (close-ended). However, if a problem is open-ended and has a number of potential solutions, start to form some creative ideas and discuss them with others.

IGNORING RIDICULE

When you put forward a creative idea, you stand the risk of being called foolish. No one wants to look foolish in front of their peers and this innate fear often prevents people from voicing their ideas. Do not be deterred by the fear of being ridiculed – have confidence in yourself when you express your ideas.

RISKING RIDICULE ▶
This assistant is sharing an idea with his team. He does not let their ridicule deter him from explaining the idea.

Colleague laughs at assistant's idea

Assistant presents an abstract idea

Manager listens attentively

CHANGING YOUR APPROACH

To be able to increase your inventiveness, you need to learn how to tap into your mind's creative resources. Practise changing your natural approach to problems until the new method becomes instinctive. Take the time to exercise your mind.

27 Recognize that developing creativity takes time and practice.

28 Think about the change you would like to make and how you could initiate it.

PREPARING TO CHANGE

The way you do things is determined by your values – your beliefs. These are influenced by the culture you grew up in and they are also affected by your character. Thus, if you enjoy structure, you will tend to resist changes that appear to cut across your desire for order. If you prefer a flexible lifestyle, you will resist changes that threaten to impose order on you. Recognize that adapting your behaviour requires practice, until the change in your approach becomes a "natural" impulse.

LEARNING TO CHANGE

Change is one of the few constants in life. Some people fight it, some embrace it, others "wait and see". But no one can avoid it. Try following a set process to move from a current behaviour to a new one. For example, for some people, being overweight is a lifestyle problem. Changing this situation means following guidelines (a diet) and having regular weight checks (feedback) to create new eating habits. Identify the change you want to make, commit to the change, resolve any potential obstacles in your path, and then take action.

MAKING CHANGES ▶
It is useful to follow a structured process to help you create a change in a behaviour pattern. Take a step-by-step approach and ask a friend to give you regular feedback on your progress.

RECOGNITION
Understand the reason for making a change

DECISION
Be committed to making the change

PERMISSION
Gain consent from other parties involved

ACTION
Take the necessary action to make the change

EXERCISING YOUR MIND

Developing your creative potential means freeing up your mind. Just as someone who is used to a sedentary life and decides to take a walking holiday needs to get fit before the trip, so you need to train your mind to work in new ways before you can develop your own creative potential. Try exercising your mind. For example, imagine where you would like to be in a year's time. Focus the image so that you can touch, hear, and feel it. Develop a plan that will help you achieve this aim.

29 Remove your self-imposed mental roadblocks by carrying out creative exercises.

▲ **DOING EXERCISES**
Carry out some simple exercises to stimulate your creative thinking and teach your mind to think in new ways.

PRACTISING DIFFERENT THINKING STYLES

THINKING STYLE	ACTIONS TO TAKE
CONSIDERING CONTEXTS	Think about something that you habitually do, for example, you always go on a beach holiday. Make a list of different holiday ideas. Then, think about what you are seeking from your usual holiday and see if any of the options satisfy this need in a way that you had not considered before.
SEEKING ALTERNATIVES	Choose an idea or object that you would like to explore. For example, think about a board writer pen. How many different uses could it have? Make a list. Then, review your ideas to see if any of them provides another use that might be interesting.
MAKING CONNECTIONS	Choose a product or idea and see how many different situations you can connect it to. For example, think about the potential uses for a boat's sail. When you have exhausted your ideas, examine the connections to see what new insights they provide.

COACHING FOR CREATIVITY

Many organizations use coaching to help their staff acquire new skills or develop existing ones. Understand the coaching process, see how you can use it to improve your creative potential, and set yourself goals to work towards.

30 Use coaching to help you change your current thinking patterns.

31 Ask a colleague you admire for advice on how to improve your creative skills.

WHAT IS COACHING?

Coaching is a useful tool that can help you develop your strengths and improve your skills. There are a number of ways that coaching can be carried out, for example, through observation and feedback or through organized sessions with a personal coach. Coaching sessions, in which the coach provides leadership and a framework for generating creative ideas, is the most suitable method for developing creativity. The coach is able to support and guide the individual being coached (the coachee), and offer advice when necessary. By the end of the sessions, the coachee is also in a position to coach others – such as members of his team.

FINDING A COACH

Coaches lead by example. Thus, to be an effective creative thinking coach, the individual must understand how creativity works in practice. He or she must also have a good knowledge of the various techniques that can help develop creative thinking. Find a suitable professional coach and set up a series of coaching sessions. Alternatively, ask a friend to act as your coach. Before you have the first session, think through what you want to achieve during the coaching process. For example, decide that you want to learn how to deal with problems in a more creative way.

32 Set a fixed amount of time for a coaching session.

33 Form clear goals to work towards during a coaching session.

Coach talks through agreed action steps

BEING COACHED

During the first session, the coach should take the lead. He or she may ask you questions about your normal thinking processes or your reactions to particular situations. Discussing these issues will help you pinpoint what you could start to do differently. Allow the coach to prompt you to make suggestions. Then, set yourself achievable weekly targets and draw up an action plan. Agree how these will be monitored and set a date for the next coaching session.

▲ **WORKING WITH A COACH**
Take notes during the coaching session and put your agreed action plan in writing. Schedule a date by which these tasks will be achieved – discuss timings with your coach to make sure they are realistic.

COACHING TECHNIQUES

In order for coaching to succeed, make sure that you adhere to a structure during your coaching sessions. If necessary, divide your allotted time into sections. Spend the first five minutes discussing the problem you want to resolve. Spend the next ten minutes identifying your goals. Move on to discussing possible solutions, before taking ten minutes to write down your action plan. Always leave a coaching session on a high note, with concrete goals set out and scheduled.

34 Recognize that coaching is an effective means of changing your current patterns of behaviour.

DOS AND DON'TS

✔ Do be open to suggestions and feedback.

✔ Do be realistic about the targets you set yourself.

✔ Do treat coaching as an investment in your personal development.

✔ Do set yourself small steps − then you can achieve each one with ease before moving on to the next one.

✘ Don't expect immediate results.

✘ Don't expect your coach to have all the answers.

✘ Don't use a coaching session as a chance to express your worries.

✘ Don't set yourself goals that you cannot monitor − make sure that you and your coach can assess your achievements.

STIMULATING CREATIVE THINKING

There is a wide range of tools that you can use to stimulate creative thinking processes. They are simple to use and effective in practice. Familiarize yourself with the different creative tools and start to understand how you can apply them.

35 Pinpoint what you want, so that you can set about achieving it.

36 Think in terms of the results you want to achieve.

37 Focus on questions rather than predicting answers.

CLARIFYING THE OUTCOME

In many situations, your reaction to a problem is instinctive. You may not even think about what outcome you actually require, and the results you finally get are therefore not always what you want A useful way to approach a problem is to define the outcome before you start the problem-solving journey and then apply your creativity to achieving it. In this way, you will have reference points against which to evaluate your ideas. For example, if your desired outcome is to gain a new customer, focus your creative energies on achieving that.

CASE STUDY
John was a manager for a large supermarket. Stock deliveries took place three times a week, but it was becoming increasingly difficult to deal with the number of lorries arriving at the store at the same time. Deliveries were causing congestion, the lorry drivers were becoming frustrated about delays, and the shop staff were having difficulties dealing with the influx of goods.

John saw that a solution could be to receive deliveries five days a week – this would reduce congestion. However, he then saw that this would cause stock-control problems.
He realized that while he wanted to reduce congestion, he wanted to retain three delivery days. His solution was to create a loading times rota. By clarifying what he wanted to achieve, John was able to resolve the problem without causing any unwanted changes.

◀ **DEFINING AN OUTCOME**
In this example, a manager was faced with a problem. Although an obvious solution sprang to mind, he realized that this proposal could cause other problems. He clarified his goals, and then he was able to work through to a creative solution.

USING PHYSICAL ACTIVITY

Certain types of physical activity can provide the right conditions for creative thinking. This is because, when you exercise, your motor senses are occupied with the basics of keeping your body functioning effectively. This frees the creative part of your mind to explore ideas. Choose a sport that you enjoy and make it a regular part of your routine – take advantage of the time to think.

▲ **BENEFITING FROM EXERCISE**
When your body is engaged in a repetitive physical activity, such as swimming or jogging, your mind is free to explore complex issues and come up with creative solutions.

38 Learn to cross the natural barriers in your mind.

USING MIND MAPPING

This process is designed to help you change the way you look at complex problems. When you are faced with a problem, impose it on to a "model" so that you view it in a different way. For example, draw the shape of a tree. Write down the main parts of the problem next to the large branches; note smaller aspects of the issue against the secondary branches, and so on. Once you have separated out the problem in this way, apply your creativity to each part of the issue, rather than trying to tackle the problem as an unwieldy whole.

Annotates tree with aspects of problem to be solved

Manager thinks about problem to be solved and breaks it into separate issues

◄ **BUILDING A PICTURE**
Mind mapping provides a logical frame for analyzing problems by separating problems into manageable parts.

USING THE "HELICOPTER" APPROACH

Most of our behaviour is sub-conscious. We tend to react to people's body language automatically, rather than thinking about what that behaviour means and responding accordingly. Adopt what is known as the "helicopter" approach. When you are talking to someone, consciously interpret his or her non-verbal behaviour before responding. This will give you an insight into the other person's feelings, and help you create better mutual understanding.

Colleague makes her point with strong feeling

He realizes that she feels strongly about issue

Manager interprets colleague's non-verbal signals

Manager shows understanding and situation is defused

Manager feels disconcerted by colleague's behaviour

Manager takes offence at colleague's aggressive body language

USING A "HELICOPTER" ▲

In this example, a manager must consider what his colleague's brusque behaviour signifies before he responds, so that he can build understanding between them. If he instinctively reacts in a negative way, their discussion will break down.

IMPOSING A CONDITION

When you impose an external condition on a problem, you change the way you look at it. For example, perhaps you want to buy a new house, but you have a budget problem. Instead of asking "What can I get for my money?" ask, "How can I change my home without spending any money?" This might lead you to think of solutions you had not previously considered, such as re-mortgaging.

RECOGNIZING THE ISSUE

A good solution to the wrong problem only creates more difficulties. Sometimes we get stuck on a problem, but we are not looking at the real issue. The "Five Whys" process helps you get to the root of a situation. When you are faced with a difficulty, ask yourself why it is a problem. Each time you respond to the question, ask "Why?" again, up to five times. This process will help you explore the deeper reasoning behind what you assume to be the problem. It will force you to evaluate your basic assumptions and reveal gaps in your thinking. Work to find new insights into seemingly unresolvable problems.

39 Ask yourself why you perceive an issue as a problem.

POINTS TO REMEMBER

- Understanding what others are feeling enables you to actively manage your relationships.
- When you have a difficult deadline, you should try and imagine what will happen if you fail to meet it.
- You should examine the real root of a problem, rather than assuming that you know what the issue is.

40 Remember that problems are opportunities for change.

◀ **ANALYZING PROBLEMS**
This manager has financial problems and wants to increase her salary. Using the "Five Whys" process, she changes the focus of the problem and finds a solution.

Manager works through problem step by step to reach a new perspective

I need to earn more money to cover my debts
PROBLEM

I am in debt because my outgoings are high
WHY?

My outgoings are high because I bought a car
WHY?

WHY?

WHY?

I bought the car, so that I had reliable transport for work
WHY?

I could sell the car and find alternative transport instead
SOLUTION

179

CHANGING THE WAY YOU THINK

In order to be creative, it is necessary to change the way you think. Learn to let go of your preconceptions. Understand the different ways you can re-programme your mind so that you can see things in different, more productive ways.

41 Question and challenge ideas, rather than just accepting them.

THINGS TO DO

1. List and review your main routines.
2. Consider whether these meet your current needs.
3. Make constructive changes to these routines.

DOING THINGS DIFFERENTLY

Telling yourself to "do things differently" is simply an internal prompt that can be used to optimize your personal effectiveness. Notice your usual ways of doing things, such as morning routines; travelling to work routines; job routines; problem-solving routines; relationship-management routines. Analyze these patterns in a creative way and think about how you could change them.

UNFREEZING YOUR MIND

Sometimes your mind freezes and you cannot find a solution to a problem. Disengage from the problem and allow your sub-conscious mind to work on the issue, undisturbed by the conscious search for a solution. Try going for a walk, thinking about something else, or making a cup of coffee. Use the method that works best for you.

42 Let your sub-conscious mind find solutions.

▼ **FINDING SOLUTIONS**
Sleeping on a problem can often help. Go to bed with a problem, leave your sub-conscious mind to work at it during the night, and wake up with the answer.

DRAWING TO CREATE IDEAS

Many people find visual images are a greater stimulus to creativity than words. Some people find it easier to express themselves by outlining an idea on paper and getting others to comment on what they see. Drawing can also free up your mind to think in a creative way. Get a sheet of paper and draw how you see the solution to a problem. Show it to others and ask them what they see. Use their feedback to help you crystallize your ideas.

◀ **DEVELOPING IDEAS**

The Italian Renaissance artist Leonardo da Vinci drew detailed drawings of his many imaginative inventions, such as his ideas for flight.

USING A NEGATIVE CONDITION

Applying a negative condition means creating a situation from which you then have to recover. For example, imagine that your competitor has halved his prices. Having decided on this negative scenario, think of as many ideas as you can for dealing with the situation. Use your creativity to see how you could overcome the problem.

43 Invest time in learning to do things differently, so that you can identify new opportunities.

QUESTIONS TO ASK YOURSELF

Q Could I handle this task differently?

Q In what ways could I improve this process?

Q When did I last make a significant change?

Q Do I feel threatened by new ideas?

Q Am I satisfied with my current routines?

Q Am I willing to make changes?

Imagine that an unforeseen problem has arisen

⬇

Think of lots of ideas for combating the situation

⬇

Categorize and write your ideas down

⬇

Review these ideas to see if they offer any useful insights

⬇

Use your insights to identify any current weaknesses

▲ **IMAGINING A PROBLEM**

Test your creativity and build your confidence in your ability to deal with problems by working through imagined negative scenarios.

USING A CREATIVE APPROACH

There are many ways of applying creativity in your everyday life and many different techniques that can help you do this. Start to use creative thinking in practice.

SELECTING THE APPROACH

Not all situations respond to a creative approach. Some are too simple to warrant the time and effort involved, others need to be reframed first. Understand the decision-making process and how creative thinking techniques can be implemented.

44 Tackle open-ended problems with creative thinking.

45 Consider whether a problem requires creative thinking or whether a solution is clear-cut.

DECIDING TO BE CREATIVE

The decision to use a creative approach or not depends on the problem. If the problem is simple for example, you are about to cross a busy road, there is no need to be creative. In fact, being creative could be counter-productive because you need the full power of your logical thinking process to get you safely across the road. However, if you are looking at ways of reducing the number of road fatalities that occur, this is an open-ended problem and a creative approach will offer you more solutions to consider. Recognize the situations where a creative approach would be beneficial.

CATEGORIZING PROBLEMS

Once you have identified that an issue is open-ended, the next step in the process is to categorize it and form a problem statement. Problems can be grouped into three categories: personal, such as an illness; professional, such as a career change opportunity; or they can involve a third party, for example, an issue that you want to help someone else to resolve. Having categorized the problem, define it and rephrase it – this will help you look at it in a different way.

PROBLEM STATEMENT ▶
Re-stating a problem allows you to see it from a different perspective, so that you can find fresh solutions.

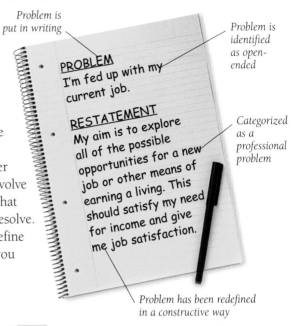

Problem is put in writing

Problem is identified as open-ended

PROBLEM
I'm fed up with my current job.

RESTATEMENT
My aim is to explore all of the possible opportunities for a new job or other means of earning a living. This should satisfy my need for income and give me job satisfaction.

Categorized as a professional problem

Problem has been redefined in a constructive way

UNDERSTANDING CONTEXTS

During the creative process, it is important to identify all the parties who have a stake in the solution of the problem. This is so that the solution matches the needs of everyone involved. For example, at an international level, there is no point looking at the political issues in the Middle East without considering the Western concerns about oil. If this is not taken into account, it is unlikely that a suggested solution will gain agreement.

46 Identify your desired outcome, so that you can work towards achieving it.

VISUALIZING OUTCOMES

Now that you have prepared your problem statement, imagine the outcome that you want to achieve. Visualizing your goal will help you clarify what you want to achieve through the creative process, and it will also help you judge the ideas you generate. Imagine actually achieving your goal. Think about how you will feel – will you feel pleased, relieved, or still uncertain? Your response is an indication of whether you really do want the outcome and it will also help to make your goal very compelling. Think about how well this outcome fits in with your other goals. Does it fit in with the direction you want your life to go in?

CHOOSING THE RIGHT TOOL

When you have clarified the desired outcome, the next step is to select the appropriate creative tool to help you achieve it. Like choosing the right club in golf, choosing the right tool is crucial to the success of the creative process. Sometimes you will need to use a combination of tools; for example, you might choose a "mind map" to clarify a problem, and then try "imposing a negative condition" to help you generate ideas. Once you have come up with ideas, use "logical thinking" to analyze them.

47 Use creative tools to help you think in more productive ways.

48 Learn how to select the right tool to achieve the best result.

USING A CREATIVE TOOL▼
Once you have decided that a problem requires a creative approach, choose the appropriate tool and use it to help you find an effective solution.

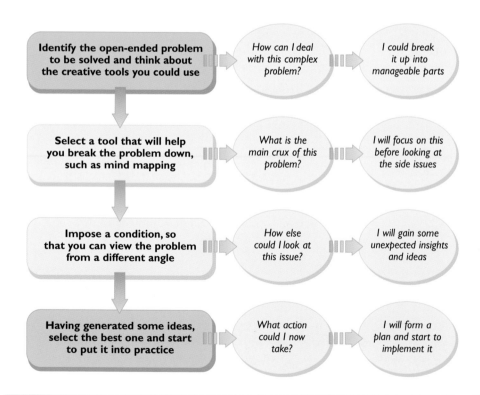

Identify the open-ended problem to be solved and think about the creative tools you could use	How can I deal with this complex problem?	I could break it up into manageable parts
Select a tool that will help you break the problem down, such as mind mapping	What is the main crux of this problem?	I will focus on this before looking at the side issues
Impose a condition, so that you can view the problem from a different angle	How else could I look at this issue?	I will gain some unexpected insights and ideas
Having generated some ideas, select the best one and start to put it into practice	What action could I now take?	I will form a plan and start to implement it

CHOOSING THE RIGHT TOOL FOR THE PROBLEM

TOOL	PROBLEM TYPE	APPLICATION
MIND MAPPING	Suitable for problems that have many parts, such as buying a house.	Provides a framework for breaking down a complex situation and enabling creative thought.
USING A NEGATIVE CONDITION	For problems where you need to generate creative ideas.	Changes your perspective and helps you generate new ideas on a topic by imagining a negative scenario.
PHYSICAL ACTIVITY	For problems that need quiet reflection, such as communicating bad news.	Frees up your mind for mental "hedge hopping".
THE "HELICOPTER" APPROACH	Useful when you want to understand what others are really feeling.	Lifts you above your problem, so that you notice non-verbal behaviour and respond appropriately in a situation.
IMPOSED CONDITION	Suitable for finding a new paradigm, like managing a life change.	Changes the shape of a problem. Provides a different perspective and allows new ideas to be evaluated.
THE FIVE WHYS	Useful for dealing with problems that have hidden agendas.	Helps you "drill down" into a situation to find the real problem, clarify issues, and form creative solutions.
DOING THINGS DIFFERENTLY	For situations in which you are seeking to make improvements.	Helps you find ways of improving personal effectiveness, and focusing your mind on what could be done differently.
OUTCOME THINKING	Useful when you want to focus on what needs to be achieved.	Enables you to clarify desired outcomes before the start of the problem-solving process.
UNFREEZING	For problems where you cannot think of any more ideas.	Helps you when your thinking process is blocked or shut down and you cannot find any solutions.
DRAWING	For problem solvers who feel happier expressing themselves graphically.	Empowers your ability to express yourself. An essential tool for people who think in a visual way.

APPLYING YOUR CREATIVITY

When you generate creative ideas, it is necessary to check that your ideas meet your needs. Make sure that you are clear about what you want to achieve. Check your ideas are relevant, and then refine them, so that they are ready to share.

49 Believe there is a better way to do things and then find out what it is.

RECOGNIZING THE NEED

New ideas are born out of the need to change something. Human beings are motivated to satisfy their needs and, when a need is not being met, they search for a solution to resolve this situation. Recognition of a need occurs when you identify your current situation with a preferred alternative and find the latter attractive. Having recognized this need, you are in a position to find a satisfactory solution.

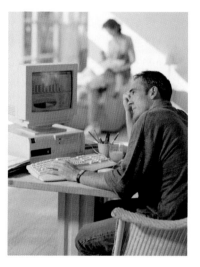

◀ **IDENTIFYING YOUR NEEDS**
This manager finds that he has to take work home in order to achieve deadlines on a project. He realizes that this causes him stress so he decides to renegotiate his schedules with his seniors.

BEING CREATIVE

It is relatively easy to go out and find a new job when you are dissatisfied with your current one; this is a logical approach. But is it the answer for you? Maybe not. Most people who change jobs are not really any more satisfied than they were before. This is because they did not clarify the need they were really trying to satisfy, and they did not creatively explore the opportunities open to them. Clarify what you really want, for example, more interesting work, more freedom, less routine. Use the Five Whys approach and then use an "alternative thinking" approach to generate ideas.

50 Write down your ideas and start to evaluate them.

51 Think about what you would like in an ideal world.

USING REFRAMING

Reframing is a useful way to clarify your needs and help you generate new solutions. For example, perhaps you are unhappy in your job. Instead of thinking about finding a new job, start to think about how you could feel more fulfilled at work:

❝ I would feel more valued if I was given more responsibility and had greater challenges. ❞

❝ I enjoy working with others, so I should concentrate on developing team projects. ❞

❝ I would enjoy my job more if I was able to change my working hours and have more time to myself. ❞

❝ I would find my job more satisfying if I received feedback from my boss – I will ask for a review. ❞

ANALYZING IDEAS

Once the ideas have been produced, they need to be evaluated. This means applying a logical process. Identify "must" and "want" criteria. "Must" criteria are the things that have to be achieved by the decision. For example, if you were considering a change of job, a "must" criteria might be to maintain your income at a certain level. A "want" could be to earn more money in the long term. Start to assess your ideas against the criteria.

52 Be clear about your goals and ideas when you explain them to others.

THE FOUR Ps

When you present an idea, start by outlining your Position – provide an overview of the background to the situation. Discuss why the situation is a Problem and highlight any quantifiable data. Outline the Possible courses of action. Mention the advantages and disadvantages associated with each possible choice. Put forward your Proposal, and highlight its benefits.

SELLING YOUR IDEAS

All ideas have to be presented to someone at some stage in the process in order to gain approval for action. The way a presentation is made can determine the success of a proposal. There are varying ways of structuring a presentation but one of the best known and most effective is called the "Four Ps" method. Introduce your idea and outline your Position. Then, define the Problem, detail the Possible courses of action, and put forward your Proposal.

IMPLEMENTING IDEAS

Creativity has value only if it is turned into action. Understand the process by which creative ideas are turned into realistic plans. Make sure that you are able to monitor progress, and always be ready to deal with difficulties should they arise.

53 Recognize that ideas that are left unimplemented have no value.

54 Write out an action plan, so that you can begin to put your ideas into practice.

DEVELOPING A PLAN

Once an idea has been accepted, the next step is to produce an action plan. A formal plan will provide you with a structured and thorough approach. It will also enable you to communicate your ideas to others. List the activities that are required for the implementation of the idea. Prioritize the actions. Estimate the time that each activity will take and produce a plan.

ALLOCATING WORK

When the plan has been agreed, the next step is to allocate the tasks. If you are implementing the project alone, do the tasks in the planned order. However, if you have the task of managing a team, for example, to develop a new product, the tasks need to be delegated. Use the "Prime Model" to help you guide your team through a project.

USING THE PRIME MODEL ▶

When you are putting proposals into action, use a structured approach. Make sure that you have all the necessary resources. Then, delegate tasks, monitor progress, and evaluate results.

55 Make sure that all your team members are clear about the goals of the project.

PREPARATION
Collect the necessary materials

READINESS
Organize your resources

IMPLEMENTATION
Carry out and delegate work

MONITORING
Keep checking progress

EVALUATION
Ensure you achieve the goal

MONITORING ACTION

In order for your ideas to be implemented successfully, you need to have the means of comparing actual results against planned outcomes. Make sure you have clear, measurable objectives. "Hard" objectives" are easy to measure, such as winning a key account within three months. A "soft objective", such as improving your organization's efficiency, is more difficult to measure. However, you might measure it in terms of an increase in production. Assess how you will measure success.

THINGS TO DO

1. List individual tasks in a logical order.

2. Estimate the time each activity will take and the resources required.

3. Form and brief a team and monitor progress.

56 See how action plans help you work with others.

REVIEWING PROGRESS ▼
Meet with your project team each week, so that you can discuss progress. Work together to find creative ways to deal with unexpected problems.

MANAGING PROBLEMS

Even in the best-managed projects, problems occur. Think of problems as opportunities to be creative. If, for example, the idea for a new product or service runs into a roadblock, look for an unplanned solution. Anticipate any potential problems and be prepared to deal with them. Keep comparing the current situation against your plan and take the necessary action to correct any deviation, either before or after it occurs.

Co-ordinator discusses an unexpected problem

Assistant thinks of ideas

Manager notes down any possible solutions

INVOLVING CREATIVE PEOPLE

Sometimes we need to employ people with acknowledged creative talent to help us find the solution to our problems. Recognize the benefits of working with specialist creative people, and provide the right environment for them to thrive in.

57 Manage creative people by being open-minded and flexible.

WORKING WITH MEN AND WOMEN

It can be beneficial to work with mixed gender teams. This is because women are thought to be more creative than men. They are conditioned to have greater psychological freedom and to think in unconventional ways, whereas men are traditionally conditioned to think logically. This combination of thinking can be very effective.

SEEKING ADVICE ▶
From time to time, we need the help of creative professionals, such as office planners, to help us find new solutions.

58 Evaluate creative ideas before you judge them.

CREATIVE PEOPLE

Some people are naturally creative because they have open minds, intense curiosity, and high levels of energy. They may "see" more than the rest of us. For example, artists can often see colours and shapes in much greater detail than other people can and they instinctively know how to convey three-dimensional information in one dimension. Recognize the situations where you would benefit from employing a creative person to help you find solutions to complex problems. It is often time and money well spent.

CHOOSING THE RIGHT PEOPLE

The creative professional you choose to seek advice from will depend on the problem you are dealing with. If it is personal, such as you are looking for a new challenge, seek advice from someone who has a lifestyle you would like to emulate. If the problem is professional, such as you are unfulfilled in your current job, consult a recruitment agency. If the problem is organizational, for example, low productivity, invite a consultant with a track record for finding creative solutions to productivity problems to come and present his or her ideas.

POINTS TO REMEMBER

● Creative people are always looking for a better way.

● Informal meetings are more suitable for creative expression.

● It is important to be open-minded to ideas and suggestions.

59 Avoid rejecting ideas without considering them.

BUILDING A ▶ PICTURE

In this example, a large clothes retailer began to lose its customer base. By recruiting an innovative design team and creating a new range of clothes, the retailer was able to restore its flagging profits.

CASE STUDY

A large clothes retailer found itself in difficulties. Its products and image had become outdated and its traditional customers were deserting it. The end of year results were poor.

The organization tried a number of different ways to help improve its disappointing results, including changing its top management and looking for alternative suppliers, but all without success.

The management team then took a close look at what they actually wanted to achieve, so that they had critieria against which to measure success. They wanted to get their results back on track, and to do this they realized they needed to win their customers back. They recruited two new design teams to improve their product. The designers completely remodelled the main product line, and the retailer went back into profit.

60 Always involve positive people in your decisions, as they often produce the best ideas.

MANAGING CREATIVE PEOPLE

Truly creative people tend to see themselves as gifted and in a class of their own. They need a degree of freedom in order to work effectively. Provide them with an informal framework within which to work. Give them clearly defined outcomes for their activities and supply the necessary resources. Involve them at the forefront of the decision-making process.

WORKING WITH OTHERS

Although we all have ideas that we incorporate into our daily lives, it can be difficult to encourage others to follow us. Develop ideas with others and build consensus and commitment.

WORKING TOGETHER

Creativity is stimulated when ideas are shared with others. Recognize that people will be better motivated if they are involved in generating the ideas that lead to decisions. Support others and be ready to show them how to use creative techniques.

61 Remember that collective thinking can reap many successful ideas.

62 Acknowledge that everyone has something to offer.

GAINING CO-OPERATION ▼
If people are involved in looking for ideas, they are committed to the task and motivated towards a resolution.

INVOLVING OTHERS
All ideas need the support of others to become reality. The best way of gaining this support is to discuss your ideas with everyone who will be affected by your decisions. Involve other people in developing new ideas, rather than trying to get them to accept your own ideas. Co-operate with others in order to gain their commitment for agreed actions.

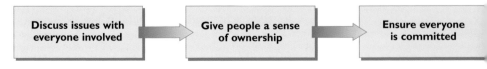

| Discuss issues with everyone involved | → | Give people a sense of ownership | → | Ensure everyone is committed |

SUPPORTING EACH OTHER

Constructive debate empowers people in a meaningful way. When people all have the same opinion, ideas can stagnate. We need new ideas and these can come only from proactive people who are not afraid to speak up. When everyone else is saying something is not possible, be the person who says, "Why not?" Use creative tools to help optimize the creativity of others and to provide a structure around which you can all generate and then analyze ideas.

THINGS TO DO

1. Encourage your team to think of ideas.
2. Ask them to put forward as many ideas as possible.
3. Work with them to assess ideas and agree on the actions you will take.

UNDERSTANDING TOOLS

Before you use creative tools with a team of people, study the applications of all the tools, and select the best one for your needs. If you have not used the tool before, find someone who has and ask for his or her advice. Get a small group together and organize a practice session before you do the exercise for real.

63 Learn how to use the necessary creative tools.

64 Aim to develop a team's creative potential.

PRACTISING USING A TOOL ▼
In this meeting, a manager is acting as a coach and observing how a team uses a creative tool. At the end of the exercise, the coach reviews how it went and makes suggestions.

Co-ordinator listens to coach's suggestions

Coach offers feedback

Assistant takes notes for team to refer to after meeting

Sales manager acknowledges points made

193

SETTING UP TEAMS

The most effective way of capturing your staff's innate creativity is to work in teams. Identify who will be affected by any decisions you make, be ready to bring the best out of other people, and start to put your creative team together.

65 Notice how a team environment gives people confidence.

66 Share ideas so that you can fine tune them.

67 Remember that open debate produces consensus.

GATHERING INPUT

To decide whether you need a team or an individual approach to a problem, ask yourself, "Will I need the commitment of others to implement my solution?" If the answer is "yes", make sure you involve the necessary people in the problem-solving process. For example, a decision to refurbish the office will affect the majority of employees and they will all expect to be consulted. Take everyone's views into account.

▼ INVOLVING OTHERS

This manager asks his staff how they feel about a departmental restructure. He listens to what each has to say, and he will incorporate their views into his decisions.

Manager asks his team for comments on restructure

Takes notes on feedback he receives

Team member has comments to make

LEADING CREATIVE TEAMS

As the team leader, you have the task of taking your team through the process of generating ideas. At "ideas meetings", be ready to adopt a different style of leadership from the one you would normally use at operational meetings. Think about how you will structure the creative meeting and how you will encourage everyone to contribute.

POINTS TO REMEMBER

● The creative process should focus on generating ideas, rather than assessing them.

● The team is responsible for the work and the results – the team leader acts as the guide.

● The joint mental capacity of many people is superior to the brains of a few.

▲ A GOOD TEAM LEADER
When you are managing creative teams, make sure that you brief your team well. Show others how to use creative tools and lead creative exercises effectively, so that you get excellent results.

Presents recommendations

Selects appropriate tools

Organizes resources

Analyzes results

Leads the exercise

Briefs the team

FORMING CREATIVE TEAMS

When you have identified who will be affected by your ideas, start to form your team. The optimum group size for a creative exercise is seven or nine people, so if 100 people will be affected by your decision, choosing a team becomes more difficult. You could repeat the exercise ten times with ten separate groups or ask each group of ten to appoint a representative, and invite these representatives to meet with you.

◀ BRIEFING TEAMS
Just as a football coach will brief his team and offer it guidance, make sure that everyone on your creative team is clear about the goals you have set.

68 Make sure the composition of the team is appropriate for the problem.

195

FACILITATING THE PROCESS

Teams can solve problems on their own but, with a good leader, they will also gain the full benefit of this learning experience. As team leader, make sure that your team is well briefed and create the right conditions for them to generate ideas.

69 Ensure that the team understands the aim of the creative meeting.

ORGANIZING THE PROCESS

Arrange the necessary accommodation for the creative meeting. Choose a large room with comfortable chairs and provide light refreshments. Make sure that there will be no disruptions and remove any telephones. Think through the goals of the meeting. For example, if the problem is a customer complaint, your meeting goal could be to, "Find a solution to the problem and ensure that it does not recur".

BRIEFING THE TEAM

Supply your team with information about the meeting in advance and make sure that they understand the goals of the exercise. For example, the meeting may be taking place to find a solution to a customer satisfaction problem. Outline what creative tool you have chosen to use and make sure that everyone understands how this tool works. State that everyone will have the chance to present their ideas and that these ideas will then be reviewed before a course of action is decided upon.

70 Make sure that you prepare your meeting well.

Manager sends brief to team via e-mail

SENDING AGENDAS ▶
Before the meeting, e-mail your team a clear agenda so that they know what to prepare for. Explain the process and the goal.

PREPARING TO RUN A CREATIVE SESSION

Ideally, a creative session should last no longer than an hour. During the session, at least 30 minutes should be dedicated to the generation of ideas. To run a successful creative session you will need the following:

● A large room with no telephones or other distractions.

● A flip chart, lots of paper, marker pens, and adhesive tape.

● A "U" shape seating layout around the flip chart.

● A group of people, most of whom should be closely involved with the issue in question. Ideally, the session should also include two or three people who are "outside" the problem – they will be invaluable for stimulating new ideas and for offering different perspectives on the issues.

● A problem to be addressed, and a clear goal to work towards. This should be written up on the flip chart, so that the focus of the meeting is always in view of everyone. If the meeting veers off its course, you can steer people back to the issue in question by pointing to the flipchart.

LEADING THE EXERCISE

The leader's role is to support the creative process by adopting an open style of leadership. This means providing a structure that frees people from their usual behaviour patterns. Encourage less vocal team members to speak up, and challenge unconstructive behaviour. Inspire the sharing and the sparking of ideas by asking open questions and discouraging team members from being judgmental. Be neutral about suggestions and value all contributions.

71 Listen carefully, and make notes you can refer to.

CULTURAL DIFFERENCES

In some countries, such as Japan and India, employees have a tendency to follow the lead of their managers, rather than taking the initiative themselves. In Western countries, such as the United States, organizations tend to encourage all their staff to offer their points of view and come up with creative ideas.

DOS AND DON'TS

✔ Do take every suggestion seriously – take ideas to their logical conclusions.

✔ Do help, support, and guide the process of creative thinking.

✘ Don't reject ideas just because they seem drastic or ridiculous.

✘ Don't influence the group by expressing your own ideas and opinions too freely.

BRAINSTORMING

This team technique is ideally suited for solving open problems. It is a simple means of generating a large number of ideas from a group of people in a short space of time. Teams enjoy the process because it is interesting and it makes people feel valued. It helps provide new solutions to old problems – take full advantage of all the ideas that are gathered.

Assistant puts forward idea

All team members are fully involved

72 Just call ideas out, rather than thinking about them first.

▲ **A BRAINSTORMING SESSION**
Brainstorming sessions can be run in a number of different ways, but they should always be lively, fun, and informal. The atmosphere should be conducive to spontaneous creativity.

Write the problem down – try stating it in several ways

⬇

Select the best statement of the problem

⬇

Begin to brainstorm the problem – call for ideas

⬇

Identify the best ideas and brainstorm them further

⬇

Categorize ideas and identify instant winners

RUNNING THE SESSION

Start a brainstorming session by outlining the task or problem to be worked on. Explain what is expected of everyone and how the process will work. Write the problem on the flip chart. Phrase it in constructive terms, such as, "How can we reduce the production time?" Then, work your way through the brainstorming process.

73 Suspend judgment, encourage the generation of ideas, and let other people's thoughts inspire you.

◄ **THE BRAINSTORMING PROCESS**
Work through the brainstorming session in a structured way. If ideas are slow in forthcoming, encourage further input. Leave the evaluation of any ideas until the end of the meeting.

USING DATA DUMPING

Data dumping is a highly visual method of producing ideas and it allows group consensus to be formed. The results are also much easier to evaluate than they are in a brainstorming session because the ideas are categorized. Start a data dumping session by stating a problem. Give each participant a set of sticky notes and ask them to write down his or her ideas in capital letters, using key words only. Each idea should be written on a separate sticky note. Participants should take it in turns to present their ideas while others ask them questions. As the leader, identify common themes and mark them on the flip chart. Tell the participants to put their notes under the appropriate headings – in this way, ideas are categorized. At the end of the session, agree on the action to be taken.

Leader asks assistant to clarify point

Sticky notes are placed under category headings

Assistant outlines her idea

Team member thinks of an idea in response to what his colleague says

Leader directs session and makes sure team stays focused

FORMING IDEAS ▲
During a data dumping session, make sure that each team member is given the opportunity to explain his or her views.

ANALYZING YOUR IDEAS

Ideas need to be analyzed to make sure that they are workable and meet your specified criteria. After a creative session, evaluate all the ideas against your goals. Identify instant winners, categorize ideas, and decide what could be implemented.

74 Remember that data only becomes information after it is categorized.

75 Pinpoint the ideas that are obviously instant winners.

76 Choose the easiest ideas to implement initially.

RECOGNIZING WINNERS

An instant winner is an idea that can be put in place immediately, providing instant benefits. For example, in a major management attitude change programme, the idea was to provide training for 800 managers from five different sites. Conventional training sessions were considered impractical so a "brainstorm" was held to find a solution. Analysis of the results produced an instant winner idea: "Train them all at once". The result was a training session held in a local hall capable of holding a large number of people, with successful results.

CASE STUDY
Jane was a product manager for a sports goods company. Products were sold by a directly employed sales force through local distributors. Jane started to notice that the number of orders she received in some months was very low, while other months showed strong sales. Jane raised this issue with her managers, and the problem was brainstormed at the sales conference. The aim was to create more stable sales figures. It then emerged that the real problem was that when the sales people saw they were having a poor month, they made it very poor by moving orders into the following month, thus ensuring their next month's bonus.

One suggestion was that commission should be paid against an annual sales target instead of monthly ones. This idea was put in place and sales began to meet targets.

◀ **IMPLEMENTING YOUR IDEAS**
In this example, a manager noticed that sales figures were fluctuating month by month. The issue was brainstormed at the sales conference. One of the suggested ideas was implemented and sales figures started to become more consistent.

CATEGORIZING IDEAS

With the exception of brainstorming, categorization is an integral part of the process of all the creative tools. After a brainstorming session, however, you are generally left with a large amount of random information. This then has to be captured and analyzed. The most effective way of doing this is to form categories. Once you have done this, list the ideas under the category headings. Highlight the ideas that are easy to implement and make sure that radical ideas are included in the list.

77 Choose categories that will help you manage the data.

Problem that was brainstormed

Improving Productivity

People
- Sack lazy people
- Pay better bonuses
- Improve training

Ideas have been sorted under appropriate headings

Technical
- Update machinery
- Improve maintenance
- Remove all quality controls

Radical ideas are included

Products
- Simplify design*
- Copy competition
- Improve handling

Finance
- Link pay to performance*
- Stop overtime
- Delay payments

Ideas that are easy to implement are highlighted

Ideas are summarized

SORTING IDEAS ▶

After a brainstorming session, categorize the ideas under different headings so that they can then be analyzed.

78 Judge ideas on their achievability and their value, and rate them on a scale of one to ten.

ASSESSING CRITERIA

Now that you have categorized the ideas, you can begin to rate them. For example, if the brainstorm ideas were focused on improving productivity, judge ideas by considering their potential impact on performance. Assess all of the ideas against this criterion. Once you have identified the ideas that meet the need, rate them in terms of achievability and value using a ten-point scale. Then, select the ideas you will implement.

STIMULATING IDEAS

People can find generating ideas difficult, especially when it means moving into the unknown. Try to find best practice examples to help inspire your team. Lead people with confidence, and ask questions that open new avenues of thought.

79 Try changing the way that you look at a problem.

Identify an area
for improvement

▼

Select a "best practice"
example as a comparison

▼

Brainstorm the characteristics
of the selected best practice

▼

Compare these characteristics
with the area to be improved

▼

Identify areas that offer
opportunities for improvements

▼

Carry out a detailed assessment
and form an action plan

80 Empower people to generate solutions.

MAKING COMPARISONS

Provide your team with a structure for creating out-of-the-box solutions to existing problems. To help generate and assess ideas, try comparing the features of something you would like to improve against a best practice example. This method is known as Metaphor Analysis. Begin by thinking in general terms about what you want to achieve and then ask yourself, "Where in business, sport, or nature is this already done well?" Then ask, "What are the features that make it successful?" Compare your current situation against the best practice situation, and start to generate ideas.

◀ **USING METAPHOR ANALYSIS**
This method helps to refresh and stimulate tired minds. It encourages people to break down conventional procedures and move towards a new and more desirable future.

DOS AND DON'TS

✔ Do work through ideas with your team.

✔ Do notice how other organizations deal with similar problems.

✔ Do seek inspiration from different sources, even if the connection seems oblique.

✘ Don't force ideas if you are not in the mood.

✘ Don't reject comparisons without giving them due consideration.

✘ Don't assume that there is only one right answer.

BEING ASSERTIVE

Our interpersonal behaviour can be characterized as either directive, passive, or assertive. Directive behaviour, which involves telling people how to do things, is designed to get things done in the way we would like. Passive behaviour is the acceptance of someone else's directions. Assertive behaviour is based on questioning what we do, as well as seeing new and better ways of doing things. Be assertive when you lead others, so that you open the door for suggestions and ideas.

81 Set a good example to your team by being proactive.

▼ **ASSESSING BEHAVIOUR**
Passive behaviour is fine in an unchanging world, but assertive behaviour holds the key to the future.

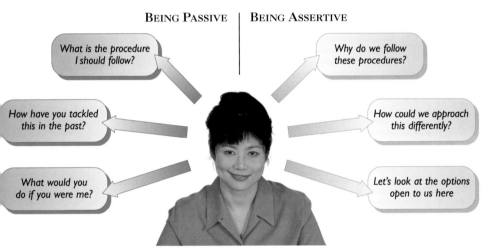

BEING PASSIVE | BEING ASSERTIVE

What is the procedure I should follow?

Why do we follow these procedures?

How have you tackled this in the past?

How could we approach this differently?

What would you do if you were me?

Let's look at the options open to us here

82 Use questions that challenge accepted thought.

83 Use closed questions to access information.

ASKING QUESTIONS

There are two types of question: open questions – those that seek general information while also generating dialogue; and closed questions – those that ask for specific information and discourage discussion. Open questions are those that cannot be answered with a straight "yes" or "no" response. Recognize that these types of question are the lifeblood of creativity. Use open questions to encourage your team to think creatively and explore ideas. Help them "get outside the box" of accepted thought.

BEING SPECIFIC

Sometimes it is useful to use closed questions, for instance when you want to find out some specific information. There are two main types of closed question. There are those that produce definite "yes" and "no" answers, such as questions that begin with, "Did you…?", "Can you…?", "Will you…?" And there are those that seek specific answers and facts, such as, "How old are you?" or, "What is your name?" – these provide reference information. Once something specific has been identified, explore it by using open questions.

RESEARCHING DATA ▶
Closed questions can be used to find specific answers in surveys, such as market research questionnaires.

84 Be polite when you ask people questions.

QUESTIONS TO ASK YOUR TEAM

Q How do you think we should deal with this?

Q What do you think could be done to improve the current situation?

Q Why do you believe that it is not possible to change things?

Q How do you think it would be possible to benchmark our performance?

Q What would you do if you were in charge?

USING OPEN QUESTIONS

Open questions result in answers that give you clues about the other person's feelings. Such questions might be, "What do you hope to do when you have finished at college?" or, "What did you think about that film?" The answers to these questions provide a broader response, as well as an insight into the attitude of the respondent. The easiest way to ask an open-ended question is to begin the sentence with a specific request such as, "Please outline your views on…" or, "Please tell me a little about…". Use phrases that indicate that you want to hear an opinion.

85 Use closed questions to start a discussion, and then develop it by asking open questions.

Challenge a proposal	→	Outline a proposal that you feel unsure about
Explain your aim	→	Explain that the aim is to test the decision
Design questions	→	Ask participants to list questions they want to ask
Discuss the proposal	→	Ask participants to present their questions
Write up ideas	→	Categorize suggestions on a flip chart
Question decision-maker	→	Put ideas forward to the person who made the proposal
Record the results	→	Look at whether the decision has been improved

▲ ASKING QUESTIONS

This questioning process is used to help you challenge a proposal. It is a valuable way of adapting ideas, but it should be carried out tactfully in order to achieve the best results.

EXAMINING IDEAS

Use a process to help you challenge your own or other people's ideas. Then you can test proposals and pinpoint possible improvements. Bear in mind that people can feel threatened when their ideas are scrutinized and that they may take criticisms personally. Be diplomatic, or your questions will be counter-productive. If you have suggestions to make, use examples from another unrelated situation. Be ready to listen and learn from other people.

POINTS TO REMEMBER

- When pressed to make changes, some people may harden their position.
- Sometimes it is necessary to push for change gently.
- Change means letting go of the past in order to embrace the challenges of the future.

86 Be sensitive when asking questions – avoid making people feel as if they are being interrogated.

REVIEWING IDEAS

Organizations waste a great deal of money every year on new ideas that fail because they have not been challenged and examined objectively. Use the different perspectives of your team members to test the potential of ideas.

87 Challenge ideas in order to fully understand what they represent.

88 Decide whether you are a dreamer, a realist, or a critic.

89 Notice what roles people in your team tend to play.

EMPLOYING A STRATEGY

The Disney Strategy is based on a method that Walt Disney used to solve problems. His philosophy was to integrate creative and logical thinking so that they took place in a sequence. In this way, ideas could be properly examined and problems effectively solved. He said that every meeting should have a "Dreamer", a "Realist", and a "Critic" present. Each of these types of thinkers has an important role to play in the examination of ideas. Identify what kind of thinker you and other members of your team are.

RECOGNIZING DIFFERENT TYPES OF THINKERS

THE DREAMER
This is the role of a person who is not bound by convention or restricted by tradition. This person is excellent at coming up with visionary ideas for his or her organization.

THE REALIST
This person takes a concept and asks questions like, "How would this work?" He or she approaches plans in a practical way. Sometimes he or she takes action before all the outcomes have been assessed.

THE CRITIC
This person thinks logically. He or she can see the vision, accept the workable details, and can also see the pitfalls. The critic can be over-cautious, but he or she makes sure that the realist's plans are feasible.

- An objective is something you want to achieve, and a strategy is how you plan to realize it.
- When you choose to play a role, do it with conviction.
- Ideas can be accepted only if they are openly challenged and openly defended.
- You can eliminate risks if you take the time to research the situation first.

USING DISNEY STRATEGY

Bring together a team of people and ask for volunteers to be the Dreamer, the Realist, and the Critic. Present the group with a problem to be solved and give them ten minutes to think about it. Let the Dreamer present ideas, ask the Realist to consider plans, and let the Critic identify the possible pitfalls. At the end, review the results.

▼ LISTENING TO DIFFERENT THINKERS

Different types of thinker can give varying perspectives on an old problem – there is room for a dreamer, a realist, and a critic on every creative thinking team.

Ask the dreamer to come up with ideas	Let the realist analyze the possibilities	Allow the critic to find potential problems

USING ROUNDS

One of the major problems with working in a team is that it can be easy for the powerful to dominate the weak. Using "rounds" enables the leader to manage the group in a democratic way, so that the weak can be as powerful as the strong. Any participant can stop the discussion and ask for a round. Each participant must then state his or her view on the subject, without fear of being interrupted.

90 Make sure that everyone has the chance to speak.

Sales assistant has her say

Leader sets example by listening to each team member

CALLING FOR A ROUND ▶

In this example, the sales assistant asks for a "round" and states her view. Each person then gives his or her view on the issue.

IMPROVING YOUR PROCEDURES

For organizations to remain competitive, they need continually to develop what they do and the way that they do it. Apply creative methods to analyze procedures and review your organization's practices to make sure that they are efficient and up to date.

91 Keep reviewing and questioning to stay ahead of the game.

92 Analyze your current procedures to see how they can be improved.

REVIEWING PROCESSES

The profitability of organizations is determined by the effectiveness with which they convert customer orders into goods and services. This "conversion" is achieved though a series of inter-related operational processes. These determine how effectively things get done. Process re-engineering is a method of assessing procedures and adjusting them if necessary. Use it to review and update your organizational processes.

REVIEWING VALUE

Organizations that wish to remain competitive must regularly review their products, processes, and materials. Value re-engineering is used to reinvent or update the products organizations make or the services they deliver. The aim is to ensure that all products and services are subjected to regular reviews to assess how they can be improved in the light of new technology, new materials, and new methods. For example, it may be possible to substitute new plastic materials for the metal parts used in a product, or it could be more cost-effective to subcontract a process rather than carrying it out "in-house".

CULTURAL DIFFERENCES

Optimizing the value of an organization means aligning the values of everyone involved – such as managers, employees, suppliers, and customers. The Japanese achieve this by holding reviews. In the United States, market research surveys are put in place to gain feedback on goods and services.

USING TOOLS TO REVIEW PROCESSES AND VALUES

TOOL	STAGES	ACTION
	1. Select the process.	Choose a process you want to review.
	2. Choose your team.	Involve people from all departments.
	3. Outline the process.	Produce a map of the current process.
PROCESS RE-ENGINEERING	4. Identify issues for review.	Look at flaws, blockages, or gaps.
	5. Outline a desired goal.	Show the process as it should be.
	6. Make recommendations.	Explain how to implement ideas.
	7. Monitor action.	Put in place monitoring procedures.
	1. Choose the product.	Review all products regularly.
	2. Select the team.	Involve a cross-section of people.
	3. Discuss the product.	Decide on the aspect to be reviewed.
VALUE RE-ENGINEERING	4. Provide information.	Ensure that product data is available.
	5. Review.	Look at ways of improving the product.
	6. Agree changes.	Analyze and decide on changes.
	7. Make recommendations.	Outline necessary improvements.

EVALUATING RESULTS

Good proposals need to be refined to make sure that they will do the job they were designed to do. There will always be people who oppose creative solutions, so identify the strengths and weaknesses of your ideas and then present your proposals with confidence.

93 Inspire people to accept any changes that you propose.

94 Recognize that poor presentation skills kill ideas.

95 Ask your team to offer ideas on how processes can be improved.

SELECTING PROPOSALS

All creative exercises produce multiple ideas that need to be "waste weeded" and then further refined to enable objective choices to be made. The ranking and rating method is a very effective way of doing this. It can be carried out either by individuals – the resultant data is then analyzed to reach a consensus – or by a team. Start with a list of alternatives. Ask your team to rank each idea in order of preference from one to ten. Then, ask them to rate ideas from one to five, to reflect how effective they believe the chosen solution will be. Record individual rankings and produce a list showing the most valued ideas.

EXAMINING A PROPOSAL

When you are discussing ideas with your team, ask questions that will help develop potentially good ideas further and also find out if there are any potential causes for concern. Here are some examples of things you could say:

❝ Imagine that this change has been put in place. How will it affect our customers? ❞

❝ If we took this idea a step further, what other implications would there be? ❞

❝ If this idea is so good, what is preventing us from putting it in place immediately? ❞

❝ How could we suggest this change in procedure to our suppliers and distributors? ❞

ANALYZING CHOICES

The tool most commonly used to analyze choices is the SWOT Analysis. The process, usually carried out by a small group, is to analyze a decision in order to identify its Strengths, Weaknesses, Opportunities, and Threats. Analyze the strengths of a proposal. What benefits will it bring? Assess the weaknesses. Could there be potential problems? Will we need new investment? Identify any possible opportunities. What markets will it open? Examine the threats. Is there a risk that we will lose our existing customer base?

96 Review the implications of your decisions.

97 Consider your ideas from every possible angle.

THINGS TO DO

1. Define your proposition – state what you want to do.

2. Identify positive and negative factors.

3. Use ranking and rating to see which forces will have the greatest impact.

4. Develop an implementation plan that builds on the positive forces and minimizes the negative.

ASSESSING PROS AND CONS

Force field analysis is a technique for identifying the elements that will help or hinder a proposal. If, for example, you want to introduce an annual review system, you will need to recognize who will actively support the process and who may be against it. For example, employees may approve of review sessions because it will make them feel valued. However, some managers may see reviews as time consuming and pointless. After these factors have been considered, develop a plan to harness the positive support and reduce the impact of resistance. In this way, you will increase your chances of success.

98 Be convincing when you present your ideas.

PRESENTING IDEAS ▶
Once you are confident in your ideas, present them, explain the benefits, and outline how you can deal with problems.

211

IMPROVING TEAM EFFECTIVENESS

We can improve the way we work only by reflecting objectively on our performance, identifying the areas for improvement, and than taking action. Aim to continually improve your own creative performance and that of your team.

99 Remember that a team is only as strong as its leader.

100 Use feedback to help you improve your skills.

101 Avoid taking criticisms personally.

DEVELOPING SKILLS

It is always worthwhile investing in your own skills and personal development, as well as those of your team members. At the end of each project hold a review and look at how you could have worked more creatively. Notice areas where you could have achieved better results if you had had the necessary know-how, such as technical training or better people-management skills. Keep up to date with developments within your industry, and make trade journals available to your team members, too.

ANALYZING PROJECTS ▼
Review projects with your team and discuss how you could have dealt with issues differently.

Assistant suggests change in procedure

Colleague agrees with assistant

REVIEWING PERFORMANCE

At the end of a project, assemble your team and say that you would like some feedback on your performance. Prepare a questionnaire and distribute it. Ask all team members to complete the form and fill one in yourself. Then, note the key questions on a flip chart and ask participants to say how you scored. Seek explanations for the marking. After the meeting, consider the feedback you received and compare it with your own views on your performance. Identify areas for improvement and decide on actions you will take.

QUESTIONS TO ASK YOURSELF

Q Did I run that project well, or did I tend to seek quick solutions, instead of taking the time to think creatively?

Q What areas of my performance do I need to improve?

Q Have I noticed failings in others that I can also see in myself?

Q Does my analysis of my performance match the views of my team?

▼ ASSESSING YOUR PERFORMANCE

After a creative session, for example a brainstorming exercise, prepare a questionnaire and ask your team to give you feedback on your performance as a leader.

Questionnaire is typed up

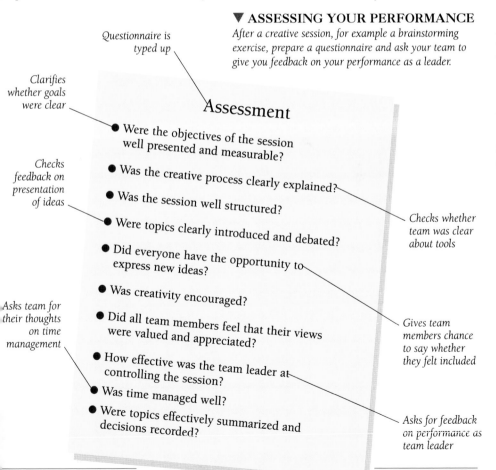

Clarifies whether goals were clear

Checks feedback on presentation of ideas

Asks team for their thoughts on time management

Assessment

● Were the objectives of the session well presented and measurable?

● Was the creative process clearly explained?

● Was the session well structured?

● Were topics clearly introduced and debated?

● Did everyone have the opportunity to express new ideas?

● Was creativity encouraged?

● Did all team members feel that their views were valued and appreciated?

● How effective was the team leader at controlling the session?

● Was time managed well?

● Were topics effectively summarized and decisions recorded?

Checks whether team was clear about tools

Gives team members chance to say whether they felt included

Asks for feedback on performance as team leader

213

ASSESSING YOUR CREATIVITY

*E*valuate *your current levels of creativity by reading the following statements, and then choosing the option that is closest to your experience. If your answer is "never", circle Option 1; if it is "always", circle Option 4, and so on. Be honest with yourself. Add your scores together and refer to the analysis to see how you scored. Use your answers to identify areas that need improvement.*

OPTIONS
1 Never
2 Occasionally
3 Frequently
4 Always

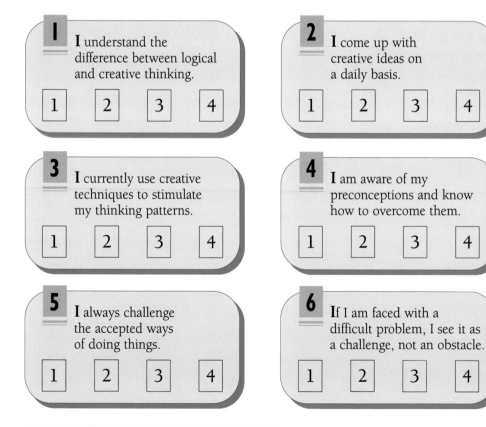

1 I understand the difference between logical and creative thinking.

| 1 | 2 | 3 | 4 |

2 I come up with creative ideas on a daily basis.

| 1 | 2 | 3 | 4 |

3 I currently use creative techniques to stimulate my thinking patterns.

| 1 | 2 | 3 | 4 |

4 I am aware of my preconceptions and know how to overcome them.

| 1 | 2 | 3 | 4 |

5 I always challenge the accepted ways of doing things.

| 1 | 2 | 3 | 4 |

6 If I am faced with a difficult problem, I see it as a challenge, not an obstacle.

| 1 | 2 | 3 | 4 |

7 I believe that I am able to think outside the box of convention.

| 1 | 2 | 3 | 4 |

8 I am good at searching my mind for new solutions to old problems.

| 1 | 2 | 3 | 4 |

9 I often wake up in the morning with new solutions to problems I face.

| 1 | 2 | 3 | 4 |

10 I always make the time to think creatively before analyzing ideas logically.

| 1 | 2 | 3 | 4 |

11 I review processes and procedures regularly, rather than just accepting them.

| 1 | 2 | 3 | 4 |

12 I believe that the impossible is possible if I want it badly enough.

| 1 | 2 | 3 | 4 |

13 I am not ashamed to suggest ideas, even if others may see them as foolish.

| 1 | 2 | 3 | 4 |

14 I regularly question my assumptions to ensure that I am being realistic.

| 1 | 2 | 3 | 4 |

15 I am always willing to listen to someone else's ideas.

| 1 | 2 | 3 | 4 |

16 I always take opportunities to do new things.

| 1 | 2 | 3 | 4 |

17 I accept that others may have difficulty with new ideas and adapt accordingly.

1 2 3 4

18 I regularly visualize my goals, and I find this helps me to solve problems.

1 2 3 4

19 I can see, hear, and feel my world and am happy with my position in it.

1 2 3 4

20 I question decisions if I think that this will lead to better results.

1 2 3 4

21 I sometimes find that people around me find my ideas threatening.

1 2 3 4

22 I keep looking for new ideas, even when I have found a potential solution.

1 2 3 4

23 I understand the value of using creative tools to solve problems.

1 2 3 4

24 I believe that even good habits can be a barrier to creativity.

1 2 3 4

25 I try to adopt a different way of doing something every week.

1 2 3 4

26 I believe that it is necessary to adapt in order to survive.

1 2 3 4

27 I know that being creative may make me unpopular with others.

1 2 3 4

28 I always ask people for their views before I make any decisions.

1 2 3 4

29 I believe that it is possible for everyone to be creative.

1 2 3 4

30 I think that it is necessary to take time out to be creative.

1 2 3 4

31 I believe that people who are not involved in an issue can still offer insights.

1 2 3 4

32 I take pride in being creative, and I encourage others to be creative, too.

1 2 3 4

ANALYSIS

Now that you have completed the self-assessment, add up the scores and check your performance by referring to the evaluation below. Identify your weakest areas, and refer to the relevant chapters in this section to hone your creativity skills.

32–64: There are many areas of your creativity that you need to work on. Concentrate on changing your preconceptions and set time aside to think more creatively.

64–95: You have a good grasp of how to be creative, but you need to improve your skills further.

96–128: You are well versed in the use of creative techniques and are fully equipped to get the best from your team, too. However, there is always room for improvement.

INFLUENCING PEOPLE

INTRODUCTION

The ability to form mutually respectful relationships with others and to succeed in getting your ideas heard is a vital element of being a good manager. Having influence enables you to gain support and commitment for your proposals, and therefore increase your potential for success. Influencing People will help you build your communication skills, improve your ability to engage the interest and co-operation of others, and develop an authoritative and reliable reputation. Practical advice, including 101 concise tips, shows you how to develop influential attitudes and become someone to whom colleagues will look for advice and leadership. Finally, a self-assessment test at the end of the section enables you to evaluate your skills as an influencer.

UNDERSTANDING INFLUENCE

When you succeed in getting your ideas heard and accepted, you are exerting influence. Recognize that your powers of persuasion contribute directly to your ability to achieve your goals.

BEING INFLUENTIAL

Effective influencers are convincing and trustworthy, and both these qualities require self-management. In order to persuade others to accept your point of view, it is necessary to present a clear case that matches their needs.

I Order your thoughts logically before you present an idea.

THE ART OF PERSUASION

Over 2,300 years ago, the Greek philosopher Aristotle summarized the skills required to become a successful influencer in his book on rhetoric. He defined persuasion as the ability to convince others to adopt your ideas. A good influencer is able to speak logically, fluently, and confidently. He or she is able to motivate and inspire others by appealing to their hidden interests.

◀ THE ROOTS OF INFLUENCE
Aristotle wrote that to be convincing, you need to learn how to win over minds with logic, to win over hearts with emotion, and to manage yourself, so that you are seen as authoritative.

2 Study the techniques of public speakers.

3 Improve your credibility by being well informed.

WINNING HEARTS AND MINDS

You win people's hearts when you respect their aspirations, interests, and concerns. In order to persuade people of the merits of a proposal, you will need to demonstrate how your ideas meet their needs. Let your enthusiasm for your ideas show, without letting it blind you to other people's views. In order to win minds, you must research your subject and present a good case. If someone has his or her own ideas, it will be necessary to negotiate a solution that meets their needs and yours.

MANAGING YOURSELF

Good influencers manage their emotions well. You can develop your confidence by noticing when you feel anxious, and then channelling this emotion in a positive way. For example, if you are nervous before a meeting, recall past successes and then imagine yourself doing well now.

HAVING INFLUENCE ▶
Effective influencers look and sound confident, well-rehearsed, and polished. They are alert to the feelings of others and adapt what they say accordingly.

CASE STUDY
Jan was a regional manager in an international organization. Her analytical approach to situations enabled her to win debates with her operating managers. However, she tended to call formal meetings to discuss issues, rather than having more informal chats. Other staff found her unapproachable.

She began to notice that her colleague James was more influential within the company than she was, and consistently achieved better results. She realized that James spent time with his operating managers outside work hours and showed an interest in their personal values. The close relationships he built enabled him to exert influence and to reach agreements quickly.

Jan began to invest more time in her relationships with other managers and tried to understand their needs. Her ability to influence her colleagues began to improve.

◀ DEVELOPING INFLUENCE
In this case study, a manager found that she was not as successful as her colleague at forming agreements and achieving results. She watched to see how her colleague's techniques differed from her own, and discovered how she could improve her influencing skills.

223

BUILDING COLLABORATION

All effective influencers cultivate collaboration with others and work to form productive relationships. Aim to be aware of people's needs and interests, so that you can work together to reach mutually beneficial goals and solutions.

4 Understand that effective influence stems from two-way dialogue.

SEEING OTHER PEOPLE'S POINTS OF VIEW

Influence is not about forcing other people to accept your ideas – this would lead to resentment. It is about achieving the support of others to work towards mutually desirable goals. If you are in a discussion with a group, imagine yourself in their shoes: see, hear, and feel their response to your message. Adapt your ideas to their needs, so that you will engage them more effectively. Seek their opinions before asking them to accept your ideas.

BEING ADAPTABLE

Prior to a one-to-one discussion, a meeting, or a presentation, make a list of the reasons why you think people will or will not go along with your ideas. Build these points into your communication, so that you appeal to the other party's motivations and pre-empt any objections. When you start talking, describe your goals in general terms and then ask your listeners what they feel is the most important consideration. Probe their views by asking questions. When you receive an answer to a question, give yourself time to reflect on it, and take it into account before you explain your idea in more detail. Adapt your ideas, so that they incorporate the other party's views rather than persisting in your own proposals regardlessly.

5 Notice other people's body language when you suggest an idea.

6 Be flexible in your approach and consider the concerns of others.

QUESTIONS TO ASK YOURSELF

Q What do I want to achieve from this partnership?

Q What does my counterpart want from our relationship?

Q How can I dovetail these wants so that we are both happy?

Q What can I give up without sacrificing my overall goal?

Q What can my counterpart offer that may not be immediately obvious?

Q What new solutions serve our common goals?

FORMING PRODUCTIVE RELATIONSHIPS

Influence goes hand in hand with agreements. For example, in order to persuade someone to follow a course of action, you need to make agreements about what is to be done and by whom. Positional bargaining is where one side sets out a case and the other responds with a stronger argument in favour of his or her own position. Such competition leads to conflict in which the side with the most power wins and the loser resents the loss. Be creative and work to reach agreements that serve the interests of both parties, because this will be more beneficial in the long run.

WORKING EFFECTIVELY WITH OTHERS

COMPETITION

"I want this deal and I am not going to compromise."

COLLABORATION

"What can we both gain from this deal?"

Look for areas of shared interest

"My idea is the only workable one."

"How can we make both of our ideas work?"

Pool ideas and start to form mutual goals

"I'd rather lose out than shift on this."

"Let's find ways to ensure both goals are achieved."

Work together to achieve top results for everyone

THE PURPOSE OF INFLUENCE

Good managers work with others to create agreements, build relationships, and achieve results. Be clear about what your aims are. Then, work with your senior managers, colleagues, and team to find shared interests and reach mutually desirable goals.

7 Understand how influence helps you create agreements with others.

INFLUENCING TO ACHIEVE A GOAL

Before you can satisfy mutual goals, you need to be clear about your own goals. This will help you focus your message. For example, before you introduce yourself to someone, think about what you want from the contact. If you want information, pinpoint what you want to know. If your aim is to interest others in your ideas, rehearse what you will say.

"SMART" GOALS

The mnemonic "SMART" will help you clarify your goals:

● Be *Specific* about what you want.
● Make sure that you can *Measure* results.
● Ensure that your goal is *Achievable*.
● Ask yourself if the goal is *Relevant*.
● Consider the *Timing* – when does your goal need to be accomplished by?

CREATING INTEREST

Appeal to people by adapting what you say to their culture, needs, and attitudes. If you are addressing people junior to you, it may be necessary to take the lead; with senior managers, you may only be required to deliver a brief. Before a discussion with someone, think about the approach you will take.

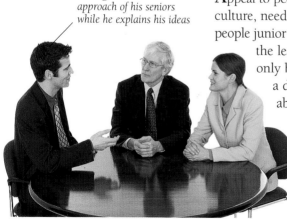

Manager matches relaxed approach of his seniors while he explains his ideas

◀ **ADAPTING STYLES**
In this example, a manager matches the formal dress and informal manner of his senior managers, so that they are more likely to react positively to his ideas

REACHING AGREEMENTS

You can only get the support of others to help you achieve your goals by reaching agreements with them. Types of agreements may include customer service agreements or a joint resolve to co-operate on a project. Your ability to influence others will increase if you are able to be firm, yet flexible. Establish the interests you have in common with the other party and aim to meet their needs as well as your own.

8 Review and update your goals regularly.

▼ FORMING AGREEMENTS
Outline your proposals clearly and decisively, support them with evidence, and take into account the views of others.

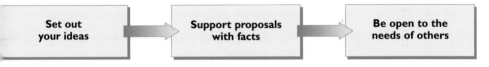

| Set out your ideas | Support proposals with facts | Be open to the needs of others |

UNDERSTANDING THE PURPOSES OF INFLUENCE

PURPOSE	METHODS
BUILD RELATIONSHIPS Create mutually beneficial relationships with others.	● Gain rapport. ● Dissolve fruitless conflict. ● Create mutual respect.
FORM AN AGREEMENT Agree on a solution that both parties are satisfied with.	● Ask questions to find out the other party's needs. ● Co-operate to find solutions that meet mutual goals. ● Incorporate other people's needs into your ideas.
WIN CUSTOMERS Put forward a proposal to a potentially new client.	● Work to understand the needs of your customers. ● Express your proposals with confidence. ● Present information that appeals to your listeners.
MOTIVATE TEAM MEMBERS Inspire team members to achieve top performance.	● Understand what drives each individual in your team. ● Outline the benefits for everyone involved in achieving team goals.
IMPROVE CAREER PROSPECTS Develop your career so that you can achieve your top potential.	● Understand your own ambitions and aims. ● Influence the senior managers in your organization. ● Build a network of useful contacts.

SWAYING OPINION

Research shows that opinions can be swayed by a variety of aspects, such as negotiation, debate, the presentation of facts, the credibility of the speaker, and the emotional appeal of the message. Combine as many of these methods as possible, adapting your message to suit whoever you are speaking to. In this way you can motivate individuals to achieve their goals; energize team members to work towards a common aim; get support for your ideas from your colleagues; or secure the backing of senior managers. To sway opinion in small groups or with individuals, make your message intimate and specific; to persuade larger groups, make your message more wide-ranging in scope.

STYLES OF SPEECH

After the battle of Gettysburg, Abraham Lincoln rekindled the morale of his men with a speech that began: "Four score and seven years ago, our fathers brought forth on this continent a new nation, conceived in liberty and dedicated to the proposition that all men are created equal...." His approach appealed to emotions and united his men in a common cause.

9 Win the respect and trust of your senior managers.

10 Tailor your points to suit the decision makers.

INFLUENCING YOUR SENIOR MANAGERS

The first step to influencing senior managers is to develop your confidence in your ability to get your ideas across in a decisive way. You can do this by being clear about your goals. Take every opportunity to demonstrate to your senior managers that you can be trusted with challenges and authority. Exercise your powers of persuasion through maturity of judgment, a command of the issues, and the ability to put your ideas across clearly and dynamically.

DOS AND DON'TS

✔ Do identify the interests and concerns of those you wish to influence.

✔ Do be aware of other people's responses to your communications.

✘ Don't miss the clues that tell you that your approach is not working.

✘ Don't continue with a suggestion regardless of the affect you are having on others.

11 Be confident when you telephone your customers – this will build their trust in your abilities.

12 Consider what motivates you in your work.

13 Make sure that you listen as well as speak.

INFLUENCING COLLEAGUES

Everyone has a good reason for being in their chosen occupation, whether this is a regular salary, convenient working hours, or the chance to be creative. Find out what motivates people, because the key to influence is knowing what people value. Ask your colleagues to think about how they could link their goals at work to their personal values so that they could increase their motivation levels. Then, link these values to your proposals so that you will be more likely to gain your colleagues' co-operation on a project.

INFLUENCING TEAMS

To build a top-performing team, you must first discover the shared values of your team members and outline a common purpose. This will prepare the way for the next influential step: to mobilize the shared energy of team members. Ask your team to consider how their inspirational goals could be achieved. Develop an action plan. While your team is working towards these goals, be available to defuse conflicts and motivate individuals.

MOTIVATING TEAMS

Establish the purpose of the team

Identify and summarize immediate goals

Discuss how these goals can be achieved

Form a plan and allocate responsibilities

Outline any aims for the future

Listens to feedback about progress

◀ BUILDING A TEAM

When you are creating a project team, take the lead, brief the team well, and allocate responsibilities. Listen to feedback, and be available to offer advice and support as projects progress.

MANAGING YOURSELF

Good influencers look, sound, and act convincing. Take steps to increase your confidence, improve your ability to empathize with others, and build trusting relationships.

BUILDING SELF-ASSURANCE

People will place greater trust in your ideas if you communicate with confidence. Learn how to increase your poise and self-assurance, develop the ability to recover quickly from your mistakes, and build on your personal strengths.

> **14** Make it your goal to talk to new people wherever you go.

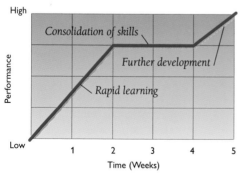

▲ **DEVELOPING SKILLS**
When you are improving performance, there is an initial period of rapid learning. Skills then need to be practised before they improve further.

TAKING SMALL STEPS

If you are new to an organization or to the arts of influence, develop your confidence one step at a time. This will allow you to achieve each task you set yourself and reinforce what you learn. For example, approach colleagues from other departments and ask them to brief you on what is going on in their field. Begin to make more contributions at meetings, and work up to more ambitious presentations. Tolerate nervousness as the price you pay for progress.

MAINTAINING POISE

Relaxation is your most important aid, because when you are relaxed you can think clearly and respond to challenges. Learn to stay calm, whatever the situation, by practising relaxation techniques until they become second nature. If you make mistakes, see them as learning opportunities. Detach yourself from the situation and ask, "What did I learn from that?" Learn to switch off negative self-talk such as, "I am no good at this".

Posture is upright and positive

15 Become a natural optimist – look for solutions rather than dwelling on problems.

▲ **BEING COMPOSED**
Always retain your composure so that you are better able to deal with any difficult situations that may arise.

BUILDING ON YOUR STRENGTHS

STRENGTH	DEVELOPMENT
ENERGETIC	Always be decisive when you outline your ideas to other people.
ORGANIZED	Make a point of planning your contributions to meetings or presentations meticulously.
FRIENDLY	Consistently put people at their ease with some well-chosen words, a compliment, or a smile.
KNOWLEDGEABLE	Keep up with current affairs and organizational matters, and subtly display your in-depth knowledge.
AMBITIOUS	Push yourself to take opportunities to lead meetings and make presentations to senior managers and customers.
ANALYTICAL	Think through your ideas from every angle and consider every objection.

DEVELOPING INFLUENTIAL ATTITUDES

Effective influencers usually have a mission. They are motivated by their values and so they are able to lead others effectively. Identify your needs, hopes, and values, cultivate your leadership abilities, and start becoming more proactive.

16 Observe what good leaders do and aim to follow their lead.

FINDING YOUR MISSION

Take some time out to think about your talents, strengths, and long-term goals. What interests you most about your work? It could be writing, planning, or human relations among many other things. In the long run, you are more likely to be successful at your job if you are interested in what you are doing. Be clear and realistic about your limitations. Ask yourself what support you need from others and then set about getting it.

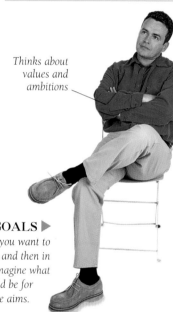

Thinks about values and ambitions

17 Ask a friend for feedback about your strengths, weaknesses, and abilities.

ANALYZING GOALS ▶
Think about where you want to be in a year's time, and then in five years' time. Imagine what your initial steps could be for achieving those aims.

DOS AND DON'TS

✔ Do believe in your abilities to achieve more in the future.

✔ Do welcome new challenges.

✔ Do continually aim to improve your skills.

✘ Don't feel defensive when others criticize your work.

✘ Don't shy away from more responsibility.

✘ Don't allow yourself to become complacent.

CULTIVATING LEADERSHIP

Leaders are people who can inspire others to participate in a vision. They are adept at balancing the need to get the job done with the need to maintain good relationships. The first step is to be clear about your purpose: this will give you an underlying strength that others will sense. The next step is to be clear about your organization's purpose. What needs to happen in order to overcome the obstacles to success? Once you have identified what needs to be done to achieve results, you are in a position to exert influence.

18 Decide what your first step towards leadership will be.

19 Understand that setbacks will happen.

Develop high expectations of yourself and others

Establish what is important for you and others to achieve

Define your intermediate and long-term goals

Harmonize your goals with your organization's goals

Gather ideas from others and get their support

Deliver a vision of the way things could be

Find ways to use others' strengths to achieve the vision

BECOMING PROACTIVE

To be an effective influencer, you need to do more than just wait for opportunities to come to you. Putting yourself at the forefront of projects that are going forward and taking every chance to make contacts is central to influence. People who back away from challenges are usually reactive – they see themselves as powerless to influence events. Become more proactive by acknowledging that you are responsible for what happens to you and always assume that life is what you make it. Interpret events in a positive way and take the initiative in making things happen. Learn from your mistakes and ignore situations that you cannot influence.

20 Recognize that influence comes from developing good relationships and sharing creative ideas.

◄ **DEVELOPING INFLUENCE**
Establish what you want to achieve personally and within your organization. Make your vision more realistic by defining how you and others can work together to build a successful future.

EMOTIONAL INTELLIGENCE

The ability to manage oneself and to build better relationships with others is vital for a successful influencer. Be aware of your own emotions, be sensitive to the feelings of others, and always act with honesty and openness.

21 Listen to your instincts when you are making difficult decisions.

ACTING WITH EMOTIONAL INTELLIGENCE

The author Daniel Goldman states that you act with emotional intelligence when you are aware of, and regulate, your own emotions and when you are sensitive to the emotions of others. Get to know your own moods well. Pay attention to the emotional state of other people, so that you can time your assertions sensitively.

Motivated

Self-aware

Self-regulated

Empathetic

Influential

▲ EMOTIONALLY INTELLIGENT
An emotionally intelligent person understands his or her own strengths and weaknesses. He or she knows that it is more productive to manage emotions rather than be led by them.

POINTS TO REMEMBER

● It is more productive to act with poise and determination, rather than to act out of fear or anger.

● By interpreting other people's non-verbal responses, you can gain insights about their feelings.

● Deal with other people's fears by exploring their assumptions.

22 Be aware of other people's preconceptions.

MATCHING BEHAVIOURS

When people have rapport, they are mutually responsive. As one leans forward, the other will too; as one speaks slower, the other does too; when one relaxes, the response is mirrored. Build rapport by matching your counterpart's body language and voice tone. Then, to find out if you really do have rapport, subtly mismatch by leaning forward or speaking faster. If the other person copies you, it is a sign that you have good rapport and that the other party is open to your influence.

LEARNING TO READ NON-VERBAL SIGNALS

Important clues to people's emotions can be found in non-verbal behaviours, such as gestures and facial expressions. By paying attention to these you can fine-tune your approach. Watch out for non-verbal signals that may indicate a person is drawing away from you. Look for behaviours that show you when someone is moving towards your view.

23 Match voice tones with others to build rapport.

▼ NOTICING SIGNS
Folded arms and a lack of eye contact indicate withdrawal. A positive expression and an open posture signal interest.

Lack of eye contact shows indifference

Tense posture indicates withdrawal

Folded hands indicate defensiveness

Foot is pointing away from speaker, suggesting resistance

Legs are crossed, forming barrier with speaker

WITHDRAWN

Direct eye contact indicates interest

Forward-leaning posture shows attentiveness

Clasped hands suggest eagerness

Feet are facing forward, showing attentiveness

ATTENTIVE

QUESTIONS TO ASK YOURSELF

Q How would I feel in that situation?

Q Am I being honest about my own feelings here?

Q Do I have a tendency to hide my own views on issues?

BEING OPEN WITH OTHERS

People are more likely to open up to those who act with sincerity. Be ready to share your emotions and values on a project and encourage openness in return. For example, if a colleague is discouraged by setbacks, speak about your own feelings of frustration in similar situations. Then explain how you overcame them.

235

DEVELOPING EMPATHY

Empathy *is the ability to read a person's responses by imaginatively putting yourself in his or her place. Develop this skill by listening, and by asking questions that get to the root of concerns, so that you can lead discussions in a positive way.*

24 Try to interpret people's intentions, as well as listening to what they say.

BEING INTUITIVE

Gifted communicators have the ability to sense what others are thinking. When you are listening to someone, be intuitive Use your imagination and your past experience of similar situations to give you some clues as to what the other person is feeling. Imagine that you are the other person and try to understand his or her needs.

◄ **INTERPRETING CAREFULLY**
Professional influencers, such as counsellors, aim to understand the assumptions and needs behind what is being said, so that they can start to solve issues.

GAUGING CONCERNS

When people tell you about something that is worrying them, they often talk around a subject instead of getting to the crux of the matter. If you feel that worries are not being aired, use questions that will help bring clues to the surface:

❝ *If you had the choice, what would you most like to happen now?* ❞

❝ *Can you give me five aspects that concern you about this issue?* ❞

❝ *What do you consider to be the fundamental thing that we should aim to achieve?* ❞

❝ *Are there any other issues that are worrying you about this situation?* ❞

LISTENING WITH "EARS"

Empathize with the person you are speaking to → Step into the other party's shoes

Acknowledge his or her interests and needs → Use non-verbal markers, such as a nod of the head

Reflect on his or her concerns → Use key words in your questions and suggestions

Summarize the key points made → Ask whether you have understood correctly

ACTIVE LISTENING

Develop the art of structuring a conversation, so that the other person feels heard, while you find out what is really at the heart of his or her concerns. Use the mnemonic "EARS" to help build rapport and understanding with another person, and to help you keep track of the key points being made. Listen for key words that express values, needs, hopes, goals, concerns, and interests.

25 Avoid giving advice unless you are asked for it.

QUESTIONS TO ASK YOURSELF

Q What assumptions are being made here?

Q Where else have I heard people voicing similar types of concerns?

Q Have I experienced a similar situation in the past?

Q What would it be like to be this person?

Q What else do I need to understand?

Q Is there something that I have missed, or have I got to the root of the issue here?

LEADING ON

Once you have developed empathy, you are in a position to lead a conversation in the direction you want to take it. Through empathy, you will have picked up some clues about the other person's thoughts and feelings. Having gathered this information, summarize what you have understood. Pause for a moment to check that your summary is accurate, then lead on with a question or a suggestion, such as, "Would it be useful to…?"

26 Check whether your intuitions are accurate by asking questions on the relevant points.

CREATING TRUST

People are more likely to be influenced by an individual they trust. Build a reputation for trustworthiness by speaking from a position of knowledge, keeping your promises, supporting others when they are in difficulty, and working through differences.

27 Remember that people respond well to honesty and courtesy.

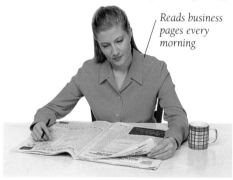

Reads business pages every morning

▲ KEEPING WELL-INFORMED

Get to know as much as you can about your line of business. Read trade journals and keep up to date with current affairs.

DEVELOPING YOUR KNOWLEDGE

When you know your subject area well, others will pay attention to what you say. Knowledgeable people breed confidence. Recognize that the more answers you have to questions, the more people will come to you when they need advice. Knowledge on a smaller scale is also useful when you are holding meetings. Brief yourself thoroughly on every issue that is to be discussed. Be ready to take the lead in briefing others.

KEEPING COMMITMENTS

People place trust in, and are influenced by, those they see as being reliable. People who do not keep their promises lose the trust of others quickly. Before you commit to new obligations, be sure that you can fulfil them. If you are not certain that you can, then say so; it is better to disappoint at this stage than later on. If, despite your best efforts, you are likely to miss a deadline, then call the other party and explain what has happened.

28 Say "No" to demands that may overstretch you.

▼ BEING RELIABLE

Before you agree to new obligations, check that you have enough time to do them and keep your promises.

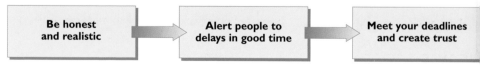

Be honest and realistic → Alert people to delays in good time → Meet your deadlines and create trust

CREATING EMOTIONAL BANK BALANCES

An emotional bank balance in your favour arises when the "gifts" you have given a person outweigh the ones you have received. Such gifts may include help, advice, information, or support. They also include those signs of personal interest that are so well appreciated: remembered personal details, such as a family event or a partner's activities; a smile; a shared lunch; or a phone call. Offer support sooner rather than later – do not wait to be asked before offering it.

29 Keep a record of things that you have agreed to do and check it daily.

▼ **ANALYZING ATTITUDES**
Think about your behaviour patterns at work – imagine how they influence the way your colleagues view you.

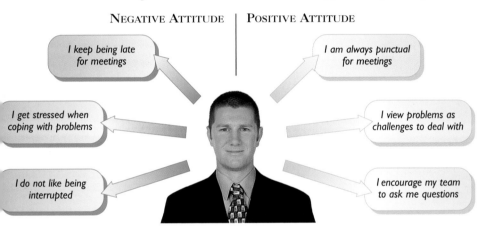

NEGATIVE ATTITUDE | POSITIVE ATTITUDE

I keep being late for meetings

I am always punctual for meetings

I get stressed when coping with problems

I view problems as challenges to deal with

I do not like being interrupted

I encourage my team to ask me questions

THINGS TO DO

1. Be open about your wants and needs.
2. Make allowance for the weaknesses of others.
3. Acknowledge your own shortfalls.
4. Be quick to make amends for your mistakes.

WORKING THROUGH DIFFERENCES

If mistrust has arisen, bury the hatchet by first being open and honest about what has happened. Make amends for your own mistakes and ask what can be done to rectify them. Voice your own concerns sincerely and listen carefully to the concerns of the other party. Learn to tolerate and explore the reasons behind differences in opinions because opposing views can often spark the best and most creative ideas. Explore agreements, but allow for different points of view.

LOOKING THE PART

The way you present yourself in your dress and in your body language affects the way people perceive you and react to you. Make a good impression by dressing to match the business culture you work in and by emanating confidence.

> **30** Notice the way that successful people in your organization dress.

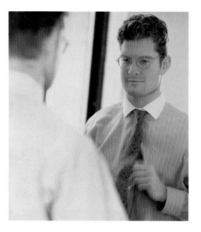

MAKING AN IMPACT

Research shows that people tend to form their first impressions within three minutes of meeting newcomers. They will be guided by dress, voice, handshake, grooming, facial expressions, and accent. First impressions are very difficult to eradicate. In order to increase your influencing skills, notice the impact that you make on others.

◄ **CREATING THE RIGHT IMPRESSION**
If you take care with your appearance, you will create a favourable impression, and you will be seen as someone who is reliable and authoritative.

MATCHING THE CULTURE

Dress code in many businesses has undergone a quiet revolution. For example, the suit has been discarded in favour of informal wear in some industries. Adapt what you wear to match the organization in which you work, because the way you dress will affect how you are perceived by colleagues, senior managers, and clients. Be ready to adapt to match the practices of customers too.

> **31** Find out a customer's dress code before a meeting and adapt your clothing to match.

WHAT TO WEAR

Codes of dress vary between businesses and industries as well as between countries. For example, established industries such as banking, accountancy, and consultancy are generally more formal in their dress style – most staff wear suits. Meanwhile design companies, publishing, and the media often favour a more casual approach to dress.

CREATING THE LOOK

Pick out your clothes carefully, because they will contribute to the impression that you make. For example, wearing a red shirt with a dark suit can make you feel more dynamic, while yellow can inspire mental stimulation. Neutral colours are very approachable and are particularly suitable if your job is very people-orientated. As well as taking care with your dress, focus on your body language too. Retain a relaxed, upright posture. Never slouch or lean on furniture. Relax your face muscles so that they are ready to break into a smile. When greeting people, ask how they are and be ready to enquire how their families are, too.

32 Allow enough time for "grooming" each morning.

33 Choose clothes that are well co-ordinated and stylish.

Bright suit is dynamic and projects confidence

Hair is regularly cut and well-groomed

Clothes are casual but well-pressed

Blouse is neat and well-fitting

FORMAL

CASUAL

Dark suit suggests integrity

Posture is upright and gives positive impression

DRESSING ▶ FORMALLY

Choose well-fitting suits in quality materials. Make sure that you feel confident and relaxed in what you wear.

◀ CREATING A CASUAL LOOK

Wear clothes that you feel comfortable in. Choose simple styles and avoid loud colours or patterns.

PRESENTING IDEAS

Your ability to persuade others rests on your ability to present a well-argued, logical case backed by evidence. Make your arguments attractive and engage your listener's interest.

FRAMING YOUR IDEAS

In order to persuade someone to your point of view, your ideas should be structured and well thought-out. Present your proposals in a logical way, and phrase suggestions carefully, so that you can guide discussions effectively.

34 Give your proposal a catchy name, so that it grabs people's attention.

ENGAGE
Outline the benefits

INFORM
Describe the facts

EXPLAIN
Talk through the process

PROJECT
Visualize the result

STRUCTURING YOUR IDEAS

People respond positively to proposals that are well organized. Catch people's interest from the start by letting them know why acting on your proposals will benefit them. Then, describe the underlying principles of your ideas so that the basis for your proposals is clear. Show how your idea will work in practice. Ask people to imagine ways in which they could apply your ideas, too.

◀ **PRESENTING IDEAS LOGICALLY**
Use this template to help you present ideas. You will soon find that the method becomes automatic, and you will be able to order your thoughts, even when you are speaking off-the-cuff.

USING FRAMES

Give structure to discussions by putting a clear "frame" around your communication. For example, using a "goal frame" means that you specify what you want to achieve. The purpose of a frame is to let people know the intent behind your words and to focus people's thinking. Preface remarks with a simple statement of purpose, such as, "Let's turn our minds to solutions" (a "solution frame") or, "Let's see how many new ideas we can come up with" (an "idea frame").

35 Change someone's perspective on a problem by adopting a different type of frame.

USEFUL FRAMES

TYPE OF FRAME	EXAMPLE
GOAL FRAME Specify what is wanted.	"Let's move on now and look at our goals." "What do we want to achieve?"
CREATIVE FRAME Generate ideas to solve a problem.	"Let's create a space for creative thinking." "This is the right time for a brainstorming session."
ACTION FRAME Set deadlines and allocate responsibilities.	"Now we've got some options open to us, let us look at who will do what and by when."
CRITICAL FRAME Identify pitfalls in a suggestion.	"Let's take a moment to consider the pitfalls of this proposal."

POINTS TO REMEMBER

- It can help you stay positive if you replace the word "but" with "and".
- A timely joke or an anecdote can often help change the frame.
- It is important to focus on positive issues, rather than being side-tracked by problems and negative points.

CHANGING THE FRAME

You can help people to see ways out of blind alleys by changing the frame they are currently in. Do this by finding another angle on the issue and then presenting it. For example, if people are bogged down in detail say, "Let's step back from the detail for a moment and consider the big picture". If someone is swamped by old problems, switch from a past to a future frame. Ask, "How will this need to be different a year from today?"

ENGAGING INTEREST

To influence people effectively, you need to find a connection between your goals and their needs and wishes. Find out what the other party wants, and use key words that emphasize these benefits as part of your proposals – draw your listener in.

36 Take the viewpoint of the person you want to influence.

ASSESSING BENEFITS

Describing how your idea, product, or service meets the needs of the people for whom it is intended is a powerful tool. Selling a fast car illustrates this idea. The fast car's powerful acceleration is a benefit for someone who enjoys driving quickly. But for a sedate driver, this confers no benefit at all. Identify your customers' needs, then focus on how they can benefit personally from the product or idea.

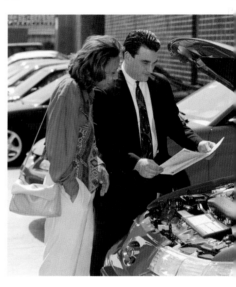

ANGLING YOUR SALES PITCH ▶
This car salesman recognizes that his customer is concerned about maintenance of the car, so he emphasizes this aspect in his sales pitch.

37 Notice what people are enthusiastic about.

38 Ask focused questions to help identify needs.

ESTABLISHING BENEFITS

The needs that people express in their own words have more credibility to them than the needs you tell them they have. For example, you may want to convince your manager to implement a new procedure. Ask him or her what he or she likes about the current methods. The answers you receive will tell you what needs to be preserved or improved by your proposal. Relate the new method specifically to your manager's needs. For example, if he or she likes the reliability of the current approach, emphasize this aspect in your proposal.

IDENTIFYING A HOOK

A hook is an aspect of your idea that meets the most important need of the listener – the key benefit. Use a hook to grab people's interest. In selling the new production method, for example, your manager's most important need may be increasing production rates to meet increased sales. So, your hook could be: "I want to propose a way to increase production and satisfy sales demands."

GAINING INSIGHTS ▶
If you want to influence a customer, it can help to gain as much background information as possible, so that you can understand their values.

39 When you sell an idea, highlight the key benefits only.

KEY WORDS

To help you engage people's interest, choose words that make your ideas connect. Visual words include "notice", "bright", and "pinpoint". Auditory words include "click", "tune", and "resonate". Feeling words include "grab", "hunch", and "impress". For example, "Using my plan has *clear* benefits that are in *tune* with our strategy, and will have an *impact* on production."

MAKING A CONNECTION

Influential people create compelling images of the benefits their listeners will derive from the ideas they advocate. They let us know what we will see and hear, and how we will feel. You can do this by using words that create pictures, sounds, and feelings to make your ideas connect with the person you are talking to. So, for example, you could express the "hook" for the production improvement as follows: "I want to *show* (visual) you how we can *beef up* (feeling) production, *harmonize* with sales (sound), and relieve the *pressure* (feeling) on us all."

QUESTIONS TO ASK

Q What do you like about the current situation?

Q What would you like to change?

Q What is most important to you?

Q How can this be useful?

Q What do you need from this?

Q Do you have a particular preference for a course of action?

GAINING CO-OPERATION

Effective influencers are open and constructive communicators. Always aim to keep discussions objective and positive by taking care over the words you choose, focusing on the essentials, and creating a reputation for openness.

40 Use "we" rather than "you" when seeking the support of others.

41 Take a deep breath before you react to a criticism.

STATING THE OUTCOME

When people know what you are asking for, it becomes easier for them to make a decision. This means making your requests in terms of what you do want rather than in terms of what you do not want. For example, instead of saying, "We never meet deadlines" say, "Let's get this done by December 31st". Remember that managers who continually state things in the negative are often thought of as moaners.

BEING POSITIVE ▼
Managers who phrase things positively, and who specify what benefits are in it for others, inspire action and loyalty.

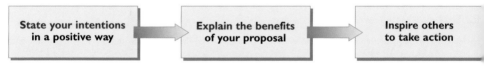

| State your intentions in a positive way | Explain the benefits of your proposal | Inspire others to take action |

EXPLAINING YOUR REASONS

Research shows that when people link their requests with a reason, they are much more likely to get a "yes" response. Try to phrase your requests carefully, so that you get the response you require:

❝ *Will you let me chair the meeting? I have some announcements to make.* ❞

❝ *Can you approve the report today? My team are keen to get started as soon as possible.* ❞

❝ *Would you finish the project by Friday? The customer made a special request for it.* ❞

❝ *Can you meet with me soon? Then we can get the project moving.* ❞

FOCUSING ON REASONS

When you put forward a proposal, choose one or two powerful arguments in your favour and concentrate on them. You risk diluting your case with weak arguments if you identify too many reasons. For example, you could come up with many reasons to convince your boss to allow you to work at home for a few days each month. Instead, choose two strong arguments to form a more convincing case. For example, point out that if you work at home, you will be able to clear twice as much work and will therefore have time to improve team performance.

PRESENTING THE FULL PICTURE ▼

This manager is presenting an idea to her team. She is precise and specific about the problems that need to be overcome, but she also explains how it will be possible to deal with these. Her enthusiasm and positivity gain her the co-operation of her staff.

42 Bring contentious issues out into the open.

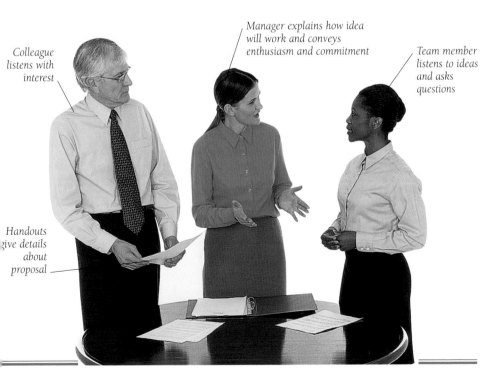

Colleague listens with interest

Manager explains how idea will work and conveys enthusiasm and commitment

Team member listens to ideas and asks questions

Handouts give details about proposal

SELLING YOUR PROPOSAL

When you are presenting an idea to another party, it is important to describe the steps by which the action plan will be accomplished. Explain how the process will work, and talk about what will be done to deal with any difficulties.

43 Keep the end goal in mind when you are explaining ideas.

44 Distribute handouts during a presentation – these should highlight your key points.

SPECIFYING THE PROCESS

Whatever your proposal, it needs to be accessible to the other party, whether this is one person or many. When you are explaining your ideas, keep to the point and avoid getting distracted by details – you can hold another meeting or take questions by e-mail once the other party has had a chance to think things through. Your main object at this stage is to show that your ideas are valid.

IDENTIFYING KEY INFLUENCE POINTS

PROPOSAL	EXAMPLE OF KEY INFLUENCE POINT
REALLOCATE ROLES	Explain how the new roles make the most of each team member's strengths.
DEVELOP NEW PRODUCTS	Talk about how the proposed products will effectively meet customers' needs.
CHANGE PROCEDURES	Explain how the new procedures will improve the effectiveness of administrative tasks.
INTRODUCE NEW SYSTEMS	Point out the benefits that new technologies will bring.
IMPLEMENT TRAINING	Show how training will reflect well on your organization's commitment to its staff.

BEING LOGICAL

When making your proposal, take your listeners step-by-step through to the final goal. Mention who will be involved, over what period of time, with what resources and support, and where the action will take place. You will come across as naturally influential when you demonstrate that you have thought things through. Show confidence in your ideas and handle objections with ease.

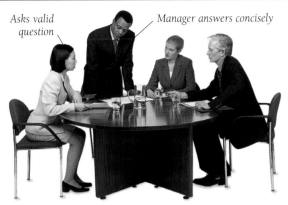

Asks valid question

Manager answers concisely

▲ OUTLINING PLANS
Describe exactly how a project will progress, detail any possible problems that will need to be handled, and answer any questions that arise. Your confident attitude will inspire trust in others.

45 Acknowledge the limits of your proposal.

46 Make your explanations as simple as possible.

QUESTIONS TO ASK YOURSELF

Q Would I invest money and time in this plan?

Q What is the worst thing that could happen?

Q Have I dealt with all my doubts?

Q Have I looked at the alternatives?

DESCRIBING CONTINGENCY PLANS

No plan can deal with every eventuality, but the more you anticipate, the more robust your ideas will become. Think about the likely obstacles and work out how they can be dealt with. Look at your ideas from the point of view of your worst critic. Then revise your plans until you have taken into account every contingency. If there are problems you cannot solve, say so.

▼ BEING PREPARED FOR PROBLEMS
When you are proposing an idea, do not hide the potential risks involved in your suggestion. Highlight the possible problems, but then go on to explain how these can be dealt with.

Suggest ideas for dealing with potential problems

SOLUTIONS
- Plan response to unavoidable risk
- Allocate resources

Highlight possible obstacles

RISKS
- Predict potential problems
- Identify known risks and threats

249

PROJECTING THE FUTURE

Inspire individuals or teams so that they are motivated to achieve the goals you have set out. Engage the imagination of others by encouraging them to consider the practical, far-reaching, and exciting implications of your ideas and proposals.

47 Create a mental picture of a desired future to help make it happen.

PREDICTING SUCCESS

When you are proposing something to someone, describe a future that engages his or her imagination. Imagine changes to the individual's life that your proposals could make and then describe the pictures you see, the words you hear, and the feelings you experience from his or her standpoint. Demonstrate how the person will benefit personally from your ideas.

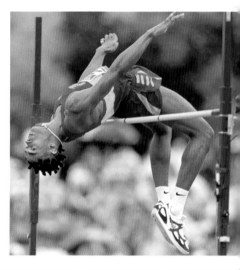

VISUALIZING SUCCESS ▶
The benefits of visualization are proven in the fields of sport and the performing arts. By imagining success, you can aim high and achieve your goals.

HANDLING OBJECTIONS WITH QUESTIONS

If someone makes an objection to your proposal, it can be useful to respond with a question. This will help you both look for solutions to problems, rather than being defeated by them. Use questions to encourage constructive thinking:

❝ *If you feel that we cannot afford the product, what can we do about the budget constraints?* ❞

❝ *If the proposal does not meet the requirements, what can be done to ensure that it does?* ❞

❝ *If we cannot begin this project now, when would be a good time to start it?* ❞

❝ *If you feel that the procedure is fine as it stands, can you outline what you like about the present approach?* ❞

IDENTIFYING SPIN-OFFS

Mention any knock-on effect your ideas will have on the team, the organization, the customers, and on the market. Think widely. These gains may seem marginal to you, but may be more central to the person you are addressing and so will sell your idea more effectively. Project a future in which your ideas are working and point out the ripple effects that they have. Engage the other person in this search for spin-offs.

48 Watch the other party's responses to your suggestions and, if necessary, change your approach.

POINTS TO REMEMBER

● If you keep your words general, your listener will have room for his or her own thoughts.

● Discuss the other party's responses with him or her and search for insights.

● It is helpful to use visual aids when you are presenting an idea, so that your listeners can picture results.

ELICITING POSITIVE RESPONSES

People will more readily commit to benefits they can see in their mind's eye. Encourage your listeners to envisage outcomes for themselves. Assume that your ideas will be turned into action. For example, say, "When we have taken the first steps…", rather than, "If we go ahead…". Ask questions that induce your listeners to think through the application of your ideas.

ENCOURAGING POSITIVE ACTION BY ASSUMING SUCCESS

NEGATIVE | POSITIVE

"If we decide to go ahead with this proposal…" ◁ **Present your project proposal to your team** ▷ "When we put these ideas into action…"

"Maybe we'll encounter some problems…" ◁ **Explain the process and ask for your team's input** ▷ "We will solve problems as they arise…"

"Perhaps you would like to think about…" ◁ **Encourage your team to imagine a completed project** ▷ "After we have completed the project…"

EXERCISING INFLUENCE

Your success as a manager is dependent on the help and co-operation of others. Engage the support of your colleagues, team, and senior managers, and fine tune your influencing skills.

FORMING NETWORKS

Building a network of supporters, allies, and potential helpers is the key to successful influencing. Make it a life-long habit to form partnerships and cultivate alliances through a genuine interest in the people around you.

49 Be confident, relaxed, and curious about the people you meet.

50 Remember that junior staff are tomorrow's bosses.

51 Start networking today – pick up the telephone.

EXPLAINING NETWORKS

Networks are loosely organized connections between people who have interests in common. An internet chat room is an example of a network. Another example is a circle of friends and acquaintances who meet occasionally at social events. Although not all of them will know everyone present, most of them will know at least one other person there. However, a network could also be a list of names in an address book. Networking involves making contact with others for two purposes: because it is fun and because business alliances can come from it.

TAKING OPPORTUNITIES

Your most common networking opportunities arise all around you, such as at lunch breaks or while you are waiting for a lift or walking through another department. Take the time to introduce yourself to people and exchange small talk about things that are happening in the organization. More formal opportunities for meeting people include training sessions and briefings. On these occasions, make the effort to get to know people.

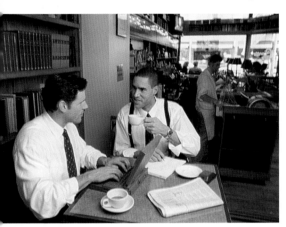

◀ **CHANCE MEETINGS**
When you are on your lunch break and you see someone you recognize from another department, go out of your way to strike up a conversation. This could be the start of a useful alliance.

52 Be open to opportunities and new friends.

INTRODUCING YOURSELF

The first golden rule is to time your entrance. Wait until people are between conversations, or pausing, before introducing yourself. If you are in a group, match what you say to what has just been said and, if at all possible, do so humorously. The second golden rule is to smile. If you are with one other person then say "hello" and give your name. Mention things you both have in common if you can, such as a mutual acquaintance.

Good listener

Perceptive

Collaborative

Friendly

Socially aware

▲ **A SUCCESSFUL NETWORKER**
This manager is an effective networker because she is able to establish mutual interests quickly, she puts people at their ease, and she finds opportunities to help others.

253

MAKING ALLIANCES

The secret of successful influence in the long term is to give more than you take. Even if your new acquaintances cannot help you now, they may be able to in the future and they may be able to introduce you to others who can help you, too. See if you have projects in common, contacts to exchange, or information to share.

INTRODUCING ASSOCIATES ▶
An excellent way to create goodwill is to introduce people to each other – this helps build alliances and shows that you are generous and supportive of others.

53 Get your name known by writing articles in journals.

54 Plan events – this is a good way to make contacts.

CREATING FOCUS GROUPS

You can start your own network by getting together some like-minded people for a weekly drink after work. This could be as an informal group or it could be one with a specific focus. Start off your group by identifying a theme that will interest as many people as possible and then contact people with that same interest.

▼ BEING PART OF A FOCUS GROUP
These managers work in different departments within the same organization, but they have agreed to meet regularly to share ideas and discuss new developments.

Sales manager talks about new customer

Product manager has some insights to offer

FOLLOWING UP

You should follow up an initial meeting with a new acquaintance as soon as possible. For example, send a short e-mail to the person to say how pleased you were to meet him or her. Be organized and keep the contact details of everyone you meet. Make notes on their work and experiences, and identify mutual interests. If the opportunity arises, invite acquaintances to the social occasions you arrange. If your relationship with a person is more formal than this, look out for opportunities to brief him or her on business matters that may be of interest.

Sends article and comments to acquaintance

KEEPING IN CONTACT ▶

This manager has seen an article in a journal that he knows an acquaintance will be very interested in, so he writes a short note and sends the article to her.

55 Keep in regular contact with your acquaintances through e-mails, telephone calls, or cards.

DOS AND DON'TS

✔ Do volunteer to lead new working groups.

✔ Do make a point of remembering names and personal details.

✔ Do be natural and open – insincerity is off-putting.

✔ Do be the first to buy a round of drinks at a social meeting.

✔ Do be the first to offer help when others need it.

✘ Don't ask people intrusive questions about their work.

✘ Don't take refusals personally.

✘ Don't worry if progress is slow – be persistent.

✘ Don't talk about your own achievements instead of taking an interest in others.

✘ Don't forget that even senior directors are people just like you.

FILING DETAILS

As your lists of contacts and acquaintances grows, develop a filing system of their details. This should include address, telephone, and e-mail details as well as any notes on correspondence. It can be useful to categorize your contacts under headings, such as the type of business they are involved in or their particular interests. Then, if you come across a useful article in a journal, for example, you can refer to your filing and quickly identify who would find the information useful.

MOTIVATING INDIVIDUALS

To achieve top performance from others, it is necessary to excite their interest in your ideas. Build trusting relationships with individuals, understand their values, involve them in decision making, secure their commitment, and give the necessary support.

56 Find out what interests team members have outside their work.

LAYING FOUNDATIONS

You are more likely to gain people's willing co-operation if you have a sound relationship with them. Look for opportunities to build mutual respect. Offer people support when they need it, and they will then be more likely to respond favourably to your requests for co-operation. When you talk to people, match their non-verbal behaviour to build rapport. It will predispose them towards giving you a fair hearing.

Manager chats to his team about his weekend

▲ **BUILDING RELATIONSHIPS**
Invest time and care in your relationships with team members and colleagues. Meet for coffee breaks, get to know them on a personal level, and respond positively to requests for help.

57 Build confidence by focusing on people's strengths.

58 Keep your team informed about developments.

SETTING THE SCENE

Always aim to engage people's interest. For example, when you give a team member a new task or an additional responsibility, give the details of the whole project, so that he or she feels involved. Knowing the big picture is motivating because people can see how they will contribute to an important outcome and this will inspire them to take an active part. Let individuals know how their contribution will affect team morale, customer loyalty, employee satisfaction, sales, profit, productivity, and so on.

ESTABLISHING MOTIVES

People are motivated to do what they like doing. They may not, however, be motivated to do what you want them to do. Discover people's values by asking them what is important to them. Then engage them by identifying how they gain personally from your plans. For example, if you know that your colleague values job security, emphasize how the new project means that there will be plenty of work for the year.

NOTICING VALUES ▶

A manager notices his employee's family photograph. He points out that if the proposal goes ahead, the employee will be able to work at home some days.

Talk to your colleague about a goal you have	Discuss what needs to be achieved and how
Identify a goal that your colleague wants to achieve	Ask questions to find out his or her motivations
Look at how this goal differs from your own	Work together to align the two goals
Decide how you can achieve your mutual goals	Let your colleague give his or her input

▲ MOTIVATING OTHERS

Discuss your mutual goals with colleagues and look at how these can be aligned. When people feel that their own input is valued, they will be better motivated to achieve results.

INVOLVING OTHERS

Participating in decision making motivates people. For example, when you talk to a colleague about how a job could be done, view it as an exercise in joint problem solving. If you have differing views, write them down. Then, brainstorm ways of closing the gap. Once you have agreed a goal, work out how to achieve it: let your colleague influence the process, so that he or she will be as committed as you are to the outcome.

59 Motivate quieter team members by asking them for their ideas.

SECURING COMMITMENT

Cement people's interest by emphasizing what they stand to gain. To check commitment, use a closed question – one that calls for a definitive answer. For example, ask, "Do you feel happy about doing what we have agreed?" Look for a clear-cut "yes" answer backed up by convincing non-verbal signs. If you see signs of doubt, work to resolve it. Ask a probing question such as, "What are your other thoughts about this?" and follow it with a question to find solutions, such as, "What do we need to do to enable you to resolve this?"

60 Look for signs of doubt, such as lack of eye contact.

61 If you cannot achieve a big goal, try a smaller one.

62 Be firm and fair when you assess others' ideas.

▼ **PROVIDING TRAINING**
To ensure the success of a new procedure, it is essential to arrange training, so that people can develop the necessary skills.

ENSURING IT HAPPENS

As well as wanting to do a task, people need to know how to do it and also have the chance to do it. Give them the best chance of succeeding in a task by providing the necessary resources. This could include giving them the necessary authority, a budget, or administrative support. If time is an issue, work with them to change priorities, reassign tasks, and improve time management.

QUESTIONS TO ASK OTHERS

Q Have you considered what steps we could now take?

Q What options are open to us at this point?

Q What one thing could you do that would make a difference to this situation?

Q What possibilities have we still not tried yet?

Q Have we neglected any important aspects?

Q How soon can we get this project moving?

Q What procedures could we put in place to help us monitor this project?

63 Show enthusiasm when you brief someone – energy is contagious.

USING PUSH/PULL STYLE

Push style of influence involves telling someone what to do. Pull style involves asking questions that presume the other person will take the initiative. A push style is useful when a person's confidence and competence is low. People look for answers because they feel more secure if they are told what to do. Use a push style with inexperienced people and gradually move to a pull style as they develop.

▼ USING "PULL" INFLUENCE

A "pull" style of influence suits most occasions. Help your team members to take the initiative by asking them leading questions and motivating them to make their own decisions.

Manager asks team member for new ideas on project

CASE STUDY

Mark was a regional manager for an American financial company. He had been sent to work in the Brazilian office of his organization for a two year period. He found that his new manager interfered with his work and did not involve him in decisions. He also resented being so far away from his family. Mark's work began to suffer, and his manager confronted him about his performance.

Mark explained what he wanted from his job. He mentioned that he had been given latitude in decision making in his past job, and he also explained that he wanted to be able to spend some time with his family. His boss was sympathetic and agreed broad parameters so that Mark could have more authority. His contract was changed to allow for a trip home twice a year. Mark's motivation levels began to improve dramatically.

◄ BEING MOTIVATED

In this example, a manager felt that his values and input were not being respected. His motivation levels fell. When he discussed his feelings with his manager, the issue was resolved and his motivation levels started to rise.

INFLUENCING TEAMS

The same principles that govern the means of influencing individuals apply to teams. However, you must also influence the relationship between team members. Define a team purpose, bring together diverse talents, and harmonize efforts.

64 Notice how the most influential person in a group is also the leader.

65 Exert influence by showing your expertise.

EXERCISING LEADERSHIP

Group dynamics are complex and can shift very quickly. If you are the manager of a team, you influence others through your authority. However unless you back up your position with a vision for the team, and by concern for your relationship with team members, your influence may be undermined If you are not the team manager, then you can exert influence through your experience and the trust you have won from others.

TAKING THE LEAD ▼
In this informal meeting, the best-informed member of the team naturally takes on the role of leader.

Business manager is impressed by what he hears

Sales administrator listens attentively to colleague

Manager is inspired by sales assistant's ideas

Sales assistant shows knowledge and leads discussion

Team leader recognizes that co-ordinator's lack of motivation is demoralizing others

Manager talks to co-ordinator and restores her sense of purpose before discontent spreads

Colleagues air grievances to assistant and discontent spreads

Co-ordinator is moaning about her work

Discontent affects colleague

DEALING WITH A LACK OF PURPOSE ▲

In this example, an office co-ordinator is complaining to her colleague about her work. The team leader must intervene to get to the root of the problem before it affects the rest of the team.

CULTURAL DIFFERENCES

In some cultures, such as Japan, subordinates tend to be subservient to their team leader. In Western cultures, such as the United States, the style of leadership tends to be more democratic. Team members are encouraged to speak their minds.

SETTING AN EXAMPLE

The model of leadership you should offer is to some extent determined by the nature of the group you are working with. For example, a team that is not achieving results may need an authoritative figure who will set a clear direction. A successful team with many talented members may need a more democratic leader, while a team in conflict may need a leader who can re-establish good relationships. However, research shows that leaders who can combine all of these skills are likely to be most influential in the long run.

SETTING A JOINT PURPOSE

To influence people to work together as a team is not easy. Your best chance is to define a common purpose that everyone can believe in. This could be high standards, recognition of good work, a community ideal, or mutual growth. Whatever it is, it has to be something people are willing to give up their time and effort to have. Look carefully at the team's function – what is its purpose? What would it mean for it to do well? Then you will be in a position to outline these values to the team.

THINGS TO DO

1. Examine the function and strengths of the team.
2. Define the principle purpose of the team.
3. Outline this purpose to your team members.

66 Ensure that each individual feels he or she is a valuable member of the team.

HANDLING DIVERSITY

Your team members may differ in their interests, needs, ages, motivations, and cultural backgrounds. Your job is to motivate them to work for themselves and for the team. Aim to create a climate of togetherness. Once you have defined the purposes of the team, establish how each member can contribute to it. Look hard at the strengths of each person and find a way that he or she could work to achieve the team's goals. Establish what each most wants to achieve and provide as many opportunities as possible for these goals to be achieved in return for teamwork

HOLDING TEAM BRIEFINGS

In order to balance the team's capacity for creativity and criticism, you will need to set guidelines for team meetings. Having set the objective or the problem to be solved, ask for creative ideas that can meet the target. It is only after these ideas have been generated that you ask the group – together – to assess them. On this basis, the best alternative can be adopted and an action plan formed. Throughout this process, influence the team to focus on each phase of the meeting, rather than rushing to a solution.

67 Involve yourself in work your team dislikes.

68 Ask your team to suspend judgment and create ideas.

STEERING A DISCUSSION

A good question can bring the team's discussion alive in a way that advice never can. After you have summarized the key points made by the team, ask an open question that leads the discussion on in a positive way. By delaying making your contribution until this time, you will not inhibit your team from putting forward their own ideas. Have some good ideas to offer at this point.

DOS AND DON'TS

✔ Do be ready to take the lead.

✔ Do take time out to review team work.

✔ Do listen to your team first, before offering your own thoughts.

✘ Don't interfere if the team is working well.

✘ Don't hang on to projects that your team could do just as well.

✘ Don't create barriers within your team.

69 Build consensus by valuing everyone's input – encourage your team members to do the same.

Define the problem

↓

Set the goal

↓

Generate and assess ideas

↓

Select the best idea

↓

Agree an action plan

▲ PLANNING ACTION
Influence your team's capacity for creativity and criticism. Direct discussions in a structured way so that you can work together to find solutions to problems and to form an action plan.

LEADING YOUR TEAM

A powerful way to direct a team discussion is to phrase things in a way that assumes something is about to happen. By subtly emphasizing the words that indicate what you want to happen, you can lead your team towards an agreement:

❝ *Before we decide on the solution, let's compare notes on what happened.* ❞

❝ *After we've discussed this, we can call the customer to let them know what we intend to do.* ❞

❝ *Have you had any good ideas yet on how we will handle this problem?* ❞

❝ *How easy will it be for you to finish this by next week?* ❞

INFLUENCING SENIOR MANAGERS

It is usually necessary to secure agreement from your senior managers for your proposals. Demonstrate confidence and foresight, identify the criteria your managers will use to assess proposals, adapt your influencing style, and avoid forcing issues.

70 Build a reliable reputation, so that senior managers learn to trust you.

71 Work to gain the respect of your senior managers.

72 Imagine how you would react to your own proposals.

CREATING A REPUTATION

Work to impress your senior managers with your ability to handle responsibility. Ideally, you should already have had some success in seeing through high-profile projects to your credit. At the very least, build a reputation as someone who can be depended on to get results, troubleshoot problems, and spot opportunities. The better your track record, the more likely that your ideas will get a respectful hearing. Recognize that people are generally promoted when they have shown that they can work at the level above the one they are on currently – talk, think, and act accordingly.

ADAPTING YOUR IDEAS

The difference between senior managers and their staff is that they have larger responsibilities. When influencing senior managers, consider their interests too – and adapt your proposals accordingly. Those in senior positions often need to take a long-term, large-scale view of an idea, such as how an idea will help the business grow. They will look beyond your ideas to assess their impact on the organization as a whole. Show that you have considered these matters also.

QUESTIONS TO ASK YOURSELF

Q Will my ideas make other people winners?

Q Is my presentation as brief as possible and have I assessed my ideas thoroughly?

Q Do I have an objective criteria for success?

Q Do my gut instincts support my plans?

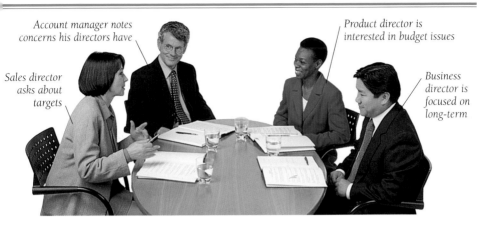

Account manager notes concerns his directors have

Product director is interested in budget issues

Sales director asks about targets

Business director is focused on long-term

ASSESSING CRITERIA ▲
By listening to the types of questions that each of his senior managers asks about his proposal, this account manager can gauge their differing criteria.

73 Anticipate the criteria of each senior manager.

IDENTIFYING CRITERIA

Success in an organization comes from the collaboration of staff and the pooling of their various skills. Department managers all have varying specialisms and concerns. For example, a financial manager will be principally concerned with accounting. However, he will also be involved in the long-term business development. Anticipate the criteria any given manager will use to evaluate your ideas, and adapt what you say accordingly.

MAKING YOUR MOVE

Once you have earned the right to be heard, studied your audience, and made your plans, it is time to make an informal approach. Timing is important: you are unlikely to get a good hearing if you approach others while they are overloaded with work. Mention that you have some ideas to share. Ask when the individual will be free to hear them, and then make an appointment.

CHOOSING A VENUE ▶
When you are introducing a proposal to a group, select a neutral venue. Arrange to meet everyone at the reception before proceeding to the meeting area.

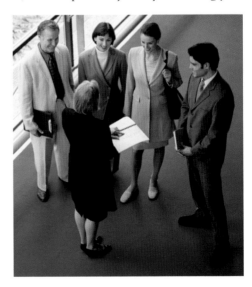

ALIGNING PROPOSALS

Get interest in your proposals by establishing ways in which they meet the objectives of the organization, the department, or the team. Start by probing for agreement. State the outcomes you have in mind and then ask your senior managers whether they agree that these aims are important. Once you have commitment to the principles, go on to show how your plans will put them into action. This will work particularly well when you mention aims that you know are dear to the hearts and minds of the senior managers involved.

74 Be assertive about asking for the go-ahead.

75 Assume success – this will give you an air of confidence.

DOS AND DON'TS

✔ Do take the opportunity to mention your ideas at informal occasions.

✔ Do look for ways to show how acceptance of your proposals will reflect well on everyone involved.

✔ Do be your own best critic – this will give you confidence.

✘ Don't appear over-eager and don't show frustration or impatience.

✘ Don't throw away old proposals – they may come in useful another time in the future.

✘ Don't forget to have facts to hand – be prepared for any challenges.

CULTURAL DIFFERENCES

In cultures where management style tends to be democratic, leaders are more likely to accept feedback in a positive way. However, in status cultures, such as Italy, suggestions or criticisms given to managers in authority can be seen as disrespectful.

76 If someone objects to your proposal, ask for their ideas on how it could be improved.

OVERCOMING OBJECTIONS

Ask careful questions to establish what the objections are. Probe for the position behind the objections. Possibly the other party is confused or uncertain rather than antagonistic. If so, ask what needs to be established before the plan can go ahead. Look for ways to minimize risk, get support from others, reduce costs, and expand benefits. It is possible that your main proposal may be rejected. If so, then have a smaller proposal ready, which preserves at least some of your original ideas.

Using Styles of Influence

Style and Use	Method
Demonstrative To give an example of your idea successfully in action.	Outline examples of the same idea at work within the organization, or in another company.
Testimonial To show the listener that the idea has the support of others.	Provide testimonials of support from others or offer to present the idea to them.
Consistent To show the listener that your proposal is in line with his or her principles.	Angle the proposal to show how it matches the needs of the listener.
Time-Aware To demonstrate how the plan will work in the long-run.	Offer to do a trial project, or to implement the plan in stages with regular reviews.
Cost-Focused To emphasize how costs and problems can be kept to a minimum.	Show how your approach resolves problems in a cost-effective way.

Exercising Patience

A lack of interest may be visible in the non-verbal responses of your seniors. If so, draw attention to this and ask for frankness in assessing your ideas. If your plans meet with criticism, do not take this personally. It is much more likely that the reasons for refusal are political and strategic rather than personal. If so, you may need to wait for the climate to change before trying again. If, despite your best efforts, you cannot gain any acceptance by reworking your proposal, then move on to something better. You will gain credit for your professionalism – and future presentations will meet with a better reception.

Points to Remember

- People are more likely to accept a smaller proposal if they have just rejected a larger one.
- You will lose respect if you do not heed feedback to your ideas.
- You should avoid being distracted by details, unless you are asked.

77 Subtly match your senior managers' non-verbal styles.

NEGOTIATING SUCCESSFULLY

It requires tact and diplomacy to handle negotiations well. Focus on interests rather than positions, prepare thoroughly, generate alternatives, remain composed when dealing with difficulties, and work to defuse disagreements.

78 Gain respect by addressing issues rather than winning arguments.

79 Take the time to think through proposals, rather than rushing to make a decision.

WORKING FROM PRINCIPLES

The classic approach to negotiation is for two sides to defend their own bargaining positions. However, if you win this battle of wills you may prejudice your relationship with your counterpart Working from principles involves a more productive approach in which you are clear about your own needs and those of your counterpart. This will gain you more influence in the long run.

CASE STUDY

Sue, an account manager for a software development house, was called in to re-negotiate a deal with a client. The buyer claimed that the cost of the product was in excess of what had originally been quoted.

Before the meeting, Sue thought through the principles that were involved. She knew her company wanted to ensure a profitable relationship, and she guessed that the client wanted a fair deal.

During the meeting, Sue dealt with the initial anger of the disgruntled buyer, and then she laid out the principles as a potential basis for agreement. She also provided evidence that her organization's prices were competitive.

Sue and the buyer agreed that the common principles underlying the deal were cost-effectiveness and a workable product. On this basis, they were then able to reach a satisfactory mutual agreement.

◀ **NEGOTIATING EFFECTIVELY**
In this case study, a manager was able to deal with a difficult negotiation by being clear about the underlying principles involved and using these as a basis from which they could form an agreement.

Identify the interests behind the other party's demands	➡	"Why is that of interest to you?"
Clarify any issues that you are not clear about	➡	"What do you mean when you say that...?"
Look for common and complementary goals	➡	"What interests do you think we share?"
Find alternative ways of meeting mutual interests	➡	"How else could we achieve our goals?"
Decide on a course of action and cement agreement	➡	"Let's form and agree on an action plan."

◀ **FORMING AGREEMENT**
Use a step-by-step process of negotiation so that you can ensure that both parties are happy with the outcome.

NEGOTIATING

Identify what you want to gain from a negotiation and then predict your counterpart's goals. Ask your counterpart to clarify these. Collaborate to identify common goals and ways to achieve mutual goals. Then, come to an agreement and write a plan, so that there can be no misunderstanding. This approach to negotiation enables both parties to achieve their aims.

80 Handle deadlocks by being firm but flexible.

COPING WITH OBSTRUCTION

Despite your best efforts at collaboration, the other party may become difficult or claim that the decision really rests with his or her managers. For example, the other party may say that if you do not give way, you will lose his or her support altogether. Refuse to be flustered and continue to press for information on facts, principles, and reasons. Avoid making concessions unless you are sure that you will get something tangible in return.

REMAINING CALM ▶
This manager remains composed, despite being faced with an irate customer. He presses for the facts of the case, and his positive attitude helps defuse the situation.

DISSOLVING CONFLICT

With the best intentions, arguments can escalate. Work to dissolve any conflict by acknowledging differences, validating other people's feelings, creating dialogue by referring to neutral criteria, and looking for areas in which you can agree.

81 Stay focused on your goals when you are faced with conflict.

NEUTRALIZING DISPUTES

Conflict can be creative if you can redirect it to find productive solutions and turn it into a platform for negotiation. If you find yourself involved in conflict, take a deep breath and focus your attention on the impersonal issues underlying the dispute. Ask a question that probes the cause of negative personal criticism, for example, "What makes you say that?" Outline the impersonal issues that you think are involved, and find out if the other person agrees.

POINTS TO REMEMBER

- It is not necessary to agree with someone about every point.
- It is easy to spot the first signs of dispute by noticing non-verbal communication.
- If a discussion becomes too heated, it may be helpful to defer it to another day or move to more neutral territory.

▲ DEALING WITH A DISPUTE

When you are faced with a dispute, aim to defuse negative emotions quickly, so that you can begin to work towards a constructive resolution to the problem.

82 Find the cause of a problem and learn from your mistakes, rather than acting defensively.

VALIDATING PEOPLE

Often the emotion involved in a dispute can be discharged if you show you understand the other person's feelings. At the very least, the person will appreciate that you have listened. This does not mean that you should accept a criticism even if you disagree with it. Make this distinction by focusing your comments on feelings. Say, "I understand that you are angry about this". Outline your interpretation of the other person's viewpoint to check that you understand and to reinforce the message that you are listening.

83 Respect diversity and everyone's right to disagree.

84 Remember that the best views are a synthesis of many.

SHOWING UNDERSTANDING ▼

In this example, this manager must act to defuse conflict by showing that she has understood all the different views, even when she does not necessarily agree with them.

Manager listens to both party's views and focuses her team on solutions

Manager acts to defuse conflict

Team members get into a heated debate

Manager fails to take control of situation and relations break down further

CREATING DIALOGUE

Once you have changed the focus of the dispute to less emotive matters, start a dialogue. The purpose of dialogue is mutual understanding: it assumes that there is no one right answer, and so it is the precursor to negotiation. Initiate dialogue by being open. If you see some way in which you may have contributed to the other person's anger, say so in a way that does not seem like a confession of guilt. For example, admit that you are sorry that a dispute has arisen and express your desire to bring the discussion back on track.

QUESTIONS TO ASK YOURSELF

Q Is there something that I have said in the past that may be at the root of this conflict?

Q Are there any areas where it may be possible to come to a mutual agreement?

Q Have I clarified the cause of my colleague's anger?

Q What alternative actions can I suggest at this point?

85 Learn from the way you dealt with past conflicts.

USING NEUTRAL CRITERIA

The use of neutral criteria enables you to move from dialogue to negotiation. Such criteria are based on precedence and standards and are independent of the views of the protagonists. For example, you may resolve a quarrel about pay by referring to human resources guidelines. Frame the discussion by suggesting that you both look through the paperwork to help cast light on the disagreement. Once you have both looked at the facts, work together to reach an agreement.

◀ PRESENTING THE FACTS
In this example, a budgetary dispute is resolved when the marketing assistant finds and produces the necessary paperwork. The figures can then be checked.

MEDIATING CONFLICT

Friction between managers, teams, and even between departments is an all too common feature of corporate life. Destructive conflicts can erode the efficiency and morale of the whole organization. By stepping in to mediate between adversaries, you will be able to defuse anger and bitterness, and restore a common sense of purpose. Remember that the key to doing this rests in helping both parties be clear about what they want, and what they are prepared to give to the other party in return for it.

86 Focus on agreements and find solutions.

87 Examine the causes of a misunderstanding.

DEALING WITH DIFFERENT SOURCES OF CONFLICT

SOURCE OF CONFLICT	WHAT TO SAY
AGGRESSION	"Isn't there a better way to come to an agreement?"
DIFFERENT PERCEPTIONS	"I can see how that happened…"
GOSSIP	"I wonder what that's based on?"
DEFENSIVENESS	"Blame is unconstructive. Let us focus on solutions."
MISUNDERSTANDING	"What causes you to think that?"
WORRY	"How can we work together to resolve this?"
BEING UNDERMINED	"I'm sorry, you should have been consulted about that."
LACK OF TRUST	"Can we put our differences in the past?"
RESENTMENT	"How can we deal with that?"
OBSTACLES	"Let's focus on the things we can influence."

REHEARSING A PRESENTATION

The difference between great speakers and average ones often lies in their preparation. To sound convincing as well as natural, practise speaking with confidence, rehearse what you have to say in detail, and be ready to deal with potential objections.

88 Keep notes on any anecdotes you hear that you could use in your talks.

Be clear about what you want to say

↓

Consider why you are qualified to speak on the subject

↓

Make sure that what you say will relate to your organization

↓

Be clear about your goals and prepare brief points

DECIDING TO SPEAK

Your decision to speak at a meeting may be spontaneous or planned. You may be asked to give a presentation, or the decision may be yours. Bear in mind that it is not necessary to say a lot to be influential; some of the noisiest people are the least influential. Before a talk, ask yourself why you are speaking on this subject. Perhaps you know your subject well or perhaps you are the most senior person there, and are expected to lead.

◀ **PREPARING TO SPEAK**
Before you speak at a meeting or a presentation, think through what you are going to say, so that you will say it with confidence and clarity. Write things out point by point.

DOS AND DON'TS

✔ Do think about what is important about the issue.

✔ Do consider what will appeal to your audience.

✔ Do outline the benefits that will follow if people act on your proposals.

✘ Don't let fear stop you from speaking out at meetings.

✘ Don't leave rehearsals until the last minute – make sure that you are properly prepared.

✘ Don't forget to include jokes and anecdotes in a presentation.

89 Think about people who present talks well and aim to emulate them.

SPEAKING WITH CONFIDENCE

There are a number of techniques you can learn that will help you speak with conviction and project yourself confidently. If you have prepared a talk, always practise it beforehand. Pretend that you are addressing someone who is standing at the back of the room you are in. Put enthusiasm into your voice, so that you will engage your audience, particularly at the start and finish. Try lowering your voice tone to demonstrate confidence – breathe deeply and start the sound of your voice in your chest, rather than in your throat. Vary your pace: slow down to make important points, and speed up to convey enthusiasm. Vary your volume: speaking quietly can make people sit up and listen, whereas a louder voice tone can be useful for making important points.

◀ **REHEARSING A TALK**
Try practising a speech in front of a mirror, so that you can take note of your body language, and make any necessary adjustments.

EXPLOITING PAST SUCCESSES

To get yourself into a positive state prior to your presentation, recall your past achievements in similar situations. If you have made successful presentations before, then recall the positive feeling you had at the time. Link this feeling to a trigger, such as a word or an image, so that imagining this word or image will automatically reproduce the positive feeling. If you have not made a presentation before, then remember a successful social occasion instead. Work on making a confident state second nature to you.

QUESTIONS TO ASK YOURSELF

Q When have I given a successful presentation in the past?

Q How did I feel at the beginning and at the end of my latest presentation?

Q In what way was that occasion similar to the present situation?

Q Are there any tactics that I used in the past presentation that I could draw on for this occasion?

90 Prepare your presentation well in advance.

91 Use positive self-talk to increase your confidence.

GETTING SUPPORT

Before a talk, ask people who will be there what their interests are, and adapt the content of your presentation accordingly. If any of the people you speak to are key decision-makers, so much the better. Having prepared what you have to say, rehearse your presentation in front of someone else. Ask your advisor to be frank with you. Do not confuse any feedback you get with criticism. Try taping your presentation beforehand and playing it back to yourself. Notice how you could adjust your voice tone or speed of delivery.

USING YOUR IMAGINATION

Make a presentation come alive in your own mind before you deliver it. Imagine that you are at the end of a successful meeting – what did you do that made it go well? Make a note of these success factors and be sure to include these during your presentation. When imagining the outcome, focus on what you will be seeing, hearing, and feeling as evidence of your success.

THINGS TO DO

1. Imagine how you will feel if your current presentation is a success.
2. Remain focused on these feelings of success.
3. Use these imagined positive feelings to increase your current confidence levels.

Manager feels happy and positive at end of her talk

◀ IMAGINING SUCCESS
Before a presentation, imagine yourself having just given a good talk, and picture the response of your audience.

Audience members appreciate good talk

ANTICIPATING OBJECTIONS

Even the best arguments meet with criticisms. To prepare for this, take on the role of your own worst critic and pick holes in your arguments. Write down your answers to the objections. An alternative course is to imagine that you are one of the influential people who will be present in your audience. What might this person say? Mentally rehearse your response to the "worst that could happen", so that you are confident you can handle anything.

▲ BEING WELL PREPARED
If you are well briefed and have carried out thorough research before a presentation, you will be able to deal with difficult questions or criticisms with ease.

DOS AND DON'TS

✔ Do read around your subject thoroughly and be well informed.

✔ Do use graphics to emphasize your key points and ideas.

✘ Don't let the thought of objections undermine your confidence.

✘ Don't be distracted from the main points that you want to make.

92 Arrive at a talk with plenty of time to prepare your materials.

CASE STUDY

Vanessa had been asked to present a key project to a party of customers. She began to prepare her material, but as the presentation drew nearer, she became increasingly nervous.. Unfortunately, during both her past presentations she had "frozen". She feared this would happen again.

She decided to work with a coach to remedy the problem. The coach helped her discover that the "freeze" response was triggered when she focused on the eyes of people in the audience. She learnt instead to focus on the sound of her own voice and on a neutral spot on the back wall.

The coach helped her set up a positive state of confidence that could be triggered by the word "calm", which she could use if she froze. However, Vanessa found that because she was well prepared, she felt naturally confident. Her talk was a great success.

◀ COPING WITH DIFFICULTIES
In this example, a project manager was asked to prepare a presentation for a customer. By learning to deal with her nerves and by preparing herself for any difficulties she might encounter, she was able to deliver a successful presentation.

SWAYING AN AUDIENCE

The way you present an idea can make or break it. Inspire and persuade people with a lively style and expressive body language. Outline your key ideas, state how your proposals will be achieved, and handle interruptions with confidence.

93 Be ready to adapt your talk to match your audience's response.

MANAGING YOUR STATE OF MIND

Once you have rehearsed, prepared your materials, and tested any equipment you will be using, begin to get into the right frame of mind for your talk. Your state needs to be confident, relaxed, and energetic. Stand for a few moments on the spot where you will be delivering your talk. Try to visualize yourself taking charge of the room and the people who will occupy it.

94 Stand in the room where you will give your presentation and think of it as your own office.

THINGS TO DO

1. Create a positive, confident mental state.
2. Prepare a hook, such as an anecdote, that will help to draw your audience in.
3. Focus on the key words that your audience will be interested in, and make sure that you are ready to emphasize these points.
4. Decide how you will vary your voice tone.

POINTS TO REMEMBER

- Even when you have prepared a talk thoroughly, always be ready to make adaptations depending on your audience's reaction.
- During a talk, breathe deeply and concentrate on staying relaxed.
- Watch out for loss of interest, and be ready to move on.
- Break up long presentations with activities or discussion groups.

INSPIRING AN AUDIENCE

Grab your audience's interest by starting with an appealing anecdote, quote, or story. Popular television programmes, celebrities, and admired figures are a rich source of stories and quotes. So are any related problems, challenges, and rewards you have experienced. Telling an amusing story (if you have one) will also get the audience on your side. But then, move quickly on to tell your listeners what your talk is about and the benefits you want them to get from it.

ENLIVENING THE PRESENTATION

If you are presenting to a group, make your presentation as visually rich as you can. Well-designed slides and flip-charts are helpful. One good image or diagram can often get an idea across better than a few hundred words. Use plenty of colours when you draw images or write bullet points. Use anecdotes to give examples for the points you are making and, wherever possible, think of a slogan to unite your material into a common theme.

Manager selects slides to use at her presentation

PREPARING VISUAL AIDS ▶
Invest the time in preparing visual aids for a presentation – slides can be a particularly effective way of keeping an audience interested in a talk.

95 Start by outlining the content of your talk.

96 Use bullet points to summarize your key points.

OUTLINING THE KEY IDEAS

There is a natural limit to the amount of information your audience can take in and remember after the event. For maximum impact, keep detail and complexity to the bare minimum. Summarize your key points and repeat these two or three times – preferably at the start and at the end of your talk. It is helpful to use an overhead projector so that your key points are visible throughout your talk. Provide direction to your listeners by telling them what the subject is, what problems it solves, and what the solution is.

CULTURAL DIFFERENCES

In the United States, public speakers often adopt an emotive style of speech. The language used is often fast-paced, and it is designed to make listeners feel personally involved in events.

In Western Europe, however, the style of public speaking is often more factually based and low-key. In the UK, speakers often use self-directed humour to break the ice and defuse tension.

97 State that you will answer questions at the end.

98 Change to a more upbeat tone when describing solutions.

CHOREOGRAPHING A TALK

It is not just what you say but the way that you say it that gets results. For example, when you stand with your weight on one foot, you come across as indecisive. However, when you stand with an upright and relaxed stance, with feet shoulder-width apart, you create an impression of confidence. Use your hands expressively to support your words, rather than simply waving them about. Move purposefully and try to present positive and negative points in different ways.

▼ USING YOUR BODY LANGUAGE

During a presentation, adapt your position and your posture as necessary. For example, when you outline a problem, stand behind the lectern. Move forwards to emphasize positive points.

Pauses reflectively

Briefly explains problem, but states that solutions do exist

Stands behind lectern

Uses right hand to list negative points

LISTING OBSTACLES

Smiles positively

Looks straight a audience

Stands closer to the audience

Counts positive points on his left hand

LISTING SOLUTIONS

99 Be ready for a range of questions about your proposal.

KEEPING IT SIMPLE ▼
A useful way to structure a presentation is to describe the present situation, say what you want to happen, and explain how.

STATING YOUR PRESENT POSITION

Be clear, precise, and specific about the problems to be overcome. The aim here is to provide feedback on what is happening now and what needs to be improved. Support what you say with facts and be ready to answer questions. If you are describing a new technique or process then talk about the problems it was designed to solve. Be positive in what you say and stress that the problems described do have a remedy.

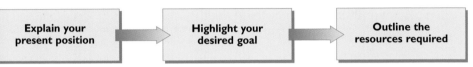

| Explain your present position | Highlight your desired goal | Outline the resources required |

STATING THE SOLUTION

As quickly as possible, move on from talking about present issues or problems and say what you propose to do about the matter. Your solution could incorporate a change in procedure, a new technique, an organizational change, a proposal to a customer, a promotion, a re-allocation of responsibility, a new product, or a call for more resources. Be sure to state clearly what your proposal will do and the goal you intend to accomplish. Make sure that you define your ideas clearly and unambiguously.

100 Respond to interruptions positively.

101 Maintain the flow of your presentation.

POINTS TO REMEMBER

● Many objections contain ideas that can improve your proposal.

● Take persistent critics to one side at the end of the meeting and ask them for their suggestions.

● Always keep your cool, no matter what the provocation – your poise will work in your favour.

HANDLING INTERRUPTIONS

Interruptions can make a presentation come alive if handled in the right way. Listen to the speaker's comments politely. Check your understanding by summarizing it in your own words. Highlight points of agreement and answer the question. If you cannot answer, then promise to get back to the speaker later. If an interruption is aggressive, ask the rest of the audience if they have other views.

ASSESSING YOUR INFLUENCING SKILLS

Evaluate your powers of persuasion by responding to the following statements and marking the option closest to your experience. Be as honest as you can: if your answer is "never", circle Option 1; if it is "always", circle Option 4, and so on. Add your scores together, and refer to the Analysis to see how well you scored. Use your answers to identify the areas that need most improvement.

OPTIONS	
1	Never
2	Occasionally
3	Frequently
4	Always

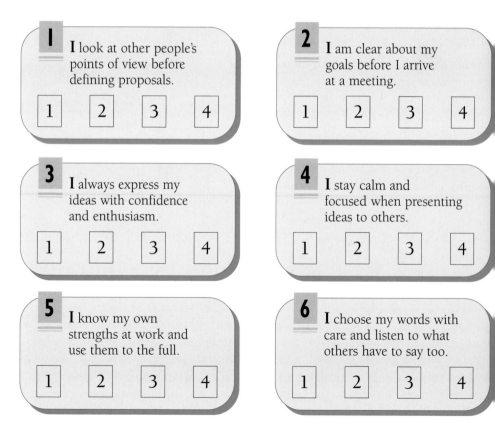

1 I look at other people's points of view before defining proposals.

1 2 3 4

2 I am clear about my goals before I arrive at a meeting.

1 2 3 4

3 I always express my ideas with confidence and enthusiasm.

1 2 3 4

4 I stay calm and focused when presenting ideas to others.

1 2 3 4

5 I know my own strengths at work and use them to the full.

1 2 3 4

6 I choose my words with care and listen to what others have to say too.

1 2 3 4

7 I handle set-backs as learning opportunities, rather than problems.

1　2　3　4

8 I ensure that I am dressed appropriately, whatever the occasion.

1　2　3　4

9 I listen carefully to opposing views before summarizing them.

1　2　3　4

10 I am proactive and always looking for new opportunities.

1　2　3　4

11 I keep abreast of developments within my industry.

1　2　3　4

12 I take the first step in introducing myself to new acquaintances.

1　2　3　4

13 I back up my ideas with reasons and hard evidence.

1　2　3　4

14 I seek the support of senior managers for my goals and plans.

1　2　3　4

15 I acknowledge the needs, interests, and values of others.

1　2　3　4

16 I rehearse my presentations thoroughly beforehand.

1　2　3　4

17 I always keep my commitments and promises faithfully.

1 2 3 4

18 I handle conflicts by looking for and identifying mutual interests.

1 2 3 4

19 I use my voice and hands to emphasize suggestions.

1 2 3 4

20 I offer support and help to others without waiting to be asked.

1 2 3 4

21 I work through differences with others openly and honestly.

1 2 3 4

22 I listen for, and use, the emotive words used by the people I talk to.

1 2 3 4

23 I make my proposals attractive by explaining their benefits.

1 2 3 4

24 I balance the big picture with the broad detail so that everything is clear.

1 2 3 4

25 I neutralize disputes by trying to understand the other party's position.

1 2 3 4

26 I am comfortable working with people who are more senior than myself.

1 2 3 4

27 I assume that there can be a positive outcome to every issue.

| 1 | 2 | 3 | 4 |

28 I am specific about asking for what I want and the support I need.

| 1 | 2 | 3 | 4 |

29 I find out what matters to the people I work with.

| 1 | 2 | 3 | 4 |

30 I test for positive responses at every step of my proposals.

| 1 | 2 | 3 | 4 |

31 I regularly mix with new people and build my contacts.

| 1 | 2 | 3 | 4 |

32 I recognize my strengths and weaknesses and always work to improve my skills.

| 1 | 2 | 3 | 4 |

ANALYSIS

Now that you have completed the self-assessment, add up the scores and check your performance by referring to the evaluation below. Identify your weakest areas, and refer to the relevant parts of this section to hone your influencing skills.
32–63: You could be more influential. Focus on being proactive rather than reactive. Concentrate on finding common ground with others, so that your self-presentation skills can start to develop.

64–95: You are influencing well and have built some good working relationships. However, expand your sphere of influence by winning over the hearts and minds of those around you.
96–128: You are a skilled influencer who relates to others well. Keep improving your abilities on your way to the top.

DEVELOPING NLP SKILLS

INTRODUCTION

The ability to develop good relationships with others and to handle situations effectively are vital elements of being a successful manager. Introducing the skills of NLP (Neuro-Linguistic Programming), Developing NLP Skills helps you to recognize the cues that give you insights into how you and others are feeling, and develop the way you approach situations so that you can achieve the highest standards. By identifying areas of your performance that you need to improve, NLP focuses on changing your thoughts, assumptions, and emotions so that you can dramatically improve the results you get. Practical advice, including 101 concise tips, shows you how to develop NLP skills and put them into practice, and a self-assessment test at the end of the section allows you to evaluate your performance levels.

THINKING ABOUT PERFORMANCE

NLP (Neuro-Linguistic Programming) helps managers to work well with others and to develop themselves. Use NLP to recognize the small changes that produce significantly better results.

KNOWING THE KEY SKILLS

The critical factor for maximizing professional performance is improving how you manage yourself and your working relationships with others. Recognize that this is something you can learn and that NLP shows you how to develop the necessary skills.

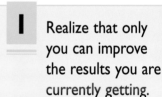
1 Realize that only you can improve the results you are currently getting.

▲ **IDENTIFYING SUCCESS**
Technical skills and IQ account for about 15 per cent of top-level performance, whereas 85 per cent of professional success is due to emotional intelligence.

15%
Skills and IQ

85%
Emotional Intelligence

IMPROVING EFFECTIVENESS
Globalization and improved communication technologies have increased the pressure on all businesses to perform, and this in turn has put pressure on staff performance. Recent research has shown that it is not primarily IQ or technical competence that determine your professional effectiveness. The biggest impact on professional success is how well you manage yourself and your working relationships with others – known as "emotional intelligence". Increase your effectiveness as a manager by identifying and developing the critical emotional intelligence skills you need.

UNDERSTANDING EMOTIONAL INTELLIGENCE

There are two aspects of emotional intelligence that determine your performance as a manager. The first is your ability to handle situations in an effective manner. Top performers use their emotions as a guide to improving what they do. The second is your ability to be sensitive to others and knowing how to make a difference to the performance of others.

WHAT IS NLP?

The field of NLP is a "tool kit" of skills used by managers to develop emotional intelligence skills and improve performance. NLP skills focus on the way you think about what you are doing that already works, what you are doing that does not work, and what you need to do differently. Change what you think, feel, and believe, and you will dramatically alter the results you get. With repeat practice, these skills become automatic and lead to a continuous improvement in performance.

2 Understand that emotional intelligence can transform your performance and career.

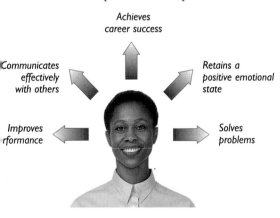

Achieves
career success

Communicates
effectively
with others

Retains a
positive emotional
state

Improves
rformance

Solves
problems

▲ APPLICATIONS OF NLP

By adopting NLP skills, you can quickly increase your effectiveness and significantly improve your performance. This has an impact on the results you and your organization achieve.

USING NLP

Many people think that emotional intelligence is a natural skill that you either do or do not have. It is, in fact, a set of skills that you can learn. Use NLP techniques to help you identify and focus on areas of your performance that you need to improve. Then, explore what to do differently, so that you can begin to improve the results you achieve. This is the first step in developing your emotional intelligence.

291

APPLYING NLP SKILLS

Much of your performance at work is probably already very effective. However, applying NLP skills will help you improve the small part of your work that limits your overall performance. Many of the skills in NLP will be natural to you already, such as goal-setting or mental rehearsal. Once you are aware of an area where you do not perform well, choose an NLP technique that will make a difference to your performance. If, for instance, you realize that you have difficulty meeting important deadlines, use the NLP skill of setting yourself daily objectives so that you are able to plan your time effectively.

3 Recognize that NLP focuses on what works.

4 Look at your work and identify any difficulties.

Gives an assured and effective presentation

Lacks confidence and composure

Takes time to mentally rehearse before presentation

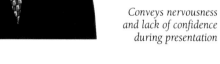

Conveys nervousness and lack of confidence during presentation

USING MENTAL REHEARSAL TO ▲ IMPROVE YOUR PERFORMANCE

This manager recognizes that he is nervous when giving presentations to his colleagues. Through using the NLP skill of mental rehearsal, he could improve his performance considerably.

QUESTIONS TO ASK YOURSELF

Q What areas of my performance am I satisfied with?

Q What aspects of my performance do I want to improve?

Q Do I know what I need to do to improve my skills?

Q What is the first action step I need to take to improve my results?

FOCUSING ON PROCESS

NLP skills are also used for problem solving. NLP looks at the content of issues or communications, while also looking at their structures or processes. For instance, it is not what someone says, but how they say it that tells you how to respond. The words spoken are the "content" of a conversation, whereas the "process" of communication is far broader. It includes all of the non-verbal messages. For instance, "That's great!" can mean opposite things depending on the context and how it is said. Learn to be flexible in your approach and assumptions.

ASSUMPTIONS TO ADOPT FOR PEAK PERFORMANCE

POSITIVE ASSUMPTIONS	REASONING
If what you are doing is not working, do something different.	If you always do what you have always done, you will always get what you have always got.
There is no failure, only feedback. It is what you do with results that matters.	Whatever happens, you can use feedback to make improvements to results.
People can access the resources they need to make whatever changes will make a difference.	There is always something that makes a difference, and it is usually inner resources.
We each create our own version and view of reality.	We perceive the world through our senses and create different models of reality.
It is easier to change yourself than it is to change others.	Changing what you do will change others' responses to you.
Using your imagination is the first stage to making real improvements.	Improvements begin as thoughts, are communicated in words, and become actions.

BOOSTING CONFIDENCE

Top-level performance requires high levels of confidence, especially in demanding circumstances. Take responsibility for how you feel and, when you need to boost your morale, use NLP techniques to develop the skill of maintaining confidence.

5 Realize that you can easily learn to build your self-confidence.

6 Avoid blaming yourself for problems, since this lowers your self-confidence.

AVOIDING BLAME

In any specific task, your abilities are related to your levels of confidence and competence. Your level of competence is often not a problem, but people lose confidence when things go wrong and then competence can fall. Your reaction may be to blame yourself or others. Realize that blaming others lowers their confidence and also damages your relationship with them. Instead, think what you could more usefully say. Then, notice how the confidence level of yourself and others improves.

SEEING YOUR ACHIEVEMENT

You may imagine the worst scenario in a situation. Thinking about potential problems is only useful if you imagine how best to deal with them. The difference between a confident and a non-confident person is their ability to imagine performing tasks well. The better you are at imagining your own successes, the better your self-image and the higher your level of self-confidence. Keep imagining your own successes until they feel "true".

DOS AND DON'TS

✔ Do believe you are good enough.	✘ Don't dwell on problems.
✔ Do practise talking confidently.	✘ Don't stamp out creativity.
✔ Do focus on your successes.	✘ Don't criticize the performance of others.
✔ Do encourage and praise good work.	✘ Don't assume your staff cannot improve.

7 Practise imagining yourself doing a task well, such as giving effective and constructive feedback.

Assess your self-doubt	→	Recall past successes	→	Boost your confidence

QUESTIONS TO ASK YOURSELF

Q Are there any occasions in the past when I was a confident decision maker?

Q Do I praise my team and pay them compliments for work that has been done well?

Q Have I examined the areas where I lack confidence?

8 Remember your experiences of peak confidence.

▲ INCREASING YOUR CONFIDENCE

Explore any self-doubt and then recall a past experience that contradicts this doubt. Imagine yourself behaving with this past confidence in the future and you will boost your present confidence.

BUILDING CONFIDENCE

Work on building your confidence. Believe in yourself and your abilities, assume you will find solutions, and feel good about outcomes. Any belief to the contrary will reduce your confidence. For example, if you believe you are a poor decision maker you will feel unconfident about decisions. Look for these barely-conscious limiting beliefs and weaken them by finding an exception. Recall a past experience that contradicts this belief and imagine yourself behaving decisively.

Shoulders are stooped, showing lack of confidence

Posture is slouched, showing dejection and low self-esteem

Shoulders are back and stance exudes confidence

Arms are relaxed, showing decreased tension

| 1 | 2 | 3 | 4 | 5 | 6 | 7 | 8 | 9 | 10 |

SCALING CONFIDENCE LEVELS ▲
Rate your level of confidence on a scale of one to ten. Imagine dropping it by a point, to make yourself feel less confident. Now increase it by two points. Notice the change in your posture and mind. Repeat this exercise to boost your confidence.

9 Maintain a positive image of yourself in the future.

295

SETTING YOUR OBJECTIVES

The process of setting objectives helps you to think through complex and changing situations. Avoid reactive "fire fighting" and use goal-setting skills. Realize that, as the skills become natural, you will find managing problems and change easier.

> **10** Set clear goals and outcomes to get the results you want.

PLANNING OUTCOMES

All successful people are clear about their goals and aims. Even though you may already set yourself goals, make sure that you use this skill regularly so that you can maximize your performance. Set goals many times a day, making sure they are achievable. Every outcome is made up of sub-outcomes, so identify the sub-outcomes as steps to achieving peak performance. For example, people improve their communication skills (sub-outcomes) in order to improve results (outcome).

◀ **SOLVING PROBLEMS**
All effective people use a version of outcome thinking regularly as a solution-focused technique for planning, and for dealing with problems or crises.

KNOWING WHEN TO PLAN

As well as developing the habit of planning your objectives thoroughly, learn to know when to think about them. Firstly, use outcome thinking every time you are planning ahead, whether it is prioritizing with a simple "to-do" list, or in strategic organizational planning. Secondly, use outcome thinking to deal with unexpected problems as they arise. Ask yourself, "Which is the central problem here?" and then run the issue through the outcome POWER model (see opposite) until you are clear about the next action step.

> **11** Remember, you can achieve more if you set goals.

> **12** Develop the habit of thinking about outcomes.

USING THE POWER MODEL TO SOLVE PROBLEMS AND PLAN EFFECTIVELY

QUESTION

EXAMPLE

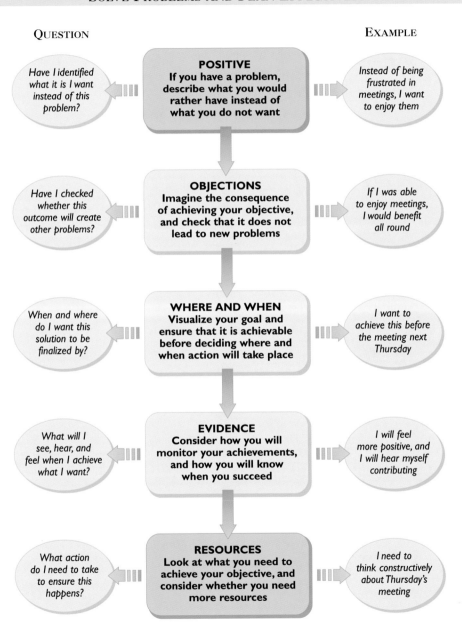

POSITIVE
If you have a problem, describe what you would rather have instead of what you do not want

Have I identified what it is I want instead of this problem?

Instead of being frustrated in meetings, I want to enjoy them

OBJECTIONS
Imagine the consequence of achieving your objective, and check that it does not lead to new problems

Have I checked whether this outcome will create other problems?

If I was able to enjoy meetings, I would benefit all round

WHERE AND WHEN
Visualize your goal and ensure that it is achievable before deciding where and when action will take place

When and where do I want this solution to be finalized by?

I want to achieve this before the meeting next Thursday

EVIDENCE
Consider how you will monitor your achievements, and how you will know when you succeed

What will I see, hear, and feel when I achieve what I want?

I will feel more positive, and I will hear myself contributing

RESOURCES
Look at what you need to achieve your objective, and consider whether you need more resources

What action do I need to take to ensure this happens?

I need to think constructively about Thursday's meeting

MANAGING PERSONAL FLEXIBILITY

Your results are determined by the way you manage yourself internally. Increase your awareness of the changes you can make in how you approach situations in order to develop the inner flexibility needed for outstanding performance.

13 Imagine how someone you respect would view a problem.

14 Be flexible in your approach to other people.

15 Adapt your approach to match particular people.

INCREASING FLEXIBILITY

Top performers choose the right methods to produce outstanding results. Develop the mental flexibility to generate high-quality options so that you can pick the best one. Think through possible approaches until you know which one is likely to work best. If you have difficulties, ask yourself, "What is the best way to view this situation?" For example, instead of viewing a colleague as "difficult", see them as a challenge. Develop your flexibility by thinking of different approaches to situations. Aim to achieve the best from others.

MAKING CHANGES

Your approach to situations is determined by your internal world – your thinking (T), assumptions (A), and emotional state (E). If you change one of these, you will change how you perceive and deal with a situation. For instance, if you have too much work, you may see only the negative points – you may be frustrated because you assume that it is not negotiable. Instead, decide which aspect of your approach is the easiest to change. You could focus on the positive (T), assume you can renegotiate (A), or feel motivated instead of frustrated (E).

THINGS TO DO

1. Watch how other people respond to you.
2. Make a note of the interactions that work.
3. Examine your thoughts, moods, and assumptions, and look at what you could change.

CHANGING YOURSELF

Develop the flexibility to handle situations at work by changing aspects of your feelings, beliefs, and thoughts. First, when you are in a difficult situation, check your emotional state and, if necessary, work on improving it. For example, remember a situation in which you did feel positive and imagine being back in it for a few seconds. Second, check your assumptions. Is what you are assuming true? Third, check your thinking. Is there a way of thinking about the situation that works better than your current approach?

▼ MAKING CHANGES

By changing any aspect of your inner world, you change the results you get. In this example, the way the manager behaves affects his employee's behaviour and directly effects the results he achieves.

Manager asks constructive questions

Problem is quickly resolved

Approaches employee to find out what happened

Manager receives a customer complaint

Manager is confrontational and employee becomes defensive – issue is not resolved

16 Think through possible approaches until you find the best option, and then proceed to take action.

Improving Your Performance

As you focus on your performance, you will notice an improvement in your results. Develop your NLP skills so that you can begin to achieve better work relationships.

Learning How to Learn

Top business performance comes from having a wide range of competencies. Recognize the key skills you need to focus on, consider how you will develop them, and learn to use the technique of mental rehearsal to consolidate what you learn.

17 Be responsible for your performance, so that you can improve it.

18 Invest in your future success by developing skills.

19 Understand that management skills can be mastered using NLP skills.

Managing Performance

There are three main areas of performance management, which include many different skills. Focus on the area you most need to work on:

- Self-management skills: These include goal setting and managing time. Your management skills will grow out of how you manage yourself.
- Project-management skills: Develop these so that you know what needs to be done and when, so you can keep projects on track.
- People-management skills: Recognize that it is your ability to communicate effectively with people that determines the success of projects.

KNOWING WHAT TO LEARN

Focus on a problem you have and decide which skill you need to develop in order to overcome the issue. For example, something that upsets you is an indication that you need to develop your emotional self-management skills. Be clear about what you are trying to achieve. If you want to remain calm in this situation, look at how to achieve this. In this case, the skill you need to learn is emotional stability.

THE LEARNING MODEL ▶

This is the process of learning a new skill so that, at each stage, you have a higher level of competence. You move from unconscious incompetence to the mastery of unconscious competence.

> **Unconscious incompetence:**
> **You are unaware of a skill**
>
> **Conscious incompetence:**
> **You are trying to learn the skill**
>
> **Conscious competence:**
> **You have to concentrate on it**
>
> **Unconscious competence:**
> **The skill becomes automatic**

TAKING ACTION

Improve your performance by focusing on only one key skill at a time. Choose and prioritize the area which has the biggest impact on your performance. Put time in your diary to clarify the specific skill needed, for example, interpersonal skills. Then, use this time to decide the actions you are going to take to develop this skill, for example, arranging a series of coaching sessions.

◀ TAKING THE TIME TO LEARN

Setting aside time for self-improvement is the only way to improve your performance. Remember that nothing is more important than developing your management skills.

REHEARSING SITUATIONS

Use repeated mental rehearsal to build skills quickly. Imagine dealing with situations better. If you find this difficult, think of someone you know who deals with situations well. Notice what they do differently and imagine yourself working in that way. For example, if you are overloaded with work, you will remain overloaded unless you know what to change. Practise thinking how you will react differently the next time someone overloads you.

20 Practise responses mentally until your new response is word perfect and becomes automatic.

MANAGING EMOTIONS

*L*earn *the skill of actively managing your emotional states, so that your working performance is maximized. Aim to manage your emotional states well at work and you will begin to thrive on challenging and potentially stressful situations.*

21 Remember you can change the way you react to situations.

POINTS TO REMEMBER

- If you allow situations to affect you emotionally, your working performance will suffer.
- Sometimes the key skill is to be aware of your own emotional state.
- It is possible to choose a different emotional state.
- Increasing your choice of emotion can transform your work.

DEALING WITH STRESS

When you get stressed, your emotional state deteriorates, affecting your thinking, judgment, and performance. For example, when you "have to" deliver something important but "cannot" because of other commitments, your mind may perceive a "dangerous" situation. This can create anxiety and poor thinking. To cope with stressful situations, you can either change your perception of the situation until it becomes a positive challenge, or, you can change your emotional state to deal with it better.

ACHIEVING "FLOW"

Top performers spend most of their time in a state of "flow" – a buzz you get from an activity you enjoy doing. This occurs when a goal is motivating and a challenge is appropriate to your level of skill. Aim to achieve this state more often. If you are bored, raise the level of challenge. If you are stressed, raise your level of competence, or increase the support you receive from others. Change your emotional state until you view a task as a chance to extend your abilities. It can help to break the task into smaller pieces to help you achieve "flow". Be aware of the state of flow of yourself and others.

Motivational level is near a state of flow

Balance of challenge and skill are optimal

▲ **FINDING THE STATE OF FLOW**
People are motivated when their levels of skill and support are equal to a challenge. A highly skilled person can become bored without a challenge and, conversely, too great a challenge can result in stress.

BECOMING AWARE

People are often unaware of their emotional states. There are hundreds of emotions you may go through in a day, such as frustration, anger, excitement, satisfaction, or relief. Once you recognize significant emotional states, treat them as signals to draw your attention to something you may have otherwise missed. For example, frustration with a project can alert you to problems that need your attention or direct you to a more useful emotional state, such as patience, because you know you have done what you can.

22 Identify your own emotional states frequently.

23 Make decisions only when you are feeling positive.

Bright eyes show confidence

Drooping eyes indicate boredom

Alert posture indicates enthusiasm

Tense jaw shows frustration

◀ **CALIBRATING EMOTIONS**
Subtle physical signs can give you clues to positive and negative emotional states. Learn to spot these small cues in yourself and others, so that you know when to intervene.

ANCHORING EMOTIONS

Instead of feeling stressed, learn to create a positive emotional state. Think of a time when you experienced a positive state, such as feeling calm. Imagine you are back in that state. Look at what was happening around you then and notice how this makes you feel now. It is possible to access this feeling in future by connecting it to a trigger, or "anchor". Squeeze the tip of your thumb and a finger together in a specific way as the feeling builds and let go before the emotion peaks. Repeat this procedure so that you build an automatic response.

Squeezes thumb and finger to trigger an emotion

▲ **TRIGGERING EMOTIONS**
Use a gesture as a link, or an anchor, to a positive state that you can trigger whenever you begin to feel stressed.

COACHING YOURSELF

Most of us have learnt to become our own worst critics. Change the way you talk within yourself so that you can turn this inner critic into an inner coach, and learn to use the three-step self-coaching process for ongoing personal development.

24 Improve your self-talk so that you can boost your performance.

25 Make sure you give yourself frequent encouragement.

26 Notice when your internal dialogue starts becoming unhelpful.

ENCOURAGING YOURSELF

Your inner dialogue will often determine your thoughts and feelings, and self-talk can often be negative. For example, when something you do goes wrong, you may say to yourself, "Why do I keep getting things wrong?" This dialogue may keep replaying a negative scene and make you feel bad about yourself. If you catch yourself doing this replace negativity with more positive self-talk. Focus on a positive aspect, however minor. Say things like, "No one is perfect. You are still learning".

▼ NOTICING EFFECTS OF POSITIVE AND NEGATIVE SELF-TALK

Recognize the different physical responses you have when you talk to yourself. Ask yourself positive and negative questions, and notice how you respond physically and emotionally.

Upright posture indicates confidence

Facial expression is relaxed

POSITIVE INNER DIALOGUE

Hunched shoulders indicate worry

Facial muscles are tense

NEGATIVE INNER DIALOGUE

QUESTIONS TO ASK YOURSELF

Q What do I need to do differently?

Q Am I running any negative self-talk instead of being positive about myself?

Q What is the most useful way to coach myself through this one?

Q What assumptions am I making that could be worth looking at again?

27 Look on the bright side, rather than always expecting the worst.

INNER COACHING VOICE

The voice that you talk to yourself with is made up of three main components: speed, tone, and volume. Alter any one of these factors if you want to change the way you feel. For example, if you feel unmotivated, speed up your inner voice and turn up the volume to increase your motivation. Try using the voice tones of whoever is best at motivating you. If you are feeling emotionally low from a work encounter, slow your inner voice down, turn down the volume, and use a caring tone so you can reach a more positive state.

DOS AND DON'TS

✔ Do remember that self-talk affects your behaviour.

✔ Do notice which self-talk works best.

✔ Do use humour in your self-talk.

✘ Don't ignore your inner dialogue.

✘ Don't dwell on negative thoughts about others.

✘ Don't be hard on yourself over an issue.

USING SELF-COACHING

You can resolve many difficulties by using the three-stage self-coaching model – problem, outcome, and action. First, identify a problem: for example, when a colleague threatens sales by neglecting a task. Second, check that you are clear on the outcome you want. You may decide to motivate the person rather than get somebody else to complete the task. Third, identify what you would do differently. Ask yourself, "What is the best way to motivate them?" Decide on the best approach and imagine yourself doing it.

28 Ensure you are comfortable with an approach before you carry it out.

▼ COACHING YOURSELF
Focus on developing positive self-talk habits through self-coaching, and benefit from the improvement in your confidence levels.

| Use positive self-talk | → | Consciously self-coach yourself | → | Benefit from more confidence |

VISUALIZING FOR EFFECTIVENESS

Visual thinking is a major tool in effective management, helping in meetings, negotiations, and problem solving. Optimize your visual thinking for mental rehearsal and creative management so that you can achieve more with less effort.

29 Practise visualizing regularly so that you become better at it.

MAKING DECISIONS

AUDITORY STRATEGY
Ask yourself what the best possible options are

VISUAL STRATEGY
Imagine and visualize the possible options

KINESTHETIC STRATEGY
Notice your gut reactions and feelings about the options

YOUR VISUAL BRAIN

The three main languages of the brain are auditory, visual, and kinesthetic (feelings). These modes of thinking have different strengths and weaknesses. Increase your effectiveness by having the three modes working together, each in their strength areas. Visual thinking is best for imagining a lot of possibilities very quickly. This will work only when your visual thinking is driven by your inner dialogue (auditory internal dialogue) asking quality questions. Your kinesthetic sense is good for deciding which options are best. Utilize these languages to help you make quality decisions.

◄ USING
VISUALIZATION
In this case study, an account manager found that if she substituted unnecessary self-talk with a visualization technique, she could dramatically increase the speed of her thinking processes.

CASE STUDY
An account manager, Julia, had problems with the amount of reports she needed to read in a short space of time. No matter how hard she tried, she could not speed up her reading, and this affected her performance. She approached a friend of hers who had trained as an NLP practitioner. In a single session, the practitioner discovered what the problem was and subsequently her reading

speed started to improve. It turned out that Julia was saying the words to herself in her head as she read. This, of course, meant that the speed of reading was limited by the speed of speech. The practitioner showed her how to curl her tongue back to switch off this internal self-talk. At the same time, she learnt how to visualize the meaning of the words directly. This method is considerably quicker than the speed of speech.

CHANGING THE MIND'S EYE

The way you visualize makes a difference to how you feel and the results you get. You can increase or reduce your feelings by making changes in how you visualize. Suppose you feel worried about a project. You realize that you have an overwhelming image of all the potential problems. Take an image of one problem at a time and make it smaller. Push it into the distance. Notice when the problem stops feeling overwhelming. Alternatively, when you want to feel more motivated to achieve a positive goal, make your image of the goal larger, closer, and more colourful. Notice when you feel more motivated.

30 Practise visualizing events in a number of different ways.

31 Change visual images so that you can change your emotional state.

WORKING WITH YOUR VISUALIZATIONS

VISUAL ELEMENT	FACTORS TO CONSIDER
SIZE	How large is the problem you are visualizing? Make the problem grow smaller by visualizing it reducing in size.
VIEWPOINT	Do you see yourself in the picture, or are you an observer? Imagine yourself taking positive control of the situation.
COLOUR	Are you thinking of the task in colour or in black and white? Motivate yourself by visualizing the task in bright, vivid colours.
MOTION	Is the image motionless or moving, and is it at normal speed? Slow down images when you reach critical issues.
DISTANCE	How far away is the image from you? Bring an image closer to make it more important.
PERSPECTIVE	Does the image have depth as it would appear in real life, or is it flat like a picture? Motivate yourself with full, 3-D images.

REHEARSING MENTALLY

The visual skill of mental rehearsal is crucial for maximizing performance. It helps you practise your part in critical situations, such as interviews, until you achieve a high standard. Imagine playing a video of yourself in an important situation. Notice the part you feel anxious about. Keep playing, looking at different ways of improving performance until you are satisfied with your results. Imagine the scene more realistically – step inside the image of yourself. Notice weaknesses in your performance and imagine improvements until you are satisfied.

THINGS TO DO

1. Imagine how you could deal with any difficulties a new task presents.

2. Practise imagining different responses to the situation.

3. Choose the best solution from your various options.

DEALING WITH TASKS ▼
You can handle a difficult task effectively if you feel well prepared. Make sure you are mentally prepared so that you do not run into difficulties.

32 Imagine various ways you could respond to a difficult situation, so that you are prepared beforehand.

Can you see yourself dealing with a difficult task well?
YES NO

Mentally rehearse. Run the task as if it was a video. Do you feel confident?
YES NO

Notice difficulties. Re-run approaches until you find a solution

Is the task important enough to rehearse more thoroughly?
YES NO

Rather than taking time perfecting the task, carry it out now

Imagine yourself in the video, resolving the issue. Are you satisfied?
YES NO

Re-run the difficulties until you resolve them, then carry out the task

Carry out the task

REHEARSING REALISTICALLY

Your mind stores images in two different ways so that you can differentiate between reality and imagination. First, think of something you did today, then imagine something you could have done instead. Notice how the real images are different from the imagined ones in terms of their size, colour, brightness, and clarity. Now, pretend your imagined event is real. The images will probably become big, bright, and moving. Aim to rehearse in the way your mind thinks of real events.

33 Avoid imagining situations in the form of daydreams.

34 Build personal flexibility by rehearsing options.

QUESTIONS TO ASK YOURSELF

Q What is crucial to my overall performance now?

Q Would it benefit me to rehearse this?

Q Can my unconscious mind start rehearsing this?

Q Has my mind learnt to rehearse automatically?

KNOWING WHEN TO REHEARSE

Some events are crucial to your overall performance, whereas others may not be. Regularly ask yourself which events are strategically most important to achieving your objectives. This tells you when to spend time on mental rehearsal. When something is critical, you usually have a growing feeling of anxiety or excitement. Focus on spotting these first signs, and then rehearse.

CREATING YOUR RESOURCE ROOM

Expand your visual capabilities further by developing the visual-thinking skills that complement mental rehearsal. First, visualize your ideal setting. It may be by the sea, or in a spaceship. Think what you would want in this ideal "resource room". This may include a library of books; a comfortable chair and viewing screen; a device that improves emotional state; a way to materialize any mentor of your choosing. Go to this imaginary room when you need to think things through.

▲ FORMING A RESOURCE ROOM
Whenever you have a creative task to do and need some inspiration, picture yourself in your ideal setting and tap into your internal creativity.

FINDING THE BEST APPROACH

Turning around difficult situations using a positive approach, or "frame", allows you to keep yourself and others more motivated. Learn to be more positive at work – your satisfaction level will increase and the productivity of your team will rise.

35 Be aware of your negative approaches and change them.

36 Change resentment towards work to an appreciation of self-development opportunities.

FINDING POSITIVE FRAMES

Remember that events only have the meaning you give them. For example, do you see a glass of water as being half-full or half-empty? Your response tells you a lot about the way you "frame" situations. The same goes for your attitude to work. You may either look at work as a never-ending succession of problems, or as a string of exciting and challenging opportunities. Maintain your positive attitude in any situation and your satisfaction with your working life will improve.

REFRAMING SITUATIONS

Treat negative thoughts in yourself or others as opportunities to think about things in a more useful way. For example, an employee may say that every time a working procedure is changed, he or she becomes confused. Reframe this problem by making constructive points:

❝ It is good that you have noticed you get confused, because now we can clarify the procedures. ❞

❝ You may be confused now, but it will all become clear when you have learnt the new skills. ❞

❝ If we understand what is causing the confusion, we can look at how to present changes differently. ❞

❝ Your confusion is evidence that you are learning something new and changing your normal routine. ❞

PREPARING FOR PROBLEMS

A good way of carefully phrasing statements so that you elicit the best response is preframing. Anticipate an employee's response to an issue and guess their main objection. Then consider the best approach to the subject in view of their objection, and imagine yourself dealing with it in this way. For example, you are about to give somebody some extra work. You guess their main issue will be not having time to plan effectively. "Preframe" the extra work by saying, "Some extra work has come in and, fortunately, we have enough time to reorganize."

37 Decide on the most useful and constructive ways to approach different situations.

PREFRAMING PROBLEMS

Consider your employee's possible objections to a project

⬇

Focus on the objection that will be the main barrier

⬇

Imagine the best light in which to present the project

⬇

Present the project positively, preframing any possible issues

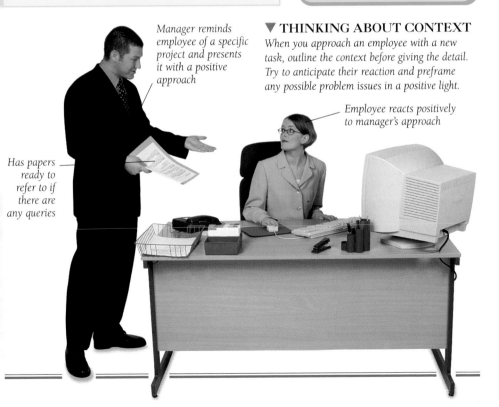

Manager reminds employee of a specific project and presents it with a positive approach

Has papers ready to refer to if there are any queries

▼ THINKING ABOUT CONTEXT

When you approach an employee with a new task, outline the context before giving the detail. Try to anticipate their reaction and preframe any possible problem issues in a positive light.

Employee reacts positively to manager's approach

FREEING UP YOUR INNER RESOURCES

Inner conflict saps energy and motivation. If you can identify and resolve conflicts, you can free up time and effort that would otherwise be wasted. Work to resolve inner conflicts so that you are not fighting against yourself and wasting your own energy.

38 Resolve any doubts you have before you commit to an action.

Head is tilted to one side

Body posture is skewed

Facial expresssion is tense

Hands are held defensively

▲ RECOGNIZING YOUR PHYSICAL UNCERTAINTY

There are mental and physical signs of doubt. Recognize signs of your physical uncertainty, so that you can act on them.

39 Watch yourself on video and look for signs of uncertainty.

RECOGNIZING INNER CONFLICT

There are many types of internal conflict that are relatively common and easy to spot, such as your own interests versus those of your colleagues, or professional demands on your time versus family demands. Internal conflict often shows up as mixed feelings. For example, when someone puts pressure on you to do something, you hear yourself saying "Yes" while noticing a small, uncomfortable feeling. Realize that this feeling shows you that you have an inner conflict. Pinpoint these feelings so that you can start to resolve any conflicting issues.

QUESTIONS TO ASK YOURSELF

Q Do I recognize subtle feelings of doubt in myself?

Q When I notice I have doubts, do I act to resolve the underlying issues?

Q How do my feelings of doubt differ from my feelings of certainty?

Q What do I feel when I am certain about an issue?

Q Have I identified any work issues I routinely have doubts about?

Q Do I see how these feelings of doubt can be used to make positive changes?

40 Make a list of any conflicting interests at work.

RESOLVING ISSUES UNCONSCIOUSLY

You may often find that problems get resolved after a good night's sleep. This is because your unconscious mind works on problems while you are asleep. Use the potential of your unconscious mind. When you cannot resolve a problem, turn it into a question for your unconscious mind to think about. For instance, an employee may be underperforming and you are unsure what to do. Ask your unconscious, "Come up with some options. Let me know when you have got the best?"

RESOLVING ISSUES CONSCIOUSLY

A conflict implies two aspects of yourself fighting each other. For example, if you want career success but feel you can only achieve this at the expense of other people, you have a conflict. Think about how these parts can work together and imagine what each part wants. Ask the "success" part what it wants – you realize it wants recognition. When you think about the "expense of others" part, you realize it wants better results. Think about how they can work together. Imagine a future "you" that can improve both results and recognition. Recognize that you can achieve both by spending time supporting others.

TIME

MONEY

> **You want to make more money, but you also want to have more free time**

> **Look at ways to merge these ambitions into one, workable aim**

> **Imagine a future "you" who is focused on the positive intentions of both ambitions**

> **You will start to have ideas to help you achieve more money and more free time**

SEEING POSSIBILITIES ▶

Visualize two seemingly contradictory possibilities you want to work towards. Imagine the future resolution of the conflict by spending time looking at the positive intentions behind each "part". Think how each part could help the other achieve mutual aims.

313

LEARNING TO BREAK BAD HABITS

Bad habits can prevent you from getting things done with ease, but it is relatively easy to change a habit by replacing an old behaviour with a more productive, new one. Remember that this is one of the easiest ways to continuously improve performance.

41 Know how to spot and change habits that limit your effectiveness.

42 Understand that being aware of bad habits is the first step towards changing them.

UNDERSTANDING HABITS

Habits are ways of automating a bundle of thought and behaviour sequences. For instance, when you think to yourself "collect e-mail", you press all the computer keys automatically, without conscious effort. Unfortunately, your brain is as good at running bad habits as useful ones. Realize that if you continue to think the way you have always thought, you will continue to get what you have always got. If a bad habit is automatic, it will keep occurring because it is outside conscious awareness.

RECOGNIZING HABITS

Blind spots about your limitations can limit your professional development. Be willing to admit your own weaknesses so you can look objectively at your own bad habits. Watch out for some of the most common habits that hinder you from achieving the highest standards. Notice yourself using these habits so that you will know what to change for the better. Extend your concept of positive habits to include any thoughts or behaviours that will boost your effectiveness. Remember, nearly everything you do, whether thought or behaviour, becomes habitual once you have repeated it a few times.

POINTS TO REMEMBER

- Remember that the level of your performance is related to the effectiveness of your habits.
- People's personalities consist of the habits that they keep running over and over again.
- Generally, people change their habits when an alternative seems more appealing.
- Your habits need to change when you are no longer getting the results you want.

EXAMINING GOOD AND BAD HABITS

HABITS WORTH LOSING

EXPERIENCING STRESS
Feeling pressured causes stress and anxiety.

PROCRASTINATING
Wasting time is inefficient and saps motivation.

SELF-CRITICIZING
Being hard on yourself undermines confidence.

BEING A VICTIM
Not being assertive lowers your potential.

HABITS WORTH HAVING

FEELING IN CONTROL
Focusing on your strengths is empowering.

SETTING DAILY GOALS
Working towards set goals is motivating.

EXPECTING THE BEST
Having high standards results in good returns.

REMAINING PERSISTENT
Being determined increases your confidence.

USING THE "SWISH PATTERN"

Identify and focus on a bad habit you want to change. Visualize it

↓

Imagine your ideal self in the future having broken the habit. Visualize the new, ideal habit

↓

Replace the first image with the second, then look away. Repeat 5 times

↓

Recall the first picture and check that it now starts to change itself automatically

CHANGING HABITS

Once you have spotted a habit you want to change, such as getting frustrated with a colleague, use the NLP "Swish" pattern to change it. Re-run the experience of being frustrated. Identify what you see when you begin to become frustrated. Magnify this image. Now, give your mind something more useful to aim at. Imagine an ideal image of yourself in the future having handled the issue well. Expand this image over the original one. Shift your attention elsewhere. Now repeat this process five times until the second image replaces the first automatically. Do this regularly until the new habit is automatically triggered whenever the old habit tries to run.

43 Remember that all top performers have spent years building the habits of success.

ANALYZING PROBLEMS

Problems are often seen from a limited perspective, whereas the answer may lie outside the "box", or problem space, in which you are thinking. Increase the size of your thinking box, so that you can get to solutions you would not otherwise reach.

44 Identify the level at which a problem needs to be addressed.

45 Avoid getting stuck on one limited viewpoint.

46 View problems as puzzles that you need to work on to solve.

EXPLORING LEVELS

Managers often get stuck by tackling problems at the wrong level. When you are exploring a problem, make sure you consider the six possible levels. When you personalize your desk, for example, you are making an environmental level change. Saying "thank you" to people more often is a behavioural change. Going for higher targets is a change in the level of expectation. Developing a new skill is a change in capability. Promotion can bring about change at an identity level. Shifting focus from the bottom line to staff development represents a change at the level of values.

EXPLORING VIEWPOINTS

Once you have explored the level of a problem, think through all the viewpoints involved, including those of your colleagues, customers, and business. Understand the viewpoints so that you can find the best solution for all. Whenever there is a problem, ensure you can describe it equally well from each party's viewpoint. If you are not sure, ask them. Suppose a customer does not care about cost, only about delivery deadlines. To keep costs down, the business uses postal delivery. However, you are worried that the material will not arrive on time. Ask the customer if they would rather pay for a special delivery. This could satisfy all parties.

QUESTIONS TO ASK YOURSELF

Q How can I think about this problem in a different way so that I can come to a solution?

Q What is the most useful and productive way to think about this?

Q Does this problem exist only in my head?

Q When is the best time to think about this problem?

Q Is there an angle that I have not yet examined?

ASSESSING THE DIFFERENT ASPECTS OF AN ISSUE

FACTOR	ASPECT	POSSIBLE SOLUTION
LEVEL	VALUES	If a different meaning and purpose were perceived, could this transform the situation?
	IDENTITY	Could a change in someone's self-perception be the key to solving the problem?
	CAPABILITY	Is learning a new skill the best way forward in this situation?
	EXPECTATION	If someone had a different assumption, could this make the difference?
	BEHAVIOUR	Would one difference in what somebody does be the answer?
	ENVIRONMENT	Can a simple change in where something happens solve the problem?
TIMESCALE	PAST	What personal resource from the past would be most effective in resolving this issue?
	PRESENT	What is the smallest thing that could be done right now to make a start on this issue?
	FUTURE	What solution becomes obvious when you imagine a future where the problem is solved?
VIEWPOINT	SELF	Is there something you need to do differently for this not to be a problem?
	OTHER	Does someone else need to do something differently in order to solve this problem?
	OBSERVER	What solution is obvious only from an outside point of view?

OPTIMIZING YOUR TIME

The way you spend your time will determine your overall performance, and this in turn will have an effect on your team. Couple time-management skills with what really motivates you, and you will immediately start to boost your results.

47 Make sure you spend some time every day focusing on priorities.

48 Show your staff the difference between what is important and what is merely urgent.

KNOWING THE BASICS

The key to success at work is knowing the difference between what is important and what is just urgent. For instance, developing your management skills is important, but it is too often squeezed out by the pressure of urgent, but less vital, matters. Reallocate your time to important issues. Ask yourself, "Is this the most useful thing I could be doing now?" Focus on tasks that are important to you, and you will be better motivated

PRIORITIZING IMPORTANT TASKS OVER URGENT TASKS

URGENT / IMPORTANT
If you spend time stressed and in crisis management, these are symptoms that you are allowing urgent tasks to dominate important tasks.

IMPORTANT / NOT URGENT
If you take the time to plan your goals and development, you are using your time well and allocating time to important tasks.

URGENT / NOT IMPORTANT
If you are interrupted by office gossip and personal calls, you are not prioritizing your time to matters that are important.

NOT IMPORTANT / NOT URGENT
If you waste time reading junk mail, you are spending time that you could better spend on important tasks.

MANAGING YOUR TIME ▼
Begin by refocusing on your core values. Review them, and then reprioritize your work to align with these values.

ASSESSING VALUES

One reason you may not be practising time management is because you are losing sight of the personal reasons for doing what you are doing. You are unable to see the wood for the trees. Refocus on your core values to help motivate yourself. Do this by asking yourself, "What is important about work?" Then, free-associate by writing down the different thoughts that come into your head. This will surface your work values. Common motivating values include satisfaction, career success, recognition, helping others, and financial rewards. Once you have ten or more, rank your top three core values.

Refocus ➡ **Review** ➡ **Reprioritize**

MOTIVATING YOURSELF

If you tend to think of time management as being either a boring chore or something that reminds you of everything you have been putting off, then you will never do it. If, on the other hand, you begin to think of time management as the shortest route to achieving more of what you really want, it becomes compelling. Avoid work overload by breaking your time into smaller tasks and get into the habit of doing this on a daily basis. It is easier to enjoy accomplishing one task at a time, and it is motivating and satisfying as you tick off each task on the list.

▲ **MANAGING YOUR TIME**
To avoid overload, break your work into bite-size chunks that are as easy and as satisfying to do as possible. The tasks inevitably feel more achievable and you will feel motivated to tackle them.

49 Learn to understand what matters to you so that you are better motivated in your work.

HELPING OTHERS IMPROVE

Increasingly, the competitive edge in an organization depends upon people's interpersonal skills. Use NLP skills to help you get the best from other people.

RELATING NON-VERBALLY

*M*ost business results are generated *through good working relationships between people. Understand and adopt the basic principles and skills of non-verbal communication, so that you can enhance your working relationships.*

50 Learn to see your behaviour from other people's perspectives.

55% Body Language

38% Speech

7% Words

▲ IMPACT OF COMMUNICATION
Research shows that, in face-to-face communication, voice tones and body language have a far greater effect in terms of how people react and respond to each other than words themselves.

GETTING ON BETTER
Working relationships are like a dance. If you alter your behaviour, other people change theirs accordingly. To be an outstanding manager, learn to practise essential attitudes. Assume people are doing the best they can from their point of view. Believe improvements will come if you work out what you can do differently to get the best out of your staff. Support them and spell out clearly what they need to do to succeed, and then make it possible for them to do it.

PACING AND LEADING

When you communicate, it is important to acknowledge what is being said in some way. "Pacing" can be done non-verbally, by nodding your head in response to a point, or verbally, by summarizing each point made. The person you are talking with then feels confident that you are listening to what he or she is saying and will be more receptive as you "lead" with a question or comment. This helps you redirect the flow to the next most useful place.

ADAPTING STYLES ▶

In this example, the manager has adapted her body language and voice tone to match the employee's. Her behaviour affects the response she receives from the employee and helps create a rapport.

MATCHING BEHAVIOURS

When people have a rapport, they tend to match each other's body language and voice tone. Tune in your body language and voice to other people's preferred styles. Notice the way people express themselves and shift your style so that it is similar. Listen to voice tones and notice when someone speaks faster or quieter. Speed up or alter your volume accordingly. If someone makes a lot of fast gestures, speed up and increase your gestures to help increase rapport.

Matches voice tone

Has calm voice tone

Sits in matching position

Feet are crossed

AVOIDING MISMATCHING

Beware of sending powerful negative messages non-verbally, such as by frowning when someone suggests an idea. This "mismatching" can damage relationships and performance. Even though you may not intend to give this signal, your unconscious communication affects the response that you will get. For instance, if you do not look up when someone talks to you, you may be sending a dismissive signal. Prevent this by becoming aware of your own unconscious mismatching and increase the quality of attention you give to others.

51 Remember, it is not what you say, but how you say it.

52 Aim to always bring out the best in others.

EVALUATING PRIORITIES

In every aspect of business, such as in customer service, staff retention, and performance management, people have priorities that need to be satisfied. Learn how to identify key needs, so that you are in a position to be able to satisfy them.

53 Practise listening for people's personal criteria in all situations.

54 Focus on issues that directly affect performance.

55 Keep a written note of customers' main priorities.

UNDERSTANDING CRITERIA

One cause of failure in business stems from staff not being clear about the needs they are trying to fulfil. Develop the habit of automatically identifying the criteria that has the most effect on your results (key performance criteria) to ensure that you and your team focus attention on the most productive issues. For example, realize that it is more cost-effective to retain existing customers than to win new ones. In your own organization, encourage your staff to become more aware of customers' priorities.

NOTICING EMPHASIS

Listen for other people's most important criteria, or ask them what they consider to be important. Sometimes their words alone will tell you. Notice the way they "mark" out their key criteria among a flow of apparent needs. They may say, "We need you to get back to us soon". The key word "soon" may be marked out with a verbal emphasis or a hand gesture. Identify the key criteria and check it by repeating it back.

Hand gesture emphasizes point

A raised voice tone underlines an important issue

EMPHASIZING A POINT ▶

What someone else considers as important may be different from your view. Watch the way people show what they consider relevant through their gestures and voice.

CLARIFYING OTHER PEOPLE'S NEEDS

When you are responsible for delivering results to others, clarify their main criteria. NLP skills will help you identify and satisfy needs. Ask, "If we can deliver X at this price by next week, is that what you want?" If there are no problems, agree to line up the next action steps. If there are problems, ask questions to find out what is going to cause the difficulty for you or them. Then discuss it to find the best way forward for both of you.

Colleague listens to points of view

Manager asks what is important about an issue

Employee leans forward to make his point

CLARIFYING INTERNAL NEEDS

When you rely on your team to be responsible for delivering results, first be sure that you have made the performance criteria clear. For example, there is little point in asking people to improve quality if you have not said which aspects of quality need improving, and to what standard. First, ask your team if they are clear about what is wanted. If you are not convinced they are clear, ask them to repeat back to you what is wanted. Secondly, make sure they are able to deliver what you want.

▲ LISTENING TO VIEWPOINTS

Take the time to ask your team members about their priorities on a project, so that they feel respected, and so that you can ensure that everyone is clear on the goals.

56 Keep clarifying to your team what is important in each situation.

WORKING WITH PERSONALITY TRAITS

In most situations, there are some ways in which people will behave consistently. Recognize these consistent patterns in yourself and others, so you increase your effectiveness and ensure you avoid the same problems repeating themselves over and over again.

57 Prevent problems by understanding your colleagues' behaviour patterns.

58 Learn to recognize patterns in yourself, as well as in others.

59 See how every mental habit can be a strength.

LOOKING AT DIFFERENCE

There are mental habits (or "meta-programs") that we all use in different situations. For example some people follow a set procedure to achieve the goals, and others prefer to have options. Evaluation can be based on people's own opinions, or on those of others. Some people initiate action, while others are reactive. Some aim to achieve positive goals, and others want to avoid negative problem. Some people think in overview, and others focus on fine details. People may also look for how things are similar to, or different from, each other

ADAPTING TO DIFFERENCE

Two people with different meta-programs can find it hard to communicate, and this can be damaging in business. Learn to recognize different patterns of behaviour in your team members, and work with these differences to maximize performance. For example, when you delegate a task to people who favour "options" to achieve their aims, as opposed to a set procedure, avoid telling them exactly what to do. They are likely to feel you do not trust them. Tell them the goal and let them decide on the best way of achieving it.

QUESTIONS TO ASK YOURSELF

Q When I delegate tasks to someone who favours procedures, do I make sure they know what to do?

Q Does this person focus on the positive or is he or she more focused on avoiding the negative?

Q Have I designed this job to suit this person's strengths?

APPLYING DIFFERENCES

Try to differentiate between people with different personalities in your team. Improve performance by ensuring that people's characteristics fit their job specifications. For example, an account executive is likely to perform better if he or she is naturally proactive, whereas a telesales person will excel if she or he reacts well to customers. Human Resources specialists use "meta-program" profiles to clarify the characteristics of top performers to recruit the best candidates.

60 Make sure people's natural personality preferences are well matched to the tasks that they perform.

WORKING WITH DIFFERENT PERSONALITY TRAITS

META-PROGRAMS	EMPLOYEE DISCUSSION	MANAGER'S VIEW
PROACTIVE	"We just need to get this done."	"Good points. If *you* start on it right now, *you* can deal with issues that come up."
REACTIVE	"Let's wait until we know more."	
BIG PICTURE	"You are not seeing the overview."	"You are both right. With no overview, we will get lost and without fine detail, we fail."
FINE DETAIL	"The fine detail is just as important."	
PROCEDURE	"This is the way it is done here."	"If *you* keep things going, I would like *you* to consider the best options."
OPTION	"Yes, but we need fresh approaches."	
SELF	"I want to make the decision here."	"Maybe we need more details about the customer's wants before you make a decision."
OTHER	"Will the customer buy it?"	
TOWARDS	"I really want to meet this deadline."	"If *you* plan how to meet the deadline, *you* can make sure we do not repeat mistakes."
AWAY FROM	"We can't make another mistake."	
SIMILARITY	"We have had this problem before."	"Let's see what worked last time and tailor it to what is different."
DIFFERENCE	"The pace of change is different."	

GETTING THE BEST DEAL

Not everyone has the same approach to negotiations – in fact, there are five main styles that people use unconsciously. Understand your own approach and learn to recognize other people's, so you get the best results for all parties in your negotiations.

61 Treat the other party's interests with the respect you give your own.

▲ MAKING A DEAL
Find a way to work towards the best results through bargaining, so that all parties will be pleased with the result.

UNDERSTANDING STYLES

Learn to recognize negotiation styles in yourself and others. A compromise style splits the difference, although both parties could have achieved more. A coercive style relies on being dominant regardless of consequences. Emotional negotiation assumes that appealing to feelings will get the best results, while rational negotiation supposes arguing a point of view will change people's minds. A bargaining style, however, is the most beneficial, because it finds the trade-offs that get the best value for all.

RECOGNIZING NEGOTIATING STYLES

NEGOTIATION STYLE	DISCUSSION
COMPROMISE	"We need a fair deal." "Maybe we can agree to split the difference."
COERCION	"Can we negotiate that?" "No, when we make demands, you should jump."
EMOTION	"Will you extend our credit terms?" "That would cause difficulties for me."
RATIONAL	"Do you see that if we can agree now...?" "But it is sensible to finalize the schedules first."
BARGAINING	"If you can deliver next week, we agree." "We will deliver next week, if you sign the deal now."

DEVELOPING THE SKILLS

Recognize occasions that could be negotiation situations. Before a negotiation, be clear on your outcomes and your bottom line. Make sure you plan and research carefully beforehand, and think through what your best alternative to a negotiated agreement is. This might be to go elsewhere. During the negotiation, maintain a steady emotional state – if you find this difficult, take a deep breath and change the focus of your thinking. Every move should get you closer to a win-win deal or the realization that no deal is the best option.

THINGS TO DO

1. Before a negotiation, try to imagine the other party's possible sticking points.

2. Gather any useful information on them.

3. Mentally rehearse the parts of the negotiation that you anticipate will be difficult.

62 Know you are only as strong as your weakest moves.

63 Work to achieve a good deal for both parties.

BENEFITING THE BUSINESS

Expand your negotiating skills and reap the future rewards in your own performance. Remember that if a party is unhappy with the results of a deal, long-term relationships may be damaged. Review every negotiation with the benefit of hindsight and look at what you could do differently in future. Practise in your imagination and make it a goal to improve relationships with every deal. Also, take stakeholders into account with each negotiation, so that your business thrives in the long term. This is win-win-win thinking.

NEGOTIATING ▶ SUCCESSFULLY

In this example, a major organization used negotiation with its suppliers to position itself as a market leader in environmentally friendly furniture. Excellence in negotiation allowed the organization to put together deals that its competition could not match.

CASE STUDY

A leading furniture retailer decided to treat increasing concerns about the environment as an opportunity rather than a problem. Initially its suppliers were resistant to making environmentally friendly changes. The retailer negotiated improvements with each supplier in order to create alternative processes that reduced environmental damage. The suppliers in turn had to renegotiate with their supply chain. This was not an overnight process. Additionally, the retailer decided not to advertise this policy, but to let people hear of it through word of mouth. This method had higher credibility and saved on advertising. The policy was a win-win-win move as customers received sustainable quality products at good prices; the organization grew rapidly because of its reputation; and the environment benefited from reduced waste.

DETECTING AND PREVENTING PROBLEMS

It is best to avoid problems before they occur. Learn to anticipate them by recognizing subtle cues in other people's behaviour. Be sensitive and aim to spot other people's potential issues, even before they are aware of them themselves.

64 Recognize that every problem was once a solution to another problem.

65 Remember, it is more cost efficient to prevent problems, rather than waiting until they happen.

RECOGNIZING POTENTIAL PROBLEMS

Learn to spot problems in advance. Sometimes someone is aware of a problem, but it may not be at the front of his or her mind. This incongruence can affect his or her behaviour and can influence others. Begin to recognize signs of this and pick up on subtle signals. First, spot your own uncertainties, such as nagging doubts, and act on them. Second, notice mixed messages in others and ask questions so that you can detect a problem before it happens.

KNOWING SELF-CERTAINTY

When you are about to make a decision, you need to have a way of recognizing your inner certainty. Unless you are certain, you could make a decision that you regret. Think of a time when you did have a feeling of certainty or inner congruence, and it turned out to be accurate. Focus on the inner feeling so that you can describe it in terms of size, shape, or location. Now compare this with a time when you were uncertain. Be aware of the differences between when you feel certain and when you do not. Then, check your certainty before you make a decision.

QUESTIONS TO ASK YOURSELF

Q How certain is this person about what they are saying?

Q How sure am I about what I am saying?

Q What do I need to ask to clarify these feelings of doubt and uncertainty?

Q How will I know when this person is certain?

Q How congruent am I feeling about this decision?

Touches face,
indicating doubt

Stance is
confident

Body posture
is open and
positive

Body posture
is skewed

Feet face
person he
is talking to
and are still

CERTAINTY UNCERTAINTY

▲ MEASURING CERTAINTY

Listen and watch carefully when people respond and notice your gut feeling about their level of certainty. When someone is certain, their verbal and non-verbal behaviour say the same thing.

RESOLVING THE PROBLEM

Surface any hidden concerns, so you can find a way of resolving problems. Notice a concern and decide whether it is worth picking up on. If it is, say, "You don't seem to be clear about 'X'. If there was a problem with 'X', what would it be?" Once the issue has surfaced, and if it seems to be significant, ask, "Do you know how to resolve that?" If they say "Yes", check for congruence. If they are incongruent, ask them again what the issue is. However, if they say "No", ask "What has to happen for us to resolve this?"

CONVERSATIONAL CALIBRATION ▶

To measure congruence, ask a colleague two questions. First, ask a question that you know your colleague knows the answer to. Then ask one you know he or she is uncertain about. Notice the differences. Rate their congruence on a scale of 1–10.

FINDING DOUBT IN OTHERS

When someone is certain, their words make more sense, their voice tone tends to be deeper, and their body language more confident. When someone is uncertain, there will be a small element of doubt or hesitation in their behaviour – their body language is sending a message of uncertainty. Concerns will show up in subtle shifts in tone of voice, facial expression, skin colouration, or pupil dilation. Learn to watch for subtle incongruities of body language.

*Employee's voice tone
and gestures are emphatic*

RESPONDING WITH CONFIDENCE

*Employee hesitates
and looks away*

RESPONDING WITH DOUBT

SHAPING MEETINGS

By knowing how to make meetings work effectively, you can transform personal and organizational productivity. Improve your meetings skills so that meetings are always a constructive forum, where issues can be discussed efficiently and effectively.

66 Keep summarizing where the meeting has got to and where it is going.

PREPARING MEETINGS

Ensure you are clear about the aim of a meeting. Ask yourself what you want to achieve by the end of the meeting. Break this into outcomes, such as decisions made and tasks allocated. Think about what you will see or hear to let you know that your goals have been achieved. For example, you will see people nod agreement to a decision; or you will hear someone offering to do a task. Finally, check that each person needs to be there for most of the items on the agenda, or schedule another meeting.

▼ KEEPING A MEETING FOCUSED
Write down your meeting goals on a flipchart so that everyone present can refer to it if necessary, and watch for signs that outcomes are being achieved.

THINGS TO DO

1. **Practise putting yourself in other people's positions so you can understand their viewpoint.**

2. **Work out the best way to move the meeting on.**

3. **Compliment others when they make a good point.**

TRACKING THE MEETING

Imagine watching the meeting from the corner of the room. Visualize yourself standing in a thoughtful pose in a position where you can observe the whole room. This is called 3rd position in NLP. Imagine moving into this position and notice if events are going anywhere. If they are, then continue as you were. If not, take charge and get agreement from everyone on the purpose of the meeting. Then, move into the 3rd position in your mind again. Keep checking that the meeting is progressing towards successful outcomes

KEEPING THE MEETING FOCUSED

Having started the meeting with the objectives in clear view of everyone, keep checking that the meeting is on track. If necessary, intervene. For example, if somebody is discussing something that is not directly relevant, say, "Good point, but I am not sure how that is helping us achieve our aim, here," and refer everyone to the agenda. If things become unclear, summarize the goals you have already achieved and refocus on the next one. When you encounter problems, ask, "What can we do differently?" to move towards solutions. If you become stuck with someone, guess their problem in order to find a way forward.

67 Summarize the goals achieved and refocus on the next one.

68 Identify the next action steps and who will carry them out.

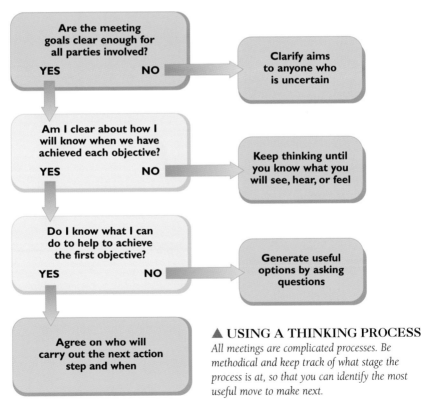

▲ USING A THINKING PROCESS

All meetings are complicated processes. Be methodical and keep track of what stage the process is at, so that you can identify the most useful move to make next.

IMPROVING WORKING RELATIONSHIPS

Managers need high levels of interpersonal skills to achieve top performance in today's pressured working environment. Learn the vital skill of knowing when and how to shift viewpoints to ensure you get the best results from others.

69 Recognize the part you play in helping your staff deliver good results.

70 Appreciate your employees' points of view.

71 Notice whether people focus more on relationships or on tasks.

LEARNING FROM WEAKNESSES

Successful managers need to achieve top results from their teams. To get the best out of people, look at what you do with people that works, and how to improve what does not work. When results are not up to standard, resist the urge to blame staff. Instead, notice your part in the results they produce. This could include things you did not do. Imagine alternative approaches that might work better next time. For example, a colleague does not seem to listen to your comments. On reflection, you realize that you told them only what you wanted, not how they should proceed.

CULTURAL DIFFERENCES

The differences between individuals are much bigger than the differences between genders. However, there are some interesting stereotypical differences between men and women. Women are often better at putting themselves into other people's shoes (known as 2nd position in NLP). Conversely, they can neglect their own needs (in 1st position). Men on the other hand are often clearer about their own needs and more assertive in satisfying them. They can, however, be weak at understanding a viewpoint that is different to their own.

MOVING YOUR VIEWPOINT

People often talk about the "real world" and forget that each of us lives in our own world. Learn to see situations from other people's viewpoints through "2nd positioning". Your own point of view is "1st position". Also, try to be an impartial observer (3rd position) and view a situation from outside any individual viewpoint. Use this perceptual position to be objective. When you are faced with a difficulty, explore all three positions.

Manager confronts an employee about a problem on a project

Sees a way to handle situation

Issue is resolved amicably

Thinks through situation from an observer's point of view

Manager has not considered other perspectives

Communication breaks down

DEALING WITH PROBLEMS

Imagine a situation with a colleague who you find difficult. Choose a word to describe how you experience the colleague's behaviour as difficult, for example, hostile. Think how they may see your behaviour as difficult. Choose another word to describe your behaviour. Imagine yourself in the situation (1st position) and note how you feel. You may be more frustrated than you realize. Focus on the person's body language and imagine being in their position (2nd position). Notice any feeling they might have that you were not aware of, such as anxiety. Then, step back (3rd position) and ask yourself, "What's the best way to handle this?"

Manager has not resolved issue and both parties feel misunderstood

▲ VALUING VIEWPOINTS

This manager must appreciate his employee's point of view from an observer position, so that he can constructively handle the situation.

RECOGNIZING THE CUES

When you are talking with someone, learn to notice which thinking style – visual, auditory, or kinesthetic (feelings) – is predominant at any particular moment. Recognize the cues so that you can fine-tune your communication to fit their style.

72 Listen for visual-, auditory-, and kinesthetic-based words or phrases.

73 Learn to recognize eye movement cues automatically.

INTERPRETING EYE-ACCESSING CUES ▼
Develop your people skills by looking for eye cues that give you insights into how people are thinking. Do this regularly until you start to spot cues automatically.

SPOTTING THE CUES
Eye movements and words are clues as to whether someone is thinking in images (Visual style), sounds (Auditory style), or feelings (Kinesthetic style). These cues are usually momentary, and people are often unaware of the phenomenon. Generally, when people look up, they are thinking visually. When they look down to their left, they are talking to themselves. When they look down to their right, they are in touch with their feelings. If someone says "I see…", this suggests visual thinking.

Constructs a visual image of something

CONSTRUCTING IMAGES

Remembers an image of something in the past

REMEMBERING IMAGES

Begins to construct a verbal response

Visualizes possibilities in his mind's eye

Recalls something said in the past

CONSTRUCTING SOUNDS **THINKING VISUALLY** **REMEMBERING SOUNDS**

Checks how he feels about something

Talks to himself inside his head

EXPERIENCING FEELINGS **INTERNAL DIALOGUE**

ADAPTING TO THE CUES

Learn to change your thinking style to match other people's. If a colleague keeps looking up and uses visual words, adapt to a visual-communication style. For example, if they say, "This project is not looking too bright", say, "Let's throw some light on it". If a customer looks down to their left and says, "I'm not sure about this", realize he or she may be talking internally about his or her concerns. Let them know you are happy to talk it through.

RECOGNIZING LANGUAGE TYPES

TYPE	EXAMPLES IN SPEECH
VISUAL	● "Bright idea." ● "We're not seeing the whole picture." ● "We need to focus on another issue."
AUDITORY	● "Sounds good." ● "We need to talk this through." ● "What he is saying does not ring true."
KINESTHETIC	● "I'm overloaded." ● "It feels right." ● "I am going to smooth it out."

SEEING OTHERS THINK

Thinking is made up of sequences, or "strategies", of images, sounds, and feelings. Spot the cues of people's thinking strategies. For instance, if your boss makes decisions by looking over different options, asking which is the best, and going on his gut feeling, take note of this for when you present him with a new project. For example, say, "Here are the possibilities I've *looked* at. Can we *discuss* which is best until you *feel* we've got the right one."

74 Spot thinking strategies so you can achieve the best from your staff and your organization.

Influencing Through Language

Effective communication will impact on your results. Recognize when to be specific with questions, and how to adapt to other people's language patterns so that you can effectively influence them. Aim to understand people's non-verbal responses.

75 Realize that by asking questions, you can direct the conversation.

76 Be aware when you brief your staff that people can react differently to the same words.

Succeeding Through Language

A manager will spend an average of eight minutes on each one-to-one interaction with an employee. What you say in this time is crucial to overall performance and results. Learn to recognize when your words get you the results you want, and when they do not. Be clear about what you want to achieve before you speak. Then compare the result your words actually produced with the result you had intended. Notice when you have to tailor the wording to suit the individual.

Choosing Your Words

Most of the time, the words you use work very well, but in some interactions you must choose your words carefully. Before these conversations, imagine watching yourself talking with the other person. Then, think through your options. Imagine the response you think they will have to each one. If they respond well in your imagination, then you know what to say to them. If they do not, imagine different approaches until you find one that works. Practise this approach several times in your mind before actually having the conversation.

77 Use sensitive and thoughtful language.

78 Learn to read people's responses as you talk.

ASKING QUESTIONS

Performance is affected by the ability of yourself and others to ask the right questions at the right time. Your team may assume that you know more about an issue than you do, and you may feel uncomfortable about asking. If you are not clear on something, decide on the question you want to ask and when to ask it. When you receive a response, it may be necessary to clarify key words (using the Meta Model), to make sure you fully understand.

QUESTIONS TO ASK YOURSELF

Q What is the most useful question to ask next?

Q What are we trying to achieve here?

Q What have we not noticed yet?

Q What do we need to change or do differently?

Q What would happen if we did this?

Q What is stopping us from doing this?

NON FACE-TO-FACE COMMUNICATION

Some people find it difficult if they cannot see the person they are talking to, and find face-to-face communication easier. Before you send e-mails, read them as if you were the recipient. On the telephone, listen closely to responses and changes in voice tone.

79 Teach yourself and your staff to ask clarifying questions.

FORMULATING CLARIFYING QUESTIONS (META MODEL)

STATEMENT	KEY WORD TYPE	QUESTION TO ASK
"You must always write *reports* better in future."	NOUN	"Which specific reports do you want me to write better?"
"You must always *write* reports better in future."	VERB	"How specifically do you want me to write these reports better?"
"You *must* always write reports better in future."	RULE	"What will the consequences be if I do not improve them?"
"You must *always* write reports better in future."	GENERALIZATION	"Do you really mean you always want me to write them better?"
"You must always write reports *better* in future."	COMPARISON	"In what way do you mean better exactly?"

REPEATING KEY WORDS

Remember that words can mean different things to different people. Listen carefully to the exact words others use – note their key words as they talk, and then use their key words in response. This will ensure that you communicate in a way that makes sense to them. Do not translate words they use. If someone says, "business performance", avoid changing it to "organizational success" because you think that is what they mean. It may not be.

▲ ASSESSING UNDERSTANDING
When you are conversing with people, be sensitive and alert to non-verbal signals so that you can be sure you have been correctly understood.

CHECKING FOR SENSE

The verbal part of behaviour is the words that people use. The non-verbal part is the body language and voice tones that tell you how to interpret what is being said. People will tell you non-verbally when what you say makes sense to them and when it does not. If it does, they may signal acknowledgment with a nod. If it does not make sense, the nods will stop, or a facial expression will shift. In this case, rephrase your information, or ask them which bit did not make sense.

**INCREASING ▶
PRODUCTIVITY**
This case study shows how even subtle changes to people's approach on the telephone can make a huge difference to the response that they get. This is especially important for call centres, which have a high proportion of customer contact.

CASE STUDY
The competition that a direct-sales organization faced had increased tenfold over two years. The managing board decided to study the differences between top-performing customer-service staff and the rest. They made some important discoveries. Top performers tended to believe that their job was primarily to help customers. They tended to make a sale only when it was in the customer's interest. This turned a sales job into a service role, which gave the staff a sense of fulfilment. Generally, it was found that top performers would shift their voice tone to try to match the customer's before leading with positive voice tones. They used more of the customer's own language. Based on these findings, the board decided to provide coaching for other staff in these critical skills. The organization's profits doubled within a year.

80 Empower your staff and benefit from good results.

81 Look for moments when artfully vague language is useful.

EMPOWERING OTHERS

If an employee's skills are limited, empower them by spelling out specifically what is required. For example, "We want to maintain a good relationship for future business. I want you to apologise to this customer and offer a full refund." When you deal with highly skilled staff, allow them to come up with their own solutions, so that you empower them to resolve issues in their own way. In this case, artfully vague language (Milton model) often works better than being specific: "Can I leave you to find the best way of dealing with this customer?"

USING VAGUE LANGUAGE (MILTON MODEL)

LANGUAGE PATTERN	DESIRED EFFECT
"You might have noticed…"	The sentence structure implies that it is okay if they have not noticed the issue.
"We're under more competitive pressure…"	This phrasing does not specify who feels what pressure, or how.
"You may or may not agree…"	This wording implies that the listeners are free to make their own opinions.
"We have to solve problems faster…"	This implies that there is a direct link between the problem and the proposed solution.
"Each new problem is an opportunity…"	This phrasing gives a positive angle to an unspecified problem.
"Have you already started to wonder…"	This sentence structure encourages people to start thinking.
"The challenge will bring out the best in us…"	The wording presents a difficult project as a chance to excel.

PROMOTING WINNING IDEAS

If you want your team to excel, you need to promote productive ideas. Use a strategy for effective thinking by separating the roles of creativity, realism, and criticism from each other and by focusing on these issues at the appropriate time.

82 Accept that it will take a lot of ideas to get to a winning one.

▲ **THINKING CREATIVELY**
If your team members are having trouble being creative, ask them to recall a time when they were resourceful, for example, on an activity weekend.

ENCOURAGING CREATIVE THINKING

Avoid criticizing people for creative thinking. Create a space in which people are clear that the aim is to be freely creative without feeling inhibited, and where all ideas are welcomed. Mark out creative thinking time. Ideally, find your own marker. For example, you might make a yellow paper hat with the word "creative" written in large letters. This hat is put on the table to remind others that their job is only to be creative. No criticism is allowed here. Use this marker regularly and people will find it easier to be creative and generate good ideas.

83 Encourage people to suggest possible improvements.

84 Check that an idea is realistic and achievable.

DOS AND DON'TS

✔ Do assume that all members of your team have something creative to offer.

✔ Do take risks when you feel an idea may be worth pursuing.

✔ Do acknowledge and pursue all positive suggestions that your team come up with.

✘ Don't criticize creative ideas, or your staff will stop suggesting their views.

✘ Don't forget to ask all your team members for their input.

✘ Don't assume that others will initiate improvements, as they often will not.

THINKING REALISTICALLY

Once ideas have been generated in the meeting, make it clear that the objective now is to discuss the implementation of ideas. This will reinforce realistic thinking. First, ask "Which are the best ideas?" Take each idea and ask, "How would you implement this?" Ask your team to think through who is doing what, how, and by when. You have a realistic plan when these questions have been answered.

Sales manager asks her team to look at practicalities of an idea

SELECTING IDEAS ▶
Once creative ideas have been aired, take the time to sort out the useful ideas from the ones that are not realistic for your organization.

POINTS TO REMEMBER

- The creative ideas meeting should be separated from the critical analysis of these ideas.
- Good ideas are not always practical or realistic at first.
- Some ideas may be workable in the future, but not the present.
- Always critically analyze ideas from a number of different points of view to test their feasibility.

THINKING CRITICALLY

If an idea is worth developing, ensure it is robust enough to work. People often get criticized for ideas before they get developed – good ideas are stopped in their tracks. Instead, know when to criticize thinking. In the meeting, make it clear that the purpose now is to troubleshoot. This prevents individuals from taking criticism personally. Then ask, "What is most likely to go wrong?" Allow your team to identify potential issues – the idea may then fail or possible problems be resolved.

ANALYZING PROJECTS

When a project is at the design stage, ensure team members know when to think creatively, critically, and realistically. Notice which role you are weakest at and aim to have someone in your team who is strong in this area. Decide which roles other people are best at. Complement their strengths by taking on their weakest role yourself. Get your team used to thinking and working in terms of these roles.

85 Form a team who complement each other's strengths and make up for each other's weaknesses.

CONTINUING TO IMPROVE

Adopting the skills of NLP is an ongoing process of self-development. Nurture the habits of continuous improvement, so that you are empowered to reach your highest potential.

LIFE PLANNING

People and organizations that set goals are more likely to achieve them than those that do not. Use regular life planning as an essential tool for keeping yourself on track in a fast-changing world. Treat plans as working directions rather than rigid goals.

86 Make a life plan so you can be sure you are working towards your aims.

CULTURAL DIFFERENCES

Increasingly in the West, people are becoming more interested in working fewer hours and having more time for leisure pursuits. Lifestyle has become a bigger concern than the standard of living. However, in the East, many people are still striving to increase their standard of living.

DECIDING ON YOUR GOALS

Failing to plan is planning to fail. Constantly think ahead in different areas of your life and over different periods of time so you have a way of keeping yourself on track. Write a list of around seven key life areas down the side of a piece of paper. These might be career, family, finance, health, enjoyment, personal development, and friendships. Choose the areas that suit you. Then, along the top, write different time scales – a month, a year, and five years. Set your own goals for each life area for each time-frame. Make sure you set goals that you are motivated to achieve.

HARNESSING YOUR MIND

When setting goals, most people under-use the power of their unconscious mind. Learn to get your unconscious mind to work for you. To do this, focus on the difference between your current reality and your goals in order to maintain a creative tension. As long as you do not try to resolve an issue consciously, your unconscious mind will continue to look for a way of resolving the tension. Use this method to help you with life planning.

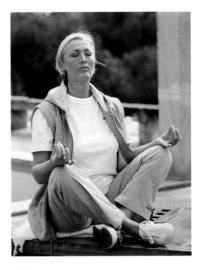

USING YOUR UNCONSCIOUS MIND ▶
Many people use meditation as part of their self-development. It can help you focus your mind by letting you observe your thinking processes instead of being caught up in them.

87 Realize the power of your unconscious mind – it is the source of your creativity.

Note down your key life areas — *Set timescales for achieving your goals*

Area	1 Month	1 Year
Career	Pay rise	Promotion
Family	Short break	Move house
Health	Take up cycling	New diet
Interests	Read book	New hobby
Self	Start diary	Do course
Finance	Begin saving	Save 10%
Others	Give to charity	Fundraise

USING TIMELINES

Make the goals you set more achievable by imagining that you have already attained them. Look at your life plan as a "timeline", to join your present to your future and past. Take your current location as the present. Imagine the future when you have achieved a goal. Move along the timeline to a goal you set and look back at the present. Walk forward and look back, or do this in your imagination. From the future, see how you achieved a goal.

Set targets for yourself to aim towards in the short- and long-term

◀ CREATING A LIFE PLAN
Every six months, review and revise your life plan, so that you adapt to changes and ensure that you are still clear about the life you want to lead.

ONGOING PERSONAL DEVELOPMENT

The way to secure long-term career and organizational success is to learn faster than your competitors. Recognize that the fast track to professional development is to work on your weakest areas, and be honest with yourself about what these are.

88 Develop your own personal and professional support systems.

89 Recognize your weaknesses so you are able to develop.

90 Make a habit of learning from other people.

KEEPING A LEARNING LOG

Build the habit of taking five minutes every day to review the key incidents of the last 24 hours. First, look at what you did that worked and congratulate yourself. Then look at what did not work. Look at what you would do differently next time. For example, you got really upset when someone blamed you for missing a deadline. On reflection, you realized you wallowed in the injustice of it. Decide that next time you will add an extra week to the schedule and focus on keeping your emotional state positive.

KEEPING A ▶ JOURNAL
Make and keep an appointment with yourself every day to write your journal, even if it is only for a couple of minutes. Write down what you achieved that day, and note down areas you need to improve on. This keeps you focused on self-development.

Thursday 24th November

Last 24 hours:
Successfully renegotiated my flexitime deal with manager.
• Key learning: Nearly forgot an appointment — set an automatic reminder on my computer next time.

Next 24 hours:
• Buy exercise book so that I can start my learning log.
• Start setting daily outcomes.
• Listen to time-management audio tapes.

Friday 25th November

Last 24 hours:
Bought exercise book and started a daily learning log

GETTING STARTED

With a personal-development activity, you must be able to motivate yourself or it will not happen. Consider using a learning log. Getting started is the hard part. When you decide to start, arrange to telephone a friend every day for the first week to let them know whether or not you have done your log for the day. A month after you have started, you may find you are getting stuck on the same issues. Get outside input for new ways of looking at these issues. Find a suitable book, or talk with a friend.

THINGS TO DO

1. Take time to reflect on your development.
2. Always aim to be learning something new.
3. Read papers and journals to keep up to date with developments.

FINDING YOUR PATH

Personal and professional development is critical to success in business. Look at ways to develop your performance. Decide on the route that works best for you: for example, a one-day course, or an MBA degree. Consider applying for organizational funding. If it is not available, look at spending your own time and money, as an investment in your success. Generally, top performers allocate 10 per cent of their resources to improvement.

91 Read at least one book a month and create a library that you can refer to in future.

CHOOSING A PERSONAL-DEVELOPMENT OPTION

TYPE OF COURSE	ADVANTAGES	DISADVANTAGES
NLP TRAINING	Complete package of skills for professional success.	The quality of these courses can vary considerably.
MBA DEGREE COURSE	A well-recognized professional qualification.	This can be expensive and time consuming.
TRANSACTIONAL ANALYSIS	Useful for understanding situation dynamics.	These are sometimes not particularly business focused.
ONE-DAY BUSINESS COURSE	Courses are tailored to the main business applications.	Changes can be hard to integrate over the long term.

COACHING FOR RESULTS

Top performers recognize they need to continually improve, and use regular coaching to turn weaknesses into strengths. Use coaching to develop these skills and increase your performance. Notice how problems can become opportunities to learn.

92 Look at problems as opportunities to concentrate on self-development.

▲ COACHING YOUR STAFF

Coach your staff to solve their own problems with your support, rather than relying on you for solutions.

JOINING FORCES

To set up a co-coaching system, find a suitable partner and agree to mutual coaching sessions on a regular basis. First, list potential partners – put them in rank order, and approach the highest first. Ask if they are willing to give it a trial run. Decide where and when suits you both best. Then decide how much time to spend coaching each other. Always have equal time each way as coach and coachee.

LEARNING TO SUPPORT

A lot of people think that they can become successful without any support. However, coaching is increasingly used by top managers because it is one of the most effective ways of improving performance. For example, if you find that you procrastinate on sales calls, you can be coached to think of these calls as a chance to build relationships rather than feeling you have to push a sale. Coaching develops your ability to support others and boosts your emotional intelligence. You can then improve your coaching of others.

DOS AND DON'TS

✔ Do reflect on what you would do differently next time.	✘ Don't think you have to know all the answers.
✔ Do informally coach people when situations arise.	✘ Don't interrupt with your suggestions unless asked.
✔ Do stay calm whatever happens in the session.	✘ Don't criticize people's thoughts and views.

93 Use coaching time as an opportunity to improve your relationships with your staff.

DECIDING WHAT TO SAY

As the coachee, focus on whatever it is most useful for you to explore. The session is for you. As coach, your job is to do what is most useful for the coachee. There are three stages to the process: exploring the issue, identifying an outcome or goal, and defining the next action step. As the coach, ask questions until the coachee becomes clearer about the issue, the outcome, and what they are going to do differently. Use your rapport skills to help the coachee feel comfortable and use your enthusiasm to "drive" their emotional state so they are more enthused to take action. At the end, ask the coachee for feedback on what worked, and what you could improve on.

94 Remember to be supportive and encouraging to your coachee.

95 Schedule another coaching session, to review the action steps taken.

USING THE THREE-STAGE COACHING PLAN

QUESTION		EFFECT
What's the most useful issue for us to focus on?	Coach and coachee decide on the key issue that is affecting the coachee's performance	Pinpoints issue that is affecting coachee's results
What do you want to achieve here and is it possible?	They set an achievable goal for the session and define how they will know it is achieved	Coachee thinks about the best way to reach the goal
Do you know what action you can take?	They discuss what needs to be done for the coachee to be able to achieve his or her goal	Coachee decides on an action and imagines doing it

347

MODELLING HIGH-FLYERS

*S*peed up your own development by
identifying the key skills you need and
by learning them from the people who have
them by replicating, or modelling, their habits.
Realize that your organization will benefit
from the sharing of the most valuable skills.

96 Understand that
performance is
a combination
of competencies.

97 Model the skills of
top performers, to
improve yourself.

98 See that emulating
others is how you
learnt as a child.

MODELLING THE BEST

High-flyers do not reinvent wheels unnecessarily.
Understand that performance is a combination
of competencies that you can develop. Use NLP
to deconstruct skills, such as decision making or
delegation, into their component learnable skills.
First, find a "model" who is particularly good at
the competency you want. This may be someone
you already know. If necessary, ask several people's
opinions before deciding who to choose as a model.
Realize you can learn anything from anyone if you
want to, believe you can, and know how to.

LEARNING HOW

Explain to your model that you
have noticed how good he or
she is at a skill and ask for a
little of their time. Aim to find
out what your model is doing
differently to you, so you can
change what you currently do
to improve your results. Look at
differences in his or her beliefs,
emotional states, and strategies
for thinking about and achieving
the results he or she gets. Note
down the differences between
your model and yourself.

*Employee asks
questions
about the
relevant skill*

*Model recalls
an example of
when he used
the skill well*

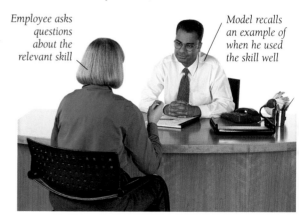

▲ HAVING A MODELLING INTERVIEW
*An employee asks a model to recall a time when he used a skill
well. She asks him why the skill is useful, what his state of mind
was while he was doing it, and what his steps of thinking were.*

DUPLICATING RESULTS

Once you know what a top performer does differently from you, begin to replicate their skills. Identify which factors make the most difference – imagine doing each one in turn and notice how much impact it has on your performance level. Imagine putting these main sub-skills together. If they work when you mentally rehearse, then begin to practise them for real. If they do not work, ask your model about any factors that are not yet clear. Then apply the new version repeatedly in real life.

POINTS TO REMEMBER

● Take every opportunity to learn from people you work with.

● Be willing to give time to others who want you to be a role model.

● Constantly look at new ways of improving your performance and your results.

● When you accept that you do not know something, you are ready to learn.

APPROACHING A MODEL

How you approach your model will affect the response you get. Choose an approach that works best for you. For example:

● "I've noticed that you're very good at presentations. Could I have a few minutes of your time to ask some questions?"

● "I liked the way you handled that client. Would you mind if I talked to you about that?"

● "I've got a problem with a client. Someone told me you would be a good person to talk to. Would that be okay?"

99 Remember that continuous learning is essential if you are to stay ahead.

IMPROVING ORGANIZATIONAL PERFORMANCE WITH MODELLING

Identify the key skills that affect results
→ For example, to manage projects on time and budget

Identify top performers with these skills
→ Look for evidence of your best project manager

Model what they do differently from others
→ Interview them to tease out the differences

Begin to coach average performers in the skills
→ Let others know what seems to work best

Review your current training programme
→ Make sure these skills are included in training

Improve your standard recruitment process
→ Update job and person specifications

DEVELOPING LEADERSHIP QUALITIES

Increasingly, NLP skills are being used to develop leadership qualities for personal and organizational success. Recognize that natural leaders have the ability to inspire and bring out the best in others, and that you too can learn to develop these qualities.

100 Find role models so you continue to improve your abilities as a leader.

101 Concentrate on developing your leadership skills so you can perform as a leading-edge manager.

MANAGING TO LEAD

We live in a world of shrinking workforces and rapid change. As a result, the managerial role is changing. There is less focus on giving orders, and more focus on leadership and coaching to bring out the best in employees. Recognize that, through skilful leadership, ordinary people can produce extraordinary results. NLP skills give you the means to become a more effective leader. Think of yourself as a leader and imagine how you would behave differently as you become a more effective leader.

LEADING YOURSELF

Start to learn the skills of leading yourself by setting yourself compelling goals and being responsible for achieving them. Welcome circumstances that stretch your skills, seek out better ways of doing things, and constantly strive to recognize and work on your weaknesses. Do this by having mentors and by using coaching sessions to develop your skills. Aim to find ways of enjoying every work project that you have. Learn to love your work, especially if you believe this is impossible.

▲ CELEBRATING SUCCESSES
Enjoy your colleagues' company and build up a good rapport. Reward yourself and your team for triumphs, to help encourage successes in the future.

LEADING OTHERS

Once you have developed leadership qualities in yourself, you will be able to lead others effectively. Remember, there is nothing that a small group of committed individuals cannot achieve. Learn to inspire and develop vision in others by appealing to their values and interests. Compulsively seek improvements and implement new initiatives and procedures. Empower others to act by giving them the resources and responsibility to deliver results. Achieve credibility by setting a good example, and lastly, reward achievements and give encouragement.

Empowers others

Seeks improvements

Encourages others

Inspires others

Sets a good example

▲ LEADERSHIP QUALITIES

To be a leader, you must earn the respect of others. Recognize the five qualities that all great leaders embody, and work on developing these in yourself.

SOLVING PROBLEMS WITH EFFECTIVE LEADERSHIP

PROBLEM	SOLUTION	MANAGER'S INTERVENTION
An employee feels a lack of motivation.	Focus on vision and motivation.	Find out more about what matters most to them. Clarify positive values and find creative "win-win" ways to satisfy these.
An employee feels a problem is inevitable.	Focus on seeking improvements.	Implement new approaches to get everybody thinking about and suggesting improvements. Act on the best suggestion.
Your team talk about what they cannot do.	Focus on empowering staff.	Find out what skills and resources they would need in order to carry out what they would like to do and explore ways of making it possible.
Staff do not believe you do as you say.	Focus on teaching by example.	Only say what you mean and always follow through on it. Whatever you ask of others, make sure you are willing to do yourself.
Staff feel their work is not valued.	Focus on giving encouragement.	Aim to frequently catch people doing the right things. Develop a wide range of ways to acknowledge and appreciate their work.

EVALUATING YOUR PERFORMANCE SKILLS

*E*valuate your ability to maximize performance with NLP by responding to the following statements, and mark the option that is closest to your experience. Be as honest as you can: if your answer is "never", circle Option 1; if it is "always", circle Option 4, and so on. Add your scores together, and refer to the Analysis to see how you scored. Use your answers to identify areas that need improving.

OPTIONS
1 Never
2 Occasionally
3 Frequently
4 Always

1 I focus on being aware of my feelings, so that I can act on them.

1 2 3 4

2 I aim to choose, adopt, and maintain positive emotional states.

1 2 3 4

3 I influence other people's emotional states to improve their performance.

1 2 3 4

4 I think about how to influence other people more effectively.

1 2 3 4

5 I work to resolve potential conflicts with other people.

1 2 3 4

6 I think about how a mentor would approach a challenging situation.

1 2 3 4

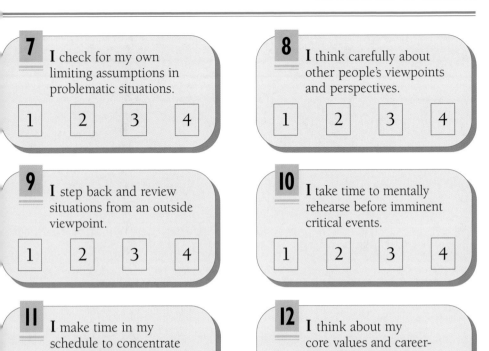

7 I check for my own limiting assumptions in problematic situations.

1 2 3 4

8 I think carefully about other people's viewpoints and perspectives.

1 2 3 4

9 I step back and review situations from an outside viewpoint.

1 2 3 4

10 I take time to mentally rehearse before imminent critical events.

1 2 3 4

11 I make time in my schedule to concentrate on self-development.

1 2 3 4

12 I think about my core values and career-development strategy.

1 2 3 4

ANALYSIS

Now you have completed the self-assessment, add up your total score and check your performance by referring to the corresponding evaluation below. Whatever level of performance you have achieved, there is always room for improvement. Identify your weakest areas and refer to the relevant parts of this section to develop and hone your NLP skills.

12–24: You have considerable potential for improving your performance by using NLP

skills to boost your managerial capabilities.
25–36: You clearly have strengths and will benefit considerably from concentrating on developing your weakest areas.
37–48: You have unusually strong emotional-intelligence capabilities but, to become a real high-flyer, you must keep developing your skills.

DEALING WITH DIFFICULT PEOPLE

INTRODUCTION

The ability to lead difficult individuals out of unproductive situations to improved performance and better working relationships is an essential management skill. Dealing with Difficult People *equips you with proven techniques and strategies to enable you to anticipate problem people, stop trouble from escalating, and help awkward staff to become fully contributing members of the team. Find out how to handle difficult people successfully by developing vital observation and communication skills, avoiding confrontation, working for co-operation, and resolving conflict. A self-assessment questionnaire enables you to measure your skill level and identify areas for improvement, while 101 tips offer practical guidance and advice. This section is an invaluable reference for anyone – from project leader to senior manager – who has responsibility for leading a team of one or more colleagues.*

UNDERSTANDING DIFFICULT PEOPLE

Difficult people stop us from achieving our goals. Understanding why people are difficult helps you to anticipate who will be difficult and take action to prevent problems and reduce conflict.

IDENTIFYING DIFFICULT PEOPLE

People who are difficult absorb your time and energy. The earlier you can identify who will be difficult and when, the better your chances will be of dealing with them successfully. In order to do this, you need to know what makes people difficult.

1 Remember that people of dissimilar ability can find each other difficult.

2 If you see the glass as being half-full, accept that your colleagues may see it differently.

UNDERSTANDING WHY PEOPLE ARE DIFFICULT

We all react differently to pressure, and we all have different expectations in life. Sometimes we may find it hard to deal with someone who has a different set of internal values to our own. By understanding ourselves and other people better, we can learn not to judge others because of our differences, to stop trying to change them, and instead to value what they bring to us.

IDENTIFYING WHO COULD BE DIFFICULT

It is possible to anticipate who is most likely to become difficult at work in two ways: from observing people's behaviour in the workplace and from your own personal knowledge of them. Are your employees clear about what is expected of them? Are they able to keep their work and home lives balanced? When you know your staff well, it is possible to avoid difficulties when pressure points arise because you can prepare in advance to offer appropriate support and development in the workplace.

3 Watch for signals that more job variety is needed.

4 Get to know your staff so that you are aware how best to help them.

5 Build a supportive culture and recognize supportive staff.

▼ RECOGNIZING WHY STAFF BECOME DIFFICULT
Employees can become demotivated and resentful as a result of poor management. An employee who continually works long, unsocial hours or who feels undervalued is likely to feel dissatisfied, which can lead to their becoming difficult.

ANTICIPATING PROBLEMS

By spotting recurrent patterns of stressful situations at work, you can reduce events in the workplace that trigger stress and prepare yourself for dealing with people who might become difficult. If employees are worried about changes to their job or rumours about redundancy, for example, insecurity and fear may push them into doing the very thing that can work against their future. You should look at your own management style as well as how you are organizing work, reviewing objectives, and developing a supportive culture, in order to prevent people becoming difficult through no fault of their own.

Job insecurity

Unclear objectives

Constant pressure

Lack of job variety

Unpredictable hours

Insufficient workload

Heavy workload

KNOWING HOW PEOPLE ARE DIFFERENT

People with different perspectives bring complementary skills to any group working together. Different perspectives can also cause conflict, however, so you need to understand individual differences if you are to deal with difficult people successfully.

6 Identify team members' skills in order to allocate them suitable roles.

7 Pick a team with varied skills to ensure harmony.

8 Know your team members' strengths and weaknesses.

EXPLAINING DIFFERENCES

People have different ways of learning. Those who are action-orientated learn best from being involved, challenged, and doing a job, while those who are more reflective are thoughtful, cautious, and good listeners. People who enjoy developing models of the world like looking at ideas or theories, while practical people enjoy learning by trial and error, suggesting quicker ways of doing things, and receiving feedback on their latest initiative. None of these people intends to be difficult. They just have different ways of looking at things.

VALUING DIFFERENT PERSPECTIVES

In any team, it is useful to have people with preferences for different ways of learning. An action-orientated member will enjoy dealing with short-term crises and performing a variety of tasks, whereas a reflective member will prefer to base decisions on data and help the group to review actions. The member with a theoretical style will draw up guidelines for action, while the person who prefers experimentation will be impatient to put ideas into practice.

Initiator kick-starts and drives the project forward

Ideas person provides input at the concept stage

IDENTIFYING LEARNING TYPES AND THEIR JOB SKILLS

LEARNING TYPES	JOB SKILLS
ACTION-ORIENTATED This type of individual likes to be fully involved, and is a visible team member who learns through experience.	● Dealing with a variety of work. ● Undertaking tasks with a short-term payoff. ● Challenging projects.
REFLECTIVE This type likes to be able to think about experiences and learns by observing, analyzing, and reflecting on what has happened.	● Research, preparation, and reading. ● Producing reports. ● Reviewing opportunities.
THEORETICAL This team member gathers and reviews ideas, concepts, and principles, and learns by integrating these into a framework for action.	● Setting objectives and developing systems. ● Teaching others. ● Analyzing best practice.
PRACTICAL This type of individual likes to test out principles in practice and learns by trial and error.	● Drawing up action plans. ● Suggesting short cuts. ● Coming up with solutions to problems.

▼ **UTILIZING TEAM SKILLS**

Successful teams have members with the different skills needed for projects. As a manager, you should set clear objectives to ensure that everyone's talents are utilized.

Expert helps to plan and provides technical insight

Networker explores opportunities and gathers resources

BEHAVING LIKE ADULTS

People are thought to approach the world from the perspective of the parent (who assumes that blame lies with the other person), the adult (who assesses situations logically), or the child (who feels he is to blame when a problem arises). Most people switch constantly between these viewpoints. Problems arise when someone communicating from one of these perspectives receives a response from someone with a different one. The miscommunication can lead to angry, upset, or withdrawn behaviour.

 9 Work to change people who always respond negatively.

THINKING ABOUT PEOPLE'S MOTIVATION

Managers need to understand what motivates difficult team members and their own role in motivating or demotivating them. Use this understanding to meet team members' needs and reach your personal goals by achieving the goals of the team.

> **10** Identify approaches that motivate the team and use them more often.

> **11** Motivate a difficult person by understanding what they need.

BEING AWARE OF NEEDS ▼
It is important to match your actions to the needs of each team member, so get to know what motivates each person.

IDENTIFYING INDIVIDUAL MOTIVATION

Team members work most effectively when they feel motivated, and become difficult when they are not. Be aware of the different ways in which people in your team are motivated, and recognize that not everyone will respond to the same reward. You need to identify which of your actions motivate the different individuals in your team, and which are demotivating, in order to enhance your team's effectiveness.

Team member is motivated by being given more responsibility

POSITIVE MOTIVATION

Team member dislikes flying and is demotivated by travel invitation

NEGATIVE MOTIVATION

MOTIVATING YOUR TEAM

Give clear direction on team aims and agree objectives with team members. Most people need a sense of achievement, and do not enjoy failing to meet objectives, so identify individual needs for training to reach the required standards. Many people welcome more responsibility when it gives them more control over their work and how it is done. Managers who support and encourage people to work together, and show appreciation for work well done, create team spirit and team members who motivate each other.

THINGS TO DO

1. Greet everyone you work with each day.
2. Go on walkabouts, ask questions, and listen.
3. Remember to praise people if you want them to repeat something.
4. Be inclusive and ask for input to decisions that affect the team.
5. Be consistent.
6. Share information and learning.
7. Coach people to develop their performance and learn new skills.

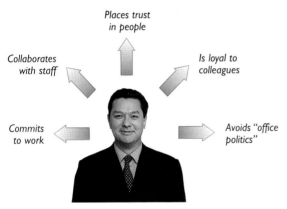

Places trust in people

Collaborates with staff

Is loyal to colleagues

Commits to work

Avoids "office politics"

A MOTIVATIONAL MANAGER

◀ **ASSESSING QUALITIES**
There are several important qualities that a manager needs to possess in order to motivate staff effectively. If any one of these qualities is absent, staff will quickly lose their motivation.

12 Make people feel that they are part of a winning team.

13 Celebrate good news and team achievements.

AVOIDING DEMOTIVATION

People do not like working inefficiently, having no control over the pace of their work, or being continually under pressure. A manager needs to be aware of the team's workload and what support individuals need in order to do their job well. If objectives are unclear and people are uncertain about what is expected from them, they can appear difficult when they do not take action or do the wrong thing. Managers should communicate and let people participate in making decisions about their roles and the way they carry out their jobs.

UNDERSTANDING THE DYNAMICS

*E*ffective communication moves *relationships forward and helps people to work together successfully. By identifying the barriers to good communication, managers can maximize the potential of their team and mobilize difficult people.*

14 Know that how you communicate is as vital as what you communicate.

SHARING INFORMATION

Check that the information is accurate

⬇

Decide who should receive the information

⬇

Choose the best method of communication

⬇

Decide who should communicate the information

⬇

Check that the information has been received and understood

⬇

Follow up to see whether action has been taken

ENERGIZING COMMUNICATION

Managers need to encourage a positive approach to communication between team members so that they support each other and become more effective as a team. Behaviour that supports good communication includes offering help, showing an interest in individuals, and acknowledging the contribution each team member makes to the team. Be honest with each other, take the time to explain why things need to happen, and share information. Being clear with the messages you send, and choosing the best way to provide information, will help the recipient to understand your meaning. Developing a positive atmosphere encourages open discussion, creates energy, avoids misunderstanding, saves time, and builds working relationships that are supportive and rewarding.

15 Be aware that when messages travel through a long chain of people, they can become distorted.

COMPARING COMMUNICATION ENERGIZERS AND BARRIERS

ENERGIZERS

- Being clear about why you are communicating.
- Thinking how your message will be received.
- Promoting open discussion.
- Encouraging people to listen to one another.
- Questioning to understand the other person's view.
- Showing an interest in what others have to say.
- Acknowledging others' input.
- Summarizing to clarify understanding.
- Building relationships by keeping channels open.
- Providing a supportive, encouraging environment.

BARRIERS

- Being unclear about purpose of communication.
- Presenting communication poorly.
- Choosing the wrong method (for example, writing a message when it should have been delivered face to face).
- Having a hidden agenda when communicating.
- Allowing strong emotions to block the message you are sending, or receiving.
- Deliberately misinforming or sabotaging information.
- Failing to provide clear channels for communication.
- Operating in a poor environment, (noise, dim lighting, etc.).

DEVELOPING EFFECTIVE COMMUNICATION

It is important to look at the channels of communication within and outside the team. Messages should be delivered directly, rather than passed down a long chain, and all team members should be told what they need to know. Any team member who feels excluded from vital knowledge may become difficult and obstruct the team's progress. Really difficult people may even sabotage a team by giving wrong information or delaying action. If a manager allows any strong negative feelings between team members to grow, a spiral of negative behaviour can quickly demoralize the team. As a result, some people may become manipulative, others may withdraw, they will not listen to each other, and the team will become demotivated and ineffective.

QUESTIONS TO ASK YOURSELF

Q Is information being shared in the most effective way?

Q Are the team clear about their goals?

Q Do I welcome ideas and take the time to listen?

Q Do I involve people in making decisions?

16 Always be positive and constructive when you are communicating.

OBSERVING DIFFICULT PEOPLE

Observing when people are about to become difficult, and having some insight into what their reasons might be, enables you to pre-empt them. Take the opportunity to turn potential conflict into an exchange of understanding and co-operation.

17 Learn to identify signs that people are about to become difficult.

18 Show people that you value their contributions.

RECOGNIZING SIGNS OF STRESS ▼

Keep a watchful eye for signs of stress in the people you work with. Some of the more common symptoms include a quick temper, a decline in personal appearance, lack of concentration, and fatigue.

WATCHING BEHAVIOUR

If someone suddenly becomes more difficult, irritable, or angry than usual, this could be a sign of emotional stress. If an individual seems depressed, frequently tearful, or just unhappy, you can gently give feedback on how he or she appears to you and ask how things are going. If the problem is personal, then you can suggest different sources of external advice. Individuals become difficult when they have lost the ability to feel or care through too much stress. Physical symptoms such as an upset stomach and indigestion, neck or chest pain, and visual disturbances can be signs of stress; some people may become difficult rather than admit to feeling unwell or under stress.

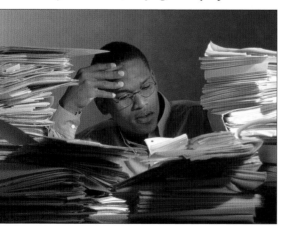

19 Define roles to reduce competing or defending within the team.

OBSERVING FELLOW WORKERS

MANAGER
As a manager, you should observe whether team members are protecting responsibilities they have acquired rather than completing tasks. Build trust between team members by defining goals and sharing views openly.

SUPERIOR
Hovering, asking questions, or going to others for information are signs that a boss is not being kept informed. You need to give more feedback on progress.

PEER
If someone is tense or concerned, ask if anything is wrong when you are alone together. Be supportive in meetings and encourage the colleague's contribution.

OTHER TEAMS
If colleagues are adopting a them-and-us attitude, improve communication by ensuring that both groups review areas where their responsibilities overlap.

OBSERVING CUSTOMERS

If you take your customers for granted, then even your long-standing clients may leave to go to a competitor. Find out how much involvement and feedback your customers need. Most customers do not enjoy complaining, but if you do not give them what they expect they will take their business away. Customers who do stay might become demanding due to a build-up of disappointment. Check that everyone in the team understands your organization's customer service standards and give recognition to those who deliver customer service well.

> **20** Encourage team members to focus on customer needs.

Team member listens attentively, noting concerns raised

Customer makes a complaint

SEEKING FEEDBACK ▶
Ensure that staff use meetings with customers to observe and listen to their views on the service being provided. If they seem demanding, find out why, and take action to deal with their concerns.

MANAGING DIFFERENT TYPES OF DIFFICULT PEOPLE

TYPE OF PERSON	HOW TO MANAGE THEM

SLUMPER
Has no enthusiasm, sighs, shrugs, but will never say that anything is wrong.

- Encourage this type to reflect on their achievements as they progress towards goals.
- Give praise when due, and check that positive feedback outweighs the negative.

DUMPER
Offloads tasks, especially the worst ones, and dumps them on others.

- Set clear objectives, project milestones, and deadlines.
- Draw up an action plan and ensure that their initials are shown against most of the actions.

JUMPER
Has no scruples; takes credit for others' work to move up the career ladder.

- Make sure that people who are responsible for projects deliver feedback themselves.
- Define responsibilities clearly and give credit to everyone involved in projects.

GRUMPER
Complains constantly about every small thing and is impossible to please.

- Hold a one-on-one meeting and ask questions to pinpoint specific problems.
- Ask them to prioritize their workload and set deadlines for achieving objectives.

BUMPER
Takes the kudos when all goes well but blames mistakes on others.

- State responsibilities clearly.
- Set stretching targets.
- Meet regularly to review progress against measurable objectives and give feedback.

TRUMPER
Always has to have the first and last word and be one step ahead of everyone else.

- Confirm in writing whatever has been agreed.
- Have an agenda for meetings, anticipate the objections a "trumper" will raise, and prepare questions and goals to challenge him or her.

THUMPER
Bullies and intimidates others and gets his own way by being aggressive.

- Stand your ground by being assertive.
- State your case calmly and ask questions to encourage the person to consider the consequences of their actions.

WORKING WITH PROFESSIONAL ADVISERS

Your professional advisers can add value by giving an objective perspective on you and your team. Observe how sensitive they are to any defensiveness in you or your team members when they are asking questions at the beginning of the project. They may be asking some questions to test how realistic you are being in your expectations. This gives you an opportunity to clarify your objectives and ask yourself what you need from the advisers. Notice how well they observe and how quickly they pick up issues as well as facts.

21 Brief advisers on the potential impact of their work on your business.

22 Be prepared to be questioned by a good adviser.

23 Be open with your suppliers and inform them of your future plans.

MONITORING SUPPLIERS

If you observe that your suppliers are becoming difficult, could it be due to something you have inadvertently done or omitted to do? Issues often arise over payment, and it is very important to have agreed, at the beginning of the working relationship, the levels of service you expect and the terms within which you will pay. Your suppliers need feedback if their service level drops in order to give them the opportunity to improve. Developing good working relationships with suppliers means they will be more likely to help you out when things become difficult.

OBSERVING YOURSELF

As a member of a team, you have to keep a balance between the tension of wanting to excel as an individual with the need to be a fully contributing team player. Observe yourself to make sure you are balancing your development as an individual with your work in the team. Continue to deliver the work you have taken on and make sure you share knowledge with the rest of the team members so that you are, collectively, more effective.

QUESTIONS TO ASK YOURSELF

Q How do other team members regard me as a colleague?

Q How often do I ask for feedback from my team?

Q What skills and strengths should I build and what are my main areas for development?

ASSESSING YOUR OPTIONS

Dealing with a difficult person successfully requires objective analysis and assessment. Consider all your options before choosing the best way to achieve co-operation and change.

PLANNING TO OVERCOME PROBLEMS

You need to understand a problem before you can decide what to do about it. Knowing how to generate and choose the best option and test possible solutions will help you to plan the way forward in order to be one step ahead of a difficult person.

24 Gather as much information as possible to analyze the real problem.

QUESTIONS TO ASK YOURSELF

Q Why is this person being difficult?

Q Is this a situation that has happened before and if so, what caused it?

Q What can I do to resolve this situation and prevent it from happening again?

DEFINING WHY THE PROBLEM IS HAPPENING

Before you can find a solution to prevent someone being difficult, you need to define why the problem is happening. Look at the situation and notice small signs of difficult behaviour. Think about questions to ask. Identify people who have been involved with this person in similar projects before. They could help you review what happened previously and assess how the situation might develop.

GENERATING OPTIONS

There is usually more than one solution to a problem and you need to choose the best option. Approach the problem with an open mind, then look at it from as many different perspectives as possible, including that of the difficult person. You must be prepared to take risks to solve problems, so suspend your judgment for a while and see what happens. Each possible solution could be captured on a memo note, or you could use images and colours in order to create a picture on a flipchart. Use your imagination to stimulate new and different ideas for overcoming the problem.

POINTS TO REMEMBER

- A problem must be defined correctly before solutions can be developed.

- Information gathered when exploring and analyzing a problem will be invaluable later when looking at possible solutions.

- Some of the best ideas come from involving others in the creative process.

- All possible solutions should be listed before evaluation starts.

TESTING SOLUTIONS

Define the main objectives a solution should achieve

↓

Score solution on how well it will achieve objectives

↓

If solution scores well, identify the risks involved

↓

Generate ideas to minimize or prevent effect of risks

↓

With contingency plans in place, assess if risks are worthwhile

CHOOSING BETWEEN POSSIBLE SOLUTIONS

The best way to make a decision and choose between several options is to think about the criteria against which the final solution will be measured. What objectives should the solution to the problem achieve and which are most important? Prioritize objectives in order of importance. Score the solutions against each objective to see which gets the highest score out of ten. High marks against the most important objectives identify your best solution. Having thoroughly analyzed the situation, and come up with the solution to achieve important objectives, gives you confidence to tackle a problem with even the most difficult person.

◀ FINDING THE RIGHT SOLUTION
Narrow your list of options by giving each solution marks out of ten for how well it achieves objectives. The highest score will suggest the best solution.

AVOIDING CONFRONTATION

When timing is not right, or the costs of confrontation are too high, avoiding confrontation with a difficult person may be an appropriate option. Understanding how to avoid confrontation enables you to choose the best response at any given moment.

25 Recognize that difficult behaviour can become a habit if not tackled early.

26 Be aware of your own emotional response.

27 Give yourself time to look objectively at a situation.

WALKING AWAY

If the difficult person is shouting at you, then there is little point in continuing to try to talk. If the person is too upset or angry to listen, then sometimes it may be wiser to walk away. This gives an opportunity for angry feelings to subside and for you to think through how best to tackle the problem objectively. If you suspect that you are postponing tackling the problem, however, then either determine to deal with it immediately or make an appointment to meet with the other person at the earliest date possible.

WORKING ROUND A DIFFICULT PERSON

If everyone else in the team is co-operative and works well together, it is tempting to work round the difficult person. This could, however, be the wrong thing to do because, by working round that person, you are, in effect, rewarding his or her difficult behaviour. If you need to get something done in a hurry, then once or twice it might be expedient to ask someone else to do the work, but if it happens again it means a precedent has been set. The difficult person may then be regarded as not being part of the team, and so not sharing the same responsibilities, which has a poor effect on the rest of the team.

CULTURAL DIFFERENCES

Britons, Americans, and Europeans may find it difficult to discern whether someone from a more reticent culture has been offended or is not going to co-operate. In Japan, for example, it is important to check whether someone is happy with a course of action or is just being polite, because their body language is different and less easy to read.

LOOKING THE OTHER WAY

Pretending not to notice the bad behaviour of a difficult person may work if that person wishes to remain part of the team. Withdrawing your eye contact can indicate your disapproval of what is going on. Sometimes this is enough to signal that the behaviour is unacceptable and needs to change. If, however, the bad behaviour continues, then ignoring it allows the individual to behave in an uncontrolled manner and this will distance him or her from the team. In some cases, looking the other way will cause that person to become more difficult as a way of regaining your attention. Avoidance tactics may work once or twice in the short term but are not a successful long-term strategy.

▼ USING AVOIDANCE TACTICS

Working closely with co-operative team members and ignoring a difficult colleague can move a situation forwards. Either the difficult team member will join in, or he will move away totally, in which case confrontation at a later date becomes inevitable.

- Any kind of confrontation in an open meeting should be avoided whenever possible. Discussion can be encouraged afterwards.

- In order to avoid antagonizing a difficult person, an open body posture should be maintained.

- Looking down at your notes can help you avoid a hostile gaze.

- Turning your attention to someone else can discourage an individual intent on talking at you.

28 Bear in mind that avoidance tactics are a short-term solution.

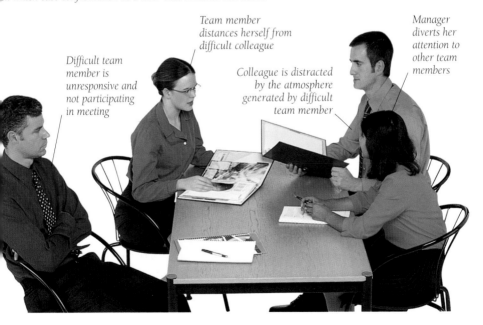

Difficult team member is unresponsive and not participating in meeting

Team member distances herself from difficult colleague

Colleague is distracted by the atmosphere generated by difficult team member

Manager diverts her attention to other team members

BEING ASSERTIVE

In order to remain calm, even when the difficult person confronting you may be angry and aggressive, you need to be assertive. Encouraging others to be aware of whether or not they are being assertive can help a difficult person move towards agreement.

29 Identify whether a difficult person is being aggressive, passive, or assertive.

30 Respect the rights of others and compromise when appropriate.

31 Listen to others if you want to be listened to yourself.

FACING AGGRESSION OR PASSIVITY

Aggression means being immovable on facts and being hard on people. A difficult person may react to criticism by being aggressive and obstructive, which can have a destructive effect on a team. Passivity means being soft on facts and being soft on people. A difficult passive person will not take action to resolve a situation and will make no effort to confront people. Although less likely to have acted hastily or upset others, a passive individual is more likely to have omitted to take action. This is often harder to find out about than an obvious mistake but can have a similar impact.

ENCOURAGING ASSERTIVENESS

When facing either aggression or passivity, you need to encourage the difficult person to be assertive while remaining assertive yourself. Assertiveness means being firm on facts and flexible with people. It is saying directly to others what you want, need, or feel. It is being honest with yourself and with others and recognizing that other people, including the difficult person, have the right to be heard and to have an opinion. Setting this example for your team will enable you to achieve better performance from difficult people.

POINTS TO REMEMBER

- The best way for your team to understand what assertive behaviour looks like is to observe you at work.
- Self-awareness and honest feedback should be encouraged so that team members are able to see assertiveness being demonstrated by others.
- Just as you have the right to be heard, it is important that the same respect should be shown to others.

USING DIFFERENT TYPES OF ASSERTIVE STATEMENTS

TYPE OF STATEMENT	EXAMPLES
FACTUAL A straightforward statement that gives facts, feedback, or information and makes clear your wishes, needs, wants, beliefs, opinions, or feelings.	● "As I see it, the system is working well." ● "I'd like you to be here by nine o'clock." ● "I feel very pleased with the way the situation has been resolved." ● "I liked the diagrams you included in your report."
EMPATHETIC A statement showing sensitivity that can be used to pre-empt an aggressive person, followed by an expression of your needs and wants.	● "I can see that the new procedure means extra work until you are used to it. However, I'd still like you to keep on working with it to give it a fair trial, please." ● "Although I know you're very busy at the moment, I need to ask you something, please."
DIVERGENT A statement that can establish whether there has been a misunderstanding between what was previously agreed, and what is actually happening.	● "As I recall, we agreed that Project X was top priority. You seem to be giving more time to Project Y. Can we please clarify which has top priority?" ● "We said we would hold meetings weekly. They seem to be fortnightly or monthly. We need to establish them regularly – every fortnight or every week as agreed."
EXPRESSIVE A statement expressing your negative feelings, letting other people know the adverse effect their behaviour is having on you, without becoming over-emotional.	● "When you're late back from lunch and the phones are busy, I feel annoyed you're not here to help. I'd like you to come back on time and take your turn on the phones." ● "I feel aggrieved when you ask my staff for answers. I'd like you to check with me first and if I can't provide answers, I'll direct you to the right person."
CONSEQUENT A statement that can be used as a warning when other people have failed to act, letting them know the consequences for them if they do not change their behaviour.	● "I'm not going to let any of my staff work on this project with your people, unless you give them access to the same training that your team was given." ● "This client's order is worth thousands. If we fail to respond to queries quickly enough and lose the account, it will have an adverse impact on the department."
RESPONSIVE A statement or question to find out the other person's views, needs, wants, or feelings, and to make sure that there is no misunderstanding between you.	● "What problems might that create?" ● "What would you prefer to do?" ● "I'd like to hear your views on this." ● "Which approach do you think is best?" ● "What are the plus and minus points from your point of view?"

CONFRONTING DIFFICULT PEOPLE

Confronting difficult staff becomes necessary if avoidance has not worked. It then becomes an opportunity for change, but you need to think beforehand about how you are going to deal with the situation successfully and move people forward.

32 Check that difficult people understand the full impact of their behaviour.

33 Avoid prolonged eye contact in a confrontational situation.

CONFRONTING DIFFICULT PEOPLE

It is essential to remain calm, listen carefully, and be assertive. Empathize with the difficult person. Perhaps their anger is with themselves and not with you. Think about the words you are going to use. Aim for an 80/20 ratio, with you talking only 20 per cent of the time. Outline the situation as you see it and ask them if they can see the problem. If they cannot, then you will not be able to move on until you get them to see that there is a problem. Once you can agree on that, you can move on to agree actions to rectify or change the situation.

USING BODY LANGUAGE ▼

Body language is important when confronting difficult people. An open posture looks relaxed and friendly, whereas a closed posture can look unwelcoming.

Open arms, chin up, and desk at an angle to avoid creating a barrier

POSITIVE BODY LANGUAGE

Arm folded across chest, chin down, seeming unwilling to be interrupted

Cluttered desk gives the impression that the manager is too busy to talk

NEGATIVE BODY LANGUAGE

KEEPING SAFE

Confrontation may provoke emotional language or even physical aggression in a difficult person. It may also provoke an aggressive or uncharacteristic reaction in you. Think about how you are likely to react if the pressure builds, and plan what you are going to do. Be aware of your organization's disciplinary policy and recognize your role as its representative. Remain impartial and listen. Sometimes listening is all that is needed to help the person calm down and start thinking clearly. If you need to understand more, ask questions in a non-threatening tone. Make sure your body language and voice do not provoke further aggression.

MOVING PEOPLE FORWARD

When confronting difficult people, you are giving them feedback they may not want to hear. If they do not want to change, then they will bring up problems and barriers as excuses to prevent change. Listen to the problems and then plan how these can be overcome in future. Keep questioning until you have a clear agreed action plan. Then focus your questions on achieving the actions you have agreed between you so that you can move them forward.

DEALING WITH CONFRONTATION

Outline the situation as you see it

Listen carefully to other person's view of situation

Gain agreement that a problem exists

Use questioning to identify ways of rectifying the problem

Agree an action plan

Focus other person on achieving actions

◀ FOCUSING ON THE FUTURE

By asking questions, John moved Susan forward from dwelling in the past to focusing on future opportunities. By agreeing actions that would make a difference, John succeeded in helping Susan to feel motivated and in control.

CASE STUDY

John, an engineer, had observed how Susan, his secretary, had recently become more difficult to motivate. At their next meeting, John asked whether there was a problem. Susan kept bringing up issues such as delays in IT training and upgrading her computer plus missed weekly meetings, all issues that had been resolved months ago. John felt aggrieved that Susan could not see how things had improved. He resolved to remain assertive and calmly to ask open questions to understand the problems from Susan's perspective. He asked Susan what was happening now and what she would like to see in future. They agreed an action plan to solve problems on ordering procedures and Susan took responsibility for the process. John followed up a week later and Susan confirmed that the new procedure was working well.

HELPING DIFFICULT PEOPLE THROUGH CHANGE

Helping people to accept that change provides opportunities is the starting point for reducing resistance to change. By anticipating it and planning ahead, you can manage it – rather than just reacting to the change and the responses of difficult people.

34 Make sure that you take the time to plan ahead for change.

35 Identify factors that help to drive change forwards.

36 Identify factors that restrain the pace of change.

IDENTIFYING REASONS FOR RESISTANCE

The most common reason for resistance to change is concern for self above other people. When you introduce change, consider the "What's In It For You?" (WIIFY) question to enable you to present the benefits of change that will overcome this attitude. Complete a forcefield analysis to see what will help and what will hinder change. Think what the difficult person's fears might be. If they have a low tolerance to change, emphasize what will remain unchanged while change is happening in other areas. They may misunderstand the purpose of change. The key to managing resistance is to communicate the benefits of the changes to come.

◀ **COMPLETING A FORCEFIELD ANALYSIS**
Create a table listing factors for change (driving forces) and those against it (restraining forces). Rate driving forces on a scale of plus 0–20, and restraining forces minus 0–20. Then add both scores to assess how likely a person is to accept the change. In this example, the change is the relocation of a key team member. Driving forces outnumber restraining forces, so the change should be accepted.

Restraining forces	Driving forces
Happy as is	
	Bus door to door
Walk to work	
	Great relocation package
Children changing school	
	Can buy bigger house
Local friends	

-20 -15 -10 -5 0 +5 +10 +15 +20
Restraining forces = -42 Driving forces = +45

WINNING SUPPORT FOR CHANGE

Enlisting the help of influential advocates of change can help you win over those who are opposed to it. In order to do this, you need to:

● List people who might be involved in, or affected by, change (known as stakeholders).
● Prioritize stakeholders according to how great an influence they have on others.
● Identify which stakeholders will support

the change and which are likely to oppose it.
● Consider the likely objections of influential opposers, identify the benefits of change from their perspective, and start lobbying them.
● Involve influential supporters early so that they use their influence with others. Explain the advantages of the change clearly, and keep them abreast of progress so that they know what needs to be communicated.

MANAGING RESISTANCE

When planning change, consider how to clearly communicate your vision for the future. When people can visualize what change will look like when it is complete, they will be inspired to commit to it. Clear signs of improvement along the way to show that change is happening successfully need to be communicated. Conduct a stakeholder analysis to identify who will be your advocates for change. They will help you gain sufficient support to outweigh your critics. Understand that people's reactions to change tend to follow a recognized pattern and give them the time they need to move through the stages towards acceptance.

QUESTIONS TO ASK YOURSELF

Q Who is directly affected by this situation?

Q Who is in a position to influence others?

Q Who is likely to react badly or be displeased?

Q Have I prepared difficult people for change by involving them in planning for future scenarios?

REACTING ▶ TO CHANGE

In response to change, people tend to go through a series of emotional reactions. Shock and denial typically give way to a pining for the past and anger, which in turn leads to depression, and finally to acceptance. The duration of this process depends on the particular situation.

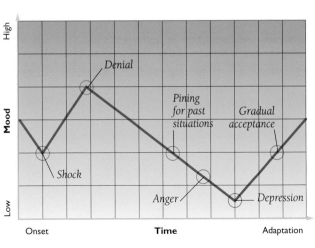

379

KNOWING WHEN TO STOP

If you cannot change a difficult person, you may have to change your attitude. It is sometimes better for the organization if you learn to live with, rather than continue to try to change, the individual. Alternatively, he or she may need to accept that it is time to leave.

37 Review a difficult person's overall performance to avoid hasty action.

38 Recognize when performance is standing still.

39 You may achieve results faster by changing your own behaviour.

ACCEPTING THE DIFFICULT PERSON

If the difficult person adds sufficient value to the organization, it may be that you will have to change your approach. Make an assessment to see if the person's strengths outweigh the weaknesses. Think about building on the strengths and putting in training or support to strengthen the weak areas. Ask yourself if you have looked objectively at that person's overall performance and taken full account of any achievements and contributions. Is it because he or she takes a different approach to your own and you find it difficult to handle? Accept that it can be extremely useful when problem-solving to have someone with a different perspective in the team.

◀ **CHANGING YOUR ATTITUDE**
Roy saw management meetings as a contest in which he was losing every round. This was affecting his self-confidence and his credibility with management colleagues. Using visualization, Roy changed his attitude to the meetings and his colleague. He was well-prepared each time and meetings became more productive.

CASE STUDY
Roy's colleague, Jane, was difficult and competitive. At management meetings, Jane frequently made suggestions as to how Roy's department could be improved. She would state her view aggressively, and Roy found it difficult to respond, although he could always think of an answer later. When he suggested that they meet regularly to discuss any problems between their two departments, Jane declined, saying she was too busy. Roy decided to change his attitude to Jane. Before meetings, Roy would visualize Jane criticizing his department on aspects he was working on improving. He visualized himself responding constructively to her comments and her more positive response. As a result, issues were resolved far more quickly and effectively during meetings, which was of benefit to the entire management team.

CHANGING YOUR OWN ATTITUDE

Empathizing with a difficult person can change your attitude to him or her. Place two chairs facing each other – one for you and one for the difficult person. Put a third chair at least 5 metres (16 feet) away, at a 90-degree angle to the other chairs. Sit opposite the difficult person's chair and state your point of view. Now sit in the other person's chair and state what you think is his or her point of view. Now stand on the third chair and look down on the two "people" facing each other. What new insights has this exercise given you into the difficult person's perspective? How will you change your approach in the light of this new information?

Manager rehearses own view

Manager imagines the discussion from both sides

5 metres (16 feet)

Manager imagines what difficult person's position will be

◀ **REVIEWING YOUR APPROACH**
Distancing yourself from the situation and looking at it from the other person's perspective can help you modify your approach accordingly. For example, you may realize that you are being overly emphatic, which can lead you to soften your approach.

REFUSING TO ACCEPT THE SITUATION

If a difficult person's behaviour is having a demoralizing effect on the team, you must manage the individual out of the situation. Look at the facts carefully. If this is the first time the person has gone beyond the limits you have set with the team, then ensure that your response is reasonable. If you have not been clear in communicating the limits, then you should now state them clearly to that person and specify how they can put the situation right. If the person cannot change in the time you specify, then you need to move them one step nearer to leaving the organization, according to normal disciplinary procedures.

40 Aim to improve performance – it is more cost-effective than dismissal.

41 Set realistic time scales for staff to demonstrate improvement.

WORKING FOR CO-OPERATION

A manager's primary aim is to gain the co-operation of difficult people. Plan your approach and use good communication skills in order to negotiate the best outcome for all parties.

PREPARING FOR CO-OPERATION

Knowing that you have planned and prepared carefully for a difficult meeting helps you feel more confident about it. Try initially for co-operation rather than conflict with a difficult person by aiming for a solution that benefits you both equally.

42 Note that a positive approach is sometimes all that is needed.

43 Plan to listen to objections before you respond by stressing benefits.

PLANNING FOR CO-OPERATION

A positive approach is often enough to win you co-operation from even the most difficult person. Prepare yourself to overcome objections to your proposals. Brainstorm what the objections might be, then think of the advantages of your proposals, including those that benefit the difficult person. Ask "If we could get round that, is there anything else that could stand in the way of this project?"

OVERCOMING OBJECTIONS

Exhaust all objections, then explain all the benefits

⬇

Ask difficult employee to rephrase any new objections

⬇

Offer further reassurance

⬇

Ask employee if he or she will support your proposals

⬇

If their answer is "No", ask why the suggestion is still not right

⬇

Outline further benefits and agree on future goals

SETTING GOALS FOR CO-OPERATION

Agreeing objectives with team members, customers, and other stakeholders reduces the risk of people becoming difficult because they failed to understand exactly what was asked of them. Goals should state what is expected in ways that mean something to people. Encourage people to write down goals in their own words so that they understand them clearly and will know when they have attained them. Set clear, well-defined objectives to ensure that people will not become difficult at a later stage because the goals set were unrealistic.

DOS AND DON'TS

✔ Do list all the benefits of what you are proposing before you have a discussion with a difficult person.

✔ Do make sure that some benefits answer the question "What's in it for me?" from the difficult person's point of view.

✘ Don't set objectives without agreeing deadlines and how they will be measured.

✘ Don't assume that you are both thinking the same thing – if you have any doubts, seek clarification by asking questions.

SETTING SMART OBJECTIVES

To help you set effective objectives, follow the SMART rule. This management acronym defines objectives as:

● Specific: they should clearly and unambiguously state requirements;

● Measurable: they must be quantifiable in terms of time, quality, quantity, and cost;

● Achievable: they should be within the

employee's capability, taking into account the resources available and authority levels;

● Relevant: they should be appropriate for the job/project and within the individual's control;

● Timely: they should have a realistic timescale for completion.

PREPARING FOR DIFFICULT SITUATIONS

Sometimes people are difficult when a situation is stressful for them. Learn how to prepare for interviews, inductions, and appraisals so that you can offer encouragement and reassurance to prevent someone from becoming difficult.

44 Ease nerves in difficult situations by asking easier questions at first.

45 Greet a candidate and accompany them to the room.

46 Prepare by reading an interviewee's CV carefully.

INTERVIEWING PEOPLE

Concentrate on putting the candidate at ease, since this will help them perform at their best. If a candidate wants a job very much, he or she may overreact by talking too much, or not enough, or by becoming defensive at perceived "trick" questions. Encourage the person to answer your questions directly. If an interviewee strays off the subject, bring them back to the point or explain why you want a specific piece of information. If the interviewee is reticent, rephrase some of your questions or probe further on the point.

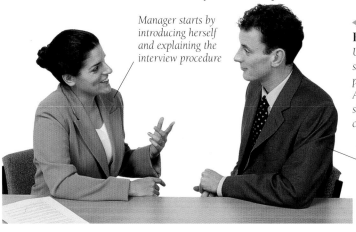

Manager starts by introducing herself and explaining the interview procedure

◀ **BUILDING RAPPORT**
Use open body language and smile encouragingly to help put the interviewee at ease. Avoid sitting on opposite sides of a desk, as this will create a barrier between you.

Interviewee has time to relax and settle into the interview

CONDUCTING APPRAISALS

Give a potentially difficult team member time to prepare for the appraisal. Ensure that they know exactly what to expect, and prepare your questions thoroughly so that the appraisee does most of the talking. Illustrate your praise with examples of real achievements and focus your constructive criticism on areas that need development. Your appraisal should reflect a 2:1 ratio of positive feedback to constructive criticism. Create an action plan together to build on strengths and develop those areas that need improvement.

THINGS TO DO

1. Confirm the date and location of the appraisal at least two weeks in advance.

2. Provide the appraisee with guidance and the means to self-assess.

3. Read through current job description and last year's appraisal and action plan.

4. Note down training undertaken, project results, and any other achievements.

5. Plan the sequence of the appraisal.

6. Prepare questions to ask.

Appraisee notes actions arising from discussion

◀ **APPRAISING EFFECTIVELY**

Use the appraisal to focus staff on the future, identifying development needs and aspirations, giving direction, and agreeing expected contribution.

POINTS TO REMEMBER

● Preparation is the key to dealing with difficult situations effectively.

● Making checklists of the preparation needed for interviews, appraisals, and induction saves you time in the long run.

● Putting yourself in the other person's situation will help you to anticipate difficulties.

● An effective manager follows up on all the actions agreed.

INDUCTING NEW RECRUITS

An induction can be stressful for a new employee who does not understand the culture of a new organization. Yet new recruits can often provide fresh and invaluable perspectives on your way of working. Value a new employee's honest opinion rather than seeing them as difficult and unlikely to "fit in". Their feedback can help you develop your team and make induction more effective. Think who could act as a mentor to the newcomer. If there is someone who also views questioning as a learning process, the benefits will be two-way.

Managing for Co-operation

People may become difficult if they feel that they are being poorly managed or are working without clear direction. Develop your own management skills and learn to adapt your leadership style in order to win co-operation from difficult individuals.

47 Develop an open culture in which staff give each other feedback.

48 Recognize that new staff may need more support.

49 Encourage initiative in experienced team members.

Managing Effectively

Effective management involves carrying out tasks successfully by deploying resources efficiently to achieve the results required. Check that you have defined roles and objectives clearly, planned and organized resources according to your priorities, and agreed the controls you will use. If someone is still being difficult, you may not have involved that person sufficiently at the planning stage. To keep the individual on board with the rest of the team, make sure that you carry out reviews of progress together.

Managing Projects

Ensure that everyone involved understands at the outset the project's objectives and constraints, its key milestones, who is responsible for what, and who will be involved at which stages. By doing this, you avoid the risk of team members becoming difficult later as a result of not being given all the information they need. Reviews, planned in advance and held frequently throughout the project, can then help you to maintain the balance between quality and performance within budget and to the agreed timescale.

Questions to Ask Yourself

Q Do I consistently set fair objectives for team members?

Q Do I monitor each individual's overall performance?

Q Have I anticipated and removed any barriers to achieving objectives?

Q Are there any recurring problems that indicate a need for me to develop my skills?

50 Delegate to show trust in people – this can help to prevent them from becoming difficult.

LEADING PEOPLE

Be prepared to adapt your leadership style with someone you find difficult, because the style you find comfortable will not work in all situations. Avoid telling someone how to do things – instead say what needs to be achieved and why, letting him or her work out how to reach the goal. A leader must also delegate well or risk overload or stress that affects the team, who may react by becoming difficult. Brief delegates on the outcomes and standards required, giving them the authority needed, and agreeing when you will review progress.

PROVIDING FEEDBACK

Feedback helps people to see themselves as others see them. Without feedback, a team member may continue to perform in a way that is no longer effective. However, feedback can be seen as a threat. Someone who expects negative criticism may become withdrawn or defensive. Give feedback regularly until it becomes accepted as the usual routine. Focus your feedback on behaviour or results rather than the person, and on what is important and within his or her control to change.

51 Give constructive feedback in order to encourage staff.

▼ **COMPARING FEEDBACK**
Feedback can have a positive effect or a negative one. Positive feedback is constructive and concentrates on what is important. Negative feedback is judgmental, overcritical, or irrelevant.

POSITIVE FEEDBACK

Is given as soon after the event as possible

Is delivered one to one

Is constructive, factual, and specific

Is balanced and of future benefit to the recipient

NEGATIVE FEEDBACK

Overwhelms the recipient with too much information

Is delivered in front of other people

Is overly judgmental, critical, or tainted with emotion

Dwells too much on the past

HANDLING POOR PERFORMANCE

*E*mployees who are under too much or too little stress may under-perform. Spot the signs early so that you can help a difficult person operate at constructive stress levels. If performance fails to improve, you may have to dismiss the difficult individual.

52 See that people develop through overcoming challenges.

53 Watch for changes in someone's behaviour.

54 Set an objective to stretch a difficult person and observe what happens.

IDENTIFYING STRESS

Everyone needs a certain amount of stress to fuel performance and experience the personal satisfaction that comes with overcoming challenges. If a difficult person seems lethargic, bored, and has no enthusiasm for the job, then he or she is not being challenged enough. Alternatively, if the person appears angry and seems to be sabotaging his or her own performance, then these could be signs of too much stress. Whatever the problem, you need to review the team member's role with them and set clear objectives. Discuss all possible courses of action that can be taken. For example, if the individual is under too much stress, it may be possible to delegate aspects of their role to someone else.

◀ **UNDERSTANDING THE STRESS CURVE**
This diagram shows how performance is affected as stress levels change. A lack of stress at one end of the curve, and a serious overload of stress at the opposite end have the same effect: performance deteriorates drastically.

Best performance

Not enough challenge

Too much pressure

In comfort zone

In panic zone

Performance

Rust out

Burn out

Pressure or stress

EXAMINING POOR PERFORMANCE

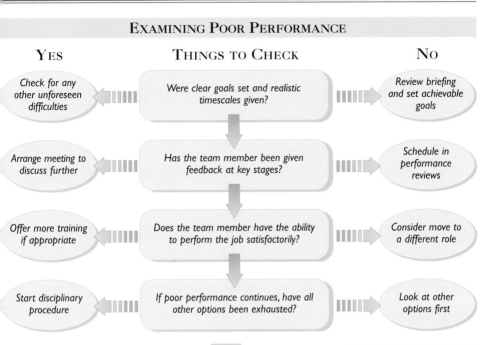

YES	THINGS TO CHECK	NO
Check for any other unforeseen difficulties	Were clear goals set and realistic timescales given?	Review briefing and set achievable goals
Arrange meeting to discuss further	Has the team member been given feedback at key stages?	Schedule in performance reviews
Offer more training if appropriate	Does the team member have the ability to perform the job satisfactorily?	Consider move to a different role
Start disciplinary procedure	If poor performance continues, have all other options been exhausted?	Look at other options first

DEALING WITH POOR ▲ PERFORMANCE

When you are dealing with poor performance, make sure that the person knows exactly what is expected and has every opportunity to rectify the situation.

55 Before dismissing someone, check that you have offered all reasonable support and encouragement.

DISMISSING PEOPLE

If all your attempts to help the difficult person to perform well fail, then he or she will have to leave. If the problem is lack of ability, then try to move the person to a more suitable position within the organization. If the problem is persistent difficult behaviour or poor performance, then you need to follow your organization's disciplinary procedure and give the person notice of dismissal. This is always written, but also needs to be delivered face to face. Prepare what you will say carefully, because the reasons you give for dismissal may be quoted in any unfair dismissal claim.

POINTS TO REMEMBER

● Emotional rejection of the job and the organization should be confronted as soon as it becomes apparent in an individual.

● The organization's role in creating the problem should also be taken into account.

● Make sure that you read up on your organization's disciplinary procedure and guidance notes.

● In some cases a professional career counsellor may be needed.

BEING OBJECTIVE

When dealing with difficult people, it helps to stay objective. Being objective demands a high level of self-awareness. Knowing your own biases and personality helps you understand what stands in the way of your working effectively with other people.

56 Avoid allowing your judgment to be clouded by a single issue.

57 Be aware that everyone listens selectively.

58 Respond to the person in front of you, not someone they remind you of.

RECOGNIZING YOUR OWN BIAS

Your background, your education and training, past experiences at work or school, childhood influences, parents or friends, and groups to which you belong all play a part in shaping your view of the world. Recognizing that we all look at the world through our own filters helps you to empathize with a person who, at first, appears difficult. Unconsciously, you may both be finding that the differences between you are forming a barrier to effective communication and to viewing issues objectively.

MAKING ASSUMPTIONS

By being aware that your viewpoint may be biased, you are less likely to make assumptions about people based on your subjective opinion alone. To avoid making wrong assumptions, keep an open mind and listen to the views of others. Take notes and summarize to ensure that, in any conversation with a difficult person, you both leave with the same understanding. Avoid forming an opinion first and then choosing the facts to support it. Instead, question to clarify and gather facts, then use these facts to make your decision. Base your decisions on behaviour and performance, not on personality or background.

CULTURAL DIFFERENCES

People from different cultures may perceive each other differently. Americans and some Europeans, for example, often greet newcomers as if they were old friends, which can appear insincere or disrespectful to people from more reserved cultures, such as in Asia and the Middle East.

OVERCOMING DIFFERENT TYPES OF BIAS

TYPE OF BIAS	HOW TO OVERCOME IT
HALO/HORNS Allowing one or two favourable or unfavourable qualities to influence your judgment of the whole person.	● Make sure that you have established the facts on the individual's performance. ● Assess how important the problem is in the light of the team member's total performance.
"SIMILAR TO ME" A tendency to favour – even recruit and promote – people you see as being similar to yourself.	● Identify the individual's strengths. ● Look at development areas for the individual. ● Determine what skills or experience are needed for the job or project.
PREJUDICE Letting background or culture cloud your judgment about people or a person who reminds you of someone.	● Ask yourself who the individual reminds you of. ● Identify what it is specifically about their behaviour or performance that is the problem. ● Assess what preconceptions you might have.
DISTORTED CONCEPTS Making assumptions based on misuse of psychology, such as assuming that all salespeople have to be extrovert.	● Identify the requirements of the job. ● Decide how much experience and which qualifications or skills are really needed. ● Ask yourself what your assumptions are based on.
STEREOTYPING Having a mental image of the ideal worker, then assessing people against this rather than on actual strengths.	● Look at what must be achieved in the job or project. ● Check that the objectives you have in mind are realistic. ● Identify the essential/desirable characteristics that will enable an individual to do the job.

EVALUATING INFORMATION

Knowing that you may have your own stereotypes about good workers, and that you can give too much weight to your similarities with people who appear to have much in common with you, helps you to evaluate difficult people more objectively. It is important to assess the difficult person and his or her behaviour overall. Make sure you are not just remembering the most recent example of difficult behaviour and overlooking previous co-operation and achievements. Ask yourself whether you did anything, perhaps unintentionally, that may have led to this change in behaviour.

59 Make sure that you avoid jumping to conclusions too quickly.

60 Ask questions and listen actively to avoid making wrong assumptions.

QUESTIONING AND LISTENING

Asking the right questions, at the right time, will speed communication by getting the response you need quickly and effectively. The key skill is listening to the response and looking for clues as to what your next question should be.

61 Be aware that silence has the same effect as a probing question.

62 Prepare questions in advance and listen for clues as to what your next question should be.

USING OPEN QUESTIONS

The best way to find out why an individual is being difficult is to ask them diplomatically. Use open questions to encourage a difficult person to open up and reveal what is causing the difficulties (work-related or personal). By using open questions you avoid leading someone into stating what you assume is the problem and encourage them into thinking through a reply. The opposite of an open question is a closed one, such as "Did you…?", which elicits only the answer "Yes" or "No".

ASKING OPEN QUESTIONS

There are many ways of phrasing an open question. Try asking questions that start with words such as "What…?", "Who…?", "When…?", and "How…?", which demand a more detailed response. Here are a few examples.

❝ *What do you think is the cause of the current situation?* ❞

❝ *What do you think would be a better way?* ❞

❝ *When could that be done?* ❞

❝ *Who else could we bring in to help with this?* ❞

❝ *How can we resolve this problem quickly?* ❞

❝ *What are your ideas on this?* ❞

ALLOWING TIME TO RESPOND

Open questions give the difficult person time to think and form a response. If you suspect that the individual has not thought an issue through, then you can ask a question to help them weigh up the pros and cons of proposed actions, such as "What are the advantages and disadvantages of…?" or "What benefits and pitfalls do you foresee if…?". If you need time to consider the team member's response, say something like, "That's an interesting point, I'd like to take time to think about that." A pause gives you time to reflect, and the other person may fill the silence with the very information you wanted.

STAYING IN CONTROL ▶
When a difficult team member attempts to badger a response from you, avoid answering before you are ready. Pausing to consider what has been said shows that you are taking their views seriously.

63 Use pauses often to give you both time to think.

Manager asks for a minute to consider the points raised

Team member demands an opinion on a sensitive issue

64 Avoid asking "Why?" too often; it can be stressful.

65 Remember not only to listen but to show that you are listening.

LISTENING ACTIVELY

Encourage a difficult person to keep talking, without having to agree or disagree with what is being said, by employing non-committal words in a positive tone of voice. For example, you can use "Uh huh…", "Ah…", and "Please tell me more…" as prompts. Think of something to say that links to what has been said earlier, using the individual's own words, to show that you are listening actively, for example, "You said earlier that you found that challenging. In what way…?" Paraphrase, summarize, and restate the other person's comments in your own words to demonstrate active listening.

USING LISTENING SKILLS

TYPE OF LISTENING	USING METHOD EFFECTIVELY
MIRRORING Using the same words as a difficult person to elicit information and help your understanding.	Imagine yourself in the other person's position, and show understanding by talking little and encouraging with nods and words.
EXPLORING Noticing words given extra emphasis or unusual words that indicate strong feelings.	Use open questions to discover the reasons behind a person's statements. Observe body language as well as voice.
AFFIRMING Reflecting ideas and feelings expressed by the person and summarizing the facts agreed.	Check for the difficult person's agreement and build on their suggestions to guide the conversation towards the desired result.

LISTENING TO VOICE AS WELL AS WORDS

If you wish to establish a real rapport with the difficult team member, you need to listen to the pace at which he or she is speaking and mirror that pace. If the individual is speaking thoughtfully and slowly, then a quick, staccato question from you will sound like gunfire and will cut them short, rather than encouraging openness so that you can understand why they are being difficult. Listen to the pitch and tone of the voice. If someone is very nervous or uptight, then their pitch will tend to be higher and more strained. If their tone is shaky and uncertain, then the team member might be indicating doubts.

> **66** Listen for defensive strategies being used to deflect you.

▼ REACTING TO PACE AND PITCH

Judge how an individual is feeling according to the pace and tone of their voice, and use the same pace and tone yourself to build rapport.

Manager listens patiently to slow speech and plans a calm, reasoned response

67 Notice repeated or unusual words that indicate areas to probe.

POINTS TO REMEMBER

- A manager who listens to his or her team encourages individuals to perform at their best.

- Criticizing ideas without consideration should be avoided if you are to encourage people to contribute suggestions.

- Many constructive discussions are destroyed by failing to focus on what is important.

- Maintaining eye contact, looking enthusiastic and seeking to learn from the conversation helps aid concentration while listening.

IDENTIFYING HIDDEN AGENDA

Once you have asked the right questions, listen to what is being said and pay special attention to repeated words or phrases that indicate what is really bothering the difficult person. If he or she is repeating words or phrases like "too difficult…", "daunting…", and "not my fault…", these indicate a lack of confidence in their ability to achieve the task in hand. Stressing words such as "important to me…", "challenging…", and "vital…", indicates that these are key issues for the individual. Listen, too, to what is not being said, because this can give you similarly important clues as to which questions to ask to find out whether or not the team member has a hidden agenda.

68 Note that emphasized words indicate what is really important to the individual.

FOLLOWING THE FIVE POINTS

Check that you are responding to a difficult person in the most constructive way by running through the following Five Points or Five Ps in your mind as you are speaking:

- **Pace:** am I speaking too slowly or too quickly? Do I seem unsure or hesitant?
- **Projection:** is my voice raised or is it mumbling or quiet? Do I need to speak more loudly/quietly?
- **Pause:** how many pauses for thought are there? Am I talking at the individual or taking time to consider?

- **Pitch:** does my voice sound strained? Is it higher, tighter, or more nervous than normal?
- **Pronunciation:** am I enunciating properly and speaking each word clearly?

HEARING ▶ YOURSELF

Listen to your voice to ensure that you are being clear and conveying the right message.

COMMUNICATING NON-VERBALLY

A difficult person will understand your approach through non-verbal communication long before you speak. Being able to observe the other person's non-verbal signs, to know when a person is about to become difficult, puts you one step ahead.

69 Be responsive whether you like or agree with people or not.

70 Notice non-verbal warnings of the response to come.

71 Build rapport with a difficult person by using mirroring.

PROJECTING THE RIGHT MESSAGE

You can use Neuro-Linguistic Programming (NLP) to increase your rapport with a difficult person. Research indicates that communication is 55 per cent understood through body language, 38 per cent through tone of voice, and only 7 per cent through actual words themselves. NLP provides some useful techniques for successful non-verbal communication. Act in a confident manner and you will start to feel confident. You can also use NLP to build rapport and trust with another person. By adopting an alert but relaxed posture yourself, you encourage a difficult individual to mirror your positive body language, which can help them to participate more fully.

Manager leans forwards slightly, appearing alert, relaxed, and ready to listen

◀ **PROJECTING THE RIGHT MESSAGE**

To demonstrate that you are interested in what the other person is about to say, make eye contact and sit well back in your chair, with no crossed legs or arms, leaning forwards about five degrees from vertical.

INTERPRETING EYE MOVEMENTS

CONSTRUCTING IMAGES
A person looking up and to their right is usually using their imagination or picturing something in their mind.

REMEMBERING SOUNDS
Someone looking to their left is usually remembering a sound or recalling something that has been said in the past.

REMEMBERING IMAGES
Someone looking up to their left is often summoning to mind a remembered image from the past.

INTERNAL DIALOGUE
A person looking down to their left is likely to be hearing an inner voice as he talks to himself inside his head.

CONSTRUCTING SOUNDS
A person looking to their right is likely to be concentrating on forming a verbal response in their mind.

HAVING FEELINGS
Someone looking down to their right is in touch with their emotions, and is checking how they feel about something.

72 Note that eye movements show you how to build rapport.

POINTS TO REMEMBER

- Listening for visual, auditory, and kinaesthetic words or phrases enables you to adapt to the cues.
- Folded arms indicate that you are touching on a sensitive issue.
- Responding with similar sensory words to those being used by a difficult person builds rapport.

USING THE SENSES TO INTERPRET INFORMATION

When people think and communicate, they tend to use three main senses: visual (seeing), auditory (hearing), and kinaesthetic (feeling). If you observe the eye positions and speech of a talking person, you can guess that person's way of processing information and use it to build rapport. For example, if someone is looking upwards and using visual words such as, "I don't see what you mean", respond with similar language such as, "Let's look at it this way…". If a person is expressing themselves in an auditory way, such as by saying "I don't like the sound of this", respond with a phrase such as "Let's talk it through…". If someone says, "This doesn't feel right", try phrases such as, "Let's take care of any concerns you may have…".

EXPLORING SOLUTIONS

Searching for solutions needs skilful questioning and an innovative approach. You need to be able to find solutions that even the most difficult person will want to put into action. Exploring ideas together will help you to achieve this.

73 Ask questions to understand the other person's needs and ideas.

74 Look for points of agreement to keep the discussion constructive.

ENCOURAGING OPEN DIALOGUE

You can encourage two-way dialogue and openness with the difficult person by signalling what you are going to say next. Use phrases such as "Can I suggest…" and "I would like to ask…". If you disagree about some things, do not emphasize them. Instead summarize the points you can agree on to underline a positive approach. If you do have to disagree, give your reasons first.

SPOTTING INFLUENCING STYLES

COERCIVE
This style involves using a more compelling, authoritative approach, even coercion, in order to gain results.

PARTICIPATORY
Influencing by participation requires an encouraging, sharing approach that inspires trust and confidence.

PERSUASIVE
People using the persuasive style of influencing will use logic and emotion in order to achieve their objectives.

INFLUENCING DISCUSSIONS

Influencing means being able to understand another person's needs and matching them with a corresponding benefit of doing what you propose. Influencing can be subtle, for example you can influence by using the word "suggest" instead of "propose", or it can involve sophisticated questioning to explore needs and find out what motivates the other person. Most people have a preferred style of influencing, and might view a person with a different style as being difficult.

SEEKING COMMITMENT

You will be able to tell from an individual's body language and tone of voice which possible solutions he or she favours. Ask the person to summarize the key actions that you have agreed. If the team member has not really agreed to some of these solutions, he or she will change their wording or miss them out altogether. If they appear enthusiastic and start to add detail to the plan you have agreed, you have gained the team member's commitment.

75 Encourage the person to use active verbs for actions, such as "save", instead of vague words like "liaise".

ENSURING ACTION

Ask questions such as, "What needs to be done, how well, by when, and by whom?" The action plan that results should identify the goal, the activities (mainly the other person's) that are needed, the resources (including who else might be involved), milestones on the way, a realistic timetable, and the outcome expected.

GAINING COMMITMENT

Establish purpose of meeting: to explore solutions together

Agree agenda of items for discussion

Open two-way dialogue

Agree action plan

Ask team member to summarize agreed actions

▼ PRODUCING AN ACTION PLAN

Always draw up an action plan to provide a record of actions you have agreed. It can be simple or detailed, but it should state clearly who should be doing what and by when.

Date agreed for completion of action

Initials of person responsible for the action

Detailed description of action planned, including any measures agreed

ACTION PLAN

No	Key Actions	Who	When
1	Draw up a graph showing the sales results over the last three quarters	CM	End April
2	Look at the sales strategy and identify potential areas for growth	LT	End June
3	Generate 350 new sales leads per month	SL	End July
4	Commission new corporate logo in line with brand values	CM	End Sep

NEGOTIATING SOLUTIONS

Finding and negotiating the right solutions demands creativity and flexibility. You need to look for solutions that will work for the difficult person and represent a winning situation for you and your team. The key is to find out first what the difficult person wants.

76 Explain why you are asking questions to allay suspicion about your motives.

QUESTIONS TO ASK YOURSELF

Q Have I shown and encouraged flexibility and creativity in suggesting solutions?

Q Can I hold my ground in the face of tough opposition?

Q Have I taken notes of the key points agreed?

Q Am I conceding something that will create an awkward precedent with other people?

Q Do I review every negotiation to identify how to improve?

FOCUSING ON HIGHER GOALS

If you cannot get a difficult person to agree to an objective, use questions to elicit a higher goal on which both of you can agree. For example, if you want to expand the team and your colleague wants to keep the team as it is, you need to move on from this stalemate with a goal that satisfies both of you, such as increasing the team's output. You can then ask questions to explore what benefits the other person would like, and other possibilities may arise from this discussion.

▼ GAINING AGREEMENT
In order to move from stalemate to a situation of mutual co-operation, you need to ask lots of questions and seek out a higher goal on which you can both agree.

Team member refuses to agree to objective

| Seek out a higher goal on which you can both agree | Establish good rapport while agreeing new goal | Ask what benefits the other person would like |

Manager asks more questions

Both parties agree on a new goal

NEGOTIATING THE BEST SOLUTION

When exploring solutions, many people view the negotiation as a tug of war with four outcomes. In fact, the only outcome you should aim for is the win-win scenario or one in which, rather than trying to take a bigger slice of cake from the other person, you look instead at how you can make the cake bigger for both of you. Ask questions that will expand the options for you both by generating other possibilities. Only when you have generated and explored a variety of possibilities together should you move towards making a decision. Explore areas of agreement to identify a solution to which you can both commit. A difficult person is more likely to agree to your proposal after you have explored all the options together.

POINTS TO REMEMBER

● To negotiate a mutually beneficial solution, open questions should be used to find out what the other person hopes to achieve.

● A manager who is willing to challenge past practice makes a good negotiator.

Manager is fair and assertive

Manager is too passive

▲ **I WIN/YOU WIN**
The ideal outcome is achieved by acknowledging the rights of both parties and searching for ways in which both can win.

▲ **I LOSE/YOU WIN**
An unsatisfactory solution is reached by passive manager who admits defeat, allowing the other person to "win".

77 Identify where you disagree while negotiating to avoid trouble later.

Manager is too aggressive

78 Summarize to clarify that you both have the same understanding.

Manager is too combative

▲ **I WIN/YOU LOSE**
Complete disregard is shown for the other person by a manipulative manager who seeks to win at their expense.

▲ **I LOSE/YOU LOSE**
Both parties lose out because a manager seeks to avoid or obstruct negotiation rather than let the other person win.

AGREEING THE SOLUTION

*I*n order to achieve long-term success with a difficult person, he or she needs to accept ownership of an action plan. There also needs to be continued co-operation throughout the life of the project, or until all the action plan points are completed.

79 Ask an individual to summarize their action plan to help them commit to it.

▲ OBSERVING BEHAVIOUR
A person who has accepted ownership of a project or plan will be enthusiastic, keen to put ideas into practice, and happy to discuss their work with colleagues.

ASSESSING OWNERSHIP

Observing behaviour will help you assess whether the difficult person has accepted ownership of the plan and is committed to it. As the individual summarizes and notes down the actions you have both agreed, note the language and tone of voice used. Are they looking forward to completing the actions and sounding enthusiastic about the solution agreed? Explore any reluctance or uncertainty and ask the person to summarize any further actions you both agree may be needed as a result. Having noted all the action points, together with any support you agreed to give, the team member should copy the action plan to you for your next review together.

IMPLEMENTING AN AGREEMENT

Check that the difficult person is clear about his or her responsibilities. Using the BOB CARD checklist, review the background, including any sensitivities or history to the project. Assess what will or will not be included, analyze the constraints that limit what can be achieved, review your assumptions, such as the availability of help from others, agree reporting requirements (setting review dates), and specify the deliverables. The plan needs to be comprehensive but also easy to understand and use.

THINGS TO DO

1. Ask the other person to suggest a realistic timescale for reviewing progress on agreed actions.

2. Check that actions agreed at the last review have been completed.

3. Praise your team member for what has been achieved.

USING THE BOB CARD CHECKLIST

The BOB CARD is a useful management tool that can help you to transform an agreement into an implementation plan.

- **Background:** review how this point was reached.
- **Objectives:** what is needed in terms of quantity, quality, time, and cost.
- **Boundaries:** the scope of the job or project – what will be included or excluded and authority levels.

- **Constraints:** usually resources such as time, people, or cost.
- **Assumptions:** check that the plan is based on realistic assumptions – if guesses are wrong, change the plan.
- **Reporting:** decide at the planning stage how to control and report on the work.
- **Deliverables:** describe what will be delivered by each phase and on final completion of the project.

CHECKING THE SOLUTION IS SAFE

Agree a solution that is Suitable, Acceptable, Feasible, and Enduring (SAFE). An agreement is suitable if it fits the current situation and the timing is right. How acceptable will it be to the rest of the team or any other stakeholders? What resources and budget will be needed to see it through? Given the time and resource constraints, how practical or feasible is this idea? How long will it take before the perceived benefits are realized? This could have an impact on how enduring the agreement will be. When you have satisfactory answers to each of these questions, you will know that the proposed agreement is SAFE.

▼ CHECKING TIMING

Look at timing in advance to highlight any potential pitfalls at the earliest opportunity, enabling changes to be made that turn the agreement into a realistic implementation plan.

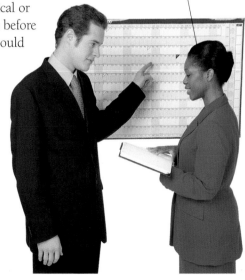

Manager checks overlap of project priorities with team member

80 Identify activities, resources, roles, and deadlines in your plan.

DEALING WITH CONFLICT

When faced with a difficult person who refuses to perform, it is important to have coping strategies in place. Learn how to work through conflict successfully.

MANAGING YOUR OWN RESPONSES

When coping with a difficult person, a manager may need to contribute much more than 50 per cent to the communication process. Only by being highly self-aware and in control of your own responses will you be able to manage those of the difficult person.

81 Be aware of your own responses and their effect on the other person.

POINTS TO REMEMBER

- Your own body language should be checked to ensure that it is not provoking a difficult situation.
- If a difficult person has tensed any muscles, this should be observed and mirrored.
- Eye contact should be maintained and words, tone, and pace of voice should be matched.

STAYING IN RAPPORT

When you do not immediately understand what is going on because a person is sending out confused signals or seems resistant or hostile, staying in rapport is vital. Maintain eye contact and mirror the person's body language. Try to speak at the same pace and in the same tone and volume, and match your breathing. Use the same language. As rapport grows, you will feel more empathy until you can begin to predict how the person will respond.

THINKING AHEAD

To gain a better understanding of the points of view of the situation, first move into deeper rapport to empathize better with the difficult person; second, check your own point of view; and third, mentally distance yourself to observe the two of you occasionally. As you move from observing back to empathy, what new insights do you have on the situation? What advice can you give yourself now for handling the difficult person more effectively? Decide on the options you think will be most useful to you and try one on the difficult person. Observe the response. If the option did not work well, revisit the three points of view and try other options until you get a positive response.

▼ DISTANCING YOURSELF

Take a step back from the conversation to examine your own point of view, then imagine that you are observing the situation from a distance. This gives you space to decide what to do next.

Manager deepens rapport to empathize more

Manager mentally distances himself still further in order to observe

Manager takes a mental step back to check his own point of view

82 Check rapport by changing posture and observing if it is mirrored.

83 Empathize with the other person to maintain rapport.

DOS AND DON'TS

✔ Do describe outcomes you want in a positive way, for example, "Continue doing…"	✘ Don't be negative when describing outcomes you want, for example, "Don't stop…"
✔ Do be aware that your own gestures can signal tension or distract from your message.	✘ Don't stare but note that people who avoid eye contact may have something to hide.
✔ Do persevere – coping with conflict requires patience and persistence.	✘ Don't put your hand over your mouth – it looks as though you are hiding something.

TAKING THE HEAT OUT OF THE SITUATION

When a difficult person is behaving aggressively, you need to know how to take the immediate heat out of the situation. Only when you have calmed the person down will you be able to regain his or her attention and move forward into productive discussion.

84 Avoid interrupting or prejudging; just listen and evaluate what is being said.

85 Take time to analyze the facts of a situation.

▼ **DRAWING UP A PROBLEM TABLE**
Create a problem table to enable you and the difficult person to identify the difficulties involved and work on devising a solution.

CREATING A DIVERSION

Asking a question that requires thought to answer is the simplest diversion of all. Ask the person to write down the advantages and disadvantages of what he or she proposes. Immediately, the person will look at the problem one step removed from both of you. If he or she needs further time to calm down, work through a problem table together. By gathering facts, the focus moves from the issues between you to actions that need to be taken.

PROBLEM TABLE

Analysis	Scale of problem	Current situation	Ideal situation	Action
Consolidated group report is never completed in time for monthly board meeting	A total of 12 divisional reports containing month-end figures need collating and summarizing by 5th of the following month to form group report	Fastest consolidation was by 10th of following month. Board is growing increasingly impatient	Board receive the consolidated group report to read 5 days before their board meeting takes place on 10th of the month	Cut-off date for monthly management accounts to be moved forwards to 25th of month to enable earlier production of month-end figures for divisional reports
Describe problem as fully as possible	*Detail size, duration, timescale, frequency, etc.*	*Outline the situation as it stands now*	*Describe what you want to see happen*	*Record actions agreed to rectify the problem*

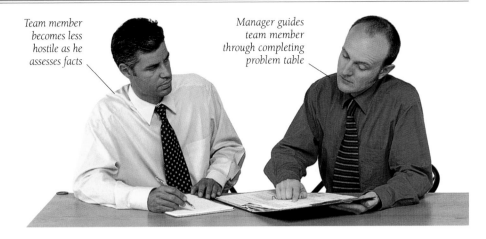

Team member becomes less hostile as he assesses facts

Manager guides team member through completing problem table

LEADING THE DIFFICULT PERSON

To lead the difficult person, use mirroring and empathize with his or her current state. Decide on the behaviour that you wish to cultivate in the person and gently change aspects of your own body language to encourage it. Check whether the person's body language and words are consistent. If the individual mirrors you, then you have established rapport and can move the person away from a negative attitude by adopting body language that indicates a positive state.

▲ WORKING THROUGH A PROBLEM TABLE

Filling in a problem table with a difficult individual encourages you both to look at the facts of a problem rather than emotive issues surrounding it. It also promotes co-operation and collaboration.

86 Avoid cutting someone short by saying "Yes, but…"

POINTS TO REMEMBER

- Discussion of a problem should happen at the right time and in the right place.
- Time out may need to be taken if either party becomes heated and needs to cool down.
- A person's body language should be matched until they are ready to follow your lead.
- If there are options you can live with, the other person should be allowed to choose from these.

LEAVING AN ESCAPE ROUTE

It is important to avoid cornering a difficult individual and leaving them no way out other than to fight past you. Unless you leave them an escape route, you risk jeopardizing your finding a solution together. Allow the difficult person the freedom to set his or her own goals and timescales within a broad framework you both agree. Always leave at least two options so that the person still has an element of choice as to which way to go and therefore a way of saving "face".

AGREEING GROUND RULES

Starting with an agreement on ground rules for working together is often easier to achieve than agreeing on the solution to the problem between you, and is a positive first step towards working more effectively with difficult people.

87 Use ground rules to set boundaries for one person or all team members.

88 Always set a time limit for discussions.

ESTABLISHING RULES▼
Ground rules help you to deal with any number of difficult people within the team. If people are to explore solutions together, everyone must abide by the rules or the meeting will lose its positive momentum.

DEFINING GROUND RULES
Ground rules are guidelines or limits within which you agree to work. The first rule that focuses two individuals on coming to a solution is to set a time limit for the discussion. Other useful rules include listening to each other, looking at the benefits of other people's proposals rather than for reasons why they will not work, maintaining confidentiality, not interrupting each other, and taking turns to speak. Agreeing the ground rules at the beginning of a meeting can put a check on everyone's behaviour.

Difficult team member reacts defensively to colleague's interruption

Manager reiterates rule that everyone must listen to each other

Difficult team member interrupts colleague with criticism

DEVELOPING A CHARTER

A person can be difficult if he or she does not understand how to interact with others in different situations. If someone deals with customers, for example, he or she must know what you promise your customers so that they understand customers' expectations and the part they have to play in their delivery. Draw up a customer charter setting out the level of service that the customer can expect. If the person is being difficult about doing the same as the rest of the team, a guideline on what you expect from team members will help.

At World Trading
we are committed to:

1

Answering your telephone call courteously within 3 rings

2

Responding immediately to any complaints by telephone and in writing within 24 hours

3

Ensuring a high level of expertise in our Customer Service Advisers through a programme of continuous training and development

A. Smith

A. Smith
Managing Director

◀ **SETTING CUSTOMER CARE STANDARDS**
Ensure that staff know the level of service they are expected to provide by drawing up a customer charter. The charter should state what your organization is prepared to do to guarantee customer satisfaction and quality care.

WRITING A SERVICE LEVEL AGREEMENT

If whole teams or departments view each other as difficult people, then a service level agreement between teams or departments may be needed. This outlines the service standards or performance levels that each department or team can expect from the other. Service level agreements minimize areas of potential difficulty because the levels of performance that each party can expect are laid down. The agreement can also contain penalties for non-compliance. Enter into such an agreement positively, recognizing that the benefit of an agreement that has been well thought through is that it will clarify for everyone exactly what it is important to achieve and maintain. Having a clear statement of service levels also makes the review process simpler and variations can more quickly be brought back on track.

89 Check that everyone knows what the service standards are.

POINTS TO REMEMBER

● Writing ground rules on a flipchart ensures that everyone is able to see and agree them.

● Charters or service level agreements clearly set out the standards expected.

● Being clear about what you expect from the outset reduces potential for conflict.

WORKING THROUGH CONFLICT.

View conflict as a chance to understand the needs of the difficult person and how to influence that person to achieve the result you need. By facing up to conflict and acknowledging there is a problem, you have an opportunity to solve the problem together.

90 Describe behaviour that is causing problems and the effect it is having.

FACING THE CONFLICT

It is important to deal with the behaviour you are confronted with at that moment. Behaviour is not constant, it stops and starts, improves and grows worse, so you need to adjust your response in a measured way. Face conflict openly by giving feedback on the effects of what you are observing, whether it is passive resistance, active resistance, or serious aggression. Use your problem-solving skills to help the person understand the cause of the problem and search for solutions with you.

Manager sits down with colleague and uses open questions to discover her deeper objections to the plan

Unhappy about plans to change working procedures in her department, angry team member confronts manager

Manager is frustrated that team member is being difficult and fails to probe for the real reasons for her behaviour

91 Suggest how someone can take a more positive approach.

ADMITTING THAT PROBLEMS EXIST

You will be unable to move forwards together until both of you admit that problems exist. If the difficult person cannot see that there are issues, you must give feedback and ask questions until they can. It is unlikely that the team member will make a commitment to solving the problem until he or she can see the impact it is having on the objectives of the team, on the organization, or on the customers. Use open questions to explore what caused the problem and who else might be involved.

▼ **RESOLVING CONFLICT**
This scenario shows two possible outcomes. By working through conflict effectively, the manager improves his working relationship with the previously difficult team member. A failure to resolve the conflict leads to the loss of a valuable team member.

Manager discovers that employee doubts her ability to meet new targets when plan is implemented

Together they explore ways to help employee meet new targets

92 Keep an open mind – you may not be aware of the facts.

EXPLORING TOGETHER

Ask questions that pinpoint the real causes of the problem, then generate ideas to solve it. Ask the person to summarize the actions agreed between you to put the problem right. This allows you to check the person's understanding of the actions needed and his or her commitment to seeing them through. Exploring problems as they arise, and agreeing on actions, starts a more positive way of working together. Exploring your complementary strengths and weaknesses will help you build on this further.

Stressed employee fails to meet new targets when plan is imposed and decides to leave the organization

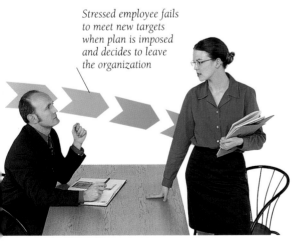

411

93 Steer discussions to future actions as opposed to past.

94 Acknowledge other people's points of view.

MAKING REQUESTS

If you tell people what to do, some people will do as directed. If you suggest what to do, twice as many people are likely to do what you want. Make your needs clear. Be direct and keep it short. Give the reason why you are asking, without trying too hard to sell the idea. Resist appealing to the person's emotions or using flattery. Respect the person's right to say "No". Put your energy into solving the problem and floating other suggestions rather than begging the person to say "Yes".

EXPRESSING YOUR VIEWS

Disagreements happen, but if you can express your views assertively, they are more likely to be handled constructively by a difficult person. Use logic and facts, and express your own opinions and feelings if you want to influence the person assertively. Suggest proposals that are positive and forward-looking and that start discussions moving. Say what you think or feel and use "I" more than "You" when giving your views. If you disagree with the person, then state this in a constructive way. First state what you agree with, then, in the same matter-of-fact way, state the reasons why you disagree with the other views or suggestions before moving on to say what you would like.

Team member begins to think about what manager is saying

Manager states views assertively, but not aggressively

BEING ▶ ASSERTIVE

By expressing your opinions in an assertive, constructive way, you encourage a more assertive response from a previously nervous or defensive person. Make sure that you recognize their views while suggesting your own.

SAYING "NO"

When you need to say "No", give the real reason for it. Avoid giving a long list of reasons or apologizing profusely for refusing. If the difficult person is persistent, repeat your reason for refusing rather than searching for a better one. Keep repeating the same message calmly and assertively until the person understands that you cannot change your decision: "I am happy to review the situation again in six months. What I cannot do is change the decision. We can arrange a review in mid-April". Eventually even the most aggressively persistent and difficult person will get the message, even if he or she does not like it.

95 Ensure that you show respect for others if you want it shown to you.

Team member tries to persuade manager to say "Yes"

Manager listens with open expression

GIVING WEIGHT ▶ TO A REFUSAL

When a difficult person is exhorting you to say "Yes", listen with an open expression and maintain good eye contact to demonstrate your assertiveness. Speak calmly and factually when you say "No".

CASE STUDY

Sandra managed a lively team in a busy agency. The team worked and played hard and in return Sandra was flexible about time off. Recently Sandra felt that they were prioritizing their social lives above meeting deadlines. Having stayed late several times to finish urgent jobs for clients, she felt angry that tasks had been left for her to complete. Sandra called a team meeting and calmly and assertively stated how she felt

about the team's behaviour. She explained that in taking on their work, her own work had not been completed on time, putting potential new business at risk. Sandra asked the team for ideas to solve the problem. They all agreed that with privileges on time off came responsibilities for seeing jobs through. Sandra was able to complete her own work and rely on her team to take their responsibilities seriously.

◀ RESOLVING CONFLICT

By stating how her team's behaviour had affected her, explaining what she wanted to happen instead, and exploring ideas to overcome the problem, Sandra helped her staff to appreciate how she felt and accept the facts. After this session, thinking ahead and ensuring that nothing was left for Sandra again became a matter of pride with the team.

USING MEDIATION

If the situation with a difficult person has become too stressful and time-consuming to deal with yourself, then using mediation can be a cost-effective option. A mediator has a responsibility to be impartial and neutral to help you both to reach agreement.

96 View involving a third party as a positive step, not a failing.

97 Talk through areas of disagreement constructively.

USING A MEDIATOR▼
The mediator is someone whom the manager and team member trust. She hears both sides, and helps both people to analyze the problem. She may put an opposite point of view to both parties, while still commanding respect and trust.

HEARING BOTH SIDES

A mediator could be someone inside your organization who will listen and take a balanced view, and who has the sensitivity, maturity, and integrity to carry out this difficult role. If there is any chance that either you or the difficult person may doubt the neutrality of the mediator, engage an external mediator or consultant whom you are both confident will be impartial. The mediator will be present to manage the emotions and tension in a difficult situation constructively and to help you to listen to each other.

Mediator's body language is neutral

Difficult person trusts the mediator's impartiality

Manager states his views and what he hopes to achieve

SELECTING A MEDIATOR

Decide on the results you want to achieve from the process

Look at mediators with relevant training and experience

Ensure that mediator is someone whom the other party will respect and trust

Check the time limit and budget for the style of mediation chosen

RESOLVING THE ISSUES

A good mediator provides a means for resolving issues between you, and enables you both to retain a sense of control by being actively involved in decision-making. In very difficult situations, perhaps between customers or stakeholders in a contract, two mediators may be needed, one for each side. The outcome of mediation is never imposed on either party, so that both sides voluntarily enter into an agreement, feeling fully informed and heard. The agreement is more likely to be followed through if both parties have been actively involved in framing it. This is because no one will be left feeling aggrieved that a solution was imposed.

98 Find out whether a mediator needs both parties to describe the situation in writing before meeting.

DRAWING UP THE AGREEMENT

Before you start mediation, think about the results you want from the process. These should form the framework for the mediation and your agreement with the mediator. When you are selecting possible mediators, ask about their training and experience. Think about the kinds of skills, values, and style you expect. If issues exist between teams or departments, or between individual employees within an organization, the resulting agreement is usually psychological, written but not legally enforceable. Between customers and organizations, however, mediation to resolve disputes can lead to agreements that are legally enforceable.

CULTURAL DIFFERENCES

It is important to recognize that mediating between people of different cultures and backgrounds can be more difficult because of language barriers and misunderstanding of cultural nuances. If it is important to either party that they have someone of their own race, sex, or culture present, then this should be considered.

LEARNING FOR THE NEXT TIME

E*very time you come into conflict with a difficult person, you can learn how to handle the situation better for next time. To develop your skill at dealing with difficult people, review how conflict arose in the first place, and how co-operation was gained.*

99 Review what went well and what skills you must develop for next time.

QUESTIONS TO ASK YOURSELF

Q Did I listen? How many of my questions were open?

Q Was my behaviour assertive throughout?

Q Did I achieve an action plan from the difficult team member?

Q Did I let the team member summarize their own actions?

Q Have we arranged future sessions to review progress?

REVIEWING DEVELOPMENT AREAS

It is important to review yourself critically after every confrontation with a difficult person to see if you can identify your strengths and any areas that need development. Ask yourself questions about your performance, and make a list of any aspects that you would like to improve for the next time. Were you focused on the result you wanted? If not, set yourself a learning objective for the next time you confront a difficult person so that you will be clearer about what you want to change in yourself.

INVOLVING THE DIFFICULT PERSON IN REVIEWS

When you have worked with a difficult person over a period of time, review how you are working together. Ask for and give specific positive feedback on your working relationship and also on what you feel needs to change or be developed. Praise the behaviour you want repeated and give feedback on what you hope will change. Agree a ground rule that you should both give twice as much motivational feedback as developmental feedback.

100 Praise good behaviour that you would like to see repeated.

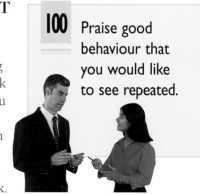

CREATING YOUR DEVELOPMENT PLAN

Reviews give you an opportunity to create a development plan for yourself. Identify the strengths you use with difficult people that you need to build on with practice. Look at the skills you need to develop, and decide whether practice alone will achieve the learning objectives you have set yourself, or whether you need training. Note what you want to be able to do and how well by the end of your next practice or training course.

PERSONAL DEVELOPMENT PLAN

Name: BARRY TURNER

What	When	How	Results
To improve my observation and interpersonal skills to negotiate and communicate more effectively with difficult people at work	August	Training workshop (2 days) on communication and negotiation skills to be provided by external training provider Value: £850	● Learned to observe body language and my effect on others ● Performance improved as a result of using negotiation and assertiveness techniques to reach agreements with difficult people

Define needs plus outcomes you expect from training

Plan the best time for development activity or training

Describe cost of activity or training, duration, and provider

Record outcomes achieved from training or activity once completed

▲ DOCUMENTING DEVELOPMENT

You can encourage difficult people to create a Personal Development Plan for themselves and you can draw one up for yourself too. Include results as well as aims.

 101 Agree on what you could both do better next time.

CREATING A JOINT DEVELOPMENT PLAN

If you have involved the difficult person in building the working relationship between you in reviews, you can both reflect on your achievements and identify your strengths as you build confidence in each other. You can also use reviews to recognize and plan further joint development needs and to improve your performance continuously. You will be surprised, in time, that you have changed your view about the difficult person you knew before.

ASSESSING YOUR ABILITY

A good knowledge of techniques to anticipate and manage difficult people is essential if you are to achieve consistently excellent performance from your staff. Test your skills by answering the following questions. If your answer is "Never" circle option 1; if it is "Always" circle option 4, and so on. Add your scores together, and refer to the analysis to see how you fared and to identify areas that need improving.

OPTIONS

1 Never

2 Occasionally

3 Frequently

4 Always

1 I know my staff well and understand what motivates them.

1 2 3 4

2 I observe my team members and monitor their workloads.

1 2 3 4

3 I identify the strengths and weaknesses of all my team members.

1 2 3 4

4 I understand that people have different ways of learning.

1 2 3 4

5 I create a working environment that builds trust and confidence.

1 2 3 4

6 I set measurable objectives with realistic timescales for achievement.

1 2 3 4

7 I greet all the people with whom I work and go on walkabouts daily.

1 2 3 4

8 I encourage staff to give feedback both to me and to each other.

1 2 3 4

9 I share information with my team and check their understanding.

1 2 3 4

10 I encourage people to focus on internal and external customer needs.

1 2 3 4

11 I ensure that everyone understands what is expected of them.

1 2 3 4

12 I understand my own strengths and weaknesses and plan my development.

1 2 3 4

13 I define a problem and plan how to overcome it by looking at several options.

1 2 3 4

14 I give myself time to think and prepare before meeting with difficult people.

1 2 3 4

15 I am assertive, and not passive or aggressive.

1 2 3 4

16 I always listen carefully to others.

1 2 3 4

17 I encourage people to move forwards rather than dwell in the past.

1 2 3 4

18 I identify reasons why people are unwilling to accept change.

1 2 3 4

19 I know when to confront difficult people and when to avoid confrontation.

1 2 3 4

20 I observe body language to give me advance warning of problems.

1 2 3 4

21 I know how to overcome objections to my suggestions.

1 2 3 4

22 I always follow up on actions agreed.

1 2 3 4

23 I set consistently fair objectives and standards for team members.

1 2 3 4

24 I give feedback on what behaviour should continue and what needs to change.

1 2 3 4

25 I evaluate information carefully and am aware of my own biases.

1 2 3 4

26 I ask open questions and listen more than I speak.

1 2 3 4

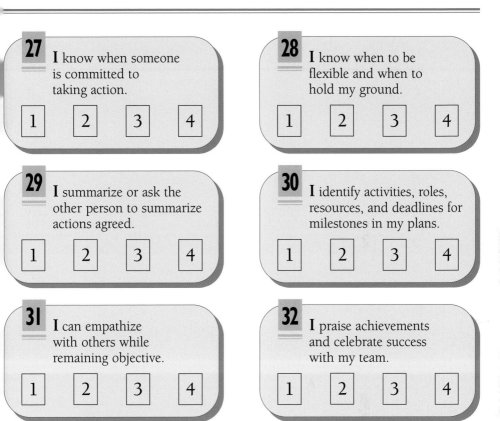

27 I know when someone is committed to taking action.

| 1 | 2 | 3 | 4 |

28 I know when to be flexible and when to hold my ground.

| 1 | 2 | 3 | 4 |

29 I summarize or ask the other person to summarize actions agreed.

| 1 | 2 | 3 | 4 |

30 I identify activities, roles, resources, and deadlines for milestones in my plans.

| 1 | 2 | 3 | 4 |

31 I can empathize with others while remaining objective.

| 1 | 2 | 3 | 4 |

32 I praise achievements and celebrate success with my team.

| 1 | 2 | 3 | 4 |

ANALYSIS

Now that you have completed the self-assessment, add up your total score and check your performance. Whatever level of success you have achieved, there is always room for improvement. Identify your weakest areas, then refer to the relevant parts of this section, where you will find practical advice and tips to help you establish and hone your skills.

32–63: You may still be surprised by difficult people. Practise your observation skills and give yourself time to prepare to handle difficult people more effectively.

64–95: You are aware of how to deal with difficult people in some more familiar situations but need to identify areas for further development.

96–128: You are able to achieve considerable success with difficult people. Develop your skills by asking for regular feedback.

APPRAISING STAFF

INTRODUCTION

The ability to use appraisal to develop and motivate employees is a core management skill. Regular, constructive feedback on performance is vital if staff are to build on their strengths, achieve their full potential, and make the maximum contribution to their organization. Appraising Staff equips you with all the skills and techniques you need to conduct successful appraisals. It clearly explains the key aims and benefits of the appraisal process, and leads you step-by-step through the preparation, management, and follow-up of the appraisal interview. The section is packed with advice to help you encourage open discussion, interpret body language, build confidence, deal with performance problems, and more. With 101 practical tips scattered throughout and a self-assessment quiz that allows you to evaluate your skills as an appraiser, this is an invaluable guide to appraising effectively.

UNDERSTANDING THE PURPOSE

Effective appraisal is at the heart of successful management. Understand how the appraisal process works, and recognize how a well-managed system benefits employees and organizations.

DEVELOPING PEOPLE

Regular feedback develops staff and helps them to achieve their objectives. Create an environment in which people welcome continuous feedback, and use the appraisal interview as a formal round-up of these on-going, informal reviews.

1 Encourage people to work to their full potential for successful results.

2 Praise good performance when you see it to motivate people to do even better.

PROVIDING FEEDBACK

All employees want to know how their performance is viewed by their manager. It is important to provide this feedback continuously, whether it is positive or negative. Proper feedback helps team members identify where they need to improve their skills, knowledge, and attitudes. Even highly successful achievers need feedback to help them sustain their performance. On-going feedback improves morale, since people know exactly where they stand, and enables managers to express concerns rather than storing them up.

APPRAISING FORMALLY

Formal appraisal interviews, held on a regular basis with your team members, are a culmination of continuous informal feedback. If on-going feedback has been effective, this formal meeting will not contain any surprises for appraisees, and the atmosphere should be positive and business-like. There are two parts to the formal appraisal: the performance review and the developmental review. The performance review enables you to gain agreement from an employee on how well he or she has done in achieving objectives, and developing skills and knowledge, during the period under review. The developmental review is aimed at pinpointing what needs to be done in future to sustain achievement or meet new objectives. This part of the appraisal helps you to continuously improve an appraisee's capabilities and prepare them to take on more responsibility. Do the two parts in one appraisal session to emphasize the link between them.

GETTING THE MOST FROM APPRAISAL

An effective appraisal system has many benefits. Use it to:

● Sustain motivation and commitment;
● Continuously improve performance;
● Give direction and agree expected contributions;
● Set targets in line with organizational and team goals;
● Review development so far;
● Identify training needs;
● Celebrate successes and learn from disappointments;
● Understand career aspirations and assess potential;
● Gather ideas for change.

| Provide continuous informal feedback | → | Formally review performance | → | Formally review development |

▲ DEFINING APPRAISAL

Effective appraisal relies on the provision of regular feedback. This feedback is then formalized in a two-part review of a team member's performance and development.

3 Make sure that people know how important they are to the organization.

APPRAISING EFFECTIVELY

Think carefully about how you will give feedback both formally and informally. In order to build for the future, it is important to be constructive in what you say and to focus on the future in the way that you say it. Make sure that all feedback is two-way, and that discussions are honest and open. Consider how you will put your points across, since people will react to the manner in which you provide feedback. Bear in mind that criticism can be difficult to take, even when an individual is aware that it is justified.

DEFINING APPRAISAL TYPES

There are three distinct types of appraisal, each involving a different approach to evaluating performance. Understand the purpose of top-down, peer, and 360-degree appraisals, and why self-assessment must feature in them all.

4 Ensure that staff understand how they will be appraised.

5 Find out how others in your organization view an appraisee's performance.

APPRAISING TOP-DOWN

Top-down appraisal means that the appraisee's immediate manager, who knows the appraisee best, is responsible for their appraisal and has the authority to agree a development plan for the future. Some companies use a "matrix" approach in which one manager appraises an individual in terms of their contribution to a specific office or region, while another manager appraises their input to their specfic area of work. A human resources specialist, for example, with an objective of putting employees on new contracts, would be assessed by a manager with human resources or legal expertise.

USING PEER APPRAISAL

In this type of appraisal, people at the same level appraise their peers, so that each appraiser can use his or her expert knowledge of the appraisee's role and responsibilities to give an authoritative opinion on their skills. Peer appraisal is often used in the professions, where specialist knowledge of issues such as ethics or technical competence is important. By monitoring colleagues as part of the appraisal process, changes in practice can be fed back to the profession, and improvements made to the way in which members behave and carry out their work.

POINTS TO REMEMBER

- Peer appraisal enables colleagues to act as mentors to one another, helping to improve performance all round.
- The exchange of open feedback among staff must be actively encouraged to ensure the effectiveness of peer appraisal.
- A combination of top-down and peer appraisal is often used to broaden the scope of feedback.

UNDERSTANDING 360-DEGREE APPRAISAL

In this type of appraisal, the appraiser seeks feedback from everyone who has worked with the appraisee, including customers, their peer group, and members of their own team. Generally, the appraiser will send out forms or questionnaires, such as customer satisfaction review forms, and then take comments into account when preparing for the formal interview. There is a growing trend towards this type of appraisal, since knowing how an appraisee's manager, peers, internal customers, external customers, and others view his or her performance often provides valuable insights.

6 See that questions on customer forms provide useful feedback.

7 Evaluate feedback carefully to ensure its value to the appraisee.

USING SELF-ASSESSMENT

Self-assessment encourages employees to play an active role in the appraisal process. The fact that people tend to be hard on themselves in a self-assessment can make the appraisal more successful. As their manager, you are likely to be less harsh, and can focus on positive aspects of their answers, praising achievements and strengths. Self-assessment questions should be framed to ensure that they help the appraisee to analyze their performance effectively. Answering the questions set should enable the appraisee to prepare for the appraisal itself, and to uncover any need for change. Avoid posing questions designed to lead an appraisee into giving evidence to support your own preconceived opinions. This will not result in a constructive appraisal.

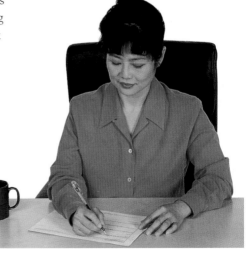

◀ ENCOURAGING REFLECTION
Self-assessment helps staff to feel included in the appraisal process. It prompts them to consider where they are going and how they are doing.

SETTING OBJECTIVES

Appraisals provide the opportunity to establish objectives in line with an organization's strategy. Bear in mind that up-to-date job descriptions are vital if you are to use appraisals to discuss, revise, and align objectives to your organization's aims.

8 Plan ahead and make allowances for any future changes.

9 Ensure that you are prepared for the arrival of new employees.

PRIMING NEW EMPLOYEES

The process of setting objectives will begin as soon as a new member of staff joins your team. Induction sessions should be used to introduce newcomers to the aims of your organization, and follow-up meetings should be held afterwards to ask new employees for feedback on the induction, agree job descriptions, and set performance objectives. If you fail to hold this meeting, a new recruit could be working for months before appraisals take place. Use the meeting to pinpoint training needs, identify other members of staff to be met, and plan future development needs.

DOCUMENTING OBJECTIVES

Every team member needs an up-to-date job description so that they understand what is expected of them and what their objectives are. The process of agreeing and documenting job descriptions can be done separately from the appraisal to enable team members to see where they need guidance or training to perform well. Be aware that roles may change between appraisals, since an individual's talents or interests in different aspects of their job can change its very nature. Appraisals enable you to update job descriptions and ensure that a team member's focus is in line with that of the team and the organization.

POINTS TO REMEMBER

- Setting aside a little time every couple of months to check through and update job descriptions makes it easier to spot any changes.
- Job descriptions should clearly define overall work objectives, broken down into key areas of activity.
- Job descriptions should be as succint as possible – ideally fitting on to one A4 page – and should list main responsibilities rather than detail daily activities.

DEFINING THE PROCESS OF SETTING OBJECTIVES

> **Induction session is held to introduce new staff to organizational objectives**

> **Follow-up meeting is held to define responsibilities and individual/team objectives**

> **Job descriptions are agreed and documented to provide focus and direction**

> **Job descriptions are reviewed regularly to maintain team and organizational focus**

> **Appraisals are used to discuss and refocus individuals if their job emphasis has changed**

> **Job descriptions are updated if necessary, and new objectives agreed**

11 Try to turn good intentions into actions.

PLANNING FOR DEVELOPMENT

Just as there is a strong link between the objectives of teams in an organization, so there is a connected set of training plans. By reviewing training and development needs at each appraisal, you will be able to match an individual's requirements to those of their team and the organization. The appraisal and each development plan are important sources of information for organizations to plan training requirements. Personal development plans (PDPs) should specify the results you want to achieve, so that people develop in a way that helps them to achieve their objectives.

10 Use appraisals as an opportunity to ensure that people are realistic about their potential.

ESTABLISHING LONG-TERM GOALS

In addition to focusing on today's results, appraisals will help you to plan for the long term. By considering the potential of each team member, and discussing their career aspirations with them, you will be able to create a picture of your team in the future and produce a succession plan. Use the appraisal to identify when it is time for an individual to move on. Consider what you will do if someone is suddenly promoted off your team, or there is a change to your role. By planning ahead, you avoid the risk of failing to deliver results during a period of transition. You also ensure that other team members are not disrupted by change and are able to maintain consistent performance.

ACHIEVING OBJECTIVES

In addition to setting objectives for every employee, appraisals help to focus people on achieving them. By agreeing challenging, realistic, and quantifiable performance measures, you and your team members will be clear on how progress will be assessed.

12 See that measures of performance are challenging but achievable.

13 Set stretching but realistic targets that will motivate your staff.

14 Use objectives as a way of getting the team to focus and work together.

SETTING PERFORMANCE MEASURES

A key aspect of the appraisal is to communicate objectives with measurable criteria. Make sure that performance is measurable in numeric or percentage terms to provide appraisees with specific targets, and give them a sense of achievement when they surpass them. Encourage appraisees to come up with their own ideas as to what they should accept as a challenge. They will be more committed if they declare what is feasible themselves. Bear in mind that appraisees will often set themselves bigger challenges than those presented by an appraiser. People will rarely suggest a target that is well below what they believe they can achieve.

MAKING OBJECTIVES SMART

In a good appraisal environment, objectives are tested to ensure that they are specific, measurable, agreed, relevant, and timebound (SMART). Make your objectives SMART by ensuring that they:

● Clearly explain what the individual is meant to achieve – setting out exactly what must be done, how, and by when;

● Are measurable in terms of efficiency (resources used) and effectiveness (quality of result);

● Are proposed by the appraisee and agreed by appraiser after discussion;

● Are well within the appraisee's capabilities and control;

● Have a clear, unequivocal, and agreed timescale for completion.

SELECTING APPROPRIATE CRITERIA

Some performance measures cannot easily be translated into quantitative targets. Outcomes can be expressed in a number of ways, which means that it is important to select criteria that are appropriate to the individual and the particular objective. For example, in setting a performance measure for the writing of a report, an appropriate qualitative measure might be that the recipient would be able to make a confident decision after reading it. A qualitative objective, such as fast response to customer queries, may become a quantitative one if you decide to measure how many times the telephone rings before it is answered. An alternative qualitative measure could derive from a customer questionnaire that seeks feedback from customers as to whether they are satisfied with the standard of service they receive. In order to help you and the appraisee find the correct measure, ask yourselves the question, "What will success look like or feel like?"

QUESTIONS TO ASK YOURSELF

Q Do I understand what our customers expect from the appraisee?

Q When we agree a qualitative measure of performance, will we easily see later whether or not it has been met?

Q Is there any way we could turn a qualitative measure into a quantitative one?

Q Are we agreeing new measures that expect performance to improve in the future?

15 Be prepared to be flexible, if necessary, should a situation change.

◄ AGREEING MEASURES

Although Sally was set the objective of improving the standard of her report writing, she was unable to raise her level of performance because Tom had failed to provide her with sufficient information. By agreeing clear measures and expectations, he provided Sally with qualitative and quantitative measures to aim for, and her performance improved dramatically.

CASE STUDY

Tom, a marketing manager, was concerned that reports written by his assistant, Sally, were poorly structured and inaccurate. He often found himself correcting her drafts several times. During her appraisal, it was agreed that Sally should work to improve her report writing. However, after several weeks, Sally's work was still not up to the standard Tom required. He realized that in failing to set performance measures, he had not given Sally the guidance she needed to achieve her objective. He sat down with Sally and together they agreed that in future Sally's reports should follow a set template, starting with a 500–600 word introduction and ending with a summary of the main points. They also agreed that Sally would check all facts so that Tom need make no more revisions to her drafts. As a result, Sally began to produce highly professional reports.

EMPOWERING STAFF

Team members must be committed to objectives if they are to carry out their tasks successfully. Use appraisals to empower staff through delegation, to gain their commitment to actions, and to encourage them to use their own initiative.

16 Work on the basis that everyone will want to do a good job.

DELEGATING CONTROL OF OBJECTIVES

Agree objective with team member

Allow team member to plan activities

Agree team member's plan

Ask team member to suggest options if plan needs to change

Agree performance measures with team member

17 Ask team members for their views on the way ahead.

EMPOWERING PEOPLE

By delegating responsibility to team members, you increase their control over what is achieved. This is because effective delegation involves the manager and team member agreeing on a specific and unambiguous statement of the objective and responsibility. The team member is then able to work on their own to achieve the objective, using their initiative to solve any problems along the way. Build an empowered environment by encouraging your team members to be less dependent on you as their manager. This will increase their effectiveness and save you time. Stress that you would prefer people to come to you with solutions rather than problems, particularly during the appraisal interview. Encourage them to analyze difficult situations, to consider ways of resolving them, and to recommend appropriate actions.

DOS AND DON'TS

✔ Do allow people to learn from their own mistakes.

✔ Do encourage people to think of different options for solving a problem.

✘ Don't assume you will always have the best answer to a situation.

✘ Don't allow people's mistakes to cause them to fail in a significant objective.

MAXIMIZING OWNERSHIP

CLARIFYING RESPONSIBILITIES ▼

During the appraisal, encourage the team member to take notes of what needs to be done. They will then be able to refer to their notes to help them summarize their action plan at the end of the meeting.

Once the achievement of an objective has been delegated, the appraisee must fully accept its value and be committed to seeing their action plan through to success. When agreeing objectives and plans at the appraisal, you must both be clear what the outcome of actions should be. Without commitment, you risk the appraisee delegating the task back to you, perhaps just before the deadline. If someone is reluctant to take on responsibility, you will need to find out why they have reservations. If an appraisee doubts their capabilities, consider how to alter the objective so that they feel able to achieve it, or organize training or guidance to build the person's competence and enable them to do the job confidently.

ENCOURAGING INITIATIVE

Use the appraisal to establish how you would like the appraisee to approach their work. You will not be getting involved in discussions on how they are going to go about achieving their objectives, but you should be concentrating on what needs to be achieved. You should let the appraisee know that you have faith in their ability and make it clear that you will be expecting them to use their own initiative. You will be setting agreed milestones to review progress so that you avoid continually asking for updates. Remember that it is important to give praise when staff make appreciable progress. "Thank you" and "Well done" are two of the most motivational phrases in the workplace.

POINTS TO REMEMBER

- People who feel able to achieve an objective in their own way will take more responsibility for that achievement.

- Good team leaders praise their people for finding new ways of getting results.

- The decision to do something is not complete until the first action is taken.

- People will take a more active part in the process of delegation if they are encouraged to question briefs and ask for more delegated responsibility.

REWARDING SUCCESS

Effective appraisal enables you to reward achievement and encourage continuous improvement. Plan to use appraisals to discuss rewards that satisfy the needs of the individual and the organization, rather than focusing on pay reviews alone.

18 Make sure that rewards are in keeping with your organization's goals.

19 Always deliver rewards that have been earned by team members.

PRESENTING PRIZES ▼
Awarding prizes or holidays is a good way of celebrating and recognizing achievement. Find out from team members during their appraisals how they would like to be rewarded for good performance to give you more ideas for non-financial rewards.

BREAKING THE PAY LINK

There is a link between what an employee is paid and their value to the organization. You may need to make judgments about the effect of a person's performance on the pay rewards they receive. To encourage excellent performance, find other ways to reward high achievers. These people are motivated by feedback and may well become de-motivated if they see low achievers receiving the same rewards. However, if the appraisal is seen as a hurdle that must be jumped in order to win a pay increase, an appraisee is likely to become defensive. For this reason, appraisals are often timed separately from pay reviews.

Team member receives prize as a reward for meeting objectives

Colleagues feel motivated to follow good example

ANALYZING NEEDS ▼
This simplified model of pyschologist Abraham Maslow's hierarchy of needs illustrates the importance of satisfying needs at the lower levels before motivating people at higher levels. A car, a social need, may be motivational, but it will not be so until physiological needs have been met.

Self-actualization needs (development of own potential, finding self-fulfilment)

Self-esteem needs (approval from others, recognition, achievement)

Social needs (acceptance from others, affiliation, belonging)

Safety needs (feeling of security, not fearing danger)

Physiological needs (basic requirements of life, such as food and drink)

MOTIVATING PEOPLE

Appraisals give you an opportunity to reward your team by thanking and motivating them. The fact that you are spending time alone with them and discussing their work is in itself encouraging. People like to know that their work is being observed by their manager. Most are also motivated by a sense of autonomy, where they feel responsible for achieving a result rather than just carrying out tasks. This helps them to feel more in control of their jobs. To keep your team motivated, delegate wherever possible. If a team member achieves success in a delegated task, their sense of achievement is a great morale-booster. Finally, think about what will motivate each individual, since everyone has different needs.

BUILDING ON SUCCESS

Use appraisals to develop your team by discussing past successes and achievements so that they can be repeated and even surpassed. Consider building on achievements by promoting a team member, or giving someone the chance to take part in development activities. In addition to rewarding the appraisee, this will also enhance their value to your organization and their ability to meet objectives. Review the period since the last appraisal and discuss how the appraisee has used the activities in their previous development plan to improve their capabilities. This discussion helps the individual to understand the value of the development activities they have undertaken and shows them how they are improving their ability to contribute to the team and organization.

20 Find out what it is that motivates each member of your staff.

21 Remember that success often breeds further success.

PREPARING TO APPRAISE

Good preparation is an essential part of appraising effectively. Plan every aspect of the discussion thoroughly and ensure that appraisees are well prepared to ensure a successful outcome.

BEING PREPARED

The appraiser and appraisee have specific responsibilities in an appraisal. To ensure that the discussion is focused and controlled, understand your own role and brief appraisees on their responsibilities so that they, too, can prepare effectively.

22 Make the most of your appraisal time by thinking about it in advance.

23 Plan to talk about the job – not about the person.

24 Always check that you have all the documentation you need for appraisals.

DEFINING THE APPRAISER'S ROLE

The role of the appraiser is to encourage and guide the appraisee through the structure of the appraisal. You should be a conduit, or a catalyst, not a judge or interrogator. Plan the logistics of the meeting at least two weeks in advance. Note down the topics you wish to discuss in order of importance, so that you know in advance what you need to cover. Think of questions that will encourage the appraisee to talk. Read any guidance notes that accompany the appraisal documentation issued by your organization.

POINTS TO REMEMBER

● An appraisee should be aware that he or she may need to make notes during the appraisal.

● Formal appraisals are more effective when the appraisee knows what to expect.

● A formal appraisal is very important to the appraisee, and the appraiser must prepare to meet those high expectations.

▼ HELPING APPRAISEES TO PREPARE

Self-assessment questions should be carefully framed to help appraisees prepare for discussion. Ensure that staff have ample space to be able to answer the questions as fully as possible.

UNDERSTANDING THE APPRAISEE'S ROLE

For the appraisee, the appraisal meeting offers an opportunity to discuss jointly their performance, their progress, their future, their objectives and focus, and their approach to the job. To help them prepare for this discussion, issue appraisees with a self-assessment document and give them plenty of time to complete it. Ask them to come up with examples of high and low points, and to think about areas for improvement. Have there been any changes to their job, or aspects that have become more or less important since the last review? Encourage people to report back on projects they have worked on, or suggest worthwhile projects for the future.

SELF-ASSESSMENT FORM

Name:

Date of appraisal:

Job title:

1. How successfully did you meet your objectives for last year? What achievements are you particularly pleased with and what strengths have you shown?

2. In what areas could you develop your performance and how could this be achieved?

3. What changes have there been to your role in the past 12 months and what changes do you foresee for the future? Are there aspects of your work in which you would welcome further guidance or training?

4. What problems or challenges did you encounter in carrying out your role last year? How did you overcome them? Are there still barriers to achieving all your objectives?

Promotes reflection on what is important to the individual

Allows appraisee to identify areas for development

Prompts the appraisee to think about how their role has changed

Encourages appraisee to think about their successes and how to overcome obstacles

EVALUATING PERFORMANCE

Preparing for appraisal involves looking at an overview. Evaluate an appraisee's progress since the last review – in terms of performance and development – to help you set new objectives and plan activities effectively for the period ahead.

25 Align the job description with the organization, not the person.

26 Look for the causes of under-performance.

REVIEWING JOB DESCRIPTIONS

Examine the appraisee's job description to ascertain whether roles or responsibilities have changed since the last appraisal. Ensure that any alterations are in the interests of the organization, and not just the appraisee. If, for example, a team member dislikes cold calling on the telephone, they may have moved the emphasis of the job towards serving existing customers instead of finding new ones. Rather than allowing the change to the job description, consider training the appraisee in telephone or tele-marketing techniques.

27 Review the facts and disregard rumour or hearsay.

EVALUATING PROGRESS

Review the achievements of the appraisee against their specific objectives. Pick out good aspects of performance so that you can praise them, and encourage the appraisee to keep up their high standards. Have they approached their work positively? Have they planned, co-ordinated, and organized successfully? Where performance falls short of what is expected, consider the possible reasons. Ask yourself whether the area of under-performance is truly important. Negative feedback may not be necessary if an issue is minor, particularly when excellent results have been achieved in other areas.

THINGS TO DO

1. Check that the action plan agreed at the last appraisal was carried out.

2. If actions have not been completed, find out why.

3. Ascertain whether the appraisee has been rewarded and/or praised for carrying out tasks successfully.

28 Check whether staff have had the time to focus on development.

REVIEWING DEVELOPMENT

Having gathered information on an appraisee's job performance, review the benefits and effectiveness of their development activities. This is important not only to ensure continuous development, but also to confirm that the investment of time and money in developing the appraisee has been worthwhile. Ascertain whether the development objectives set at the last appraisal achieved what was expected. Check that the activities improved performance to a level that affected business results. Finally, review the performance of coaches and training organizations involved to ascertain how successful they were.

Appraiser finds out how team member has benefited from training in new software program

◀ **CHECKING FOR QUALITY**

Follow up on courses by seeking feedback from staff on their effectiveness. Invite them to demonstrate what they have learned and consider whether the team might benefit from a similar presentation.

IDENTIFYING PROBLEMS

When planned development activities have not been carried out, investigate why. Perhaps an appraisee was unable to attend a course because there was a crisis in the office. If so, find out whether losing the cancellation fee and wasting the trainer's time was truly warranted. Consider whether the appraisee still needs to carry out the activity. Could the need be met differently in the future? Assess whether the development activities were appropriate for the individual. For example, if after watching a video or reading a book, the information received was not applied, the appraisee may benefit from a different method of learning.

QUESTIONS TO ASK YOURSELF

Q Is the reason for any problem the appraisee may be having outside the appraiser's control?

Q What barriers restricted performance?

Q Were the objectives sufficiently clear?

Q Does the under-performance expose a development need?

Q Is the person capable of developing enough to perform to standard?

IDENTIFYING GOALS

Having evaluated performance, the next stage of preparation is to pinpoint areas for improvement and set objectives to achieve strategic business goals. Identify current levels of performance, and look for ways of developing skills and knowledge.

29 Bring objectives in line with the goals and policy of the organization.

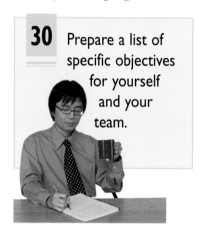

30 Prepare a list of specific objectives for yourself and your team.

FOCUSING ON TARGETS

Challenging yet achievable targets are essential if people are to feel motivated to improve performance and sustain high standards. Prepare for effective objective-setting with the appraisee by considering key result areas for their job. List these areas in order of importance, focus on up to six areas at the top of your list, and draw up suitable objectives for each. Phrase objectives carefully, using specific, active language, such as "sell" and "produce". Avoid vague or ambiguous terms such as "liaise" or "improve".

PREPARING MEASURABLE OBJECTIVES

Assign measures to each objective, ensuring that you will be able to access the information you need to monitor performance against those measures. Look, too, at team and organizational objectives and how these are measured. Consider the contribution that each team member must make towards this. For example, if the team's revenue target amounts to £2,000,000 and there are ten team members, you may wish to set everyone an objective of achieving £210,000. This divides the task evenly and ensures that if one person misses the target but everyone else achieves it, there is a good chance that the team will achieve its aim.

31 Be ambitious and always aim high when setting objectives.

32 Always try to be consistent in your expectations of other people.

SETTING STANDARDS

It is important to set standards, covering both the job and personal behaviour, by which competency can be measured. To help you do this, imagine what ideal performance would look like. In a customer service environment, for example, you may wish to see that staff have developed an efficient process for following up with customers as promised. Next, think how a high performer would typically behave – perhaps he or she would have the ability to listen actively and empathetically. Avoid focusing on the people who are currently doing the job and concentrate on the job itself and the desired results. Assess whether the appraisee is meeting the standards so that you can discuss development or praise progress in the appraisal.

33 Focus on what would be ideal, not on what is being achieved now.

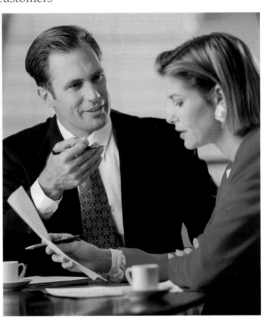

GAINING AN INSIGHT ▶
Find out more about the levels of competency needed to do a job successfully by talking to people with experience in the role. Speak to staff who have done the same work effectively or refer to outside experts in the field.

ASSESSING DEVELOPMENT NEEDS

Consider whether the requirements of a team member's role are changing and plan to prepare people for impending change before it occurs. If altering roles means that additional skills are required, assess whether the team member has already demonstrated those skills sufficiently, or whether there are any areas where they are lacking skills. If you identify a need for development, plan which activities would be appropriate. Prior to the appraisal, check that resources, such as a budget for training, will be available for the planned activities. Ensure, too, that you will be able to release the team member from normal duties during the training period.

PLANNING AHEAD

Effective planning for an appraisal involves anticipating an appraisee's needs and considering how best to respond to them. Be clear on what you are able to agree, and consider timing, resources, and allocating responsibility for agreed actions.

34 Have a good grasp of company policy on career development.

QUESTIONS TO ASK YOURSELF

Q Will I be able to make decisions on pay, time off or other rewards?

Q Am I in a position to promise that someone will be promoted or trained for further career progression?

Q Am I able to agree training and development and the budget necessary for it?

Q Do I have the authority to organize job transfers, secondments, or work experience on different projects or sites?

Q Will the human resources department agree that I have selected the best method of developing the individual?

DEFINING AUTHORITY

Make sure that you know what you will be able to agree on your own authority, and what needs authorization. If you are unsure about this when you come to conduct the appraisal, you risk reducing your credibility as a manager by raising an appraisee's expectations and then dashing them later. You may also lose the appraisee's trust if you are forced to renege on a promise that cannot be resourced.

Manager re-reads her organization's appraisal policy to check that she has not missed anything

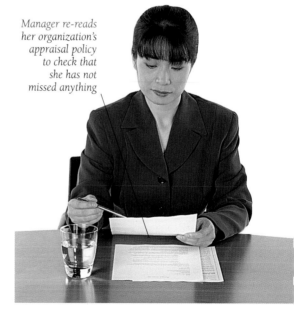

BEING THOROUGH ▶
Familiarize yourself with company policies on matters such as holiday and expense allowances so that you will be in a position to answer questions on these issues. Be clear, too, on your organization's and team's aims to ensure that any objectives agreed will be in alignment.

35 Promise only things you can genuinely deliver.

36 Identify problems that may prevent an appraisee from achieving objectives.

PLANNING TIME AND RESOURCES

Estimate the duration, and start and finishing times, of the tasks necessary to achieve the objectives you have prepared for the appraisee. This will help you to ensure that what the appraisee suggests is realistically attainable. Estimate how much time is needed for development activities and assess whether you will need cover while the appraisee is away. Plan the resources needed both to achieve objectives and undertake development activities. Consider equipment, materials, and facilities such as working space. This well-prepared "project" plan will provide a starting point for your appraisal discussion.

ALLOCATING TASKS

Consider in advance who will be responsible for carrying out proposed actions after the meeting. For example, who will monitor any milestones agreed on the way to the objectives? Consider how exceptions or shortfalls could be reported. This task may be taken on by the appraisee, or you might take responsibility yourself, or ask a third party. After the appraisal, who should be responsible for researching and organizing development work, such as training? Finally, bear in mind that if the appraisee is to take ownership of the objectives, achieving them must be within their direct control.

37 Check that people have the time to lend their support.

Manager asks senior team member to act as a mentor to appraisee

ORGANIZING SUPPORT ▶

If there are members of staff who may be able to assist the appraisee in achieving their performance or development objectives, approach them before the appraisal to enlist their support. During the appraisal you can then let the appraisee know what level of assistance they can expect.

CREATING A POSITIVE ENVIRONMENT

A conducive appraisal environment encourages openness, receptiveness, and discussion. Build your credibility, create an atmosphere of trust, and pay attention to the layout of the meeting room to help the appraisee relax and feel comfortable.

38 Show respect for issues discussed in confidence with the appraisee.

39 Avoid telling an individual one thing and saying something else to another.

MAINTAINING CONFIDENTIALITY

To create an atmosphere in which both appraiser and appraisee can talk freely, it is important to stress that complete confidentiality is expected on both sides. Prior to the appraisal interview, make sure that you let the appraisee know which aspects of the discussion will be kept between the two parties, and what needs to be passed on to others, for example the Human Resources department. Having agreed to keep certain matters confidential, keep to your word and do not discuss them with anyone else.

BUILDING TRUST

Trust grows over time, and the stronger the relationship between appraiser and appraisee, the more effective appraisals will become. Earn your team's trust by putting into action decisions made during the appraisal. The reputation of an appraisal system can be ruined if what is said in the appraisal room turns out to be a series of good intentions that are never followed through. You will need to be assertive as a manager, but you should always be seen as honest, consistent, and fair.

POINTS TO REMEMBER

- Trust can take a long time to build, yet it can be destroyed within seconds.
- If an appraisee suspects that confidentiality might be broken, significant items may be held back.
- Taking a few moments before the appraisal to imagine yourself in your appraisee's shoes will help you to be on their wavelength.

SETTING UP THE ROOM

Create a relaxed ambience by choosing a suitable room and arranging office furniture so that there are no barriers between yourself and the appraisee. Make sure that the room is private so that you are not overheard, and that it does not have glass doors or panels – you do not want to be distracted by people walking past and looking into the room. Careful preparation of the meeting room shows the appraisee that you are genuinely interested in their achievements and development. Conversely, an unprofessional atmosphere will make the appraisee feel isolated and unimportant. Check that lights will not be shining in the appraisee's eyes or silhouetting you against the window so that they cannot see and read your expressions.

40 Plan to start the appraisal as you mean to continue – in a positive tone.

▼ ARRANGING THE DETAILS

When planning seating arrangements, aim to create the most informal, comfortable atmosphere possible. Using the corner of a desk is friendly, informal, and practical. It is easy to maintain good eye contact and is far less confrontational than sitting opposite one another.

Work at the same level by sitting on chairs that are of a similar size

Clear the work surface so that paperwork does not form a barrier between you

BEING OBJECTIVE

A manager's personal approach to an appraisal meeting is critical to its success. Prepare yourself for the discussion by considering how you will encourage ideas, avoid bias, and focus on the important aspects of the job.

41 Ensure that you hold an objective appraisal – not a subjective review.

POINTS TO REMEMBER

- A manager who encourages his or her team to come up with ideas will get more from them.
- To build a creative environment, all ideas should be heard and treated with respect.
- Many seemingly foolish ideas can lead to sensible solutions.
- Ideas should never be criticized in public, since this will discourage people from voicing their suggestions.

ENCOURAGING IDEAS

Remember that you are aiming to encourage people to come up with their own ideas and opinions. You will learn little about your team members, or their ideas, by simply telling them what to do. Frame questions that will prompt appraisees to voice their ideas and take ownership of what is agreed. For example, you could ask what difficulties they have faced and how they might overcome them next time. Your staff are likely to be far more knowledgeable about their jobs than you are. You also want to hear their opinions, not simply a reflection of your views.

AVOIDING BIAS

One of the key attributes of a good appraiser is the ability to stand back and think about an issue before making a decision. This is especially important when conducting appraisals, since it is vital to avoid jumping to conclusions based on superficial information. Many people tend to form opinions of others based on their past experiences of them, or may assume that an individual who shares one attribute with another person also has other qualities in common with them. There are a number of well-known types of bias that a good appraiser should learn to recognize to ensure that they are in the best position to avoid them.

QUESTIONS TO ASK YOURSELF

Q Am I treating all my team members equally and fairly?

Q Do I work hard to avoid unfair treatment of individuals whom I may not particularly like?

Q Have I identified my unfair biases, and am I avoiding them successfully?

Q What am I doing to build rapport with people whom I like less than others?

RECOGNIZING TYPES OF BIAS

TYPE OF BIAS	RECOGNIZING THE SIGNS
HALO/HORNS	A tendency to allow one or two favourable or unfavourable personal attributes to colour your judgment, such as assuming that an attractive and articulate individual is also intelligent.
PREJUDICE	The judgment of an appraisee is clouded by personal views of a particular group or type of people, or the fact that they resemble or remind you of an acquaintance.
"SIMILAR TO ME"	A tendency to like people we see as being similar to ourselves and therefore to recruit, and even promote, in our own likeness. This leads to unbalanced teams, where all members have the same strengths.
DISTORTED PERSONALITY THEORY	The inclination to base an evaluation of appraisees on distorted personality traits, such as assuming that someone needs to be extrovert in order to be a good sales person.
GOOD WORKER	The propensity to have a mental image of a good worker, and to favour only those appraisees who match that image. This can result in unfair criticism of appraisees who fail to fit the stereotype.

42 Aim to ask an appraisee to express what success would look or feel like to them.

BEING RESULTS-ORIENTED

Make sure that the appraisal will be focused on what is important. If you discuss side issues at length, you risk misdirecting a team member's productivity by leading them to think that these are important. You should also avoid subjective or judgmental comments. Having set targets and standards for what is important, allow appraisees to express results in a way that makes sense to them. An appraisee's success criteria can be just as valid and motivating for them as quantitative criteria. Nevertheless, it is vital for you both to agree on what is to be measured, so that there are clear indicators of what has been achieved.

PLANNING THE STRUCTURE

A good appraisal is well structured. Establish the order of proceedings, and plan to get the meeting off to a positive start. Then consider how to focus the appraisee on key areas for discussion and deliver feedback effectively.

43 Make sure that every appraisal follows the same six-step structure.

STARTING POSITIVELY

Always aim to begin every appraisal with a strong motivational statement and an easy question to ease the appraisee into the session and help them to relax. Next, you should agree on the purpose of the meeting, and outline what will be covered. Plan to say that you will review progress on each objective, one at a time. Aim to give the appraisee the chance to comment first, with questions such as, "How do you think your performance went in this area?" You will have the facts in front of you, both in terms of what has been achieved and of the feedback you are expecting to give. However, by allowing the appraisee to speak first, you encourage the process of self-assessment, and in identifying where you have different perceptions, you can explore the reasons why.

FOLLOWING THE SIX-STEP APPRAISAL STRUCTURE

Introduction — Establish the positive purpose of the meeting

Agenda — Agree items for discussion with the appraisee

Discussion — Initiate two-way communication

Action plan — Agree actions needed to achieve objectives

Summary — Ask appraisee to summarize agreed actions

Follow up — Monitor action plan and objectives

SETTING THE AGENDA

There is a limit to the number of issues you can effectively tackle during the appraisal, so plan to focus the appraisee on key areas so that you can agree a measurable number of objectives, say six. You may have other items to review, such as special projects, and the appraisee is likely to have their own items for discussion. It is important to remember that the appraisal is not the time to catch up on operational matters. You will be holding the discussion not as part of your day-to-day management of the team, but to review the individual's overall performance and skills, set new objectives for the period ahead, and agree a development plan. Any other business, such as a disciplinary matter, is outside the scope of the meeting and should be left out.

44 Try to cut your planned agenda in half to see if that improves the focus.

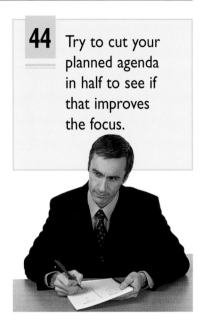

45 Focus on matters that have a direct impact on performance.

BEING CONSTRUCTIVE

If you have to give negative feedback, do so constructively, encouraging people to look forward, not backward. Avoid demotivating a potentially good appraisee by sounding over-critical. If performance has suffered, look first at your own leadership. Have you misjudged their level of skill, or failed to provide support? If there are no external reasons, then the appraisee needs to understand the impact of the problem. Plan how to tackle the issues constructively. How will you get them to acknowledge that a problem exists? Think of questions that will prompt the appraisee to find solutions. He or she will be more committed to resolving matters if the idea is their own.

MAINTAINING A POSITIVE TONE ▼
Aim to "sandwich" critical remarks between positive points of praise so that you keep the ratio of two expressions of praise to one expression of criticism.

| **Praise** | **Criticize** | **Praise** |

MANAGING THE APPRAISAL

Managing the appraisal involves careful choreography of the discussion. Become an effective appraiser by following a set format while remaining flexible at all times.

INTRODUCING THE SESSION

The start of a meeting sets the tone for what is to come. Launch the interview successfully by putting the appraisee at ease. Build their confidence, agree what will be discussed, and explain how the meeting will be conducted to give them time to relax.

46 Make sure that the appraisee knows exactly what to expect.

47 Put the appraisee at ease as quickly as possible.

48 Stress that the appraisal will have a positive result.

BUILDING CONFIDENCE

Many appraisees feel nervous and apprehensive at the start of their appraisal. Help them to overcome their anxieties by creating a welcoming, encouraging atmosphere. Address any uncertainties by stressing the positive purpose of the meeting and informing them how long you expect it to last. To build trust and confidence, begin with a motivational statement that conveys faith in their ability. Then ask an easy question to start them talking. Do not launch abruptly into the session by asking a challenging question early on, since this will cause the appraisee to feel defensive.

49 Check that you both set off in the same direction.

AGREEING THE PURPOSE

Establish the purpose of the appraisal interview to clarify why you are both there. Set out what you need to achieve from the appraisal, focusing on the advantages to the appraisee, so that staff truly believe that the appraisal will ultimately benefit them. Explain that you will be agreeing an agenda first, reviewing the previous period, discussing progress on objectives and how development needs were met, and pinpointing any further needs that have arisen. Establish that you will be agreeing objectives for the period ahead and then identifying any development needs linked to new objectives or responsibilities.

USING AN APPRAISAL DOCUMENT ▼

Ask the appraisee to fill in an appraisal document as you progress through the appraisal. This will save the time and effort of transcribing notes later. If it has been decided that you should fill in the form, show the appraisee what you have written and gain their assent on every category.

Purpose of job should be clearly defined in a brief summary

APPRAISAL DOCUMENT

Overall purpose of job:
To plan and design engineering projects to meet client specification within budget/time estimates.

Key areas of responsibility	Objectives	Deadline	Review comments on outcome
1. To manage the X Port development project.	1. To keep in touch with clients at agreed frequency and chair steering meetings.	Jan – Feb	
	2. To submit proposal by Feb 12 and obtain project by end of March.	March 31	
	3. To source project support to within 90% of requirements.		
2. To develop communications within design team.	1. To hold monthly meetings to review projects and communicate results within one week.	Review in April	
	2. Evaluate clarity of drawings and communicate results to staff twice a week or as required.	By June	

Responsibilities will be broadly summarized

Objectives should be described in a brief but specific statement

Dates for progress review meeting need to be recorded

453

AGREEING THE AGENDA

*F*or an appraisal to run smoothly, both parties must agree on the items to be discussed. Alter your agenda to include some of the appraisee's ideas, explain how you will agree future objectives, and check that you have included all the important issues.

50 Focus on issues that are relevant to the objectives of the entire team.

51 Avoid being sidetracked by excessive or minor detail.

SEEKING INPUT

To ensure that the appraisee feels involved in the discussion you are about to have, ask them to add their own points to the agenda. Compare the importance of your agenda items with the topics that they wish to cover, and be prepared to change your agenda to accommodate them. Even if you regard their issues as less important, you must tackle some of them. If you ignore their concerns, they will feel that you are uninterested in their problems. By agreeing to include their points at this stage, you will also avoid problems later. An appraisee who has an axe to grind is likely to continue to attempt to bring the subject up, distracting you from your agenda. Be fair. If they are right, change the agenda.

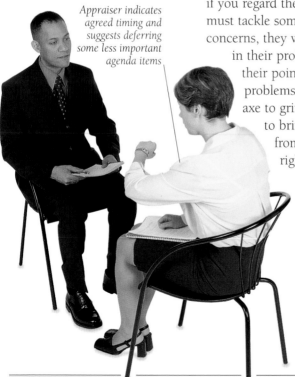

Appraiser indicates agreed timing and suggests deferring some less important agenda items

◀ DISCUSSING TIME CONSTRAINTS

It is unlikely that there will be time to discuss all the items tabled. Make sure that you agree at the outset which items will be included on the agenda, and which points will not be covered, so that you can arrange a meeting to handle outstanding matters at a later date.

DEVELOPING OBJECTIVES

The aim of the appraisal is to develop a set of objectives that the employee is committed to achieving. Agree with the appraisee that you will discuss each previous objective in turn to identify what went well, what did not go so well, and what the appraisee can do about it. This may simply be to continue to maintain high standards, or to develop their skills in order to improve their performance. Establish that you will be setting future objectives in the form of a jointly agreed action plan, with criteria to measure success. You will also agree on the importance of objectives to the team, to the organization and, most importantly, to the appraisee if they are successful.

52 See that the appraisee participates fully in creating the agenda so that they feel included and involved.

ASSESSING THE AGENDA

Check that the agenda focuses on the appraisee's performance as it stands now. Do not assume, for example, that he or she will see the link between success in a past project and using the same skills on a new and different future project. Do not duck issues – you risk setting objectives that the appraisee will accept with no hope of achieving. Ensure that the agenda includes finding out what the appraisee believes is achievable. They may feel they can achieve more than you thought possible. You will discuss this and identify why your views differ. You may find that you think more is achievable than they do, and will need to plan support and confidence-building activities.

ORDERING ITEMS FOR DISCUSSION

Review previous objectives

Praise achievements

Give constructive feedback

Identify development needs

Praise additional achievements

Agree new objectives

Agree further development needs

Plan and agree actions

Summarize

ENCOURAGING DISCUSSION

In a successful appraisal interview, the appraisee should be doing most of the talking. Encourage staff to take a leading role in the discussion by adopting good questioning techniques, then listening actively to the answers.

53 Keep asking questions to gain the appraisee's involvement.

54 Avoid interrupting once an appraisee has started talking.

55 Consider how to turn most of your closed questions into open ones.

ASKING QUESTIONS

Good questioning techniques are essential if you are to discover an appraisee's true opinions. When you understand how an individual feels, you can use this knowledge to help them improve their performance. By asking the right questions you encourage an appraisee to bring issues into the open, rather than harbour a problem so that it festers and hinders performance. Use questioning in a genuine attempt to find out how the appraisee feels about all aspects of their job. Listen to their answers. Avoid cross-examining the appraisee or asking leading questions in a bid to confirm a pre-conceived notion in your own mind.

USING OPEN QUESTIONS

An open question encourages an expansive answer, as opposed to a closed question, which typically prompts a one-word "yes" or "no" response. Frame open questions by starting with the words, "What", "When", "How", "Which", "Who" or "Why". If you ask open questions, such as, "What were the main learning points?", an appraisee is far more likely to express their ideas than if you ask a closed question, such as "Did you achieve this objective?" Look at the objectives you will be reviewing and come up with an open question to start the discussion on each one.

56 If an appraisee looks confused, ensure you are not using jargon that they do not understand.

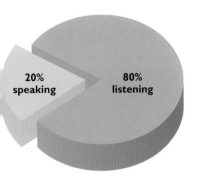

▲ LISTENING PROPERLY
Ideally, you should aim to spend about 80 per cent of the appraisal time listening, and only 20 per cent of the time speaking.

▼ SHOWING INTEREST
The appraiser in this example is an active listener; his body language demonstrates that he is giving his undivided attention to the appraisee and is concentrating on what is being said.

LISTENING ACTIVELY

Once you have encouraged the appraisee to start talking, listen actively to their answers. If you are listening actively, you will be able to glean far more from what is being said. Look at the appraisee and maintain good eye contact – but try to avoid staring. Bear in mind that even if you glance over their shoulder or out of the window, you will give the impression that you are not paying proper attention to what is being said. When the appraisee pauses, or draws to a conclusion, help them to build on their ideas by asking further questions. Be aware of the tone of voice that they are using, and listen out for subtleties of speech that may provide clues on what they truly think about their performance. This will enable you to build joint solutions by asking more questions such as, "What will help you to achieve even better results?"

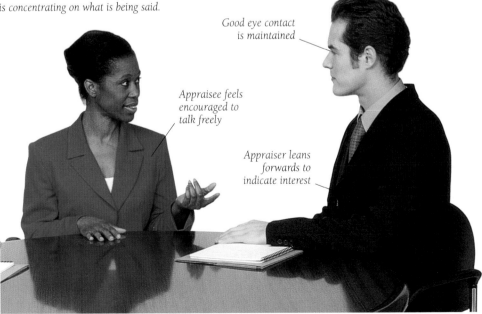

Good eye contact is maintained

Appraisee feels encouraged to talk freely

Appraiser leans forwards to indicate interest

BEING PRACTICAL

There may be a long list of issues to discuss in an appraisal, most of them with significant implications for the future. Ensure that you keep to the agreed timing, tackle all the important items, and prompt appraisees to reach realistic conclusions.

57 Aim to stick to the time allowed for the appraisal meeting.

58 If an appraisee hints at any problem, address it immediately.

KEEPING TO THE POINT

Stick to the agenda and focus on essential issues by controlling the discussion so that it does not stray from the appraisee's previous important objectives or those for the future. It is important to complete the appraisal in the time allocated or you risk spending longer than you can afford on appraising the entire team, and may be forced to postpone some appraisals. If a discussion on one point has overrun, consider which agenda items you can shorten, miss out, or deal with at a later date.

COVERING VITAL ISSUES

If, as a result of time constraints, you are unable to discuss an important issue in sufficient depth, agree to have another conversation on the topic at a later date – and keep to that next date. Avoid using this as an excuse to postpone difficult issues; the sooner these are out in the open, the better. If there is a hint that an appraisee is experiencing difficulty in any part of their job, discuss it immediately. Failure to address the situation is likely to worsen it. Avoid taking action that may alleviate a problem in the short term but compound it in the future. By offering to complete the task under discussion yourself, for example, you will not equip the appraisee to cope if the same circumstances recur.

POINTS TO REMEMBER

● If an issue has a high impact on performance but is not urgent, it may be dealt with later.

● If an issue is urgent but has little impact on performance, it may also be left for another day.

● Issues that have a high impact on performance and are urgent must be dealt with immediately.

59 Keep the tone relaxed but avoid time-wasting chat.

DOS AND DON'TS

✔ Do allow people to learn from their own mistakes.

✔ Do encourage people to think of ways of solving a problem.

✔ Do make your feedback and your agreements for the future absolutely clear.

✔ Do clarify the situation if an incorrect assumption has been made.

✘ Don't assume that you will have the best answer to a situation.

✘ Don't allow mistakes to cause people to fail in their objectives.

✘ Don't allow an appraisee to leave with an unrealistic view of their ability.

✘ Don't waste time discussing skills that the appraisee does not really need.

60 Under-promise during an appraisal and over-deliver afterwards, rather than over-promise and regret it.

CONSIDERING IMPLICATIONS

Bear in mind that what you say to an appraisee may have repercussions beyond the hour or so you spend with them. It is important to avoid agreeing to any action that may have an adverse effect on the team or on the organization itself. If, for example, you agree that an appraisee should attend an external training course to obtain qualifications that are not directly relevant to their job, this could create a precedent. The result of this may be that you find yourself being pressured by other members of the team to be given similar advantages.

MOVING FORWARD

At some point, both parties need to draw a line on the past and think of the future. This is particularly true if the past has been inherited and has left legacies that cannot be changed. When you come to the natural end of a discussion of the past, signal the time to move forward by talking about the action plan. Focus on future objectives and what you both think will work from now on. Talk about future milestones and deadlines that have to be achieved. Ask the appraisee to summarize the actions you have agreed, to check that you both have the same understanding of what has to be done.

FOCUSING ON THE FUTURE ▼
Encourage the team member to look to the future and motivate them by explaining how future action plans will benefit the appraisee, the team, and the organization.

Manager points out that time management course should put an end to having to work late

READING THE SIGNALS

Some people struggle to raise concerns in a straightforward manner. Understand the role that body language plays so that you can read an appraisee's body posture and facial expression to gauge whether they are holding back or responding positively.

61 Avoid reading too much into a single gesture – look for clusters of them.

62 If an appraisee looks tense, ensure that you look relaxed yourself.

IDENTIFYING ANXIETIES

You may need to coax an appraisee into speaking their mind, particularly if they are worried about what you will think, or do not know you very well. Begin with questions about easy and positive issues. Smile and maintain good eye contact. Watch for agitation and concern; this could imply that the conversation has turned towards issues they would rather hide. Listen to the content of replies and to the tone of voice used. Keep asking questions to get to the bottom of the matter, even if you are covering the same ground again.

WATCHING FACIAL EXPRESSION

When two people have a good rapport, they will look at one another throughout their conversation, turning away only to blink or think. The level of eye contact provides many clues to how your appraisee is feeling. If, for example, the appraisee avoids eye contact, there is probably a reason. Perhaps he or she does not wish to discuss the issue, is having difficulty in facing it, or is not telling the whole truth. Watch for changes in facial expression. If an appraisee looks away at a particular point, ask questions in that area to discover what is troubling them. Avoid taking notes when an appraisee is discussing an important point, since this will interrupt eye contact and prevent you from gauging their expression.

Head held straight but relaxed shows confidence

▲ SHOWING OPENNESS

By maintaining direct eye contact with you, this appraisee is signalling that a good rapport has been established.

CHECKING CONFIDENCE

Watch how an appraisee reacts to taking on each action as you proceed through the agenda. Look for any signals that they are not totally comfortable with what you are asking of them. It is important that the appraisee does not have reservations that will prevent them from achieving their objective. For example, if you are asking the appraisee to take on a new project or task, question them to assess their understanding of the task and their plan for carrying it out. You should be able to determine their level of confidence from their tone of voice and facial expressions as they answer. If the appraisee says "Yes", but in a hesitant fashion, this signals an undisclosed concern, or barrier, to achieving success. Use open questions to explore this area until you achieve the response of an unqualified "Yes", delivered in a firm tone of voice. Look out for phrases such as, "Yes, but ..." and "Fairly happy ...", since both indicate a lack of confidence. Continue the discussion until you receive unqualified agreement.

> **63** Watch an appraisee's eye movements – they can give a lot away.

CULTURAL DIFFERENCES

The Japanese tend to behave more formally than Europeans or Americans, which makes their body language more difficult to read. In the United States, body language is used to build rapport quickly, which may appear over-friendly and therefore be thought insincere by Europeans, who are more restrained.

Expression indicates undisclosed feelings

Tensing of the muscles around the eyes shows contemplation

Questioning expression indicates a lack of commitment

▲ HAVING RESERVATIONS
By looking downwards while thinking, this appraisee indicates that he may have some doubts, which you will need to explore.

▲ FRAMING A RESPONSE
This appraisee is looking straight ahead but not necessarily in focus, suggesting that he is visualizing how he should respond.

▲ FEELING UNCOMFORTABLE
By her expression, this appraisee is signalling that she lacks commitment to doing what has been asked of her.

ADOPTING THE RIGHT POSTURE

Always maintain an open posture, keeping your hands relaxed at your sides or in your lap. By being relaxed yourself, you will encourage the appraisee to relax, too. Make sure that the room is neither too hot nor too cold, but is at a comfortable temperature that encourages both of you to sit comfortably. Avoid crossing your arms, since this suggests either defensiveness or that you are putting up a barrier, and avoid leaning an elbow on the desk, which could be interpreted as an aggressive gesture. Remember that you are leading the discussion, so it is important to work at looking relaxed, even if you, too, are nervous at the outset.

CULTURAL DIFFERENCES

Body language conveys varying messages in different countries. In Latin cultures, for example, touch is used as a way of establishing and maintaining rapport. In more formal cultures such as in Japan, Scandinavia, and northern Europe, this would be considered an invasion of private space. A nod in Middle Eastern countries would signal disagreement rather than assent.

64 Remember that body language speaks more than words.

65 Be aware that if an appraisee leans back and crosses their hands, it signals reluctance.

NOTING AN APPRAISEE'S POSTURE

Look at the appraisee's posture. If he or she is perched on the edge of their seat, this suggests nervousness or anxiety. Relax them by using a friendly tone of voice, a smile, and plenty of open questions. If an appraisee places their elbows on the table, or clenches their fists, they could be feeling suspicious or even aggressive. Keep your own body language open, but neutral, and stress to the appraisee how the appraisal will benefit them.

DOS AND DON'TS

✔ Do observe what happens when you alter your body posture or expression.

✔ Do check that an appraisee's body language matches their words.

✘ Don't interrupt or use a judgmental or condescending tone of voice

✘ Don't look down at your notes for long periods, since this can reduce rapport.

MIRRORING BODY LANGUAGE

The study of Neuro-Linguistic Programming (NLP) provides further insights into the meaning of body language. One premise of NLP is that if two people are enjoying a good rapport, they will mirror one another's postures and use similar gestures. When one party leans forward slightly because they are interested in what is being said, the other party also tends to lean forward. When first-class rapport occurs, people may even mirror one another's breathing patterns. You can use NLP techniques to create empathy and ease tension by subtly mirroring an appraisee's posture. NLP practitioners also observe that people move their eyes according to what they are thinking. Thus you can gauge an individual's inner feelings by watching their eye movements.

66 Be aware of your own body posture at all times.

67 Encourage an appraisee with a friendly smile.

▼ INFLUENCING POSTURE

You can use mirroring techniques to alter the posture of an appraisee. By adopting a relaxed but alert posture yourself, you encourage the appraisee to mirror your positive body language.

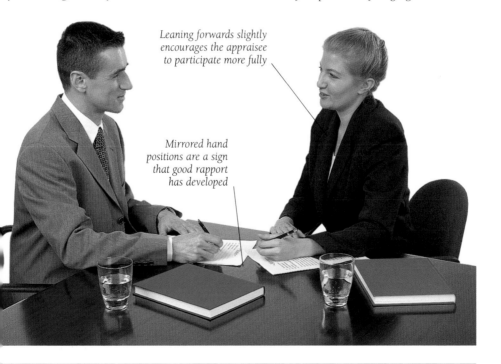

Leaning forwards slightly encourages the appraisee to participate more fully

Mirrored hand positions are a sign that good rapport has developed

ASSESSING COMMITMENT

People turn good intentions into achievement when they are committed to taking action. Check that appraisees take full ownership of their objectives before, during, and after the appraisal. If commitment is lacking, take steps to find out why.

68 If you spot doubts, question until you gain an appraisee's commitment.

POINTS TO REMEMBER

- An appraisee who is not committed to taking action will nevertheless find ways to avoid saying a direct "No" to their appraiser's suggestions.
- The detection of a lack of commitment early on makes it easier to avoid problems later.
- An appraisee who feels that they have been pressurized into agreement is unlikely to be truly committed.

ANTICIPATING COMMITMENT

If you know an appraisee, you will be able to anticipate their level of commitment more easily. Consider whether they have agreed to undertake a task in the past but failed to deliver. Do they keep you up to date with progress regularly, or only when you intervene to ask for information? This knowledge will help you to decide how assertive you need to be to ensure that the appraisee is committed to carrying out action plans. If an appraisee is new to your team, you should make these judgments during the appraisal.

OBSERVING COMMITMENT

It is important to observe the degree of enthusiasm and commitment the appraisee shows towards agreed objectives and performance levels throughout the appraisal. There are a number of signs that an appraisee is becoming committed to the task. If, for example, they begin to elaborate on plans for achieving an objective, or start asking questions about implementation and who should be informed about the objective, these are positive signals of commitment. To test commitment, use a closed question aimed at prompting an unequivocal "Yes". If an appraisee is unwilling to commit, he or she will ask more questions, or voice doubts.

69 Watch how keenly an appraisee accepts responsibility.

70 Practical questions or suggestions indicate readiness to commit.

AGREEING REVIEW DATES

Encourage the appraisee to suggest an appropriate time to review progress in achieving milestones. In setting dates themselves, they take control of their own progress and will be more committed than if review dates are imposed. Before agreeing dates, take the appraisee's experience into account: more frequent reviews may be needed for inexperienced staff. Make clear any exceptions to the timetable, such as the need to be informed of any issues that could put a critical deadline or project at risk.

71 Stress that you will not interfere – but that you expect to be kept advised.

72 Be careful to avoid accepting a glib "Yes".

RECOGNIZING COMMITMENT ▼

Committed appraisees keep their manager well informed of progress, ask for help when needed, and discuss their tasks with colleagues. Uncommitted appraisees tend to avoid their manager and all discussion of the task at hand.

REVIEWING COMMITMENT

An appraisee who is committed to a task will prioritize it. If they find that they cannot achieve a date, they will try to negotiate extra time or suggest dropping less urgent actions in order to complete the task. If an appraisee has no intention of performing the task, you are unlikely to find out until after the deadline for completion. To review commitment, consider whether the appraisee approaches you with problems in good time. If you have to chase an appraisee, you must address why they have not taken ownership of their task.

POSITIVE COMMITMENT

Shows enthusiasm

Solves problems

Reports on progress

Displays initiative

POOR COMMITMENT

Displays resignation

Ignores problems

Maintains silence

Lacks initiative

HANDLING DIFFICULT SITUATIONS

An appraisal is almost certain to cause staff to worry, since their capabilities are under discussion and their future is at stake. Be prepared to deal with the unexpected, and learn how to handle difficult situations with authority and sensitivity.

73 Try to anticipate negative responses and plan how to deal with them.

HANDLING UNEXPECTED CHALLENGES

It is important to deal with challenges when they happen if you are to retain your credibility. If an appraisee challenges your authority, or your facts, try to deal with this at once. When you need time to think, use open questions to press the person to clarify their point. Should an appraisee reveal information of which you had no prior knowledge, or that sheds new light on a situation, check whether this affects the feedback you had planned.

Manager takes a long pause before calmly responding to challenge

Appraisee airs grievances and challenges manager's facts

Manager listens while appraisee speaks his mind

▲ DEALING WITH DIFFICULT PEOPLE

This illustration shows how, by remaining calm and framing her response with care, the appraiser was able to instigate a more productive discussion and agree actions to which the appraisee was fully committed.

RECOGNIZING YOUR LIMITATIONS

During the appraisal, your team member may reveal information that could affect their ability to do their job. You could discover, for example, that they have a serious illness which they had kept to themselves. Maintain a balance in your aims as manager. While it is important to motivate and build relationships with individuals, you must consider the success of your team and organization. Be sympathetic, but do not start altering the existing sickness policy at the appraisal.

74 Recognize when to seek guidance from colleagues or professionals.

75 Endeavour to remain calm and in control at all times.

Appraisee recovers and the discussion is concluded successfully

When progess is reviewed, appraisee is successfully carrying out action plan

Manager becomes irritated and interrupts appraisee

Appraisee reacts angrily, appraisal is stopped, and his performance begins to deteriorate

STOPPING THE APPRAISAL

In some circumstances, your only way forward may be to stop the appraisal. First, do all that you can to defuse a difficult situation. If an individual is upset, allow them to recover their composure and continue when you can. Be sympathetic if tears are genuine, but be wary of tears designed to deflect you from your feedback. Try to move on and get them to focus on the next agenda item, which, if you are following the praise, criticize, praise principle, should be more positive. If the appraisee has stopped listening, however, there is little point in continuing. Set a date to finish the appraisal as soon as possible.

DEALING WITH PERFORMANCE PROBLEMS

Tackling poor performance effectively is a challenge for all managers. Gain acknowledgment that a problem exists, then you can deal with it constructively by identifying causes and asking appraisees to come up with effective solutions.

76 Use good questioning techniques to explore solutions.

77 Avoid discussing problems that do not affect performance.

GAINING AGREEMENT

Before you can correct a problem, the appraisee must acknowledge that a problem exists. It is important that they realize the adverse impact of their actions on meeting their objectives, or they will not commit to solving the problem. Explain how their performance has affected that of their team or the organization. Ask questions to check that the team member has now accepted that there is a problem. Make sure that they fully understand where they have gone wrong and the impact of allowing the situation to continue.

IDENTIFYING CAUSES

Having gained agreement that a performance problem exists, explore the reasons and look for ways of resolving it. Ask the appraisee to analyze the cause; he or she may provide valuable insight into what has gone wrong. Some problems have multiple causes. If a person is falling behind with their work, for example, there may be a need for skills training. But are there other factors to consider? Watch out for excuses or blaming other departments – make sure that the appraisee takes the responsibility they should.

QUESTIONS TO ASK YOURSELF

Q Could problems with organizational processes be contributing to a shortfall in performance?

Q Is the machinery being used adequate for the job?

Q Is an insufficient budget holding the individual back?

Q Are the materials being used appropriate for the job?

ADDRESSING PERFORMANCE PROBLEMS

PROBLEM	WAYS TO ADDRESS IT
CAPABILITY The inability to perform the job as defined, perhaps as a result of a selection error or lack of experience.	● Provide support and training to enable the appraisee to tackle the job effectively. ● If training is not the answer, consider transferring the employee to a more suitable role.
TRAINING A lack of necessary skills or information that is preventing the employee from performing to standard.	● Identify gaps in knowledge, skills, or approach, and select appropriate development activities to help the appraisee meet required standards. ● Set objectives for continuous improvement.
MOTIVATION A decrease in effectiveness due to under-stimulation, or boredom, or stress resulting from too great a challenge.	● Identify development activities that will re-energize the appraisee in their role. ● Review tasks that have been delegated to the appraisee – are you over-stretching them?
DISTRACTION An inability to concentrate and be effective at work, perhaps due to a personal problem that is claiming an individual's attention.	● Be sympathetic. If necessary, agree time off work so that problems can be attended to. ● Recognize when to refer an appraisee to experts if performance fails to pick up.
ALIENATION A rejection of, and feeling of non-involvement in, the job and organization where there is a history of long-term frustration.	● Find out how the problem has arisen: is it the result of lack of challenge or neglect? ● Consider referral to a career counsellor to help the employee to resolve their issues.

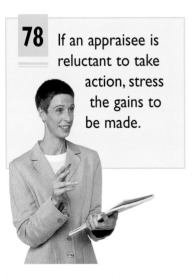

78 If an appraisee is reluctant to take action, stress the gains to be made.

FINDING SOLUTIONS

The best solutions are those that appraisees discover themselves. Ask the appraisee to come up with a plan to resolve or avoid the problem next time. Offer your own ideas only if necessary. Discuss the options before making a decision. If their solution is unrealistic, prompt them to discuss its advantages and disadvantages, or ask them to consider the risks associated with their proposal. By asking such questions, you can help the appraisee to choose a more workable plan of action. Finally, agree a short- and long-term action plan that will immediately bring performance into line, and then continuously improve it.

DISCUSSING DEVELOPMENT

Training and development activities are aimed at helping appraisees to achieve their objectives and improve both short- and long-term performance. Choose activities and methods of learning to suit the appraisee, then agree on learning objectives.

79 Keep the long term in mind when planning development.

80 See that personal development plans are dynamic and kept up to date.

DOCUMENTING DEVELOPMENT ▼
Ask the appraisee to record their training needs and learning objectives on their personal development plan as you discuss them. Details of the activity should be recorded by the appraiser.

DEFINING DEVELOPMENT

Training and development activities are designed to continuously improve team members' skills and capabilities in their current roles, and to develop their future potential. They help staff to welcome and learn from change, work more effectively, and take on wider responsibilities. Activities are documented in personal development plans (PDPs), which map out current and future development goals. To agree activities positively, first talk to the appraisee about their strengths to show that you value their contribution. Then discuss areas where development is needed.

PERSONAL DEVELOPMENT PLAN

Name: NORMAN JACKSON

Development need	Activity	When	Learning objective	Results
To understand how to prioritize tasks, allocate sufficient time to each, and achieve tasks by deadline Tools and tips to help organize myself better would be very useful.	1 day time management workshop Value: £220 externally provided by external training provider	October	I will be able to plan my time more effectively and achieve what is important	● Learned tools and techniques to organize and plan my day more efficiently ● My performance has improved in that I can more effectively focus on important priorities

Appraisee should summarize training requirements

Appraiser describes activity with details of cost, and provider

Appraisee should define what he hopes to gain from activity

Appraisee should record outcome of training activity once completed

CHOOSING A METHOD OF DEVELOPMENT

Training is often conducted on the job, with an appraisee being coached by their manager or a colleague, but other methods can be used to accelerate the learning process. Discuss the options with the appraisee to identify what is best for them. What is their preferred method of learning? Do they learn faster by doing a job themselves, or by having the job demonstrated to them? Do they enjoy reading, or would they gain more from computer-based learning? Decide on the method, when training should take place, and then plan the dates and make the necessary arrangements.

81 Ascertain what type of previous training has taught the appraisee most.

82 Encourage people to take up every opportunity for development.

SELECTING ACTIVITIES

The following are examples of possible development activities:

- Coaching and mentoring;
- Shadowing a colleague;
- Reading journals/books;
- Attending courses or workshops;
- Taking on delegated tasks;
- Attending project meetings;
- Being rotated in a role or transferred to a new job;
- Going on secondment;
- Attending conferences, briefings, or seminars;
- Studying for professional or work-related qualifications, such as first aid, health and safety, or business management.

WRITING LEARNING OBJECTIVES

Just as you agree clear business objectives with measures of success for appraisees, so you also need to establish what they should learn from undertaking training courses or other development activities. Defining learning objectives gives direction to training and allows you to monitor whether activities are meeting the needs of the team and its members. Consider what you want the learner to be able to do by the end of the activity, and how well you want them to able to do it. This gives you learning objectives with two constituents – a verb and a standard. For example, if you plan to send an appraisee to learn more about the service you offer to customers, a learning objective might be that at the end of training, the appraisee will be able to answer customer queries on three of your products. Even on formal training courses that already have general learning objectives, you should still tailor objectives to describe your appraisee's particular needs.

DISCUSSING ASPIRATIONS AND POTENTIAL

Most people aspire to take on more senior roles and further their careers. Take the opportunity to discuss an appraisee's future aspirations and potential so that you can help them prepare for advancement in the future.

83 Talk about long-term prospects as well as short-term objectives.

PLANNING FOR THE FUTURE

Find out about an appraisee's aspirations for the future so that you can plan the support and development they need. Use open questions to explore how they envisage their current role changing over the next year. Then ask what the appraisee would like to be doing in, say, one to two years' time. Aim to identify development needs for both time frames. There are many ways of meeting development needs, such as special projects, site visits, or preparing to present to colleagues, that will enable an individual to gain more experience or skills.

Recognizing his potential, manager arranges training to help him further his career

Appraisee outlines his hopes of being promoted to a more senior role

▲ BUILDING CAREERS
This illustration shows how training an appraisee who is able to take on more responsibility benefits the organization, and how, when aspirations are not realized, the individual becomes frustrated and decides to leave.

ANTICIPATING CAREER MOVES

Be aware of your organization's policy on career development. Look at the career paths that other people in your organization, or team, have followed. This will give you a better idea of the career moves that might be possible and enable you to answer an appraisee's questions on the subject. If an appraisee is ambitious and has the potential, a move in one or two years may well involve transferring to another part of the organization. Even if you support it, do not agree to a potential move if you are not in a position to help it happen, or if it is not in line with company policy.

Appraisee's aspirations are realized when he is promoted to lead a new project team

Appraisee receives no training, becomes demotivated, and decides to find a new job

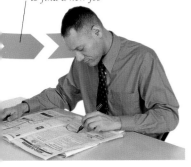

BENEFITING YOUR ORGANIZATION

It is important to keep the needs of your organization in mind throughout the appraisal. Complete any career development documentation, and make sure that the human resources department and senior managers know about people in your team who have potential. Avoid trying to keep people on the team for as long as possible because you have trained and developed them: remember that new recruits inject new ideas. Remember, too, that senior management prefers "net exporters" of team members to managers who hoard their own people. Aim to become known as a manager who develops and encourages people, since this will result in more people wanting to join your team.

DOS AND DON'TS

✔ Do look for ways of promoting people who are capable of doing more.

✔ Do plan how to replace people who are promoted off your team.

✘ Don't pass poor performers onto colleagues in other departments.

✘ Don't assume that your staff will be happy to remain in their current jobs.

PLANNING ACTION

*I*n order for an appraisee to achieve
objectives, it is vital that they know
who is responsible for which actions and
the deadlines for carrying them out. Agree
and document a detailed action plan that
sets out what needs to be done.

84 Ensure that someone is accountable for every action.

85 Always carry out your own commitments on time.

CREATING AN ACTION PLAN ▼

*Draw up an action plan to provide
a record of actions agreed. It may be
no more than a simple note of chasing
up information, or it may be a
more detailed rundown of new
responsibilities or projects.*

DOCUMENTING ACTIONS

Write down actions that arise from your discussion about objectives to ensure that you have a record of what has been agreed. This will avoid any misunderstandings or disagreements later. Use a prepared form, or ask the appraisee to use a notepad. Be careful to avoid dictating an action plan, since this will not encourage the appraisee to commit to it. As the appraiser, you may also be responsible for a few actions, primarily those concerned with resourcing training and development, or informing people in other areas of your organization that the appraisee has your authority to act.

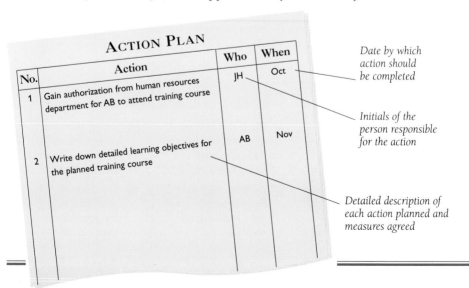

ACTION PLAN

No.	Action	Who	When
1	Gain authorization from human resources department for AB to attend training course	JH	Oct
2	Write down detailed learning objectives for the planned training course	AB	Nov

Date by which action should be completed

Initials of the person responsible for the action

Detailed description of each action planned and measures agreed

Planning a Project

A project is a series of activities designed to achieve a specific outcome to a set budget and timescale. Some of the objectives you agree may well constitute a project. If you assign a project to the appraisee during the appraisal, help them to use the discipline of project management to improve their performance. Make sure that you can measure success quantitatively and qualitatively. Finally, if you have any doubts about the appraisee's ability to complete the project successfully, address them. Decide how the appraisee can overcome the skills gap, or close it with training and development.

Planning Diaries

To help the appraisee use their own initiative and take ownership of their objectives, it is important that you keep the actions that you agree to in an appraisee's action plan to a minimum. However, there may be issues that are beyond their control, such as ensuring that they are given the authority to manage a project or work towards an objective. Let the appraisee know what you need to do, so that you can both note the dates by which actions will be completed. After the appraisal, allocate the time and resources you need to enable you to support the appraisee's achievement of their objectives without doing their job for them.

AGREEING DATES ▶
Make sure that there are no discrepancies regarding what actions are expected to be done when, and by whom, by writing dates in both the appraiser's and appraisee's diaries.

Assigning a New Project

Establish the overall purpose of the project

↓

Define the objectives of the project in detail

↓

Outline constraints and find ways to tackle them

↓

Ask the appraisee to list key milestones of the project

↓

Agree on how achievement of milestones will be measured

↓

Check that it is feasible for the appraisee to succeed in project

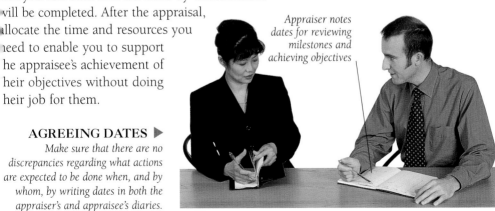

Appraiser notes dates for reviewing milestones and achieving objectives

SUMMARIZING THE APPRAISAL

*D*ocumenting a summary of the appraisal provides a vital record for both parties, and for the organization, of what has been agreed. Agree a detailed summary with the appraisee as a final check that they are committed to their action plan.

86 Listen carefully to what an appraisee says, and observe how they say it.

87 Avoid dictating to an appraisee – allow them to use their own words

INVOLVING THE APPRAISEE

Using their notes, or the form that they have filled in, let the appraisee summarize what has been agreed as a final check that they are committed to the action plan. If the appraisee finds it difficult to sum up the action plan in their own words, this indicates that they have not fully understood what needs to be done. Discuss those areas that are causing uncertainty to ensure that you both take away the same result from the appraisal.

CASE STUDY

Nigel's manager, Helen, had run out of time at the end of his appraisal. As a result, she had not asked Nigel to summarize the last action plan in his own words. The appraisal over, Helen was expecting Nigel to choose some stationery and order it from their usual supplier as part of a long-term contract. However, Nigel thought that he had been asked to choose the stationery and then approach several suppliers for a quotation. The misunderstanding came to light the following day when Nigel explained to Helen that stationery could not be delivered on time. Helen asked why, and explained that it was not necessary to go out to tender. She then asked Nigel to state the actions he was going to take to meet the schedule. This avoided further misunderstanding and the stationery duly arrived just before it was needed.

◀ SECURING CONFIRMATION

By failing to ask Nigel to summarize an action in his own words, Helen paved the way for misunderstanding. Fortunately, the miscommunication came to light the next day, when she was able to rectify her oversight. This time, she asked Nigel to state exactly what his subsequent actions would be, clarifying the situation for them both, and ensuring the prompt delivery of the stationery.

CLEARING UP MISUNDERSTANDINGS

If an appraisee omits a vital point from their summary, or misinterprets an issue, respond immediately. The appraisee may have altered the content, or the tone of what was said, perhaps to avoid taking action. Do not allow a misunderstanding to continue, since it will be difficult to raise the issue again without damaging the credibility and trust you have built up. If you need clarification, ask the appraisee to repeat the point, or give your own summary and check that you are both on the same wavelength.

POINTS TO REMEMBER

● Misunderstandings are often caused by wishful listening – hearing only what you want to hear.
● It is best to get things right the first time.
● People should be allowed to express and summarize action plans in their own style.
● Misunderstandings that are allowed to continue can often result in a loss of trust.

88 You should both leave the appraisal with the same understanding.

SEEKING CONFIRMATION

Aim to end the appraisal with an agreement that is satisfactory to both of you. If there is no time to reach total agreement on important areas, arrange to discuss the issues again later. You have now completed the appraisal form, the personal development plan and/or the action plan. Produce copies of these for yourself, the appraisee, and, if required, for the human resources department.

GETTING FEEDBACK

In order to develop your own skills, immediately after the appraisal ask the appraisee to give you feedback on how valuable the session has been for them. Find out how well the person thought you listened and whether the output, including action plans and personal development plans, has been worthwhile. Ask an open question such as, "How useful has this appraisal been?" Ask which parts were most useful and what could be improved upon. Giving honest feedback to an appraiser can be difficult, so observe their body language and listen to their tone of voice to ascertain whether they are being open, or keeping opinions to themselves. If you doubt their positivity, probe further until they voice any misgivings they were concealing. Ask for an additional evaluation later on (perhaps at a review session) with the question, "What results do you attribute to our last appraisal?"

FOLLOWING UP THE APPRAISAL

Following up after an appraisal is key to maintaining motivation and progress. Monitor activities and development, and evaluate the appraisee's and your own ability to benefit from the process.

MONITORING PROGRESS

To ensure that appraisals result in the long-term benefits they set out to achieve, progress must be closely monitored. Hold the correct types of review at the appropriate time, and understand how to conduct them effectively.

89 Hold a short review, even if an appraisee is making good progress.

90 Ensure that you understand how people are feeling.

91 Try to anticipate problem areas for the appraisee.

USING REVIEWS

Hold reviews to check that milestones are being achieved between appraisals, to identify strengths and recognize shortcomings, and to build confidence. Staying in touch with an appraisee's progress will motivate them to keep improving. Choose a type of review that is appropriate to the appraisee, according to their progress and competence level. Allow experienced staff to meet deadlines on their own as far as possible, but hold more frequent reviews for newcomers, those who have taken on challenging new responsibilities, or those whose objectives are particularly stretching.

DEFINING TYPES OF REVIEW

TYPE OF REVIEW	WHEN TO USE IT
QUICK UPDATE A spontaneous, short, and informal review with no agenda.	This is useful when people are handling a new task or role, or if something has just happened with implications for the staff member or project.
AD-HOC REVIEW A 10–15 minute review with the purpose of discussing a specific topic.	This is held if the appraisee or appraiser are concerned that an objective may be under threat and need to plan how to tackle the problem.
CHECKPOINT REVIEW A pre-planned meeting to monitor milestones as agreed with the appraisee.	This is used to check that progress is on target, objectives are being met, and all is progressing according to plan.
EVALUATION REVIEW A formal meeting held at the end of every project to assess its effectiveness.	This provides an opportunity to find out what has been learned, to check that objectives were met, and that they were appropriate.

CARRYING OUT REVIEWS

While it is important that you build in checkpoints to ensure that the expected progress is being made, avoid interfering to deal with minor mistakes. Instead, use reviews to ensure that both you and the appraisee understand the nature of progress to date. Ask open questions to encourage the appraisee to admit to problems, if they exist. Assess their level of confidence, and listen for unsolicited comments that might signal doubts that they can achieve what is required. If there is a problem that the individual is finding difficult to put right, offer your support, but do not press them to accept it if they turn it down. Your aim is to encourage them to take ownership of the activity, think problems through, and only then offer solutions. Avoid becoming too involved in detail, since this will result in too much of your time being taken up in review meetings and cause the appraisee to think that you do not trust them.

QUESTIONS TO ASK APPRAISEES

Q What has been achieved and what have we learned?

Q How well do you think that we have worked together?

Q Which factors have helped your progress and which have hindered it?

Q What further development needs have you identified?

Q How do you think what has happened so far might change the way in which we work together in the future?

Q Are you happy to take responsibility for carrying this improvement action forward?

Q Can you foresee any problems that could hinder your progress in the future?

IMPLEMENTING DEVELOPMENT PLANS

To help staff develop their skills and knowledge as agreed in the appraisal, consider which development activities are most suitable. Review development plans frequently, and help appraisees to monitor their progress as they implement them.

92 Promote the sharing of insights and experience among your team.

93 It is never too late for anyone to learn new skills.

DEVELOPING YOURSELF▼
Learning should be a continuous process, no matter what your age. The more skills and experiences you acquire, the more confident and knowledgeable you become.

PROMOTING LIFELONG LEARNING

Each team member has a unique set of skills, knowledge, and experience that shapes their attitudes and behaviour. Your team members may be aware of at least some of their strengths, but the feedback that you give during appraisals helps people to recognize all the skills, knowledge, and experience they have acquired. Realizing what they have learned, and continuing to learn new skills, increases confidence and promotes a willingness to use more initiative and take risks.

Discuss the development plan you agreed during the appraisal with each individual, so that they take ownership of it and become familiar with the continual process of learning and self-development.

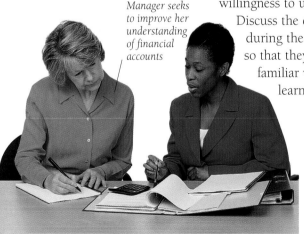

Manager seeks to improve her understanding of financial accounts

94 Encourage people to greet new challenges with enthusiasm.

IMPLEMENTING AND REVIEWING THE PLAN

Look for development activities that benefit the organization, the team, and the team member. If, for example, you know that the appraisee is keen on outdoor activities, such as climbing and sailing, it may be appropriate to send them on an outward-bound style course to learn how teams form and develop. Encourage team members to refer to their personal development plans and review the results of development activities frequently. Help them to develop transferable skills that they can apply to a wide range of situations. Agree changes to development plans that enable the appraisee to react to changing circumstances and customer demands.

EVALUATING DEVELOPMENT

Review agreed learning objectives with the appraisee

↓

Assess whether those objectives were achieved

↓

Ask appraisee how they have applied new skills to their work

↓

Identify actions that have taken place as a result of learning

↓

Evaluate specific improvements to performance

↓

Record results of development on personal development plan

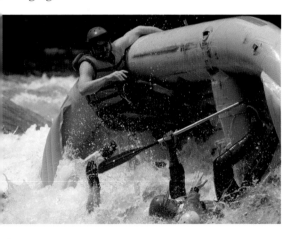

▲ BUILDING TEAM SKILLS

By sending adventurous staff on courses in an environment that they will enjoy, you are helping them to learn team-building techniques that will be useful to their team and their organization. They will also improve their skills as a team member or leader in their favoured leisure pursuits.

EVALUATING TRAINING

Hold a de-brief session immediately after development activities to discuss how well learning objectives were met. De-brief after every type of event, including on-the-job coaching. If there is a gap between what was expected and what was achieved, discuss how to close the gap and update the development plan with that action.

ENCOURAGING TEAMWORK

The six-step appraisal system works just as well when used for teams as it does for individuals. Develop the skills and improve the performance of your team as a whole by holding regular team appraisals and integrating training needs.

95 Help people to realize how much they can learn from one another.

96 Praise team efforts to show that you value the fact that they pull together.

USING THE SIX-STEP PLAN

The six-step plan not only provides a framework for individual appraisals but is also useful in the team environment. Prepare the key issues for discussion, and call the team together for a combined appraisal on how well they are working together. Explain the purpose of the session and establish what team members' roles are. If there are issues that involve one or two people and not the whole group, postpone these to a separate meeting. As you work through the agenda, ensure that people write down their actions. Finally, ask everyone to summarize their own action plans to check their understanding and commitment.

USING TEAM APPRAISAL ▼
Focus team members on the objectives that they are seeking to achieve as a unit. Negotiate the agenda for the meeting, and be prepared to drop items that you have outlined for discussion in favour of better suggestions from team members.

Manager concentrates on discussing items that are of interest to the whole group

Team member prepares to summarize her own action plan at the end of the meeting

Team member notes actions for which he is responsible

97 Involve the whole team in planning its development for the future.

98 Get the most from a training budget by sharing resources.

ENCOURAGING TEAM FEEDBACK

Extend the use of the appraisal process to improving teamwork skills. Ensure that the entire team are clear about their objectives and how they are linked to other teams within the organization. As well as encouraging people to give and receive feedback during their own appraisal, help them to be open and constructive with each other. In the open environment encouraged by an effective appraisal, team members should be encouraged to share information and knowledge to build support and trust. Use team meetings to solve problems, build good working relationships, and review how the team is progressing against objectives.

INTEGRATING TRAINING

Group individuals with common training and development needs together so that training courses will be more economical. Keep a record for senior management of who have been attending courses, on which subjects, and the benefits. This will allow the management team to assess whether their investment in training and development is paying off in terms of business objectives. If senior managers are convinced by the business case for developing their staff, they will continue to invest. Future development plans are more likely to be approved if they build on past successes.

POINTS TO REMEMBER

- Just as consistency is needed within a single team, an organization requires consistency throughout all teams.
- Peers are often the best advisers to their colleagues.

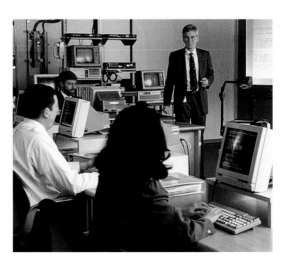

**ORGANIZING ▶
GROUP TRAINING**
Plan to group people with similar training needs together. This is both cost-effective and strengthens staff relations, since team members can share learning experiences.

EVALUATING YOURSELF

For the appraisal system to work successfully, managers themselves must improve and develop skills alongside their staff. Evaluate your performance as an appraiser and ask your appraisees for feedback in order to become more effective.

99 Act as your own critic – but remember to be constructive.

100 Take every opportunity to learn and practise new skills.

101 Check that appraisals have win-win outcomes for all involved.

MONITORING PROGRESS

To ensure that appraisals have contributed to your team's continuous improvement, examine the results that each team member is achieving after the appraisals have taken place. Allow a period of, say, three months to see a noticeable improvement in performance. Check that the objectives set are consistent with the standards set for all individuals on your team. To help you do this, ask staff in similar jobs on other teams to give you a benchmark for performance. Ensure that the team's action plan has been implemented and that you have provided the promised support and resources. Finally, plan review sessions that are focused on performance improvement. Do the reviews demonstrate that clear progress is being made?

DEVELOPING YOUR APPRAISAL SKILLS

A valuable method of developing your appraisal skills is to practise role playing. Ask a colleague who understands the appraisee and his or her work situation to role-play how the appraisee might behave. If you have practised the answer to a difficult question, you will be able to answer it more authoritatively in the real meeting. Consider attending a training course on conducting appraisals. These generally tend to feature role playing quite heavily. If you do attend a training course, prepare notes on staff members you will have to appraise so that you will be able to use them as examples without breaching confidentiality.

EVALUATING THE LONG TERM

Review the entire appraisal process and all the appraisals you have conducted over the period of the past year. Reflect on what you have learned about yourself as an appraiser and how appraisal has helped you to achieve results. Only when you are slightly removed from the event will you be able to see patterns clearly and identify your development needs as an appraiser. Perhaps you need further training to be able to give feedback that is motivational, even when its content makes difficult listening for the appraisee. Perhaps you need to clarify roles or make objectives more measurable. Look at your timetable for appraisals and assess whether you allowed sufficient time for preparation, the appraisals themselves, and following up afterwards. Do you need to start earlier next time? How fair were the appraisals, and were they consistent for all individuals on your team? What have you learned about appraising over the year and, for that matter, about yourself?

QUESTIONS TO ASK YOURSELF

Q How well did I prepare: did I gather all the facts and have all the necessary documentation ready?

Q What percentage of the time was I speaking and how well did I listen?

Q How balanced was my feedback: was it mainly positive and motivational with appropriate developmental feedback?

▼ SEEKING FEEDBACK

To develop your skills as an appraiser, ask team members to give you honest feedback on your performance and the usefulness of their appraisals. Find out whether they were happy with the feedback they received, and if there are any aspects of the appraisal process that they feel could be improved.

Manager seeks feedback on the time allowed for staff to prepare for appraisals

ASSESSING YOUR APPRAISING SKILLS

E*valuate your ability to develop people through feedback and appraisal by answering the following questions as honestly as you can. If your answer is "Never", circle option 1; if it is "Always", circle option 4, and so on. Add your scores together, and refer to the analysis to see how you scored. Use the answers to identify the areas that need improving.*

OPTIONS
1 Never
2 Occasionally
3 Frequently
4 Always

1 I build an environment where people expect me to give them feedback.

1 2 3 4

2 I use self-assessment to help people prepare for appraisals effectively.

1 2 3 4

3 I consider the team and the organization when planning objectives.

1 2 3 4

4 I plan appropriate measures to evaluate performance.

1 2 3 4

5 I delegate responsibility to my team members wherever possible.

1 2 3 4

6 I encourage people to come to me with solutions rather than problems.

1 2 3 4

7 I carefully consider which topics should be raised during an appraisal.

1 2 3 4

8 I prepare notes on the appraisee's past performance prior to their appraisal.

1 2 3 4

9 I identify ways of developing people when I prepare for their appraisal.

1 2 3 4

10 I am aware of what I can agree on my own authority in an appraisal.

1 2 3 4

11 I conduct appraisals in an atmosphere of trust and confidentiality.

1 2 3 4

12 I treat all staff equally and am fair and objective with every individual.

1 2 3 4

13 I plan how to deliver feedback constructively.

1 2 3 4

14 I explain the format that the interview will take at the start of the appraisal.

1 2 3 4

15 I agree the agenda at the beginning of the appraisal.

1 2 3 4

16 I listen far more than I speak during an appraisal.

1 2 3 4

17 I understand that what I say to an individual may have implications for others.

1 2 3 4

18 I am able to discover what is at the heart of people's anxieties.

1 2 3 4

19 I use my body language to help an appraisee to relax.

1 2 3 4

20 I ensure that appraisees are committed to carrying out their action plans.

1 2 3 4

21 I anticipate challenges that may occur in appraisals.

1 2 3 4

22 I ask appraisees for ways to solve problems before offering my own ideas.

1 2 3 4

23 I agree learning objectives before anyone attends a course.

1 2 3 4

24 I encourage people to consider wider opportunities throughout the organization.

1 2 3 4

25 I ensure that appraisees write their own action plans.

1 2 3 4

26 I ask an appraisee to give their summary of an appraisal first.

1 2 3 4

27 I review people's development plans on a regular basis.

1　2　3　4

28 I know which outside interests my appraisees enjoy.

1　2　3　4

29 I discuss the effectiveness of a training course shortly after it is held.

1　2　3　4

30 I consider whether individuals' training needs can be grouped together.

1　2　3　4

31 I use the six-step plan as the agenda for team appraisal meetings.

1　2　3　4

32 I ask for feedback on my skills as an appraiser after each appraisal.

1　2　3　4

ANALYSIS

Now that you have completed the self-assessment, add up your total score and check your performance. Whatever level of skill you have achieved in conducting appraisals, there is always room for improvement. Identify your weakest areas, then refer to the relevant pages of this section, where you will find practical advice and tips to help you refine your skills.

32–63: Your appraising skills are not yet sufficient to succeed in getting the best from people. Check that you are preparing as thoroughly as you should.

64–95: You are a reasonably proficient appraiser but you should identify areas for development and incorporate them into your personal development plan.

96–128: You are a good appraiser. Avoid complacency by seeking feedback from appraisees.

MANAGING PUBLIC RELATIONS

INTRODUCTION

Public relations comprises a set of practical skills and strategies designed to enhance the reputation of an organization, help strengthen its relationships with key audiences, and enable it to deal with crises from a position of strength. Whether PR is the main focus of your work, or merely an add-on to your job description, Managing Public Relations will guide you to success. Covering the principal aspects of PR, including the vital skills of using the media, organizing events, and producing persuasive publicity material, this section shows you how to ensure the well-being of your organization. Use the self-assessment questionnaire to measure your skill level and identify areas for improvement, and follow the hints, guidance, and advice to help you build and develop your PR skills. Backed up with 101 tips, this section is an invaluable guide to the skills you need for an essential business discipline.

UNDERSTANDING PUBLIC RELATIONS

An organization's reputation is one of its most critical assets. Understand how public relations builds and enhances a good image and why a strategic approach ensures success.

DEFINING PUBLIC RELATIONS

Public relations, or PR, is a powerful tool that can make a vital contribution to organizational success. Learn to distinguish between effective PR and cheap publicity gimmicks in order to build a solid, respected reputation with your key audiences.

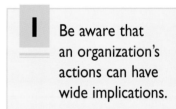

1 Be aware that an organization's actions can have wide implications.

UNDERSTANDING THE BASICS

Public relations describes the way issues and messages are communicated between an organization and the public. It is the discipline that looks after corporate reputation. The aim of PR is to win understanding and support from, and to influence the opinions and behaviour of, an organization's key audiences. This is achieved through a planned, sustained set of activities.

2 Make certain that all PR claims can be substantiated.

3 Remind colleagues that they all have a PR role, regardless of their job title.

BUILDING REPUTATION

The true purpose of PR is to create a well-deserved reputation. That may involve offering excellent customer care, communicating effectively with your audiences, and showing social responsibility towards your workforce, the local community, and the environment. Cheap publicity gimmicks designed to deceive the public, or glitzy activities aimed at diverting attention from poor organizational behaviour give PR a bad name and have no place in an effective PR campaign.

ANTICIPATING EVENTS

Effective PR is about anticipating tomorrow's issues, rather than apologizing to staff and the public for poor decisions that have been made. By harnessing PR skills you will not only be able to act to improve the reputation of your organization, but you will also be able to show your colleagues what PR can do to make their jobs easier. Demonstrate how PR can help the human resources department improve employee communications. Prove the worth of PR in supporting marketing activity. Ensure that the chief executive knows that good PR can build better investor relationships and thereby help the share price.

4 Know that averting bad publicity is as crucial as attracting good publicity.

▼ ACHIEVING A GOOD OUTCOME
The outcome of effective PR is a good, well-deserved image based on a genuine commitment to provide excellent service and to be a good, caring employer and a responsible organization. Cheap publicity creates an image without substance.

POSITIVE OUTCOME

"I like that organization"

"The staff are genuine and I trust them"

"It deserves its good reputation"

POOR OUTCOME

"That company always hypes its achievements"

"This is just another cheap PR stunt"

"It uses glossy publicity to hide its shortcomings"

USING PR WITH MARKETING

The differences between PR and marketing may seem blurred, yet each has its own part to play in organizational success. Use PR to support marketing activity and co-ordinate these two distinct disciplines for maximum impact.

5 Use both editorial and advertising to secure positive media coverage.

FITTING PR INTO THE MARKETING MIX

Marketing involves developing the right product at the right price, getting it to a place where consumers can buy it, and promoting it so that they know about it. These components are known as the marketing mix, or the four Ps: product, price, place, and promotion. PR is often seen as the fifth P of the mix, standing for perception. Consumers prefer to do business with organizations they hold in high regard, and effective PR builds positive perceptions, creating a fertile environment for successful marketing.

WORKING WITH THE MARKETING TEAM ▼
Attend marketing meetings, explain to marketing colleagues how PR can support their campaigns, and point out any negative PR implications that may result from their planned activity

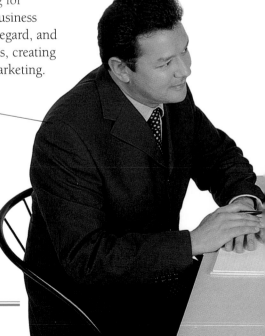

Marketing manager looks for ways of attracting media attention

6 Plan a day away with colleagues to improve team dynamics.

SUPPORTING MARKETING OBJECTIVES WITH PR

MARKETING OBJECTIVE	SUPPORTIVE PR ACTIVITY
To build stronger and more lasting relationships with clients.	● Organize a corporate hospitality event. ● Produce a quarterly customer newsletter.
To increase the public's awareness of the organization.	● Secure positive media coverage. ● Organize an open day.
To promote a new range of products more widely.	● Secure editorial in trade and consumer press. ● Organize in-store tastings or trial sessions.

7 Ask for a copy of your organization's marketing strategy.

WORKING TOGETHER

For maximum impact, PR and marketing activity should be co-ordinated. When the marketing department advertises new products and services, reinforce the campaign by attracting favourable editorial coverage. Use your company website as a marketing tool as well as a PR vehicle. Create an area for journalists with press releases, background information, and press photographs for down-loading. Combined PR and marketing campaigns can be worth far more than the sum of their individual parts.

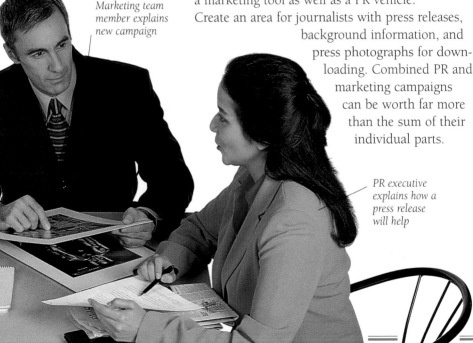

Marketing team member explains new campaign

PR executive explains how a press release will help

COMMUNICATING EFFECTIVELY

Public relations is sometimes known as communications because effective dialogue lies at its heart. To ensure success, make sure that communication is a two-way process, and be aware of non-verbal and unintentional messages.

8 Examine the way in which your customers perceive you.

9 To communicate well, be prompt, accurate, and comprehensive.

UNDERSTANDING COMMUNICATION

Good communication enables you to build lasting relationships with your target audiences, transform difficult relationships, and avert misunderstanding that leads to ill will. Poor communication leaves customers feeling ignored and disinclined to do business with you again. Assess the effectiveness of all your communication methods, such as letters, e-mails, face-to-face talks, and publicity materials.

ENSURING TWO-WAY COMMUNICATION

Remember that communication is a two-way process. As well as sending out the right messages, an organization must establish mechanisms to receive them from others, including staff, customers, suppliers, and the public. Make it easy for people to communicate with you. Send out questionnaires to seek feedback. Use comment cards and suggestion boxes. Include an e-mail reply device on your website. When you receive messages, show that you value dialogue by replying promptly to those who took the trouble to contact you.

10 Know when to listen – effective communication is about more than just talking.

SENDING THE RIGHT MESSAGES

Ensure that any messages you convey are by design rather than accident. Burly security men guarding doors; signs curtly stating rules and regulations; or unfriendly, unhelpful, or untrained staff are powerful but negative messages. They send out signals of an unwelcoming or uncaring organization. Do not overlook the impact that actions of staff, or policies and procedures, can have in conveying an unfavourable image. Look at your organization as if for the first time. What is your impression? Gather first impressions from new staff, new customers, or first-time visitors to your premises. Listen to what they say and act to eradicate unintentional negative messages.

QUESTIONS TO ASK YOURSELF

Q Do we always inform customers of delays?

Q Do we always tell customers about changes to arrangements?

Q Do we tell customers about relevant internal news, such as new staff appointments?

 Ensure that the message sent is the message received.

A lack of eye contact implies a lack of interest

NEGATIVE

A smile shows pleasure in dealing with the customer

A smart appearance communicates a professional image

POSITIVE

UNDERSTANDING ▶ NON-VERBAL MESSAGES

Non-verbal messages are very powerful. In these two scenarios, a customer receives very different signals. An uncaring, unfriendly message from a staff member damages her faith in the company, while helpful and considerate body language instils goodwill.

TAKING A STRATEGIC APPROACH

Long-term, strategic PR planning is far more effective than unco-ordinated flurries of activity. Map out your public relations campaign so that your purpose is clear, activity can be planned, progress monitored, and outcomes measured.

12 Ensure that PR strategy supports both corporate and marketing strategies.

13 Use PR proactively to anticipate and avert bad publicity.

14 Take the offensive rather than be on the defensive.

UNDERSTANDING STRATEGY

To achieve a proactive approach to PR, you will need to produce a PR strategy. Your strategy must support your organization's corporate strategy, as well as linking with your company's marketing strategy. Because of this, it can be helpful to involve those responsible for corporate and marketing strategy when planning PR strategy. They can help explain the organization's wider strategy, while you can explain to them how PR can be used to support corporate goals.

SETTING OBJECTIVES

The first step in strategic planning is to establish objectives, a set of goals that define what you want to achieve. These might focus on improving your organization's reputation, raising its profile, or building stronger relationships with key groups, for example. Clear objectives will help you to reach your target, to chart progress, to measure results and to assess effectiveness. Set objectives at the outset, but make sure that you allow ample time for this. All PR activity that you undertake will be aimed at achieving these goals.

POINTS TO REMEMBER

- Objectives should be clear, specific, unambiguous, quantifiable, and incorporate a time frame.
- To ensure that they remain relevant, objectives should be revised periodically.
- If objectives are to be effective, they should be demanding yet achievable.

15 Use PR persuasively to help shape the way others see your organization.

IDENTIFYING TARGET AUDIENCES

Most organizations will have several audiences or "publics", so a strategic approach to PR involves clearly identifying all of them. Some will be regarded as more important than others. Audiences might include:

- customers;
- staff;
- media;
- public;
- investors/shareholders;
- market analysts;
- other stakeholders;
- the local community;
- local, regional/state, or national/federal government.

16 Define messages to promote what you value and find ways to convey them.

DEFINING KEY MESSAGES

Every organization will have key corporate messages that need to be conveyed. You might, for example, want to tell everyone how innovative your organization is, or how caring. In addition to these, there will be a sub-set of messages personalized for each principal audience. When launching a new product, for example, investors will want to be told of any impact on the share price. The media and the community's focus of interest may be on the environmental impact. Try to give each audience information tailored to its particular needs and viewpoint.

▼ REAPING THE BENEFITS

In developing a strategic approach and setting aside time for PR, Eileen made a major contribution to the success of the business. Sales continued to increase, and PR came to be regarded as a vital and valued part of the organization's work.

CASE STUDY

Eileen worked for a medium-sized engineering firm. Part of her job was to take care of the company's PR. However, she was so busy with her principal tasks that PR was very much an afterthought. Most of what took place was reactive and defensive, and outcomes were never measured. Thanks to this chaotic, ad hoc approach, PR bore little fruit, confirming a general feeling that PR was a waste of time. Eileen decided

to undertake some PR planning. She drew up a strategy and set aside time to implement it. Within a few months, media exposure in the trade press had increased dramatically, leading directly to an upturn in orders. As a result of improved internal communication, production staff felt renewed motivation and accepted new working arrangements in order to meet their bulging workload. Faith in PR grew and Eileen was given a full-time PR role.

 17 Consider inviting key colleagues to strategic planning meetings.

PLANNING FOR SUCCESS ▼

Ask the team to suggest effective ways of communicating messages to your principal audiences. Choose a channel that is appropriate to your audience, the message, and the urgency of conveying it.

ACHIEVING OBJECTIVES

Strategic PR involves considerable research, planning, and discussion. How will you meet your objectives? What ideas do you have for conveying the desired messages to your principal audiences. Draw up a series of ideas to help you meet each of your objectives. Calculate the cost of each idea, decide which ones you will implement, then produce an activity timetable. Include details of who will be responsible for each activity, with start and completion dates. Hold regular meetings with those involved in implementation so that you can chart progress and solve any problems.

PR manager favours combining methods for maximum impact

Team member suggests holding an exhibition to promote message

DOCUMENTING THE PLAN

A PR strategy is a written document, not a set of ideas to be carried around in your head. Writing down your strategy also helps you to focus on what you need to achieve, how, and when. Record details of your key publications, along with the principal messages per audience. You will also need to include your objectives, and – in broad terms – your ideas for achieving them. Specify what measures you will use to evaluate success and set a date for an interim evaluation. The final part of the strategy is your activity timetable.

 18 Review your PR strategy every six months.

 19 Ensure PR activity is geared towards achievement.

ASSESSING EFFECTIVENESS

Measuring effectiveness is an important element of strategic PR. The aim of measuring is to assess whether or not objectives have been achieved. Use questionnaires, focus groups, and other research methods to measure whether your messages have reached their target and achieved the desired outcome. You may need to conduct research before a PR campaign, as well as afterwards, to obtain an accurate measure of shifts in behaviour or attitude. Use evaluation to learn which tactics and techniques worked, and which did not. This knowledge will help you to be more effective next time.

20 Good PR can reduce staff absenteeism.

21 Look for creative solutions to PR problems.

MEASURING THE EFFECTIVENESS OF A PR CAMPAIGN

INDICATOR	HOW TO MEASURE EFFECTIVENESS
REACH	● How well did the message reach the target audiences? ● What is the proof?
KNOWLEDGE	● How well informed and educated is the audience about the company and its products? ● How do we know?
UNDERSTANDING	● Has the audience grasped the message? ● How can we tell?
PREFERENCE	● Has favour increased with the target audience? ● How do we know?
ATTITUDES	● Has the audience's view been altered in a positive way? ● Is there any evidence of this?
OPINIONS	● Have people's opinions changed in the way that was intended? ● How do we know?
BEHAVIOUR	● Has target audience behaviour altered in the intended way? ● How do we know?

DEVELOPING
PR SKILLS

Improving staff communication and customer care, dealing with crises, and organizing events and campaigns are key PR skills. Learn how to become an accomplished PR practitioner.

COMMUNICATING WITH STAFF

Good PR starts at home. Committed and helpful staff create a good image, so regard employees not just as a workforce, but as a principal target audience. Nurture staff commitment through effective employee communication involving genuine dialogue.

22 Ask staff for their ideas on how communication can be improved.

23 Communicate well to reduce staff turnover and boost morale.

KEEPING STAFF INFORMED

Use PR techniques to help you achieve a genuine and meaningful relationship with staff. Employees need to know what is going on in their organization and should be kept informed at an early stage of developments that will affect them. Tell employees about new staff, promotions, job opportunities, new products and services, high-profile marketing activity, financial results, and future plans. Effective internal communication is in everyone's interests.

CREATING REAL DIALOGUE

Recognize the benefits of sharing information and create a genuine, open, two-way communication channel between staff and management. Staff are sometimes sceptical of internal communication because it is often used merely to deliver bad news, such as redundancies. Distrust is understandable if staff receive nothing but company propaganda. Staff want to hear all news, good and bad, presented in a straightforward and honest way. Ensure that the information flow is two-way. All team members can provide valuable insights. Encourage them to feed ideas to managers.

24 Present information in a way that is easy to understand.

25 Avoid using euphemisms in an attempt to dilute bad news.

QUESTIONS TO ASK YOURSELF

Q What are the different categories of employee?

Q What does each group need to know?

Q What is the preferred manner of communication?

Q How can we improve the ways in which we communicate?

UNDERTAKING A COMMUNICATIONS AUDIT

You may be surprised at how staff regard the effectiveness or otherwise of your organization's internal communication. Find out what your staff think. Where are the information blockages? Are you telling staff too much or too little? Do they understand and believe the corporate messages? Demonstrate to staff that their views are important. Send out a questionnaire, phrasing questions so that you can identify where the problems are. Act on the findings. Draw up an action plan, share it with staff, then implement it.

◀ **BEING OPEN**
Spike's reluctance to discuss bad news with staff led to fear, insecurity, and the loss of a team member. By talking to his employees, Spike put an end to all the worrying and ensured their continued support.

CASE STUDY

Spike owned and managed a small record production company employing 25 staff. A former artist was taking him to court over a disagreement about royalties. Upset about the court case, Spike kept this news to himself. But gossip in the industry eventually reached Spike's employees. They began to worry about the future of their jobs: rumour suggested that the legal action could bankrupt Spike. One staff member who was offered a job elsewhere decided to accept because of the feared uncertainty of her current job. Overhearing the office gossip, Spike realized that a wholly inaccurate story was circulating. He called a meeting to explain the situation. Staff learned that Spike was the wronged party and stood an excellent chance of winning his court battle. Morale improved and staff were able to support Spike through this difficult time.

MANAGING YOUR CORPORATE REPUTATION

A *good corporate image is founded on substance, and its creation should be more than a cosmetic exercise. Assess your current image carefully, draw up an action plan to tackle weak areas, and then work hard to maintain your reputation.*

26 Tackle complaints from customers promptly and considerately.

27 Always aim to exceed customer expectations.

▼ **CREATING AN IMAGE MATRIX**
This sample shows a simple matrix that you can adapt to suit your needs and use to help you plan action after undertaking an image audit within your organization.

CONDUCTING AN IMAGE AUDIT

Find out how your audiences perceive you, using research methods such as questionnaires and focus groups. Combine this with an audit of your main methods of communication. Look for unintentional messages. What message is conveyed by a dirty delivery van, for example? Examine every aspect of your work that communicates something about your organization, including premises, policies, and customer care. Ask yourself, "With only this to go on, what would I think of us as an organization?"

	ITEM 1	ITEM 2	ITEM 3
Item examined	Lobby area	Promotional brochure	Delivery waiting times for customers
Image conveyed	Dowdy and old-fashioned	Cheap and unprofessional	Inefficient and unprofessional
Desired image	Welcoming and stylish	Attractive, professional, and upmarket	Fast, efficient, and customer-orientated
Action required	Redecorate and replace chairs	Produce new brochure with good design	Explore recruiting more casual and part-time packers
Budget	£1,200	£18,000	Unknown
Delegated to	Melanie	Stephen	Mark
Start/completion	Feb/March	March/June	Feb/March

ENGENDERING TRUST

Organizations with good reputations are trusted. It pays to engender trust because:

● People are more likely to do business with you;

● They are more likely to buy your shares;

● You attract better staff;

● The media and the public trust you to tell the truth;

● You are more likely to be believed in times of adversity.

PRODUCING AN ACTION PLAN

Having identified the shortcomings in your image, you now need to tackle these weaknesses by devising practical ideas and incorporating them into a workable action plan aimed at improving perceptions. Ensure that every action in your plan is assigned to a named person with the skills, the authority, and the time to carry it out. Give those responsible for implementation a sufficient budget, and agree a start and a completion date. Bring them together for a briefing; they need to be able to see the big picture and understand the reasoning behind the need for action. Ask for progress updates so that you can monitor implementation.

MAINTAINING A REPUTATION

It can take years to build a good image, but a reputation can be destroyed in seconds. Work to maintain your hard-won image. Show staff that you value them, treat them well, and communicate openly with them. Unhappy staff tell their friends how dissatisfied they are, thus damaging your reputation as a good employer. Disaffected staff also tend to provide poor service, which will erode your good image. Provide excellent customer care so that people have no cause to complain; when complaints do occur, make sure that you handle them swiftly, fairly, and courteously.

▼ CREATING AN OVERLAP

To maintain a successful reputation, there must be an overlap between the identity that an organization seeks to create and the image it has with the public, so that their experience of the organization tallies with the way in which it is publicized.

Radio safety campaign promotes the image of a caring organization

CARING FOR CUSTOMERS

*E*xcellent customer care is at the very *core of effective PR. Your reputation depends upon it. Aim to attain 100 per cent customer satisfaction by training staff, introducing a customer charter, and taking prompt action to rectify mistakes.*

28 Try to ensure that your customers have nothing to complain about.

29 Turn dissatisfied customers into advocates.

30 Try to see matters from a customer's perspective.

DELIVERING EXCELLENT SERVICE

One of the best ways to build or enhance a good image is to work hard at getting your customer care right. Conversely, ignore customer care and you will damage your reputation. It is surprising how few staff seem able to provide good service naturally. Most need training. Additionally, they must feel committed and motivated. Check that staff know what is expected of them. Produce a set of measurable service standards and incentivize staff to meet them.

DEVELOPING A CUSTOMER CHARTER

Draw up a customer charter that tells customers what they can expect from you and what you will do if you fail to keep your promise. Provided that you deliver on your customer charter commitments, this can be an excellent way of enhancing your reputation and giving people confidence in you. Specify how quickly you will answer the phone; reply to letters, faxes and e-mails; and deliver orders. Produce a clear, fair complaints procedure and a returns policy for faulty or unwanted goods. Make sure that you give people confidence to do business with you time and again.

QUESTIONS TO ASK YOURSELF

Q Do our customers have strong reasons to recommend us to others?

Q Have we reassured customers with guarantees of what we will do should things go wrong?

31 Make customer satisfaction the goal of all staff.

BEING ACCOMMODATING

Adopt a "can do" attitude. Sometimes an organization's rules and regulations, policies, and procedures get in the way of good customer service. Insisting that all enquiries are submitted in writing is an example of an inflexible and unfriendly rule. Check your own rules for customer friendliness: are they entirely necessary? Be prepared to be flexible where you can. Train staff to be genuinely helpful and to accommodate all reasonable customer requests. Go that extra mile to make a customer happy. Total customer satisfaction should be the goal of all staff.

POINTS TO REMEMBER

● Policies and procedures should never be used as an excuse not to help a customer.

● The value of "people passion" should never be underestimated: staff who genuinely care make a huge difference to reputation, and a passion for their work will enhance an organization's image.

● Staff who are treated well will be champions of an organization; those who are treated badly will become critics.

32 Avoid passing customers from one department to another.

Team member learns how to ask a customer if they need help

Trainer intervenes in role play to suggest a more helpful approach

Colleague gives feedback in her role as customer

◀ INVESTING IN CUSTOMER CARE

Expert customer care training is an investment, not a cost. Remember that all new staff should undergo training in the organization's customer care programme, and existing staff may need refresher training every two or three years.

PLANNING A CAMPAIGN

Campaigning is becoming increasingly popular as a method of raising an organization's profile and building a positive image. Plan your campaign carefully, launch it in a blaze of publicity, and know how to sustain it until your objectives are achieved.

33 To be sure of success, plan your campaign with military precision.

34 Work out your budget carefully – campaigning can be expensive.

ADDRESSING THE FUNDAMENTALS

Organizations may campaign in support of a consumer issue, or they may join forces with other organizations to mount a trade campaign to promote their industry or to lobby local, national, or international government on an issue that affects their industry. Before contemplating a campaign launch, consider all the issues. Decide on your objectives (what you want to achieve); target (whom you want to influence); and tactics and techniques (how you will achieve your objectives). You should also examine the strengths and weaknesses of your case, gather your facts, and anticipate opposing arguments.

RECOGNIZING A GOOD CAMPAIGNER ▼
The hallmarks of a good campaigner are easy to spot. They are creative, committed, and highly effective individuals with logical minds and often with infectious enthusiasm. These qualities will stand them in good stead when charged with running a campaign.

Articulate

Honest

Persuasive

Familiar with arguments for and against

Organized and effective

Believer in the cause

Well informed

NAMING YOUR CAMPAIGN

It is always advisable to name your campaign. This can help turn a rather nebulous set of objectives into an entity with its own distinct identity, making it easier for supporters to identify with your cause. Campaign names should be apt, memorable, and preferably short. Add further character to your campaign by designing a logo and visual identity that can be used on stationery and other materials to help promote and reinforce the campaign aims. A slogan that encapsulates the campaign aims in a snappy way is also a good idea.

POINTS TO REMEMBER

- Names for international campaigns should be checked to ensure that they do not translate into something inappropriate.
- A long name could be reduced to a pronounceable acronym.
- The addition of a strapline could help to reinforce your campaign name.
- Brainstorming can be a good way of generating campaign names.

35 Publicize campaign successes to rekindle interest.

36 Organize a campaign launch and invite the media along.

PRODUCING MATERIALS

Most campaigns require some type of literature aimed at informing and educating, persuading and winning support, and publicizing aims. This might include a campaign leaflet setting out your case; posters and other promotional material; and balloons, badges, pens, and carrier bags stamped with the campaign slogan. A campaign video is a good way of spreading the word. If you wish to encourage supporters to join in the campaigning activity, produce a campaign pack outlining how they can demonstrate their support, and provide factsheets containing the information they will need when speaking out in your favour.

SUSTAINING INTEREST

By mapping out campaign activity well into the future, you will ensure that your campaign does not peter out after a successful launch. Make a timetable of the activities you will undertake in the weeks and months after the launch. Create opportunities to attract publicity and spread the campaign message. Do research and publicize the findings. Think of ideas for photocalls. Mount displays and exhibitions. Start a petition.

37 Use creativity and inventiveness to keep your cause in the limelight.

ORGANIZING EVENTS

Much PR activity is event based, making event management a fundamental PR skill. Come up with a creative idea for an event, select your venue with care, and plan down to the very last detail to ensure a day to remember.

38 Involve helpers at an early stage in the planning of a new event.

39 Try to be original when planning an event in order to make it memorable.

40 Choose a venue or celebrity guest to link with the theme of your event.

PLANNING AN EVENT

There are all manner of PR events that you may consider planning, from product launches and factory, store, or new premises openings to parties, open days, corporate entertainment, exhibitions, open days, press conferences, and media trips. Events are organized to profile-raise, build customer loyalty, and enhance reputation. Some events require no more than organizational skills; others call for creativity, too. On occasion, you will need to come up with interesting, original, and appropriate ideas for memorable events. This might involve booking an unusual venue – such as a waxworks museum, film studios, or butterfly farm – or using a celebrity sportsperson, film star, or pop singer.

SETTING THE DATE

The date of an event may be predetermined, such as your organization's anniversary. Often, though, you will be able to influence it. If you are able to dictate when an event will occur, aim to make it coincide with another linked or topical occasion. An event for couples may benefit from being held on Valentine's day, for example. Beware of competing events; it would be unfortunate if someone else's high-profile occasion stole the limelight from your own.

41 Avoid setting an adverse date, such as an outdoor event in winter.

THINGS TO DO

1. Set a date that will not clash with other big events.
2. Choose an appropriate venue for your launch.
3. Decide who to invite – this may include supporters, politicians, and the media.
4. Decide on the form of your launch – press conference, photocall, seminar, or other.

SELECTING A PLANNING COMMITTEE

Small events can easily be managed by one person, but you will need the help and support of others when planning major events. Establish a planning team for significant events, involving people with the time and skills to assist. Look for helpers who are well organized and enthusiastic, and involve them at the earliest stage so that they have a stronger stake in your event's success. It is easy when event planning to overlook small but vital issues, so list what needs to be done to the last detail and ensure that a team member is given responsibility for each item.

BRIEFING KEY PARTICIPANTS

If you are asking people to perform a function at an event – such as giving an after-dinner speech or officiating at an opening – provide a comprehensive brief. This is especially important if they are unfamiliar with your company. The better informed they are, the better they will do the job. Explain, preferably face-to-face, and followed up in writing, what you expect from them. State clearly the purpose of the event, what you want them to do, and who will be there. Specify when they are to arrive, and when they can expect to leave. If necessary, include some background information on your organization, a map, and car-parking details.

▼ **PREPARING MATERIAL FOR A GUEST SPEAKER**
Provide your guest speaker with a full script well in advance of the event, setting out the main points to cover. He or she will then be able to prepare notes to make sure that the speech is delivered smoothly.

Speaker uses notes based on organizer's draft to ensure relevance

42 Check speakers' credentials to ensure they have the right expertise.

BOOKING A VENUE

Draw up a list of possible venues so that you can compare the advantages and disadvantages of each, bearing in mind costs, location, capacity, and facilities. Think about the type of atmosphere you wish to create: will it be a serious occasion, or a fun, informal one? The venue will set the mood of your presentation. Consider whether the venue is accessible to your guests – is it within easy reach of public transport, or will you need to organize transportation?

43 Select a venue that complements your corporate image.

▼ CONFIRMING DETAILS

Whenever you book anything – equipment, speakers, venues, food, and so on – always confirm your booking and all requirements in writing. Keep a record of all correspondence and phone calls.

Dear Janet Smith,

I am writing to confirm the details we discussed when I visited you earlier this week.

I would like to book the function suite and the two connecting syndicate rooms at the Grand Hotel for our annual seminar on August 20. We will need the rooms from 9 a.m. to 5 p.m. We will also have sole use of the banqueting suite from 12.30 p.m. to 1.30 p.m. and from 3 p.m. to 3.30 p.m.

Specify all dates and times

There will be 150 people in total, 140 guests plus 10 staff. We require tea, coffee, and biscuits for 150 people to be available on arrival of delegates (9.30 a.m., although I will arrive at 9 a.m.). Your staff will serve this in the main function room. As agreed, herbal teas will also be available. Tea, coffee, and biscuits will be served again at 3 p.m. in the banqueting suite.

Confirm any special requests

Delegates will move to the banqueting suite at 12.30 p.m. for lunch. We would like menu B. One week before the event I will contact you to confirm the nature and number of special meals. In addition, you will have five surplus vegetarian meals available on the day for delegates who have not booked one in advance. One bottle of red house wine will be served to each table of four people. Two bottles of mineral water will also be available per table. Each table will have a centrepiece posy of pink carnations.

State any equipment you want the venue to provide, and check that any equipment you want to bring is acceptable

We will need an overhead projector and screen in each of the three rooms, as well as a flipchart stand, pad, and pens in the two syndicate rooms. We will supply name badges, pads, and pens.

Please could you write to me within the next seven days to confirm that you agree to these arrangements.

Always ask suppliers to write confirming that they agree to providing your specified arrangements

I look forward to hearing from you.

Yours sincerely

Paula Wilson

Paula Wilson
PR Manager

PLANNING THE KEY COMPONENTS OF AN EVENT

KEY COMPONENT	HOW TO PLAN EFFECTIVELY
VENUE The location of an event. This must be chosen carefully to suit the type of function.	Check that a proposed venue can accommodate your needs, that it is large enough for your requirements, and that it can meet any special needs of your guests, such as providing disabled access or an induction loop.
CATERING Food and refreshments provided during the event. Quantity, quality, and price are main considerations.	Shop around, as prices vary considerably. Look at sample menus and ensure that people with special dietary needs – vegetarians, vegans, people with food allergies, etc. – can be catered for. Check that the venue allows outside caterers.
GUEST LIST A list of all invitees, including staff such as photographers, and a reserve guest list.	Keep a reserve list so that if a guest is unable to attend, you can diplomatically fill the place with someone from your back-up list. Design and print invitations for everyone on the guest list and distribute them in plenty of time.
ENTERTAINMENT Musicians, singers, dancers, comedians, or other performers or activities planned for the event.	Try to see any entertainers in action before you book them. Find out what facilities entertainers will need, such as a dressing room, a public address system, lighting, backing music, or a nearby power supply.

BEING PREPARED

Draw up a checklist of facilities and equipment needed for your event. This might include: a public address system; portable toilets; tables and chairs; slide or overhead projectors; television and video recorder; lighting; a lectern; badges; tents and marquees; or barriers and signage. You may need staff such as marshals, technicians, and parking attendants. Pay attention to detail and ensure that nothing is overlooked.

DEALING WITH LEGAL AND SAFETY MATTERS

When you organize an event, you are responsible for the safety of people attending it and must take all reasonable steps to protect them. Investigate what is required to ensure that your event is safe and legal. Local and national laws may apply, perhaps requiring you to obtain a licence for public entertainment or the serving of alcohol. Police permission may be needed for certain types of event. There are possible food hygiene laws to consider. You may need stewards and first aiders. Safety barriers may be necessary. Take care to remain within the law, gain sufficient public liability insurance, and seek the necessary permits. If you are planning a large public event, consider seeking advice from a professional event manager.

EXHIBITING AT EVENTS

*A*n *exhibition provides the opportunity to present your message to the public and inform them of your work. Decide what you want to achieve, select your showcase with care, and undertake careful planning to ensure that you make the most of the event.*

44 Consider carefully what you hope to achieve by exhibiting.

QUESTIONS TO ASK YOURSELF

Q Why do we want to stage an exhibition or mount a display?

Q What are our main objectives?

Q Is this the best way of achieving them?

Q Will our chosen showcase enable us to reach our target audience?

SHOULD YOU EXHIBIT?

Exhibitions aimed at attracting sales – at trade fairs, for example – are usually organized by the marketing department. Exhibitions aimed at persuading, educating, promoting an image, or raising your profile are the domain of PR staff. Buying a stand at an exhibition, staffing it, and producing attractive display boards can be expensive but provides an excellent opportunity to reach your target audience face-to-face and to engage them in discussions about your work.

CHOOSING A SHOWCASE

The key to successful exhibiting is to select the right venue: one that will attract your target audience. If you plan to display at a major exhibition, ask the organizers for detailed audience profiles to help you decide whether this is a suitable showcase for you. Ask who else will be exhibiting there. Find out about the organizer's promotional strategy (advertising, editorial, leaflets, and so on) for publicizing the event. Be sure that it will attract a big enough turnout of the right kind of people.

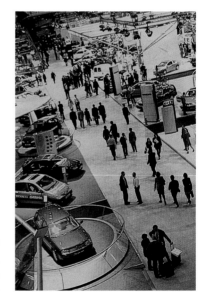

LOCATING YOUR STAND ▶
Visit a venue in advance to check the location of your stand. Make sure that your stand occupies a bright, central position, where it will attract the maximum number of visitors.

Staff member presents visitor with a promotional bag containing an information pack and gift

STAFFING YOUR STAND

While informative display boards in your chosen location will promote your message well enough, staffed stands are a more effective (albeit more costly) way of communicating. Select staff who are outgoing, happy to talk to people, and at the right level for the occasion. For example, a stand at a conference for chief executive officers should be staffed by high-ranking individuals who can talk comfortably and knowledgeably with CEOs. Brief staff thoroughly so that they know what message they are promoting, and can answer any likely questions. Organize a staffing rota to cover rest breaks so that your stand is staffed at all times.

◀ **DELIVERING YOUR MESSAGE**
Instruct staff on what to do with visitors once they are over the threshold, whether it is to talk through the display or show a video. Visitors should leave the stand carrying your message in their hand or in their head.

ATTRACTING PEOPLE TO YOUR STAND

Staffing a stand can sometimes be a dispiriting matter. People may wander past, but it can be difficult to get them to come over and take a look. Consider how you will attract visitors to your stand. Perhaps you could organize a prize draw, provide free refreshments, or offer a free consultation. What can you place on your stand to act as a people magnet? Interactive computers, demonstrations, talks and participative workshops can all be used to entice visitors in. Design your stand carefully to ensure that it is accessible, with no barriers to entry, and that it looks attractive, colourful, and appealing. Friendly and approachable staff can also make a big difference to attendance at your stand.

POINTS TO REMEMBER

● Negotiating before paying for a stand will help you to ensure a better deal.

● Your stand and contents should always be insured.

● There should be sufficient supplies of company literature.

● All leads should be followed up after the event.

45 Avoid overstaffing your stand. It will deter visitors.

IMPROVING YOUR PRESENTATION SKILLS

Effective public relations demands first-rate communication skills, whether one-to-one, or one to 100. Learn to prepare your presentations with care, conquer your nerves, and appraise your performance honestly after the event.

46 Prepare cue cards to remind you of your main key points.

47 Avoid a rushed ending by pacing your speech.

48 Deliver your talk in a style that will be appropriate to your audience.

PREPARING TO PRESENT

Few of us are gifted with a natural talent for public speaking. For most people, a successful presentation relies on careful planning and preparation. Start by finding out as much as you can about those you will be addressing, so that you can pitch your talk at the right level. How large will your audience be? Will participants be there by choice? Do they have knowledge of the subject? What is their age and sex? Do they have any relevant affiliations? Think about your style of delivery: should it be light and anecdotal, or serious and academic?

RESEARCHING THE DETAIL

To help you face your audience with confidence, research your venue. Find out how the room will be organized. Will seating be set out theatre-style, around a table, or in a horseshoe shape? Having done your research, concentrate on your speech. Define the purpose and intended outcome of your talk, decide on a theme, gather the facts you need, and organize them into a logical structure. Break the talk into manageable chunks. Prepare notes or cue cards and organize handouts or visual aids.

POINTS TO REMEMBER

- If public speaking is a significant part of your job, a training course in presentation skills may be worthwhile.
- Great care should be taken with style and appearance (they account for around 92 per cent of the impact you make).
- Visual clues from the audience should be acted upon.

THINGS TO DO

1. Find out if you are being asked to make a speech, give a talk, or lead a discussion.

2. Find out whether the event is formal or informal.

3. Ask how much time you will have.

4. Find out how large the audience will be.

DEVELOPING YOUR OWN STYLE

Truly successful speakers have a strong presence and unique style, and it can be tempting to try to emulate them. However, it is important to develop a style that is natural for you. If you feel comfortable, you will come across as sincere, which will help you win over audiences. Ensure that your style is not patronising. Use everyday words and phrases. Try to be yourself and imagine that you are talking to just one other person, not a crowd. Speak with immense enthusiasm, even passion. Convey feeling. Remember that enthusiasm is contagious, so spread it to your audience.

Eye contact establishes positive rapport

Relaxed body language conveys confidence

Open jacket presents an image of honesty

Open hand gesture indicates integrity

▲ **APPEARING CONFIDENT**
A confident stance establishes credibility. Speak at a natural pace and aim to maintain eye contact with your audience.

▲ **LOOKING AND FEELING AT EASE**
Relaxed body language conveys honesty and openness. Pause between main points to gauge reactions to your speech.

▲ **USING HAND GESTURES**
Open-handed gestures can help to emphasize key points. Make good use of them to draw the entire audience into the presentation.

49 If you are using a microphone, avoid hiding behind it.

50 Remember to smile – but only when it feels natural to do so.

COPING WITH NERVES

It is natural to be nervous at the prospect of facing an audience, however small. In fact, the rush of adrenaline that results from nervousness helps you cope with the stresses of a presentation. However, excessive nerves need to be dealt with. Confidence in your knowledge of the subject can act as a nerve-calmer. Rehearse beforehand to help reassure yourself that you can do it. Practise relaxation breathing techniques so that you are able to control and steady your breathing when the adrenaline kicks in. Use some of your nervous energy to enliven your speech. Take a deep breath before you begin, and have a glass of water at your side to deal with dryness of the mouth. Sometimes it can help to tell your audience that you are feeling a little nervous; this can act as an ice-breaker and assist in winning their goodwill.

FACING THE AUDIENCE

The first few minutes of a talk are the most difficult. Survive these, and it can only get easier. Welcome your audience and establish a rapport. Make eye contact to help establish and maintain their interest. Run through the proposed content as part of your introduction. Tell your audience when you will finish, whether there will be any breaks, and whether you will be providing handouts and taking questions. Pace yourself. By the time you complete your introduction, your nerves will have calmed. Immediately after your talk, assess your performance. What did you do well? Where could you improve? Follow up any undertakings made, such as sending out further information.

51 Begin by showing your warmth, friendliness, and enthusiasm.

DOS AND DON'TS

✔ Do dress for the occasion.

✔ Do adopt a positive and confident pose.

✔ Do speak up so that the audience can hear you clearly.

✔ Do finish on time.

✘ Don't use distracting mannerisms.

✘ Don't ramble.

✘ Don't use jargon that is unfamiliar to the audience.

✘ Don't use too many statistics.

USING VISUAL AIDS EFFECTIVELY

VISUAL AID

POINTS TO NOTE

OVERHEAD PROJECTORS
Colourful images for overhead projectors are easily created using inexpensive software. These are useful for showing text, but photographs may not reproduce so well.

- All overheads should have a similar visual style for clarity and cohesion.
- Lower-case lettering is far easier to read than capitals.
- A transparency should be informative, but not crammed with too much detail.

FLIP-CHART
A useful supplementary aid, this is ideal for recording an audience's brainstorming contributions, summarizing action points, and explaining ideas visually.

- Sheets should be prepared in advance, using illustrations to explain key points.
- Important points can be emphasized with colour.
- Everyone in the audience must be able to see the flip-chart clearly.

SLIDE PROJECTOR
This is useful when you need to show high quality photographs, since slides are clearer (and more costly) than transparencies.

- Slides should be arranged in order in a slide box prior to your speech.
- Lower lighting levels are needed than for an overhead projector.
- Operating a projector may require some practice prior to your presentation.

LAPTOP COMPUTER
A personal computer with presentation software enables you to prepare visuals and accompanying speaker's notes and handouts in a few easy steps.

- A laptop can be connected to a special projector, enabling slides to be displayed at the click of a mouse.
- High quality graphics may be quickly and inexpensively prepared, and existing slides amended with ease and speed.

VIDEOS
These can be a powerful supplement to a talk. Use videos to show short, live-action images, as well as to spark discussion and debate.

- A video should not take the place of a presentation.
- Videos should be kept short, lasting no longer than about 10 minutes.
- The decision to show a video before or after the presentation may affect its impact.

521

DEVELOPING AN INTERNET SITE

With literally millions of people logging on to travel in cyberspace, a website is fast becoming an essential communication tool. Establish an informative, persuasive site to help you communicate with your target audiences.

52 Keep an eye on other websites and adapt ideas for your own.

53 Ensure that any graphics used are fast-loading.

54 Make sure that you include your website address in all publicity.

ESTABLISHING A WEBSITE

A professional website can improve your image and enhance communication. If your organization does not already have a website, give some serious thought to creating one. Your public might draw unflattering conclusions from the fact that you are not represented in cyberspace. Although you can buy or download software that will help you create a site, remember that your site will form an important part of your corporate image, so it should look professional. Avoid creating a site that could be seen as amateurish. Unless you have the skills in-house, commission a professional website designer.

**BRIEFING A ▶
WEB DESIGNER**
Decide how you intend to use your site. Do you want to inform or educate, build awareness or campaign on an issue? The purpose will dictate the content. Brief your designer on the purpose of the site so that it can be tailor-made for your needs.

PR manager points out website features she would like to see incorporated

DEVELOPING AN INTEGRATED WEBSITE

Website content is often seen as the domain of the marketing department, making it consumer- and sales-driven. Ensure that your organization's website is also PR-driven. Create an area for the media with press releases, downloadable pictures, and background information. Many journalists look first to the internet to find out about an organization. Make access easy (and content relevant) for analysts and investors. Help your marketing colleagues see that your website can be used to persuade and influence a wide audience. Ensure that your website design exploits the interactive nature of the internet and enables a two-way flow of messages. Listening to your target audience is as important as talking to them.

DOS AND DON'TS

✔ Do ask your target audience what they want from your site – and keep the information on it up to date.

✔ Do feature changing attractions to tempt visitors back to your site.

✘ Do not allow graphics to dominate at the expense of content – a website is a communications tool.

✘ Do not overload your home page with information; it will deter visitors from exploring your site.

CREATING AN EFFECTIVE WEBSITE

Commission website design

↓

Test the new site for usability

↓

Go "live" and publicize the site

↓

Collect feedback on the site

↓

Amend your site accordingly

↓

Refresh and update the website regularly

WRITING FOR THE INTERNET

Reading on-screen is much harder than reading text on paper. Tests have shown that on-screen reading is, in fact, 25 per cent slower. Bear this is mind when writing material for your website. Use short, uncomplicated sentences. One-third to one-half of a page of A4 paper can be seen on-screen at a time. Make your site more enticing by breaking up text into manageable chunks and by using plenty of bulletpoints. Surfers dislike scrolling through dense screeds of text.

HANDLING CRISES

Crisis management is an essential PR skill. A well-managed crisis can result in an enhanced image rather than a damaged one. Identify potential crises, draw up contingency plans, and you will be able to keep a calm head should disaster strike.

55 Issue frequent briefings to dispel rumour and speculation.

56 Produce a comprehensive list of potential crises.

57 Decide whether you will need legal advisers to guard against litigation.

BEING PREPARED FOR CRISES

Every organization is a target for crisis. It may come in the shape of fraud; a leak of sensitive information; a hostile takeover bid; robbery; a dangerous product or design fault; sabotage; blackmail; kidnapping; boycotts; natural disaster such as flooding; environmental damage and pollution; or accidents, such as a fatal factory fire. Crises can strike at any time, yet, despite their unpredictable nature, they can be planned for. Examine your vulnerabilities and take pre-emptive action to reduce risk by strengthening your organization. Identify all the things that could go wrong within your organization, however unlikely.

DRAWING UP A CRISIS PLAN

Plan for every contingency and be ready to respond proactively. Take your list of potential disasters and draw up a crisis plan for each scenario. Include information on what action will be taken by whom to inform relevant staff, official bodies, the media, and the public. Do not limit training to head office staff; if a crisis happens in another location, staff there will have to cope with the initial impact. Plan for every eventuality.

Team member makes note of who to contact in an emergency

THINGS TO DO

1. Show genuine sympathy to victims, families, and friends if there has been any harm to people.
2. State your concern if there has been harm to property.
3. Promise a full inquiry.
4. Outline the steps that you have taken to rectify the situation.

▼ PLANNING FOR A CRISIS

Bring together members of your crisis team to present roles and responsibilities and discuss necessary action. Such in-depth planning can increase your chances of a positive outcome.

IMPLEMENTING THE ACTION PLAN

However carefully you have planned, when disaster strikes, stress levels will be far higher than experienced during dry-runs. It is important to select members of a crisis team for their ability to remain calm and in control while under pressure. This skill may be stretched to the limit. Every member should have a copy of the crisis plan and be aware of what is expected of them, what the boundaries are, and who is in charge. You may need to set up freephone helplines; organize a product recall, including media advertising and mailshots to product owners; or you may need to hold a press conference at very short notice. Your crisis manual should contain details of how to implement these key crisis actions, making your task more straightforward and enabling you to carry it out with minimum delay.

Team member is allocated role of official spokesperson in the event of crisis

Manager explains each step of crisis action plan

58 Use your website to commmunicate during a crisis.

ACTING PROMPTLY▼

Protect your reputation by letting the public know what steps you have taken to rectify any errors on your organization's part – such as poor procedures, or unsafe or unacceptable practices. Demonstrate that you have made improvements and show an appropriate amount of regret.

MANAGING THE MEDIA

Disasters make news. Little-known organizations can suddenly find themselves thrust into the limelight for all the wrong reasons. Effective media handling during a crisis is essential if you want to get your message across and help shape a positive image for your organization, even in adversity. Media attention in a crisis may be unavoidable. Draw up a protocol stating who may and may not comment to the media and make staff are aware of this before a crisis occurs. Dealing with aggressive, probing journalists is difficult, so ensure that all spokespeople have undergone media training and know how to field difficult questions. In your crisis manual, list likely tricky questions, as well as good answers to them. Decide how you want to handle the media. You may want to hold a media conference or briefing, or just issue press statements and news releases. Your approach may be proactive, or you may choose to reactively respond to media enquiries. There is no one right way because each crisis demands its own approach.

PR manager reads newspaper allegations that her organization has handled crisis unsympathetically

Manager is pleased with the good press her company has received

59 Learn from other companies that are managing crises.

BENEFITING FROM ▶ CRISIS TRAINING

Having been trained in how to deal with a crisis, Tom, Caitlin, and Peter knew exactly what to do when a serious situation occurred. As a result, the crisis was dealt with swiftly and effectively, with no long-term damage to the company's reputation.

CASE STUDY

Tom, a night-time security man at a biscuit factory, received a telephone call from a journalist seeking a response to a report that glass had been found in one of the company's cookies. Tom contacted Caitlin, the company press officer, at home. She immediately issued a holding statement, which had been pre-cleared by the company lawyers and chief executive. Next she contacted everyone on her crisis list to inform them, including Peter, the production manager. Peter halted production, notified wholesalers and organized a product recall. Caitlin placed ads in the national press asking people to return packets labelled batch 201, issued press releases, and posted instructions on the company website. Customers returning packets gave their details and were sent a personalized letter of apology and an impressive goody bag as compensation.

LOOKING AFTER EMPLOYEES

Staff are an important audience in their own right, so make sure that you keep them informed during a crisis. Brief employees during a major crisis so that they are up to date on what happened and why. Hold regular briefings to keep them updated on the situation. Use the company intranet, issue memos, or hold meetings. When the crisis has abated, do not overlook the possible effects of crisis upon staff. Depending on the nature of the incident, they may be upset and traumatised. Assist employees in dealing with what may have been a difficult or anxious situation. If appropriate, offer some time off work, provide stress counselling, or find other ways to assist affected staff.

MANAGING CRISES EFFECTIVELY

Identify potential crises and take pre-emptive action

Draw up crisis action plans for every scenario

Train relevant staff in crisis management skills

Rehearse for crisis situations and test procedures

When crisis strikes, implement your action plan

Review procedures and rebuild any damage to reputation

60 Following a crisis, be sure to debrief staff and review and refine your crisis procedures.

WORKING WITH THE MEDIA

Media management is a core PR skill. Build strong relationships with journalists, organize successful media events, and monitor coverage to ensure that your message is being conveyed.

MAKING FRIENDS WITH THE MEDIA

Good media contacts often result in better media coverage. Get to know key journalists, and make sure that they know you. Then use your contacts ruthlessly to help you secure excellent coverage for your organization.

61 Understand how people in the press, radio, and television work.

62 Familiarize yourself with the news coverage of target publications.

SECURING ATTENTION

Adopting a proactive approach to media management enables you to build and enhance your profile, promote products, put your case, or simply inform the public, politicians, and trade and professional audiences. Reactive media relations leave you responding to other people's stories. Get to know who's who: once media people start looking to you for help with stories, you'll know you have established a good relationship.

BUILDING RELATIONSHIPS

Organizations with good media contacts and strong, long-term relations with media personnel attract more coverage in general, and more positive coverage in particular. Watch television, listen to the radio, and read newspapers and magazines so that you are familiar with the style of language used and the types of stories covered.

Identify programmes and publications likely to be good outlets for your news. Get to know the editor of your local or trade publication. Contact journalists who specialize in your field of work. Find out who runs the newsroom at your local radio station and TV newsroom. Recognize that a good relationship is mutually beneficial. Always be helpful to journalists: return their calls, keep their deadlines, and be nice to them to keep them on your side.

▼ MAKING MEDIA CONTACTS

Draw up a list of journalists and correspondents to make contact with and then telephone to introduce yourself. Invite journalists to lunch or out for coffee so that you can get to know them better. It is important to work hard to create and sustain relationships with your target media.

ORGANIZING MEDIA VISITS

Consider organizing a formal media visit to which you can invite reporters you want to get to know. Organize site or factory visits to demonstrate your work in action. Draw up a programme that includes lunch with relevant staff. Brief staff on what they can and cannot say over lunch, bearing in mind that many reporters pick up their best stories thanks to loose talk over a bottle of wine. Line up a good story for them to take away, along with a goody bag containing any of your products, or a bottle of wine or whisky. You should not bribe the media, but being mildly generous can help to make them feel better disposed towards you.

POINTS TO REMEMBER

● Journalists are busy people. They need to go away with a good story.

● All journalists like exclusive news, but good stories should be shared, rather than all given to your favourite reporter.

● Journalists may often waste your time, but wasting theirs is never an option if a good relationship is to be maintained.

● Deadlines are vitally important to the media and should be treated with the greatest respect.

ATTRACTING COVERAGE

Favourable media coverage can enhance the reputation of your organization and build credibility with key audiences. Identify newsworthy stories, issue effective news releases, and put together useful media packs to guarantee that you make the headlines.

63 Ask the features editor to consider doing a piece on your organization.

64 Note that letters pages can be an important publicity platform.

65 Use wide margins on releases to give journalists room to make notes.

UNDERSTANDING NEWS RELEASES

The principal way to get on television, radio, or in the press is to issue a news release. A news release is simply your news story, written in a journalistic style. Print and broadcast journalists rely on these releases to help them compile reports, features, and programmes. On receiving your release, a news editor will glance at the headline and first paragraph to get the gist of your story. If what he or she sees fails to attract the all-important attention, it will be discarded. It is estimated that this happens to up to 97 per cent of releases. To create an attention-grabbing release that will stand out from the hundreds of others received daily, make sure that your story is interesting, unusual, controversial, unique, unexpected, or significant.

HITTING THE HEADLINES

To ensure good media coverage for your organization, issue a news release to publicize anything positive that is likely to attract media attention. This might include:

- new products and services;
- product and service enhancements;
- new staff and promotions;
- the winning of awards and honours;
- new outlets and premises;
- important announcements, such as the creation of new jobs, or the opening of a new head office;
- breakthroughs and advancements;
- expansions and takeovers.

Unless you are placing an embargo on your release, type the words "For immediate use" here

Begin with an interesting story angle

Include any background information in a "Notes to editors" section at the end of your release

Include two contact names with work and home numbers

NEWS RELEASE

For immediate use Monday, July 27th

WORLD'S FIRST ARTIFICIAL SKY

The world's first artificial sky has just been switched on. A London company, LonGlass Limited, has produced an £800,000 artificial sky for the London offices of New York bank NYCorp.

Computerized lighting behind a glass ceiling creates brightness in the East during the morning, gradually moving West as the day progresses, thus mimicking the real movement of the sun. The whole effect aims to simulate the natural daylight that was lost when a glass atrium at the offices of NYCorp was filled in to create more office space on the floors above.

Charlie Anderson, Managing Director of LonGlass, says: "This project was not only a major engineering feat, it was a major logistical one too. Because of the bank's need to maintain continuous trading, it was necessary to carry out the work 'after hours' – at night and at weekends."

NOTES TO EDITORS:

1. LonGlass Limited, which this year celebrates its 50th anniversary, has a turnover of £18 million. Further information about the company is available from its Web site: www.longlass.co.uk
2. NYCorp was given planning permission to infill the atrium subject to their replacing the lost natural daylight. An artificial sky was the solution.
3. Photographs of the artificial sky, and other projects, can be downloaded from the LonGlass Web site.

FOR FURTHER INFORMATION CONTACT:
Jenny Mark, PR Manager, LonGlass Limited, on 020 7177 5433 (office) or 020 8943 4322 (home) or Charlie Anderson, Managing Director, on 020 7177 5434 (office) or 020 7755 4793 (home)

Insert the date of distribution

Use a factual but interesting headline

Use double spacing for the body of your release

Include a quotation to make your release look like an authentic media interview

Direct journalists to your website, where they can download relevant photographs and useful background material

▲ CREATING A SUCCESSFUL RELEASE

A good release may be used as the basis for a report in the media, or it may trigger a call from a reporter wanting to find out more. Ensure your release is cleared for issue by your chief executive or other authorized figure.

66 Cover all the facts and keep your releases succinct.

COVERING THE FIVE "Ws"

Having created a news angle to give your story newsworthiness, make sure your release contains the five "Ws", or key facts around which your story is based. Check that you have covered the following:

● WHO will be doing the activity? It may be an individual, an organization, or both.
● WHAT will they be doing? It may be an activity or an announcement.
● WHEN will they be doing it? State the date and, where appropriate, the time.
● WHERE will the event take place?
● WHY are you doing it? What is the reason?

ISSUING YOUR RELEASE

Once your release has been completed, checked, and authorized by the relevant manager, issue it to your target media. If you are unsure where to send it, look for local media addresses in a telephone directory. For national, trade, technical, and consumer titles, plus radio and TV programme details, obtain a specialist media directory. These are expensive, but invaluable if you intend to use media relations as a core plank of your publicity strategy. The directories vary enormously. Some are organized by geographic area, others alphabetically by category (such as aviation, banking, beauty, coin collecting, and so on). Some cover only trade and technical publications, others list only consumer or business titles. Certain directories specialize in the broadcast media, listing programmes, names of producers, and brief details on programme content.

67 Staple releases to prevent pages from being mislaid in a busy newsroom.

68 Make sure that your release arrives in time to meet deadlines.

POINTS TO REMEMBER

- Releases should be addressed to a named person if they are being sent by post. Alternatively, they should be marked for the attention of the news editor or other relevant job title.
- If time is short, or a release or media pack is accompanied by an item such as a product sample, it may be advisable to use a courier service.
- Faxes often go astray in large buildings, so this method of issuing releases should be used only if you have a dedicated fax number of the newsroom or relevant journalist.
- IT reporters will prefer to receive releases electronically.

PRODUCING A MEDIA PACK

If you are mounting a campaign or launching a new product, you may need to give journalists a lot more information than can be contained in a single news release. In such cases, you should organize a media pack. Place in the pack a copy of your news release and any other information that will be useful. For example, you might choose to include background information on your organization, campaign, or product. Case histories, biographies of key personnel, factsheets, a list of frequently asked questions (with answers), and photographs can all form part of a press pack. Product samples, too, can be included. Media packs can be sent to journalists or handed out at a media event such as a news conference, press visit, or photocall.

SECURING COVERAGE FROM DIFFERENT MEDIA

MEDIUM	WAYS TO SECURE COVERAGE
TELEVISION This is a fast-moving, visual medium screening only stories that work well on the small screen.	Aim to create interest with children, animals, costumes, props, and colourful backdrops or interesting venues. Select TV spokespeople with care, since some people are more "telegenic" than others.
RADIO As an aural medium, radio relies on the spoken word and on sound effects.	Think how your story will sound, and what you can do to enhance its listenability. Local stations will want local stories, while national ones usually want material with nationwide significance.
PRESS National papers use national stories, or highly unusual local ones. Local papers look for a strong local angle.	Secure national coverage by stressing the scale or significance of your story. For the local press, look out for ways to identify and emphasize the local angle, perhaps by quoting a local manager.
MAGAZINES Stories have a relevant consumer focus or, for specialist titles, one that will appeal to its specific market.	Avoid technical data and concentrate on the significance to the public or the special interest group. Make an early approach, since these publications usually have long lead-in times.

ORGANIZING A NEWS CONFERENCE

Arrange a conference only when your news is likely to generate considerable media interest – when you are announcing widescale job losses, for example, or announcing significant good news, such as a new factory with an accompanying jobs boost. The idea is to bring everyone together – the media and key representatives from your company – so that you can deal with the announcement and any follow-up interviews at the same time. Have quiet rooms available for media interviews after the event, and ensure that staff giving interviews are fully briefed. Organizing a news conference is time-consuming, and the event itself can be stressful, so ensure that yours will be justified before calling one. If a news release will do the job just as well, send the release – and save time and trouble.

69 Avoid jargon in news releases, unless for the trade press.

70 List your company's experts, and areas of expertise, for your target media.

GIVING MEDIA INTERVIEWS

Being interviewed by the media can be a nerve-wracking business. Prepare well and learn how to respond to difficult questions to ensure that your interview presents you and your organization in a professional and favourable light.

71 Write notes for radio interviews on cue cards – paper will rustle.

72 Avoid distracting mannerisms, such as fiddling with your clothing.

73 Speak in usable, distinct soundbites to help get your message across.

PREPARING FOR A RADIO OR TV INTERVIEW

Broadcast interviews often cause more anxiety than press interviews, but generally there is no need for the extra fear that they tend to generate. Unless an interview is being broadcast live, you do not need to worry too much because it is usually possible to have a question re-asked and re-recorded so that you can offer a more succinct, or a more comprehensive, answer. On most occasions, the interviewer wants to show you at your best, so it is in their interest to relax you and to help you give good answers. Only if you are the villain of the piece will you be given a hard time. Run through likely questions with a colleague in preparation for an interview and to help build confidence.

◀ MANAGING A HOSTILE INTERVIEW
Sometimes your organization will attract media attention when you would rather it did not. It might be that you are making staff redundant, closing a factory, or that some crisis has occurred. When faced with cameras, tape recorders, and hostile reporters, keep calm, make sure that you put your key points across, and then bring the interview firmly to a conclusion.

HANDLING DIFFICULT QUESTIONS

Interviewers generally ask questions designed to get interviewees to respond in an interesting, illuminating, lively, animated, or entertaining way. Rigorous or aggressive questioning may be encountered when your organization has done something unacceptable. Decide in advance what you are willing to say and what you will not reveal. Consider how you will handle difficult questions and practise your answers. When posed a tricky question, never say "No comment". This indicates that you have something to hide. Avoid sounding evasive. Concentrate on getting your points across, if necessary by re-interpreting the interviewer's questions. If asked how you feel about making employees redundant, focus on the positive, such as the help you are offering staff in securing new jobs. Stress, for example, that all employees will receive paid time off to attend job interviews, as well as free out-placement advice.

POINTS TO REMEMBER

- Appropriate dress should be worn for TV, or press interviews where you will be photographed.
- Key points that you would like to get across should be decided on beforehand and opportunities sought during the interview to convey them.
- "Off the record" interviews are inadvisable unless you know and trust a reporter 100 per cent and have very good reasons for speaking off the record.

▼ RECOGNIZING A GOOD SPOKESPERSON

Most organizations have at least one official spokesperson. Make sure that anyone who will be speaking on your company's behalf has the requisite skills and the appropriate personality to do a good job.

GOOD SPOKESPERSON POOR SPOKESPERSON

GOOD SPOKESPERSON	POOR SPOKESPERSON
Confident	Nervous
Empathetic	Arrogant
Genuine	Aggressive
Knowledgeable	Ill-informed
Calm	Angry

GETTING PHOTOGRAPHS PUBLISHED

A good photograph is an excellent publicity vehicle. Learn how to create a viable photo opportunity by identifying the elements that comprise a good photo story. Then contact picture editors to "sell" the idea, or commission your own press shots.

> **74** Whenever your company creates news, consider its picture potential.

ORGANIZING A PHOTOCALL

A photocall is an event that you organize in order to try to attract press photographers. TV cameras may be invited too, if the event merits it. Produce a photocall notice and send it to the picture desk at your target publications about one week before the event. If a paper regards your photo opportunity as worth considering, it will include it in its picture diary. Bear in mind, however, that this is no guarantee of attendance, particularly if a more newsworthy event occurs in the intervening period.

WRITING AN EFFECTIVE PHOTOCALL NOTICE ▼
To invite photographers to attend a photocall, send them a photocall notice. Shown here is the type of photocall that would merit TV coverage. In this case, radio would be invited too, as the material – music and screaming fans – would make excellent listening for pop stations.

PHOTOCALL Issued July 10

CHART-TOPPING BAND LIGHTENING TO OPEN RECORD STORE
The chart-topping band Lightening will be in Anytown, performing their hit single *Heartbreak* to shoppers, and opening a new high street record shop.

PROGRAMME
10 a.m. Band arrives by stretch limousine, to be greeted by screaming fans
10.30 a.m. Band performs hit single *Heartbreak* on the pavement outside Vinyl Groove
10.35 a.m. Johnny Splitz, lead singer with Lightening, will officially open the shop
10.40 a.m. The band will sign autographs in the store for the awaiting fans

Date: Tuesday, July 18th Time: 10 a.m. start
Venue: Vinyl Groove Record Store, 27 High Street, Anytown

YOU ARE INVITED TO SEND A PHOTOGRAPHER

For further information contact: Jenny Stone, store manager, Vinyl Groove 0160 122 5567 (store) or
0160 556 3232 (home) Zak McClone, agent for Lightening 0998 678 4356 (office) or 0770 765438 (mobile)

Include a factual headline

Begin with a short paragraph explaining what is happening and why

If appropriate, include a programme of events

State where and when the event will be

ISSUING YOUR OWN PHOTOGRAPHS

Local newspapers, trade publications, and some consumer magazines will consider using high quality photographs that are supplied to them. To ensure that your photographs are of an acceptable quality and composition, make sure that you use a professional freelance press photographer who thoroughly understands the needs of the print media. Where appropriate, issue photographs with news releases. Alternatively, state in your news release that photos are available for downloading from your website. Ensure that any photos you issue are clearly captioned on the back. State who or what is shown on the photograph, listing people left to right. Never write directly on the back of the photograph, as this may damage it. Always write your caption on a sticky label and then attach it.

75 Avoid shots of products on their own, unless for trade publications.

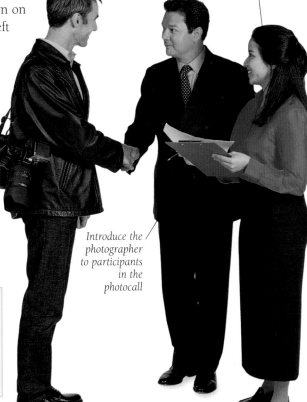

If you have a news release explaining the story, give a copy to the photographer

Introduce the photographer to participants in the photocall

GETTING THE BEST ▶ FROM A PHOTOCALL

Greet photographers when they arrive at a photocall, explain the purpose of the event, and tell them who or what is available to be photographed.

76 Use props or backgrounds to make pictures more interesting.

MONITORING MEDIA COVERAGE

Having succeeded in getting news stories into print or onto film, the next step is to ensure that your organization is being publicized consistently in a positive light. Keep notes of any media contact, track media coverage, and evaluate your work.

77 Research specialist software that can help you evaluate media coverage.

LOGGING MEDIA CALLS

The harder you work at raising your company's profile, the more likely it is that you will attract an increased number of calls from the media. Aim to log these calls so that you have a reliable record of reactive media responses. Take a note of who calls, the publication or programme they represent, and the nature of their enquiry. Also record your response or any statement issued. Ask when the piece is being run and when it appears, check that you have been represented fairly.

Write down what the journalist wants to know and why

MEDIA LOG

Name of journalist Publication/programme
Contact phone number Contact fax number
Date of call Time of call
Call taken by Response needed by
Nature of enquiry

Response

Response issued by Method

Ask when a response is needed to avoid missing media deadlines

Make a note of what you said in response to the call – if you issued a written response, attach it to the log

Insert name of person providing the response

State whether the call was dealt with there and then, or handled in a follow-up phone call, by post, e-mail, or fax

TRACKING COVERAGE

Every time you issue a news release or photocall notice, keep a copy for your files. Attach to it a distribution list and compare actual media coverage against this list to work out your "hit" rate. If most of your releases are being used, you are probably being highly effective. If only a small percentage of releases are being published or aired, investigate why. Are you missing deadlines, issuing weak releases, or targeting the wrong media? Call some names on your distribution list and see if you can find out.

78 Consider using a press cuttings bureau to help you monitor the coverage you receive.

79 Video TV news to see if key messages are well conveyed.

80 Keep a scrap book of press cuttings for your archive.

USING A BUREAU

Consider outsourcing media monitoring to a specialist bureau. These bureaux will issue press cuttings, audio tapes of radio coverage, video tapes of television coverage, and transcripts of broadcast coverage. Many also offer an evaluation service. You may need one bureau for press and another for broadcast monitoring, as not all bureaux handle both. Press cuttings bureaux often charge a monthly retainer or reading fee, and an amount per cutting. Broadcast monitoring firms do not usually charge a retainer.

EVALUATING COVERAGE

Organizations once used quantitative rather than qualitative measures for assessing their media effectiveness. A thick bundle of press cuttings represented success. Today, this measure is seen as one-dimensional since it fails to distinguish between positive and negative coverage. Your evaluation should assess each piece of media coverage to ascertain whether the messages conveyed are positive, negative, or neutral. Also take into account the value of successfully keeping potentially damaging stories out of the media. Effective evaluation relies on the analysis of a combination of factors, namely: frequency (how often the story is repeated); circulation (how many people were reached); and readership (whether the readership is a key audience for your organization).

539

PRODUCING PUBLICITY

Effective printed materials are key to successful PR. Learn to write powerful copy, commission strong design and photography, and organize quality printing to ensure persuasive results.

THINKING ABOUT PUBLICITY

Producing a PR document, such as a promotional brochure, from scratch can be daunting. To produce publicity material that will attain maximum impact with the minimum of stress, plan throroughly and allow plenty of time.

81 Avoid rushing key decisions – focus on getting them absolutely right.

82 Remember to allow time to evaluate any quotes submitted.

IMPROVING RESULTS

The key to producing effective publicity materials is to adopt an organized approach. Make sure that you allow sufficient time by creating a production schedule setting out deadlines for copy, proofs, and final artwork. Circulate a copy to appropriate colleagues, making it clear who is responsible for each task. Build in leeway to allow for delays, and seek competitive quotations from suppliers such as copywriters, photographers, and printers.

▼ PLANNING PUBLICITY

It is easier for the team to produce effective publicity if everyone has a clear vision of what they are aiming for. Work with the team to form a concept for your material, and then explain your ideas to copywriters, designers, and illustrators.

PR executive explains his concept to team members

UNDERSTANDING AIDCA

Every item of publicity you produce should attract attention. Make your publicity attention-grabbing using colour, layout, illustration, and text to create an unmissable piece of publicity. Next, maintain interest by holding the attention of the reader with captivating, persuasive, clear, and readable copy. Ease the reading process with thoughtful design and navigational layout. Then create desire. Decide what reader-response you want, and produce publicity designed to elicit that reaction. Having appealed to the heart, now use hard and persuasive facts to build conviction. The final test of successful publicity material is its ability to prompt action. These five stages are known by the acronym AIDCA, standing for attention, interest, desire, conviction and action.

USING YOUR PUBLICITY

It is not uncommon for organizations to spend considerable sums of money producing quality publicity material, only to leave much of it stacked, unused, in a storeroom. Ensure that your brochures and other materials are distributed to your target audiences. Draw up a distribution plan, and be ready to activate it as soon as your material is ready. Check that staff are aware of new materials and have sufficient supplies to hand out. Take your publicity materials to talks, seminars, and exhibitions. Leave supplies where they will be picked up by your target audience. Aim to make your materials work hard for you.

QUESTIONS TO ASK YOURSELF

Q What publicity material do we need?

Q Why do we need it: is there anything else we can use?

Q How will we use it: will we send material out in mailshots, or simply hand it out?

Q What is purpose of the material: is it meant to publicize or persuade?

Q Who is publicity aimed at, and is there a target delivery date?

WRITING COPY

A few well-chosen words can stir the emotions and even persuade people to adopt a different viewpoint. The art lies in choosing the right words. Effective copy remembers the reader, uses straightforward language, and employs meticulous planning.

83 Write with a real person, rather than an abstract category, in mind.

84 Practise writing copy until you feel more comfortable with the style.

UNDERSTANDING COPY

Publicity material should be written in a totally new and different language. It is neither business writing nor traditional composition but a style that is creative and rule-breaking. Certain grammatical strictures can be abandoned in the language of copy. As long as communication is not being impeded, it is acceptable to adopt a more relaxed style of writing, something more akin perhaps to the spoken word.

DIFFERENTIATING WRITING STYLES

BUSINESS WRITING	COPYWRITING
Uses a formal style and is traditional in its language.	Is informal in style, using contractions such as "you're" and "we'll".
Often uses the "third person", for example "the organization" and "the customer".	Usually makes use of the first and second person, for example, "we" and "you".
Often uses business or company jargon.	Uses plain English at all times.
Often comprises long tracts of text.	Comprises short, readable chunks of text.
Follows strict grammatical rules.	Breaks grammatical rules in a controlled way.
Uses the passive voice.	Uses the active voice.

GETTING STARTED ON YOUR COPY

Jot down your thoughts and ideas

Organize your ideas into clear themes

Arrange your themes in a logical order

Decide on what goes where and the space it should occupy

Sit down and write a first draft

Revise your draft and polish your finished work

85 Identify your audience before setting pen to paper.

CULTURAL DIFFERENCES

Although English is a global language, usage and style differ from one country to another. If expressing dates in numerals, for example, 2.6.01 would be interpreted as June 2, 2001, in the United Kingdom but as February 6, 2001, in the United States. Similarly, the French and Germans use a period to group digits in numbers and a comma as the decimal separator, whereas the Anglo-Saxon countries do the opposite, that is 1,000 could mean one (to three decimal places), or one thousand. In Germany and Scandinavia, writers often emphasize points by indenting them on a separate line rather than underlining or italicizing them, which is how important points are often emphasized in the U.S. and the U.K.

USING PLAIN ENGLISH

Organizational jargon is an extremely useful shorthand when confined to communication in-house or with fellow professionals who, as it were, speak the language. However, publicity materials are generally produced for an external audience and so should avoid jargon. Jargon-free writing is known as "plain English". It features short, everyday words and brief sentences; unnecessary technical terms and officialese are avoided. Plain English follows a clear and logical order that takes into account the needs and interests of the reader. It is a straightforward and transparent style, not a pompous, self-important, and opaque way of writing. Replace cumbersome and clichéd phrases with succinct words: "now" rather than "at this point in time", for example.

86 Use headlines and subheads to break up your body copy.

87 Avoid using dense screeds of text, as this will deter readers.

APPLYING COPYWRITING TECHNIQUES

Professional copywriters use a number of techniques to add interest and life to their prose. Rhyme is a much-used technique, as is alliteration (where two or more neighbouring words begin with the same sound). Puns (witty plays on words), too, are a popular technique. Good copy has rhythm. A mix of short and longer sentences can help your copy flow. An occasional one-word sentence will provide interest and unexpectedly alter the rhythm in a way that holds a reader's interest. Avoid monotony by inverting sentences and creating a new word order. For example, rather than writing "This year's catalogue features a wider range of products than ever and is unmissable", try "With a wider than ever range of products, this year's catalogue is unmissable".

FINDING INSPIRATION

When you are under pressure to produce a piece of publicity, it can be difficult to come up with a good idea. The harder you try, the more elusive the idea becomes. Look out for other people's good ideas and build up a collection of inspirational publicity material. When inspiration is lacking, look through your collection to see if it can spark a few ideas. Analyze effective copy and try to identify the techniques the writer has used. See if those techniques can be re-interpreted and re-deployed in your own work. Sometimes inspiration can be found in unexpected places: children's books, giftwrap, greetings cards, and magazines have all served to stimulate creativity. If inspiration still eludes you, try a brainstorming session with colleagues. This may free your mind and help release a good idea.

▼ COLLECTING IDEAS
Build up a scrap book of inspirational publicity that you can refer to when you need to think up new ideas. Bear in mind that inspiration can sometimes come from unexpected places, such as children's books or greetings cards.

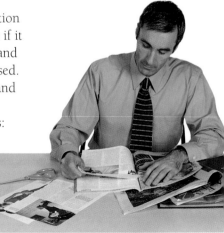

REVISING YOUR WORK

Produce a first draft of your publicity material, then put it aside for a day or two. Return to it fresh and your chances of spotting its shortcomings will be increased. Identify areas for improvement, then redraft as necessary. Repeat this process until you are happy with the result. When revising your work, look out for: clichés; repetition of words or phrases; jargon; and redundancy (unnecessary words). Check for lack of consistency. Avoid verbosity, ambiguity, and pomposity. Aim for clarity and brevity. Having reached a version that you feel content with, test your text on a small number of people representative of your target audience. Ask for feedback and amend your copy as necessary.

▼ MAKING CORRECTIONS

Each time you make revisions, read through your copy carefully, checking for consistency and clarity as well as for any mistakes in spelling or punctuation. The more professional your publicity is, the more seriously it will be taken.

PR executive cuts extraneous words to tighten up her copy

USING A COPYWRITER

Regard copy as one of the most vital elements of successful publicity materials. Unless you have the utmost confidence in your ability to write good copy, commission a professional copywriter to do the job for you. Copywriters know how to attract and maintain readers' attention and are skilled in translating complex ideas into lively, readable text.

DEALING WITH WRITER'S BLOCK

All writers experience writer's block occasionally, but it is an affliction that strikes inexperienced writers particularly frequently. The main symptom is an inexplicable inability to concentrate or to write. If you do suffer from writer's block, try one of the many techniques guaranteed to help you get started – or finished. Take a break, get some fresh air, or try a change of scene. Find a quiet place to work, or take your writing home with you. Boost your energy levels by running around the block or eating a snack. You will probably be more alert earlier in the working day, so timetable your copywriting for the morning if writer's block remains a problem.

DESIGNING PUBLICITY

Attractive publicity design is as important as well-written copy. Tackle design in-house, or use a professional graphic designer or illustrator. Know how to brief a designer, check proofs, and assess the effectiveness of the design.

88 Choose a point size large enough for people to able to read easily.

89 Check that the eye can easily follow the design.

KEEPING YOUR LAYOUTS SIMPLE ▼
Desktop publishing enables users to create professional publicity materials that reinforce corporate identity. Avoid using too many effects and opt for clear, simple layouts.

DESIGNING IN-HOUSE

With desktop publishing software, basic design is within the realms of any organization. Materials such as invoices, in-house manuals, order forms, and price lists may be easily designed to a professional standard in-house. Keep it simple. Limit yourself to one or two fonts (type faces) and point sizes (type sizes). Use ready-made templates as your basis, but personalize them to fit your corporate style. Attend a desktop publishing (DTP) course if necessary. Technical competence should be accompanied by a good eye for design.

POOR EXAMPLE

Layout is chaotic and difficult to follow

Too many fonts and point sizes look confusing and messy

Overuse of clipart and heavy borders gives amateurish feel to design

Dark paper detracts from message

Press release

THE WORLD'S FIRST artificial sky has just been switched on. A London company, LonGlass Limited, has produced an £800,000 artificial sky office ban

"This project was no major engineering fe major logistical one Because of the Bank maintain continuous was necessary to car

Computerized lighting behind a glass ceiling creates brightness in the East during the morning, gradually moving West as the day progresses, thus mimicking the real movement of the sun. The whole effect aims to

GOOD EXAMPLE

❄ PRESS RELEASE

First artificial sky

THE WORLD'S FIRST artificial sky has just been switched on. A London company, LonGlass Limited, has produced an £800,000 artificial sky for the London offices of New York bank NYCorp.

Charlie Anderson, Managing Director of LonGlass, says: *"This project was not only a major engineering feat, it was a major logistical one too. Because of the bank's need to maintain continuous trading, it was necessary to carry out the work 'after hours' – at night and at weekends."*

Computerized lighting behind a glass ceiling creates brightness in the East during the morning, gradually moving West as the day

1

Layout and text are clear, readable, and easy to follow

Using fewer fonts and point sizes helps keep the message clear and easily accessible

USING "OVERPRINT" STATIONERY

Overprint stationery enables you to have attractive and professional design without the expense of commissioning original design. Specialist suppliers produce attractive designs of letterheads and business stationery, menus, invoices, leaflets, posters, and other publicity material. This is then overprinted on a laser printer or photocopier with your own text, address, and other information. Slightly more costly are personalized "empty belly" leaflets or posters. Similar in principle to overprint stationery, these are designed just for you and may incorporate your logo and corporate colours.

90 Check that your logo appears on everything you design.

91 Use personalized stationery for professional and quick results.

FINDING A DESIGNER

It is important to use designers wherever possible, since poor design will reflect badly on your reputation. Professional training and know-how enables them to do a better job than even the keenest amateur. If you do not already have a good relationship with a designer, find one you can work with. Use either a design consultancy or a freelance. Some designers charge significantly more than others, but quality and price do not always go hand in hand, so shop around. Ask about fees during any initial discussions. Most designers will show you their best work, usually to be found in high-budget, lavish productions. Ask to see examples of both low- and mid-budget work too. Their ability to tackle a low-budget commission well is a good indicator of their general ability and creativity.

MEETING DESIGNERS ▼
Arrange to see three or four designers and look through their portfolios. Select a designer you feel you can work with. Choose one whose work you like, whose style is varied, and who seems to have a good feel for what you are seeking.

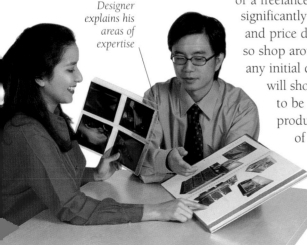

Designer explains his areas of expertise

PROVIDING A COMPREHENSIVE DESIGN BRIEF

KEY AREA	WHAT TO COVER IN YOUR BRIEF
AUDIENCE	Explain who the publicity is aimed at. Try to paint a picture of the type of person who will read it.
STYLE	What style are you looking for? Nostalgic? Contemporary? High-tech? Lavish? Explain your ideas fully.
EXTENT	Inform your designer of the number of pages and what size they should be (for example, whether they are A4 or A3).
ILLUSTRATIONS	State whether charts, tables, and other illustrations are required, and tell your designer of photography requirements.
COLOURS	State how many colours should be used, and whether there are certain colours to include (such as corporate colours) or avoid.
PAPER	Explain your requirements for a particular type or colour of paper, asking your designer for advice and samples if necessary.
SPECIAL EFFECTS	Discuss any special effects required, such as die cutting, spot varnishes, or foil blocking, and ask for your designer's input.

92 Choose artwork that is appropriate for your audience.

93 Use the local art college as a source of design talent.

COMMISSIONING ILLUSTRATION

Graphic designers take text and produce layouts using special computer design packages. Illustrators provide designers with drawings, paintings, and other illustrations, usually produced on paper. Your designer should be able to put you in touch with an illustrator who can produce the style of artwork you are looking for. Like artists, illustrators have their own distinct style – perhaps very detailed and lifelike, or bold abstract work. Ask to see an illustrator's portfolio to satisfy yourself that you like their style.

94 Spot misspellings by reading from right to left.

95 Look through brochures and collect design ideas that appeal.

ESTABLISHING A HOUSE STYLE

To ensure that all your material is seen to come from the same stable, establish your own house style. Specify the font and colours to be used. These will probably be taken from your corporate identity. State how large your logo must be (or how small it can go) and where it should be positioned. House style can cover words as well as design. Produce guidelines to ensure consistency. Explain, for example, what the acceptable writing style is, or how words with alternative spellings should be spelt. Give copies to anyone responsible for writing or designing material.

CHECKING PROOFS THOROUGHLY

When checking proofs, there is plenty to watch out for. Often you will find that a word has been repeated. Spelling mistakes may occur. A word may be missed out altogether. That is why it is important to read what is there, not what you think is there. Avoid speed reading. Pore over every word. Look for awkward breaks in words. Words may have two spellings: take co-ordinate (hyphen) and coordinate (no hyphen). You may use British 'ise' endings, as in 'utilise', or American 'ize', as in 'utilize'. The golden rule is to be consistent.

ACHIEVING ►
CONSISTENCY
Read all proofs to ensure consistency and accuracy throughout. Correct any spelling variations or inaccurate punctuation, and make sure that any photos and captions have been correctly paired.

Trade show attracts record crowds

This year's popular three-day National Garden Furniture trade show attracted record crowds of 45,000 at the Central Arena in Lower Hadley Upon the Mill. One hundred of the country's leading garden furniture manufacturers took part and exhibited their latest designs at the show which was organized by Wooded Cane and Company and promoted by A Tree and Sons. Johnathan Smith, Managing Director of Wooded Cane and Company, said: "It is only the third year we have organized this national event and we are all delighted by the record attendance figures. Work is already underway planning next year's show when we hope to introduce new facilities for our exhibitors and our visitors with more on-site catering outlets."

Highlights of this year's designs included a glass and plastic multi-coloured five-piece table and chair set as well as a more traditional alpine chalet-styled shed, complete with verandah.

Over 40,000 people visited the National Garden Furniture show.

COMMISSIONING PHOTOGRAPHY

Whether you are using pictures on your website or on your publicity materials, products, premises, and people will look their best when photographed by a professional. Build up a stock of good quality photographs that reflect your work.

96 Bear in mind that good photographs can speak louder than words.

97 Ask to see evidence of a photographer's area of expertise.

FINDING A PHOTOGRAPHER

Photographers excel in different areas, so you may have to use different people for different assignments. Some are excellent press photographers, others excel at studio work, and others have a talent for photographing people. Ask about a photographer's area of expertise, look at their portfolios, and judge for yourself.

BRIEFING YOUR PHOTOGRAPHER

Give your photographer a full brief. Begin with the assignment. State locations (and whether indoor or outdoor) and, where necessary, draw up a schedule. List who or what is to be photographed and what you hope to show or to achieve with each shot, then state when you want the job completed. Provide some background material on your company to help the photographer understand your work. Always confirm details in writing, and ask the photographer to assign copyright for pictures to you, also in writing.

▼ DISCUSSING FORMAT
Specify the format that you want your photographer to use, for example colour transparencies. If you are unsure, explain how you want to use the photos and ask what would be the best format.

USING YOUR OWN PHOTOGRAPHS

Look for opportunities to use your photographs. Incorporate them into exhibition and display boards. Include relevant shots in press packs, use them to illustrate your website, and provide downloadable pictures for media use. Make good use of photographs in publicity materials and incorporate slides into talks and presentations to bring them to life.

98 Ask photographers to confirm shoot details in writing.

USING PICTURE LIBRARIES

You can obtain professional photographs from picture libraries, which provide a choice of literally millions of high-quality images. This is a useful option if you are looking for top quality photos that would be uneconomical to commission yourself, perhaps because an exotic location is required, or models, or special props. Simply describe in as much detail as possible the type of image you want and leave the library to source a selection. Often a small search fee is charged, which is waived if you "buy" the image. Generally, you pay for permission to use an image once, with the fee depending on factors such as where it will appear and how large it will be. Buying sole rights to use a photo is expensive and probably unnecessary. Most picture libraries produce CD-ROM catalogues that give an indication of the pictures they stock. Bear in mind that these contain only a sample of what is on offer, since a CD has room for only a limited number of images.

COMPARING PRICES

Although price should not dictate which photographer you use, it may influence selection to some degree. When asking photographers about their charges, check the following:
- Rate – this may be charged hourly, daily or half-daily, or per assignment;
- Materials – you may be charged extra for film, developing, and contact sheets;
- Expenses – ask what expenses are charged and at what rate, such as mileage and meals;
- Prints – ask the price of different sized prints.

Work out the approximate overall cost of different photographers. A low hourly rate may not ultimately produce a smaller bill.

POINTS TO REMEMBER
- Premises should always be tidied before a photo shoot.
- Photographs should be as interesting, creative, and imaginative as possible.
- Shots of large crowds or people in meetings should be avoided.
- Photographs should not contain too many different elements.
- A photographic budget can be stretched by anticipating need and taking shots that could be used in the future.

GETTING PUBLICITY PRINTED

Every PR executive needs a good working knowledge of print production. Ensure that you know how to select the right printer for the right job, and learn which factors influence cost and how to make savings by undertaking your own print-buying.

99 Check proofs carefully before signing them off for printing.

OBTAINING COMPETITIVE QUOTATIONS

Prepare a short-list of printers

⬇

Draw up a specification detailing your needs

⬇

Ask for a written quotation and samples

⬇

Select a printer based on price and quality

⬇

Confirm the job in writing, and state the delivery date and delivery address

CHOOSING A PRINTER

Whenever you use a supplier, make sure that you shop around – not only for the best price, but also for the most appropriate provider for your needs. Most large printing firms employ sales representatives who will be happy to visit you. Find out what equipment and machinery the print firm uses and what it is capable of. Ensure that the representative brings samples. Check that the quality is good. Are colours true? Are documents folded neatly? Are pages stapled, or wire stitched, with precision? Are pages cut square? Usually a rep can arrange for you to visit and to see the printshop in action. This is a good opportunity to introduce yourself to the processes and the jargon, and to ask questions.

DOS AND DON'TS

✔ Do get three quotes for every print job, and tell printers you are doing this.

✔ Do ask for a fully inclusive and itemized quotation that also covers any extras.

✘ Do not give work to a printer if you are unhappy with the quality of their samples.

✘ Do not use a printer who took too long to prepare a quote – this signals unreliability.

BUDGETING FOR PRINT

Many factors affect print prices. Internal factors – such as how busy the printer is, or how much they want your business – will have an influence. Then there is the specification or "spec". Certain processes will add to the cost. Full-colour printing costs more than two-colour printing. The number of pages (extent), the number of copies (run), and the type of paper used (stock) will also affect cost. Special effects and finishes, such as metallic inks, die-cutting, varnishing, laminating, and embossing will inflate the bill. There will be a charge for scanning (converting photographs into a form that enables them to be printed) and for the provision of cromalins (special photographic proofs).

POINTS TO REMEMBER

- Extra charges for collating, folding, stitching, and delivery will need to be taken into account.
- Unusual and non-standard papers will be likely to attract a premium.
- While heavier paper may look attractive, it could increase postage costs if you are intending to mail publicity.
- It is far less expensive to have a few extra copies printed if you think you may need them than to reprint materials at a later date.

100 Negotiate print quotes downwards to ensure that you get the best deal.

USING DIGITAL PRINTING

Traditional printing performed on a printing press is ideal for runs of at least 500: the larger the run, the lower the unit cost. However, for short runs – especially short full-colour runs – digital printing is more cost effective. With a press, the main cost is in setting up the machine, making small runs uneconomical. Digital printing has no set-up costs, so the unit cost for one copy is little different to the unit cost for 1,000. Many printshops offer both forms of printing. Ask which is best for your needs.

UNDERTAKING YOUR OWN PRINT-BUYING

If you do not have time to arrange your own printing, or if print-buying is a new area and you would prefer to gain some experience first, you can ask a graphic designer to organize it for you. In the long term, however, it is cheaper to do your own print-buying. It is standard practice for designers to mark up the cost of printing, usually by about 15 or 20 per cent, as a kind of handling fee.

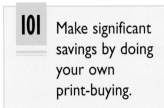

101 Make significant savings by doing your own print-buying.

ASSESSING YOUR PR ABILITY

A thorough understanding of PR techniques will help you to build a good image and protect the reputation of your organization. Test your skills by answering the following questions. If your answer is "Never", circle option 1; if it is "Always", circle option 4, and so on. Add your scores together, and refer to the analysis to see how you fared. Use the answers to identify areas that need improving.

OPTIONS

1 Never

2 Occasionally

3 Frequently

4 Always

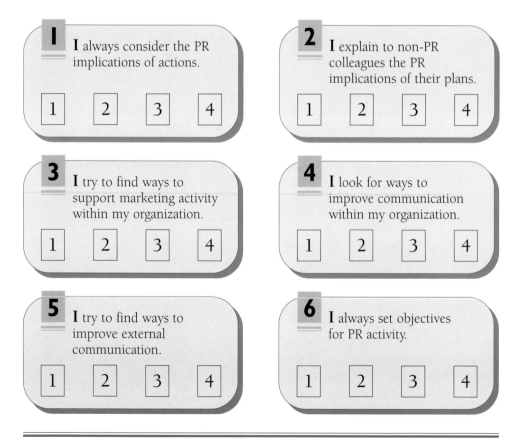

1 I always consider the PR implications of actions.

1 2 3 4

2 I explain to non-PR colleagues the PR implications of their plans.

1 2 3 4

3 I try to find ways to support marketing activity within my organization.

1 2 3 4

4 I look for ways to improve communication within my organization.

1 2 3 4

5 I try to find ways to improve external communication.

1 2 3 4

6 I always set objectives for PR activity.

1 2 3 4

7 I select communications channels with care.

1 2 3 4

8 I define clear messages for each PR initiative.

1 2 3 4

9 I seek to measure the effectiveness of PR activities.

1 2 3 4

10 I ensure that staff information is presented clearly and honestly.

1 2 3 4

11 I consider the impact of all our activities on our reputation.

1 2 3 4

12 I pay attention to the smallest detail when organizing events.

1 2 3 4

13 I select event venues with great care.

1 2 3 4

14 I provide written briefs for event participants.

1 2 3 4

15 I consider the legal and safety issues of any event.

1 2 3 4

16 I set aside time to plan and prepare for talks and presentations.

1 2 3 4

17 I evaluate my performance after giving a presentation.

1 2 3 4

18 I look for opportunities to attract positive media coverage.

1 2 3 4

19 I work hard to build and maintain good relationships with the media.

1 2 3 4

20 I check press releases to ensure that the five "Ws" are covered.

1 2 3 4

21 I prepare thoroughly for media interviews.

1 2 3 4

22 I try to anticipate tricky media questions.

1 2 3 4

23 I examine events for their photo opportunity potential.

1 2 3 4

24 I log all media calls.

1 2 3 4

25 I calculate the hit rate of news releases.

1 2 3 4

26 I evaluate media coverage.

1 2 3 4

27 I allow sufficient time for publicity production.

1 2 3 4

28 I produce a production schedule for new publicity materials.

1 2 3 4

29 I produce a distribution plan for each new piece of publicity.

1 2 3 4

30 I write publicity materials in an appropriate style for the target audience.

1 2 3 4

31 I commission professional design when necessary.

1 2 3 4

32 I check design proofs with care.

1 2 3 4

ANALYSIS

Now that you have completed the self-assessment, add up your total score and check your performance. Whatever level of success you have achieved, there is always room for improvement. Identify your weakest areas, then refer to the relevant pages of this section, where you will find practical advice and tips to help you establish and hone your PR skills.

32–63: You need to take a more organized, systematic, sustained, and proactive approach to improve the effectiveness of your PR activity.

64–95: Some of your PR activity is having a positive impact on your organization's reputation, but you need to develop your skills to become more strategic in approach.

96–128: You are thorough, professional, strategic, and are achieving considerable success. Keep it up.

PUTTING CUSTOMERS FIRST

INTRODUCTION

To maximize business performance in the future, managers must focus on their most valuable assets – their customers – today. Putting Customers First *helps you build your customer-orientated skills, plan effectively to meet customer requirements on time, and give customers the benefits they want. From gathering information that will help you and your team understand your clients to building successful working partnerships with them, every aspect of the customer-first approach is clearly explained. With 101 practical tips and a self-assessment questionnaire to help you evaluate your customer service skills, this section is an invaluable reference to achieving market-led success.*

UNDERSTANDING CUSTOMERS

A thorough understanding of your customers is essential if you are to serve them well. Identify and learn about your best customers so that you can plan how best to satisfy them.

WHY PUT CUSTOMERS FIRST?

For an organization to thrive, it must keep pace with its customers' changing needs and succeed in satisfying them. Put customers first, and you will ensure that you meet and anticipate their demands and expectations, and so continue to win their business.

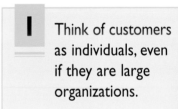

1 Think of customers as individuals, even if they are large organizations.

2 Encourage staff to analyze all their activities from the customers' point of view.

MEETING CUSTOMERS' REQUIREMENTS

By adopting a customer-first approach, you ensure that you provide the right products and services to the right people now and into the future. If you enable your customers to drive which products and services you provide and how you provide them, you can be certain that you are meeting their needs. This is vital for long-term profitability, since customers will pay only for what they want.

ANTICIPATING NEEDS

Government policies, consumer fashions, new technologies, economic conditions, and hence customers' needs are changing all the time. As a result, it is vital that you understand your customers thoroughly, listen to them regularly, watch for developments or events that could affect them and their business, and then plan how to meet their new requirements. You will then avoid the risk that they will go elsewhere because you have failed to identify that their needs have changed or that competitors are offering superior products and services.

MEETING CHANGING REQUIREMENTS

> Conduct research into customers' wants

> ↓

> Design product or service to meet need

> ↓

> Gather feedback to measure customer satisfaction

> ↓

> Assess how competitors are meeting customers' needs

> ↓

> Evaluate findings and make changes if necessary

3 Every time you meet customers, make a point of talking about their future requirements.

SATISFYING EXPECTATIONS

Today's customers expect first-class service. If they sense that you are not putting them first, they will feel disappointed. Be aware that your customers will not only assess your performance against that of your competitors, but they will also judge you against what they promised to deliver, and what they believe to be acceptable standards. If you anticipate missing a deadline or failing to deliver exactly what was promised, inform your customers as early as possible.

Team member calls customer to ask how she can be of more help

EXCEEDING ▶ EXPECTATIONS

Put customers first by always striving to improve your service. Remember that all customers have choices, and your objective is to ensure that they choose to keep doing business with you.

FOCUSING ON YOUR BEST CUSTOMERS

Some customers will be more important to your organization than others. Some who are important in the short term may not be so valuable in the long term. Identify your best prospects so that you can focus on serving them well in the future.

> **4** Make a list of your top ten customers and talk to them frequently.

> **5** See that your team know who their best customers are.

> **6** Keep in regular contact with your customers.

DEFINING "BEST" CUSTOMERS

Whether your customers are internal to your organization, outside individuals or companies, or representatives of other organizations, some will be better prospects than others. Your best customers are not necessarily the ones who bring you the greatest profits now, but those who will want more of your services in the future. It is far more cost-effective to retain existing customers than attract new ones, so focus on customers who are likely to provide the best returns in the future.

Acts as a good reference for other prospects

Has real need for your products or services

Is not threatened by external economic forces

Appreciates the value of your products/services

Has potential to grow

Is commercially worthwhile

◀ **IDENTIFYING A WORTHWHILE CUSTOMER**
There are several important qualities that can make a customer particularly valuable, and some will be more important to you than others.

EXAMINING TRENDS

To identify customers who will be most important in the future, look at the underlying trends within your industry. If, for example, you currently serve customers in an industry that is in decline, consider changing the focus of your efforts. You may also need to change your focus to cater for seasonal or fashion trends. An ice cream manufacturer who sells ice cream to children during the summer, for example, might decide to sell frozen desserts to adults in the winter. Change your focus before sales or revenue fall by anticipating, rather than reacting to, an economic trend. Look for signs of new trends and seek out growth areas, then alter which customers you target, or your products and services, to meet this challenge.

7 Always ask your customers how their business is progressing.

8 Study the trade journals for each of your customers' industries.

9 Help your customers succeed and you will succeed too.

RETAINING LONG-TERM CUSTOMERS

Selling more of your products or services to existing customers is far more cost-effective than selling to new prospects. It therefore makes sense to retain your best customers by anticipating new economic conditions and helping current customers to adapt to them. Make sure that you are prepared to help your customers make the most of opportunities when new markets open up.

◀ **BUILDING RELATIONSHIPS**
Meet customers informally and demonstrate your knowledge of their industry and specific needs. Inform them of events or developments that may affect them adversely in time for them to take appropriate action.

Team member brings customer's attention to negative market report

Customer learns of market trend going against him

UNDERSTANDING THE END CUSTOMER

An important part of preparing to serve your customers well is to gain an understanding of what their customers want. Find out from your customers how you and your team can play your part in keeping the end customer satisfied.

10 Remember that the end customer is the life blood of your organization.

11 Serve your internal customers well to keep external customers happy.

UNDERSTANDING CUSTOMER EXPECTATIONS

If you are part of a large organization, you are likely to be working for other people inside your organization. These people are your internal customers, and they will have expectations that need to be satisfied. However, it is important to understand their aims. They, in turn, will be responsible for satisfying their customers, and the chain goes on until it reaches the end customer outside the organization. To ensure that you are providing the right service in the right way, you need to know how your internal customers want to serve their customers.

CASE STUDY

Tom, an administrator, was responsible for providing information to internal customers. He collated data for Sally, the manager of a team providing a maintenance service to an organization's computer department, on the length of time it took for an engineer to respond to each Type A (fast-response) problem. Sally explained that this was no longer how the external customer measured her team's performance. They were now more interested in the time it took for an engineer to fix the problem. By making a small change to the engineers' logging system, Tom was able to provide Sally with this information relatively easily. This not only saved Sally the time it would have taken to make the calculations herself, but also impressed the end customer, who noted the team's fast, efficient response to the new requirement.

◀ **RESPONDING TO CUSTOMER DEMANDS**
By talking to Sally about the changing requirements of the external customer, Tom was able to improve the quality of service he delivered to her, which in turn improved the level of service her internal team provided externally.

12 Talk to everyone who acts as a link between you and the end customer.

13 If you are unsure how to link what you do to the end customer, ask your superior for guidance.

LINKING TO YOUR ORGANIZATION'S STRATEGY

Most organizations have a strategy that defines which products or services are sold and delivered to which groups of customers, and sets out how this should be done excellently and competitively. Ensure that you are familiar with both your own organization's strategy and your customers' goals so that you can tailor the way in which you provide your services to fit in with them. If, for example, your team is responsible for designing brochures for the sales department, your internal customer, your organization's strategy will set out overall which external customers should be targeted. The sales team's more specific goals will have been set in line with this strategy. You will need to understand both sets of aims in order to meet the wants and needs of external customers and ensure that you are presenting one consistent strategy to them.

CONNECTING EVERYONE TO THE END CUSTOMER

Encourage your team to think about the end customer as they go about their daily business. If they have always followed the same routine, stress the importance of evaluating what impact their method of working has on current customers, and the impact it might have on future customers. Does it actually benefit customers? If there is no perceived gain for customers, team members need to think about changing or dropping the process in question. Customers will have a number of requirements. Some requirements are "must haves" and some are "would be nice to haves". Address both of these, and remember that if you do not meet their "must have" requirements, you will lose loyal customers.

POINTS TO REMEMBER

- Everyone should be interested in how well you are meeting external customer needs.
- If a customer requirement changes, be prepared to change your process or system too.
- Customers buy your products and services because of the benefits they offer them.

14 Find out what your end customer thinks of your service.

FINDING OUT WHAT CUSTOMERS WANT

There are several effective techniques that can help you discover exactly what your customers want. Gather useful information from a variety of sources, and use focus groups, questionnaires, and customer feedback to substantiate your findings.

15 Keep detailed records of any customer research you carry out.

16 View every customer as a useful source of information.

Customer explains why he bought the product

GATHERING INFORMATION

In order to focus on addressing your chosen customers' needs and wants, you must understand what those needs and wants are. Unfortunately, the type of information held about customers by organizations is often lacking. It is of limited use, for example, to know how many purchases of a particular product a customer has made. You also need to know *why* they bought the product if you are to provide the right products and services in the future. Gather information that provides you with the intelligence you need rather than collating data just because it is easy to record. You can use your company resources, but make sure that you back up this information with external facts and feedback from the customers themselves.

◀ CONDUCTING MARKET RESEARCH
Use market research to help you build a clearer picture of your customers, and find out how they perceive your organization and the products or services it provides.

IDENTIFYING SOURCES OF CUSTOMER INFORMATION

SOURCE	FACTORS TO CONSIDER
COMPANY RESOURCES Your own organization's historical data on customers.	Existing information will give you numbers and details of the products and services your customers have bought, why they bought them, and the benefits received.
INDUSTRY BODIES Umbrella organizations representing different industries.	These bodies usually publish journals or newsletters, and often have websites to which you can refer to find out more about customers in specific industries.
COMMISSIONED REPORTS Produced for a fee, these contain information requested by a client.	Usually written to a very specific brief, these are often made public so that you can read reports produced for other companies as well as commissioning them yourself.
CUSTOMER FEEDBACK Includes meetings, focus groups, and questionnaires.	This is an extremely important source of information about your customers' needs and wants since it comes directly from the customers themselves.
STATUTORY BODIES Regulatory bodies holding data on company figures and performance.	This information can be helpful in building a company profile of your typical customer based on factors such as size and turnover.

SEEKING EXTERNAL FACTS

Look for information from a variety of external sources, such as industry publications, government statistics, and analysts' reports. Commissioned reports, such as those produced by marketing consultants, may also provide useful insights. These can be expensive unless you obtain them from a local library or professional institution. Whenever possible, back up external findings by monitoring internally. If, for example, an external exit poll at a supermarket shows that customers like the new self-service checkouts, use internal monitoring to check that the number of customers passing through them has actually increased.

17 Make it your business to know your customer's business.

18 Look into research conducted by other people – it may prove useful.

569

HOLDING FOCUS GROUPS

One of the most effective techniques for finding out what your customers really want is to bring a group of them together for a discussion that focuses on their concerns. This kind of meeting is known as a focus group. The success of a focus group depends on getting the right people to attend and asking the right questions. Make sure that focus group members are representative of your customers. You may have to offer people an incentive to join the group, such as free samples of your products. The atmosphere should be as informal and friendly as possible. Aim to invite between six and eight people. This means that you get a range of views with everyone having ample opportunity to speak.

QUESTIONS TO ASK YOUR CUSTOMERS

Q What is most important to you when deciding what to buy?

Q Why did you buy this product/service?

Q What benefits are you getting from your last purchase?

Q How do you see the situation changing in future?

Q Is our service satisfactory and how would you rate it?

19 Make sure that you listen to what focus group members have to say.

▼ RUNNING A FOCUS GROUP

Encourage focus group members to reveal their true feelings, attitudes, and motivations by asking open questions such as "Why do you like this?", "Can you explain how you go about choosing?", and "How do you think your opinion will change in the future?" Seek opinions from all present.

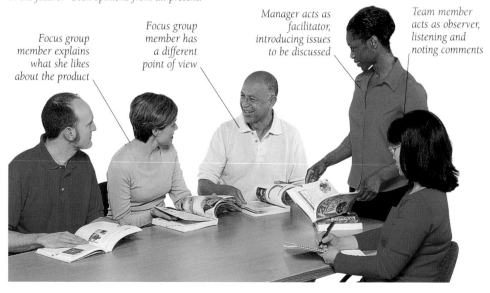

Focus group member explains what she likes about the product

Focus group member has a different point of view

Manager acts as facilitator, introducing issues to be discussed

Team member acts as observer, listening and noting comments

USING QUESTIONNAIRES

Questionnaires are a good way of reaching a large number of customers. Plan the topics you want to cover carefully, the information you require, and which questions will reveal that information. Before including any questions, consider how the answers will be used. If you cannot use an answer to a particular question to help improve customer service, delete it. Test your initial questionnaire with colleagues to make sure that the questions are easy to understand and that the answers will not be ambiguous.

GETTING FEEDBACK

Feedback helps you not only to understand your customers but also to know when their needs have changed. Tick-sheets of multiple-choice questions can provide a good indication of customer opinion and identify new trends. Broader questions that need more than a "Yes" or "No" answer will generate more information. When you have received feedback, use the information to look for ways in which you can improve your service.

20 Ask clear questions so that feedback is unambiguous.

▼ LOGGING FEEDBACK
Collate and maintain records of customer feedback so that you can refer to them in future, such as when planning to develop new products or enter new markets.

Contact name for each customer

First point of contact

Subsequent point of contact

Date	Customer name	Complaint	Dealt with by	Passed to	Report no.
Sept 6th	Richard Main Ace Industries	Monthly invoice has an incorrect charge	Tina Mills	Ben Langdon, Accounts	CB1061
Sept 9th	Susan Delves Lea Newsagents	Delivery of the wrong books	Tina Mills	Mike Peters, Warehousing	CB1062
Oct 15th	Jane Copeland Stationery First	Return of batch of glue guns due to breakages	Tina Mills	Sue Childs, Purchasing	CB1063
Nov 3rd	Martin Johnson Clips 'n' Things	Late delivery of October order	Tina Mills	David Bruce, Dispatch	CB1064

Problem as described by the customer

Reference number of report detailing action taken

UNDERSTANDING CUSTOMER GROUPS

If customers are to come first, they must all be treated as individuals. Divide your customers into groups to help you better understand their different needs, group your products or services, and then establish where your current and future priorities lie.

21 Look at what your customers have in common to help you group them.

22 Consider grouping customers by region, size, or growth potential.

GROUPING CUSTOMERS AND PRODUCTS

It is unlikely that all your customers behave in the same way or want the same things. Families and teenagers, for example, look for different holiday facilities from the same supplier, even from the same resort. By dividing your customers into groups, you can tailor products and services to appeal to particular groups. Identify groupings for your products and services, too. Group products and services by appropriate criteria, such as complexity. A simple group, for example, will require minimal after-sales support; a complex one may need substantial follow-up.

▲ APPEALING TO CUSTOMER GROUPS
Identifying groups of customers enables you to focus more closely on the aspirations and desires of a specific group, such as retired senior citizens. In this way, you can present the benefits of your products or services to appeal exclusively to them.

23 Ensure that you offer customers the products or services they want.

24 Ask an objective colleague to give you feedback on your groupings.

DOCUMENTING THE SEGMENTS

Once you have decided on the best ways to group your products and customers, create a product–customer matrix to document these segments. List the product groups down the side of the matrix and the customer groups along the bottom. Each product–customer segment will have different needs and wants. Consider what you have to do in order to be successful with each product–customer segment. It is important to think creatively rather than simply accept that you will continue in the same way with the products and customer groups you have been dealing with up until now. As you discuss one of your groups of customers with colleagues, you may define a new way of taking products and services to them.

ESTABLISHING CURRENT PRIORITIES

It is important to establish which product–customer segments should take priority in order to avoid offering the same product to everyone in the same form and satisfying no one. Look at the current position first. You may decide that the most important group is the one that is likely to bring in the most revenue, or you may rate priority according to the amount of activity (high, medium, or low) that you currently put into each segment. Take time to prioritize in order to ensure that your products and services are appropriate to each customer group. If, for example, you were to provide a technology help desk to a large organization, one customer group might be data entry operators and another group computer systems experts. You would therefore need to plan very different levels of support to meet the needs of the two groups.

THINGS TO DO

1. Check that the product–customer segments you focus on will continue to grow for another two years.

2. Discuss your priorities with everyone involved.

3. Agree on levels of resources to put into each group.

25 Encourage debate on priorities as a way of improving team focus.

USING A MATRIX FOR INTERNAL CUSTOMERS

The product–customer matrix can be used for internal customers in the same way as for external customers. When documenting your product groups and internal customer groups, consider whether you could also serve other parts of the organization.

Your knowledge of your organization's strategy for serving its end customers may help you to identify potential new areas or internal customers, and provide a basis on which to organize your product–customer matrix.

26 Be realistic: resources for new areas must come from somewhere.

AGREEING FUTURE EMPHASIS

Having identified the current relative priority of each segment, involve the team in anticipating what the priorities will be in the future. Moving a product–customer segment from low to high priority requires considerably more effort and expense than sustaining an already high-priority segment, so this needs to be planned for. You may also need to conduct further research into some segments in order to make a final decision. If, for example, it costs too much to reach a particular segment, you may have to reconsider whether it is worth focusing on. Document plans to upgrade or downgrade emphasis on a product–customer matrix, and check that everyone involved in servicing the segments agrees with the priorities set.

DOCUMENTING FUTURE EMPHASIS ▼
Devise a product–customer matrix showing where you plan to upgrade and reduce emphasis on products or services in the future. The team can then use this for easy reference.

	Customer group A	Customer group B	Customer group C
Products/Services 2	H > L	M > L	L > H
Products/Services 1	M > H	0 > M	0 > M

Key

H *High level of activity, that is, occupying many staff and other resources*

M *Medium level of activity*

L *Low level of activity*

0 *No activity at all*

> *Estimated change of emphasis from now to the future*

CHANGING EMPHASIS

The emphasis you agree on now is likely to change over time, perhaps in response to a change in customer needs, or as a result of one segment performing significantly better or worse than expected. Customers are also unlikely to remain in the same group forever, so make sure that you and your team watch for this and respond flexibly and quickly. For example, if a distributor supplies its retail customer with own-branded products and the customer changes strategy to sell higher-margin branded goods, the distributor must change the products it supplies. A failure to do so may result in the loss of the retail customer. However, if the change is made effectively, the distributor stands to gain a larger, more profitable client.

27 Remember that it takes time and effort to secure new customers.

▼ **GAINING COMMITMENT**

If there is a need to change emphasis and focus on a new product–customer segment, explain to the team why the change must happen. A new focus may have an impact on their roles and responsibilities, so discuss the implications of a change and address any concerns in order to make sure that everyone is fully committed.

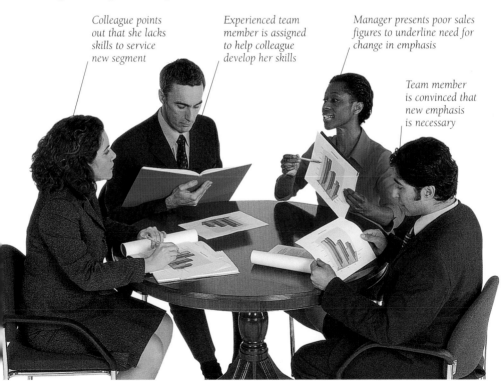

Colleague points out that she lacks skills to service new segment

Experienced team member is assigned to help colleague develop her skills

Manager presents poor sales figures to underline need for change in emphasis

Team member is convinced that new emphasis is necessary

UNDERSTANDING THE BUYING PROCESS

For even quite simple products and services, a customer's buying process can be complex. In taking your product or service to the customer, you need to understand the detail of this buying decision and what the customer is looking for as the ideal.

28 Bear in mind that no product or service will stay the same forever.

29 Realize that few buying decisions are made on the basis of price alone.

IDENTIFYING BUYING CRITERIA

When customers are deciding whether to buy, they will first consider whether the key areas of product, service, relationship, and price meet basic criteria. In each area, different customers will have more specific criteria. For example, while one group might be looking for next-day delivery, another may require flexible delivery times. These criteria form the basis for customers' buying thought processes.

UNDERSTANDING BASIC BUYING CRITERIA

KEY AREAS	CUSTOMER CRITERIA
PRODUCT OR SERVICE Bought by customers to meet a perceived need.	● Will the product or service do what I want it to do? ● Can I obtain the product or service when I want to, and will there be adequate support if I need it?
RELATIONSHIP The way in which the product or service is delivered.	● Do I like and trust the people who are providing the product or service? ● Will my colleagues also find it easy to work with them?
PRICE The charge for the product or service.	● Does the product or service offer value for money? ● Is the price competitive? ● Would I be better spending my money on something else?

KNOWING THE IDEAL

Find out what your customers regard as their "ideal" level of performance. This will help you understand your customers better and identify gaps between what you are offering and what they actually want. Once you know where the gaps are, you can plan how to close them. For example, if delivery time is important to your customers, ask yourself what the best possible scenario would be. Perhaps they would ideally like delivery within seven days and at a predetermined time of day. How close can you come to that? Bear in mind that if you do not come as close as possible to your customers' ideal, a competitor probably will.

30 Remember that different customers will buy from you in different ways.

31 Identify the ideal so that you can provide it to customers.

32 Learn how to deal with customers by noting how they buy from you.

RECOGNIZING THE CONCEPT OF FAIR VALUE

Not all buying criteria are equally important. The relative weighting each customer group gives to different criteria is also likely to vary. When choosing a mode of transport, for example, business people are likely to be more concerned about how quickly they can get from A to B than about prices, whereas for students, cost is likely to be all-important. Once you have assessed your products and services to see how well they meet your customers' various needs and wants, you must ensure that they also represent what customers consider to be fair value. Make sure that you understand what customers regard as fair value, and plan how to supply it.

▲ UNDERSTANDING FAIR VALUE
Busy professionals may be willing to pay extra for speedy service when choosing a business lunch venue, but if prices are too high, they will not feel that they are getting fair value.

REVIEWING YOUR APPROACH

A business operation must be run to suit customers rather than the organization. Create a customer-focused plan, and improve systems and processes so that they truly benefit customers.

SETTING CUSTOMER-FIRST OBJECTIVES

In a customer-first environment, your team's objectives need to reflect your customers' aims. Set objectives that will bring benefits for your customers once you achieve them, and establish how to measure performance in your customers' terms.

33 Remember that everyone likes to get value for money.

34 Ask customers to confirm that your purpose statement will help achieve their goals.

We will provide quality system support to sales so that they can process orders within 72 hours.

FOCUSING PURPOSE STATEMENTS

A purpose statement is a clear and succinct definition of a team's future goals. Learn about each of your customers' purpose statements, and ensure that your own statement refers to them as the final aiming point. If your customers do not have purpose statements, discuss this matter with them and use what you learn to revise or create your own team's purpose statement.

DEFINING OBJECTIVES

Once your purpose statement puts customers first, you can define objectives that are also driven by your customers' aims. Test the effectiveness of each objective by asking the question, "If we achieve this objective, will it help our customers to carry out their purpose statement?" Each objective must state the benefits for customers once it is successfully achieved. If it is difficult or impossible to determine how an objective will benefit your customers, rethink it.

35 Ensure that your purpose statement says what you will do for customers.

SELECTING INDICATORS

To determine whether you are on target to achieve your objectives, you will need to select indicators to measure your performance. To help you set customer-first indicators, think how customers would measure your progress. For example, a customer receiving reports from a finance department might measure performance based on three key factors: how promptly the report is delivered, how easy it is to understand, and how accurate it is.

PLANNING WITH CUSTOMERS IN MIND

Define your purpose to reflect customer needs → Focus on your customers' final aiming point

Set objectives that bring benefits for customers → State clearly the benefits customers can expect

Select indicators that are meaningful to customers → Agree performance measures with customers

Check that indicators have real benefits for customers → Seek customer feedback on value of indicators

Document objectives and indicators on a performance scorecard → Agree objective/ indicator priorities with customers

ALIGNING INDIVIDUAL OBJECTIVES AND INDICATORS

When setting individual targets and performance measures, make sure that these tie in with the customer-first objectives of the team. If your staff are able to see their own targets in terms of benefits to the customers, they will be encouraged to keep customers in mind as they go about their everyday work. See that everyone is equipped with the skills to achieve their objectives. If necessary, plan training or development activities to enable people to perform successfully.

SEEKING FEEDBACK ON INDICATORS

Discuss your performance indicators with customers to check that they reflect what your clients truly need and that you are putting effort into activities that really help them. In this way, you will avoid wasting time on issues that have little impact on customers. Ask your clients whether there are areas in which you could offer more assistance. Look particularly for improvements that you could make relatively easily that would considerably boost your customers' performance. A small change that you make may result in a major benefit to your customers.

36 Make sure that you set realistic targets to measure progress.

37 Concentrate on aspects of performance that help customers.

REVISING ▶ INDICATORS

By discussing a performance indicator that was causing problems with his customer, John was able to find a better way of working. He also ensured that he avoided disappointing the customer by taking the initiative at an early stage, rather than waiting until he missed his targets.

CASE STUDY

John was in charge of restocking vending machines in his customer's office block. One of his performance indicators was that he check and restock all the machines in the building every two days, but he was finding this very difficult to achieve. Rather than risk missing his targets, he decided to discuss the problem with the customer's catering manager. The catering manager suggested that, since some machines were used far less often than others, it was not necessary for John to visit these so often. They agreed which machines were less important, and decided that John would visit the less-used machines only once a week to save time. Having his performance indicator revised in this way by the catering manager gave John more time to visit the priority machines, and so he was able to meet his restocking targets more easily.

DOCUMENTING YOUR OBJECTIVES

To complete the process of focusing objectives on each customer, summarize the indicators you have agreed on a performance scorecard. You will then be able to use the scorecard to check progress on a regular basis. Make sure that you have between four and eight indicators: less than four means you are not thinking widely enough; more than eight is too many to be able to focus on effectively. Agree the relative priority of each indicator with the team and with the customer. Plan to check performance regularly, at least once a month, or more frequently if the team is new or is involved in new activities.

QUESTIONS TO ASK YOURSELF

Q If I meet all my indicators, will the customer be satisfied?

Q Are the indicators that I put in place last year still relevant?

Q Are all the targets I have set myself feasible?

Q Are all the targets stretching and worth achieving?

Q Do the indicators focus on the customer in the main?

38 Imagine that you are your customer when reviewing your performance scorecard.

▼ CREATING A PERFORMANCE CHART

Document your objectives and indicators on a performance scorecard. Agree the priority of each objective with your customer on a rating of 1–10. Add a status column with green, amber, and red colour coding to focus attention on areas for improvement.

Summary of objective

Priority of objective

Urgency rating of red, amber, green

Objective	Indicator	P	Target	Current	Status
Improve sales of standard products	Increase volume of orders	10	7.5 million	5 million	●
Improve the speed of decision-making	Reduce time to respond to a customer request for information	8	4 weeks	8 weeks	●
Improve the efficiency of preparing customer quotations	(a) Reduce time spent on preparing quotations (b) Cut number of days spent on product training courses	6	(a) 2 days p/m (b) 0 days p/y	(a) 4 days p/m (b) 5 days p/y	● ●

Measure of the objective's success

Desired level of performance

Current level of performance

IMPROVING YOUR BUSINESS PROCESSES

*I*t is vital to deliver what is expected, when it is expected, and at an agreed price by operating consistently using up-to-date business processes. Review your procedures regularly to ensure that every one of them puts customers first.

39 If performance falls, analyze whether a process is at fault.

40 Always do what you say you will do.

CHANGING PROCESSES ▼
If you currently bill your customers for large amounts, consider whether this system benefits them. It may suit them better to pay smaller, more regular sums.

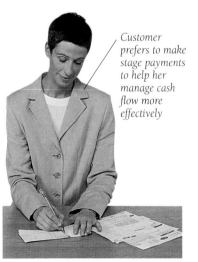

Customer prefers to make stage payments to help her manage cash flow more effectively

IDENTIFYING PROCESSES

Make a list of the procedures or business processes your team currently uses and those it will need to use in order to achieve its objectives. Some processes, such as the handling of sales orders, will involve the customers, while others will be more specific to the way in which you and your team operate, such as the methods you use for recording and accessing information. There may also be regular business activities that could be grouped together as identified processes. It is important to identify all your business processes to ensure that each one puts the customers first.

EVALUATING PROCESSES

Review all your processes to ascertain which have the most impact on your customers' and your own success so that you can focus on improving these core processes first. Examine each process, even if it is only the process by which the team answers the telephone, and ask, "What impact does this have on the customers' ability to achieve their objectives?" and "How much impact does this have on our performance against our objectives?"

FOCUSING KEY PROCESSES ON CUSTOMERS

KEY PROCESSES	HOW TO FOCUS ON CUSTOMERS
CUSTOMER SUPPORT The assistance provided for customers once they have taken delivery of your product or service.	● Check that the support you offer is as convenient as possible for customers. ● Establish procedures to maintain regular contact with customers and keep them informed of all developments.
PRODUCT DEVELOPMENT The method used to make changes or improvements to your products or services.	● Decide what you have to deliver and make sure that new products are relevant to customers. ● Change your products and services to meet customer needs.
USE OF INFORMATION The way in which data about customers is gathered, collated, and distributed.	● Gather information from a wide variety of sources and check that it is presented in a useful format. ● Ensure that customer feedback is comprehensive and accessible to the right people at the right time.
PRACTICE IMPROVEMENT The usage of tools and techniques to improve the way in which you do business with customers.	● Use templates to promote consistency and draw attention to significant information in dramatic ways. ● Make templates and tools available to people who need them, including internal customers where appropriate.
DECISION-MAKING The logical process used by the team to make key business decisions.	● Build customers into your decision-making process by using their ideal as your aiming point. ● Consider all the options before deciding which one represents the best solution for customers.

UPDATING PROCESSES

Watch for processes that have been in place for a long time, because if they have not been altered to keep up with customers' changing requirements, they are unlikely to put customers first. If, for example, you have always coded invoices in a way that is meaningful to you but incomprehensible to your customers, this procedure should be revised as soon as possible.

41 Think about how you could start to work differently.

DEVELOPING CUSTOMER-LED PROCESSES

Every business process involves delivering something to somebody. Make sure that you deliver what your customers want by involving them in developing processes. If, for example, you are to build an exhibition stand for the marketing team, identify and agree milestones along the way when you will show progress to date. You can then move on to the next phase of the project knowing that you have kept the customer informed, so reducing the risk that they will want major changes as the project ends.

DOS AND DON'TS

✔ Do let customers know beforehand if you are going to be late completing a milestone.

✔ Do review processes with customers regularly to keep them informed.

✘ Don't give customers any surprises, welcome or unwelcome, when you deliver the goods.

✘ Don't leave in place any process that does not benefit customers.

42 Review your customer-led processes to keep them up to date.

43 Involve your customers when planning your business processes.

▼ INVOLVING CUSTOMERS
When managing a project, examine the processes you will use with your customer to ensure that they are of benefit to them. Explore areas for improvement together, and change your project plan if necessary.

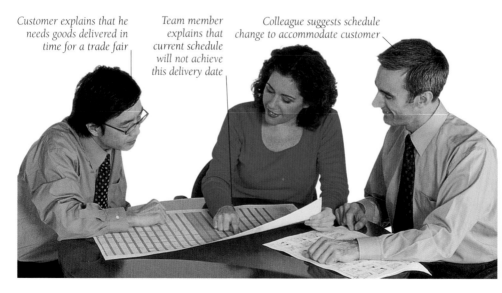

Customer explains that he needs goods delivered in time for a trade fair

Team member explains that current schedule will not achieve this delivery date

Colleague suggests schedule change to accommodate customer

DOCUMENTING PROCESSES

Once you have identified all your processes, document them so that people can quickly understand what their role is in the process. If you document processes well, it will be easy to introduce a new member into the team. Check the completed documents with other people or teams involved in them. They may suggest improvements in the way the process works.

POINTS TO REMEMBER

● The most successful organizations communicate openly between different departments.

● Once a process has passed to another team, it will still need to be monitored if it affects your customers.

● Documenting processes always leads to their improvement.

● Computer systems have a vital role to play in standardizing processes.

44 Consider how you can streamline a process so that you achieve the same goal in less time.

▼ USING PROCESS MAPS

Document your team's procedures to help you operate more consistently and more productively. This will also ensure that you avoid situations where an individual involved in the process thinks that someone else is handling an issue when others think that they are.

CUSTOMER
Receives replacement product

Contacts customer to arrange delivery time

STOCK CONTROL
Organizes delivery of replacement product

Customer details passed to stock control department

Passes on request for product recall

CUSTOMER SERVICE
Contacts customer to notify them of fault

CUSTOMER SERVICE
Receives complaints about faulty product

Customer service representative passes details to production

PRODUCTION
Runs product test and finds problem

Faults are referred to development team

PRODUCT DEVELOPMENT
Checks specification and finds component fault

PROVIDING CUSTOMER SUPPORT

Effective, efficient service and support is key to building customer loyalty. Show customers that they are valued by keeping them informed, and ask clients for feedback to help you continuously improve the level of assistance and care you provide.

> **45** Remember that if you delay things, a problem can turn into a crisis.

KEEPING CUSTOMERS INFORMED

Monitor how successful customers have been in implementing your services by keeping in touch and asking for feedback, even when you are not trying to increase the business you are doing with them. Send out feedback forms on a regular basis and be proactive about contacting customers to check that they are happy with your service. If customers request information, provide it straight away, or let them know when they can expect it. If you propose a change to your existing service, or are introducing something new, relay this information in your customers' terms by explaining the benefits of the change. If the change is major, or likely to be disruptive, meet customers to discuss alternative options.

> **46** Let customers know when you make changes.

▼ WARNING CUSTOMERS OF DELAYS

In this scenario, the customer who is kept informed suffers minimum disruption. The team member who fails to inform the customer loses the business and incurs damage to his organization's reputation.

Team member discovers that supplier is behind schedule

Customer signs sales order and is promised delivery within seven days

CONNECTING TO THE VOICE OF THE CUSTOMERS

Put in place a process by which all members of the team talk directly to customers from time to time. They will bring new insights that the team leader might miss, because they are in a routine with the customers. The team is also more likely to work towards the customers' goals if they have met them and listened to them talking about their aims, strengths, and weaknesses. If you deal with customers regularly on the telephone, it might also be useful to have regular face-to-face meetings.

THINGS TO DO

1. Ask team members when they last met a customer.
2. Ensure regular meetings are arranged.
3. Plan meetings between yourself and customers.

47 Make customers feel that you are on their side.

48 Take responsibility for meeting customers' expectations.

Customer receives goods and her goodwill is restored

Customer receives letter the next day and is able to make contingency plan

Team member writes promptly to customer to inform her that goods will be late

Angry customer hears nothing and cancels order after goods fail to arrive

IMPROVING SYSTEMS

Make sure that you provide the most convenient service possible to your customers. Minimize the amount of paperwork they have to do, and organize delivery times to take account of their needs. If you have always waited for signed orders from customers before starting delivery, for example, you could change the process to make it more customer-friendly. Perhaps you could arrange to take orders electronically to reduce the amount of time customers have to wait between ordering and receiving the goods.

DEVELOPING PRODUCTS AND SERVICES

In order to maintain customer satisfaction, products and services must be developed with customers' needs in mind. Emphasize the benefits to customers of what you provide, and take their individual needs and lifestyles into account when making changes.

49 Find out how your competitors are improving their products/services.

50 Brief your team to highlight product or service benefits, not features, when talking to customers.

HIGHLIGHTING BENEFITS

Any product or service feature will be of value to customers only if they have a need for it. For example, if the feature of a monthly report to customers is that it compares two previous months' data, it may benefit them only once they have accumulated several reports and converted them into graphs that enable them to analyze a trend. Changing the content and presentation of such a report would ensure that it is immediately seen as a benefit. List the features of your products or services now, and see how many you can turn into customer benefits.

DISTINGUISHING FEATURES AND BENEFITS

FEATURES OF A NEW KETTLE	BENEFITS OF A NEW KETTLE
"Uses the latest microchip technology."	Switches off automatically at boiling point.
"Has a concealed element."	Easy to clean; boils small quantities of water.
"Spout contains a filter."	Keeps limescale out of drinks.

STANDARDIZING PRODUCTS

All customers are individuals and may have very different requirements in terms of the features and benefits they are looking for in the products or services you provide. However, it would be impractical to provide a unique product or service to every customer. Analyze what individual customers want by building up a profile of their characteristics as you collect information about them. Once you know what their special needs and interests are, you can then look for overlaps and common requirements and decide where to offer standardization. The characteristics you identify for external customers may include age group, sex, income, personal goals or aspirations, or level of education. If your customers are internal, it may be useful to draw up a profile of their characteristics so that you can decide how best to serve them.

51 Make sure that a product feature is of real use to customers.

POINTS TO REMEMBER

- All customers like to feel special and dislike being taken for granted.
- As your knowledge of your customers increases, you will be able to give a better and more tailored service.
- People buy things that conform to the image they want to give to other people.

CULTURAL DIFFERENCES

The same product may have to reach different markets, so it is vital to take into consideration the needs of different parts of the world. In Scandinavia, managers tend to keep their mobile phones on all the time, so that they are available if decisions have to be made. In the US, people use their mobiles more to call people than to be called, and switch them off when working. This affects the products and service the mobile phone operators have to provide.

CONSIDERING LIFESTYLES

When designing or altering your products or services, look further than your customers' needs and take into account how they want to live and be perceived. Elderly customers, for example, are unlikely to be attracted to psychedelic packaging. You should also consider how customers will use the product or service. If you are selling mobile phones, you may need to appeal both to young people, who want to make local calls to friends, as well as to sales people, who regularly call long-distance. It is unlikely that the same pricing structure will suit both groups. Consider the lifestyles of internal customers, too. If, for example, your customers are sales representatives who are rarely in the office, ensure that the products you provide do not sit on their desks for protracted periods of time. Take steps to provide the product where they need it.

USING CUSTOMER INFORMATION

Customer-focused processes must be backed up with the right information, in the right place, at the right time. Use your information to check that you are still achieving customer satisfaction, and exploit opportunities through increased knowledge.

52 Encourage the team to share information and insights.

53 Learn about your competitors' customers as well as your own clients.

GATHERING IDEAS ▼
Ask team members to seek out new sources of information to improve their knowledge of customers and competitors.

COMPARING CUSTOMER INFORMATION

Develop a range of sources of customer information to make sure that your knowledge is based on a wide variety of views and to avoid making assumptions based on data from a single source. In addition to seeking customer feedback on a regular basis, check relevant technical or trade magazines for possible insights into how the market is changing. Look at competitors' websites to find out how they are approaching their prospects and customers, and for defensive or proactive ideas. Ask team members to attend relevant exhibitions and conferences, and encourage them to speak to people in other organizations, even in different industries, to get new ideas.

Team member directs colleague to website listed in trade magazine

Colleague finds valuable new source of information

CHECKING THAT INFORMATION IS USEFUL

Examine the information you gain from your customers at the point of sale, and check that it is really providing the facts you require. Then assess whether it is in a format that makes it useful. If, for example, you are monitoring the number of telephone enquiries from internal customers, it may be more useful to calculate from which departments most calls are coming.

54 Avoid recording irrelevant details that could obscure important facts.

MAKING CUSTOMER INFORMATION ACCESSIBLE

Once you have set up a good process for obtaining customer information, make sure that it is accessible to the team so that they can react to it. A change in customer requirements that one person discovers in one location should be available to other people so that they can be forewarned that their customers' needs may change in the same way. Look at how team members will make use of the data, and make it accessible in that way. If people in a finance department, for example, would benefit from knowing how long each customer takes to receive their invoice, design a report that gives them that information.

55 Realize that information can be shared globally.

◀ MAKING DATA ACCESSIBLE
Check that customer information is easily accessible to the team, and that it is presented in a format that is useful to them.

Files are clearly labelled and colour coded

Team member knows where to find the report she needs

56 With the facts to hand, you are more likely to make the right decisions.

591

USING BEST PRACTICES

There are various tools and techniques that can be used to promote consistency in your dealings with customers and help you learn from past experience. Make use of templates and best practices to help you work more effectively.

57 Use electronic templates to speed up communication.

58 Ensure that you record your team's success stories.

59 Ask successful team members to explain how they serve customers.

USING TEMPLATES TO AID ANALYSIS

Encourage all team members to contribute to the process of obtaining and using customer feedback by asking them to document the information they collect in a consistent manner in a template. This is a form that can include numerical information, for example the score out of ten that a customer has awarded to a particular aspect of the service, as well as comments and suggestions made by customers. If everyone has access to a computer, the most effective method is to use electronic templates, which can then be stored and made available to relevant staff throughout the organization.

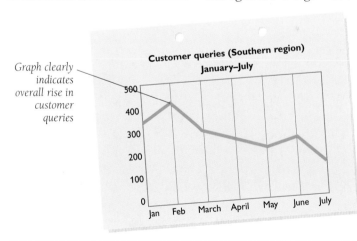

Graph clearly indicates overall rise in customer queries

Customer queries (Southern region)
January–July

◀ PLOTTING CUSTOMER REACTION
Make use of software packages to present customer information in a graphical way. This will enable team members to see at a glance whether there are problem areas or issues that need their urgent attention.

ASSESSING FUTURE RISKS

Use a simple tool to help you think ahead and assess the risks of your current plans. If, for example, you are planning to increase your prices, there is a risk that you will lose some of your customers. Consider the impact that this would have on performance. If there is a high probability that you will lose customers and that this will have a high impact on performance, change your plan. Encourage team members to conduct and document these risk assessments in the form of a template so that their colleagues are able to learn from their work.

60 Assess the risks attached to any decision that you or your team take.

61 Learn from other people's assessment of risk and prepare to change plans.

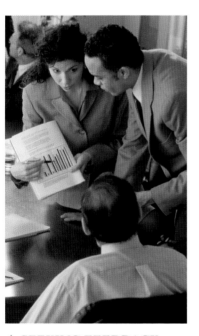

▲ **SEEKING FEEDBACK**
Show the templates you are using to store information to your customers in order to obtain their feedback. Ask them for adverse comments as well as suggestions for improvement, and then act on them.

DOS AND DON'TS

✔ Do involve your customers in your use of tools and templates where appropriate.

✔ Do make sure that you capture the insights of any team members who may be leaving the team.

✘ Don't expect a tool to remain suitable without change for a long period.

✘ Don't forget to build a library of completed templates that team members can use to learn from.

FOLLOWING THE SAME ROUTINES

The templates you create are often called "best practices" because they describe the best way of getting something done. Once you have identifed best practices, use them as a matter of routine in a variety of circumstances, from preparing handouts for a conference to building a sales order processing system. Once you have followed a routine several times, you will become so familiar with it that you will find yourself following best practice automatically. For consistency's sake, encourage other people to use the same routines.

Making Customer-Focused Decisions

If customers are to come first, they need to be considered as a matter of course every time the team makes a decision. To ensure that you make the right decisions for your team and your customers, establish a logical process that you follow every time.

62 Ensure that you identify all the options before making a decision.

63 Always look at the facts of an issue.

Using a Process

Following the same customer-first process in making every decision has several benefits. The team will become faster at decision-making, since if everyone knows the process, they quickly eliminate customer-unfriendly options and come to the most suitable alternative. In addition, any team members who are opposed to a decision are more likely to accept it if it has been reached by consensus. Imagine that your customers are present at a decision-making meeting, and consider what they would add to the discussion.

64 Consider how a decision will affect customers.

Defining the Ideal

The team must agree on the criteria against which they wish to measure a decision. Consider the criteria that your customers would use. Suppose, for example, you need to choose between two suppliers of office equipment. Ask the team to brainstorm what the ideal solution would be from both the customers' and the team's point of view. Ask the questions "What do we want this equipment to do for our customers and the team? What benefits should we look for?" This list then gives the team a way of filtering options and comparing alternatives.

- It is better to consider more than one option so that sufficient thought goes into making the best decision.

- When a team does not have time to think about a decision but takes the only option they can think of, they are fire-fighting.

- Successful teams get out of fire-fighting mode and start to make decisions ahead of time.

- When suggesting a decision to your manager, be prepared to justify why your option is the best.

EVALUATING OPTIONS

With the team's help, identify which criteria are most important to customers. You may find that three or four stand out as vital. Now measure all your options against the ideal agreed for each of these important criteria. The process is logical, but good creative thinking is still needed to evaluate the options effectively. Having carried out this evaluation, you may find that the decision is obvious. If not, take the next most important criterion and repeat the process. Continue until one option stands out, or until the team is certain that, say, two options have nothing between them. Where that is the case, choose the option that is best for your customers.

▼ CONSIDERING OPTIONS

In this example, a team discusses the option of engaging a new supplier. The manager encourages the team to weigh up the options from both the customers' and their own viewpoint before making a final decision that puts the customers first.

Manager identifies problem with current supplier

Team member looks at effect on customers of taking no action

Colleague points out best and worst outcomes of hiring new supplier

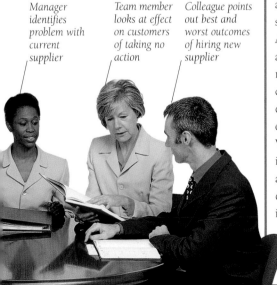

MAKING SAFE DECISIONS

What would be the impact if you made a wrong decision? If it lost you a customer it could be catastrophic, so use the SAFE criteria (Suitable, Acceptable, Feasible, and Enduring) as a final test. Ask yourself "Is the decision really the most suitable one given the current customer situation? Is the decision acceptable to the customer and everyone else who has an interest in it? Will it be feasible and practical to implement the decision given the time and resources available? Will the decision endure in the long term, or will it become invalid or unacceptable to the customer?" Use the SAFE criteria as a quick check for any decision made by teams or individuals.

DELIVERING SATISFACTION

Satisfied customers are likely to be loyal customers. Develop an environment in which everyone recognizes that customers' best interests must come first in all aspects of their work.

PROMOTING A CUSTOMER-FIRST ATTITUDE

Keeping customers' needs in mind at all times is key to being able to meet their requirements. Promote a customer-first attitude by encouraging others to focus on customer needs and recognize the importance of the market over internal issues.

65 Realize that staff must be able to empathize with customers.

66 Ask team members to bring a number of customer-first ideas to relevant meetings.

Introduce loyalty scheme awarding discounts to our high-value customers

KEEPING CUSTOMERS VISIBLE

Help team members to look outwards by creating a customer satisfaction notice board – a prominent visual display that charts their successes and problems with external customers. You might post sales figures on a board, show how much repeat business is being won, or give the team an indication of their market share. Make sure that you highlight any problems, too.

ALLOWING CUSTOMERS TO DEFINE QUALITY

Make sure that the quality of the products or services you provide meets your customers' expectations, not just your own internal quality targets. Look for a balance between performance (what your products and services do for the customer), price (your customers' views on the cost they have to pay), and timescale (how quickly they would like products or services delivered, or requests for support dealt with). Post these indicators on to your customer satisfaction board. If you are an internal team some way from the outside customer, talk to your sales colleagues or other teams with direct customer contact to ensure that your quality indicators are accurate.

▼ DISPLAYING INFORMATION

Use your customer satisfaction board to draw attention to customer care issues. Ask team members to pin up relevant customer information, such as magazine articles, complaints, and letters.

Team member adds note of what is being done to rectify a customer complaint

QUESTIONS TO ASK YOURSELF

Q Are our products and services good enough?

Q Is our knowledge based on our customer feedback?

Q Does the customer satisfaction board show how well the team are serving external customers?

Q Do I encourage and gather suggestions for improvements from my team members?

Q Do we know what customers will want in one year's time?

DRIVING THE MARKET

Organizations that anticipate changes in customer requirements can be described as driving the market rather than simply responding to it. These organizations are successful because they attract customers away from rivals who react only when challenged by a customer or a competitor. Can you remember when a team member last made a suggestion aimed at anticipating a change in customer requirements? If not, you need to encourage the team to look for ways of improving customer satisfaction and to think of changes that will be welcomed by customers and enable you to stand out against the competition.

DEVELOPING A CUSTOMER-FIRST CULTURE

A customer-first culture should permeate every level of an organization. As a manager, you should take steps to promote this culture by example and check that your team's activities are aimed at satisfying and motivating people to remain as customers.

67 Thank clients for their custom to make them feel valued.

68 Ask dissatisfied customers how you can win back their business.

69 Help customers understand how well you are serving them.

PROMOTING THE RIGHT CLIMATE

Ensure that you and your team always do the right thing for customers. If someone makes a mistake, they should contact customers immediately to explain the error. Waiting for a complaint or hoping that customers will not notice the mistake constitutes poor service. Avoid cutting corners simply to save time. Imagine how you would like to be treated as a customer. If you are providing a first-class service, your customers will have faith in you and the products you provide.

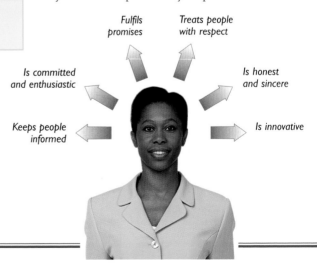

Fulfils promises

Treats people with respect

Is committed and enthusiastic

Is honest and sincere

Keeps people informed

Is innovative

LEADING BY ▶ EXAMPLE
This manager fosters a customer-first culture by demonstrating to her team the qualities that she expects them to model when dealing with customers.

FOCUSING TASKS ON CUSTOMERS

To ensure that team members are working in the most appropriate way to satisfy customers, bring them together to review all their tasks and assess the impact and benefits of each one on customers. Use this opportunity to change any activities that do not have tangible benefits for customers. For example, if a customer is sent a regular newsletter, there is little point in this activity unless it contains information that is useful to them.

REVIEWING TASKS

> **Make a list of all the tasks undertaken by the team**

> **Decide which tasks have an impact on customers**

> **Discard activities that have no impact and are unnecessary**

> **Where tasks have an impact, assess benefit to customers**

> **If tasks have no benefit, change them so that they do**

DOS AND DON'TS

✔ Do answer customer questions quickly, before they become complaints.

✔ Do treat customer concerns as important; after all, they certainly are to them.

✘ Don't create a situation where customers are passed from person to person before they get an answer to a question.

✘ Don't overload customers with information.

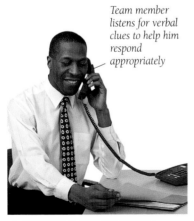

Team member listens for verbal clues to help him respond appropriately

▲ BEING RESPONSIVE

When customers telephone, think about the impression you are making on them. Make sure that your body language and voice reflect your concern to provide a first-class customer service.

MAKING CUSTOMERS FEEL GOOD

Ask yourself how a customer would feel after dealing with you or your team. Can you be certain that they would be left with a positive impression? If, for example, you ran a help desk in the information technology department, what would be the response if a customer were to call with a problem of their own making that you had solved the week before? It is most important that the team respond sympathetically so that the customer is not made to feel humiliated for calling again. Be as helpful as possible in solving the problem for a second time. Then politely suggest how the customer may be able to tackle the problem should a similar situation arise in the future.

FORMING PARTNERSHIPS

Since customers are the lifeblood of your team, they should be treated as part of it. Make sure that team members do not view customers as outsiders, but that they work with them to build mutual trust and lasting commitment on both sides.

70 Remember that customers' trust should never be breached.

71 Introduce new employees to customers as early as possible.

72 Try to find areas of similarity between you and your customer.

WORKING TOGETHER

Ensure that team members recognize that they each have a part to play in building long-term partnerships with customers. Explain the importance of understanding and responding to customer needs in order to build trust and mutual respect. Check that everyone sees their role, objectives, and tasks in the context of satisfying customers, particularly new recruits who may be unused to a customer-first environment. Stress that customers should be treated as part of the team; they should be as aware of what is going on as they would be if they were working alongside you.

Senior team member directs new recruit to customer satisfaction board

Manager explains needs of internal customers

New recruit sees her role from the customer's point of view

BRIEFING ▶ NEW RECRUITS
Explain to new employees that what customers expect from them is of primary importance, and that learning organizational procedures and systems is of secondary importance.

THINGS TO DO

1. Smile and greet customers in a friendly manner.
2. Remember customers' names and use them when talking to them.
3. Use positive words and body language to show customers that you value them.
4. Always thank your customers for doing business with you.

ENCOURAGING LOYALTY

Avoid treating customers as people who will use your product or service only once. To ensure that customers want to return, plant the seeds of partnership as soon as they make contact with you, whether they are placing an order worth thousands of pounds or simply asking for information. Make every customer feel valued and appreciated. Remember that people notice small details, particularly when forming first impressions of a supplier. If someone is reading a newspaper while serving them, they may well resolve never to come again. If greeted with a friendly smile and a show of polite interest, they will feel welcome and are more likely to return as a result.

73 Start building trust by arriving at customer meetings a few minutes early.

BUILDING LASTING PARTNERSHIPS

Help the team realize that providing customer satisfaction can bring enormous job satisfaction. Explain how much easier it is to work by agreement rather than in conflict, and stress the importance of maintaining regular contact with customers. Make sure that everyone prepares thoroughly for customer meetings, since this is one of the most important elements of putting customers first and building an enduring partnership. Customers appreciate suppliers who can answer questions at meetings because they have anticipated that they will be asked.

Customer outlines an idea

Team member listens carefully and takes selective notes

▲ LISTENING TO CUSTOMERS

An important part of relationship-building is the ability to listen actively to your customers rather than doing all the talking. Concentrate, listen for ideas rather than just words or reactions, and ask questions to clarify your understanding.

HANDLING CHANGE EFFECTIVELY

Change must be expected and tackled positively. Handle change well by understanding when your customers require you to do things differently, and by ensuring that your team accepts the need for change and welcomes the improvement it brings.

74 Ask of every change, "How will this affect our customers?"

75 Listen for chance remarks that could signal a customer's desire for change.

IDENTIFYING THE NEED FOR CHANGE

To help you determine the need for change, keep in contact with your customers and update your customer information regularly. If feedback reveals that customers are unhappy with any aspect of your products or services, you will need to make changes. Ask your team to report back on what customers have to say, and to monitor the activities of competitors who may be talking to their customers. Watch for developments in the market you serve, and the products and services you supply, by reading relevant books and magazines. Be aware of any changes occurring in your customers' environment, even if they do not appear to affect you directly. If, for example, a trade journal reports that one of your customers is planning to open new call centres to deal with client queries, think how you could change to help them do this, and approach them with the idea.

USING FEEDBACK TO ▼ HELP PLAN CHANGE
This pie chart is based on feedback illustrating the different problems that customers experienced with a telephone service. Bad sales service and faulty equipment accounted for most customer dissatisfaction, so these areas became the main focus of change.

Poor sales service 30%

Billing problems 15%

Slow and poor repair 15%

Faulty equipment 30%

Inefficient installation 10%

ACTING DECISIVELY

Once you have recognized that customers want you to change something, act decisively. Customers often give little advance warning that they need something different, so you may need to make a change quickly. With the team and other key people, such as customers themselves, produce and agree on a step-by-step plan to implement the change. Ensure that your plan sets out what the benefits of the change will be for the customers, the timetable for change, and how progress and success will be measured.

Passive resister leans back and folds arms, indicating a barrier to change

Doubter sits back and places hand on chin

Active resister uses hand gestures to reinforce his objections

Manager leans forwards, showing sympathy and an interest in colleague's opinions

▲ DEALING WITH NEGATIVE REACTIONS

Watch for signs of resistance from team members when discussing change, and try to interpret them. Active resisters may use their voices and hand gestures, passive resisters may lean back and cross their arms or legs. Be sympathetic towards resisters and seek to address their specific fears in order to win them round and gain their commitment to the change.

MANAGING RISKS

If the change is a major one, examine the risks involved. For example, if you introduce new software for an internal customer, there may be a risk that staff would be unable to work at full capacity initially. Identify any risks, and then plan to minimize the likelihood of the risk happening, and reduce the impact if it does. In this example, you may decide to have a period when both the old and new systems are available.

SUCCEEDING WITH E-BUSINESS

The internet can be used to help you get closer to your customers and provide a better service than that offered by your competitors. Ensure that your systems are customer-friendly and focus on building long-term cyber relationships.

76 Ask someone to assess your website for ease and speed of use.

▲ REACHING CUSTOMERS
Customers will feel encouraged to return to a website that offers support features such as discussion groups, mailing lists, and text-based contact with support staff.

77 Keep a note of any problems that you have in navigating your own site.

IMPROVING EFFICIENCY

Use internet technology to give customers the most convenient, cost-effective, and efficient service possible. Make sure that your site is fast-loading to avoid frustrating people. Check that it is easy for customers to place an order on-line. Then make sure that they are able to track progress towards delivery. Test your system by logging on as a customer and making a purchase. Look at any forms as a customer would – for the first time. Are they easy to understand and simple to complete? Make a detailed note of any difficulties you encounter so that you can take steps to improve your system.

DOS AND DON'TS

✔ Do recognize and investigate the potential that technology offers.

✔ Do ask the question, "What is in this for my organization?"

✔ Do use technology where it has an impact on the customer.

✘ Don't accept solutions just because they exist.

✘ Don't implement a solution unless it benefits the customer.

✘ Don't stop reviewing how and where technology can improve customer satisfaction.

INTRODUCING NEW TECHNOLOGY

Consider using a pilot scheme and phased implementation to introduce new technology at a pace that suits your team and your customers. Think through the objections that customers might have to changing their way of doing business with you, and reflect those concerns in the design of the system. As well as helping customers use new technology, make sure that you train your own team, who may also be fearful – perhaps because they see it as a threat to their jobs. Work at a pace that your customers find acceptable, but do not hold up those who want to make the change to technology as fast as possible by offering two routes to implementation.

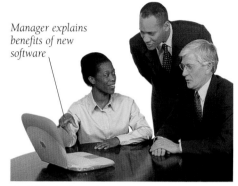

Manager explains benefits of new software

▲ **CHANGING IN PHASES**
Help customers to feel comfortable with new technology by offering support to enable them to make the changeover if necessary. Consider allowing people to use the old method of working until they feel confident with a new system.

78 Be creative in using the internet to improve customer relations.

THINGS TO DO

1. Improve your on-line skills by attending a course.
2. Use the internet regularly to learn your way around it.
3. Learn from the way other people use the internet.

BUILDING CYBER RELATIONSHIPS

As increasing numbers of organizations go on-line, it is vital to stay ahead of the competition. Bear in mind that there is little loyalty on the internet, since customers can move to your competitors' sites with just the click of a mouse. Monitor the way that customers use your site to find ways to improve it. Use the internet to facilitate communication with customers, and encourage vital feedback by making it simple for them to e-mail you with their comments. Plan how to make your website more customer-friendly. Perhaps you could offer two routes through the site, one for first-time customers and another for those making repeat orders. How about recommending other relevant products, giving special offers for bulk buying, or offering discounts for buying on-line?

COMMUNICATING CLEARLY

Effective communication is essential if you are to keep customers satisfied. Examine the style and content of your correspondence to check that it is customer-friendly, that it promotes your team's brand qualities, and that it sets realistic expectations.

79 Ensure that customers' names are always correctly spelt.

CULTURAL DIFFERENCES

People in Asia have a heightened fear of "losing face" in front of others. In communicating with them, therefore, it is wise to use language that in no way implies that they have made a mistake. The French have a reputation for communicating in a rather visionary way and are not afraid of abstract thoughts. The British, by contrast, like communication to be clear and simple. North Americans are quite comfortable with introducing fashionable words and modern jargon.

IMPROVING YOUR CORRESPONDENCE

Make sure that the team's correspondence to customers, from letters to brochures to order forms, is easy to understand and to the point. Avoid using your own organizational jargon, although you could include your customers' jargon after hearing it in conversation or having read it in their company literature, since this will make it clear that you understand them. Take note of the degree of formality that your customers use in written documents, and use the same style when corresponding with them. Avoid clichés, watch for repetition, and delete unnecessary words.

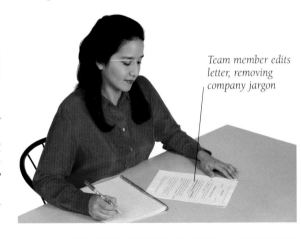

Team member edits letter, removing company jargon

REVIEWING ▶ CORRESPONDENCE
Look at the correspondence you send to customers and imagine that you are the recipient. How would you react? If you have written an item yourself, it may be useful to seek an objective opinion from a colleague.

PROMOTING THE TEAM AS A BRAND

Just as customers become loyal to their favourite product brands, you can encourage loyalty by presenting your team as a brand. Think what it is that you and your team do that is different and express this in a phrase or short branding sentence. Then emphasize this differentiation when you communicate with customers. Make sure that the way in which you communicate reflects your brand. If, for example, you wish to emphasize your team's reputation for efficiency and speed, use short sentences and words such as "Urgent" and "Do it now". Note that brands take time to build, but can be destroyed instantly if someone acts in a way that contradicts your brand values.

▼ PROJECTING AN IMAGE

In this example, two types of statement are sent out by teams that promote themselves as efficient and caring. A long, confusing statement contradicts the team's image and fails to impress the customer, whereas a short, comprehensive analysis is what he expects and requires.

Too much information is confusing and unnecessary

A concise statement is easy to understand

LONG STATEMENT SHORT STATEMENT

POINTS TO REMEMBER

- Regular communication between you and your customers should prevent problems from building up.
- Your company literature should be used as a means of selling your team to customers.

80 Avoid small print and hidden clauses or conditions.

SETTING EXPECTATIONS

Make sure that in all your communications with customers, you give them a realistic expectation of the benefits they will receive from your product or service. This will avoid the risk that customers will expect more than you deliver, which will result in their feeling disappointed and dissatisfied. Your company literature must obviously present benefits, such as reductions in costs, that you would expect the majority of your customers to achieve. You must also appear to be offering products and services that are competitive. Remember, however, that if you promise to supply a benefit to a customer and then fail to deliver it, you will lose their business.

DEALING WITH COMPLAINTS

Complaints provide opportunities to learn what customers really think. Welcome complaints as a chance to impress your customers and encourage their loyalty, while looking for ways to prevent similar problems from occurring again.

81 Accept that a complaint is also an opportunity for change.

82 Start by apologizing that your customers feel the need to complain.

WELCOMING COMPLAINTS

A complaint should be viewed as an opportunity to learn, improve your service, and find out what customers really want. Customers who go to the trouble of complaining are usually interested in giving you a chance to put matters right. This means that if you tackle the complaint effectively, you are more likely to retain your customers and improve your relationships. Even when one of your customers may be at fault, for example if they could have avoided the problem by buying more of your products or services at an earlier stage, avoid implying this. Resolve the issue, and then suggest, if appropriate, that the customer does more business with you. If the customer could make a change that would reduce the likelihood that the problem would recur, point this out in a friendly way. But be sensitive. Unless the customer is 100 per cent convinced that their problem has been fully resolved, they are unlikely to agree to increase their business with you, and your suggestion could do more harm than good.

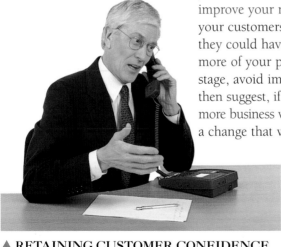

▲ RETAINING CUSTOMER CONFIDENCE
When handling a complaint, make sure that you apologize for any inconvenience, take charge of the problem, and let the customer know what you are doing to resolve the matter.

IMPLEMENTING A COMPLAINT-HANDLING PROCESS

STAGE	ACTION TO TAKE
RECORDING Listen to and/or log written complaints to provide reference when planning action.	● Make sure that you pay full attention to what is being said, avoid interrupting, and take notes. ● Show a sympathetic interest and make it clear that you are on the customer's side, even if they are angry.
QUESTIONING Find out details of the situation by asking appropriate questions to give a complete picture.	● Ask probing questions to pinpoint whether there has been any misunderstanding that can be easily resolved. ● Question in a genuine attempt to understand the situation; avoid leading questions or cross-examination.
RESOLVING Propose and agree on a solution that is acceptable to the customer.	● Ensure that any solution is specific so that the customer is left in no doubt as to how the issue will be resolved. ● Ask the customer to sign a document or confirm by telephone that they agree with the proposed action.
IMPLEMENTING Carry out an action plan to rectify a situation to agreed standards and schedule.	● Summarize what you plan to do to ensure successful implementation, and actions for the customer, if any. ● Include and gain agreement to any actions that need to be carried out by staff in other departments.
FOLLOWING-UP Ensure that the complaint has been resolved to the customer's full satisfaction.	● Check that the customer is satisfied and ask whether there is anything more you can do for them. ● Examine the underlying cause of the complaint to ensure that it does not occur again.

BEING CONSISTENT

Whenever you make a proposal or suggest a solution to a problem, always present your case with the customer in mind. Encourage the team to use the same systematic approach so that it becomes common language. Document the process in the form of a template so that team members can refer to it at first. After a short time, they will start to use it automatically.

POINTS TO REMEMBER

● A well-handled complaint is an opportunity to strengthen customer relationships.

● One complaint will often reveal others that customers have kept to themselves.

● Dissatisfied customers may complain to senior management.

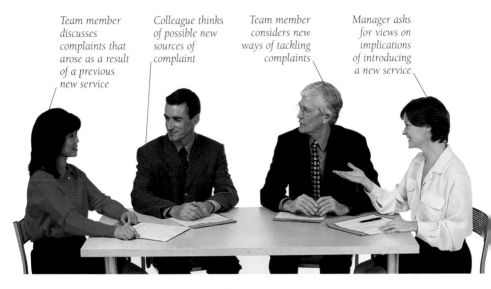

Team member discusses complaints that arose as a result of a previous new service

Colleague thinks of possible new sources of complaint

Team member considers new ways of tackling complaints

Manager asks for views on implications of introducing a new service

DISCUSSING ▲ COMPLAINTS

Handling complaints can sometimes be difficult, particularly for inexperienced team members. Hold regular sessions to discuss complaints from the past and think of those that could arise in future.

83 Practise handling complaints within the team before meeting customers to discuss them.

HANDLING THE WHOLE PROBLEM

A complaint is not only a customer situation that you must deal with but is also a sign that something is going wrong. When you have dealt with the complaint and re-established customer satisfaction, find out the causes of the problem. Until you have understood the underlying reasons for the complaint occurring, you will not have resolved it successfully. Whether you discover that there is a fault with the product itself, or a flaw in your organizational procedures, ask yourself, "How can we make sure that this does not occur again?" Look for solutions that will resolve the issue once and for all.

POINTS TO REMEMBER

● If more than one or two people make the same complaint, the problem may be widespread.

● An unusually poor response to an advertising campaign could suggest that there is a customer satisfaction problem.

● A large number of complaints could indicate that the people providing the service are experiencing a morale or stress problem.

● Complaints also suggest a deficiency in, or a lack of training of, the supplier.

ENCOURAGING COMPLAINTS

People often accept a product or service that does not quite meet their needs or expectations in order to avoid the trouble it takes to make a complaint. When someone does complain, they will often raise other issues they have had in the past as well. This is helpful feedback and you should encourage it. Ask people if they are satisfied in other areas than the original complaint; you need to know of any other unsatisfactory areas.

BEING PROACTIVE

When customers have an issue with your service, they may complain at a time when the issue does not appear to be critical or to have much impact on their performance. However, it is important to avoid complacency and to look for issues that, if unresolved, will certainly become crises later. Try to anticipate which customer issues are likely to have a high impact on their performance, either now or in the future, and resolve these as a priority. Deal with a high-impact problem immediately, before it becomes urgent.

84 Encourage clients to point out your deficiencies.

85 Look for trends in complaints and analyze the results.

MONITORING COMPLAINTS

Previous complaints provide vital information for planning the development or expansion of your products and services. Use a computer system to log the complaints. You may need to put code numbers on each type of complaint to identify their nature; this enables you to analyze the number of occurrences of different types of complaint.

◀ RECORDING COMPLAINTS
Use a template to log complaints systematically. Make sure that the information is accessible to the team, since it can provide valuable insights into what they need to do to make products and services more attractive to customers.

Complaint log No:

Date: _____ Time: _____ am/pm

Source: _____

Nature: _____

Dealt with by: _____

Response time: _____

Issues: _____

Method of follow up:
Letter ☐ Telephone ☐ Fax ☐
E-mail ☐ Face-to-face ☐

IMPROVING PERFORMANCE

An organization succeeds in the long term by keeping pace with market changes and evolving customers' needs. Make sure your team is building for the future, especially with key customers.

LOOKING FOR LASTING BENEFITS

Success in the long term depends upon customers continuing to receive real benefits from your products and services. Maintain your customer focus to ensure that your customers and your organization reap the rewards as you achieve your objectives.

86 Ensure that your customers continue to get benefits from your service.

87 Convince your team that their success depends upon creating lasting gains for customers.

CHECKING INDICATORS OF SUCCESS

Most teams focus on meeting their own targets and contributing to the success of the organization. However, you need to check that achieving your goals also results in benefits to the customers. Review the indicators you set to measure your success, and check that each one also brings gains for your customers. If there is no gain, change the indicator so that it benefits the customers.

WORKING WITH OTHER TEAMS

If other teams in your organization serve the same customers, it is vital that everyone works together for the benefit of the customers. Meet with your colleagues and discuss how you can pool resources and present a united front to customers. Discuss your different objectives and indicators of success and consider how, together, you can achieve the best results for your customers. Consider how you can create lasting gains for everyone by asking two key questions: "If we all perform to the time targets set in our indicators, will the customers receive the benefits they need in time?" and "Will the customer benefit be enduring?"

▼ **ALIGNING TEAM AIMS**
Hold regular meetings with other teams who serve the same customers. Align your objectives to avoid inter-team conflict and ensure that you work together as partners with one common aim: to achieve the best possible results for your customers.

88 Think how you would sum up the way in which you benefit customers.

89 Focus the efforts of your team on improving customer benefits.

SUMMARIZING THE BENEFITS

Once you are certain that you are working towards building a long-term, mutually beneficial relationship with your customers, summarize the benefits your team brings to customers in a short statement. Set out what is special about the way you provide those benefits. Ask yourself, "If I found myself in a lift for a very short time with a customer or a potential customer, how would I sum up what we offer and why we are the best team to deliver on that offer?" Make sure that everyone in the team agrees with this "ten-second lift pitch" and would summarize it in the same way. Use this statement to keep the team focused as they carry out their work.

BUILDING A LOYAL CUSTOMER BASE

People are more likely to remain loyal if they find it easy to do business with you. Help customers prepare a case for buying your products and services, and arrange to plan jointly for the future to strengthen business ties and build trust between you.

90 Help your customers make positive business decisions.

91 Learn how your customers prepare their cost/ benefits analyses.

PREPARING BUSINESS CASES

Most organizations require that before a manager or a team spends money, a business case is prepared to show the costs and benefits of the project. In most organizations, this cost/benefits analysis then has to pass the test of "return on investment". The buyer may, for example, have to work out how long it takes for the benefits gained to exceed the costs being spent. Every company has its own way of doing this, so find out how your customers do it. You will be able to help them build a positive business case if you understand their process.

◀ **JUSTIFYING A PURCHASE**
By working on a cost justification exercise with his customer, Sam, Harry was able to prove that the new franking equipment would save money for the organization. Harry's solid business case was then accepted by the purchasing manager.

CASE STUDY

Harry, a salesman for a firm of stationery manufacturers, had a verbal agreement with Sam, post room manager for a large organization, to supply a franking machine for each of their 14 office locations. Later, he received a call from Sam apologizing for the fact that the purchasing department had turned down the request. Harry asked to see Angela, the purchasing manager. He asked her why she had turned down the request and was told that the purchase had not been cost justified. Harry and Sam sat down and looked at the current costs of stamping outgoing mail and compared it with the proposed use of franking machines. They proved that it was cheaper to buy the machines and that there were further benefits from changing. Angela accepted the business case they had made and placed an order for the machines.

92 Use a joint planning session as an opportunity to agree on objectives.

POINTS TO REMEMBER

- Knowing in advance what your customers have in mind makes it easier to meet their requirements.
- Planning together is a good way to strengthen customer relationships.
- A joint planning session allows customers to take your products and services into account as they plan their future.

AGREEING TO PLAN TOGETHER

Move your relationships with customers forwards by assisting them to realize the financial benefits, as estimated in their business case, that will accrue from using your products or services. Lay the foundations for successful working partnerships by suggesting that you hold joint planning sessions. Stress the benefits of planning together by explaining that if you are to offer exactly what they need at the time they need it, the earlier you are involved in their plans the better. Make it clear to customers that it is important to your team to improve what they offer continuously. Explain that understanding your customers' future plans means that you will be able to take them into account when you are planning your own business development.

PREPARING FOR A JOINT PLANNING SESSION

Once a customer has agreed to attend a joint planning session, prepare for it carefully. Decide who needs to be there from your organization. For example, should you involve people responsible for the development of new products and services? Perhaps someone from marketing could make a useful contribution? The objective of a planning session is to translate the customer's and your objectives into a series of goal-focused activities. Allow enough time for the meeting. You may need to set aside a day or half a day to plan effectively, depending on the complexity of your products and services.

▼ INVITING ATTENDEES
Consider who will be involved in carrying out actions that will result from a joint planning meeting, and invite them along. If necessary, meet colleagues to discuss their input before the planning meeting.

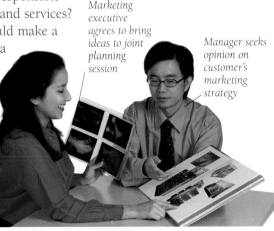

Marketing executive agrees to bring ideas to joint planning session

Manager seeks opinion on customer's marketing strategy

USING ANALYSIS

Start the planning session by asking the customer to outline their statement of purpose – a single sentence summarizing their role and aims – for everyone present. As a basis for the joint plan, encourage the customer to summarize their strengths, weaknesses, opportunities, and threats, which is known as SWOT analysis. Contribute by commenting on your experience of working with the customer. However, your main role at this stage is to listen and learn about the issues at the heart of your customer's activities.

93 Agree some goals that benefit you and your customer.

ASSESSING YOUR CUSTOMER'S SWOT ▼
A SWOT summary details the customer's strengths, weaknesses, opportunities, and threats, often in the form of a matrix. The chart below highlights questions to ask to help you decide which key elements from your analysis belong under which headings.

SETTING MUTUAL GOALS

Define goals that aim to increase the probability that your customer will achieve their business targets by removing their weaknesses, exploiting opportunities, and avoiding threats. For example, if a weakness threatening the customer's business is a lack of financial information, they need to set a goal to improve their financial processes. Your team can then set goals to assist them to do this, if applicable. Set a timescale for goals and recognize that while some goals belong only to one party, many overlap. Where there is an overlap, set goals for which you take joint responsibility.

UNDERSTANDING YOUR CUSTOMER'S SWOT

STRENGTHS
What is the customer competent at? What is the customer really good at?

WEAKNESSES
Where is the customer short of resources or capabilities? Where do they have competitive disadvantages?

OPPORTUNITIES
How could the customer boost their sales to customers and improve their service? Where are there new markets?

THREATS
How might your customer's business be overtaken? Which markets are declining?

ESTABLISHING ACTION PLANS

Once you have an agreed set of goals, begin defining the tasks that your team or the customer needs to carry out to achieve those goals. Make sure that each action is described clearly and unambiguously, and assign a time for the action to be completed and a person to be responsible for each individual task. Keep a record of actions, responsibilities, and timescales.

94 Make sure that every planning session ends with an action plan.

Team member agrees to take responsibility for action

Customer suggests timescale for action to be completed

Senior team member summarizes action

▲ AGREEING ACTION

If four people or more are involved in the planning session, divide into groups to establish and agree on action plans. Appoint senior team members to lead smaller groups of two or three people, since this will speed up the process.

95 Avoid agreeing to actions that will be impossible to achieve.

IMPLEMENTING THE PLAN

Agree with the customer that you (or one of your team members) are responsible for implementing your part of the plan. Arrange to hold regular meetings to update the plan, to check that it is still relevant, and to deal with areas where there are difficulties in carrying out the original ideas. If there is a lot to do following the original meeting, hold progress meetings on a weekly basis. As actions are completed and goals achieved, hold monthly meetings. Aim to have a major review (like the original joint session) on an annual basis for each of your most important customers.

LEARNING AND INNOVATING

Customer expectations change constantly, which is why organizations must be innovative in order to stay ahead of the competition. Review your plans to keep pace with change and ensure that team members share and learn from their experiences.

96 Learn from your successes as well as from your mistakes.

97 Realize that if you stop learning, you will soon stop being effective.

ENCOURAGING INNOVATION

Stress to the team that today's performance will not be good enough for tomorrow. You need to find new things to do, new ways of doing them, and encourage innovative ideas. Encourage individuals to discuss issues that have gone wrong so that they feel confident enough to allow other team members to learn from their mistakes. Motivate the team by rewarding good ideas, encouraging suggestions, and organizing competitions to select the best improvement or innovation suggested. Reward people by publicly thanking them and/or giving them a gift of some sort. Learn from past experience and change your processes or systems to reflect new experience.

Team member is thanked for her efforts

Colleague is motivated to aim for similar achievement

◀ **REWARDING STAFF**
People respond well to praise and encouragement. Make sure that you publicly reward team members' innovation and effort.

Q Have profits increased since our plans were implemented?

Q Have we seen an increase in our customer base?

Q Have we attracted a greater number of orders, or larger individual orders?

Q Has the number of product/ service enquiries risen?

Q Has awareness of our organization and its products or services increased?

THINKING STRATEGICALLY

It is important to accept the fact that, in today's changing world, you will have to review the fundamental basis of your plans from time to time, going back to the basic questions: "What products and services do we provide, to which groups of customers, and where should our focus be?" Ask yourself again on what basis you intend to compete for the loyalty of your customers. Plan to hold this type of review at least once a year – but bring it forwards if circumstances require it. If, for example, a competitor has approached one of your customers with a novel way of providing the service you are responsible for, call the review session immediately, because it may be too late if you wait for the normal time of review.

98 Be prepared to change your plans in the light of new circumstances for you or your customers.

▼ REVISING OBJECTIVES
The world is not static. Things within your organization or within your market are likely to change over time. If they do, you might need to redefine your objectives. Review objectives every six months or annually to check that you are still on track.

YES	CHECK OBJECTIVES	NO
Carry on with action plan	Are your customer-first objectives still relevant?	Revise objectives
Consider adding new objectives	Have you achieved any of your objectives yet?	Carry on implementation
Devise new objectives	Have new issues arisen that require new objectives?	Carry on implementation

EVOLVING TOWARDS FUTURE CUSTOMERS

As markets evolve, it is essential to move with them. Consider who your future customers will be and, based on an honest appraisal of past results and your in-depth understanding of your current customers, plan how to satisfy their needs.

99 Imagine who your customers will be in two years' time.

100 When you close a sale, analyze why you have been successful.

LEARNING FROM EXPERIENCE ▼
In this scenario, a team fails to sell a proposal to a new customer. By analyzing and improving their presentation, they go on to close their next deal. A failure to rectify what went wrong results in the loss of another potential client.

IMPROVING THROUGH EXPERIENCE

When seeking to attract new customers, it is important to analyze where your team members have been successful in selling a proposal, and examine why you have lost potential customers who have found your proposals less attractive. Stress that this exercise is designed not to apportion blame but to make sure that the team learns from these events. As a manager, it is essential that you move away from a blame culture and encourage the team to share experiences if you are to help them act more honestly and improve through learning.

New customer is unconvinced by proposal

Team member hears that customer has gone to a competitor

101	Seek to improve what you have to offer on an ongoing basis.

Improved presentation leads to winning new customer

Team meet to analyze why presentation failed to convince

They deliver the same proposal and lose another customer

Team fails to address reasons for losing customer

PROVIDING GREATER BENEFITS

Seek to combine products and services in creative ways in order to provide greater benefits to customers. If, for example, you lead a purchasing team and are conducting research into buying new supplies for one internal customer, you may consider passing on the information to other internal customers who might benefit from your research. Where you are dealing with different market groups and find ways of improving performance in one market, pass these insights on to others where appropriate. For example, if an IT team has helped the production department with a particular software package, they should assess whether it is relevant to other departments.

THINKING CREATIVELY

When looking for ways to improve customer service, avoid being restricted by the way things have been done in the past. Think creatively and challenge your team to come up with new ways of providing the services your customers require. Even when day-to-day pressures make it difficult, take time out to give people the opportunity to stop and think creatively. Look at what other organizations in your industry are doing by visiting them and attending cross-organizational conferences and events. Finally, look outside your own industry, since it is quite possible that in a different environment, other teams have discovered new ways of building customer loyalty.

ASSESSING YOUR CUSTOMER-FIRST SKILLS

*E*valuate your ability to develop a customer-first environment by responding to the following statements, marking the option closest to your experience. If your answer is "never", circle Option 1; if it is "always", circle Option 4, and so on. Be honest with yourself. Add your scores together, and refer to the analysis to see how well you scored. Use your answers to identify the areas that most need further development.

OPTIONS

1 Never

2 Occasionally

3 Frequently

4 Always

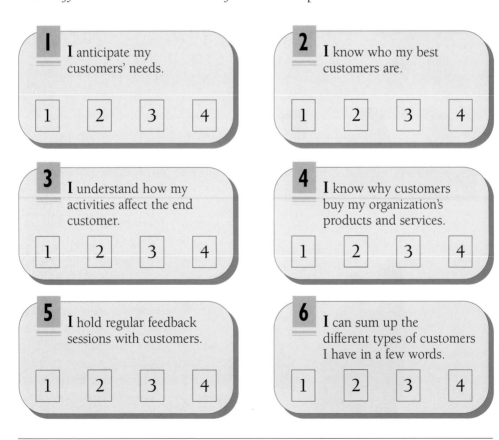

1 I anticipate my customers' needs.

1 2 3 4

2 I know who my best customers are.

1 2 3 4

3 I understand how my activities affect the end customer.

1 2 3 4

4 I know why customers buy my organization's products and services.

1 2 3 4

5 I hold regular feedback sessions with customers.

1 2 3 4

6 I can sum up the different types of customers I have in a few words.

1 2 3 4

7 I know where the emphasis of my activity needs to be.

1 2 3 4

8 I understand how my customers make the decision to buy.

1 2 3 4

9 I make sure that I am guided by the customer's aims when setting objectives.

1 2 3 4

10 I have clear measures of success for each of my objectives.

1 2 3 4

11 I focus my key business processes on the customer.

1 2 3 4

12 I have a document describing my key processes.

1 2 3 4

13 I always keep my customers well-informed.

1 2 3 4

14 I understand the benefits my customers receive from my products or services.

1 2 3 4

15 I ensure that customer information is accessible to everyone who needs it.

1 2 3 4

16 I assess the risk in every decision I make.

1 2 3 4

17 I am aware of what my customers would ideally like.

1 2 3 4

18 I make sure that the customer is very visible to my team.

1 2 3 4

19 I promote a customer-first culture by setting an example.

1 2 3 4

20 I prepare thoroughly for customer meetings.

1 2 3 4

21 I act decisively when change is needed.

1 2 3 4

22 I make good use of electronic communication in serving my customers.

1 2 3 4

23 I check that written documents are easy to read and understand.

1 2 3 4

24 I see every complaint as an opportunity.

1 2 3 4

25 I keep detailed records of complaints.

1 2 3 4

26 I work well with other teams who have the same customers.

1 2 3 4

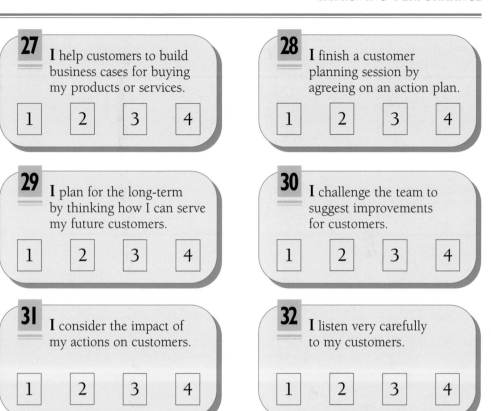

27 I help customers to build business cases for buying my products or services.

1 2 3 4

28 I finish a customer planning session by agreeing on an action plan.

1 2 3 4

29 I plan for the long-term by thinking how I can serve my future customers.

1 2 3 4

30 I challenge the team to suggest improvements for customers.

1 2 3 4

31 I consider the impact of my actions on customers.

1 2 3 4

32 I listen very carefully to my customers.

1 2 3 4

ANALYSIS

Now that you have completed the self-assessment, add up your total score and check your performance. Whatever level of success you have achieved, there is always room for improvement. Identify your weakest areas, and then re-read relevant sections to develop and refine your skills in putting the customer first.

32–64: You are not yet operating in a way that puts the customer first. Go carefully through each page of chapter two.

65–95: You are putting the customer first in most cases but need to address some weak points.

96–128: You consistently put the customer first. Avoid complacency by continuously reviewing your performance and requesting feedback from your customers.

MANAGING GLOBALLY

INTRODUCTION

O*rganizations from every part of the world are reaching out beyond their domestic markets to become international players. Not only is this very demanding on the businesses themselves, but it also creates a challenge for individual managers who must cope with working across geographic and cultural borders. Managing Globally teaches you how to succeed in this new world. It provides clear systems and approaches to help you manage global networks and teams, and it examines the skills needed for dealing with different cultures. Practical advice, including 101 concise tips, helps you to achieve the best results for you and your team. Finally, a self-assessment exercise enables you to evaluate and improve your global management skills.*

SUCCEEDING AS A GLOBAL MANAGER

For an organization to succeed on a global scale, a radical shift in business procedures is required. To become a successful global manager, aim to develop a global outlook.

WHAT IS GLOBALIZATION?

There are many definitions of the term "globalization". Develop an understanding of what it is in terms of business and why it is important to your organization in particular. Be ready to deal with the challenge of global complexity.

 Become the best informed person on globalization that you know.

▲ SHRINKING THE WORLD
One of the most rewarding aspects of being a global manager is the chance to make close business relationships with people from all over the world.

DEFINING GLOBALIZATION

In business, globalization is the trend toward an integrated worldwide economy. It is seen increasingly in markets, finance, production, and logistics. Politics has created global opportunities, economics has provided the incentives, and technology the means. In a broader sense, globalization is a process in which local lives are increasingly influenced by global forces, leading to greater cultural interaction.

2 Use all the technology available to you so that you can communicate globally.

CO-OPERATING GLOBALLY

Globalization has evolved slowly. In the twentieth century, new forms of economic co-operation between advanced industrial nations were instigated as a result of the two devastating world wars. These included the World Bank, International Monetary Fund (IMF), and General Agreement on Tariffs and Trade (GATT). Later, the fall of the Berlin Wall (1989) and the collapse of the Soviet Union (1992) triggered the spread of democracy, along with deregulation of markets.

LOOKING AT MARKETS

New and emerging markets provide opportunities for businesses to improve their revenues. While every country has its own unique culture, many new and emerging markets have growing middle classes who are willing and able to spend money on global brands. Think about how your organization could enter new markets and reduce costs, for example by increasing the scale of the production or by moving it to a lower cost location.

Communicates effectively

Embraces technological developments

Understands different cultures

Looks for opportunities in new markets

Remains open-minded

THINKING GLOBALLY

3 Keep up to date with new technology.

4 Be prepared for sudden and rapid changes.

ADOPTING NEW TECHNOLOGIES

On-going developments in transport and communication are dramatically increasing the flow of people, goods, capital, information, and ideas across borders. Previous constraints of time and space have dissolved in a world shaped by the internet, intranets, satellite television, and mobile telecommunication. Understand how a new technological infrastructure can redefine your ideas of what business can be done, and from where, when, and how.

UNDERSTANDING THE GLOBALIZATION PROCESS

A global manager needs to know what point his or her organization has reached in the globalization process, and where it wants to go. Understand the process and recognize the strategies that will give your organization a global advantage.

> **5** Find out about your organization's plans for global development.

OPERATING NATIONALLY

A national or domestic business is based solely in its home market. Such a firm has not made any Foreign Direct Investment (FDI) to set up international operations. However, it can enter the international marketplace by licensing its products and services, by franchising, or by exporting. Be aware that in free-trade economies, a domestic business is always in danger of losing its home market to more competitive global firms.

OPERATING INTERNATIONALLY

When a domestic organization's international activities reach a certain size, it will probably establish an international division to monitor cross-border transactions, such as the licensing of rights, the setting up of franchise operations, or the exporting of products. Then, a sales office may be opened in another country, or a joint venture partnership established with a foreign business. Consider how partnering can help you gain access to new markets – it can significantly reduce the amount of research you need to do in order to succeed in a new territory.

> **6** Identify your organization's global potential.

> **7** Make sure that your management team shares a global vision.

CREATING A MULTINATIONAL

As an international business expands, it develops a physical presence (subsidiaries) in multiple countries. It might do this through mergers and acquisitions or by creating new operations. Power tends to be distributed geographically, with each country unit focused on doing business and performing a range of functions, including sales and customer service, in its own territory. The challenge is to co-ordinate product development and manage brands across geographical borders.

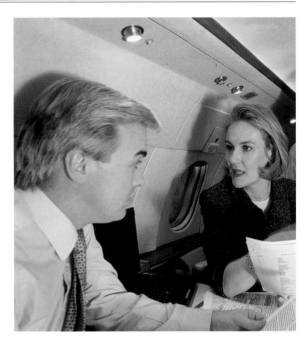

8 Identify how your organization intends to reach its global targets and what obstacles are in its way.

▲ **BEING PREPARED**
Before an overseas business meeting, take some time to refresh everyone's minds on the main aims of the trip, so that your team is focused before the meeting.

EVOLVING INTO A GLOBAL ORGANIZATION

The next challenge is to integrate the subsidiaries into a fully functional network: a global organization must think and act as one business worldwide, while also maintaining local responsiveness. At this stage, power usually moves from country units to worldwide business groups, responsible for global product and brand strategies, research, and development. Recognize that excellent cross-border co-ordination is a critical business advantage, and will give your organization capabilities that competitors cannot easily match.

QUESTIONS TO ASK YOURSELF

Q Where can I find up-to-date information on my organization's global strategy?

Q How can I help my staff and myself to develop a global outlook?

Q What can I do in my area to support global co-ordination of the business?

Q Are our operating methods in line with best practices from around the world?

IDENTIFYING GLOBAL BUSINESS CAPABILITIES

Every global manager needs to develop the vision necessary to succeed in the integrated world economy. Understand your market, develop a clear focus, refine business processes, form a talented team, and aim to conserve your organization's identity.

9 Challenge all your existing assumptions about doing business.

Q Am I keeping up to date with changing customer needs and wants worldwide?

Q Do I look for the global potential in local innovations?

Q Am I recruiting people who can handle the complexities of global business?

Q Am I rewarding my staff for identifying local and global risks and opportunities?

CUSTOMER RELATIONS ▶
As your organization achieves success in global markets, the balance of its customer base is likely to change. Local and regional customers may have less impact on your business than global ones.

10 Look for niche-market opportunities.

SCANNING THE MARKET

Monitor the global business environment to identify any opportunities and risks that could affect your organization. You should be particularly aware of industry trends, changes in your customer preferences, competitor moves in products and pricing, new technology, legal and regulatory changes, relevant government policy changes, new methods for marketing and distribution, and new supply sources. Gather information so that you can ensure that strategic and tactical policies are based on fact, not speculation.

KEY ■ Local ■ Regional ■ Global

11 Compare your organization with its competitors.

12 Examine every aspect of your business.

DEVELOPING A FOCUS

In formulating global strategic goals, a business must have certain information. Make sure that you know who and where your customers are and how they are changing. Look at your products and services to consider which have the best potential to succeed, while requiring the least adaptation. Study strategic markets to see how they can be entered into or expanded. Finally, look at the strategies of global and local competitors: think about how they could be bettered and beaten.

LEARNING FOR COMPETITIVE ADVANTAGE

To improve its strategies, and to be able to develop and sustain its sources of competitive advantage, a business must be in a continuous state of learning. Recognize that global competitive advantage comes from at least three sources: 1) technical excellence – an ability to create, absorb, and apply knowledge across the organization, 2) operational excellence – an ability to develop world-class systems and processes, and 3) relational excellence – an ability to work effectively with culturally diverse customers, colleagues, and partners.

▼ USING AN INTRANET
This manager is searching on the intranet to identify people in her organization who have the expertise to be part of a new global product development team.

POINTS TO REMEMBER

- Similarities in global customer preferences present opportunities for greater economies of scale.

- Global customers like to deal with suppliers who can fulfil their needs around the world.

- Focus attention on capabilities that make your organization distinctive in the global market.

MAXIMIZING VALUE AND MINIMIZING COSTS

A business consists of value-creating activities, such as product development and marketing. Your organization must decide where to locate each of these activities in order to maximize value creation and minimize costs. Allocate responsibilities and transform your business structure into a global network by putting procedures in place to co-ordinate areas such as budgeting and reporting.

MANAGING FOR RESULTS

One of your critical responsibilities as a global manager is to attract, develop, and retain world-class talent. Remember that talented workers are attracted to the worldwide business arena by the opportunity to perform challenging and creative work, and by the chance of professional development. They also value programmes that reward results. Ensure that collaboration across borders is possible, and that your organization has processes for capturing, disseminating, and integrating new knowledge and best practices.

 13 Remember that a talented workforce is crucial for global success.

▼ PRIORITIZING PEOPLE
Successful globalization depends on talented people. Employ the best people, extend their expertise, and give them the necessary incentives to stay with you.

| Attract | Develop | Retain |

ATTRACTING TOP-QUALITY EMPLOYEES

INCENTIVE	ADVANTAGE
CHALLENGING WORK	Well-designed jobs and international project assignments create a real sense of accomplishment and fulfilment.
FAMILY SUPPORT	Ongoing support enables staff and their families to manage the demands of living and working across borders.
GLOBAL OPPORTUNITIES	Work in different environments provides the opportunity to gain a rewarding global business perspective.
PROFESSIONAL DEVELOPMENT	Opportunities to gain cutting-edge skills and knowledge increase personal effectiveness and satisfaction.
REWARD AND RECOGNITION	Formal compensation programmes and career advancement arrangements show that global experience is valued.
WORLD TRAVEL	Adventurous individuals appreciate the chance to explore the world and experience different cultures.

RENEWING FOR GROWTH

A business must work continually to create its own future in the global market. It does this by scanning the marketplace constantly and creating new opportunities beyond the current vision of the consumer. Make sure that your team of employees is diverse enough to cope with the challenge of a global market: remember that diversity promotes innovation. Ensure that your organizational culture is an incubator for top-quality ideas.

Team member suggests idea for how to develop a product

Manager reacts positively to new idea

▲ SHARING IDEAS

This manager recognizes the value of fostering and sharing ideas. He arranges regular meetings where team members can express and discuss their views.

14 Compare, assess, and rank your organization against its global competitors.

STAYING COMMITTED TO CORE VALUES

While it is important to be prepared to change in a dynamic global marketplace, it is also important to conserve what is of long-term value. A global organization needs to identify those features of its business that should not be changed or may be changed only very slowly. An organization's commitment to its core values, for example, will show its integrity and reliability to its customers and partners. These consistent values will also provide diverse stakeholders around the world with a clear view of what they can expect when dealing with your firm. Recognize that your successful global brands also need conserving – these help generate recognition and confidence.

THINGS TO DO

1. Share strategic information with staff worldwide.
2. Keep local managers involved in identifying global solutions.
3. Seek out and eliminate obstacles to global co-ordination.
4. Establish global performance indicators for the business.
5. Look for talented and creative staff.

IDENTIFYING PERSONAL SUCCESS FACTORS

The global manager must be flexible and open-minded. Be ready to adapt your habitual attitudes and behaviour so that you can enjoy successful working relationships with people from other cultures and from different geographical locations.

15 Be open to advice from managers who have more global experience.

16 Learn about different cultures and lifestyles.

17 Believe in your abilities but be open to change.

MANAGING YOURSELF

Cosmopolitan attitudes are essential in global managers, who must behave as global citizens as well as national citizens. Learn how other cultures do business, and be prepared to adapt to altering circumstances. Think about ways you could approach new situations. Challenge your existing mental perceptions and biases, and be open to other people's points of view, even if they differ considerably from your own. Set realistic expectations for yourself and others when working across borders and persevere even in conditions of high uncertainty and ambiguity.

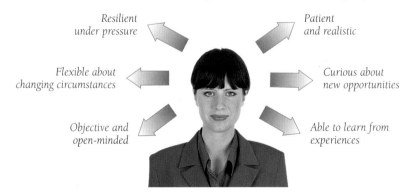

Resilient under pressure

Patient and realistic

Flexible about changing circumstances

Curious about new opportunities

Objective and open-minded

Able to learn from experiences

QUALITIES OF A GOOD GLOBAL MANAGER

MANAGING RELATIONSHIPS

Global managers need to collaborate effectively across borders so that they can develop synergies throughout the global business. Work at finding routes to shared understandings, despite language barriers and other cultural differences. Learn to see the world from the point of view of another culture. This, in turn, will enable you to build better relationships and increase your persuasiveness. It will also help you to recognize and adapt to different bargaining and conflict-management styles. Finally, create an extensive web of relationships inside and outside your organization and benefit from the support and knowledge you gain through them.

POINTS TO REMEMBER

● There will be gaps in your local management capabilities – analyze these honestly.

● Learning to manage successfully in a global economy is a continuous process.

● It is important to be receptive to international opportunities, and to be willing to take risks.

 18 Be an example to others in how to develop oneself.

DEVELOPING GLOBAL MANAGEMENT COMPETENCIES

TYPE OF APPROACH	ACTION
CONCEPTUALIZE	Identify patterns in the global environment that will help increase your understanding and effectiveness.
BUILD A CULTURE	Create an inclusive business culture in which people from diverse backgrounds can contribute their best work.
SCAN THE ENVIRONMENT	Detect and assess all possible risks and opportunities in the global marketplace.
INTEGRATE	Think beyond either/or answers to generate both/and solutions to complex problems.
OPTIMIZE	Look for a balance between global and local needs to generate the best possible results.
PARTNER	Discover potential alliances with competitors, related businesses, suppliers, and distributors.

MANAGING YOUR GLOBAL CAREER

A *global career offers you numerous opportunities. Identify the different roles and options open to you and then devise a clear focus for your career. Aim to gain the necessary experiences you need so that you can form your career path.*

19 Find a person with international experience to be your role model.

20 Let your boss know that you would like to take on international assignments.

LOOKING AT GLOBAL GENERALISTS

Usually located at the corporate centre, global generalists have experience in a number of the organization's strategic businesses and markets worldwide. They understand how the businesses, customers, partners, suppliers, and distributors work together. Their role is primarily strategic and they take decisions based on their broad knowledge of global opportunities and risks. They are also responsible for ensuring that the next generation of global leaders is developed.

LOOKING AT GLOBAL SPECIALISTS

Global specialists are experts in their business or functional area. For example, they might be a global product manager or a global human resource manager. Typically based at the corporate centre, they may complete assignments in local territories, bringing with them global knowledge and expertise. They may also act as integrators, identifying and transferring best practices worldwide. Their primary role is to ensure that the business operates to a world-class standard.

21 Develop a career plan and work toward realizing it.

22 Make continuous learning your top priority.

UNDERSTANDING LOCAL GENERALISTS

Country managers are experts in their territorial businesses and markets – they are known as local generalists. They need to understand how their operation fits into the total global enterprise. Key to aligning local and global strategies, they must make sure that the drive for global efficiencies is achievable and realistic at a local level. Given their pivotal role in translating global strategies into local tactics, they are in a strong position to become future global leaders.

▲ KEEPING INFORMED
A global manager needs first-hand knowledge of the way the business works at the local level, and to understand the perspective of local employees.

QUESTIONS TO ASK YOURSELF

Q What kind of global management career do I want?

Q How can I educate myself in international business?

Q What can I do to develop a network of global contacts in the organization?

UNDERSTANDING LOCAL SPECIALISTS

A factory manager, for example, is a local specialist – he or she is an expert within a local operation. While their primary focus is local, they are likely to deal with global processes. They may also be involved in regional or global teams, because they are able to supply a global business team with valuable insights about local issues.

GAINING THE RIGHT EXPERIENCE FOR YOUR CAREER

GENERALIST	SPECIALIST
GLOBAL	**GLOBAL**
● Take every chance to gain experiences in different businesses and multiple markets.	● Look for ways to gain specific business, product, or functional expertise.
● Seek opportunities to develop expertise in strategic thinking.	● Apply your knowledge and skills in the organization's strategic markets.
LOCAL	**LOCAL**
● Gain multiple experiences within local businesses and functions.	● Become an expert in a local business, product, or function.
● Make the most of any opportunities to work on global teams.	● Make sure that you align yourself and your business with global standards.

MANAGING THE GLOBAL ASSIGNMENT

G*lobal management careers involve a range of international assignments – short-, medium-, and long-term. Before a stint abroad, make sure that you prepare yourself properly so that you can adjust to what can be a dramatic change in lifestyle.*

23 Avoid comparisons between your home and your host cultures.

24 Be honest with yourself about any fears that you have.

ADAPTING WELL ▼
To be able to cope in a new environment, be understanding, avoid preconceived notions, and be flexible.

PREPARING YOURSELF

To succeed on an international assignment, you must be able to accept that each culture makes sense to the people who live within it. Appreciate each culture's potential value, and be ready to integrate what is of value into your way of working. Learn about the culture you will be visiting by reading, seeking cross-cultural training, developing friendships with overseas colleagues, and travelling.

Be respectful	Keep an open mind	Be ready to adapt

Consultant briefs manager on etiquette and values

Listens attentively to experienced advice

Notes key points

◄ SEEKING ADVICE
Before an international assignment, this manager meets a consultant so that she can find out about the country she is visiting and be made aware of any potential difficulties.

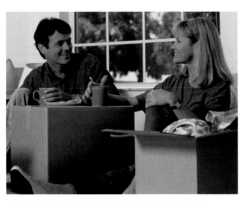

CONSIDERING FAMILY

Before you and your family leave for a lengthy assignment abroad, it is vital that you are all well-informed. Make sure that your family members feel totally involved in preparations for moving and that you discuss any concerns that they may have. Prepare your family for differences in everyday life, such as shopping, transport, postal services, and recreation. Find out about education and health care services in the country you will be living in. If you can, try to visit your host country with your family before committing yourself to going.

▲ INVOLVING YOUR FAMILY
When you are about to embark on a long-term assignment abroad, remember that your whole family is affected and that you will all be making the move. Work together as you prepare for your trip.

MAKING ADJUSTMENTS

While you are abroad, you may find that cultural differences cause frustration. You can fight, flee, or go with the flow. The latter will help you to see how the host culture operates. This enables you to make adjustments and begin to adapt. Help yourself adjust by regularly contacting friends at home. Get to know other expatriates and make a point of continuing ordinary family rituals.

25 Be adaptable, but be clear about the lines you are not prepared to cross.

THINGS TO DO

1. Set yourself modest goals and celebrate successes.
2. Share your thoughts and feelings with your family.
3. If you have a negative response to a new environment, avoid blaming the local culture.

RETURNING HOME

After the initial pleasure of getting home from a period of work abroad, you may feel an anticlimax. You are not the same person that you were, time has not stood still at home, and, often, few people are interested in what you have done. Counter any disappointment with some adjustment strategies. At work, set up sessions to communicate what you have learned and to highlight any valuable practices used in the country you have been living in. Encourage your family to reflect on the experience of having lived abroad.

MANAGING RELATIONSHIPS

A global manager appreciates the impact that culture has on business. Aim to understand cultural differences, develop your relationship skills, and overcome communication barriers.

UNDERSTANDING CULTURE

Groups of people see the world through their own set of assumptions, beliefs, values, and attitudes. Learn about your culture and how it has shaped you, and aim to understand how other cultures work so that you can be an effective global manager.

26 View a difficult cross-cultural interaction as part of a learning curve.

27 Experiment with new routines and rituals.

28 Be aware of your cultural habits and assumptions.

WHAT IS CULTURE?

Culture may be defined as the inherited ideas, beliefs, values, and knowledge of a group. As well as providing a sense of shared identity and belonging, culture helps us solve three types of problems: physical (how we feed, clothe, and shelter ourselves); philosophical (the meaning and purpose of life, and understandings about right and wrong); and relational (how we behave towards other members of our group and with other groups). Remember that our cultural solutions to these problems are learned, not innate, and are passed on through generations.

CULTURAL INFLUENCES

As a cultural group, our solutions to life's fundamental questions are influenced greatly by the natural environment in which we live, and our history, religion, and language. Individually, a mixture of formal and informal influences shapes us. Look at how national, local, organizational, professional, and functional cultures all have an effect on our outlook. National influences include institutions like the family, schools, churches, peer groups, and the media. Organizational influences include value statements, policies and procedures, and reward and recognition systems.

▲ DIFFERENT CULTURES
Culture influences every aspect of our lives – from the way we dress to the way we conduct business.

29 Remain open-minded, flexible, and ready to learn – even when other people are not.

ANALYZING CULTURES

Cultures are often said to be like icebergs. Above the surface are the characteristics that can be seen, heard, touched, smelled, and tasted, such as food, dress, art, and the use of gestures. Below the surface are the largely unconscious assumptions, attitudes, and beliefs that shape decision-making, relationships, conflict, and so on. Recognize that it is the below-the-surface aspects that cause the most problems when doing business across borders.

UNDERSTANDING CULTURES

Your first challenge is to become aware of the reality of cultural diversity. Next, you must develop appropriate attitudes for working cross-culturally – including respect, openness, and a willingness to learn. Seek knowledge of other cultures through first-hand experience and/or research. Translate your knowledge into specific skills that you will be able to use, such as international negotiation techniques and leading global teams.

BARRIERS TO CULTURAL COMMUNICATION

There are many factors that can be a barrier to cross-cultural communication:
● A belief that we are all the same.
● A perception that you have nothing to learn from others.
● An attitude that your way is best.
● The opinion that those who are culturally different to you need to be developed.

IDENTIFYING CULTURAL PATTERNS

The shared assumptions, values, and beliefs of a group form a cultural pattern. Teach yourself how the pattern fits together – its underlying logic – so that you can adapt to new environments quickly and effectively in your role as a global manager.

30 Start by understanding, and being honest with, yourself.

31 Learn as much as you can about other cultures.

32 Get to know individuals from other cultures.

CULTURAL COMPLEXITY

Although each culture is unique and complex, being made up of internal tensions, contradictions, and variations, it is possible to identify three main cultural "types" – autonomy, consensus, and status. Cultural types are very broad generalizations and should be treated with caution. They are useful guides, but they must be open to modification: if they are used to form stereotypes, they become destructive. Avoid allowing stereotypes to block your sensitivity to, and understanding of, individual exceptions.

RECOGNIZING AUTONOMY CULTURES

Members of autonomy cultures seek individuality and independence. A person in this type of culture is expected to determine his or her own identity, and dependence on other individuals or institutions is seen as a weakness. Conformity is expected only to the degree that it allows the society to function with some cohesion. Areas associated with this cultural type include Australia and New Zealand, Canada and the United States, and many parts of northern and western Europe.

POINTS TO REMEMBER

● In reality, cultures are a unique mix of cultural types, although one type will tend to be dominant.

● Study and careful observation are needed to help you understand a culture.

● The internet is a useful resource for cultural information.

● The more time you spend in a different culture, the more complex it will appear.

UNDERSTANDING CONSENSUS CULTURES

Members of consensus cultures are driven by the need for harmony, at least on the surface. The individual's personal identity is closely bound to that of a larger group, which maintains its identity by encouraging homogeneity and conformity. Great importance is placed on stability within the group. Becoming alienated from it can be very traumatic for the individual. Many parts of Asia have consensus-type cultures, including Japan, and, to a lesser extent, China and Korea.

33 Note that not all cultures work in the same way.

34 Inspire others to learn about different cultures.

35 Treat every model of culture as a generalized idea, not a fixed reality.

OPENING YOUR MIND ▼
A manager who refuses to learn and listen has a very limited view of the world. He must develop a more cosmopolitan and open-minded outlook.

IDENTIFYING STATUS CULTURES

Honour and respect, both for the individual and the group, drive members of status cultures. In this type of culture, an individual's identity is closely connected to that of the group, which can be an extended family, class, clan, or tribe. The shared heritage of group members is important: group survival and pride are of supreme value. Loyalty to strong leaders who are representative of the group is essential. Areas associated with status-type cultures include southern Europe, South America, Africa, and the Middle East.

This manager has fixed opinions and is not open to other people's views

When he notices himself behaving in this way, he tries to stop himself from making quick judgments based on his own cultural assumptions

He finds that by listening to others, he can find new inspiration and ideas

ADAPTING TO CULTURAL DIFFERENCES

Global managers must realize that many of the business practices which work successfully in their home culture will not be appropriate in another country. Ensure that you are able to adjust your approach to suit different cultural contexts.

36 Find a middle path between being yourself and adapting to others.

37 Respect and use the customary formalities that are valued by your host culture.

ADAPTING SUCCESSFULLY

To be effective, you need to be able to adapt in a new environment. However, adaptation does not equal adoption. For example, you are not trying to switch from being English to being Italian – this would make you appear foolish and manipulative. Adapt to show respect for another culture and to build relationships. For example, in a consensus culture, communicate in an indirect way, because this will make your hosts feel most comfortable.

SUCCEEDING IN CONSENSUS CULTURES

Relationships and long-term business goals are important in consensus cultures. Invest time in building lasting relationships and respect the formalities. For example, do not make someone "lose face" by criticizing them in public. Be patient and do not try to rush decisions. Also, be prepared for questions about yourself and your organization.

Accepts business card

SHOWING RESPECT ▶
In this example, a manager greets someone from a consensus culture by offering his card. He does not realize that it is respectful to offer a card using both hands.

SUCCEEDING IN AUTONOMY CULTURES

Members of autonomy cultures tend to be pragmatic, task-focused, and driven by quick results. They will like you to be flexible, but also decisive and action-oriented. Try to demonstrate optimism, confidence, and initiative when you are in this environment. Show how you can help individuals reach their goals, by selling yourself and your ideas. Time is money in such cultures, so be punctual and meet deadlines.

38 Be prepared to work outside the comfort zone and customs of your own culture.

SUCCEEDING IN STATUS CULTURES

Business in status cultures is usually highly personal. Work at building trust, and show respect for your colleagues and your superiors. Be aware that a hierarchy exists and be careful not to cause unintentional offence. Always accept hospitality, because it is tied to honour. Expect lots of small talk – get down to business only when your counterpart gives you some cues. Expect many interruptions and be patient. Stay focused on timing rather than timekeeping.

CULTURAL DIFFERENCES

Some issues that you take for granted may be viewed very differently in another culture. Where different cultural expectations are not properly understood, deals can be lost and products can fail. For example, in Africa it is customary to illustrate food packaging using an image of the product inside. Thus it is inappropriate to put a picture of a baby on a jar of baby food.

▼ **RESPECTING CULTURES**
In this example, a manager working in a different culture to his own found that his assumptions about acceptable behaviour were challenged. He adjusted accordingly.

CASE STUDY
Peter is from England. He was working in a status culture in Europe, where he saw some inefficiencies in his department's processes. He decided to take the initiative and produced a report on what he saw as the department's problems and he suggested some solutions. When he presented the report to his boss, he expected some praise and encouragement. Instead, his boss glared angrily, and over the next few weeks, treated him with suspicion.
A colleague pointed out to Peter that he had insulted his boss. Within a status culture, the boss is perceived to be the expert, the problem solver. It was as if Peter had said to his boss, "You're not doing your job properly!" Next time Peter noticed an issue, he subtly brought it to the attention of his boss – who then saw him as an ally.

DEVELOPING RELATIONSHIP ADVANTAGE

A vital challenge for the global manager is to build good working relationships across geographical and cultural borders. Recognize that strong, trusting relationships are the foundation of successful collaborations in a diverse business network.

39 Develop a strategy for building strong global relationships.

IDENTIFYING ADVANTAGES

You can gain advantage over your competitors in three main ways. The first is in intellectual capital, such as knowledge and copyrights. The second is in operational systems, including best processes and systems. The third is in relationships – the ability to develop strong personal and group links across geographical, business, and cultural borders. Be aware that relationship advantage is very difficult for a competitor to replicate. Good feeling across the global network cannot be manufactured.

DEVELOPING PARTNERSHIPS

Global businesses are dependent on their ability to forge international joint ventures and alliances. Most partnerships fail because of cultural neglect. Too many managers assume that if the economics look good, success is guaranteed. Beyond studying the spreadsheets, be prepared to develop cultural understanding. Let go of "there is only one way" thinking and alter from "either/or" to "both/and" working methods, to create business methods that give the best results for all parties. Encourage others on your team to do the same.

THINGS TO DO

1. Think about your global relationships – customers, partners, and colleagues.
2. Identify their needs.
3. Implement initiatives to meet these needs.
4. Review these relationships regularly to make sure that they are working well.

FOCUSING ON COLLEAGUES

Global organizations aim to draw on the talent and expertise within their worldwide networks. New initiatives in product development, marketing, and delivery are often dependent on cross-border collaboration. Many businesses also expect fresh perspectives to be generated through their diverse employees. Make sure that employees around the world are able to share ideas.

40 Learn to see your organization's products in the same way that your diverse customers do.

Meet your partners and agree on shared business objectives

Identify tasks that need to be done to meet those objectives

Identify how each culture would carry out those tasks

Analyze the advantages of each approach in a specific context

Decide on the best approach, or mix of approaches, to use

BLENDING DIFFERENCES ▶
Create a culture of inclusion in which differences are respected, but are not the primary focus. Instead, use these differences to create value for customers and the business.

CONNECTING WITH THE CUSTOMER

It is vital to understand your customers in their cultural context. Only by learning what factors influence their diverse perceptions of value, quality, and service is your business able to develop products that will meet their needs. For example, cost is a key concern to customers in northern Europe, but not to such an extent in Latin America, where people are more interested in value. In southern Europe and Asia, high levels of service will encourage repeat purchases, but will not have the same effect in northern Europe. Standardization must be balanced with responsiveness to local conditions. For example, a global beefburger chain opened a kosher restaurant in Jerusalem, and used lamb instead of beef in India.

RESEARCHING CUSTOMER VALUES ▶
Your customers hold the key to your organization's success as a global competitor. Gather data so that you can begin to build a picture of your customers in all your different markets.

MANAGING YOURSELF

To be a successful global manager, you must learn to manage yourself successfully. Be aware of your typical responses to a variety of situations, and start to develop those responses that increase your managerial effectiveness.

41 Remind yourself of other adaptations you have made in your life.

ANALYZING YOURSELF

Commit yourself to self-understanding

↓

Detach yourself from your perceptions of "yourself"

↓

Observe yourself in action in different contexts

↓

Analyze your ways of thinking, feeling, and behaving

↓

Create new options that increase your adaptability

↓

Aim to act deliberately, instead of habitually

MANAGING FEELINGS

Working across cultures can trigger a range of intense feelings: fear, superiority, helplessness, anger, anxiety, disgust. If these influence your work and interaction with others, they can be destructive. Acknowledge them, compartmentalize them, and examine them objectively. Remember that tasks can be repeated and decisions reversed, but relationships are very difficult to repair.

QUESTIONS TO ASK YOURSELF

Q How do I think and act in new situations?

Q How do I handle difficult situations?

Q Would these strategies work for me in all cultures?

Q What causes me the most stress and why?

Q Have I had positive feedback that I could act upon?

Q How can I increase my self-awareness?

MANAGING THOUGHTS

Everyone learns thought patterns that provide short-cuts to understanding. Stereotyping, where we sort the world into categories and put new information into one of these, is an example. Learn to manage your thinking so that you can handle greater complexity. Resist taking shortcuts – and making quick, often false, assumptions – and learn to tolerate different situations and beliefs.

MANAGING BEHAVIOURS

Awareness of the underlying cultural influence in how you speak and behave is a critical step towards self-management. If you are from a culture that values hierarchy, you will communicate some form of deference in your speech and body language. Realize that although this is acceptable in your home environment, your deference may be perceived as weakness when you work in a culture that values an open, democratic leadership. In this new context, manage your behaviour by becoming more assertive and explicit so that you increase your effectiveness.

42 Ask someone to comment on your behavioural traits.

43 Set yourself small goals and work to achieve them.

◀ **BEING AWARE OF BODY LANGUAGE**
This manager's open gestures may create an impression of honesty and friendliness in a Western culture. However, it may be viewed as disrespectful in Asian cultures.

ANALYZING YOUR SELF-MANAGEMENT CAPABILITIES

CAPABILITY	POSITIVE ASPECTS	NEGATIVE ASPECTS
MANAGING FEELINGS	● Able to handle stress ● Optimistic, self-confident ● Good self-awareness ● Flexible and co-operative	● Always on guard and abrasive ● Cynical ● Judgmental and self-righteous ● Ethnocentric
MANAGING THINKING	● Reflects on experience ● Quick thinking and creative ● Honest and non-conformist ● Able to improvise	● Tendency towards denial ● Not a team player ● Egotistical and gullible ● Needs definite answers
MANAGING BEHAVIOUR	● Observes and listens ● Sociable and easy going ● Patient and realistic ● Criticizes constructively	● Averse to risks ● Fearful of losing face ● Needs to be in control ● Unable to criticize self

BUILDING GLOBAL RELATIONSHIPS

Strong relationships are built on trust and influence wherever you are in the world. Focus on developing trust, and show interest in and respect for other cultures. Learn to see the world from the perspective of other cultures, rather than just your own.

44 Ask yourself: "Am I reading this behaviour correctly?"

45 Notice which communication channels your colleagues prefer, and use them.

FORMING RELATIONSHIPS

Culture affects how quickly relationships can be formed and what obligations are assumed from these relationships. In European cultures, where mobility has traditionally been low, communities are guarded about sharing personal information: relationships tend to be formed slowly. Trust is only earned over time. In mobile societies like the United States, relationships tend to be developed quickly before people move on.

DEVELOPING TRUST

It is vital not to misread cultural signals, because this can undermine trust. In the office, character, competence, and confidence are key to trust, but it is possible to misread signals in these areas:

● Character – people who are used to explicit communication can confuse indirectness with lying and begin questioning someone's integrity.
● Competence – in some cultures, family connections influence position, but this does not mean that these managers lack expertise.
● Confidence – an individualist working with someone from a harmony-driven culture might confuse modesty with weakness.

QUESTIONS TO ASK YOURSELF

Q What do people in this culture expect of a relationship?

Q Are relationships in this culture traditionally built quickly or slowly?

Q What will make a good impression?

Q Is trust assumed, or must it be earned over time?

Q What needs to be done in order to keep the relationship strong?

Showing Interest

A quick way to build relationships is to show a genuine interest in the other person's culture. Many Westerners focus on getting work done, and only then – time allowing – work at building relationships. To other cultures, this appears impersonal. Typically, people everywhere are happy to talk about their culture. When you are on a business trip, show an interest in your surroundings. For example, "On the way from the airport, I saw people singing and dancing. Can you tell me what the festival is about?"

46 Keep a record of your contacts in the global network.

47 Make relationship-building a pleasure, not a task.

48 Keep in touch with colleagues – do not wait for a business need.

Developing Networks

Global organizations depend on deep and strong collaboration across borders. Consider sponsoring cross-border events, such as training workshops. Think about creating global bulletin boards on the intranet, where people can share international experiences. Intranets are useful for producing learning modules on cultural awareness, and for networking and teamwork.

Assessing Communication Styles

Communication Style	Advantages
Meeting Face to Face	● It is helpful to gauge people's feelings through their body language and facial expressions. Strong relationships can result.
Video-conferencing	● The technology allows members of the global business to discuss issues in real time and put faces to names with their overseas colleagues.
Conversing by Telephone	● Talking to overseas colleagues, instead of corresponding in writing, ensures that any misunderstandings can be clarified instantly.

Understanding Cross-Cultural Communication

Some cultures communicate most readily via written messages, while others prefer talking. To relate successfully, understand what communication is, how it works, and how to tailor it to the cultural context into which it will be received.

49 Create the right conditions for open cross-cultural dialogue.

Questions to Ask Yourself

Q Who should be communicating and with whom?

Q What information should the message contain?

Q How should it be designed for the best effect?

Q When is the best time to send the message?

Q Where is the best place to deliver it?

Understanding Communication

When we "deliver" a message, we assume that we have "communicated". But it is often the case that what has been said is not the same as what has been heard. Although the communicator may feel in control, it is the receiver who determines whether communication takes place. Remember that the outcome of successful communication is agreement about meaning. This can be difficult to achieve in cross-cultural communication where some degree of misunderstanding is inevitable.

Modelling Communication

In a simple model of communication, a sender encodes a message using symbols, words, pictures, and/or gestures. It is then sent to the receiver via a message channel (face to face, telephone, e-mail). The receiver decodes the message (interprets its meaning). Typically, the receiver sends a message back to the sender, and becomes the encoder. The original sender becomes the decoder. Be aware of cultural influences in how the sender encodes the message and how the receiver decodes it.

50 Always check for shared understanding.

51 Remember, talking louder does not help understanding.

CULTURAL DIFFERENCES

In relationship-focused cultures, such as those in Asia, words only convey a small part of the message; the listener infers the rest, based on their knowledge of the speaker, the setting of the conversation, and any body language. Task-focused cultures such as Germany or the United States, prefer to use words as the key form of communication.

UNDERSTANDING COMMUNICATION STYLES

Autonomy cultures prefer explicit and precise communication, with little use of body language. Consensus cultures tend to be more indirect: meaning depends on the wider context, such as who says what to whom. In status cultures, communication tends to be rhetorical and emotional, using exaggeration and repetition.

52 Make sure that your intent is to learn from communication, rather than to compete or control.

MANAGING ATTITUDES IN A CROSS-CULTURAL DIALOGUE

NEGATIVE | | POSITIVE

The dialogue is viewed as a debate	**Understand each person's expectations**	The object is to reach a mutual understanding
Rank, coercion, and power games destroy openness	**Be aware of different attitudes towards status**	In the dialogue, everyone has an equal status
Stereotypical thinking blocks understanding	**Be open-minded and listen to all points of view**	Different views are appreciated and understood
Assumptions are taken for granted	**Find out what assumptions each person holds**	Participants examine their assumptions
Judgments make participants defensive	**Do not allow judgments to block mutual agreement**	Potential judgments are turned into enquiries

OVERCOMING COMMUNICATION BARRIERS

The barriers to communicating across cultures must be recognized and managed. Be aware of all the pitfalls of communication so that you avoid sending or receiving the wrong messages, and always try to see other people's points of view.

53 Empathize with your foreign colleague's needs and wants.

54 Always consider whether your body language is helping or hindering a discussion.

MISINTERPRETING SIGNS

It is easy to misinterpret someone's behaviour by assuming that they share our understanding of it. For example, many Westerners interpret direct eye contact during conversation as a sign of sincerity, whereas in Asian cultures, a lowering of the eyes communicates respectful deference. The Asian may consider the Westerner's behaviour as aggressive, even hostile, while the Westerner sees the Asian's behaviour as insincere. The result – instant distrust between the parties.

READING BODY LANGUAGE

Along with eye contact, body movement (facial expressions, gestures, handshakes, bows, and posture) is an important form of non-verbal communication. People from all cultures use their bodies to reinforce the meaning of what they say, to communicate something that they have not said, or even to oppose what they are saying. Be aware of your body language and learn about the body language used in other cultures. For example, pointing a finger to emphasize a point can be seen as rude, rather than emphatic, in some Asian cultures.

Two managers are involved in heated debate

AVOIDING ETHNOCENTRISM

Making the standards of one's own group – what is considered right, reasonable, and rational – the standards for the rest of the world, is known as ethnocentrism. It is usually accompanied by feelings of superiority. Everyone experiences ethnocentric feelings. Acknowledge them for what they are: destructive responses to the unfamiliar. Stay constructive and try to see things from the other person's point of view. Ask yourself: "What is causing such a strong reaction in me?" and "Am I being objective?" Look for what is interesting and valuable in the way the other person sees things.

55 Stay open to an issue, even if it appears to go against your values.

Mutual understanding is reached

Manager considers colleague's point of view

He realizes that they are both ultimately aiming for same goal

Managers will not listen to each other's reasoning

Communication breaks down completely

◀ **SHOWING UNDERSTANDING**
In this example, two managers are arguing about how to deal with a procedure, and their conversation is quickly deteriorating. To try to prevent the discussion breaking down in animosity, the managers need to follow the golden rule of communication: listen first, think second, and then talk.

RECOGNIZING GENER ISSUES

Manager greets customer warmly

It is widely thought that women face more prejudice than men in the international workplace. In fact, many women report a "halo effect" when working in some male-dominated cultures. The men recognize that women managers are rare, and so think those that do exist must be outstanding. However, remember that some cultures demarcate strongly between male and female roles and this can make it difficult for women to succeed.

BUILDING RELATIONSHIPS ▶

It has been suggested that women are more successful than men in international business because they pay more attention to building and maintaining positive relationships.

POINTS TO REMEMBER

- Keep your language simple and present only one idea at a time.
- If you do not understand a point, do not pretend that you do.
- Be prepared to ask questions.
- If you make a telephone call, follow it up with an e-mail.
- Speak slowly and clearly.

USING CLEAR LANGUAGE

The key to communication is to put yourself in your reader's or listener's place, while paying attention to some basics. Be careful to avoid slang, jargon, acronyms, buzzwords, clichés, and colloquialisms. Make sure that you are literal and specific; vague, abstract language will confuse and frustrate your customer or colleague. Provide adequate contextual information. Do not simply count on others knowing what you mean.

WOMEN WORKING GLOBALLY

Women working on an assignment in a different culture to their own can be faced with a variety of challenges. There are ways to help overcome any potential difficulties:

- Find a consultant who can brief you on values and norms of behaviour.
- Display professionalism in how you dress and respect local customs.

- Be very well prepared (more than your male colleagues) and make your presentations direct, with few qualifiers.
- Demonstrate your decision-making power and authority.
- Do not take male-dominated cultures personally or react to them by becoming aggressive.

BEING SENSITIVE

A general rule in successful communication is to stay clear of subjects such as sex, politics, and religion until trust is established. Initially, discuss neutral topics like your journey, the weather, and holidays. Wait until you know someone better before talking about families. Take your cue from them as to when this might be appropriate.

A sense of humour enables you to put your cultural mistakes into perspective. However, beware: jokes rarely translate well, because they often rely on local knowledge.

56 Avoid potentially controversial topics at the beginning of a relationship.

BEING PREPARED ▶
In this example, an American businessman realized that he needed to adapt his behaviour and body language in order to gain respect and achieve success in a different culture.

CASE STUDY
An American businessman visited a bank in Tokyo. He walked into the meeting room and threw himself into his chair. He sat back and crossed his legs casually. The Japanese bankers said nothing but exchanged quick glances with one another. They knew instantly that their bank would not want to do business with this rude man.
Realizing his mistake, the next time the American businessman planned a trip to Japan, he took the time to learn about Japanese habits and manners.
When he arrived in Japan, he greeted his hosts with a small bow and exchanged business cards with both hands. He sat formally in his chair and did not rush to talk about business, but discussed his trip and his interest in Japanese current affairs. He also exchanged small gifts with his hosts. He was received positively.

57 Keep your sense of humour, but leave your jokes at home.

58 Make your interpretations tentative until they are confirmed.

AVOIDING STEREOTYPES

Stereotypes are relatively fixed generalizations made about others and they leave little room for identifying and adapting to individual differences. Stereotypes can be negative ("all… are lazy") or positive ("all… are clever"). Both types are empty statements with no value. One of the most important tasks facing any global manager is to examine your, largely unconscious, stereotypes. Any generalizations that you do make must be very tentative and open to change. Keep in mind that you do not interact with a whole culture, but with individuals from within it.

MANAGING GLOBAL ETHICS

Globalization increases our exposure to different ethical norms. Be sensitive to other people's cultural perceptions of what is right or wrong, and understand the systems your organization has for dealing with ethical issues.

> **59** Be clear about your own moral values – and adhere to them.

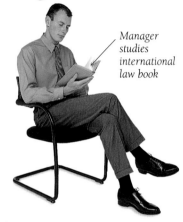

Manager studies international law book

▲ STUDYING THE LAW
Make yourself fully aware of how your organization views ethical matters. Read up on the legal situation at home and abroad.

STUDYING ETHICS

Ethics is about morality – identifying acceptable standards of conduct. There are many daunting ethical issues that a global manager might have to deal with, including payments made to foreign officials or businesses to win contracts, insider trading, employee discrimination, environmental abuse, working conditions, counterfeiting, and piracy. Seek help at corporate and local levels to deal with these. Make sure that you understand the legal framework of your home culture, and the ethical codes of your organization. Never rush to judgment. Be sure that you appreciate fully the potential consequences of any action you may take, for the business and for those involved.

AVOIDING IMPERIALISM

Perceptions of right and wrong vary. Bribery in one culture may be seen in another as the price for doing business. In one country, hiring relatives may be perceived as the rational thing to do (relatives can usually be trusted), whereas in another it would be considered nepotism. Even if general agreement exists on values such as human rights and environmental protection, specific definitions and overall priorities will differ. Avoid trying to impose your own standards because this may lead to accusations of ethical imperialism.

> **60** Make sure your organization has ethical guidelines.

> **61** Study examples of previous ethical dilemmas.

QUESTIONS TO ASK YOURSELF

Q Am I comfortable with living with the results of this action?

Q What if everyone acted in this way?

Q Would I want my children to do this?

Q Would I want this to happen to my family?

Q Would I want my family to see this in the newspaper?

ANALYZING OPTIONS

You can deal with ethical issues with either absolutism or relativism. In reality, ethical issues are complex, and solutions are not either/or. Applying absolute principles may have unintended results. For example, some American businesses withdrew their manufacturing sites from Bangladesh because of the use of child labour. Fearing the loss of more business, the factory owners dismissed 30–50,000 children. Many of these children then went into more dangerous jobs. Always look at a situation from several viewpoints.

BEING PROACTIVE

Organizations should be proactive in ethical issues, creating specific codes of conduct. These need to be reinforced by being included in performance evaluations and promotion criteria. Use training to introduce employees to different ethical norms and your organization's ethical expectations. If violations do occur, carry out an audit to find the causes – organizational culture, ineffective leadership, or inadequate reporting procedures may all be underlying problems.

62 Remember that good ethics lead to good business.

▼ USING TRAINING
Discuss a selection of ethical dilemmas likely to be encountered in global business with your team.

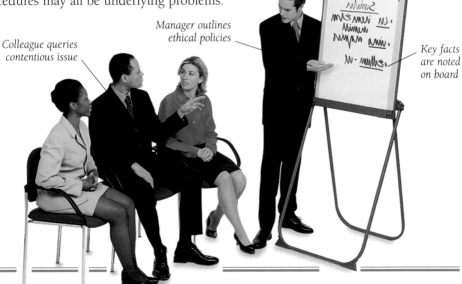

Colleague queries contentious issue

Manager outlines ethical policies

Key facts are noted on board

WORKING PRACTICES

When you begin working globally, all your managerial techniques will need to be adapted. Be prepared to adopt new practices to achieve your goals in a multicultural environment.

ASSESSING LEADERSHIP

Each culture has a perspective on what it means to be a good leader. Understand the different leadership styles that you may encounter, study respected leaders in other cultures, and be ready to adapt your leadership styles in different contexts.

63 Remember that one leadership style will not be appropriate for all.

64 Find a balance between tasks and relationships so that you can lead effectively.

ASSESSING POWER

How much power a leader has, and how it is used, varies between different cultures. In autonomy cultures, it is distributed widely – the hierarchy in organizations tends to be relatively flat. Decision-making is bottom-up and top-down and everyone can contribute ideas and opinions. In consensus and status cultures, power is concentrated in a few hands and there is a large gap between those who have power and those who do not. In these cultures, decision-making is top-down, although input may be gathered from employees who are lower down in the hierarchy.

THE PEOPLE DIMENSION OF LEADERSHIP

In autonomy cultures, leaders often have technical expertise and an impersonal approach. They tend to focus on the task to be done and rely on processes and action plans. Relationships are more important to leaders in consensus and status cultures, because they believe these will help get the job done. Leaders in consensus cultures take advice from the wider group and offer guidance. In status cultures, leaders are often strong, charismatic figures who rely on a close group of advisors.

65 Develop leaders in all levels and areas of your business.

66 Find someone to be your leadership mentor.

POINTS TO REMEMBER

- You should aim to lead your team with vision.
- Your team will be better focused if you provide it with a clear strategy.
- Learn what influencing techniques will be most effective in a particular culture and keep this in mind when you form a strategy.

IDENTIFYING STYLES

After taking into account the influence of power and relationships, research has identified four major leadership styles worldwide. The democratic leader provides a structure, consults widely, and empowers others. The collaborative leader becomes involved as a team player and negotiates shared solutions. The autocratic leader controls, and demands loyalty. The paternalistic leader is a parental figure, looking after the group's interests.

FLEXING STYLES

To get the best out of people, find out about their expectations of leadership. Employees who are used to an autocratic or paternalistic style of leadership may get confused if you use a more democratic style. To them, you may appear to lack authority and confidence. Make sure that you can adapt while also appearing and feeling natural.

PRACTISING STYLES ▶

This manager is receiving advice about leadership styles from a consultant: he is practising leading democratically.

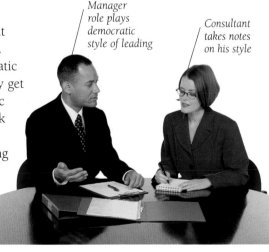

Manager role plays democratic style of leading

Consultant takes notes on his style

MOTIVATING ACROSS CULTURES

A global manager needs to identify the needs of individual employees, within the context of the culture in which he or she is working. Recognize the personal priorities of the diverse individuals in your team and apply the appropriate motivational tools.

67 Take note – the factors that motivate someone can change.

68 Remember that money is not the main motivator for everyone – family may be the priority.

FOCUSING ON MOTIVATION

People worldwide work to satisfy their needs and wants. These vary according to the circumstances of the individual, and on factors such as cultural values. It is difficult to generalize, but research suggests that professionals in a range of countries value challenge, autonomy, and the opportunities to use their skills. Not surprisingly, lower level workers place high importance on security, earnings, benefits, and working conditions. Make sure that you are sensitive to the different priorities of the individuals in your global team.

RECOGNIZING MOTIVATION

Beyond personal circumstances, individuals are influenced by wider cultural values. For example, in Latin America, job status and a good personal life are key motivators. In Saudi Arabia, family esteem is more important than public recognition. In one country, a job may be viewed as an economic necessity, in another country it may be tied to self-identity. Be aware of the values of different cultures.

▼ MATERIAL POSSESSIONS
Some people are motivated by expensive material possessions which show that they are successful in their work and have achieved a high standard of living.

LOOKING AT A MODEL OF MOTIVATION

This model of motivation focuses on the three basic needs that occur in any workforce. These are: the desire to achieve independence and personal accomplishment; the wish to affiliate and attain harmony; and the desire to have power and control decisions. These general motivations must then be looked at in the context of particular cultures:

- Autonomy cultures tend to be motivated by the desire to achieve.
- Consensus cultures are usually motivated by the wish to gain affiliation.
- Status cultures are often motivated by the desire for power.

To understand fully what motivates an individual, take personal circumstances into account and allow for cultural changes.

69 Ensure that you fit the right motivator to the culture and the individual.

USING TOOLS

Local knowledge enables a manager to determine the best motivators in the culture. In autonomy cultures, individual incentives are the most suitable. Use praise, promotions, and pay raises. In consensus cultures, group-based incentives work best. Distribute bonuses, formal recognition, competitive awards, and holiday awards throughout the team. Recognize that anything that enhances respect is motivational in status cultures – these include titles, position, flattery, gifts for the individual and the family, and bonuses.

DOS AND DON'TS

✔ Do tailor your reward programmes to suit local cultural values.

✔ Do monitor the priorities of your employees, and make adjustments.

✘ Don't assume that the same things motivate all groups in a country.

✘ Don't assume that what has motivated people in the past will motivate them now.

THINKING ABOUT MOTIVATION

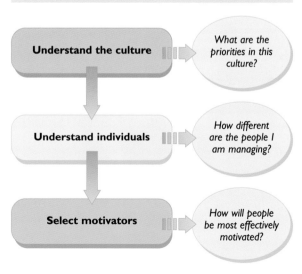

Understand the culture → What are the priorities in this culture?

Understand individuals → How different are the people I am managing?

Select motivators → How will people be most effectively motivated?

Giving Feedback

Managers need to give and receive feedback on performance. There are various methods of providing feedback, some more direct than others. Choose the appropriate method, depending on the culture in which it is being received.

70 Observe how other people in the culture give feedback.

Discussing Performance

Formal, direct feedback is typical in autonomy cultures. The focus is on the performance and personal strengths of the individual. Use two-way communication so that the employee can give his or her point of view and negotiate new goals. Bear in mind that autonomy cultures vary in their directness. In Britain and the United States, for example, encouraging words are said at the beginning and end of a performance review. In Germany, criticism is more direct.

Manager discusses employee's views

▲ **COMMUNICATING OPENLY**
Feedback in an autonomy culture is expected to be an exchange of views and a negotiation of new goals. Both sides will communicate equally.

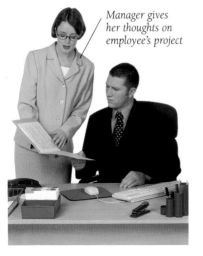

Manager gives her thoughts on employee's project

One-Way Feedback

Performance feedback in status cultures tends to be spontaneous and only one way: two-way communications could undermine the authority of the manager. Reputation is critical so some problems may need to be skirted around to prevent a manager appearing to have failed. Negative feedback could be conveyed via an intermediary. As well as performance, emphasize the employee's characteristics, including civility and loyalty.

◀ **STATING VIEWS**
Managers in status cultures tend to give feedback and express their opinions on the spur of the moment, rather than initiating a formal review session.

BEING INDIRECT

Indirect feedback is common in consensus cultures where preserving reputation, or "face", is critical. The manager counsels and guides. Feedback is likely to be relatively informal and continuous, with its focus being on how well an employee performs in the team. Try to speak to a group rather than an individual, tell hypothetical stories about yourself to illustrate a problem, and increase a person's responsibilities to show your approval.

71 Be careful to avoid causing someone embarrassment.

▼ **ADDRESSING A GROUP**
To help someone save "face", feedback may be given to the whole group, rather than solely to an individual.

Manager gives critical feedback to whole group

Employee listens to feedback, but has not lost face in front of his colleagues

SAVING "FACE"

"Face" is an individual's reputation, the degree of respect in which he is held by others (known as *kao* in Japanese and *mianzi* in Chinese). There are a number of things you can say to prevent someone from losing face during a difficult debate or negotiation:

❝ *I didn't want to say anything in the meeting, but perhaps we could have a word in private.* ❞

❝ *Perhaps we could save that question until we have all had a chance to look at the specifications.* ❞

❝ *You should be very proud of your company. It has a wonderful history of reliability and customer service.* ❞

❝ *Let's not look to assign blame to anyone. We will solve this together through patience and goodwill.* ❞

MAKING PRESENTATIONS

Global managers are often called upon to make presentations to customers, employees, and joint venture partners. To give a successful presentation, make sure that you know your audience, and be clear about your key message and objectives.

72 Make it easy for your audience to understand your key points.

QUESTIONS TO ASK YOURSELF

Q Do I know my audience and what they will expect of me?

Q Am I clear about what I want to communicate?

Q Am I able to adapt if I am losing the audience's attention?

Q Should I have my presentation translated or use a translator?

ASSESSING AN AUDIENCE

Imagine your presentation as it will be seen by your audience. Consider the following points: the potential benefits your presentation offers them; how they will perceive you; what they will think of the subject matter; their cultural expectations about presentations. The more you know about your audience, the more confident you will be in delivering your message. Do not, however, let confidence appear as arrogance.

PLANNING PRESENTATIONS

A successful presentation needs to connect with the needs and wants of those who are going to be listening to it. Find out about the business situation of members of the audience, their cultural values, and what they will see as the benefits of working with you – such as cost, suitability for their culture, proven reliability, and long-term perspective. Identify your key messages and link them to these benefits in a logical sequence. Choose a presentation style that is appropriate for your intended audience, for example, adjust it to be formal or informal.

FORMING A STRUCTURE ▶

Give your presentation a structure, but research where the emphasis is required. North Americans, for example, will prefer you to get to the point without too much background information.

TERRITORY
Give background information

ISSUE
Focus on the specific point

POSSIBILITIES
Outline the available options

SOLUTION
Give your recommendation

USING TOOLS AT A PRESENTATION

TOOL	HOW TO APPLY
PRESENTATION MAP	At the outset, give an overview of the structure of the key message that you will be delivering.
CHANGE SIGNALS	Indicate clearly when you are changing topics. For example: "I will now talk about...."
VISUAL/VERBAL HOOKS	Use images, graphs, charts, or spreadsheets to highlight points, and emphasize key words.
HANDOUTS	Prepare copies of the presentation and any relevant supporting material.
PACING	Alter the speed of your presentation to suit the fluency of the audience.
BODY LANGUAGE	Be aware of cultural differences and omit gestures that might be confusing.

THINGS TO DO

1. Consider what thoughts you want to leave your audience with.
2. Brainstorm ideas on content, flow, and methods.
3. Identify your key messages and adapt them to suit your audience.
4. Rehearse the presentation several times beforehand.

ADAPTING PRESENTATIONS

Consensus cultures like a relatively low-key, formal presentation with a lot of background information, visuals, and handouts. The audience will be attentive, but not very participative. Autonomy cultures tend to like short, well-structured, and dynamic presentations with a relatively small amount of context. Supporting data is important. Expect many questions. Status cultures like a warm, personal touch, and a "soft-sell" approach. They are likely to interrupt regularly and want to engage in dialogue. Gently guide them back to the topics you want to discuss. They will appreciate your flexibility.

671

Conducting Negotiations

Negotiating is a critical skill for global managers. To be effective at cross-border negotiation, find ways to work around cultural differences so that the outcome is acceptable to all parties. Use well-tried tactics and be well prepared.

73 Be clear about what you will accept and what you will concede.

Points to Remember

- Most cultures want to feel they are winning a debate.

- In many consensus and status cultures, a written contract will be less important than a handshake. In these cultures, overly legalistic contracts may be perceived as a lack of trust.

- In many parts of Asia, a contract is never final. It is always open to renewed negotiation as circumstances change.

Adapting Your Style

Cultural style influences the pace of negotiations, as well as the strategies, decision-making, and contractual arrangements used. Negotiations in autonomy cultures tend to be fast, but are tied up with legalities. Negotiations in consensus cultures are often slow, and require trust, which is built up over time. Contracts are likely to be broad, and subject to change as circumstances alter. People in status cultures also like to take time to form trusting relationships. They may become impatient with overly legalistic contracts.

Considering Factors

Before a negotiation, ask yourself some questions:
- Why? – List the risks and opportunities for both sides in the negotiations.
- When? – Consider the factors, such as budget cycles or the market, that will influence timing.
- Where? – Think about the advantages and disadvantages of specific locations.
- Who? – Look at the status, age, and gender of those involved. Consider including a third party.
- How? – Judge the amount of time that should be spent on task versus relationship issues.

Cultural Differences

The Western tendency to be direct can be perceived as confrontational by those in cultures that put great value on relationships and prefer indirect communication. The respectful deference of an Asian can be seen as a weakness by a Westerner.

THE NEGOTIATION PROCESS

PREPARATION
Identify objectives, cultural differences, and shared interests

⬇

STRATEGY
List questions to ask and determine team roles

⬇

OPENING
Introduce yourself and create a positive atmosphere

⬇

UNDERSTANDING
Listen more, talk less, and look for common ground

⬇

BARGAINING
Emphasize mutual interests and make concessions slowly

⬇

CLOSING
Reiterate agreements and follow them up in writing

74 Take a break if you have reached a deadlock.

PREPARING YOURSELF

Make sure that you understand the context of the negotiations that you will be taking part in. Gather fundamental information about the other party and its country of origin. Assess the decision-making style, hierarchy, and underlying interests of the organization. Gauge the economic development, and the monetary, fiscal, and trade policies of the country it is based in, as well as the telecommunication and transport networks. Understand the country's political ideologies and foreign policies, and make a point of studying the legal tradition and business law. Make sure that you appreciate the values and beliefs, language, and customs of the country too.

NEGOTIATING SKILLS

Keep your language plain and simple and make sure that everyone understands the meaning of what you have said. Minimize surprises, because these will put the other party on the defensive. Focus on all parties' mutual underlying interests. If you see the situation as a problem that you all want to solve, you will avoid getting into a deadlock. Never rush: patience beats impatience every time. Build trust, and always focus on a win-win result.

Emphasizes key point

BEING ▶ CLEAR
Keep reiterating shared interests, even though your opening positions seem far apart.

MANAGING CONFLICT ACROSS BORDERS

Working across a variety of cultures increases the chance that there will be misunderstandings and clashes of opposing interests. Accept the challenge and adapt your strategies so that any conflict is constructive, rather than destructive.

75 Think carefully before adopting your usual way of handling conflict.

CULTURAL DIFFERENCES

In Japan, leaders are expected to preserve *wa* (harmony) and to avoid open conflict through co-operation and a caring attitude. In the United States, conflict is expected to emerge naturally when different interests compete.

CULTURES AND CONFLICT

Generally, autonomy cultures expect conflict. Individual interests will often clash with one another and with the organization. The best ideas and people are thought to emerge out of competition. Consensus cultures typically avoid open conflict, although confrontation can occur when there is no risk of damaging the group or of losing face. Although feelings are openly expressed in status cultures, there is a dislike of conflict and aggressive, adversarial styles.

COPING WITH CONFLICT

There are five strategies for managing conflict, ranging from passive to active. Passive strategies include avoiding (keeping the conflict under the surface) or yielding (letting the other party have their way). Active strategies include competing (demanding your way) or creating (collaborating to find a solution). Bargaining to find a compromise is a middle path between active and passive.

USING PERSUASION ▶

This manager is bargaining with a customer. He is appealing to his customer's emotions and relying on their good relationship to help him reach an agreement on a contract.

ADAPTING STRATEGIES

Managers tend to rely on one or two conflict-management strategies. However, when you work globally, you need to be able to use all five. Using only avoiding and yielding will not help you in autonomy cultures, where the emphasis is on competing and creating. Relying on a competitive strategy will not succeed in consensus cultures, where avoidance and indirectness are valued. To gain credibility in status cultures, be ready to compete, but be prepared to bargain, which is often accompanied by emotional appeals to friendship.

76 Adapt your strategy, depending on the context.

77 Avoid mistaking emotion for hostility.

LEARNING FROM CONFLICT

Conflict can be constructive when it results in deeper learning about one another, and an improvement in communication. Turn every cross-cultural conflict into a learning experience for everyone involved:

● Make sure that the rules for handling conflict are understood by everyone.
● Do not allow personal attacks.

● Use conflict to bring cultural differences into the open.
● Make sure that you demonstrate your appreciation of these differences.
● Look for ways to highlight shared interests and opinions.
● Encourage open communication and dialogue.

A LEARNING ▶ EXPERIENCE
In this case study, it is the manager's ability to make apologies, even when she did not know what she had done wrong, that allowed the dialogue to move forward in a way that was satisfactory to both parties.

CASE STUDY
Mohammed, an employee in Cairo, telephoned his manager Linda in New York. After saying hello to him, she immediately asked him what he was calling about. Mohammed, thinking that he had disturbed her when she was busy, tried to end the call, saying he would phone again another time. Linda realized that she had upset him and apologized. She asked him how she had caused offence. He then admitted that in his culture it was customary to engage in some talk about personal matters and the family before getting down to business, and that her unintentionally brusque attitude had upset him.

With Mohammed feeling more able to communicate under his own terms, they began the conversation again and it was concluded successfully. Their relationship was stronger as a result of their mutual understanding.

LEADING GLOBAL TEAMS

A well-led global team can produce cohesion in geographically dispersed organizations. Understand the dynamics of teamwork, foster good communication, and lead a high-performing team.

RUNNING GLOBAL TEAMS

To run a successful global team, it is necessary to ensure that it is flexible, responsive, and innovative. Ensure that your team is culturally diverse, and includes members whose business activities span the globe and who work well together.

78 Be very clear about how your global team can work together.

▲ USING TECHNOLOGY
When your team members work in different countries, use communication technology, such as video conferencing, so that staff feel part of a larger team.

WHAT IS A GLOBAL TEAM?

A global team brings together people with the experience, knowledge, and skills to fulfil an organization's goals. For example, strategic global teams identify or implement initiatives that put the business in a better position in the marketplace. Operational teams focus on the efficient and effective running of the business across the whole network. They include information technology teams and head office teams.

79 Be very positive about your team's capabilities.

80 Make every team member feel valued.

EXAMINING ROLES

Culturally diverse global teams perform three valuable roles. First, they create a global view of the business, while having a sound knowledge of local realities. Second, they have the potential for generating creative ideas and making fully-informed decisions. Third, teams representative of the organization's international base are in a better position to ensure that new procedures are implemented throughout the business. Understand that no one person has all the answers in a global environment, and develop a "collective" intelligence.

ASSESSING DYNAMICS

Global teams can produce exceptional results, but they can also be dysfunctional. Dysfunction can be caused by many factors: if there are too many people of one nationality, they may dictate to the rest; language difficulties can result in the exclusion of one or more people; over-politeness may mean people repress real views. Recognize these issues and work to counteract them.

81 Make sure that your team is able to share ideas and information effectively.

EXAMINING THE FUNCTIONS OF GLOBAL TEAMS

Team members who are based in various locations around the world can bring together specialist knowledge and insights. Together, they can produce a unique and valuable overview of the global market. Their roles may include:

- Analysis of external and internal risks to the business.
- Alertness to new opportunities, such as possible new markets to enter.
- Co-ordination of global projects, activities, and processes.

- Development of global strategy, products, services, and training.
- Responsiveness to new trends in the market, such as increased competition.
- Experimentation to generate radically new ideas and to test them.
- Integration of business activities to create efficient interaction.
- Transference of technologies, best practices, and knowledge.
- Assessment of diverse customer needs in key markets.

DEALING WITH
TEAM EXPECTATIONS

Cultural background shapes expectations about the role of a team. It also affects how members relate to each other and to you as team leader. Integrate the team and make sure that you satisfy the requirements of each individual team member.

82 Recognize your own cultural expectations of teamwork.

83 Look at how teamwork styles might complement each other.

FOCUSING ON TASKS

Teamwork in autonomy cultures is task-centered and the team has specific objectives. Members are often individual specialists with particular roles and responsibilities. Meetings tend to have clear agendas and produce tangible results. Spend time on tangential issues, but guide the discussion back to the agenda. Recognize that tension lies between the pursuit of results and the need to provide the rewards, such as recognition, expected by individual members.

ALIGNING THE TEAM ▼
A leader needs to understand the different perspectives of team members and work towards building common understanding.

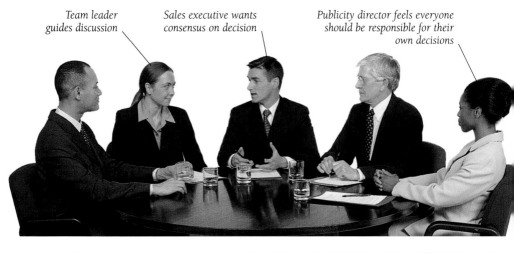

Team leader guides discussion

Sales executive wants consensus on decision

Publicity director feels everyone should be responsible for their own decisions

WORKING AS A COMMUNITY

In consensus teams, results are achieved via well-ordered relationships. Total team agreement is the intended outcome after thorough deliberation of all the perspectives. Competition within the team is not expected, but strong rivalry between teams is typical. Bear in mind that much of the contentious work could be done outside of meetings. Use meetings to exchange information or affirm decisions already made. Make use of group protocols and well-defined agendas.

WORKING AS A CLAN

Because of the need to maintain differences in rank, teamwork in status cultures can be difficult. An autocratic/paternalistic leader will control all decisions, while other members simply express opinions. Loyalty, personal allegiances, and obligations play significant roles in what is done, how, and by when. Be aware that the team's purpose is often defined over time, and agendas will be relatively free-flowing. Although outcomes may be unpredictable, remember that a successful meeting will reinforce team relationships.

84 Balance tasks with building relationships.

85 Use differences to spark greater levels of creativity.

REINFORCING TEAM RELATIONSHIPS

Your management challenge is to create an inclusive team, with a common vision and mission, in which everyone can contribute their best work. Always aim to allow individuals to maintain their identity. Use expressions like:

We will succeed as a team by allowing our differences to complement one another.

Whatever our differences, it is important to remember that we share the same goals.

Let's learn from each other the ways we can create better value for our customers.

We're in this as a team, and together we can solve any problem that comes our way.

ASSESSING GLOBAL TEAMS

Global teams bring together all the ingredients for success, but also for disaster. Accept that it is your responsibility to help your global team work well together, identify and improve its strengths, and be prepared to tackle its weaknesses.

86 Be flexible about how you expect team members to contribute.

VALUING PEOPLE

Successful team players contribute to a team in three ways. First, they recognize cultural differences and are willing to collaborate across them for the advantage of the organization. Second, they have the necessary strategic expertise and market experience. Third, they have the requisite communication and interpersonal skills.

Communicative

Open-minded

Empathetic

Experienced

Flexible

A GOOD TEAM MEMBER ▶
Look for people who will be prepared to put the interests of the team above their own personal interests, and who will stay open to learning.

87 Create a database of good global team players.

88 Give your global team direction and purpose.

FOCUSING ON A PURPOSE

A strong sense of purpose helps bring together a culturally diverse team because it provides the necessary elements of cohesion and direction. Make sure that everyone on your team agrees about the words used to describe this purpose, and that they understand its meaning. Form a team purpose that consists of two parts: an engaging vision and a clear mission. Vision provides the overall sense of what the team is about. Mission consists of the specific goals and objectives that will enable the team to achieve the vision.

GAINING PARTICIPATION

Everyone on the team needs to contribute to the work and the final outcome. Create suitable conditions for this to happen, taking into account language and any other cultural differences. Remember that cultural background will shape how individuals on the team like to participate. For example, Americans are comfortable with brainstorming, but many Asians find this practice akin to not thinking about what you are saying. They would prefer to think through their ideas carefully before presenting them. Be capable of enabling different styles of participating to coexist and complement one another.

FOSTERING PARTNERSHIPS

In successful partnering, the team generates more than the sum of its parts. Cultural differences can ignite vital energy within a team, producing a "hot" group that performs above expectations. Poor partnering decreases energy, because differences create fragmentation and disorder.

ANALYZING THE ATTITUDES OF DIFFERENT TEAMS

TYPE OF TEAM	ATTITUDE	OUTCOME
POSITIVE TEAM	Team members value cultural differences.	Trust
	Team recognizes their interdependence.	Collaboration
	They interact in an honest, respectful way.	Mutual support
	They share views and and are open to learning.	Innovative ideas
NEGATIVE TEAM	Members see cultural differences as liabilities.	Mistrust
	They value their interests instead of the team's.	Unhealthy rivalry
	They interact in a suspicious or defensive way.	Blame
	They keep information to themselves.	My way or no way

DEVELOPING GLOBAL TEAMS

Teams – global or domestic – typically develop through a series of phases, the sequence of which may be affected by change, for example, a member joining or leaving. Recognize what phase your team is in, and guide your members forward.

89 Promote team differences as assets, rather than liabilities.

90 Accept conflict among your team as a path to understanding and deeper learning.

FORMING TEAMS

Prepare yourself for team leadership. Be clear about team objectives and learn about each individual. During the first meetings, focus on relationships before tasks. Help everyone relate to each other as individuals. There may be an initial honeymoon period, when differences are treated as interesting novelties – be prepared for this to end. Keep checking for understanding about vision, mission, roles, and responsibilities.

DEVELOPING TEAMS

As work starts, team members will experience the impact of cultural diversity. Make sure that they all understand that differences are expected and welcomed. Express support for variations in expectations about leadership, communication, and so on. When differences emerge, use them to learn about each other and as resources for creativity. If stereotyping emerges when things get stressful, challenge it. Recognize that conflict is expressed and handled differently across cultures. Give time for differing views to be debated. Otherwise, all you will achieve is superficial agreement rather than learning and commitment.

QUESTIONS TO ASK YOURSELF

Q Am I demonstrating an appreciation of the differences on my team?

Q Am I being empathetic to the difficulties others might be experiencing?

Q Am I enabling everyone to participate fully?

Q Am I coaching team members to collaborate effectively?

Q Have I allowed for differences in language fluency and comprehension?

WORKING AS A TEAM

As team members develop shared working practices, ensure that you encourage common ground, but allow for exceptions. Avoid voting on procedures because voting creates majorities and minorities, and builds resentment. Put in writing any agreements that are reached and use these as a reference point. This is useful for reviewing what has been learned, and for sharing it with other teams.

▼ SHARING WITH OTHERS

Create a collaborative team spirit by listening, sharing your knowledge and expertise, and by being open to all ideas.

Team leader guides input of team

POINTS TO REMEMBER

- Encourage competition between ideas, not among team members.
- Celebrate successes, because this will generate strong group feelings and commitment.
- All team members should benefit from any feedback.

BEING PATIENT ▼

This case study reveals why patience is an asset in a global team. Without it, the whole team can make the wrong decisions.

91 Be a role model for openness – you will find that your team will be frank with you in return.

PERFORMING AS A TEAM

When the team has achieved its expected potential, it should then aim for even higher performance levels. As the leader, monitor and communicate results to your team. This will help to build pride in team achievements, which will revitalize the team's energy and commitment, especially if it meets infrequently. Work to keep everyone involved and motivated to the end of the project. Make sure that any new members are socialized quickly in the shared methods and culture of the team.

CASE STUDY

Juan from Spain was on a predominantly native English-speaking team. His English was adequate, but not fluent. The team had been put together to test launch a new product in southern Europe.

During the brainstorming sessions, Juan attempted to communicate his ideas but the others got impatient and kept interrupting him. The native English speakers wanted to put a launch plan together quickly.

By the end of the meeting, a plan had been established, but Juan looked frustrated and confused. He tried to speak to the team leader, but was brushed off, "Sorry Juan, I have another meeting."

Two months later, the test launch had been a failure. In a review meeting, one of the members said to Juan, "I now know what you were trying to tell us. We've wasted a lot of time by not listening and by rushing ahead."

LEADING A TEAM

Global teams bring together multiple sets of skills and diverse working methods. Strong and effective leadership is required for such teams to work well. Be ready to adopt different leadership styles for the various phases of team development.

92 Reduce your team's feelings of uncertainty, without over-directing.

COMMUNICATOR
Explain the team's purpose, roles, and responsibilities

FACILITATOR
Create opportunities for deeper team understanding

INTEGRATOR
Support the development of common working ground

CHALLENGER
Proactively seek higher levels of achievement

COMMUNICATING WITH YOUR TEAM

In the team-forming stage, there will be a lot of uncertainty among team members, who may ask lots of questions. Why has the team been formed? Why am I here? What are the expected results, and when must they be achieved? You might not have all the answers, but communicate what you know honestly and directly. Also, encourage team members to find their own answers, otherwise they may become passive. For example, if someone asks why they are on the team, ask them to say why they think they have been chosen.

◀ **LEADING ROLES**
As the team develops, the team leader must adopt different roles to help it increase its effectiveness. Keep alert to changes in the team's performance, and alter your leadership accordingly.

ACTING AS A FACILITATOR

In the developing phase, help facilitate differences within the team. Rather than demand compliance, help bring differences in perception and style to the surface, where they can be understood better and managed more effectively. Promote better team interaction through open-ended questioning and help members see shared interests and perspectives. Be prepared to offer guidance for finding a joint way forward.

POINTS TO REMEMBER

● The key challenge for the leader is to emphasize the value that differences bring to the team.

● Help new team members by sharing all the information that they need to succeed.

● Ask for ideas from the team before expressing your own, so that you achieve more input.

93 Be prepared to challenge signs of complacency.

94 Help to bring differences to the surface, where they can be faced.

INTEGRATING A TEAM

As the team begins to work together, you, as the leader and integrator, must help it to balance diversity with cohesion. Help the team develop common working ground (shared values and norms) and begin to act as a role model. Be a willing learner, thoughtful listener, and energetic collaborator. As an integrator, try to improvise with new approaches that make the most of cultural differences. For example, you might begin a meeting with American-style brainstorming, and then end the meeting by defining the course of action each person has agreed to – this more systematic approach is favoured by Germans.

CHALLENGING THE TEAM

When the team has achieved a level of self-management, you must still ensure that it is kept focused. Help it to respond and adapt to changes in the business environment. Manage unsettling internal alterations, such as members leaving or joining. While solidifying the team's performance, challenge members to reach higher levels of achievement. Consider yourself to be the agent of change, demonstrate pride in your team, and show an eagerness and enthusiasm for breakthroughs and continuous improvements.

95 Act out of choice, rather than out of habit.

Leader sets targets that will motivate his team

BEING INSPIRING ▶
By working for and with his team, this leader inspires members to overcome obstacles and to achieve more.

DEVELOPING A TEAM CULTURE

Global teams need to shape a common culture that provides all members with shared expectations and a sense of belonging together. Recognize that the team culture will evolve over time, but it can be accelerated by getting early agreement on shared values.

96 Balance diverse interests and views with a common team culture.

97 Focus on communicating and listening.

COMMUNICATING WELL

The key to great teamwork is communication. Make sure that you and team members agree to keep language plain and simple. Take time to clarify any assumptions and keep checking for differences in meaning and perception. Ensure that everyone listens to what is being said. As the team leader, keep looking out for non-verbal behaviour that indicates confusion or resistance, such as a frown. Encourage others to do the same. Set a pace that is comfortable for the whole team.

SHOWING RESPECT ▼

In this example, when a team member arrives late, the leader reminds her that the team appreciates promptness.

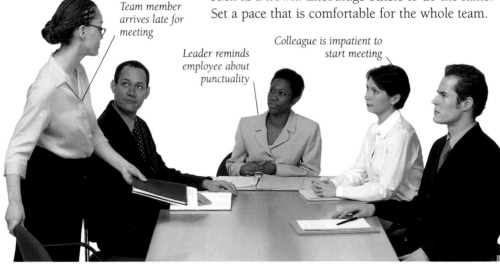

Team member arrives late for meeting

Leader reminds employee about punctuality

Colleague is impatient to start meeting

ENCOURAGING LEADERSHIP

Reaching peak performance requires leadership behaviour from everyone. This will involve team members challenging their conventional thought patterns, as well as each other's limiting beliefs about what can be done. Encourage your team to be proactive, and help them deal with any friction before performance is affected. Resist any individuals or sub-groups who seek to impose their views, but remember to focus on solving problems, not assigning blame.

> **98** Respect the values and culture of individual members, but remind them to work as a team.

SHARED VALUES

The leader must ensure a high level of trust on the team. Trust strengthens commitment. Encourage the following values:

- Empathy – have concern for the well-being of all.
- Fairness – treat each other equally, without bias.
- Honesty – relate to each other straightforwardly.
- Respect – value each other's differences and contributions.
- Sharing – share knowledge and expertise to produce the best outcomes for the team.

THINGS TO DO

1. Work with the team to agree ground rules, such as punctuality or how to handle conflict.

2. Write these rules down and distribute them to all team members.

3. Periodically review the rules at team meetings, and collectively evaluate how well the team is following them.

FOSTERING GOOD ORGANIZATION

Provide a sense of structure in your organization, so that procedures are clear. Encourage your team to define their roles so that everyone knows what is expected of them; record these definitions to avoid misunderstandings. Manage the workflow: make it clear who will receive what from whom and by when. In this way, you will help your team to manage its time and processes so that targets are achieved. Review progress regularly.

▼ **MONITORING PROCESSES**
Make sure that all your team members know their roles, and are aware of schedules and deadlines. Monitor performance, achievements, and results.

| Define roles | → | Manage time | → | Review progress |

RUNNING REMOTE TEAMS

Global businesses operate in an increasingly networked world. More and more teams consist of people in multiple locations and time zones. Recognize that the success of your team depends on developing cohesion, communication, and interaction.

99 Keep e-mail communications to the point, but retain pleasantries.

100 Always keep cultural differences in mind.

101 Follow up verbal communication in writing.

MANAGING REMOTELY

Connectivity, confidence, and commitment are critical for the success of remote teams. A strong sense of connectivity unites a team across time and distance. Be a good role model for communication. Use technology but do not neglect the "human touch". Be sure that you and your team members are confident that everyone on the team will fulfil their responsibilities. Without full commitment, morale and goodwill disappear very quickly. Both are difficult to retrieve when members are widely dispersed.

REAPING REWARDS

There are no special formulas for managing globally – all businesses are different and are constantly changing. Work closely with your global customers, partners, and colleagues to create value from your differences. Stay in touch with all aspects of your organization, from the grass roots up. It is a demanding task, but the rewards of good global relationships are priceless.

KEEPING IN TOUCH ▶
Make sure that you can contact and communicate with your team members, customers, and partners wherever you are in the world.

STRATEGIES FOR RUNNING REMOTE TEAMS

TYPE OF STRATEGY	IMPLEMENTATION
SHRINK THE DISTANCE	Hold some face-to-face meetings and establish regular communications. Set up intranet-based biographies to enable team members to learn about each other. Return phone calls within half a day.
EXPLOIT TECHNOLOGY	Choose a form of communication available to all members and appropriate for the task (e.g. video conferencing so that all the team are involved in a meeting). Follow up telephone calls in writing to ensure agreement on meaning.
SPOTLIGHT CULTURE	Before making a telephone call, remind yourself that the receiver has a different culture, and adjust your communication accordingly. Put a world map on your office wall, highlighting where your team members are located.
COMMUNICATE CONTEXT	Choose the appropriate technology for the context. Video conferencing, for example, reveals body language and voice tone, as well as facts, whereas a fax machine exchanges information only.
ENCOURAGE PARTICIPATION	Avoid feelings of isolation by establishing emotional links, such as celebration of success, between team members. Be fair to everyone, encouraging ideas from all, and never rely more on those who are physically closer to you.
MAINTAIN FOCUS	Create goals and mission statements, role descriptions, task and process charts, schedules, and reviews. Communicate regularly to prevent members being focused on local issues, thereby neglecting the global overview.

ASSESSING YOUR CROSS-CULTURAL SKILLS

*E*valuate your readiness for global management by reading the following statements, and then choosing the option that is closest to your experience. If your answer is "never", circle Option 1; if it is "always", circle Option 4, and so on. Be honest with yourself. Add your scores together and refer to the analysis to see how you scored. Use your answers to identify areas that need improvement.

OPTIONS

1 Never

2 Occasionally

3 Frequently

4 Always

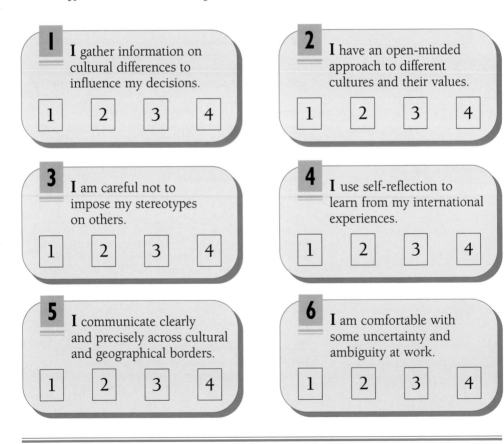

1 I gather information on cultural differences to influence my decisions.

1 2 3 4

2 I have an open-minded approach to different cultures and their values.

1 2 3 4

3 I am careful not to impose my stereotypes on others.

1 2 3 4

4 I use self-reflection to learn from my international experiences.

1 2 3 4

5 I communicate clearly and precisely across cultural and geographical borders.

1 2 3 4

6 I am comfortable with some uncertainty and ambiguity at work.

1 2 3 4

7 I am patient with other people as they learn to adapt their working techniques.

1 2 3 4

8 I look for opportunities to gain valid cross-cultural experiences.

1 2 3 4

9 I make sure everybody working with me takes cultural differences seriously.

1 2 3 4

10 I keep checking for shared understanding in cross-cultural work.

1 2 3 4

11 I adapt easily and effectively to new situations.

1 2 3 4

12 I take the time necessary to build trusting and strong relationships.

1 2 3 4

13 I listen attentively and accurately, giving plenty of time to each speaker.

1 2 3 4

14 I make sure that everyone in my team feels included.

1 2 3 4

15 I can empathize with other people so that they know they can rely on me.

1 2 3 4

16 I can recognize my own biases and work towards managing them.

1 2 3 4

17 I anticipate the effect of cultural differences on business issues.

1 2 3 4

18 I always try to integrate opposites into mutually beneficial solutions.

1 2 3 4

19 I make sure my staff members attend cross-cultural training sessions.

1 2 3 4

20 I pay attention to my global management development needs.

1 2 3 4

21 I create opportunities to talk about cultural differences with my team.

1 2 3 4

22 I seek and use feedback on my global management performance.

1 2 3 4

23 I try to create the right conditions for everyone to do their best work.

1 2 3 4

24 I pay attention to the value cultural differences can add to the business.

1 2 3 4

25 I try to understand the cultural orientation of our business associates.

1 2 3 4

26 I resist judging people if I do not understand their culture and circumstances.

1 2 3 4

27 I make sure that I show respect to others who are different to me.

| 1 | 2 | 3 | 4 |

28 I am eager to share my international experiences with others.

| 1 | 2 | 3 | 4 |

29 I nurture a sense of humour to support relationship building.

| 1 | 2 | 3 | 4 |

30 I am confident in my ability to manage in different cultural contexts.

| 1 | 2 | 3 | 4 |

31 I make sure everyone understands the organization's ethical values.

| 1 | 2 | 3 | 4 |

32 I use cross-cultural conflict to deepen our learning about each other.

| 1 | 2 | 3 | 4 |

ANALYSIS

Now that you have completed the self-assessment, add up your total score and check your performance. Whatever level of success you have achieved, there is always room for improvement. Identify your weakest areas, and then re-read relevant chapters to establish and hone your global management skills.

32-64: As yet, your global management skills are limited. Set goals for yourself so that you can improve your effectiveness.

65-95: You have a good grasp of many global management issues, but you need to develop your skills to be wholly effective.

96-128: You are a skilled global manager, but remember that the international marketplace is always changing. Stay focused on continually improving your knowledge and skills.

BALANCING WORK AND LIFE

INTRODUCTION

All too often, success is seen in terms of material possessions and financial gain. It is easy to fall into the trap of working long hours, striving to achieve a good standard of living but, in the process, neglecting relationships, self-development, leisure pursuits, and personal happiness. Balancing Work and Life will help you understand what success means to you and explains how you can live your life with renewed vision and purpose. Practical advice, including 101 concise tips, shows you how to focus on your true priorities and develop healthy attitudes to success in yourself and your team. As you begin to achieve a better balance in your work and life, you will discover new levels of creativity, fulfilment, and happiness.

ASSESSING SUCCESS

To be successful in your work and life, you must be clear about what success is. Clarify your values and goals, and understand that success is not just about hard work and no play.

UNDERSTANDING SUCCESS

To create a balance between the demands of your work and your life, you need to examine what success means to you. Start by clarifying your values, purpose, roles, and attitudes so that you have something to measure your achievements against.

1 Think about what success means to you – be honest with yourself.

DEFINING SUCCESS

People often work hard to gain "success" without knowing what success really means. You may climb a career ladder, but are you fulfilled by your work? Do you have a good home life? We receive differing messages about success – through the media, our families, and our culture. But ultimately, success comes from leading a fulfilled and balanced life. Begin to balance your work and life more effectively.

◀ RECOGNIZING SUCCESS
A successful person has a clear definition of success. This manager enjoys her job, but she leaves the office on time so that she can spend time with her family.

Build your relationships by discussing your intentions

SUCCESS
An outline of what will fulfil you

Decide on your criteria for success and then plan action

SYNERGY
The ability to get along with others

STRATEGY
A plan for achieving a balanced life

Involve the key people in your plan and gain their support

▲ **ACHIEVING A BALANCED LIFE**
Develop criteria for success so that you can focus on your priorities. Form a strategy to help you stay on track, and focus on synergy so that you have the necessary support to achieve success.

CLARIFYING VALUES

To define success, start by clarifying your values. Schedule time alone and think about what is most important to you. What kind of partner and parent do you want to be? What kind of son or daughter? What kind of friend and manager? What difference would you like to make in people's lives? Put your values at the centre of your life so that you can retain greater balance, vision, and happiness in every area of your life.

FOCUSING ON VALUES ▶
Think about the relationships you have with others and what you most value about them. Decide on the characteristics that you value in yourself.

2 Set time aside every day to focus on your values, and ensure that you remain true to them.

AIMING FOR SUCCESS

The "S³" formula will help you consider the key factors in a work-life balance. The first "S" stands for "Success" – begin to form criteria of what success means to you. The second "S" stands for "Strategy" – start to form a workable plan to achieve a balance between work and life. The third "S" denotes "Synergy" – make sure you focus on relationships and creative co-operation with those around you. Aim to be a team player and a good communicator.

CHOOSING A PURPOSE

Purpose is your reason for doing something: it is what gives your work and life meaning. Purpose is something that you choose rather than find, and it is based on what is important to you. For example, if being a loving parent and a supportive colleague is what is important to you, then your purpose may be to inspire others with your strength of character. If it is important to you to achieve certain work goals, then your purpose may be to be an effective role model to your team. Pinpoint your purpose so that you have real direction.

QUESTIONS TO ASK YOURSELF

Q What aspects of my life am I most passionate about?

Q Is being a parent the most important aspect of my life?

Q Have I recognized what motivates me?

Q What are my unique talents and my strengths?

Q What purpose would I like to give my work and my life?

| Think about how you live your life | Clarify your values | Define your purpose |

▲ BECOMING FOCUSED
Think deeply about each aspect of your life and work. This will help you reach a better understanding of your values, and enable you to focus on your purpose.

SEEING THE BIG PICTURE

The big picture is your overall vision of your work and life. It includes your values, goals, and roles. Invest time in developing your vision. Allow your imagination free rein and picture your ideal life. Picture the key people in your life – your family, friends, colleagues, and customers – and imagine all these relationships working well. Visualize your ideal work and your ideal leisure time. Write down the essence of your big picture.

3 Make the time to create a picture of your ideal life.

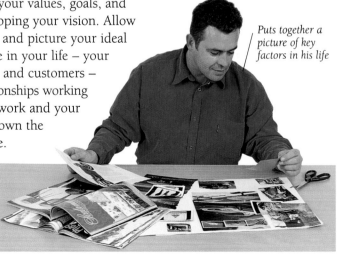

Puts together a picture of key factors in his life

BUILDING A ▶ PICTURE
Cut out photographs and images to make a blueprint of your ideal life and collate them together on a board.

RECOGNIZING SUCCESS AS A STATE OF MIND

Success is an attitude, and not just a set of achievements or financial gain. If this were not the case, then every high achiever would consider themselves successful. But, in fact, many rich, famous, and accomplished people have material success but do not actually feel truly successful or fulfilled. Understand that success is not just found in outer things, but is located within yourself. Cultivate success as a state of mind so that you stop chasing false goals and expectations, and start living your life focused on what matters to you.

4 Develop a positive attitude towards achieving success.

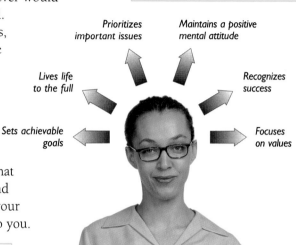

Prioritizes important issues

Maintains a positive mental attitude

Lives life to the full

Recognizes success

Sets achievable goals

Focuses on values

▲ HAVING THE RIGHT ATTITUDE

It is important to have a positive, proactive attitude so that you can live your life with purpose and vision. This will enable you to increase your effectiveness and achieve success and fulfilment.

5 Involve your family in the development of your vision.

CASE STUDY
The managing director of a clothing outlet had achieved the trappings of success. He had a lifestyle that friends admired: a substantial income, a large house, a fast car, and he enjoyed annual luxury holidays.
Unfortunately, he neither felt successful, nor enjoyed his achievements – his marriage was collapsing, his children no longer confided in him, and he was constantly under pressure to expand his business.

When he actually evaluated his definition of success, he discovered that he valued his family, friends, and leisure time more than his business.
He developed a strategy that incorporated his true priorities. He explained to his colleagues that he would be leaving work on time to see his family and pursue other interests. As he began to resolve his family conflicts and rekindle a zest for life, he found that he began to enjoy his work more too.

◀ EVALUATING SUCCESS
In this case study, a managing director saw that his family life was being damaged by his constant striving for financial success. By involving his family and friends in developing a new vision, he was able to live his life with renewed purpose.

AT WHAT COST SUCCESS?

In a fast, busy world, you pay a high price for confusing success with constant adrenaline, endless activity, all work, no rest, and no play. Avoid working long hours to meet deadlines, learn how to manage your time, and avoid falling into an activity trap.

6 Realize that if you are always busy, you may not be working effectively.

QUESTIONS TO ASK YOURSELF

Q Do I work longer hours than I need to?

Q Am I achieving something important or am I just keeping busy?

Q Do I feel guilty if I am the first person to leave the office?

Q How can I prioritize my time more effectively?

MANAGING YOUR TIME

One of the biggest traps to fall into today is the "busy culture". The major problem with this culture is that the habit of "busy-ness" eclipses real business: it gives rise to a "start early, finish late" work ethic that confuses constant effort with real effectiveness. Avoid keeping busy out of a sense of habit, duty, or guilt – these factors all reduce effectiveness, morale, and motivation. Think about how you could be less busy and more effective. How could you work smarter, not harder?

MANAGING URGENCY

If you are always busy, you may not have the time to prioritize effectively. You may waste time on urgent tasks rather than concentrating on what is important. An urgent task is something that requires immediate attention. Importance, on the other hand, has to do with the big picture, core values, and your purpose. Have the courage to put priorities first, even when you are under pressure, so that you build success in the long-term.

7 Prioritize tasks according to their importance, not their urgency, so that you always stay focused.

PRIORITIZING TIME

Recognize that you are overloaded with urgent tasks

Look at the tasks that are critical and must be done

Decide which tasks can be put on hold or delegated

Concentrate on the critical tasks and work more effectively

LIVING TOO FAST

Many results today are measured in terms of speed. However, although speed is important for factors such as strategy or service, it must not override everything. Speed of delivery, for example, must be balanced with quality of work, and an upgrade to faster technology must be led by vision and not just for the sake of change itself. Although you may enjoy living life in the fast lane, realize that there are costs in terms of your health and wellbeing. Remember that relationships can deteriorate if they are not given time and attention.

8 Remember that speed can detract from quality.

9 Be alert to the symptoms of burnout.

RECOGNIZING BURNOUT

People suffering from burnout often have identifiable characteristics, such as chronic fatigue, a short fuse, impaired vision, poor productivity, and low self-esteem. Sufferers may withdraw from family and friends, or seek escape through alcoholism, absenteeism, or illness.

THE ACTIVITY TRAP

Constant activity is a trap that erodes effectiveness at work and in life. Temper your drive to be active with moments of reflection so that you can achieve a sense of accomplishment. All too often, in an effort to achieve a result, we damage a relationship, neglect what's important, and cause unnecessary distress. Always clarify your priorities before taking action.

AVOIDING WORKAHOLISM

Workaholism is an escape from life through work. It is a compulsive behaviour that can damage effectiveness, estrange families, and impair health. A workaholic will ensure that they always have access to work. Often confused as a sign of dedication, this leads to imbalance and burnout. Be alert to symptoms of overload and focus on balancing your work and life.

▼ REACHING OVERLOAD
This manager is struggling to deal with a number of tasks at once and is unable to focus and prioritize.

Receives message from customer on his mobile phone

Cancels social plans at last minute

CREATING CRITERIA

A healthy work–life balance is achieved by establishing clear criteria for success that include work objectives, leisure plans, and aims for self-improvement. Take an honest look at your priorities and set goals that you can work towards.

10 Make sure that your work is led by your criteria for success.

11 Take your interests outside work seriously.

12 Ask your friends and family what success means to them.

SUCCEEDING AT WORK

Think deeply about your criteria for success at work. Is your criteria to get the job done at whatever cost? Does the means justify the end? What sort of work relationships do you want? Reflect upon the impact work has on the rest of your life. Does work enrich the whole of your life or has your home life become merely a rest from work? Each day, ask yourself, "How do I know if I have been successful at work or not?" Be specific. Think about the quality of your relationships. How important is your self-development and learning? Start to write down your criteria.

CASE STUDY

A manager in the hospitality industry was having difficulty coping with his work.

He decided to pinpoint his priorities and write down his goals for his work and life. He found that this enabled him to manage his workload. Even if he was faced with a difficult task, he discovered that he was able to cope because he had a clear criteria for success.

He decided that if he needed to attend his children's school, he would make sure that he was available. At the same time, he worked at maintaining good friendships. Meanwhile, his self-regulation meant that he spent more time on the important aspects of his work, such as meeting customers' needs and encouraging team morale.

Since he was now performing to his new high standards, he become a sought-after hospitality manager whilst enjoying a balanced home life.

◀ **REMAINING FOCUSED**

This manager found that strong commitment to his roles and goals, and an ability to remain focused, were deciding factors in his success.

IDENTIFYING ROLES

A role defines an area of responsibility, such as being a manager, parent, partner, or friend. To enjoy a healthy work–life balance you must define each of your roles. Be careful not to neglect your most important roles. For example, be aware that your role as a parent can be damaged if you consistently prioritize your work above your family. Your role as a husband or a wife can suffer if you spend too much time and energy on your career or your children. And friendships can be lost if you do not make the time to pick up the phone. Be clear and flexible in your roles.

Strive to be an outstanding parent

Focus on being a good colleague

Aim to be a supportive friend

▲ DEFINING YOUR ROLES
Think about the critical roles in your life. When you are setting your criteria for success, consider what you want to achieve in these roles so that you can excel in them.

13 List, prioritize, and assess the important roles you play in your work and in your life.

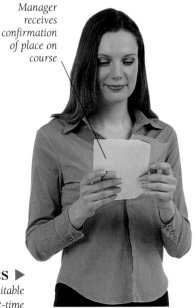

Manager receives confirmation of place on course

SUCCEEDING IN LIFE

Think about your life as a whole – your family, friends, leisure pursuits, personal development goals, and involvement in your community. How significant a part do you want to play in the development of your children? What do you consider to be success in your friendships? What are your favourite leisure pursuits? What are your personal development goals? Realize that success is about all aspects of life, and not just about work.

CONTINUING YOUR STUDIES ▶
If your priority is to further your education, look for a suitable course at a college. This manager wants to continue part-time academic studies while she continues working.

SETTING GOALS

Setting your short-, mid-, and long-term goals is essential when it comes to creating clear criteria for success. Write down your goals in three main categories: things you want to be, things you hope to do, and things you wish to have. Use the SMART formula to help you work through the process. Be Specific: state your goals precisely and clearly. Make sure they are Measurable – ensure that you can obtain proof of your progress and can check that you are on track. Set achievable Actions – state what tasks need to be carried out. Be Realistic – make sure your goals are a possible dream. Allow for Timing – allocate a reasonable time span for each goal.

SMART GOALS

SPECIFIC
Ensure your aim is clear

MEASURABLE
Define standards to work to

ACTIONS
Set yourself tasks to do

REALISTIC
Make sure the goal is achievable

TIMING
Set a time frame

LISTING A SET OF GOALS ▼
A successful manager has clearly defined her goals on paper. The act of writing these goals down focused her mind and reflected her commitment to achieving them.

Aim is made clear / Means of monitoring progress is defined / Appropriate and realistic actions are planned

	SPECIFIC	MEASUREMENT	ACTION	REALISTIC	TIMING
"TO BE" GOALS	To be a successful parent	My children always seek my advice	Discuss their needs and concerns	Yes	Ongoing
"TO DO" GOALS	To do my filing regularly	To have a clear in-tray and organized filing	Plan a system for organizing my filing	Yes	Half day
"TO HAVE" GOALS	To have a two-week holiday in Florida	To be lying on a beach, feeling happy and relaxed	Give my holiday dates to my boss and my team	Yes	Two weeks in August

Goals are divided into categories / Goals and actions are checked to make sure that they are realistic / Dates for action are scheduled

14 Think about tasks you are good at and aim to build on your strengths.

PRIORITIZING KEY ISSUES

Make sure that you prioritize your goals, your strengths, and your actions. Recognize that you cannot excel at everything and prioritize accordingly. If necessary, delegate those tasks or issues that do not complement your skills. Ask yourself, "What am I really good at?", "Where do my natural talents lie?", "What do I enjoy most?", and "What will help me advance my life's goals and vision?" Being strategic about key issues at work and in your life will make all the difference to achieving a healthy balance.

MAKING A SUCCESS STATEMENT

A success statement provides a reference point for assessing your work and life balance. Form one that encompasses your values and purpose. Include your roles and goals. The statement will become your personal constitution, the criterion by which you measure the balance of work and life. Involve a trusted friend or colleague in the process so that they can give you feedback. Let the statement inspire your decisions, influence your actions, and guide your life.

15 Write your success statement and refer to it regularly.

▼ **WRITING A STATEMENT**
In this example, a manager has written out a success statement. The statement is a live document that the manager can update and adapt regularly to ensure that it is still relevant.

MY SUCCESS STATEMENT
I choose a harmonious balance between my work and my life. I address my family's needs first, and I aim to contribute to their wellbeing, happiness, and sense of fulfilment. I am proactive in my work, and I achieve my career goals with imagination and integrity. I am known for my sense of humour and my compassion. I am a team player. I always celebrate the successes of my colleagues and partners. I am committed to learning something new every day. I enjoy quality leisure time, and I eat and sleep well. I am able to relax, and I celebrate life every day.

EVALUATING YOUR SUCCESS

Having established your criteria for success, the next step is to be able to measure it. Recognize the signs that show you that you are achieving success, ask your friends for feedback, and, if possible, work with a coach to keep your objectives clear.

16 Review your successes – make sure that you are ready to adapt.

THINGS TO DO

1. Put a date in your diary each week to review your successes.
2. Spend 30 minutes reviewing your achievements.
3. Make sure that you are meeting your criteria.

REVIEWING SUCCESS

Success is a process, not just a final goal. If you are going to achieve a balance between your work and life, you will need to monitor and review your progress constantly. Continually reflect on the big picture of your life so that you can make sure that your actions are relevant and you are using your time well. Schedule half an hour per week to review the factors that are critical to your success. Ensure that you stay committed to what is important to you.

MEASURING SUCCESS

What proof do you need to show you that you are succeeding in your work and your life? Would it involve receiving customer recognition? Does it include finishing projects and work on schedule? Would it be having a sense of purpose and fun at work? Or does it mean having time for your family and friends? Would it mean being able to play a game of golf a week? Would it involve having time for meditation? Make sure you know how you will measure success so that you remain motivated.

Director congratulates manager on successful results

RECOGNIZING SIGNS OF SUCCESS ▶
Think about how you will recognize signs of your success – this may be receiving praise from your boss if you have achieved good results on a project.

17 Ask for and learn from constructive feedback.

18 Use coaching to build strengths and overcome barriers.

RECEIVING FEEDBACK

A useful aid in measuring success is to receive feedback from colleagues, family, and friends. We all have skills we can improve, and these can often be more easily identified by others. Ask a trusted colleague to give you feedback on how to improve your effectiveness at work. Ask your partner or a trusted friend if they would give you feedback on your work–life balance. Be open-minded. Sometimes the truth is hard to hear, and sometimes new ideas are hard to adopt, but remember that positive feedback is a valuable gift.

WORKING WITH A COACH

Coaching is becoming increasingly popular because organizations are recognizing that long-term success depends on their staff – their level of commitment, expertise, and creativity. Working with a coach will enable you to clarify your work and life objectives. Realize that coaching can help you deal with difficult situations, such as work changes and personal problems. Use it to help you liberate your personal potential.

BEING COACHED ▶

Use a coaching session as an opportunity to assess your strengths and recognize your weaknesses so that you can build a successful future.

19 Think of one way you could improve your life every day and then take action.

DOS AND DON'TS

✔ Do make sure you reward yourself for your successes.	✘ Don't focus on your mistakes and ignore your successes.
✔ Do ask your friends, partner, and colleagues for feedback on your work–life balance.	✘ Don't underestimate the value of coaching in helping you to clarify your objectives.

ANALYZING YOUR SUCCESS

Find out how successful you are by responding to the following statements, and mark the options that are closest to your experience. Be as honest as you can: if your answer is "never", circle Option 1; if it is "always", circle Option 4, and so on. Add your scores together, and refer to the Analysis to see how you scored. Use your answers to identify areas that need most improvement.

OPTIONS
1 Never
2 Occasionally
3 Frequently
4 Always

1 I am clear on what success means to me at work.

1 2 3 4

3 I clarify my values and position them at the centre of my life.

1 2 3 4

5 I invest time in continuously developing my goals and vision.

1 2 3 4

2 I am clear on what success means to me at home.

1 2 3 4

4 I use my sense of purpose to inspire the decisions that I make.

1 2 3 4

6 I prioritize my work according to importance, not urgency.

1 2 3 4

7 I consider the different roles I have and prioritize them accordingly.

| 1 | 2 | 3 | 4 |

8 I set clearly identifiable goals and objectives using the SMART formula.

| 1 | 2 | 3 | 4 |

9 I have a success statement that inspires and motivates me.

| 1 | 2 | 3 | 4 |

10 I ask for feedback so that I can enhance my work and my life.

| 1 | 2 | 3 | 4 |

11 I consult a "success coach" or mentor for my personal growth.

| 1 | 2 | 3 | 4 |

12 I reward and celebrate my success and the success of others.

| 1 | 2 | 3 | 4 |

ANALYSIS

Now you have completed the self-assessment, add up your total score and check your performance by referring to the corresponding evaluation below. Identify your weakest areas, and refer to the relevant pages in this chapter where you will find practical advice and tips to help you focus on success:

12–23: You are surviving, but now it is time to thrive. You need to implement the strategies in this chapter to try something new and improve the balance of your work and life.

24–35: You are doing very well, but there is room for improvement and you can still achieve a better balance.

36–48: You are focused, well-motivated, good at motivating others, and have a clear sense of direction, both at home and at work. Keep this up.

UNDERSTANDING YOURSELF

Understanding yourself and what you want to achieve enables you to live a fulfilling life. Look at your beliefs, be sensitive to your emotions, assess your priorities, and plan action.

ANALYZING YOURSELF

*A*chieving a work–life balance involves challenging the way you think and behave. Use your beliefs, perceptions, choices, and actions in strategic ways to reach the balance you need. Think positively and take responsibility for your choices and decisions.

20 Make sure that you live your life by the values you believe in.

21 Develop beliefs that enhance your work–life balance.

WIDENING YOUR VISION ▼
Think about any assumptions you hold that may limit you, identify new options, and develop a new vision.

UNDERSTANDING BELIEFS

You have beliefs about everything, including work, life, success, and happiness. These beliefs influence your choices and actions. It is often the case that people who have a poor work–life balance have limiting beliefs such as "success must have a price", "long hours are unavoidable", and "a social life comes later". Write down any limiting beliefs you hold and be as honest as possible.

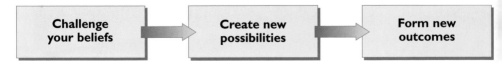

Challenge your beliefs → Create new possibilities → Form new outcomes

PERCEIVING CLEARLY

Perception is subjective and describes the way that you see things and the way you interpret experiences. Be aware that perception is a choice: there is always another way of seeing things. Change your perceptions and turn problems into opportunities, challenges into stepping stones, and setbacks into "set-ups" for greater success and happiness. Be prepared to look for solutions so that you will stand a good chance of finding them. Stay open and be flexible.

22 Think of new possibilities every day.

23 Start looking for better ways of doing things.

THINGS TO DO

1. Write down your thoughts about balancing work and life.

2. Identify the thoughts that limit your options.

3. Write down any new thoughts that you have about your life and review them regularly.

THINKING POSITIVELY

As the old saying states, "As a man thinketh, so he is". Psychologists estimate that people think approximately 40,000 thoughts per day and are responsible for choosing their thoughts. Try to put your past experiences and conditioning to one side so that you can create fresh ideas and lateral solutions – this is known as "possibility thinking". Be willing to let your old ideas make way for the new, because changing your thinking can change your life. Make sure that you help your team think positively rather than negatively too, because it will change the results they achieve.

COMPARING THINKING STYLES

THINKING NEGATIVELY	THINKING POSITIVELY
There is so much to do and there is never enough time to do it.	There is always enough time for what is really important.
People place too many demands on me. I cannot control my time.	I value my time and I can influence others to respect my needs.
I am busy, but I am not making a worthwhile contribution.	By being clear about success, I can make a real difference.

WATCHING YOUR WORDS

The most important conversations you hold in life are the ones that you hold with yourself. Notice how your "self-talk" influences your beliefs, choices, and actions. Start to listen to what you are telling yourself: listen for limiting "I can't" statements, "yes, but" affirmations, and "if only" self-talk. Make sure that you do not talk yourself out of what might be possible. Tell yourself that an effective work and life balance is a definite possibility and develop an "I can" mind-set. Adopt a new vocabulary that can help you overcome doubt, anxiety, cynicism, and tiredness.

24 Practise talking to yourself using positive language.

25 Learn to see the value of the contribution you make at work.

POINTS TO REMEMBER

● Changing your self-talk can change your life.

● The results you achieve depend on the choices and decisions that you make.

● You are responsible for the choices that you make, and you can take control of your work and life balance.

26 Think about the choices you make at work that affect your life.

MAKING CHOICES

People constantly make choices that influence their lives. It is easy to feel that you are not in control of your actions or your decisions, but the reality is that you are. For example, when your boss asks you to do something, make sure that you are in a position to carry out the request and be honest if you feel it is not feasible. Always consider the consequences of your choices for yourself and others – remember that your actions do not just affect you, they affect those around you.

Manager prepares to leave office

Boss stops him and asks him to attend meeting

TAKING CONTROL ▶
In this example, a manager is preparing to leave the office on time so that he can take his wife out for her birthday. When his boss asks him to attend a last-minute meeting, he has to act decisively.

TAKING ACTION

Taking action is about taking responsibility for your life. Do not blame circumstances, conditions, or others for your experiences. It is your choice either to wait for your life to get better, or to take action. The extent to which you are willing to act is equal to how far you are exercising your "proactivity muscle". Developing this "muscle" is comparable to working out at the gym – you cannot expect to develop strong biceps overnight. Practise creating a proactive mind-set and look for ways to enhance your life each day – then act!

Manager leaves office on time, happy with outcome

Boss understands and reschedules meeting

Explains to boss that he has commitments at home

Manager feels resentful – meeting is unproductive

UNDERSTANDING EMOTIONAL ISSUES

By improving your emotional intelligence, you can enjoy greater happiness and success in your relationships, your life, and your work. Recognize and learn from your emotions, be empathetic to others, and be ready to ask for support if necessary.

27 Recognize and understand your feelings so that you can act on them.

QUESTIONS TO ASK YOURSELF

Q Do I listen to my feelings before I make a decision?

Q Am I able to manage my feelings?

Q Do I take into account the feelings of others?

Q Are my actions always in tune with my values?

Q Am I prepared to ask for the necessary support if I need guidance?

UNDERSTANDING EMOTIONAL INTELLIGENCE

Emotional intelligence is your ability to manage your feelings and thoughts. Developing your emotional intelligence can enhance your decision-making and help you communicate more honestly, think more clearly, and act more authentically. Be aware that your feelings are a gateway to creativity, intuition, and inspiration. If you can manage your feelings, you will manage yourself and others better. Realize that emotional intelligence helps you to tap into your own wisdom and develop understanding and trust in your relationships.

28 Take the time to listen to your feelings.

Adaptable Good communicator

Intuitive Self-aware

Sensitive to others Highly motivated

EMOTIONAL INTELLIGENCE ▶
Being emotionally intelligent is the key to achieving success. By being aware of your own feelings, and the feelings of others, you can succeed in work and life.

Expression is tense

Posture is stooped

▲ NOTICING EMOTIONS
Learn to recognize the mental and physical signs of your emotions, and then you can act on them.

RECOGNIZING EMOTIONS

Take the time to record your thoughts and feelings every day – they can give you important insights. For example, monitoring your thoughts and feelings can help you see how well you are balancing your work and life. Notice when you feel confident and optimistic – this is a sign that you are doing well. Feelings of uncertainty and irritability may show that you are having difficulties. Realize that suppressing an emotion only blocks your learning and inhibits your self-awareness. Try to see something positive in all your emotions.

> **29** Be constructive and learn from your feelings, rather than ignoring them or indulging in them.

LEARNING FROM EMOTIONS

Emotions are pieces of information. They are messages that you can read and learn from to help you achieve greater success and happiness. For example, stress might be an invitation to change something; pain might be a signal to let go of something; fear might be a sign that you need extra help; doubt might be encouraging you to make a better choice; and guilt might be telling you that you are not living according to your true values. Never block your feelings – learn to read and follow them.

▼ NOTICING EMOTIONS
In this example, a manager reacted to a stressful situation without taking note of her feelings or the feelings of others. It was only when she sought advice that she understood how she could have used her feelings in a positive, constructive way.

CASE STUDY
A manager at a pharmaceutical company was under pressure to meet a deadline. She started working longer hours and demanded that her team work longer hours too.
Within a short space of time, employees were calling in sick. She started to vent her worries at home. Her husband complained that her behaviour was unreasonable and requested that she leave her concerns at work.

She sought advice from her boss, who encouraged her to use her stress to reach a positive outcome. She called a team meeting to explain her predicament. She apologized for her previous unreasonable demands, and she worked with her team to find a solution.
She reflected that if she had recognized the signs of stress in the first place, she could have been proactive about the necessary course of action rather than reacting hastily.

STAYING FLEXIBLE

The ability to be flexible is fundamental to emotional intelligence. Remember that balancing work and life is not just about logic, reason, and finance; it is about heart, soul, and relationships. Aim to see all sides of a situation so that you are less likely to repeat unconstructive habits that only hinder your progress. Learn to be flexible so that you do not succumb to doubt, cynicism, or the temptation to give up.

> Face a difficult issue that seems hard to resolve

> Stay positive and retain a flexible attitude

> Be open-minded and think about all the possible options

> Reflect on the possibilities and decide on the necessary action

BEING FLEXIBLE ▶
Flexibility encourages you to stay positive even when a desired outcome looks uncertain. It helps you reflect upon the many options available to you.

Sits back and listens to what employee is saying

BEING EMPATHETIC

To have empathy means that you are able to understand other people's positions as well as your own. It ensures greater compassion, trust, co-operation, and honesty in your relationships. Begin to identify and let go of any limiting thoughts or feelings you may have that serve to block your success. Always aim to respect and understand other people's positions.

◀ BEING AWARE OF BODY LANGUAGE
By keeping eye contact and an open posture, this manager is showing that she is listening to and acknowledging what the employee is saying. He, in turn, is being open and honest.

DOS AND DON'TS

✔ Do show others that you understand and respect them.	✘ Don't make assumptions about other people's feelings.
✔ Do be trusting and open in your relationships with others.	✘ Don't be cynical and inflexible when you are dealing with other people.

30 Recognize doubt in your team members and try to find the cause of concern.

ASKING FOR SUPPORT

It is often counter-productive to keep your feelings to yourself. When you have an emotional issue, seek guidance from a colleague, family member, or friend – someone who is an empathetic listener. Bear in mind that everyone requires support to express their feelings and then learn constructively from them. This enhances self-awareness and self-mastery – the keystones of emotional intelligence. Remember that people with greater clarity about their feelings are more in control of their lives. And if you are effective at managing your own feelings, you will be better able to support others.

31 Listen to others and get a different perspective on life.

Explains what he finds stressful in his work and life

Friend listens and makes constructive comments

▲ **TALKING ABOUT FEELINGS**
This man has made a list of the things that cause him stress in his life. Discussing them with a friend, and listening to her feedback, helps him deal with issues constructively and positively.

ASKING FOR HELP

Asking for help is a strength, not a weakness. Friends and colleagues may be experiencing similar feelings to you, and talking to them about an issue can help you resolve it. Think about ways you could phrase questions so that you get the positive support you need:

❝ *I have noticed that I start to feel stressed when I have too much work to do. How do you deal with stress?* ❞

❝ *My boss makes comments when I leave work on time. How would you deal with that situation?* ❞

❝ *I am aware that I find it difficult to balance my work and life. What strategies do you use?* ❞

❝ *My son is worried about his school work, but he refuses to talk about it. How would you raise the subject?* ❞

PUTTING TOGETHER YOUR OWN JIGSAW

Your life is like a jigsaw: it is made up of different pieces. Ensure that you make time for each important aspect of your life – your relationships, family, leisure time, work, and self-improvement – and begin to focus on your life as a whole.

32 Remember that good relationships are an essential human need.

Partners spend quality time together

ENJOYING A RELATIONSHIP

A poor work–life balance can have a detrimental effect on a relationship. Be aware that if you are unable to shake off the stress of work when you go home, this can affect your private life – and, ultimately, it can cause irrevocable differences between you and those you love. What do you want from a relationship: love, respect, communication, intimacy, fun? How important are each of these elements to you right now? Clarify what you want in your relationship and make achieving that result a priority.

◀ **SPENDING TIME WITH YOUR PARTNER**
This couple schedules time together in which they pursue their mutual interests. Valuing their relationship, they have a balanced home life and, as a result, are better motivated at work.

33 Show your family how much you value them.

DOS AND DON'TS

✔ Do seek to understand your partner's needs.	✘ Don't prioritize your work over your relationships.
✔ Do make sure that you make time to have fun with your family.	✘ Don't put off enjoyable activities due to an excessive workload.

HAVING CHILDREN

The experience of parenthood is both demanding and rewarding. Ask yourself what your priorities are in relation to children? Do you have children but want to spend more time with them? Do you want to have children but are unsure about when? Find out your company's family-friendly policies – these could be an important element in your ability to balance parenthood and a career. Recognize that a rich work life and a happy family need not conflict if you are committed to both.

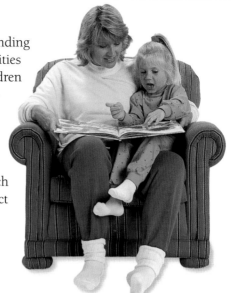

PUTTING CHILDREN FIRST ▶
If you have children, make sure that you spend enough time with them and enjoy helping them learn and grow.

34 Be clear about what kind of parent you want to be.

QUESTIONS TO ASK YOURSELF

Q How important is my family to me?

Q What are my hopes and goals for my family?

Q Do I know what my family wants to achieve?

Q What would it take to improve family life?

Q How can I show my family how much I love and appreciate them?

CARING FOR YOUR FAMILY

View your family – this includes your parents and your friends – as your bedrock. Remember that it is their support that helps you manage the other areas of your life successfully. Be careful not to fall into the trap of neglecting your family and only spending time with them when there is a problem to be resolved. If you repeatedly put work first, a breakdown in communication within the family could occur. Reflect on how important your family is to you: if it figures highly for you, then keep renewing your commitment to it. Schedule quality time together at weekends and evenings. Do not wait for holidays or a birthday before you demonstrate that you care.

35 Recognize the role your family plays in all your successes and how much you rely on their support.

MAKING TIME FOR LEISURE

Plays tennis to take his mind off work and eliminate stress

Do you allow time for your favourite leisure activities? There is a price to pay for not taking leisure time – you may experience higher stress levels, greater exhaustion, ill health, insomnia, and impaired relationships. What leisure activities do you want to do that you may have been putting off? What changes do you need to make to ensure that you achieve a balance? Realize that leisure activities enhance your health by acting as both a preventative measure against stress, for example, as well as a cure for it. A healthy amount of leisure can enrich your creativity at work, your time at home, and your friendships in life.

TAKING THE TIME TO ENJOY SPORTS ▶
Schedule time to play a sport and to take regular exercise – this will keep you healthy, help you unwind, and refresh your mind so that you are ready for new challenges.

36 Use leisure time to help you deal with stress.

37 Realize that taking time to relax will improve your productivity.

DEFINING WORK GOALS

To live a successful, well-balanced life you need to have clearly defined work goals that you can prioritize accordingly. Think about your specific career aspirations. Are you satisfied in your current position or are you planning to make changes? Review your financial aims. Do you want to stay at your current level of salary or do you want to increase your earnings? Do you need to learn new skills to maximize your potential at work? Write down your objectives and priorities.

▼ PRIORITIZING YOUR GOALS
Think about what you want to achieve at work; make a list of your objectives and put them in order of importance; and then set out a plan to work towards.

| Clarify your working goals | → | List goals in order of priority | → | Plan how you will implement goals |

IMPROVING YOURSELF

It is essential that people commit to lifelong learning in a competitive and fast-moving world. Decide what personal development goals you have. Would it be useful for you to improve skills such as leadership, motivation, communication, or confidence? If so, which ones? Make a personal development plan by listing the key skills that you want to improve and then prioritizing them. Find out what seminars, workshops, or other activities would meet your learning needs. Schedule time to attend events, read literature, and receive coaching.

38 Commit to achieving all your priorities.

39 Set time aside each week for self-development and training.

▼ PIECING A WORK AND LIFE JIGSAW TOGETHER
This is an example of a manager's work-life jigsaw. Once she had analyzed the different elements of her life, she began to understand how each aspect fitted in with the full picture of her life.

Invests time in her relationship and enjoys a balanced and loving partnership

Spends quality time with her children and plans fun days out together

Commits to spending more time with her family

Keeps looking for opportunities to develop and improve her strengths and skills

Analyzes her career aims and works towards achieving them

Schedules time for sport and leisure so that she can be healthy and revitalized

RELATIONSHIPS
CHILDREN
FAMILY
LEISURE
WORK
SELF IMPROVEMENT

PLANNING ACTION

The key to implementing good intentions is to create and follow an action plan for your work and life. Identify your objectives, clarify your goals, discuss your plans with those who will be involved in them, and set yourself achievable targets.

40 Recognize that action plans save you time, energy, and confusion.

FOCUSING ON OBJECTIVES

Be specific about a final outcome you want to achieve – your objective. Focus on what you do want rather than what you do not want. Think about how you will know that you have achieved an objective. What evidence will you require to show that you have succeeded? Think about what information you will need before you take action and make sure it will not produce any adverse consequences.

ASSESSING OBJECTIVES ▶

Identify an objective and then think through how you will achieve it before you embark on an action plan.

Clarify an objective you want to achieve	*I want a better balance between my work and life*
Look at why you want to achieve this	*I want to spend more time with my family*
Find the information you will need	*I need to find out about working flexitime*
Think about the potential consequences	*I need to discuss my new hours with my colleagues*
Make sure that you are responsible for the goal	*I am committed to achieving this goal*

QUESTIONS TO ASK YOURSELF

Q Am I clear about what I want to achieve?

Q How will I know I have achieved it?

Q Do I need more information?

Q Am I willing and able to take responsibility for my goals?

Q Have I set myself realistic goals?

Q How will I reward myself for successes?

41 Clarify your objectives and then form an action plan.

DECIDING GOALS

Having decided on your desired objectives, clarify the work and life goals that will help you reach each objective. For example, if achieving a work–life balance is an objective, what specific relationship goals will help you reach that objective? What aims do you already have in relation to children? What are your work goals? Review your current goals, or set yourself some new ones.

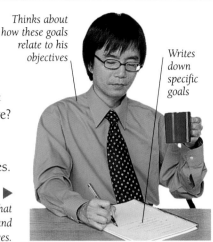

Thinks about how these goals relate to his objectives

Writes down specific goals

ASSESSING YOUR GOALS ▶

Make the time to think about your goals. Actively imagine what you will see, hear, and feel when you have achieved them and how they will help you achieve your overall objectives.

42 Read the latest developments so that all your actions are well-informed.

GATHERING INFORMATION

Before you start work on your goals, ensure that you are as well informed as possible. The right information can save you a lot of time and energy. Make use of all the resources around you, such as colleagues, a human resources manager, your friends, inspirational books, training courses, the internet, or a coach. There is no need to reinvent the wheel. Get as much information and help as you can and make every action an informed choice.

KNOWING WHO

You will achieve your goals if you ask for support from the appropriate people. Identify the key players in your situation. Discuss your plans and ask for their input when necessary. Some people can feel threatened by change – try and understand their concerns. Reassure them that you have thought through your actions, but be flexible and ready to consider other options.

INVOLVING KEY PEOPLE

COLLEAGUES
Talk to your colleagues and ask for their input and advice when necessary.

PARTNER
Discuss and agree your plans with your partner.

FRIENDS
Talk over your ideas with your friends and be open to new options.

DECIDING STEPS

It is vital to identify clearly how you will achieve each goal before you take action so that you stay focused. Break down each goal into bite-sized chunks and prioritize each chunk. The more understanding that you have about the sequence of events that will lead to an outcome, the easier it will be to achieve. Ask for a second opinion on the steps you have recognized, and if necessary, involve the appropriate people in particular steps.

43 Set a date for each of your action steps.

MANAGING YOUR TIME

Identify realistic time frames for actions so that you can pace yourself, stay focused, and measure your progress. Remember, if your ultimate aim is to achieve a better balance between work and life, it defeats the object to set unrealistic targets that create unnecessary pressure on you. Establish your key objective and then do something every day, however small, to move towards it.

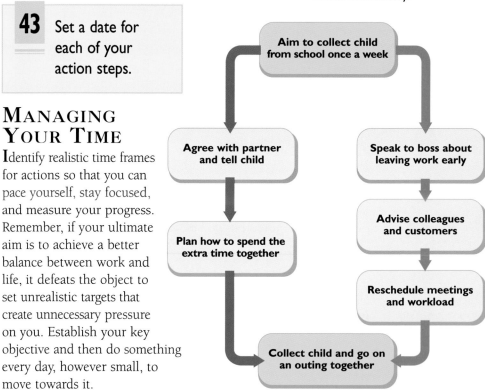

SCHEDULING ACTION STEPS ▲

In this example, a manager has decided that he wants to spend more time with his child. His goal is to collect his child from school once a week and share a leisure pursuit. He defines the steps he needs to take at home and at work, and puts them into sequence.

Key

Action steps to be implemented at home

Action steps to be implemented at work

MAKING A PLAN TO ACHIEVE WORK–LIFE BALANCE

GOAL	INFORMATION NEEDED	STEPS TO TAKE	DEADLINE
RELATIONSHIPS To work together as a team with my partner	To talk to my partner about both our needs, and look at how we could communicate more effectively.	● Arrange a romantic dinner. ● Set time aside for a frank discussion.	April 20th
CHILDREN To read them a story three times per week.	Find out what stories my children like, and make sure that I can leave work punctually to be home at their bedtime.	● Ask children what stories they like. ● Start leaving work on time.	April 15th
FAMILY To enjoy a family activity at least once a week.	To have a family discussion about what activities each of us enjoy and what types of hobbies we could do together.	● Discuss mutual interests. ● Agree on shared activities.	May 1st
WORK To spend most of my time on important tasks.	To talk to my manager to help me clarify my role and to find out what my most crucial day-to-day tasks are.	● Review my work tasks and priorities. ● Speak to my boss about my priorities.	April 10th
LEISURE To have a tennis lesson once a fortnight.	To find out about local tennis coaches, convenient times for lessons, and what prices they charge.	● Call a coach. ● Schedule regular tennis lessons and attend.	May 7th
PERSONAL DEVELOPMENT To learn meditation.	To ask my friends and colleagues to recommend a good meditation course, either near my home or my office.	● Find a convenient class. ● Schedule a meditation course.	May 14th

MAKING CHANGES

There are practical measures you can take to create a better work and life balance. Think about changes, start to put them into action, and lead your team through your good example.

ADAPTING WORK ROUTINES

To be successful in today's workplace, organizations and employees have to be open to new ways of working. Notice how globalization, new technology, and new employment trends are forcing change, and look at ways of adapting your work routine.

44 Realize that everyone benefits when you balance your work and life.

45 Set a target for the number of hours you want to work.

46 Make sure you always take all your allocated annual leave.

ACHIEVING BALANCE

Organizations who actively promote work-life strategies benefit from better recruitment and improved staff retention – their staff suffer from less stress and take less sick leave. The economy also benefits because the job market stabilizes, giving more people the opportunity to work. Society benefits because parents can more easily provide for the health and happiness of their families. Realize that a good work–life balance is beneficial for all, because individuals who achieve this balance tend to perform better, enjoy good health, and achieve sustainable success.

By law, employees are entitled to a set amount of annual leave, and maternity or paternity leave; they are also entitled to compassionate leave. An organization cannot normally require employees to work more than a set national number of hours a week – employees may choose to work longer, however.

WORKING HOURS

Decide how many working hours a week are right for you. Some people want to work fewer hours, for example, to accommodate higher education. Others may prefer to work more hours so that they can earn extra income. Clarify your objectives so that you can make better decisions about your career. Consider part-time options such as job-sharing, where two employees share one job; term-time working, where an employee has leave during school holidays; and "V" time working, where an employee works reduced hours with the guarantee of returning to full-time work later.

WORKING FROM HOME

Home working is where employees agree to do some or all of their work from home. They usually make a dedicated space for work at home and also share "hot desks" or "flexi desks" at the office. New technology has made home working more possible in recent years – it is especially suited to jobs like computer programming, market research, and journalism. Before you opt for home working, make sure that you are able to set clear boundaries between work and the rest of your life.

▲ WORKING FROM HOME
The benefits of working at home include no commuting time, more actual working time, flexible working hours, and more time with your family.

47 Find out about your entitlement to maternity or paternity leave.

WORKING FLEXIBLY

Flexible working schemes are becoming more common. "Flexitime" allows you to set your own daily working hours. "Flexi-leave" means you can break annual leave into long-weekends and half-days. "Compressed hours working" allows you to work the hours of a normal five-day week within four days. "Annualized hours" allows you to work a set number of hours each year in your own time. Find out what options are available to you.

Working Smarter, Not Harder

A common myth is that the results you achieve are directly related to how hard you work. However, greater effort does not always equal greater effectiveness. Use your time efficiently, learn to delegate, and make sure you switch off when you leave the office.

48 Value every hour of the day – make sure that you use them effectively.

49 Take full advantage of your available leisure time.

50 Schedule regular hour-long thinking sessions.

Using Time Efficiently

Sometimes a poor work–life balance is a symptom of poor time management. Realize that time is your most valuable resource: ultimately, your ability to "save time" or "waste time" determines how well you balance your work and life. Have you ever systematically recorded and assessed your work time? Do you employ an effective time-management system to plan your working week? Take a moment now to identify one "time vampire" that eats into your available time and, also, one "time saver" that can win you back some time.

Time-Setting Tips

There are habits you can develop to help you use your time more effectively at work and improve your productivity:

- Monitor and review your time at work to make sure you are working efficiently.
- Break tasks into manageable sizes, and schedule them accordingly.
- Prepare daily activity sheets to identify your key priorities, meetings, and deadlines – make sure that your team members have access to these.
- Create a diary on your computer, update it daily, and refer to it to make sure that you are on track.
- Encourage your team to make their own decisions, rather than referring to you about every issue – there is not enough time in the day.

TIDYING YOUR WORK AREA

Decluttering your work area encourages mental clarity and sharper focus so that you are better able to deal with your workload. Schedule time each week to declutter your office and master your desk. Your desk surface should be reserved only for current, high-priority projects. Get a large wastepaper bin and purge your desk-top and drawers of any unnecessary paper. Make sure that your computer filing system is up to date and easy to navigate around.

51 Set aside one hour every week to tidy your workspace.

Diary is kept up to date

In-tray is clear

Pens are tidy

KEEPING ORGANIZED ▶
Make sure your in-tray is free of paperwork – file away correspondence that you have already dealt with. If you have redundant files on your computer desktop, delete them.

Stationery is kept in drawer

Paperwork is filed

SIMPLIFYING YOUR LIFE

Success has traditionally been defined as "more" – more money and possessions, a car with more horsepower, a job with more responsibilities, a social life with more friends. Recognize that too much of "more" can clutter up your life. It can leave you over-stretched, over-committed, and overwhelmed. Avoid losing sight of your true values and real priorities. In this way, you can let go of excess and focus on what is most essential.

52 Evaluate your real priorities and focus your attention on them so that you are able to give your best.

THINGS TO DO

1. Think about what is essential to you.
2. Find out whether your colleagues' priorities conflict with your own.
3. Plan solutions that take into account everybody's particular needs.

DELEGATING EFFECTIVELY

One of the biggest blocks to enjoying a healthy work–life balance is the failure to delegate. Recognize that if you are able to delegate effectively, you will have more time and space to set your own goals and to organize, manage, and coach your team. Delegation ensures that no-one is indispensable, it gives colleagues opportunities to grow and to prove themselves, and it helps managers evaluate potential. Remember that positive delegation means that you have enough time and energy to steer your team towards its true purpose and success. It also ensures that you do not drown in over-tiredness and, in the long run, let your team down.

ASSESSING YOUR WORKLOAD

| Are you constantly overloaded with work? | → | Have the skills and confidence to delegate tasks |

| Are you doing tasks that a team member could do better? | → | Hand the task over to the relevant team member |

| Are there any tasks that can only be done by you? | → | Prioritize your time and energy on these tasks |

53 Decide whether it is necessary for you to do a task personally or if it is possible to delegate it.

CASE STUDY

John's first boss consistently disempowered his team by refusing to invest time in training them, and he always double-checked their work. John recognized that he was displaying similar managerial traits and decided to break this negative pattern.
He called a team meeting and declared his intention to make changes. He handled any sceptical queries with quiet reassurance. From then on, if staff asked him to solve a problem, he encouraged them to come up with solutions of their own first, rather than supplying an answer.
He invested time in having initial briefings followed by progress review meetings, so that his staff had clear guidelines and understood what was expected of them.
His greatest satisfaction came from hearing the positive feedback from his staff – they felt valued and motivated.

◀ LEARNING TO DELEGATE

A manager was creating a cycle in which his inability to delegate was producing a negative outcome. He consciously decided to change this habit. He found it difficult at first, but each success made it easier and he soon found that the habit of delegating became automatic.

SWITCHING OFF

Leave your work behind when you leave the office. Clearly designate what is "work time" and what is "family time", "time out", and "my time". If you do this, you will probably find you work fewer hours but produce more focused work. When "work time" is over, learn to stop thinking about it. Discipline yourself to turn off mobile phones, pagers, laptop computers, e-mail, and the internet. This will help refresh your mind and body. Aim to live more and work better.

▲ LEAVING WORK CARES BEHIND YOU
When you leave work, and are enjoying time out with your friends, leave any work issues behind you so that they cannot invade and disrupt your personal life.

Switch off ▶ Relax ▶ Recharge

▲ TAKING TIME FOR YOURSELF
When you leave the office each evening, switch your mind off from your work. Take quality time to rejuvenate, and you will feel refreshed and better equipped to deal with work the next day.

QUESTIONS TO ASK YOURSELF

Q Am I using my time effectively or is there a better way I could organize myself?

Q Is there an easier way I could approach this task?

Q Could I delegate this work to someone who would be better able to deal with it?

Q Do I spend enough time on priorities, or am I distracted by other tasks?

Q Do I create enough time and space for family and friends?

Q Do I allocate any time for reviewing, revising, and improving working practices?

ONE-MINUTE EXCELLENCE

Punctuate your daily work schedule with moments of quiet. Take one minute of excellence to review goals, strategy, and balance: one minute is often enough to give you an idea that can help you work smarter, not harder. Ask yourself questions, like, "Is this the best use of my time?" and "Is there a better way to do this?" Give yourself "time out" to make sure you are not being distracted by urgent, but unimportant, tasks.

UNDERSTANDING CHANGE

Understanding the psychology of change can help you make changes for the better. Be specific: think about the changes you could make, the people who could offer you support, the obstacles you may encounter – and then take action.

54 Have the courage to make changes in your work and your life.

CULTURAL DIFFERENCES

It is part of the Japanese culture to be adaptable to continual change. Europeans, on the other hand, are generally less open to change, although this attitude is slowly altering. In the United States, they approach change as a challenge. Australasians often initially resist change, but then tend to adapt to it very well.

BEING OPEN TO CHANGE

Change is inevitable in life, whether you actively seek it or try to avoid it. You can deal with change in two primary ways: either resist it or welcome it. Bear in mind that resistance to change usually creates more problems than it avoids. It can cause greater fear, anxiety, procrastination, and imbalance. You can feel stuck, and your life will not move forward. Recognize that resistance is not a solution, and that your life will not change if you will not change. Instead, have courage and welcome change. Take a leap of faith and make adjustments for the better by being willing to take a risk. If you adopt a proactive approach to change, it will pay dividends.

BENEFITING FROM CHANGE

To make a change happen, you must get leverage: this means that you must understand how change will affect you. You can do this in two ways. Assess the cost of not making a change for the better in your work and life balance. What will be the cost to your quality of life, your relationships, and your effectiveness at work? Alternatively, assess the benefits of making the change. How much happier will you be? How will your family and friends feel? How much more rewarding will work be? Use your answers as leverage to help motivate you to make changes.

55 Be proactive and work to make things happen.

56 Take responsibility for the changes you want to happen.

CREATING CHANGE

Identify what it is you want to change. Be specific. What is it about your work and life balance that you want to improve? Is it fewer working hours, more free weekends, less commuting? Next, ask yourself who do you need to speak to about it? Is it your manager, colleagues, customers and/or your partner? What new action will you undertake? Will you delegate more, attend fewer meetings, or stop saying "yes" to unessential tasks?

 57 Ask yourself what changes you could make to your life.

▼ **IDENTIFYING ISSUES**
Instead of thinking about a problem in a negative way, think about how you could approach it positively, and come up with a constructive solution.

THINKING NEGATIVELY | THINKING POSITIVELY

I don't like working such long hours

I must delegate work more effectively

I waste time going to meetings

I will only attend essential meetings

I spend too much time travelling to work

I could work from home more often

SAYING "NO" TO UNESSENTIAL TASKS

Many people continually find themselves overloaded with work because they find it difficult to say "no". Realize that you can change this pattern: If you know that you will not have the time to deal with something, be honest:

❝ *I would like to help you, but my current list of priorities is taking up all my time.* ❞

❝ *I understand that the schedule is tight, but my own project is delayed. Can someone else help you?* ❞

❝ *Are you absolutely sure you need my input at this stage? If not, please come back to me at a later date.* ❞

❝ *I'm sorry that I am unable to deal with your task, but I can offer advice that may be of use instead.* ❞

- Unhealthy independence can cause you unnecessary struggle and create setbacks that could have been avoided.

- People who are too independent are usually afraid to ask for help when they need it.

- It is a sign of strength, not of weakness, to ask for help.

FINDING SUPPORT

A common block to making changes is unhealthy independence. If you try to make changes entirely under your own steam, you can block yourself off from other people's encouragement, support, and inspiration. Take a moment to make a list of all the people who might be able to support you in having a better work–life balance. Make a list of other possible sources of support, such as books, training courses, and specialist networks.

RECOGNIZING OBSTACLES

Internal obstacles to change, such as fear of failure, usually outnumber external obstacles, such as an uncompromising boss. To create a change, let go of your old patterns of thinking and behaving. Let go of old doubts and fears. Once your mind is clear, you will be in a better position to address any external obstacles you may face – and these are often not as insurmountable as you imagine.

58 Ask a coach or mentor to help you deal with a change you want to make.

OVERCOMING INTERNAL OBSTACLES TO CHANGE

INTERNAL OBSTACLE	SOLUTION
SELF-DOUBT I feel awkward about initiating this change.	Acknowledge your doubts but recognize that you do not have to face change on your own.
FEELING OVERWHELMED I can only handle so much change.	Keep yourself focused on the benefits of the change you are making.
INNER FEARS I lack the confidence to make this change.	Ask for feedback from a trusted colleague to assess the reality of your concerns.
NEGATIVE THINKING In the past, changes have backfired.	Remember an occasion when you were forced to make a change, but it worked out well.

TAKING ACTION

The key to making any change is to begin: one small step is enough to start the ball rolling. Either you can act or you can wait for something to happen. Waiting for a change to happen is called procrastination, and this is a major block to change. Procrastination is a thief of time. It stops you from taking responsibility for your life. It corrupts creative thinking, decision-making, and proactive living. Decide what change you want to make, get leverage, ask for help, address the obstacles, and then decide to act. Ask yourself, "What is the next best step I could take to achieve a better work–life balance?" and "When will I take this step?" Schedule a date in your diary and stick to it.

59 See that small changes make a big difference.

60 Challenge every obstacle that you encounter.

▼ MAKING CHANGES
Once you have pinpointed a change you want to make, and have worked to eliminate any possible obstacles, you are ready to implement it.

| Decide on change | → | Overcome obstacles | → | Take the necessary action |

DEALING WITH ▶ OBSTACLES
A manager had witnessed many changes within her organization during a short period of time. She was cynical about a further change her boss had outlined, but she had to rise to the challenge.

CASE STUDY

Kim, a manager in the communications industry, was asked by her boss to increase sales, but without an equivalent increase in resources.

She was cynical about being able to increase the sales figures, but she called her team together and informed them of the position. She listened to their concerns and ensured that they felt understood. She encouraged their creative input and followed up their ideas.

Although Kim took the leadership role, she involved everyone in decision-making, because she realized that this was essential for the team's ongoing commitment. She noted how ready each team member was to the proposed change and encouraged the risk-takers to lead. Kim then kept focused on managing the change and its outcome.

Together, Kim and her team successfully achieved the seemingly impossible results.

LEADING BY EXAMPLE

Managers are most effective when they act as a role model and lead by example – in this way, they bring out the best in themselves and others. Create a good team culture, coach your team, and ensure that your staff maintain a work–life balance.

61 Be a good example to your colleagues and team members.

LEADING THE WAY

An effective manager is a good role model. Make sure you lead by action and not just words – always demonstrate what is required. Remember that people learn best by example. As a manager, you are in a position to teach and demonstrate the importance of a healthy work and life balance. Think about how you might best do this. For example, leave the office on time so that you encourage your staff to do likewise.

Exercises regularly

Enjoys work

Keeps regular working hours

Prioritizes actions

Takes annual leave

▲ A GOOD ROLE MODEL
Be an example to your team by implementing a good attitude, a strong set of values, and proactive behaviour. As you display these qualities yourself, you will inspire your team to go the extra mile.

DOS AND DON'TS

☑ Do take your full lunch break and leave work on time.

☑ Do look after your health and spiritual wellbeing.

☑ Do take your allocated holiday leave and use it constructively.

☑ Do schedule time for leisure activities.

☒ Don't book meetings after office hours.

☒ Don't always be the last person to leave the office.

☒ Don't send e-mails to colleagues at the weekends.

☒ Don't ignore your commitments to your family.

62 Make sure team members respect each other.

63 Tell your team what you expect from them.

GIVING GUIDANCE

As a manager, it is your job to steer the team culture – this is a set of agreements about how best a team will work together. When you are creating a team culture, focus on vision, values, relationships, and key issues such as work–life balance. Be explicit about what you want. Tell people you want them to be effective rather than exhausted. Make sure that your team members know that you do not require them to give their all for the job at the expense of their home lives. Reinforce a work–life balance every time you conduct interviews, give feedback, do performance reviews, or lead team meetings.

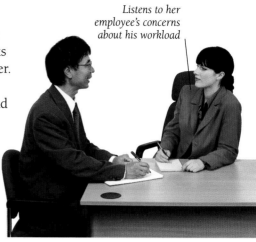

Listens to her employee's concerns about his workload

▲ GIVING A REVIEW
During a performance review, take the opportunity to talk to your team members about their work–life balance and suggest ways that it could be improved.

64 Monitor the motivational level of your team.

BUILDING HEALTHY TEAMS

It is not in a manager's interests to have a continually overworked team, because the cost of overworking is too high. Teamwork deteriorates, performance falters, relationships suffer, and the team spirit eventually dries up. Monitor the health of your team, keep gauging their energy, and be alert to the dangers of burnout. If you drive your team to exhaustion, they will not be able to produce the results you need and you will lose their loyalty. Make sure that team members are able to be creative and are given the chance to offer ideas.

◀ ENCOURAGING IDEAS
Establish a culture that supports and encourages the creativity of your team, so that team members feel valued and fulfilled by their work.

Manager listens to ideas

Sales assistant suggests possible new database

CULTURAL DIFFERENCES

In the United States and Japan, annual leave is generally shorter than in Europe. Britain has a reputation for working long hours. Meanwhile, in France, employees are not expected to work more than a 35-hour week.

BANISHING GUILT

A "guilt culture" is one of the biggest drains on personal effectiveness at work. The term refers to the pressure people feel to work long hours, work weekends, skip lunch breaks, forgo holiday leave, and miss family commitments. Guilt cultures are often perpetuated by managers and team members, but organizations pay a high price in return. Realize that overworking blunts performance and long hours do not necessarily increase productivity. Banish guilt and liberate the talent of your team.

COACHING OTHERS

For a team to work well, each team member must work to their own optimum personal effectiveness. Coach your staff to have a better work–life balance. Coaching may include one-to-one sessions, time-management training, or making helpful information available. Remember, the right balance between work and life varies between people. Build rapport, listen, understand, and then create a programme to suit individual needs.

65 Teach others what you want to practise yourself.

66 Encourage your team members to leave the office on time.

BALANCING TEAM WORKLOADS ▼

Each week, meet with your team and schedule the week's work. Let team members discuss their workload and, if necessary, share out responsibilities so that no-one is overstretched.

Sales executive explains that he foresees problems meeting deadline

Sales assistant is willing to help with workload

Manager suggests sales executive delegates work to sales assistant

COACHING TECHNIQUES

Coaching is a valuable skill that you can use in one-to-one sessions with your staff, and in your daily interactions with people. Aim to gain rapport and trust because this is the first step in good communication. Remember that the key to effective listening is being able to see situations from other people's points of view. If you are working with a coachee, help them create a well-formed action plan to follow. Make sure that you clearly outline the steps, timing, and people involved in any action.

BEING A COACH ▶
Listen to the coachee, but also give constructive feedback. Offer advice if you are asked, but let the coachee develop his or her own solutions.

RESETTING THE BALANCE

Remember that it is in your interests that your team members have healthy home lives. Of course, business does sometimes involve unpredictable change, crises, busy seasons, unforeseen meetings, difficult deadlines, weekend conferences, and travel abroad. A work–life balance is not static and is always changing – there will be times when home life suffers. Be quick to reset a healthy work–life balance as soon as possible. Don't just push on. Remember, balance is the key to sustainable long-term success.

 67 Rest when your energy is low so that you recharge.

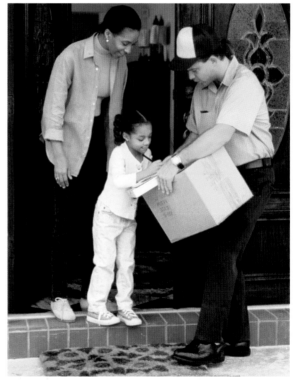

▲ ACKNOWLEDGING GOOD WORK
When your staff have worked long hours to meet a difficult deadline on a project, be quick to thank them and their families for their extra efforts – you could even send a hamper.

SUSTAINING BALANCE

Maintaining balance is the key to professional and personal success. Be sure about what you want, live a healthy and fulfilled life, stay motivated, and always celebrate successes.

REVIEWING YOUR GOALS

Regularly reviewing your goals can help you focus your time and energy on what is most important to you. Set yourself achievable goals, make sure you evaluate all your experiences, and keep checking that you are focused on your priorities.

68 Review your purpose regularly so that you remain focused.

LIVING WITH PURPOSE

Your purpose is the reason why you take action. It is like a compass that helps you navigate the way ahead. If you do not review your purpose regularly, you can lose your direction, impetus, and *joie de vivre*. Be clear about why you go to work and what you want from your life. Write down your purpose and keep referring to it. Ensure your goals and actions align with your purpose.

◀ **DISCUSSING YOUR VISION**
Discuss your purpose with friends and colleagues in order to build greater mutual understanding and support, and to learn from their experiences and insights.

Maintain positive thinking

Be innovative

Focus on your purpose

Note down daily intentions

FORMING INTENTIONS

An intention is a specific mental focus to help you achieve an outcome. Each day, set intentions for the type of person you want to be, the life you want to live, and the contribution you want to make. Let these intentions inspire your actions, choices, and thinking. On difficult days, you may need to keep reminding yourself of your intentions because it is easy to be swayed off your course.

◀ FOCUSING ON YOUR INTENTIONS
Write down your intentions. Read them before you make a phone call, type an e-mail, or go to a meeting so that you are constantly reminded of what you are aiming to achieve.

PAYING ATTENTION

There is an old saying: "some people go through life, and others grow through life". Successful people are committed to lifelong learning and growing. By being willing to learn and grow, you will not be a victim of life. Pay close attention to the results you get in life and use every experience as a learning curve. Make time to evaluate your experiences. Ask yourself, "What is the lesson here?" and, "What do I need to learn here?" Look at every problem as an opportunity and every challenge as a chance to learn something new.

69 Remember that positive thinking is more effective.

70 Write your reflections in a daily journal.

QUESTIONS TO ASK YOURSELF

Q Have my values and priorities remained the same, or are they changing?

Q Am I having enough time for myself?

Q Who could I be spending more time with?

Q Am I taking my family's views into account?

STAYING FOCUSED

Once a week, schedule time to review your work and life. Ask yourself key questions and listen to your intuition. Think about your goals and ask yourself, "Are my actions in line with my priorities?" Think about your day and ask yourself, "Am I making the best use of my time?" Think about your relationships and ask yourself, "How could they improve?" Think about your health and ask yourself, "Do I have enough leisure time?" Use the answers to your questions to sharpen your focus.

BEING ASSERTIVE

Assertiveness helps you to align your thoughts, communications, and actions. Make sure that you know what you will say "yes" to and what you will say "no" to, always be true to yourself and others, and put your assertiveness into action.

71 Be certain about what you want and what you do not want.

72 Dedicate your valuable time to your real priorities.

73 Be assertive about saying "yes" to your priorities.

SAYING "YES"

True assertiveness starts with knowing what you want to say "yes" to. Every day you are exposed to numerous opportunities, invitations, choices, advertisements, requests – all of which want a "yes" from you. Avoid trying to say "yes" to everything because you will end up unfocused and unable to fulfil your commitments. Make sure that you know what you want to say "yes" to, so that you can be effective, happy, and purposeful. Saying "yes" to your priorities commits you to what is important in your life.

▼ **PRIORITIZING LEISURE TIME**
This manager views leisure time as a priority. When a colleague approaches him and proposes a game of squash during a lunch hour, he responds enthusiastically.

Colleague suggests a game of squash

Manager agrees to play squash

SAYING "NO"

If you cannot say "no" you may lose sight of your purpose and focus. A difficulty in saying "no" can lead to confused priorities, unhealthy compromises, inner exhaustion, and general ineffectiveness. Learn to say "no" – this will save time for you and others. It will make your relationships stronger and more honest.

Colleagues try to persuade manager to join them for drink

Manager is assertive and says "no"

BEING DEFINITE ▶
When his colleagues ask this manager for a drink, he would like to join them, but he would prefer to spend some time at home.

74 Think about how you react to someone who is direct, honest, and authentic.

BEING AUTHENTIC

Many people find it difficult to say "no" because they think it will cause conflict, anger, and guilt. If, however, you never say "no" you will lose focus and respect and, ultimately, you will lose yourself. Recognize that this inauthenticity can lead to deceit and resentment. You will find that the more authentic you are, the more honest and helpful others will be in return. Be assertive so that you are authentic and true to yourself.

ACTING NOW

Assertiveness is an antidote to procrastination. Focus your attention on the present, instead of on the future. Set "present-time goals" – something that can be achieved immediately. First, decide what is important to you, such as being a good friend. Next, ask yourself questions such as, "What can I do today to be a good friend?" Think about the action you could take to achieve your goal, and put it into effect immediately.

THINGS TO DO

1. Set a "present-time goal".
2. Take immediate action so that your good intention is not lost.
3. Monitor progress to ensure that the goal is achieved.

DEVELOPING CONFIDENCE

Inner confidence enables you to make decisions and take actions that help you sustain a healthy work–life balance. Learn to value and believe in yourself, build on your strengths, and aim to be resourceful, decisive, and empowered.

75 Recognize that if you respect yourself, others will too.

POINTS TO REMEMBER

- If you treat yourself well, others will treat you well too.
- The way you view yourself is expressed in your posture and your body language.
- When you behave decisively and confidently, people will follow your lead.
- A happy, balanced life starts with self-belief and vision.

76 Make a list of your strengths and aim to add to it.

VALUING YOURSELF

It is up to you to value yourself and your life. If you will not do this, then no one else can either. Remember that you have a lot to give, but you can only do this if you appreciate yourself. One way to value yourself is to ensure you sustain a healthy work–life balance. Remind yourself that you are a valuable asset to your organization, your colleagues, your family, and your friends. Look after yourself. Remember that the better you treat yourself, the more you can achieve. People will respect you for valuing yourself, even if it feels unfamiliar to them initially.

▼ ASSESSING YOUR CONFIDENCE
When your confidence is low, your lack of self-esteem will show in your tense facial muscles. As your confidence rises, your bearing and expressions become more positive.

Facial muscles are tense and strained

Expression is composed and calm

Eyes are bright and posture is upright

LOW CONFIDENCE AVERAGE CONFIDENCE HIGH CONFIDENCE

Building Self-Belief

Self-belief immunizes you against hopelessness and feeling dis-empowered. Remember that the greater your confidence, the greater your capacity will be to take action and succeed at life and work. Develop your self-belief, and your abilities, skills, and strengths will increase too. Adopt a "can-do" mentality and you will achieve your goals. Remember, a healthy work–life balance is always possible: believe you can do it, and you can.

77 Recognize that being assertive and positive helps you sharpen your focus.

STRENGTHS
Look at what you excel at

WEAKNESSES
Analyze your weaker areas

OPPORTUNITIES
Think about possible solutions

THREATS
Predict possible obstacles

Building Strengths

The more you build on your strengths, the easier it is to build your work–life balance. Perform the SWOT analysis on yourself. Look at your strengths. What are you already skilled at? Next, identify your weaknesses. What could you improve? What fears could you let go of? Next, spot opportunities for change, growth, support, and help. Finally, look for any threats that might hamper your progress, such as procrastination and self-doubt.

◀ **USING THE SWOT ANALYSIS**
Use the SWOT analysis to help you focus. Take an honest look at your strengths and weaknesses. Look at ways you could change or grow and examine the possible obstacles in your way.

Empowering Yourself

Empowerment increases assertiveness, inspires creativity, and supports effective action. It can also help you to be decisive and resourceful when too many demands compete for your time and energy. Symptoms of dis-empowerment include lack of inspiration, low energy levels, and a sense of hopelessness. Usually you will feel dis-empowered when you are acting without purpose. When you feel this way, ask yourself, "What needs to happen for me to be empowered again?" Get support for making the necessary changes.

78 Think about what makes you feel empowered.

79 Work on your inner beliefs and they will grow.

DEALING WITH STRESS

*S*tress is an increasingly common feature *of modern living. Avoid perceiving stress as the "enemy" – think of it as a possible "friend" that can help you to sustain a work–life balance. Learn to deal with stress and anxiety, and aim to have fun!*

80 Learn to recognize the signals your body makes when you are stressed.

THINGS TO DO

1. Recognize the symptoms of stress.
2. Make a point of choosing to think positive thoughts.
3. Schedule regular exercise, to help cleanse your body.
4. If your muscles are tense, take a warm bath.
5. Find someone to talk to about your worries.

BUSTING STRESS

Stress is like a red light that appears on the dashboard of your car. It is a signal telling you that you are "running on empty" and are "out of balance". Whenever you are feeling stressed, recognize that your body is telling you to make a change for the better. If you do not take action, you will receive louder and more frequent signals. Recognize stress as a sign that your work–life balance is under threat – use it as an impetus to act.

▼ **TRACKING CAUSES OF STRESS**
Monitor the things that make you feel stressed during the week, such as giving a presentation or leading a meeting, so that you can learn to cope with these events in a more positive way.

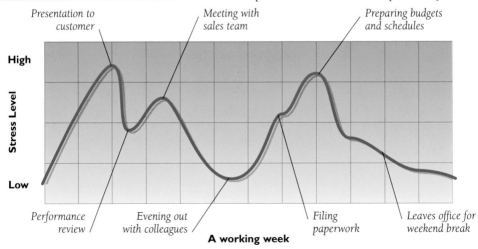

Presentation to customer

Meeting with sales team

Preparing budgets and schedules

High

Stress Level

Low

Performance review

Evening out with colleagues

Filing paperwork

Leaves office for weekend break

A working week

ALLEVIATING ANXIETY

How much anxiety does it take to solve a problem? None, because anxiety is not a solution for anything. Instead, anxiety is a sign for you to take action. Identify the cause of your anxiety. Note down what will happen to you if all you do is stay anxious. Write down the possible things you could undertake to counteract your anxiety. Decide on the appropriate action and begin it now.

QUESTIONS TO ASK YOURSELF

Q Why am I feeling anxious and what can I do to alleviate the feeling?

Q What is the root cause of this anxiety?

Q Would it help to talk to someone about this?

81 Give yourself time to relax and recentre every day.

82 Try not to take every issue too seriously.

ENDING STRUGGLE

Struggle is not always inevitable or necessary. Sometimes people struggle and they make things harder than they need to be. They invite struggle because they refuse to ask for help, make a change, or try to feel relaxed. Be aware that struggle is a state of mind. People who are continually battling often believe that struggle is an inevitable price for success and happiness. Whenever you are struggling, ask yourself how you could do things more easily. Use your imagination and intelligence to find an easier way.

HAVING FUN

The "fight, flight, or frolic" responses are three ways to deal with stress. Choose the "fight" option and tackle stress head on. For example, communicate more honestly with someone you have been avoiding. Opt for the "flight" option and remove yourself from the stress. This may involve taking a lunch break, going for a walk, or having a holiday. Choose the "frolic" option and concentrate on work, rest, and play, play, play.

▲ TAKING TIME TO ENJOY YOURSELF
If you are feeling stressed, take the time to have fun. An evening out can help you wind down and will immunize you against stress – this in turn will help you be more effective at work.

LIVING HEALTHILY

Good health is all about balance. Improve your work and your life by ensuring that you eat nourishing food, exercise regularly, and sleep well. Notice when your mind and body are feeling low on energy and take the time to rejuvenate.

83 Make sure that you keep your body properly nourished.

CULTURAL DIFFERENCES

The Japanese government advises its citizens to eat at least 30 different types of food each day so that they obtain the necessary amount of nutrients in their diet. Western governments are now aware that diets high in salt and saturated fat are a major cause of disease in their countries.

EATING WELL

Hippocrates, the father of medicine, wrote, "Let your food be your medicine, and let your medicine be your food". Make sure that you make healthy choices about your diet. Educate yourself about food, your body type, and the most healthy diet for your lifestyle. Eat plenty of fruit and vegetables during the day so that you have a rich source of vitamins and minerals. Make sure that you get the right balance of carbohydrates, protein, and fats. Limit your intake of artificial additives and sweeteners and your daily intake of caffeine and alcohol. Try to drink two litres of water per day.

TAKING EXERCISE

Either you have to take time to be healthy or you have to take time to be ill. Recognize that regular exercise is a great way to increase health, boost your energy, have more fun, switch off from work, and have an active social life. If you have not exercised for a while, a gym instructor can test your fitness level. He or she can also plan a personal programme that will help you improve your fitness level. Get into the habit of scheduling exercise sessions into your diary just as you would plan an evening out with friends. What exercise have you planned for this week? Get your diary out and book something now.

84 Ensure you eat three regular meals per day.

85 Book regular coaching sessions in your favourite sport or hobby.

*Eats banana
before going
to bed*

SLEEPING BETTER

Adults require an average of eight hours of sleep a night. In the long term, sleep deprivation can lead to mood swings and poor concentration. Are you sleeping well? Do you feel rested when you wake? A common cause of sleep disruption is a drop in blood sugar levels during the night. Try having a non-sugary snack before you go to bed.

◀ **HELPING YOURSELF SLEEP**

If you have problems sleeping, eat a banana an hour before bedtime – the fruit contains tryptophan, which has natural sedative powers that will help you relax and sleep more soundly.

RELAXING REGULARLY

Being able to relax is vital for a good work–life balance. Discover which ways of relaxing you prefer. Some people like to practise meditation, read quietly, or have long hot baths. Other people prefer more active and social types of relaxation, such as playing sports, going to the cinema, or enjoying a meal with friends. Relax regularly and you will boost your health, enjoy your life more, and improve your performance at work.

86 Relax before you go to bed – light some scented candles and have a bath.

RELAXED BREATHING EXERCISES

Try these breathing exercises before you go to sleep, or during moments of stress:

● Sit or lie down in a comfortable position. Ensure your head, neck, and spine are aligned. Close your eyes.

● Allow your breathing to become deeper, longer, and slower.

● Breathe into the abdomen area, pushing your stomach out as you breathe in and letting your stomach sink back down again as you breathe out.

● End your relaxation as deliberately as you began. Repeat when required.

RELAXING ▶

As you inhale, repeat the words to yourself "deep and long and slow". As you exhale, repeat the words "slow and long and deep".

INCREASING YOUR VITALITY

Vitality is a by-product of balance, health, and happiness. Boost your vitality by looking after yourself and by making good choices. Live your life to the full, enjoy your work and your leisure time, and have a positive and happy outlook.

87 Celebrate and enjoy the fact that you are alive each day.

THINGS TO DO

1. Commit to spending time with the people you love.

2. Schedule time with your friends in your diary and stick to the dates.

3. Choose social events you want to attend.

LIVING LIFE TO THE FULL

Do you live to work or do you work to live? Life is an adventure. Have the courage to take risks, break routines, and be spontaneous so that you can enjoy new experiences. Live for today and embrace happiness now – if you give yourself wholeheartedly to life, you will actually increase your vitality. Once you do, you will find that you work better because you will approach challenges with more energy. Remember that life is too precious to waste.

ENJOYING YOUR WORK

When work is no longer fun, it can lead to stress and unhappiness. Aim to make your work fun so that you increase your creativity, enhance your relationships, and become more successful. It may be necessary to change your job. Or try viewing your job from a positive perspective – most jobs have something to do with helping others, being of service, or making a difference. Recognize the value of your job and learn to enjoy your work.

QUESTIONS TO ASK YOURSELF

Q What aspects of my work am I passionate about?

Q What is my purpose at work, and what do I hope to achieve in my career?

Q How could I make work more enjoyable, rather than viewing it as a chore?

Q How could I be more creative at work?

Q How could I make more of a difference at work?

Q Is there a better attitude I could approach my work with?

88 Discover what you are passionate about and make sure that you try to incorporate it into your work.

ENCOURAGING LEISURE

Use your leisure time to put the zest back into your life. Schedule activities you enjoy and take the time to learn new interests. After a stressful day at the office, it can be invigorating to do something completely different. Find yourself what psychologists describe as "a third place" – a place other than home and work where you can unwind and enjoy yourself, such as a tennis club, a sailing club, an art class, or a coffee bar.

89 Plan days off work regularly so that you can recharge.

▼ ENJOYING A HOBBY
Learn a new skill, and you will feel challenged and rewarded. Your brain will be reinvigorated, giving you the energy and focus to inspire your work and life.

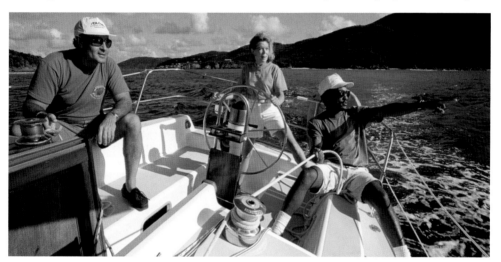

90 Develop a positive outlook and your life will be happier.

91 Notice how people react to your positivity.

CHOOSING HAPPINESS

Vitality is as much a mental attitude as a physical state. One of the biggest drains on your energy can be inner fears, self-criticism, and cynicism. By contrast, there is nothing more energizing than laughter, a compliment, or a moment of kindness. Sometimes it can be tiring if you are trying too hard to feel happy. Avoid chasing happiness. Instead, make sure you choose happiness by changing your outlook and state of mind. Make a conscious decision to be happy and to enjoy your life, and choose a better balance in your life.

STAYING MOTIVATED

It is easy to be motivated when your work and life are both going well, but it is also important to keep motivated when you are faced with challenges. Overcome any problems, ask for help if necessary, and give yourself the chance to be inspired.

92 Make sure your attitude is part of the solution, not the problem.

OVERCOMING DIFFICULTY

Everyone experiences bad times. Most people know what it is like to fail an interview, lose a customer, or argue with a friend. Success is not about the absence of failures: it is about the courage to overcome them. Try not to feel demotivated during difficult times – this can create a downward spiral of apathy and negativity. Hold your nerve and stay positive so that your attitude does not make a difficult situation worse.

Remains positive and focused, and strives to succeed

ACTION

FOCUS

ATTITUDE

BELIEF

COURAGE

STAYING POSITIVE ▶
Even during difficult situations, keep your mood and momentum upbeat. Adopt the positive qualities that will bring you success.

93 Get feedback from your colleagues and customers.

94 Look for solutions and, if necessary, ask for help.

ASKING FOR HELP

If a situation feels too much to handle on your own, it probably is. In other words, you probably need some extra help. Trying to stay motivated every day all by yourself is almost impossible. Life and work is a team game. Remain strong by being willing to ask for and accept help. During difficult times, spend quality time with people who understand you, support you, and believe in you – such as your family and friends. Realize that too much self-reliance can be a weakness.

TAKING CHARGE

During difficult times, ask yourself, "Is this something I can change?" In other words, find out if you are willing to take charge. Are you taking responsibility or are you making excuses? Are you waiting for things to get better or are you taking action? Are you blaming others or are you looking for solutions? When you are faced with a problem, reset your thoughts, choices, and perceptions and focus them on success, not on failure. Change your thoughts and you will transform your life.

QUESTIONS TO ASK YOURSELF

Q Do I know someone who could be my mentor?

Q Do I regularly read inspirational books to feed my imagination?

Q What training course could I attend next?

Q Who could give me valuable feedback?

95 Choose your thoughts carefully – remain focused.

96 Make sure that you note down inspirational ideas.

BEING INSPIRED

What do you do for inspiration? Do you listen to motivational tapes? Do you find inspiration in nature or in meditation? Most people do not get their best ideas at work. In fact, they are often most inspired when they are relaxed and detached from work. Make space in your life for inspiration. Carry a small notebook and write down any ideas as they occur to you. Book meetings and lunches with people who you admire and can learn from. When you travel, go by train instead of by car so that you can read, reflect, and relax more.

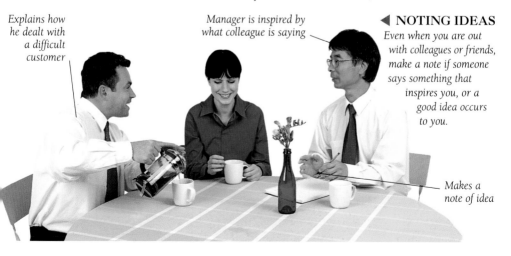

Explains how he dealt with a difficult customer

Manager is inspired by what colleague is saying

◀ **NOTING IDEAS**
Even when you are out with colleagues or friends, make a note if someone says something that inspires you, or a good idea occurs to you.

Makes a note of idea

CELEBRATING SUCCESS

When you achieve a success, make sure you celebrate it – celebration builds your confidence, increases your future resolve, and helps make success a state of mind. Recognize, reward, enjoy, and share success in yourself and others.

97 Keep a "success journal" and note down your daily achievements.

98 Recognize successes at home as well as at work.

99 Reward team members for their successes.

RECOGNIZING SUCCESS

Do you notice when you have done something well, or do you generally only notice when you have got something wrong? Are you quicker to praise than you are to find fault? The ability to recognize your success and the success of others is an essential skill for building a success-focused culture within your team. Realize that recognition is motivating. Ensure that you identify your own success and encourage your team to do the same. Start meetings by acknowledging recent successes, rather than merely discussing failures or mistakes.

REWARDING SUCCESS

Do not fall into the trap of waiting for an annual performance review or another form of systemized approach to reward success. Sometimes people feel that if they reward success too frequently, it will lose its meaning. They forget that even a simple "thank you" is an important, under-used reward that costs nothing. Ensure that you have ongoing incentive schemes that reward your employee's achievements. Monitor the schemes to make sure that they raise morale and yield the desired effect of showing that you value good performance. Reward your own successes too – buy yourself a gift, treat yourself to a meal, or go to a health spa to show that you value yourself.

THINGS TO DO

1. Notice when a team member completes a task well.
2. Let them know that their success has been noticed.
3. Set up an incentive scheme to reward staff achievements.
4. Reward yourself for your own triumphs and successes.

100 Celebrate with your family so that they feel involved in your success.

ENJOYING SUCCESS

Many people achieve successes but fail to enjoy them. There are many reasons for this. One is the tendency to push ahead so fast to the next goal or task that there is no time for celebration. Another is that they undervalue themselves and their achievements. Maybe they feel that completing a project successfully is merely part of their job description. Make sure that you enjoy your success and reward yourself with a healthy work–life balance. It is not worth having success at work if you have no friends, no fun, and no life.

SHARING SUCCESS

There is no such thing as a self-made man or woman. Success is always a team effort. When you are successful in life and in work, share your success with those who count. You can do this in many ways, such as by sharing your learning, giving others your support, and thanking people for their contribution. Helping others will remind you of your own skills. Teach others what you want to learn. Remember that a good work–life balance is achieved through mutually supportive relationships at work and at home.

101 Have the courage to choose the life you want to lead.

▲ CELEBRATING WITH COLLEAGUES

Success is an ongoing process, not a final goal. Celebrate success with your team at significant points during a project, not just at its completion, so that you sustain morale and motivation.

ASSESSING YOUR WORK–LIFE BALANCE

Find out how well you manage your work–life balance by responding to the following statements. Circle the options that are closest to your experience. Be as honest as you can: if your answer is "never", circle Option 1; if it is "always", circle Option 4, and so on. Add your scores together, and refer to the Analysis to see how you scored. Use your answers to identify areas that need improvement.

OPTIONS

1 Never

2 Occasionally

3 Frequently

4 Always

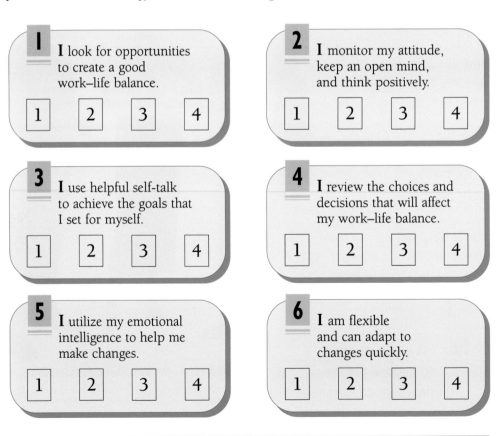

1 I look for opportunities to create a good work–life balance.

1 2 3 4

2 I monitor my attitude, keep an open mind, and think positively.

1 2 3 4

3 I use helpful self-talk to achieve the goals that I set for myself.

1 2 3 4

4 I review the choices and decisions that will affect my work–life balance.

1 2 3 4

5 I utilize my emotional intelligence to help me make changes.

1 2 3 4

6 I am flexible and can adapt to changes quickly.

1 2 3 4

7 I prioritize my loving relationships and put them at the centre of my life.

1 2 3 4

8 I spend rewarding, quality time with my family and friends.

1 2 3 4

9 I schedule a healthy amount of leisure time each week.

1 2 3 4

10 I clearly identify my key objectives before I take action.

1 2 3 4

11 I use a structured action plan to achieve my objectives.

1 2 3 4

12 I invest time and energy in communicating effectively with others.

1 2 3 4

13 I seek to understand other people's points of view.

1 2 3 4

14 I try to find solutions that are best for everyone involved.

1 2 3 4

15 I have meetings with my team to generate new and creative solutions.

1 2 3 4

16 I am proactive about making changes for the better.

1 2 3 4

17 I identify the best working options that match my objectives.

1 2 3 4

18 I avoid "starting early, finishing late" on the majority of work days.

1 2 3 4

19 I do not make a habit of taking work home to finish at night.

1 2 3 4

20 I rarely go into the office to work at weekends.

1 2 3 4

21 I use my time away from work effectively and make the most of my leisure.

1 2 3 4

22 I take responsibility for my choices and actions.

1 2 3 4

23 I recognize that I am constantly learning and developing my skills.

1 2 3 4

24 I make time for the most important people in my life.

1 2 3 4

25 I know what I want to say "yes" to in my work and in my life.

1 2 3 4

26 I believe in my ability to achieve my goals and objectives.

1 2 3 4

27 I recognize my value to my organization and my family.

| 1 | 2 | 3 | 4 |

28 I use stress as a trigger to make changes for the better.

| 1 | 2 | 3 | 4 |

29 I eat a healthy, well-balanced diet that consists mainly of fresh food.

| 1 | 2 | 3 | 4 |

30 I take exercise that refreshes and energizes me.

| 1 | 2 | 3 | 4 |

31 I schedule plenty of time to relax and enjoy myself.

| 1 | 2 | 3 | 4 |

32 I celebrate the journey of my life and enjoy all my successes.

| 1 | 2 | 3 | 4 |

ANALYSIS

Now you have completed the self-assessment, add up your total score and check your work–life balance by referring to the corresponding evaluation below. Identify your weakest areas, and refer to the relevant chapters in this section to develop and hone those skills.

32–62: You are working too hard and need to examine your priorities. Implement the strategies in this chapter to try something new and improve your work–life balance.

65–95: To make changes for the better you need to know how, and you must want to. You are doing well, but allow yourself the chance to enjoy even more balance.

96–128: You are focused, well-motivated, and have a clear direction. Remember: work–life balance is an ongoing process, so keep refining your skills.

MANAGING YOUR CAREER

INTRODUCTION

The ability to maintain a dynamic career path and develop a portfolio of skills and achievements is a must for managers. Managing Your Career shows you how to build on past experience and maximize opportunities to achieve success and fulfilment in your working life. From reviewing your current situation to exploring career options, monitoring development, and handling crises and change, all the key aspects of effective career planning are covered. With 101 practical tips scattered throughout, and self-assessment exercises that enable you to evaluate how well you have managed your career to date, this is an invaluable reference for every ambitious manager.

MAPPING THE FUTURE

Effective planning is at the heart of career success. Assess your position now, decide where you want to be, and then use your experience to help you map the best route for the future.

WHY MANAGE YOUR CAREER?

Success and happiness at work are rarely achieved by chance. Recognize that by taking a proactive approach to managing your career, you are more likely to realize your ambitions, do justice to your skills, and stay in full employment.

1 View managing your career as an exciting new project.

2 Give planning your career the time and effort it deserves.

MAKING WISE CHOICES

To make the most of all the career choices that face you during your working life, be clear about your goals, alert to opportunities, and quick to make key decisions when necessary. Effective planning will help you be prepared and focused, so that when you need to, you can make the right choices. Nobody wants to look back on their career at retirement and wish they had taken a different path or done things another way.

- A career can be likened to a journey: if that journey is to be a purposeful expedition rather than an aimless one, it will need to be managed well.

- The degree of satisfaction you gain from your work is within your own control.

3 Concentrate on career opportunities.

GAINING A SENSE OF PURPOSE

The most successful career paths have good planning, a sense of direction, and clear milestones along the way. A career path needs to be flexible but it should always be structured. If you have a "map" of your intended route, you can make sure that all the activities in your working life help further your aims and give you a sense of purpose. Managing your career does not mean closing your mind to luck and chance, but involves talking and thinking about your career in a methodical way. This will help you gain further insights and recognize any opportunities as they arise, so that you can make the most of them.

MAKING THE MOST OF YOUR EXPERIENCE

It is rare to know from your first experience of work where you want to go next in your career. Often people find out what suits them over time, learning from their reactions to different positions, environments, roles, and responsibilities. Actively managing your career will help you use all your experience effectively, so that you avoid repeating less successful events and maximize your satisfaction with your working life. You will be better equipped to foresee situations, make sensible, realistic plans, and act upon them. As a result, you will have more confidence and be clearer about your personal priorities.

4 Be prepared to look back as well as ahead.

Team member reaches milestone in career plan

Manager congratulates team member on promotion

FULFILLING YOUR POTENTIAL ▶
Taking control of your career encourages you to make the most of your capabilities so that you feel challenged and stimulated at work. Achieving career goals also brings a great sense of satisfaction.

UNDERSTANDING CAREER MANAGEMENT

Managing your career is not an option but a necessity in order to halt or prevent career drift. Be proactive in developing your career plan so that you do not miss out on the rewards that more focus, drive, and direction can bring.

5 Note that career management gives you added focus in other areas of life.

QUESTIONS TO ASK YOURSELF

Q What does managing my career mean to me?

Q What is the appeal of looking deeper into this subject?

Q How have I managed my career so far?

Q Which aspects of my career do I think need attention?

Q How would I describe my career outlook?

6 Keep your longer-term career goals private.

CLARIFYING YOUR JOURNEY

Just as you would not set off on a journey without a destination and a rough route in mind, so you need to plan in a similar way to make a success of your career. By being clear about how to achieve your goals, you will maximize your chances of success. If you are at all career-minded, then you may already be managing your career to some extent. However, there is always scope to raise your career consciousness through analysis and deliberation.

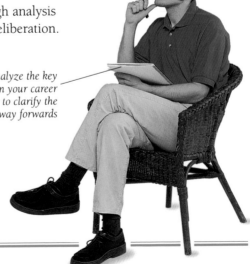

Analyze the key points in your career so far to clarify the way forwards

INVESTING IN YOURSELF ▶
The concept of career management may sound daunting, especially if you feel your life is already too busy. But taking time to consider your career in detail is a valuable investment that will enable you to enrich your working life.

WORKING TO A PLAN

Some people have an early career idea that sustains them for years and they dedicate time and effort to pursuing this single goal. What they gain in determination, however, they risk losing in not being adaptable and open to the unexpected. Other people are vague about what they want to achieve and are content to see what turns up in the way of career opportunities. These people benefit from being flexible over their career options but may not progress very fast. The best approach is to work to a structured plan to give you a sense of direction and prevent career drift, but at the same time staying flexible to help you adjust to changes along the way.

7 Aim to be active in the management of your career.

POINTS TO REMEMBER

- The results you achieve depend on the choices and decisions that you make.
- You are responsible for the choices that you make, and you can take control of your work and life balance.

8 Always look ahead, even when you are happy at work and planning seems unnecessary.

▼ BEING AN EFFECTIVE CAREER MANAGER

A career manager has a proactive approach to life, taking the initiative and making things happen. A career drifter has a passive approach, preferring inactivity and taking the easiest option.

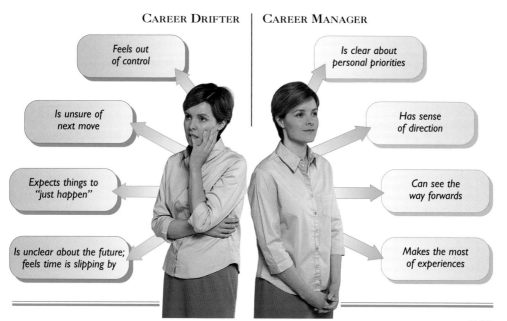

CAREER DRIFTER | CAREER MANAGER

Feels out of control

Is clear about personal priorities

Is unsure of next move

Has sense of direction

Expects things to "just happen"

Can see the way forwards

Is unclear about the future; feels time is slipping by

Makes the most of experiences

INCREASING YOUR CONTROL

Managing your career does not mean that it will become totally predictable, because there will always be certain factors beyond your control. Relocation of company premises, changes in personnel, fluctuating commercial fortunes, or management restructures are examples of decisions over which you may not have any influence because they arise from the external environment. There will also be times, such as in unexpected or difficult situations, when you cannot predict or control your own reactions. However, having mapped out your future, you will be able to focus on your longer-term goals during these challenging periods, which can help you stay objective and increase your control.

9 Remember that it is never too early or too late to start managing your career.

WHAT IS A CAREER?

A career is much more than just full-time employment. The following activities should all be considered an important part of your career:

- Permanent or casual contracts (however short)
- Freelance, consultancy, or self-employment
- Post-retirement activities
- Formal education and training
- Informal studies or self-taught material
- Development activities (work-based or private learning)
- Voluntary work or any charitable activity
- Political or public representation or involvement
- Hobbies or interests

MAKING CHOICES ▶ IN LATER LIFE

Although George had reached retirement age, he was still able to benefit from managing his career. His years of experience doing voluntary work stood him in good stead when he decided to actively pursue a new position. The church committee was happy to employ George as church warden, and he continued to enjoy his working life and develop new skills in this role.

CASE STUDY

George had been developing his voluntary activities in his local church over many years. As he approached retirement from his full-time paid employment in a bank, he realized that he was not ready to stop work completely. Approaching the church committee, he asked about the possibility of part-time work there. As a result, when he retired from working at the bank at the age of 65, he began a new career as church warden, caring for the church premises and organizing local activities. Although the salary was much lower than before, he gained great satisfaction from this new career development, which sustained him over the next decade. In addition, he felt that he was making a valuable contribution to the community while still enjoying working, albeit for fewer hours and at a reduced level of energy.

KEEPING UP TO DATE

Changes in the work environment can sometimes creep up on you when you are simply busy living your life. Just think about the developments in communications technology over the past 30 years and you have a vivid example of the pace of recent inventions. Career management involves paying attention to your own development so that you are continually learning and adding to your experience. By doing this you avoid the risk of being outrun by people whose skills are more recent and up to date.

10 Use every opportunity to learn and develop your skills.

DEFINING KEY ASPECTS OF CAREER MANAGEMENT

KEY AREAS	FACTORS TO CONSIDER
SELF-ANALYSIS Learning about yourself by evaluating your past experience.	● An honest appraisal of your career will help you draw useful conclusions about your strengths and weaknesses. ● Analysis will help you decide where you will "fit" best.
MARKET ASSESSMENT Understanding what is on offer in the employment market.	● A thorough research of the job market is a means of discovering relevant opportunities in your field. ● Consider your own contribution to the world of work.
TARGET-SETTING Establishing what you want to achieve and when.	● Setting targets will give you more focus. ● Once you have set targets, you can plan the steps needed to achieve them so that you progress smoothly.
CHANGE MANAGEMENT Tackling employment difficulties when they arise.	● Handling change effectively involves being adaptable but prepared to alter career direction if necessary. ● Involve other people if change is major.
MONITORING Keeping a check on progress towards career goals.	● Holding regular reviewing and planning sessions will ensure that you stay on track. ● Monitor new developments that may affect your career.

ASSESSING YOUR CURRENT SITUATION

We are all at different stages in our lives and you may want to take stock of your present situation because you feel you need to make a change. Check and analyze your progress to see exactly where you are now and what may lay ahead.

11 Know yourself – this is the key to managing your career successfully.

12 Ensure that you understand all the different aspects of your career.

STOPPING TO THINK ▼
Feeling bored or under-employed is a sign that you need to stop, take stock of your current position, and identify how to put under-utilized skills to better use.

CHECKING YOUR PROGRESS

Everyone can benefit from checking their career progress. If you are dissatisfied, it makes sense to stop and ask yourself why. Even if everything is going well, it is still a good idea to check that your career path is proceeding properly and that you are doing enough to maintain this progress. By taking stock of your current position, you can identify what to do next. Look at where you have resources to use and where there are gaps to be filled, perhaps by training, mentoring, or a change of career. Is there any aspect of your current position that you would like to change? For example, you may feel that you deserve more financial reward for your effort, a promotion, or a new challenge.

13 Use dissatisfaction to prompt you to plan your career more actively.

ANALYZING YOUR PROGRESS

How did you get to this point in your career? To find out, consider your career in three ways. First, pay more attention to events and changes that have occurred. Second, study closely the experiences you have gone through so that you can analyze the causes and effects of your own behaviour and that of others. Third, evaluate the consequences of particular types of behaviour and decisions that you have taken. These three tools – attention, analysis, and evaluation – can provide the information you need.

CONSIDERING YOUR CAREER

Log each change or event as it happens

↓

Analyze how the event has taken place

↓

Think how present behaviour could influence the future

↓

Use the analysis to direct your future endeavours

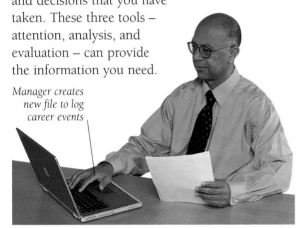

Manager creates new file to log career events

▲ EVALUATING CAREER MOVES
Get into the habit of logging events and career changes as soon as possible. Make a start by analyzing what has happened so far, using your curriculum vitae to prompt your memory.

14 Analyze the past to help you illuminate the future.

TOP TEN REASONS FOR CAREER REPOSITIONING

Here are some factors that have motivated others to start managing their career. Do any of them relate to you at the moment?
- Facing a crisis
- Reaching a career crossroads
- Having to make a crucial decision
- Recovering from a difficult period
- Needing longer-term changes
- Wanting to improve future prospects
- Looking to match the fortunes of others
- Ending a period of drift
- Feeling confused and unclear
- Wanting to take more control over all areas of life

GETTING STARTED

Sometimes the most daunting part of a project is simply getting started. Learn to see career management as enjoyable and instructive in its own right, then you will be able to learn from the process as well as focus more sharply on your future.

> **15** Take charge of your career to make it more satisfying.

QUESTIONS TO ASK YOURSELF

Q In which direction would I like to be heading?

Q Do I have an ideal career destination in mind?

Q How will I make time available to manage my career on a regular basis?

Q What resources do I need to help me?

Q What preparations should I be making at this stage?

MAKING A COMMITMENT

As with any project, to succeed you need to commit yourself fully to the idea of what you are doing and acknowledge in advance the changes that may have to be made. It will involve looking at all areas of your life and could have an impact on your private life and implications for your family. Are you prepared to be honest with yourself, to be open to all possibilities, and to be really thorough in your analysis? Making the time, generating the energy, and finding the focus to concentrate on your career may be stretching.

There may also be risks involved, but there will be rewards for those who have an open mind and a willingness to explore their career possibilities. You will soon have another management skill in your portfolio: that of career management.

Clip out any career articles that interest you

◀ **CREATING A CAREER FILE**
Make up a file of your career thoughts and ideas. Collect job advertisements and course information that interest you. Even if these items are not relevant straight away, they may be useful later. You are gathering raw material to help you in the planning process ahead. This file may also provide useful data for future job applications.

16 Invest more time in your career in order to achieve greater rewards.

POINTS TO REMEMBER

- You should always be truthful with yourself and about yourself.
- Changing your approach could change the direction that your career takes.
- It may be necessary to change your appearance or your behaviour to pursue a career.

CHOOSING YOUR TOOLS

To complete any job effectively, you need the appropriate tools that reflect your own style and personality. Some people prefer to work alone, perhaps using a computer or a book. Some prefer to use a professional adviser, or a close friend, colleague, or peer group. Sometimes a mixture of these will be appropriate. Use whichever tools you feel most comfortable with, provided they help you progress with your analysis and evaluation.

17 Realize that deciding to explore your career requires effort and application.

USING A SPIDER DIAGRAM

A spider diagram is a useful device for making notes about your career. It is a pictorial method that can help you release your creative thinking, make connections between subjects, and see patterns in your thoughts and behaviour that may otherwise remain hidden. A diagram is also more memorable than a list.

GOALS
- Salary rise
- Find out more
- Courses
- Fitness course

RESPECT
- Higher status
- Qualifications
- Study
- Distance learning

Life and career plans

HEALTH
- Use relaxation techniques
- Join fitness class
- Buy exercise video
- Walk more
- Take up yoga

MONEY
- Underpaid
- Male colleagues paid more
- Make case for salary review
- Talk to boss

TIME
- Buy electronic diary
- Leave work early
- Delegate minor tasks

◀ **CREATING A DIAGRAM**
Start by writing down a topic in the centre of the page. Then note your ideas in branch form radiating out from the centre. Work clockwise and keep to a few words for each point.

SETTING GOALS AND TARGETS

Thinking about goals involves envisaging where you want to get to and how you intend to get there. An essential first step is to focus on your ultimate aims. Then set key career markers on the way that you can view as your targets.

18 Keep your options open – it is rare to find one perfect career solution.

POINTS TO REMEMBER

- Goals may change over time but an ultimate aim should always be kept in sight.
- Most people underplay their talents rather than ask themselves if they could aim higher.
- Work can bring benefits ranging from financial to status to social rewards, so knowing what motivates you is important.
- Career goals indicate whether you are essentially happy with your course or need to make a significant change of career.

DEFINING YOUR GOALS

It may feel difficult to be clear about your ultimate career goals at first. However, you do not need to be too definite about them at this stage. Write down the first three things that occur to you as worth aiming for. Be ambitious for yourself, particularly if you are only just starting out in your career. If you are trying to establish new goals as a result of redundancy or an abrupt change of circumstance, you may initially feel uncertain or unconfident about the future. In these situations it is still important to be determined and to avoid allowing a difficult experience to hold you back.

Tells friend that she wants to be her own boss

CLARIFYING ▶ YOUR GOALS

Discuss your goals with a partner or colleague to help you make them as specific as possible. This will make it easier to work towards them. Seek to turn vague goals such as "I want more responsibility", into concrete ones such as "I want to become head of my section."

CONSIDERING BOUNDARIES

Think through the aims you have written down. Ruling out the impractical will save you time and remove distractions. Is changing location out of the question? Will you need to study? If you need to keep earning money while you study, work out how much you need to live on compared to your present income. This will clarify how flexible you can afford to be. Perhaps distance learning will enable you to continue earning while you learn? Do you have, or plan to have, a family, and does that need to be incorporated into your career management plans?

19 Consider enrolling in distance learning if studying for qualifications while working is your goal.

QUESTIONS TO ASK YOURSELF

Q Do I have at least three targets to help me reach each of my goals?

Q Are my targets both ambitious enough and achievable?

Q Have I made a serious undertaking with myself to pursue these goals?

Responds by asking what exactly she wants to do

SETTING TARGETS

Now you have identified some goals, break them down into smaller steps. In this way you will be able to move forwards. Suppose you had written down "become a leader in my field". That is unlikely to happen overnight – it will need planning and effort if it is to come true – and several things will need to occur for this career goal to be achieved. You may need to study to a higher level and establish a reputation in clinical work or on the conference circuit. You may need to publish details of your work in academic or professional journals, and you will need to have some original work under your belt. This aim, therefore, has four distinct targets to use as milestones in your career: study, establish a reputation, get published, and produce original work. As you reach each target you will know that you are nearer your goal.

20 Make sure you choose the way of working that feels most comfortable to you.

IDENTIFYING YOUR ASSETS

Assets in career terms include your strengths of personality and work achievements. Identify your assets and the skills and knowledge you have accumulated in order to provide a sturdy foundation on which to build your future plans.

21 Ask friends and colleagues for their perceptions of your character.

22 Try to evaluate how others see you to understand your own assets.

DESCRIBING YOUR PERSONAL STYLE

You need to understand the type of person you are to envisage where you would best fit into the working world. Think how your friends and colleagues would describe you at your best, and then make a list of your assets. Remember to include any positive feedback you have received during appraisals and in references, and any compliments paid to you by colleagues.

LISTING YOUR ASSETS

Use the following list of assets to help prompt you when creating your own list of attributes that describe your character. Do not worry about ordering or qualifying what you write.

- Able to work alone
- Accurate
- Adaptable
- Alert
- Approachable
- Articulate
- Assertive
- Calm
- Capable
- Cautious
- Collaborator
- Committed
- Competent
- Confident
- Co-operative
- Creative
- Decisive
- Dedicated
- Determined
- Dynamic
- Enthusiastic
- Flexible
- Friendly
- Good at deadlines
- Good manager
- Hardworking
- Humorous
- Innovative
- Lively
- Loyal
- Methodical
- Motivator
- Optimistic
- Organized
- Patient
- Perceptive
- Polite
- Proactive
- Punctual
- Quick to learn
- Reliable
- Responsible
- Self-motivated
- Sensible
- Sensitive
- Serious-minded
- Shows flair
- Steadfast
- Strong
- Tactful
- Thorough
- Versatile

23 Retrace your steps as a useful exercise in learning.

24 View your portfolio as all the elements of your career so far.

ANALYZING YOUR DESCRIPTION

Review your list of assets. Do they all describe similar strengths or do they show a very varied character? Does the list make you think of any particular work environment that would be suitable (or unsuitable) for this kind of person? Are you happy with the picture presented by this list? Do you wish you could add different words? Are there actions you could take to help you expand the list? For example, if you want to be able to add the word "assertive", could you gain more assertiveness through training? Keep a record of the list and your thoughts about it for future reflection.

COMPILING YOUR PORTFOLIO

Your portfolio should include all your skills, knowledge, and achievements gained from all your employment endeavours so far. It is important to remember all that you have achieved so that you can build up an accurate chronology of your work history for your portfolio. List the positions you have held, the places in which you have been based, and the skills you have learned. Try to fill in any gaps or sketchy details, such as missing months. Ascertaining exactly where an assignment took place, for example, may help you remember how you felt about being there.

▼ RECORDING YOUR EXPERIENCES
In a notebook, using perhaps a page for each year, enter all the different activities on which you have spent time, the skills and knowledge you have gained, and where you have been based.

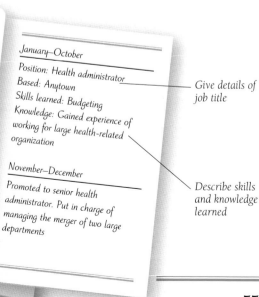

January–October

Position: Health administrator
Based: Anytown
Skills learned: Budgeting
Knowledge: Gained experience of working for large health-related organization

Give details of job title

November–December

Promoted to senior health administrator. Put in charge of managing the merger of two large departments

Describe skills and knowledge learned

Record any achievements

EVALUATING YOUR PORTFOLIO

Exploring the choices and changes you have made in the past can highlight trends and connections that have affected you. Use this new insight to see the most effective way forwards, minimize negative patterns, and maximize useful connections.

25 Try to identify any recurring themes or unexpected links.

26 Read old diaries to find out how you felt during different work phases.

LOOKING BACK

Now that you have all the information about your employment history in your portfolio, analyze how you felt about each stage. This will enable you to be clear about which elements you want to maximize and which to minimize. Constructing a timeline of your level of satisfaction at each point can help you locate patterns and themes in what you have done in the past – some may have been beneficial to your career, while others may have held you back. Plot the patterns on a graph to show the ups and downs of each stage. Accuracy is not as important as the relative high and low points. Think around the job to include the peer group, managers, and the team with which you worked most closely.

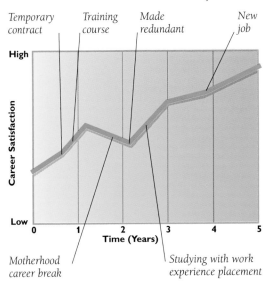

Temporary contract

Training course

Made redundant

New job

Motherhood career break

Studying with work experience placement

◀ **PLOTTING A TIMELINE**
Create a timeline to represent your career path. Can you see any patterns emerging about where and when you were most and least satisfied? What was happening in your life then? Analyze and learn from the material that emerges.

USING PHOTOGRAPHS AS PROMPTS

Photographs can be a helpful indication of your state of mind at different times. Sometimes the camera captures expressions that we are not aware of. Collect old shots of you at different stages in your career. How do you look in each – on top of things, full of pride, and with a sense of worth? Perhaps there are periods when you seem glum or depressed, where you are not taking as much care of yourself as you should? Ask friends and family if they remember you during these different phases to see if their recollections tally with your own. You could rank the photographs in order of happy appearance and see if this ties in with your memory of the satisfaction you were gaining at work at the time. Work takes up such a major slice of our lives that you will often find this to be the case.

◀ **LOOKING FOR CLUES**
Study old photo albums for insights into how your career has affected your emotional wellbeing.

LEARNING FROM THE HIGH POINTS

The times in your career when you have felt most successful will be clear indicators of situations that played to your strengths. List the happy times, detailing the position you held, the team in which you operated, the resulting achievements, and the way you felt about each situation. Which strengths were you exhibiting at which time? Assess whether the type of role you played made a difference to the way you performed. Perhaps you were given extra responsibility and lived up to expectations, or perhaps you were working as part of a tightly knit team that brought out the best in you? Or perhaps you enjoyed happy experiences because you were interested in the products or services with which you were involved, or the environment in which you worked.

QUESTIONS TO ASK YOURSELF

Q How do my career peaks and troughs help me plan ahead?

Q Can I identify helpful situations to seek out from now on?

Q Are there scenarios to avoid repeating in the future?

Q Do the answers to the last two questions point to a particular career direction?

27 Try to find reasons for the most successful periods in your career.

UNDERSTANDING THE LOW POINTS

Even in the shortest career you are likely to have spent some time feeling rather uninspired. Examine those periods now to see if they illustrate situations to avoid in the future. Were you working for employers you disliked or within teams that were dysfunctional? What effect did these periods have on you and on your general morale? Perhaps the culture of the sector in which the job was located did not match your values? How did these differences make you feel, and what, if anything, did you do about it?

28 Analyze the low points in your career and the reasons for them.

▼ LEARNING FROM LOW POINTS

In this example, a manager's experience of a festering dispute between two colleagues proves a valuable learning aid. He now encourages his team to discuss their differences and find ways of resolving them.

Team member freely airs his opinion

Manager acts as arbiter

Team member expresses her point of view

CASE STUDY

Bill, a sales manager, and Nancy, an office manager, both worked for the same manufacturing organization. Bill enjoyed his job immensely, and ran a close-knit team that strove hard to reach its sales targets. He was keen to build on his success within the organization for a couple of years, after which he planned to realize his ambitions by moving on to gain wider experience of sales management in a different working environment.

Nancy was miserable in her role as office manager. She felt stultified by the lack of interest shown in her work by her boss and often felt remote from the organization because it was difficult to see how her team contributed to the end product. There were no challenging sales targets to reach and no contact with the organization's customers. She could feel her morale falling and her confidence slowly ebbing away and knew that she must move to a new job soon.

◀ GAINING FROM EXPERIENCE

Bill's experience of working for a manufacturing organization was a very positive one. He felt integrated into the firm and was determined to learn as much as possible before moving on. Nancy learned that working in isolation was demotivating for her and decided to look for a new job before her morale fell any further.

RECOGNIZING PATTERNS

When situations crop up again and again, even if not in exactly the same form, we can learn from them. These patterns may help us move forwards, or they may block our progress. Can you see any patterns in your past? Have there been several similar incidents or working relationships? Perhaps people consistently relate to you in a certain manner or perhaps you keep finding yourself in similar situations? It may be the first time that you have looked back at your career in this way. Try to think about any aspect of your own behaviour that may contribute to the frequency of the pattern occurring.

29 Be productive in your analysis – avoid regretting past behaviour.

30 Move on if you cannot change or learn from recurring patterns.

DOS AND DON'TS

✔ Do make sure you reward yourself for your successes.

✔ Do ask your friends, partner, and colleagues for feedback on your work–life balance.

✘ Don't focus on your mistakes and ignore your successes.

✘ Don't underestimate the value of coaching in helping you clarify your objectives.

▼ **SUMMARIZING YOUR EVALUATION**
Write down what you have learned from your analysis to help increase your understanding. Think about key areas for improvement and then record what action you plan to take and by when, so that you feel you have committed to it in writing.

Joe Smith: ANALYSIS

Mistakes	Running restaurant with my brother – I jumped in too quickly.
Disappointments	Two years of low income and stressful family relationships.
Learning points	However exciting the career prospect, I must thoroughly evaluate every project solely on business grounds before I commit to it.
Areas for development	I need to improve my financial and budgeting analysis and marketing skills so that I am able to assess the business feasibility of projects more confidently.
Action	Look into college courses and aim to start studying part-time by end of year.

— Previous difficulties caused by eagerness for new projects

— Learned to temper enthusiasm with harder-edged business analysis

EXPLORING THE POSSIBILITIES

Any dreams you have had of your perfect career should not be ignored. If you have imagined career paths that would bring you great satisfaction, consider them now in more detail to check their feasibility. They may be more achievable than you thought.

31 Ask family and friends what kind of job they think would suit you.

32 Take time out to revisit forgotten plans and dream up some solutions.

DARING TO DREAM

Managing your career involves exploring dreams. Do you have a wish to improve your qualifications or an old hankering to follow a career that requires specialized skills? Perhaps you dreamed of being a ballet dancer or a brain surgeon, or following the same career path as a friend? Or you may have a few vague ideas but do not know enough to do anything about them at this stage. Be explicit about each idea and explore what there is to be gained from taking any of them further.

TAKING THE LONG VIEW

Every job has periods of stagnation. Try to avoid thinking that total happiness and continual movement forwards should be the norm. If there is still scope for progress later, treading water for a time is fine. For example, you may find that the results for your division are poorer than you expected. If you know that a new computer sales system and a thorough retraining package will soon be introduced, it may be better to wait and see what happens. Think about your career over a period of a year. It takes a good six months in any new position to feel really confident about it.

POINTS TO REMEMBER

- Beware of acting hastily. It is often a good idea to bide your time until a conclusion is clearer.
- Appealing career ideas may hint at undeveloped talents.
- Having decided that a career possibility is not for you, the idea should be discarded so that you are able to move on.
- If there is an activity you love, consider whether there is any way of fitting it into your working life.

PUSHING BACK THE BOUNDARIES

Spending time on the activities you like best can seem like an expensive luxury. However, if there are activities that you have always wanted to spend time on, it is worth considering ways of bringing them into your present working life. Many people have creative abilities that have to take a back seat because of the need to seek gainful employment. To achieve a more satisfying balance in your life, look at how you can devote more time to doing what you enjoy most.

33 Think what you want to see when you look back in 10 years' time.

Qualifies in interior design and works freelance to gain experience

DREAM	OPTIONS	ACTION
To run my own interior design and decorating business	Look at part-time college courses and career prospects once qualified	Enrol on course and help friends with redecoration schemes to test commitment

Employee reads design magazines to help with research

▲ REALIZING A DREAM

If you wish to pursue a new career direction, research any training needed to obtain necessary qualifications and look at the prospects. You can then plan your action accordingly.

DOS AND DON'TS

✔ Do think back to your earliest innovative career ideas.

✔ Do reflect on the work of people you know.

✔ Do consider occupations that you have heard of or read about.

✘ Don't be constrained by your past work history.

✘ Don't rule out options that sound unlikely without thinking about whether they could be made to happen.

✘ Don't include anything totally unrealistic.

FORMING CONCLUSIONS

Think about what you want to achieve in the future and create a plan of action to help you plot the way forwards. Do you need to find out more about career possibilities? You may need to gather more information. To help you understand your path, be clear and honest about your own motivation. What do you want to achieve in 10 years' time? Money, an expert reputation, increased status, or an improved work–life balance?

ASSESSING YOUR CAREER MANAGEMENT

E valuate your current career management by working through this simple questionnaire. Be as honest as you can and answer with the first response that comes into your mind. If your answer is "disagree", circle Option 1; if it is "agree" circle Option 4; and so on. Add your scores together, then refer to the Analysis to see what that score represents.

OPTIONS

1 Disagree

2 Slightly disagree

3 Slightly agree

4 Agree

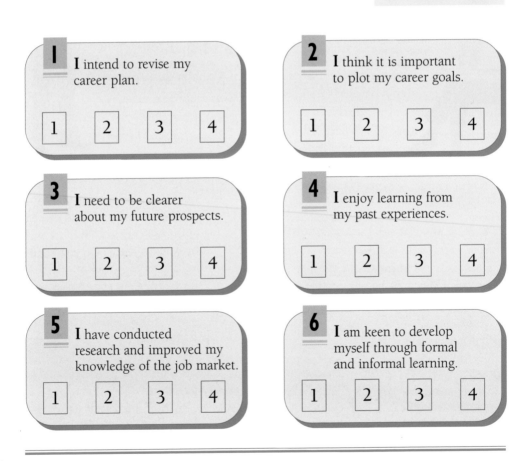

1 I intend to revise my career plan.

1 2 3 4

2 I think it is important to plot my career goals.

1 2 3 4

3 I need to be clearer about my future prospects.

1 2 3 4

4 I enjoy learning from my past experiences.

1 2 3 4

5 I have conducted research and improved my knowledge of the job market.

1 2 3 4

6 I am keen to develop myself through formal and informal learning.

1 2 3 4

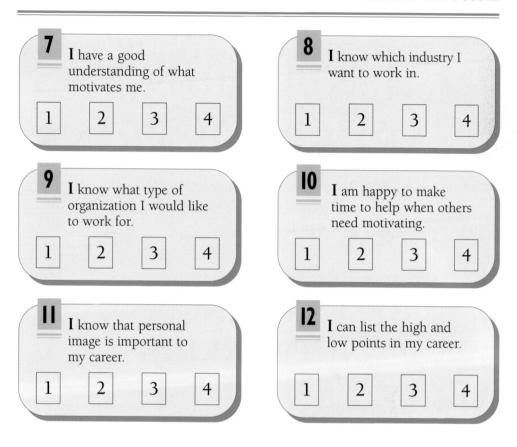

7 I have a good understanding of what motivates me.

1 2 3 4

8 I know which industry I want to work in.

1 2 3 4

9 I know what type of organization I would like to work for.

1 2 3 4

10 I am happy to make time to help when others need motivating.

1 2 3 4

11 I know that personal image is important to my career.

1 2 3 4

12 I can list the high and low points in my career.

1 2 3 4

ANALYSIS

Add up your score and check your career management skills by referring to the evaluation below. Identify your weakest areas and refer to the relevant parts of this chapter to help you refine your skills.

12–26: You seem half-hearted about your prospects. You may want to come back to this subject later when the benefits of career management are clearer.

27–39: You are learning about career management and can analyze your experience and assess your present position. Think where you are aiming in order to complete the process.

40–48: You can see how your career will be improved by thorough planning and continual personal development. You will soon be in a position to maximize opportunities that come your way.

EXPLORING CAREER OPTIONS

It is important to be aware of the kind of work that is currently available in the marketplace. Do as much research as possible and use your network of friends and contacts.

RESEARCHING AND NETWORKING

Many jobs are never advertised but are filled through word of mouth. Find out how the companies concerned recruit their staff and how you can access networks that can help you track down, and be considered for, these job opportunities.

34 Be supportive of others – you may need their help later in life.

35 Read reference or yearbooks to gain an overview of current key industry players.

ACCESSING INFORMATION

Having accurate information about companies, employment opportunities, and the work market is vital for working out your next career move. Research carefully the companies and markets in which you have an interest. Make your research formal and deliberate, and give yourself plenty of time in which to do it. Use your contacts with family, friends, colleagues, and associates to give you further insight into potential job opportunities.

APPRAISING THE MARKET

Find out as much as you can about the business that interests you. Read newspapers and magazines, tune into television or radio documentaries, surf the Web, or even attend industry seminars and exhibitions to keep you informed. Stay abreast of current market conditions and future forecasts that might affect job availability. If you are keen to work in the non-profit sector, for example, you need to be aware that government funding can have a big impact on job vacancies in this area because the level of funding fluctuates with different economic and political priorities.

TALKING TO AGENCIES ▶

Employment agencies have their finger on the pulse of demand and supply. Ask for an interview and check out the state of the market in their skill area.

36 Access websites of organizations to see how they project themselves.

37 Monitor job sites on the internet to find out where the opportunities are.

POINTS TO REMEMBER

- Finding out about an organization's working environment and culture can pay dividends when you apply for a job.

- Reading material published by organizations in which you are interested will help you find out about current priorities, policies, and plans.

- Researching professional or trade association websites and publications can illuminate unfamiliar areas of work.

Specialist describes a thriving market – but only for people with the right skills

CHOOSING YOUR APPROACH

Since organizations and sectors tend to recruit staff in different ways, you need to find out how and where they recruit, what they are looking for, and how you can apply for any vacancies. Large corporations, for example, rely mainly on press or website advertisements or recruitment agencies. Smaller firms may be more open to approaches from individuals, particularly if the person seems to meet a current need and can be hired without recruitment costs. Some organizations prefer to fill vacancies on a temporary or contract basis, which allows them more time to recruit permanent staff.

JUSTIFYING NETWORKING

Networking may sound a cold and callous way of using your friends and colleagues to further your career, but it is actually a sensible extension to your research methods. Friends have probably enquired about your work or asked you to keep your eyes open for future job vacancies at your company in the past. Most of us are only too pleased to help others in this way. Often the information you gain through networking is about more than just a specific vacancy, and this may turn out to have a greater relevance than you think.

38 Think like a careers adviser – ask people about their working lives.

Even friends' networks may prove useful

FRIENDS' CONTACTS

REMOTE CONNECTIONS

CONTACTS

ASSOCIATES

FRIENDS

FAMILY

Family and friends are the most immediate sources of networking

▲ LISTING CONTACTS
Begin by listing all the people you know who may have access to information about the kind of career that interests you. Think of all your personal and work contacts – these are your network.

ASSESSING THE JOB MARKET

Use newspapers to help you with your assessment of the job market. Look at the job vacancy advertisements to get an idea of buoyant sectors and information about the standards required for each job. Study the financial and business pages for a more in-depth focus on longer-term employment and performance trends in different sectors. Take time to digest specialist or feature articles that can give a wider picture of the world of work.

◀ READING THE PAPERS
Choose newspapers with the largest number of relevant job vacancies and study them carefully, reading articles that you would usually pass over.

DOS AND DON'TS

✔ Do think about all your contacts, past and present, and be creative about how they could be of assistance.

✔ Do show appropriate gratitude when people try to help you.

✔ Do give people the chance to say "no" should they feel it would be difficult to help you for some reason.

✘ Don't feel embarrassed to approach people on your network list – think of it as seeking and offering information.

✘ Don't overload the same people all the time – no one likes to feel responsible for another's career progress.

✘ Don't forget to support other people who may need assistance from you.

39 Add names to your network whenever possible.

40 Show an interest in others so that interaction is not all one-way.

41 Use social gatherings to meet new contacts and expand your nework of contacts.

USING YOUR NETWORK

Think about how the people you have identified in your network can help you. Depending on the nature of your association and their current position, you can plan how to enlist their support. Perhaps they worked for a competing organization? If so, they might be able to give you inside information about the fortunes of key players in the sector and current priorities and policies. Perhaps they work for the company you want to move to? Begin by calling and just having a chat. Follow up with an informal lunch to take the discussion further.

◀ **NETWORK LUNCHING**
By networking, Royston succeeded in moving one step ahead of the competition and getting the job of his dreams. He and his ex-colleague had always got on well, and Royston knew that he would be happy to help him advance his career.

CASE STUDY
Royston wanted to find a job in a national broadcasting organization. He knew that all its vacancies were advertised in the press but he was keen to get any advantage that he could. He discovered that an ex-colleague now worked for the same corporation. They arranged to meet, with Royston buying lunch. For the price of a salt-beef sandwich and a cola, Royston gained in three ways. The first was that the contact sent him the internal weekly bulletin that detailed all the upcoming job vacancies seven days before they appeared in the national press. Second, his contact told him all about the working atmosphere and how he had obtained his own job. Third, the contact directed him to an article by a key department head, detailing the kind of employees he was seeking. Royston is now working in his dream job at the corporation.

EXAMINING SCOPE AND OPPORTUNITY

To help you find the right career, you need to look at the scope and focus of different employment opportunities. Consider the sector, size, and structure of different workplaces – these may be deciding factors in your choice of employment.

42 Remember that all career exploration is an evolving process.

43 Think which type of organization you would like to be with in ten years.

EVALUATING SECTORS ▼
If you envisage working in manufacturing, monitor the performance of companies within that sector to help you assess which are likely to offer most opportunity.

CONSIDERING STRUCTURE

Study an organization's management structure to help you identify new opportunities and avoid jobs with little potential for growth. Most organizations have broadly similar management structures, whatever their size or sector. Senior management has a strategic overview of the essential business, and reporting to them are the departmental or divisional managers who set the day-to-day priorities. Middle managers or supervisors report to these managers and have an overview of the teams carrying out the work.

MONITORING SECTORS

Monitor the fortunes of sectors and the companies within them. Your options will be more limited in a declining sector and vice versa. The real growth area of recent years has been in the service sector. Read the home news and business pages in the broadsheet press to assess current economic successes and failures.

CONSIDERING THE SIZE OF AN ORGANIZATION

SIZE	ADVANTAGES	DISADVANTAGES
SMALL	• Freedom to make decisions. • Involvement in all aspects of work. • Liaison with external providers and consultants. • Direct relationship with clients or customers.	• Your actions and decisions are vital, so your responsibility is greater. • Family atmosphere but family-type pressures, too. • Limited scope for progressing up the career ladder.
MEDIUM	• Teamwork is important; close relationship with colleagues. • Opportunities to see and learn from other disciplines and functions. • Chance to input your ideas. • Financial stability.	• Too large to star, too small to allow much opportunity. • People outside the company are unlikely to have heard of it. • Less secure employment than with a large organization.
LARGE	• Many career routes may be available. • More chance of organization's investment in your development. • Higher salary levels and benefits. • Has currency in wider employment market when you want to move on.	• Organization may be so large that you feel compartmentalized. • Less chance of any one individual having an effect on the company. • Can be difficult to gain recognition or a sense of achievement.

CHOOSING PUBLIC OR PRIVATE SECTORS

The old boundaries between public and private sectors are becoming increasingly blurred. Private companies support schools and hospitals; trades unions and businesses work in partnership; government and corporations cooperate on national initiatives, and the non-profit sector is keen to learn best business practice. Public sector experience is now highly valued by companies that sell goods and services to schools and hospitals. It is important to understand the differences and similarities between the sectors to enable you to talk confidently at job interviews about the environment of your choice.

QUESTIONS TO ASK YOURSELF

Q Can I imagine myself doing something completely different?

Q Do I have a business idea that could work?

Q Do I want to move into a new sector or to a different size of organization?

Q Do I want to move higher up the management ladder?

Q Would I take a pay cut to work in a non-profit organization where I would be making a contribution to society?

Using the Job Search Process

An analysis of the work market should be followed up with more detailed research into individual jobs. Go through the process of applying for vacancies to help you learn much more about the type of role that might best suit you.

44 Rehearse your presentation before you have an interview.

Targeting Your Research

Find vacancies that interest you and request job descriptions

Study the details of each job to assess your suitability for the role

Outline the contribution you could make and plan how to present your case

Compose your job application, making it as impressive as you can

If there is more that you need to know about the job, plan questions to ask

Analyzing Vacancies

Once you have looked at the job opportunities available and assessed the suitability of different business sectors, target individual vacancies in order to find out more. If you find a vacancy that really appeals to you, dissect the advertisement and any information that the employer sends you. Find out as much as possible about the organization and its products or services. List the key points of the role to establish what the employer is looking for. By going through this selection process you will discover whether you are keen on the job, or perhaps even form a very different impression of the vacancy.

Dos and Don'ts

✔ Do apply for vacancies that stretch you beyond your present level.

✔ Do maintain a positive attitude, concentrating on your strengths.

✔ Do ask for feedback; it can help you learn from a disappointment.

✘ Don't build up your hopes too high over any particular job.

✘ Don't hold back at an interview if you are enthusiastic.

✘ Don't get despondent if and when you experience rejection.

ASSESSING SUITABILITY

Job applications may take time, effort, and a substantial investment of self-confidence, but it is always worth applying for jobs you think would really suit you. Start by matching the details of the vacancy to yourself. Do you have the relevant experience, attributes, and personality to claim this job for your own? You may decide not to continue with the application once you have considered all the information, or you may be able to improve your suitability by stressing your transferable skills. For example, if you have not managed large teams before, you could emphasize your leadership role in complex projects and your varied responsibilities.

45 Show keenness in an interview, even if you are not yet sure about the job.

Candidate learns that role is far more diverse than she thought

Manager explains what job entails

KEEPING ▶
AN OPEN MIND
Approach every interview seriously, even when you are not sure that you want the job. The selection process may lead you to change your mind.

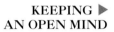

46 Keep records of all your applications and interviews.

47 Tell a company if you decide not to take the application process further.

FORMING YOUR OPINION

If you are invited to an interview, use this chance to learn more about the job and broaden your research into finding the role that is right for you. Attending the interview will enable you to look at the environment, meet people with whom you will be working, hear more about the job concerned, and seek answers to any outstanding issues. You can then make a final judgment. If you are offered the job and you liked what you saw, you can accept with confidence. If you decide not to go further with the application, view the experience as good practice. If you are not offered the position, use the process to improve future endeavours.

EXPLORING SELF-EMPLOYMENT

More and more people are considering self-employment, especially if they need to fit their work around other areas of their lives, such as family commitments. Look at the key issues of this style of working to see if it has any attractions for you.

48 Use your business networks to lead you to potential new clients.

49 Involve your family in the development of your plans.

50 Limit your initial financial investment and keep money-related paperwork.

GOING IT ALONE

Self-employment offers varied job opportunities. It is particularly appealing to parents because it gives them more flexibility to combine working and bringing up children, although it is not an easy option. Self-employment makes it easier to embark upon a new career and on very different terms from those of the employee. There is also the possibility that you may be able to develop a side-activity into your main source of income. Do you have an interest in something that you think could earn you money? Look at the local economy to see which services are in short supply.

FRANCHISING

This is a halfway house between self-employment and working for an employer: a company gives you the right to sell its product or service in return for a regular payment. Examples include make-up sold at home, fast-food restaurants, and coffee shops. You do have to pay money up front to buy into them, and they can be expensive, so make sure that the franchising company is reputable. Seek advice from statutory authorities that oversee the issue of franchises, relevant local government departments, and consumer protection agencies before you commit yourself. If possible, talk to other franchise holders before making a decision.

CONSIDERING SELF-EMPLOYMENT

BENEFITS

- Able to work at your own pace.
- Can choose not to work or mix work and domestic responsibilities.
- May decide how far to pursue business aims and invest how you want.
- Can set your own charges or fees.
- Able to experiment as you choose.
- Can share resources with others.
- Satisfaction of having control over the product or service.
- Your successes are immediately apparent.
- Work can become more creative and dynamic.

DISADVANTAGES

- Can involve working long hours, difficult to switch off.
- Requires strict self-discipline.
- Feast or famine: it is rare to have a steady stream of income.
- Need to budget carefully and plan the workload.
- Need confidence to sell and justify quality.
- Expected to be working only on each customer's particular job.
- Little financial security (unless purchased).

51 Keep three to six months' salary saved, just in case.

EXAMINING FEASIBILITY

Ask yourself a series of questions that could form the basis of an eventual business plan. The first considerations are: what would you be selling and do you have any evidence of demand? Successful businesses tend to be demand-led, where they have built up an interest in what they are selling over a period of time. Seek opinions from other people. Ask if they would buy your service or product and how much they would pay. Find out where they usually hear about such products or services. Aim to attract business before spending money on building a business profile, because without sales you will not survive.

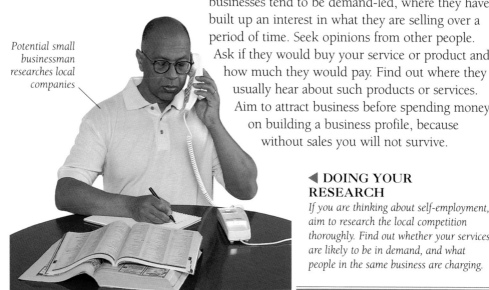

Potential small businessman researches local companies

◀ DOING YOUR RESEARCH

If you are thinking about self-employment, aim to research the local competition thoroughly. Find out whether your services are likely to be in demand, and what people in the same business are charging.

DEVELOPING YOUR CAREER

Career changes happen at intervals, but even the most determined job-changer works in a particular role most of the time. Learn how to manage your working life between these changes.

REVIEWING AND PLANNING

Developing your career involves closely monitoring your progress to ensure that future plans are still on track. Hold regular reviewing and planning sessions so that you can assess what you have achieved and what you need to do next.

52 Keep computer files on your career private, if writing them at work.

53 Gain other people's perceptions of events at work.

54 Try combining your work reviews with reviews of your life in general.

REVIEWING YOUR WORK
Establish a pattern of regularly reviewing your work in a critical but constructive way. Use this exercise to make plans for the future and learn lessons from the past. It is useful to evaluate your progress after every job change and each work project you have managed or completed. You should be incorporating normal work planning and reviewing as part of your job, but this is adding the personal career element. The results will give you raw material you can use again in future job applications and interviews as well as for your own internal job appraisals or reviews.

55 Criticize yourself constructively and be generous with self-praise.

QUESTIONS TO ASK YOURSELF

Q Can I identify aspects of my work that I would like to experience more frequently?

Q Are there aspects of my work that did not suit me that I could avoid in the future?

Q What made the high or low points of my position significant?

Q Can I improve my present situation by calling on previous experience?

UTILIZING THE PAST

Make the most of your previous experience. Analyze what has happened to you and how you feel about it, and act on it. If possible, talk to other people who were around at the time to get their views on what occurred. You are hired to do a job because you have exhibited some skills in that area in the past. As a result, you may find that you are always given the same kind of work to do, with little possibility of being given something different to try. It is often opportunities outside work that can develop you in new ways and create new talents. Perhaps there are roles in your community, part-time work that could grow into a full-time role, or self-employment opportunities that you could consider? A flexible approach to enhancing the aspects of work that please and excite you can help you maximize your satisfaction with your career.

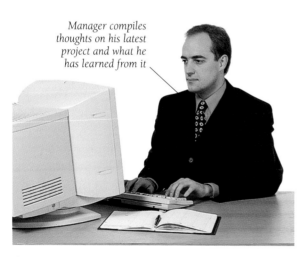

Manager compiles thoughts on his latest project and what he has learned from it

▲ RECORDING YOUR CONCLUSIONS
Keep a permanent record of your conclusions either in a specially purchased notebook or wallet file or on a computer. Date and sign your notes to give them a more formal status.

REVIEWING AND PLANNING EFFECTIVELY

Ask yourself what has happened since your last review

↓

Think how events occurred and how you feel about them

↓

Consider what you would like to happen next

↓

Decide how you will achieve a new goal

CHOOSING REVIEW DATES

Try to tie in your career reviews with a regular event. Any of the following times may be suitable for you:

- On the first or last day of each month
- As the financial year begins or ends
- At the start or end of each calendar year
- On your birthday
- After some internal changes at work
- After some personal changes

- On the anniversary of starting your present job
- When you are taking up a new position or leaving one
- When you are about to start or have just completed a project

56 Include new and challenging targets in each career plan.

WRITING YOUR CAREER PLAN

It is best to create a plan that includes both one-year and five-year targets. Write down how you see the future developing. Include some ambitious aims to keep you reaching as far as you can, and non-work issues, too, if you want your career plan to cover all your activities. Include something creative or unusual to expand your horizons and keep you trying out new subjects or skill areas. Schedule in some learning too, whether it is a formal course or a less structured programme.

MAKING A CAREER PLAN ▼

Here are some of the topics that your plan should cover. Add more according to your own circumstances: a varied plan makes for a varied career.

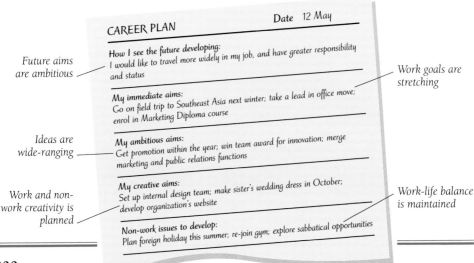

Future aims are ambitious

Ideas are wide-ranging

Work and non-work creativity is planned

Work goals are stretching

Work-life balance is maintained

CAREER PLAN Date 12 May

How I see the future developing:
I would like to travel more widely in my job, and have greater responsibility and status

My immediate aims:
Go on field trip to Southeast Asia next winter; take a lead in office move; enrol in Marketing Diploma course

My ambitious aims:
Get promotion within the year; win team award for innovation; merge marketing and public relations functions

My creative aims:
Set up internal design team; make sister's wedding dress in October; develop organization's website

Non-work issues to develop:
Plan foreign holiday this summer; re-join gym; explore sabbatical opportunities

WIDENING ▶ EXPERIENCE

Sometimes a job can offer satisfaction in some areas and not others. By weighing up what she was gaining and what she was missing, Margaret was able to take steps to compensate for the gaps. She was realistic about her prospects and prepared to spread her working contribution outside her main role.

CASE STUDY

Margaret was happy enough in her job as an editor but felt lonely. When she looked back at her previous work history she found that the times when she had felt most fulfilled were when she was working as part of a team at the centre of operations. She was unwilling to jeopardize her present post, so she decided instead to look for ways of building into her future the element of teamwork that she missed.

She found her ideal team role outside work through her interest in a campaigning organization. She asked if she could help as a trustee on the organization's management board and was accepted straight away. In her new role, she enjoys working on strategic issues and policy, while others direct the organization. She still uses her professional skills to the full in her day job and feels far more fulfilled overall.

USING YOUR CAREER PLAN

Make sure that you check your career plan regularly to see what you have achieved. Tick off targets that you have reached, noting any future work that may need to be done. For example, a work project may need monitoring in the future. Update entries that need further work with altered timescales and revised targets. What has been delaying you on these points? Finally, revisit those items where no action took place. Analyze carefully what went wrong. Perhaps you need to reframe an unrealistic goal, or perhaps you simply ran out of time? Plan how to avoid this during the next period. If the goal is still important to you, include it for another year. Otherwise, delete it and rearrange other aspects of the plan to compensate. Keep old plans to give you a sense of perspective. You will find these records of your past career management very useful when you are completing application forms in the future.

POINTS TO REMEMBER

● All the possibilities should be outlined in order to assess what is feasible.

● Hurdles that could prevent you from achieving your aims need to be identified so that you can plan how to overcome them.

57 Realize that work alone will not fulfil all your needs.

58 Talk through your career plan with family or friends.

BENEFITING FROM APPRAISALS

Regular appraisals are essential if you want to keep on top of your career. If appraisals are conducted by your employer, make sure that you learn from them and identify further opportunities to develop. Alternatively, plan to evaluate yourself.

59 Consider how you see your future developing with your employer.

UNDERSTANDING APPRAISALS

The best companies will have systems in place to help staff think about their work in terms of how they fit into the organization. A time will be booked with your manager to discuss your work since the last review and to set targets and development activities for the period ahead. Not every organization is so well run, but if you are lucky enough to be offered such an opportunity, make sure that you prepare thoroughly beforehand.

60 Be honest about past difficulties but focus on how you dealt with them.

PREPARING FOR AN APPRAISAL

Review achievements and difficulties → Decide which tasks you were best at and why

Consider present-day successes and frustrations → Identify causes of satisfaction or frustration

Anticipate future successes and difficulties → Decide what might hinder your success

Review targets and objectives → Look for the best you can contribute to your job

Think about areas that you would like to develop → Assess whether you need new skills or knowledge

PARTICIPATING IN AN APPRAISAL

Be as honest as you can about your achievements and areas for development during your appraisal. Keep an open mind about what may arise and try to react positively to feedback from your manager. Accept praise for any extra effort where it is due and listen carefully to any negative opinions. If you have prepared properly you will be able to describe your view of the situation. Try to elicit the learning points from any feedback. Summarize the main points of the appraisal and make sure that you act on any recommendations – your development needs to be driven by you.

61 Work out in advance what you will say and how you will say it.

▼ DISCUSSING DEVELOPMENT

Envisage how you would like to see your current role developing in the next year so that you can present a convincing case for any training needs.

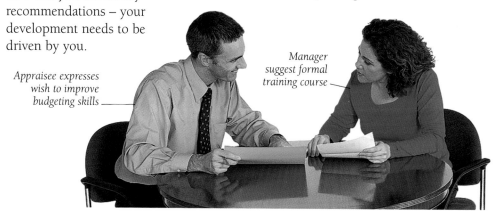

Appraisee expresses wish to improve budgeting skills

Manager suggest formal training course

APPRAISING YOURSELF

If there are no organized appraisals at your workplace, or you work alone, set up the experience for yourself. You can make it as challenging as you like, but avoid using it as an excuse to tell yourself that everything is going well and that there is no action to take. You can work alone, or you can find someone you can trust to act as your sounding board. That person does not need to be familiar with your work. In fact, since the good relationship you have with a particular colleague can easily change, it is wisest to pick someone outside your workplace. Prepare your thoughts as you would for a normal appraisal and talk or think through your answers. Write down your conclusions as a permanent record of this process for future reference.

DEVELOPING YOURSELF

You are responsible for your career development. Accept this responsibility and start making plans for your future development so that you can grow, learn, progress, and thrive in the employment market as well in your personal life.

62 Fulfil your work objectives and learn through self-development.

63 Think who might be prepared to act as your mentor.

64 Identify activities that suit the way you like to learn.

TAKING RESPONSIBILITY

Although you may get some help from enlightened employers in your career development, in the event that no assistance is forthcoming make sure that your own plans and hopes precede this. If you work for yourself or in a small group, you may feel that you cannot spare the time or money for your development, but to neglect it would be unwise. Without continuous attention to your development, even the most stimulating jobs can become stifling. Regular attention to this area will enrich both your work and your personal life.

BENEFITING FROM SELF-DEVELOPMENT

One advantage for people who take their own development seriously is that they are more confident about their own abilities. They are able to converse on a variety of subjects, seem more interested in others, and appear more interesting, too. If you have developed yourself by speaking to groups, for example, this will be revealed in your added poise when giving presentations. Being up to date on professional interests will make you a more attractive prospect to employers, and being knowledgeable about current affairs will be useful in any forum.

THINGS TO DO

1. Help yourself by reading books on aspects of management that interest you, such as motivating people or strategic thinking.

2. Enrol on some short courses that will take your knowledge further.

3. Read professional journals to keep abreast of new developments.

ENRICHING YOUR LIFE

Study is not necessarily dry, boring, or irrelevant. On the contrary, it can provide stimulation, excitement, and great leaps of understanding, but it does require hard work. If you find the right course, however, you will feel enriched by the experience. Bear in mind that development constitutes far more than formal studies. It includes all the activities that will broaden you as a person and accompany you through life. Think through areas that are ripe for development and aim to work on anything about which you feel unclear.

65 Enliven slow periods at work by reading a management or self-help book.

66 Think of ways to incorporate self-development into your career plan.

DOS AND DON'TS

✔ Do have a general idea of where your next job may be and the level at which you want work.

✔ Do plan now for what will make you suitable for the next job.

✔ Do act now to gain the knowledge you need for the next step.

✘ Don't underestimate the time needed to learn a new subject.

✘ Don't forget to explore learning opportunities that can be undertaken while working full-time.

✘ Don't neglect your development even if you feel satisfied at present.

BEING ▶ PROACTIVE

By joining a local debating society, Neera made the most of a rare chance to learn a new skill and be given direct feedback on her performance. Without this valuable experience, she might have been held back at work by her unassertive attitude to speaking in public.

CASE STUDY

Neera decided that she wanted to develop her public speaking skills. Her job as a researcher did not call for any public speaking, and she knew that her employer would not sponsor her training, so she decided to look for some opportunities outside work. She did not want to restrict herself to studying the theory, she wanted practice and feedback on her areas for development. Through her local public library she found a debating society that met near her home. Although the first session was daunting, she found others there like herself. That was three years ago. She is now Secretary of the group. Although she feels she will never be a great orator, she can now speak with passion when needed. She has also found out how to structure a speech for maximum impact and how to use humour to hold an audience's attention.

GAINING KNOWLEDGE

Continual learning does not mean that you have to register for a new evening class every term. There are many other activities that contribute to our knowledge, such as coaching, mentoring, work shadowing, job sampling, exchanges, research activities, secondments, temporary appointments, or expanding an existing job into new areas. Much of what we learn is almost unconscious – picked up by watching, reading, and hearing about new ways of doing things. Always be on the lookout for new ways to develop your skills.

67 Realize that it is never too late to learn new skills.

68 Keep your computer skills up to date – seek out training at work.

69 Avoid being held back by a fear of the unknown.

BUILDING ON ACHIEVEMENTS

It is important to build on any previous investment in your development. If you have been on a course that you found interesting at the time or which you subsequently found useful, see if you can take this to the next stage with a more advanced course on the same subject. Alternatively, there may be allied subjects that you could study, either during working hours or outside work, that would provide you with further opportunities. If you have privately undertaken a course that has proved to be of benefit to you at work, consider whether your employers might support you in further training. If you can demonstrate the benefits, they might regard the cost as an investment.

◀ USING COMPUTER SOFTWARE
The ability to use information technology is a core skill that can apply to almost every job. Make sure that, at the very least, you keep up with the latest software packages and know how to use electronic mail.

IDENTIFYING METHODS OF LEARNING

METHOD	FACTORS TO CONSIDER
COACHING Working with a trainer or senior colleague to increase skills.	This is a good way of improving confidence and learning new skills on the job, particularly if you happen to be inexperienced or new to a role.
JOB SWAP Exchanging jobs with a colleague for a fixed period of time.	This enables you to experience different priorities, needs, and methods of working. For example, private and public sector accountants might do each other's work for a week.
MENTORING Being guided by an experienced colleague on a longer-term basis.	A mentoring relationship often runs for a minimum of 6 months and can be an invaluable experience, particularly when there is a high level of commitment on both sides.
READING Studying books, journals, articles, and researching on the internet.	Reading is a learning method that can be easily fitted into your spare time. Try reading on the train or bus to work, or find a quiet spot at lunchtimes, such as a library or park.
RESOURCE CENTRES Acquiring new skills at local or corporate access centres.	These centres can help you further your education, such as by learning a new language. Courses are very popular, so you may need to book in advance.
SABBATICAL Taking time off in order to study, travel, or do other work.	In academic life, sabbaticals are paid for once they have been fully justified, but this is rare in other sectors unless the break provides clear and necessary work input.
SECONDMENT Moving temporarily to another post, department, or organization.	A short-term placement in an allied but different workplace offers variety and is a stimulating way to broaden experience and aid development.
STUDY Participating in on-the-job training, courses, open learning, workshops.	Studying will help you progress in your career. Be aware, however, that the longer the course, the higher the level of application and commitment required.
TEMPORARY PROMOTION Working in a higher position until the position is filled permanently.	This enables you to gain experience working at a higher level and to decide whether the responsibility suits you. "Acting up" can lead to permanent promotion.
WORK EXPERIENCE Gaining experience by doing paid or unpaid work for a period of time.	A formal placement involves trying out a role for a fixed period, often to a preset programme. This is a chance to experience a different job at first-hand.
WORK SHADOWING Accompanying someone who has a different job.	This is a useful way of seeing how someone else works. It provides an insight into their key tasks, related work practices, priorities, and problems.

ESTABLISHING LEARNING GROUPS

Managing other people can be isolating because it is difficult to truly be one of the team. Keep yourself motivated by establishing or joining a learning group, or learning set, so that you are able to rely on support and stimulation from your peers.

70 Make sure that all group members have the chance to contribute.

DEFINING LEARNING GROUPS

Increasing numbers of people who are interested in developing their own careers are setting up groups to plan, manage, and facilitate their own learning. Academic or professional issues can be considered and discussed, sometimes around real work problems that are affecting a member of the group. This allows true action learning: the objective consideration of the issue and possible solutions. These learning groups are run by groups of friends or colleagues who want to learn from and with each other, independent of any college or any work learning that may be taking place. Sometimes the group members will all be based in the same organization, but more often they will come from different places of work.

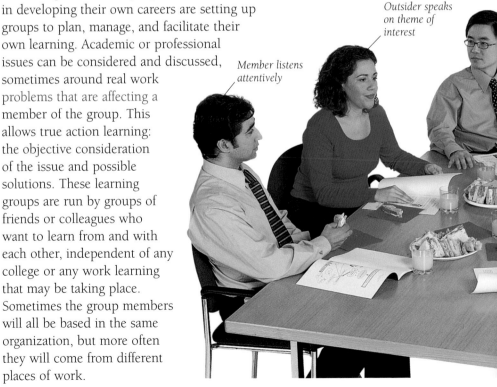

Outsider speaks on theme of interest

Member listens attentively

71 Prepare in advance to ensure thorough group discussion takes place.

ESTABLISHING A LEARNING GROUP

Form your own group from friends and associates. Try to pick a varied collection of people who will all have something special to contribute. They should possess similar outlooks and be interested in learning and helping each other to excel. Group members should initially commit to attending sessions for at least one year. Five or six people is plenty. Be open to others' needs: some people may be more interested in solving work problems or enhancing their employability; others may be seeking academic enrichment.

▼ RUNNING A LEARNING GROUP

Select a mix of people and discuss how you will work together. Ask guest speakers to attend, making sure that you cater to different styles and interests. Share good practice and learning events. Keep the atmosphere social and informal.

DOS AND DON'TS

✔ Do conduct regular reviews of your group's working procedures.

✔ Do make sure that everyone participates.

✔ Do tackle new subjects frequently.

✘ Don't have too many people from very similar backgrounds.

✘ Don't waste the time on general social chit-chat.

✘ Don't get too "safe" – introduce challenges.

Member takes responsibility for running the meeting

Member asks a question on a point that concerns him

Member sees how subject matter relates to her work situation

72 Discuss a wide range of subjects with your group.

73 Make sure that all members are accorded tolerance and respect.

ACHIEVING CAREER SUCCESS

As a career develops, twists and turns are inevitable. Be prepared to overcome obstacles, change direction when necessary, and turn events to your advantage so that you continue to thrive.

COPING WITH A SETBACK

Even with the most careful planning, career progression can sometimes be thrown off course by sudden, unexpected events. If you suffer a setback, keep calm, think positively, and plan what to do next so that you can re-establish your position.

74 Be aware of external changing circumstances that may affect you.

75 Note that a crisis can represent a turning point.

76 Adopt a calm approach to help diffuse a difficult situation.

RECOGNIZING THE CAUSES

We are all at the mercy of events over which we have little control. Common setbacks to a career include losing a job (perhaps due to being sacked or being made redundant), being demoted or moved to a new role (perhaps following a company merger or takeover), and failing to win promotion. Whatever the type of setback, it can result in a loss of dignity, demoralization, and damage to an individual's reputation. However, provided you handle such situations calmly and rationally, you can ensure that short-term obstacles do not affect your long-term prospects.

HANDLING SHORT-TERM SITUATIONS

SITUATION	IMPLICATIONS	ACTION
Loss of job provokes crisis leading to trauma and confusion.	May suffer lack of confidence, respond in an over-emotional way, and react by panicking.	Review your CV, sound out employment agencies, plan the next step.
Merger or takeover creates difficult working environment and strains relationships.	Longer-term career ideas may be disrupted, requiring re-evaluation of your plans.	Consult a career counsellor to review your future options before making any move.
Circumstances alter – perhaps the working brief changes or company fortunes fall.	Longer-term career ideas may need revising in the light of the current situation.	Keep abreast of changes, and monitor economic forces and vacancies in your field.

POINTS TO REMEMBER

● A setback is soon forgotten, but the way you reacted may not be.

● Suffering one setback after another could indicate that there is a mismatch between your career plans and reality.

● Keep a sense of perspective – work is just work and no one is indispensable.

77 Use the people you respect as sounding boards.

REGAINING ▶ YOUR COMPOSURE
Working on practical issues with colleagues can help to distract you from a difficult situation and maintain a sense of proportion until you decide what to do.

RESCUING THE SITUATION

Keep positive, look at all the facts, and see if you can find a way to get back on your original path or identify a new one. Analyze what caused a setback and try to take remedial action, such as putting progressive proposals to your superior. If you feel that you acted unwisely, try to undo any damage that you can. If you feel demoralized, perhaps as a result of having to leave work suddenly, look for ways to boost your confidence in other areas of your life while you think about your next move.

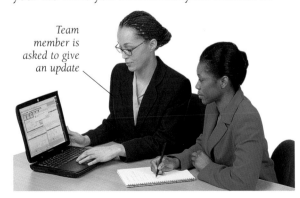

Team member is asked to give an update

IDENTIFYING THE NEED FOR CHANGE

There are times in every career when it is necessary to change direction. Keep checking that your original career plan is relevant as you develop and gain experience, and recognize the need to alter course if your circumstances or expectations change.

78 Anticipate change so that you can plan how to cope with it.

79 Be inspired by people who have hit rock bottom, and climbed back to success.

LOOKING BACK

It is important to compare what you are doing now with what you did before to see how you have changed and how your expectations and ambitions have progressed. You may have changed in ways that you had not anticipated, with the result that your original long-term career plans are no longer relevant. For example, if you have developed far more confidence after giving many presentations, you might want to take on a more visible role. Or perhaps you have discovered a new talent and would like to exploit it.

BEING PRACTICAL

Taking a new career path becomes more difficult the longer you leave it. In your 20s you are likely to have a "Why not?" attitude to drastic career changes. By your 30s you will be keen to establish yourself on a developing career path. Your 40s are likely to be your most ambitious years, while in your 50s starting a brand new career will seem highly risky. Once you have built up a track record and investment of time in one job area you will be loathe to relinquish it if that means starting all over again at the bottom of the ladder.

QUESTIONS TO ASK YOURSELF

Q Am I confident about the potential gains to be made?

Q Am I clear about the costs involved in the change?

Q Have I communicated with everyone who will be affected?

Q Have I considered possible disadvantages carefully?

Q Have I been realistic in my assessment and calculations?

EXAMINING REASONS FOR CHANGE

When a job is easy and every situation seems familiar, change is desirable. Staying in a position with no challenges can be stultifying. Perhaps you need more money or would work for less for more satisfaction. Health or family circumstances might be reasons for change, or market depression or outlook could convince you to alter your plans. You may simply feel that you have outgrown your job and it has no more to offer you. Even if you feel happy and secure, you may need to change as a result of internal restructuring or a new appointment.

80 Plan for the future to give you a head start in anticipating change.

MAKING A ▶ POSITIVE CHANGE

Roger was happy in his work but wanted to see more of his family. Rather than change jobs, he made a convincing case for flexible working hours.

CASE STUDY

Roger was becoming resentful of the long hours he was required to work. He wanted to see more of his wife and two children. He approached his departmental head with the proposal that he try out flexible working for a trial period of one year. This would involve him working one less day a week but to compensate he would have to do some work at home and work longer hours on the days that he came into the office. His employers agreed but only to a six-month trial initially. They voiced concerns that the change in his working hours might jeopardize production. However, everything worked well and the flexible pattern continued for five years. The company then decided to open up similar opportunities to all staff to recognize the need for them to be able to adapt to the changing roles facing them outside work.

POINTS TO REMEMBER

- Change is normal and desirable. A static situation is a far greater cause for concern.
- Common reasons for changing career are to earn a larger salary or have better working conditions.
- While change can provide fresh ways to work, new ideas, and stimulating contacts, new routines take time to learn and it can be difficult to rethink old habits.

UNDERSTANDING BOTH SIDES OF CHANGE

Before deciding whether to make a change, weigh up the benefits and disadvantages impartially. Discuss the issues with other people to help you think them through. For example, if you want to enjoy more flexible working, perhaps due to family commitments, you may have to accept that you will receive less financial reward. If you cannot seem to progress any further in your current role without retraining, would it be worthwhile enrolling in a distance learning course?

ENHANCING YOUR PROSPECTS

People who strive to broaden their experience are attractive to employers. Consider taking time off for study, research, or travel, look for wider responsibilities in your present role, or aim to move to new pastures in order to enhance your prospects.

81 Change perspective by working in different areas of an organization.

QUESTIONS TO ASK YOURSELF

Q What could I do with a six-month career break? Could I specialize in a new area?

Q Is there an area of interest for me to research or study?

Q Would a work break give me any new skills that would be of value to my employer?

Q Would travelling be an option, and what are the likely costs?

Q Could I survive without pay for this period?

BROADENING KNOWLEDGE

Taking time off to study or travel is known as a sabbatical or a career break. In academic life, taking a sabbatical for research or study is common, and this concept of time out to replenish professional enthusiasm and knowledge is now gaining ground in other sectors. However, not all employers will look favourably on a request for a career break, since it may be costly to keep a post open. If this is the case with your employer, decide whether you could self-finance an unpaid work break. Alternatively, consider leaving your current job and taking a break before applying for another.

TAKING ON NEW ▶ CHALLENGES
This scenario depicts two outcomes for a team leader who became demotivated at work. By following outside interests, he developed his organizational skills and gained fresh confidence and enthusiasm. This was noticed when he returned to work and he was given a more challenging role. A failure to take action led him to feel more demotivated and depressed.

Team leader receives negative feedback in his appraisal

Team leader becomes demotivated and despondent

CHANGING YOUR JOB PROFILE

If you are dissatisfied with your job, or if you are doing it because you need to, rather than because you want to, look for other areas to give you the extra sense of achievement that you are missing. Do you have an interest in other jobs in the organization? If so, why not offer to liaise between departments or sit on committees or project groups that could use your talents?

THINGS TO DO

1. Evaluate your key work tasks and decide which are necessary, optional, or habitual.
2. Stop doing unnecessary tasks and break old habits.
3. Find different ways to perform necessary and optional tasks.
4. Work hard to acquire the right reputation and image.
5. Develop a positive outlook.

82 Consider taking on an extra element of responsibility – it may bring new interests and rewards.

Relations with colleagues improve, and team leader is promoted to manager

Volunteers outside his work to help organize charity fund-raising events

Becomes more frustrated and isolated, damaging his career prospects

83 Make it a habit to try something different until it comes naturally.

Continues in the same old routine

84 Identify gaps in your life and try to find new ways of filling them.

KNOWING WHEN TO MOVE ON

Most jobs can become routine but sometimes you may feel as though you have ground to a halt. Perhaps you are desperate for each day to end because the work has become very predictable. Or perhaps you have stopped believing in what senior people say, or you have lost respect for the organization. Regularly assess how you feel about your job. Choose a subjective score from 0–10 where 0 = desperately bad and 10 = excellent. If you are frequently awarding your frame of mind lower than 5, you should consider changing your job. Consistently low scores show that you are having more negative than positive experiences. If your score is regularly at the top end of the scale, there is probably scope for you to stay in your job and make changes to improve your routine.

POINTS TO REMEMBER

● Don't wait until things have gone wrong before planning a change.

● It is always easier to get a job when you are employed than when you are out of work.

● A check needs to be kept on a changing situation – your second best option could become your preferred option in the longer term.

85 Change is a fact of life, so make sure that you plan to accommodate it.

86 Aim to leave a job that does not fulfil you before your morale suffers.

Receives invitation to a job interview

MAKING A FRESH START

If you feel unappreciated, or the essential day-to-day work does not interest you, or you believe you are being victimized, you are likely to feel cynical and frustrated. Perhaps you have experienced personal clashes with people at work, or a run of difficulties in performance. Even if these situations are not of your own making, by staying put you risk creating a bad atmosphere for everyone. You will also start to feel negative and alienated and become worn down and depressed. The best way forwards is to cut your losses, move on, and make a fresh start somewhere new.

◀ **TAKING POSITIVE ACTION**
Staying in a job where you feel unhappy will harm your career, so start looking and applying for other jobs as soon as possible. Simply taking some positive action will help you feel in a better frame of mind.

REMAINING POSITIVE

Always talk positively about your current job in subsequent job interviews. Most interviewers are able to identify a demotivated candidate who is desperate to leave a job, even if you try to hide your true feelings in your answers. Avoid showing any lack of enthusiasm in the way you describe your current job, since a candidate who decries his or her current employer will sound disloyal and give the impression that they will do the same about any future employer later on. Even if you feel you have been at a standstill, try to reinterpret your frustration by highlighting your achievements. Be as objective as you can and concentrate on what you learned. Discuss areas where you did feel that you contributed and explain why. Talk about where you would like to be heading rather than what you are keen to leave behind.

87 Find positive aspects of your last job to discuss in an interview.

▼ BEING INTERVIEWED
Be positive about your last job when talking to prospective employers. If you are critical or negative of your colleagues or the organization, you risk giving the impression that you are untrustworthy.

Candidate highlights his achievements in previous job

Interviewer notes his loyalty to former employer

88 Use the people you respect as sounding boards.

89 Think how to put the best gloss on the job you want to leave.

DOS AND DON'TS

✔ Do be positive and enthusiastic – stress what you have to contribute in the future rather than on past disappointments.

✔ Do treat each new opportunity as a blank page.

✔ Do analyze your behaviour on a regular basis.

✘ Don't develop an antagonistic or a cynical attitude.

✘ Don't get demoralized – a much more suitable job may be just around the corner.

✘ Don't dwell on your difficulties – in years to come you will struggle to remember what you were worrying about.

MAKING A CAREER MOVE

Waiting until a career decision is clear-cut can mean waiting forever. Assess the outcome of a move on a balance of probable gains and losses. Analyze what these mean to you to establish the important aspects of the options facing you.

90 Make a list of things you want from a job, then aim to get them.

QUESTIONS TO ASK YOURSELF

Q Have I established the salary, working hours, and conditions?

Q Are there any other benefits or any disadvantages?

Q What is the potential for progress up the career ladder?

Q Am I worried about how I would fit into a new kind of organization?

Q Would finding out more allay my fears?

BALANCING GAINS AND LOSSES

When you need to weigh up the advantages and disadvantages of making a career move, the quantitative factors that can be compared and contrasted are few. Having established the amount of pay, working hours, and conditions, plus daily commuting implications, the rest is simply a matter of adjudication about the quality of the benefits on offer. Use a combination of instinct, imagination, and judgment to find your way to a satisfactory outcome.

CASE STUDY

Penny was very clear about what she wanted from her career. She had summarized her key motivational factors as being attention, achievement, and acclaim. For the past five years Penny had been moving towards a job where she felt fulfilled in each of these aspects. Her current role gave her the satisfaction of two of the three, but she felt it was time to find a new position that would offer her more.

Penny applied for a job and was invited to an interview. She found that having a clear vision of what she wanted helped her talk her way through the gruelling interview process. When the company offered her the job, they said that a deciding factor was the clarity with which she could express herself and her aims. Weighing up the new role, Penny found that the benefits to be gained outweighed any worries, and accepted the position.

◀ ACHIEVING CLARITY
Penny decided exactly what she wanted from her career. Armed with this information, she was able to make sensible decisions according to her real priorities. Without this clarity, Penny could have found that each job move brought more frustration than satisfaction, and her career direction may well have become confused.

91 Trust your instincts – what were your first feelings about an issue?

USING YOUR INSTINCT

Innate impulses, often called instincts, are immediate responses to act in one way or another. Recognize these powerful feelings, note them, and then examine what might have provoked them. Sometimes they are identifying subtle indicators that cause you discomfort or interest you. Try to articulate exactly what it is that you are feeling. Perhaps talking to someone about a proposed move would help you gain clarity about the relative advantages and disadvantages?

ASSESSING TANGIBLES

Tangible factors – those that can be measured or observed – include the physical conditions relating to a job and the policies practised in an organization. Consider the salary, even if this is not your primary motivating factor, along with any other payments such as overtime, bonuses, expenses, pension contributions, or other financial incentives. The whole financial package should feel like the right rate for the job and the amount that you would need in order to accept the position. Other conditions to consider are working hours, travel time, opportunities for flexible working, and holiday arrangements.

92 Wait for written confirmation of a job offer before you resign.

POINTS TO REMEMBER

- Most people become set in their ways and need to be encouraged to try something different.
- Every change will have both plusses and minuses.
- Any decision to move should be based on objective factors rather than on prejudices.
- Making assumptions should be avoided – always check that the situation is really as you perceive it to be.

◀ **ASSESSING PRIORITIES**
Think carefully about the tangible factors of a career that are important to you. Being able to work part-time from home to reduce travel time may be a strong consideration for you.

LOOKING AT INTANGIBLES

There are also intangible factors to take into account when assessing a career change. These include the working atmosphere, the team approach, how an organization is run, quality of leadership, and career potential. Assess these by talking to staff who already work for the company. These factors, such as how motivating the environment would be, are almost completely subjective. You may only judge factors in this group, such as the degree of responsibility offered, how far creativity is encouraged, and how clearly communication takes place, from the interaction you have with a company prior to employment.

93 Assess whether the atmosphere in an organization feels right to you.

94 Weigh up tangibles and intangibles before making career decisions.

Explains that job involves working some unsocial hours

Friend talks about her experience of shift work

◀ **TALKING THROUGH YOUR OPTIONS**
If you are finding it difficult to make a decision, talk through your concerns with a trusted friend. Ask them what they would do in your shoes. They may be able to point out considerations that you have so far overlooked.

◀ **CHANGING CAREER**
After having a family, Abbi found that her career priorities changed. The benefits she gained from having more control over her working day far outweighed the higher status and salary she had previously enjoyed.

CASE STUDY
Abbi, a senior social worker, loved her work. She felt valued, useful, and enjoyed the challenges of the job. However, after having children, the demands and the long hours proved exhausting. These feelings did not diminish when the children started school. At 45, Abbi decided to change her career in order to find working hours that fitted in with her domestic priorities. She applied for a retraining grant and enrolled at college to become a teacher. Although she was sacrificing her seniority and higher salary, she was gaining more control over factors she viewed as important. Most significantly, even though the course was hard work, she started to enjoy life again, knowing that her professional skills were helping people while she was doing justice to her other priorities. She taught for 15 years until she retired and never regretted her change of career direction.

PLANNING A CAREER CHANGE

KEY ISSUES

HOW TO PLAN EFFECTIVELY

YOUR ROLE AND RESPONSIBILITY
What you expect and what is expected of you.

- Find out to what extent your skills are in demand in the marketplace. Take steps to update skills or acquire them if it would increase your options.
- Consider how you would sell your achievements and experience to an employer in a new field.

SALARY
Pay, overtime, bonuses, expenses, pension contributions.

- If it is likely that you would have to take a cut in salary, establish what your minimum income could be.
- Assess whether there is scope for achieving the level of financial reward you will need and want in the future – is there a ceiling that you need to be aware of?

CONDITIONS
Hours, flexible working, holiday entitlement, work environment.

- Think about which conditions are most important to you – are you looking for similar or much better conditions than you have at present?
- If a change will involve working longer hours to learn the ropes, are you happy to make this commitment?

LOCATION
The place, or places, where you can expect to be based.

- If you make a big change, such as from administrative to technical work, the location may shift accordingly to become site-based rather than office-bound.
- Jobs that involve travel, especially at short notice, could prove difficult if you have family commitments.

CULTURE
Atmosphere, quality of leadership, staff attitudes, and team spirit.

- Decide which intangible aspects of a workplace, such as how it feels to work there, are most important to you.
- Profit-making or non-profit organizations have different explicit aims and implicit values that you may want to take into account.

PROSPECTS
Will there be plenty of opportunity to move up the career ladder?

- If you are moving to enhance your future prospects, you will need to monitor your progress as you find your feet.
- Assess where you want to be in five years' time and find out if it is feasible to get there by changing career.

SURVIVING AND THRIVING

There are times when you will feel as though you are merely surviving at work. At other times you may feel that you are forging ahead. Learn how to handle the ups and downs of your career so that you stay on course for success.

95 Learning from failure can be just as useful as learning from success.

STAYING ON COURSE

From time to time you will be faced with circumstances, at work or at home, that may not be to your liking. These ups and downs need not throw you off course if you keep a positive mental attitude. Take the long view about progress at work to help you get through frustrating times. Short-term stagnation may be necessary for a later breakthrough. If work is frustrating, aim for successes in other areas of your life to help you feel calm and positive. Take some physical exercise. This will help you cope with pressure at work so that you can survive until you start to thrive again.

Team leader asks for feedback

Manager points out areas of improvement

◀ LEARNING FROM OTHERS

Discuss work with respected colleagues or peers and ask for advice when you are unsure how to proceed. It can be valuable to learn how people with different skills and experience might approach a problem.

96 Be prepared to ask for support from colleagues and to give them support.

*Graham still had a lot to offer
as he neared retirement. His
willingness to work without
pay at the end of his paid
employment meant that his
career continued to develop.
He used his technical and
managerial expertise to work
in an entirely different setting
for the good of others, a
rewarding encounter which
led him to further
new experiences.*

CASE STUDY

Graham, a water engineer, was nearing retirement but did not feel ready to stop work. He approached a volunteer organization that sent professionals overseas to see if they would be interested in someone of his age. To his delight, they were particularly keen to interview him because of his wealth of experience, which they realized was so badly needed in the developing world. He discovered that more than 300 of the 1,000 people they sent overseas were over 50. Six months later, Graham began a two-year placement on a water infrastructure project in a small African country. Working with the local community, he helped them improve drinking water and irrigation systems throughout the area. He returned home after extending his stay for a year and now gives talks to new volunteers to share his enthusiasm for and experience of such projects.

97 If you want to be able to enjoy a happy, fulfilled retirement, start planning for it early.

PLANNING AHEAD

These days it is not unusual for people to work until they are 70 or more. This does not mean that they carry on in the same job. The usual retirement age of around 60 to 65 often spurs people to change priorities for the active years ahead. Your career priorities will change at different stages of your life. In your 20s you can afford to explore varied jobs and roles and consider professional training courses. In your 30s you may have family commitments or be planning to travel. In your 40s you will want to be consolidating your progress and in your 50s you are likely to be reaping the rewards of earlier education and training. At 60 you may be looking ahead, perhaps even thinking about a new direction. Your career plan needs to cover these different steps in your life, which means looking ahead and reviewing progress regularly.

CULTURAL DIFFERENCES

If you plan to work abroad, bear in mind the differences between cultures. In the United States and the Far East, for example, staff are usually given two weeks' paid holiday per year, whereas in Europe and the United Kingdom, four to five weeks' paid leave is the norm. Permits may be needed to enable you to work legally in some countries, and most countries require that foreign workers pay tax.

98 Keep checking that your career and life goals tally.

INVESTING IN OTHERS

The most effective managers are as interested in developing their teams as they are in their own progress. Encourage team members to manage their own careers by explaining your own approach and the benefits to be gained from good planning.

99 Use your own career planning skills to help and inspire others.

100 Develop staff and you will improve their effectiveness.

USING PROJECT SKILLS ▼
Promote the discipline of project management so that team members learn to focus on priorities, monitor progress, overcome difficulties, and adapt to change. These skills can then be transferred to planning their individual improvement and development in consultation with you.

DEVELOPING STAFF

In addition to managing their own careers, good managers encourage their staff to take their career planning seriously. Whether your organization is large or small, or located in the public or private sector, other people in your team will benefit from your approach to career management. Talk to your team about how you manage your own career, and raise the subject at staff meetings. Highlight the benefits of people taking on new projects or moving into a new area. For example, you could stress how an individual might improve their career prospects by taking on work that could enhance their reputation or lead to a promotion. In this way staff can be inspired to welcome change and fully endorse any new developments.

Team leader reports on progress of project

Manager encourages regular reviews

ENCOURAGING TEAMWORK

The more you explain to your team the benefits of career planning and make the link between development and performance, the more you will build an atmosphere that encourages development and learning. Provide opportunities for sharing learning with others and make time to discuss staff progress. Give priority to career subjects and promote self-development for all staff. Encourage team members to analyze their performance together and to highlight development activities that could improve their work in the future. In this way you will build team spirit and ensure that staff are positive and productive.

POINTS TO REMEMBER

- Staff who have been involved in development activities should be asked to share their knowledge with the rest of the team.
- Appraisal discussions should be used to highlight progress and offer guidance on possible career development.
- Where individual effort has helped the whole team succeed, it should be celebrated.
- By investing in your staff you will be further developing your own strengths and skills.

BEING AN EFFECTIVE ROLE MODEL ▼
Your behaviour will have a direct effect on every member of every team you lead. Make sure that you always act positively to show that career success is worth working for.

101 Reward good work and celebrate innovation to inspire your team to career success.

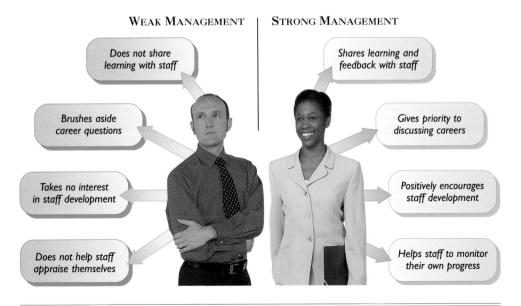

WEAK MANAGEMENT | STRONG MANAGEMENT

Does not share learning with staff

Brushes aside career questions

Takes no interest in staff development

Does not help staff appraise themselves

Shares learning and feedback with staff

Gives priority to discussing careers

Positively encourages staff development

Helps staff to monitor their own progress

ASSESSING YOUR CAREER MANAGEMENT SKILLS

*F*ind out whether you are managing your career *successfully by reading the following statements, and then choosing the option that is closest to your experience. If your answer is "never", circle Option 1; if it is "always", circle Option 4, and so on. Be honest with yourself. Add your scores together and refer to the analysis to see how you scored. Use your answers to identify areas that need improvement.*

OPTIONS
1 Never
2 Occasionally
3 Frequently
4 Always

1 I revise my career plan each year in the light of my present position.

1 2 3 4

2 I get advice from respected friends about my career.

1 2 3 4

3 I feel confident about my next career move.

1 2 3 4

4 I know how my present job fits into my overall career plans.

1 2 3 4

5 I feel that there is a good balance between work and the rest of my life.

1 2 3 4

6 I have found an outlet for my creativity in my current position.

1 2 3 4

7 The different parts of my life seem to fit together well.

1 2 3 4

8 I analyze my previous career moves and decisions.

1 2 3 4

9 I keep up to date with the current state of the employment market.

1 2 3 4

10 I network with friends and associates so that I hear about vacancies.

1 2 3 4

11 I work with others to keep my skills current and topical.

1 2 3 4

12 In each post I work at building my skills for the next one.

1 2 3 4

13 I am often involved in some type of formal learning activity.

1 2 3 4

14 I work out what I can contribute to each post I apply for.

1 2 3 4

15 I thoroughly research each new position on offer.

1 2 3 4

16 I use the internet to help me with research into employment issues.

1 2 3 4

17 I make a note of any achievements and successes when they occur.

| 1 | 2 | 3 | 4 |

18 I plan for appraisals and make full notes in advance of the event.

| 1 | 2 | 3 | 4 |

19 I try to grasp the learning points of any career disasters.

| 1 | 2 | 3 | 4 |

20 I try to learn from disappointments and keep a positive frame of mind.

| 1 | 2 | 3 | 4 |

21 I resist moaning and avoid becoming cynical about my job.

| 1 | 2 | 3 | 4 |

22 I am a supportive colleague to my peers, superiors, and subordinates.

| 1 | 2 | 3 | 4 |

23 I often read a journal that is relevant to my profession.

| 1 | 2 | 3 | 4 |

24 I am a member of my relevant professional or trade association.

| 1 | 2 | 3 | 4 |

25 I regularly read a quality newspaper, including the business pages.

| 1 | 2 | 3 | 4 |

26 I work hard because I am ambitious to fulfil my goals.

| 1 | 2 | 3 | 4 |

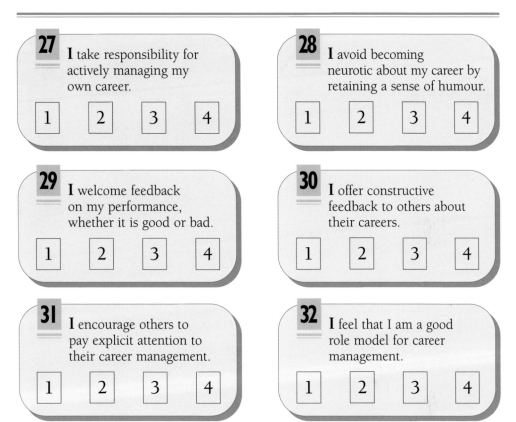

27 I take responsibility for actively managing my own career.

| 1 | 2 | 3 | 4 |

28 I avoid becoming neurotic about my career by retaining a sense of humour.

| 1 | 2 | 3 | 4 |

29 I welcome feedback on my performance, whether it is good or bad.

| 1 | 2 | 3 | 4 |

30 I offer constructive feedback to others about their careers.

| 1 | 2 | 3 | 4 |

31 I encourage others to pay explicit attention to their career management.

| 1 | 2 | 3 | 4 |

32 I feel that I am a good role model for career management.

| 1 | 2 | 3 | 4 |

ANALYSIS

Now that you have completed the self-assessment, add up your total score and check your career management skills by referring to the evaluation below. Identify your weakest areas, and then re-read relevant chapters to help you further refine your skills.

32–64: You have a passive approach to your working life and are allowing career opportunities to slip away. Develop a clearer view of where you want to get to and make realistic plans of how to get there.

65–95: You are managing your career reasonably well but could afford to take more control of the factors affecting you.

96–128: You enjoy developing your career and it shows, but do keep your mind open to the unexpected opportunities that life can produce.

INDEX

customers, putting them first (*cont'd*)
 loyalty, 601, 614–17
 market research, 568–71, 590–2
 needs, 563, 568
 new technology, 605
 objectives, 578–81
 partnerships, 600–1
 performance charts, 581
 performance indicators, 579–80, 612
 priorities, 573
 process maps, 585
 product packaging, 469
 product–customer matrix, 573, 574
 products and services, 588–9, 651
 purpose statements, 578
 quality, 597
 questionnaires, 571
 requirements, 563
 retaining customers, 565
 risk assessment, 593, 603
 SAFE decisions, 595
 strategy, 567, 619
 SWOT summary, 567, 616
 teams, 607, 613
 templates, 592, 593
 trends, 565

D

data:
 dealing with, 28
 filing, 28
 handling immediately, 60
 information *vs.* 29
data dumping, 199

decision making, 44–57
 action, 23, 56–7
 advice, 49, 55
 criteria, 51
 cultural differences, 47, 685
 customer-focused, 594–5
 focus, 45–6
 information gathering, 23
 intuition, 53, 55
 making the decision, 53, 54
 options, 52, 53
 pressures, 47
 problems, 48–9
 process, 45, 50–3
 purpose, 50
 SAFE decisions, 403, 595
 self-certainty, 328
 short-cuts, 54–5
 thinking, 44–7, 52
 VSAFE process, 54–5
delegating, 324, 434, 732
design briefs, 548
designers, 547, 548
designing publicity:
 checking proofs, 549
 commissioning illustration, 548
 design briefs, 548
 house style, 549
 in-house, 546
 "overprint" stationery, 547
development, *see* learning; personal
 development; staff development
development reviews, 427, 441, 470–1
diaries, 65, 475
dictionaries, 111

G

JK

L

M

T

W

websites, 522–3, 604, 605
withdrawn behaviour, 235
word processing, 88–9, 114–17, 546
work permits, 823
work routines, 728–33
 adapting, 729–30
 flexitime, 729
 holidays, 823
 one-minute excellence, 733
 self-employment, 796–7
 tidiness, 731
 working from home, 76, 729
 working hours, 729, 740
 see also time management
workaholism, 703
working from home, 76, 729
working hours, 729, 740
working with others, 192–213, 340
 analyzing ideas, 200–1
 brainstorming, 198
 briefings, 195, 196, 262
 creative sessions, 197
 creative teams, 195–201
 cultural differences, 197
 data dumping, 199
 delegating, 27, 324, 434, 732
 examining ideas, 205
 gaining co-operation, 192
 improving effectiveness, 212–13
 input, 194
 leadership, 195, 197
 meetings, 196, 197
 procedures, 208–9

working with others (*cont'd*)
 proposals, 210–11
 reviewing ideas, 206–7
 setting up teams, 194–5
 stimulating ideas, 202–4
 supporting each other, 193
 tools, 193
 see also teams
work–life balance:
 action plans, 715, 724–7, 745
 assertiveness, 744–5
 assessing, 758–61
 beliefs, 712
 burnout, 703
 change, 734–7, 755
 children, 721, 729
 choices, 714
 confidence, 746–7
 criteria, 704–7, 724
 delegating, 732
 emotional intelligence, 234, 716–19
 family, 643, 721
 goals, 722, 725, 742–3
 guilt, 740
 health, *see* health and fitness
 holidays, 728, 740, 823
 intentions, 743
 international assignments, 642–3, 660, 823
 key issues, 707
 leading by example, 738–41
 leisure, 722, 733, 749, 753
 motivation, 754–5
 one-minute excellence, 733
 perception, 713

AUTHORS

Moi Ali has worked as a public relations and marketing consultant for nearly two decades. She is founder and Chief Executive of marketing and PR company Pink Anglia PR, and specializes in clients with limited budgets, in particular small businesses and charities. She has written several books on PR and marketing, including Essential Managers: *Marketing Effectively* and Essential Managers: *Effective Public Relations* (Dorling Kindersley).

George Boulden is Chairman and Managing Director of ALA International Ltd., and promotes the use of Action Learning to solve business problems. He has clients across the globe and has performed consultancy work for several international agencies, including the World Health Organization. He has written a number of articles and books, including *Industrial Re-Structuring*.

Terence Brake is President of Transnational Management Associates-USA, a leading executive development consultancy focused on managing the human challenges of globalization. He travels across the globe designing, developing, and delivering global business workshops for clients in the Americas, Asia, and Europe. His previous books include *Doing Business Internationally: The Guide to Cross-Cultural Success*.

Andy Bruce is the founder and chief executive of SofTools Limited, a specialist management consulting and software company. He has a generalist business background, and has spent the last ten years helping a variety of organizations to redefine strategic direction and implement change programmes. His previous books include Essential Managers: *Project Management* and Essential Managers: *Strategic Thinking* (Dorling Kindersley).

Dr. John Eaton PhD is a Senior Partner with Coaching Solutions, an innovative company that offers executive coaching to blue-chip concerns throughout the UK. He contributes regularly to journals, including *Theory & Psychology*, *Organizations and People*, and *Training Journal*. He is co-author with Roy Johnson of several books, including *Essential Managers: Coaching Successfully* (Dorling Kindersley) and *Communicate with Emotional Intelligence*.

Robert Holden is the founder of "The Coaching Success Partnership" and "The Happiness Project" (www.happiness.co.uk). A broadcaster, psychologist, and inspirational speaker, he coaches a variety of people from entrepreneurs to sportspeople, and his work has twice been the focus of BBC1's "QED" documentary programme. Among his recent publications are *Shift Happens!*, *Hello Happiness*, and *Happiness Now!*

Roy Johnson MBA is a founder and senior partner of Coaching Solutions. He also works as a trainer through PACE, his own award-winning company, helping managers to improve performance and manage change. He has worked closely with John Eaton on several projects, from books and articles to an on-line coaching skills training service.

Ken Langdon has a background in sales and marketing in the computer industry, and has lectured on strategic thinking and planning to audiences in Europe, Australasia, and the USA. He was a pioneer in the use of project management techniques in the IT industry, and now helps companies large and small to review strategies at boardroom and team level.

Christina Osborne is Chief Executive of Business Solutions, a strategic human resources consultancy, and advises clients on how to design organizations and develop people to succeed. She has lectured in business schools and held a range of executive and non-executive board roles in the public and private sectors. She is a Fellow of the Institute of Directors and the Chartered Institute of Personnel and Development.

Ben Renshaw is a success coach, seminar leader, and inspirational speaker who has won international acclaim for his innovative work with leading businesses. He is co-director of "The Coaching Success Partnership" and "The Happiness Project", and has appeared as a relationship expert on Channel 4's "Perfect Match". See www.happiness.co.uk for details.

John Seymour is a leading authority in professional NLP training. He is an international business consultant and trainer, best-selling author, and founder of John Seymour Associates, Britain's longest established NLP training organization. He is co-author of *Introducing NLP: Neuro-Linguistic Programming*. Details can be found at www.johnseymour-nlp.co.uk.

Martin Shervington is a leading-edge international consultant, trainer, and coach, applying NLP techniques to increase levels of creativity, effectiveness, and personal development in organizations (www.martinshervington.com). An international author, he has written several books on NLP, including *Don't Think of Purple Spotted Oranges*.

Rebecca Tee is a management consultant, sought-after speaker, and former President of the Institute of Career Guidance. She has written several books on the subject of career management, including *How You Can Get That Job!*, *Preparing Your Own CV*, and *Successful Interview Skills*. She has presented a programme in Sky TV's "Basic Instincts" series.

ACKNOWLEDGMENTS

PUBLISHER'S ACKNOWLEDGMENTS

Dorling Kindersley would like to thank the following for their help and participation:

Editorial Alison Bolus, Kate Bresler, Amy Corzine, Nigel Ritchie, Mark Wallace, Fiona Wild; **Jacket Editorial** Jane Oliver-Jedrzejak; **Jacket Design** Brendan Kersey; **Index** Sue Lightfoot; **Proofreading** Polly Boyd, Sue Gordon, Hazel Richardson; **Translator** Michael Salvage, Multilingua, Guildford, UK; **Photography** Andy Crawford, Steve Gorton, Gary Ombler, Tim Ridley, Matthew Ward; **Photographic Assistance** Sarah Ashun, Nick Goodall, Nici Harper, Andy Komorowski, Lee Walsh; **Picture Research** Anna Bedewell, Cheryl Dubyk-Yates, Anna Grapes, ilumi, Franziska Marking, Samantha Nunn, Marianna Sonnenberg, Laura Roberts; **Picture Library** Neale Chamberlain, Melanie Simmonds, Hayley Smith, Lee Thompson

Models David Adkins, Tracey Allanson, Roger André, Phillip Argent, Clare Borg, Carolyn Boult, Marian Broderick, Dale Buckton, Ed Burns, Angela Cameron, Anne Chapman, Kuo Kang Chen, Brent Clarke, Jane Cooke, Celine Cordwell, Russell Cosh, Roberto Costa, Felicity Crowe, Lorraine Davies, Sander de Groot, Patrick Dobbs, Miles Elliot, Carole Evans, Lorraine Evans, Vosjava Fahkro, Jeanie Fraser, John Gillard, Ben Glickman, Emma Harris, Kate Hayward, Sasha Heseltine, Richard Hill, Cornell John, Mahesh Kanani, James Kearns, Lucy Kelly, Aziz Khan, Michael Labat, Janey Madlani, Zahid Malik, Maggie Mant, Frankie Mayers, Sotris Melioumis, Ian Midson, Sophie Millett, Brian Monaghan, Roger Mundy, Karen Murray, Chantal Newall, Steve Newell, Mutsumi Niwa, Ted Nixon, Pippa Oakes, Kerry O'Sullivan, Mary-Jane Robinson, Kiran Shah, Lois Sharland, Lynne Staff, Daniel Stevens, Kaz Takabatake, Suki Tan, Peter Taylor, Fiona Terry, Anastasia Vengeroua, Silvana Viera, Dominica Warburton, Ann Winterborn, Rebecca Woodhouse, Roberta Woodhouse, Teresa Woodward, Gilbert Wu, Wendy Yun; **Make-up** Nicky Clarke, Pauline Hudson, Janice Tee

PICTURE CREDITS

Key: *a* above; *b* below; *c* centre; *l* left; *r* right; *t* top

Allsport: 250; Mike Powell 177*t*. **AKG:** Eric Lessing 222. **Corbis:** 696–7*c*; Tony Arruza 309*br*; Bettman 181; Ronnen Eshel 628*c*; Walter Hodges 749*br*; R.W. Jones 40*cl*; James Marshall 753*c*; Premium Stock 59*br*; Steve Thornton 326*cl*; David Turnley 160; Peter Turnley 65*br*; Patrick Ward 340*cl*. **Corbis Stock Market:** 16–17, 31*bl*, 741*br*, 772*bl*; Jon Feingersh 338*cl*, 676*bl*; Charles Gupton 258; Jose Luis Palaez Inc. 402, 424–5, 560, 572*bl*, 593*bl*, 630*bl*; Ariel Skelley 220–1; Jeff Zaruba 483. **Digital Vision:** 443. **Eyewire:** 806*bl*. **Getty Images:** David Hanover 698*bl*; Paul Viant 753*cr*. **Robert Harding Picture Library:** 301*cl*. **Image Bank/Getty Images:** Barros & Barros 236; Derek Berwin 645*tr*; Flip Chalfont 641*tr*; Romilly Lockyer 516*br*; Ghislain and Marie David de Lossy 190; Patty McConville 155; Henry Sims 350*br*. **Images Colour Library:** 288–9. **Image State:** AGE Fotostock 633*tr*, 688*br*. **Nasa:** 170. **PhotoDisc:** 481; 792*bl*; 819*bl*. **The Photographer's Library:** 492–3. **Pictor International:** Robert Llewellyn 366. **Powerstock Photolibrary/Zefa:** 77*tl*, 343; Norman Jung 84–5. **Rex Features:** Axel Kirchhof 549*br*. **Stone/Getty Images:** 604, 764. Christopher Bissell 356–7; Tim Brown 211; Nick Daly 195*b*; Walter Hodges 18*bl*; Stuart Hughs 240; Joseph Pobereskin 152; Chad Slatterly 733*tr*; Arthur Tilley 643*tl*; David Young-Wolff 244. **Superstock:** 577*bl*; Jim Arbogast 534*bl*. **Telegraph Colour Library:** 742*bl*; Rob Brimson 277; John Terence Turner 253*c*, VCL/Paul Viant 186; VCL 265*b*.

All other images © Dorling Kindersley

For further information see: **www.dkimages.com**